WALTER
RALEGH

WALTER RALEGH

Architect of Empire

ALAN GALLAY

BASIC BOOKS

New York

Basic Books
Hachette Book Group
1290 Avenue of the Americas, New York, NY 10104
www.basicbooks.com

Printed in the United States of America

First Edition: November 2019

Published by Basic Books, an imprint of Perseus Books, LLC, a subsidiary of Hachette Book Group, Inc. The Basic Books name and logo is a trademark of the Hachette Book Group.

The Hachette Speakers Bureau provides a wide range of authors for speaking events. To find out more, go to www.hachettespeakersbureau.com or call (866) 376-6591.

The publisher is not responsible for websites (or their content) that are not owned by the publisher.

Print book interior design by Jeff Williams.

Library of Congress Control Number: 2019010985

ISBNs: 978-1-5416-4579-0 (hardcover), 978-1-5416-4578-3 (ebook)

LSC-C

10 9 8 7 6 5 4 3 2 1

For my sister, Sandy Gallay

CONTENTS

PART FOUR

"The land itself would wage war on them":
The Roanoke Adventure

PART FIVE

"a brave new world, That has such people in't":
Roanoke as Cultural Production

PART SIX

Fictions of Colonization: "Re-peopling" Munster

PART SEVEN

Our right existed as long as "the memory of man runneth":
Settlement and Resistance on the Ralegh Seignories

PART EIGHT

Colonization as an Economic Enterprise

PART NINE

The Colonial Impulse: Search, Discovery, Redemption

PART TEN

"The arte of Magicke is the arte of worshipping God":
Colonialism as a History of the World and Universe

ILLUSTRATIONS

NOTE TO READER

SIR WALTER RALEGH spelled his name many ways, and it has become usual now to spell it as he did in his later years.

I have retained the original spelling in quotations except for employing modern usage by reversing the *j* and *i*, and the *u* and *v*, when necessary, though not when any of this occurred in the title of books.

In the old English calendar, the first date of the New Year was March 25, though most of Europe already had adjusted to the New Style calendar, beginning the year on January 1. For the period of January 1 to March 25, I have listed the year in both the Old Style and New Style, such as February 23, 1583/84, which now we would describe as 1584. There also were eleven additional dates in September in the Old Style calendar, but I have kept the date used in the document and not attempted modernization.

In the endnotes, in referring to English government records, APC signifies Acts of the Privy Council, and CSP signifies Calendar of State Papers.

1. William Segar portrait of Ralegh, 1598

The Inventory

O n his third imprisonment in the Tower of London, an inventory was taken of "such things as were found on the body of Sir Walter Rawleigh, Knycht, the 15 day of August 1618."[1]

Ralegh might have been wearing a coat tailored of the New Draperies, the stylish, soft worsted wool used in expensive English coats, a wool suitable for a summer day in London. The coat would have had huge pockets to accommodate the myriad items recorded in the inventory.

Ralegh no longer introduced to the court new fashions as he had done thirty years earlier, but he still knew how to dress the part of England's most famous knight. In the words of one scholar, Ralegh epitomized Renaissance "self-fashioning"[2]—he created images of himself to present to the world. If anything, this understates how much Ralegh truly imagined about his world. Imagination was a powerful, creative force in his life. He used poetry, prose, music, conversation, and storytelling to create—or re-create—peoples and places, imaginary, legendary, and mythical, that were as real to him as the peoples and places he knew firsthand. He imagined himself a great colonizer of overseas lands who would earn fame on a par with Columbus and Cortés.

His pockets full of personal treasures and mementos, Ralegh also carried ores into prison, where he would assess whether they contained silver or gold in the laboratory he had built during his second imprisonment. In this laboratory, he also produced cordials to heal the sick: he carried an ounce of ambergris, the gray, waxy substance secreted by the sperm whale, highly valued for treating an array of ailments. And he wrote his wife to bring him additional ingredients. Ralegh also carried in his pocket a spleen stone obtained in Guiana more than twenty years earlier and likely used to create a curative tea. The king's officials confiscated most everything he brought except for the ambergris and spleen stone.

Ralegh spent much of his life studying, planning, preparing, and then producing. As he sailed the ocean blue, he reputedly brought with him a parcel of books. In prison, he amassed over five hundred volumes in multiple languages, including Latin, Greek, French, and Spanish. His interests ranged from geopolitics to alchemy. In the British Library can be found his handwritten recipe for barreling beef. He wrote about royal marriages, warrior women, and numerous other subjects. And he often worked under difficult circumstances. During his second imprisonment in the Tower of London, he gained international fame for the cordials he produced in the laboratory, and he penned the most renowned history written by an Englishman in the seventeenth century.

Ralegh not only became expert in myriad fields but also lived a physically active life of public service. He frequently recruited men to serve on sea and land, built and inspected fortifications, captained ships, and led men into battle. He was an adventurer—in the original meaning of the term, he "ventured" his life and his capital on numerous enterprises in the Atlantic World. Famously, he searched for El Dorado, the legendary city of gold, hoping to add the Empire of Guiana and Peru to Queen Elizabeth I's empire. As her favorite, he became one of the most despised men in England, and also one of its greatest heroes. The painting on page xiv shows Ralegh in one of his typical outfits that could carry all the many items in the inventory, and in the top left it depicts the city of Cádiz. Ralegh was the hero of the Battle of Cádiz in 1596, the cane in his right hand a reminder of the grave leg wound he received there.

In 1618, when Ralegh entered the Tower of London as prisoner of King James I of England, he was much admired as the last of Queen Elizabeth's famous knights. Today he is remembered for the apocryphal story of how he laid his cloak over the mud so Elizabeth should not dirty her shoes—the courtier *par excellence*. Dashing, witty, and handsome, he earned the queen's love and respect. She permitted him monopoly rights to found England's first colony in America, which he named Virginia in her honor.

Ralegh's pockets were filled with items reflective of his life as the foremost English colonizer of the sixteenth century. He had not only held sole patent from Elizabeth to colonize in America but also received from her the largest chunk of land in the Munster Plantation, the most significant sixteenth-century English colonization project in

Ireland. And he had pursued a thirty-year effort to colonize in South America. He stood at the center of all the major colonization projects of Elizabeth's reign, yet historians ignore their overlap and instead focus on his North American endeavors, giving scant attention to Ireland and South America. At exactly the same time Ralegh directed English colonization of North America, he undertook colonization of Ireland and sent people to South America to prepare for English colonization there. And his interests overseas were not confined to colonization. Ralegh organized and participated in naval and pirating expeditions, helped open new Atlantic trade routes, and played a significant role in England's rise as a maritime power.

Ralegh carried into prison many items related to the sea, including "a loadstone in a scarlet purse." This magnet was employed as a compass—the most appropriate tool for the "Shepherd of the Ocean," a moniker given Ralegh by Edmund Spenser, England's first national poet. Ralegh promoted the arts of navigation in England, oversaw the building of England's most advanced ship, and became the most important English naval theorist of his time. He did not need a compass in prison, but the fact that he carried one shows how important the sea was in his life.

Many of the personal items in Ralegh's pockets were set in gold and studded with diamonds. He carried a jacinth seal, likely a sapphire "with a Neptune cut in it" set in gold. Because he had another seal for official business, he most likely used the Neptune for sending letters between ships in his fleet. He also held "one gold whistle set with small diamonds," almost certainly a bosun's whistle, which had only become common in England a decade earlier. When he was much younger, he wore diamonds on his shoes and lace ruffs around his neck to make an impression. But none of these ostentations were mindless. When Ralegh pulled these useful items from his pocket, their beauty was a marker to him of their essential value. Like other "natural philosophers," Ralegh was intensely curious about the nature of material things, their character and purpose. He believed that scientific study of nature—God's Creation—increased piety. As an alchemist, he attempted to transform one thing into another; humans could improve life by altering substances. Overseas, he collected crystals, ores, and plants, and then conducted experiments on these items. Ralegh's overseas activities thus fulfilled service to the monarch and promoted his material interests while they fed his curiosity about the nature of the universe.

Ralegh carried with him into prison numerous other mementos of colonization and empire. He bore on his person many maps of the Empire of Guiana, which included the alleged route to El Dorado, plus documents about a "silver myne" in Guiana, and a "Guiana idoll of gold and copper." The king confiscated all these things, just in case Ralegh really did know where the world's richest mines were located. Though Ralegh might have carried the idol to prove the provenance of its gold, it likely also held personal meaning. Fascinated with the cultures of America, Ralegh wrote about America's Native peoples, promoted publication of others' studies, and frequently had American Indians brought to him in England (with their permission) and then returned them to their homes. In his second imprisonment in the Tower of London, he had as constant companions two Americans. They lived near the Tower and visited him daily. He subsequently visited one of them in South America.

Ralegh also wore into the Tower a diamond ring given to him by Queen Elizabeth. His life and fortune, in many ways, depended on his monarch, first Elizabeth and then James. She bestowed upon him all kinds of gifts and favors: estates, monopolies, and lands to colonize. Though much of what she gave him was confiscated by her successor, the ring remained. Ralegh, who wrote much poetry, composed an epic poem for Elizabeth during his first imprisonment in the Tower, to remind her that he had sailed the seas

> To seeke new worlds, for golde, for prayse, for glory,
> to try desire, to try love severed farr
> when I was gonn shee sent her memory
> more stronge then weare tenthowsand shipps of war[3]

Elizabeth had been dead fifteen years when Ralegh entered the Tower for his third imprisonment, but his identity remained entwined with hers, as it does to the present day. She was his queen—a goddess, actually multiple goddesses, according to his poetry. He served her in so many ways, as companion and entertainer, but also in Parliament, Ireland, Spain, France, the Low Countries, the Azores, as Governor of Jersey, and as Lord Lieutenant of Cornwall. He serenaded her on the lute, advised her, did her bidding, and bore responsibility for her protection as Captain of the Guard.

Ralegh played a key role in perpetuating the "Cult of Elizabeth," which sat at the foundation of the English Empire and turned the colonization of America into a divinely inspired national cause. Yet Ralegh's role as an architect of the English Empire has barely been recognized owing to the perception of him as a failed colonizer by subsequent generations, which have difficulty understanding how his activities and ideas paved the way forward. One problem is teleology—reading history backward from what occurred at its end and ignoring first causes. We have an idea of where colonialism and empire wound up, so we think we know how it must have begun. Instead, presented here is an origin story of empire far different from what we have imagined. It provides new context for understanding its legacies, especially in the United States and Ireland.

Even before England colonized in America, the first published proposal on what to do with the Native people provided an array of possible answers that included genocide, enslavement, and removal. Ralegh worked to prevent this form of imperialism. Though the documents showing Ralegh's opposition to abuse of Native peoples have been long available, they remain ignored. Most likely, they make no sense to later generations, which have assumed that any document generated by colonizers must be grounded in the idea of subduing the colonized. Historians and biographers consistently have failed to come to terms with a great many incongruities in Ralegh's activities and his concepts of empire because they fail to see the Tudor context in which he lived and in which the empire unfolded.

Ralegh has been the subject of many biographies. Most misconstrue the essence of the man because they do not see how various aspects of his life connected. Ralegh had so many interests—and the first stages of the English Empire were so multifaceted—that it is difficult to portray him and his colonial endeavors holistically. To assess him, too many biographers have grasped measuring sticks made of sand, so imprisoned by their own cultural concerns as to be unable to determine whether he was a hero or a Devil's minion. In trying to determine whether Ralegh worked for good or bad, evidence must not be ignored solely because it does not fit with preconceptions. To gain a clear view of the man, we must enter the Tudor world to see how their thinking conditioned their activities when they ventured overseas and how they adjusted their plans and behavior during the seminal years of empire building. I take quite seriously Ralegh's words—and others' words—not by ignoring euphemism and intent to mislead but by respecting intention and cultural meaning.

Ralegh excelled as a wordsmith. Language played a significant role in his rise in the estimation of Elizabeth and her court. Some contemporaries viewed his use of words as "art" in a negative sense, as manipulation to selfish ends. Ralegh certainly used his wit to gain advantage over others. But his mind engaged in deep contemplation of the mysteries of the universe, a task many of his peers also appreciated and engaged in. Subsequent generations have had difficulty making sense of his character, thought, and accomplishments. In the eighteenth century, Edward Gibbon, when he decided to become a historian, determined to begin by writing a biography of Ralegh. After conducting research, he gave up the task, finding "the events of his life are interesting; but his character is ambiguous." Gibbon desired "a safer and more extensive theme" and ultimately opted to write his multivolume masterpiece, *The History of the Decline and Fall of the Roman Empire* (1776–1789), leaving behind the man who deigned to write a *History of the World*.[4]

Readers desire their heroes' virtues and errors to be readily identifiable. As a courtier engaged in politics, Ralegh seemed governed by self-interest. Colonizing itself can be viewed as a selfish enterprise, and empire can be seen as one of the largest roots of evil in the early modern world. But the origin story of empire is not entirely a story of self-interest. It is true that overseas expansion was driven by material desires. Many English believed colonization was the only way to secure the nation's future. Ralegh and his peers envisioned colonization bringing them and their mother country abundance, but they also perceived overseas expansion in utopian terms: they would not abuse, enslave, and kill American Indians as the Spanish had done. They foresaw empire as creating a better world for both the colonizer and the colonized. Ralegh was dismayed to learn that his countrymen just as easily as the Spanish employed violence against America's Native peoples, but he took steps, and offered radical plans, to shape an empire where all worked together for mutual benefit. Ralegh ultimately failed in this task, but his thinking infused utopian notions into future colonial enterprises.

Ralegh's vision was inspired by the Christian philosophy of Hermeticism, an interest he shared with much of the intelligentsia of Europe. Many Hermeticists looked to end sectarian differences among Christians and between Christians and non-Christians. They steered toward a universalism that avowed religious tolerance and cultural diversity. (Ralegh even provided a theological explanation for the diversity of the universe to buttress his arguments for religious tolerance.)

Hermeticism and colonialism converged in Ralegh's mind. Hermeticists believed that in America they had the opportunity to discover secrets of the universe—of God's Creation—that could lead humanity to greater physical and spiritual well-being.

This was not a colonialism of the "White Man's Burden," whereby Europeans asserted a patriarchal obligation to bring Christianity to inferior peoples. Ralegh denied that the English were God's "chosen people," and he ultimately questioned the idea of sending missionaries to convert America's Indians. He believed there was much to be learned from the Natives. He argued that non-Christians' piety often surpassed that of Christians. These beliefs of his have confused historians, who have no notion of how Ralegh's views of colonialism and America converged with his understanding of God, history, and the nature of the material and spiritual worlds. Yet when we reconstruct Ralegh's life as a colonizer by connecting his various activities and ideas to their Tudor-Stuart context, we gain a far different picture of Ralegh and the origins of the English Empire.

WHO WAS THIS MAN that played such a substantial role in shaping the English Empire at its founding? We know little about Ralegh's own foundation, his early life; we are not even sure when he was born, though it is thought to have been between 1552 and 1554. We know that he had deep roots in South West England, where his family were gentry—untitled folk, but considered above most of the common people. Ralegh's great aunt was governess to the future Queen Elizabeth and continued to serve the queen during the early years of her monarchy, meaning Ralegh's family was of substance, for Princess Elizabeth could not have just anyone looking after her. Blood mattered. Later as queen, Elizabeth allowed some of the aunt's kin at court, where it was up to them to make a good impression.

One who made a great impression was Ralegh's much older half brother Humphrey Gilbert, who gained notoriety in service to the queen and who took Ralegh under his wing. Once Ralegh had the queen's attention, connections to others, notably to his vast male cousinry in South West England, continued to play a central role in his life. These men supported one another, particularly in maritime, political, and colonial activities. Ralegh relied on his countrymen—his cousins—in his many colonial enterprises, and he gave to them and to the southwest counties his leadership and patronage, providing them opportunities to serve the queen. Though the southwestern men had limited power on the Privy Council that advised Elizabeth, Ralegh, his kin, and neighbors played an inordinately large role in steering a new course for England in the world. They provided their expertise at sea by undertaking exploration, piracy, trade, warfare, and colonization to build an empire for their queen. They set a course for England to become a world power.

Though Ralegh's rise to prominence depended on his connections, especially to the monarch, that is not to diminish the importance of his personal attributes to his attainment of wealth and power. Ralegh possessed extraordinary talents. He had a keen ability to both lead and advise, earning respect from those he commanded and from those to whom he answered. He epitomized the Renaissance man of action—a doer and a thinker who lived the examined life while performing physical service for others. As a soldier, explorer, colonizer, politician, and bureaucrat, he displayed the pragmatism necessary to achieve success, the moral compass that directed him to look toward the well-being of others, and the cynicism of a courtier to be suspicious of men's motives.

He also looked after his own interests. Ralegh skillfully accumulated a vast estate—to be expected from one who stood so close to the monarch and performed for her so many services. By no means did he live a Spartan existence. As a courtier, he spent lavishly, reflecting his and his peers' love of beautiful things. In a manner typical of the Renaissance intellectual, Ralegh meshed his interests in the physical and spiritual worlds. He ultimately went beyond his peers in harnessing his thoughts on God and the Bible, and their relationship to material objects, colonialism and empire, and kingship. In doing so, he confirmed for many who knew him well, and for many who admitted they had misjudged him, that he possessed a large and deep vision of the history of the world.

Despite his vision, political skills, and his service, Ralegh spent a significant portion of his life in prison (and briefer periods in jail). His monarchs punished him for bad behavior, for perceived challenges to their authority. Ultimately, their treatment of him, and his scathing rebukes of their abuse of power, inspired future revolutionaries in the English Civil War to take the head of their king. Ralegh left us with a host of important legacies.

PART ONE

◄—

"Thei saw the heddes
of theyre dedde fathers"

The Foundations of English Colonialism

CHAPTER 1

Toward an Empire

W hen Walter Ralegh wrote his massive *History of the World* from prison in the early seventeenth century, he understood world history to be a story of colonialism. God, the author of all history, had "planted" the world with people, first Adam and Eve and then Noah and his children. Ralegh labeled the settlements of the book of Genesis "Plantations," a term his contemporaries used to denote settlements of their people in new lands. Thus, the English settlement in Munster, Ireland, was termed the Munster Plantation, and the settlement of English at Chesapeake Bay was referred to as the Virginia Plantation.

Plantation was nearly synonymous with *colony*. Both involved moving groups of people to new lands. But *plantation* was used by Ralegh and other English to signify settlement of distant lands to which the monarch of England had a secure claim, whereas *colonies* were established in places where sovereignty had yet to be ensured. Thus, Ralegh's attempt in the 1580s to establish English in Virginia (today's Roanoke Island, North Carolina) was a question of colonization, but when John Smith led English to the Chesapeake in 1607, it was a plantation because Ralegh presumably had made good England's claim by prior settlement in the region. The Pilgrims, too, called their new home in America "Plimouth Plantation."

For Ralegh and other English, colonization was England's future. It personified their aspirations in the present and offered a lens through which to view the past. Few public issues—except, perhaps, the Spanish threat and the queen's succession—so occupied the minds of the

English during the last decades of Queen Elizabeth's reign as overseas expansion. The Tudor government generated more documents about the colonization of Ireland than about any other subject. The largest army amassed in England in this period served in Ireland to secure the Munster Plantation and to end a revolt in northern Ireland, which led to English settlement of the Ulster Plantation. When we apprehend how thoroughly colonization infused Elizabethan thinking, we can see how Ralegh understood the Old Testament and the history of the ancient world as grounded in human migration and settlement.

—

To RALEGH, the world's ancient peoples moved to new lands either to establish a plantation or to colonize. Three historical overseas projects shaped Ralegh's and other English people's worldview: the Norman Conquest of England, the Anglo-Norman Conquest of Ireland, and the building of the Spanish Empire in America.

In 1066, the Normans, descendants of Vikings in Normandy, France, conquered England, then beat back separate Anglo-Saxon and Danish Viking attempts to retake it. In but a few years, the Normans dispossessed England's landowners of 95 percent of their land, an incredibly swift and thorough conquering and colonizing of England. Centuries later, in the Age of Elizabeth (1558–1603), English elites were quite conscious of their Norman heritage, perceiving the Norman Conquest as an illustration of how the lives of inferior peoples could be improved by conquest and the civilizing influence of outsiders. William Rastell's reedited and translated edition of his father John's multivolume *Exposition of Certain Difficult and Obscure Words and Terms of the Law* (1567) claimed that the descendants of the Normans, "although they were born in England, had yet always minds to be compted [accounted] normans than English."[1] Ralegh's friend Edmund Spenser, in his *View of the State of Ireland* (1590s), reminded his English readers that they were not inherently culturally superior to the Irish, for the English had been "civilized" by the Normans during the conquest, a service they now had the opportunity to perform in Ireland.[2] Colonization and conquest could thus be defined by the colonizer as a form of benevolence. Ralegh differed because he did not regard colonization's benevolence as a one-way street. In his career as a colonizer, he would offer an alternative to the Norman Conquest model, wherein empire would be an act of co-creation in which the colonized and the colonizer formed a partnership to mutual benefit.

The second conquest of great importance to England and the life of Ralegh occurred in 1172, a century after the Norman Conquest. In the late 1160s, the Irish king of Leinster, Diarmait Mac Murchada, challenged by numerous rivals and looking for some muscle to tip the balance of power in his favor, courted support from the Norman king of England, Henry II. Henry declined to assist but did not stop his vassal, the Earl of Pembroke, soon to be known as Strongbow, from leading his own army from Wales. Strongbow conducted a successful invasion along Ireland's east coast. Worried that Strongbow and his followers would set up independent kingdoms, Henry II followed with a huge army in 1171. By 1172, Henry had attained the fealty of not only Strongbow but also most of Ireland's leaders, Gaelic and Anglo-Norman alike. English monarchs then claimed sovereignty over Ireland, a sovereignty still insecure four hundred years later when the fortunes of Ralegh and his family became intimately tied to Irish history.

Unlike in England, where the Normans extended their control over the entirety of the land, in Ireland they dominated and settled only the east coast, particularly around Dublin, in large portions of the south (Munster province), and in central Ireland. In these places, a few large Anglo-Norman families reigned supreme, controlling governance and the land.

Anglo-Normans who settled in Ireland before the mid-sixteenth century are often referred to as Old English or as Anglo-Irish to distinguish them from those who colonized later under Elizabeth, called the English or the New English. The New English looked down on the assimilated Old English because the latter resisted Tudor attempts to transform Ireland; many became rebels but ultimately lost their lands to the New English. For hundreds of years these families had been the bulwark of the monarch of England's sovereignty in Ireland, a sovereignty that lay in the queen, because Ireland belonged to Elizabeth, not to England, its Parliament, or its people.

Reality, however, dictated that English monarchs consult the English Parliament for money to administer overseas enterprises—the military and administrative costs of maintaining Ireland extended beyond the capabilities of the monarch. To administer Ireland, English monarchs had appointed a resident lord deputy. Sometimes the lord deputy was sent from England; more often he was selected from among the Anglo-Norman lords, if for no other reason than that these lords possessed the means to raise money in Ireland to support their administration.

In Ireland, local lords jockeyed for power, their domains contracting and expanding, their private armies of kerne (Irish soldiers) and gallowglass (Scots mercenaries) buttressing them against neighbors and sometimes against the English monarch.

Occasionally, the English sent an army across the Irish Sea to secure revenue and fidelity from lords not forthcoming with funds. Sometimes an Irish Parliament (from 1297) met to raise taxes and pass laws that benefited England's monarch and settlers, though these laws also were enacted to keep English settlers in line. Money was the root of the monarchy's interest in Ireland, but revenue from the Irish dominions rarely, if ever, reached hoped-for levels. Only when the Tudor monarchs (1485–1603) took power in England was a host of measures enacted to ensure compliance with a centralizing English authority. This is not to say that the English had not tried earlier to transform Ireland. By the close of the thirteenth century, the English had begun to attempt to alter Irish culture, which they viewed as barbaric, and, even more importantly, to prevent the Old English from becoming Irish.

Commonly, Anglo-Irish lords found it politically useful for maintaining the loyalty of their people to become more Irish than the Irish. In England, much hand-wringing followed this alleged degeneration. In 1367, the Irish Parliament, at the behest of Edward III's son Lionel, enacted the Statutes of Kilkenny to halt assimilation of Irish customs and mores, forbidding English from speaking Gaelic, keeping Irish "entertainers," wearing Irish clothes, and even riding horses in the Irish manner. Although noncompliance was declared treason, the statutes had no impact. The drive to separate English from Irish led to the construction of the Pale in 1471—a series of dykes and trenches without causeways to cross them—to pen the English in and keep the Irish out (hence the saying referring to those with barbarous customs who live without law to be "beyond the Pale of civilization").[3]

Those familiar with English colonial history in America will recognize from the above discussion of Ireland how similar were English motives in America. The English intended to transform the culture of the indigenous peoples and prevent their own colonists from becoming Natives. The English hoped to alter the Native peoples' conception of property, labor, and social organization. Once it established sufficient power, England also intended to raise revenue from its colonies—or at least to have the colonies pay for their own administration.

The English understood their landholding system as the basis of civil society. Individual rights and the attainment of political privileges

2. Albrecht Dürer drawing of kerne and gallowglass

were guaranteed through property holding and one's place in the hierarchy. The English introduced common law in Ireland to alter the ways the Irish owned and inherited land and to allow for easier, systematic collection of rents by the Crown. For generations, the English tried to replace Irish pastoralism with English agrarianism to create an orderly landscape of farmers who fenced their land and adopted English common law. The Tudors also sought to "civilize" the Irish by undermining and eradicating the clan/sept system. (*Septs* refers to families or groups within clans.) Irish landholding and tenancy derived from clan membership, and clan allegiance interfered with obedience to the English monarch. The English whittled away at the great lords' power with the intention of converting Ireland into a more English society in which the lesser nobility and other men of substance claimed their landed property in an English manner. The English tried to induce the Irish to change their names, to give up the *O'*, *Mac/Mc*, *Fitz*, and *Oge* that signaled individuals' position and membership in a particular clan and thus their claim to land as a member of that clan.[4] In exchange, the English government offered to guarantee individuals their land through patents that could be passed on to heirs in the English manner. Many Irish chose this course, and not until the nineteenth century did a movement develop to restore the old-style names.

To convince the Irish to accept the common law and English culture, the English sought to provide examples to the premodern Irish of proper living in their own Irish settlements. The most potent symbol of transformation: the fence. The Irish let their livestock roam freely and presumably did little planting of crops (a lie made evident by the great crops the English destroyed during wartime as a means to wrest Irish submission). Fencing, to the English, symbolized sustained labor by cultivators who made the most of their land. Fencing represented self-discipline and the discipline of labor—a master's ability to make his servants work. Before the Protestant work ethic arrived in England—before Protestantism emerged—many English property owners already subscribed to its basic tenet of the virtue of labor and of disciplining labor to produce for those who possessed capital, that is, the land. When Elizabeth granted lands to Ralegh and others for the Munster Plantation, mechanisms were put in place to nullify grants not actually taken up and "improved" by the grantees. This policy was carried to America. Although fencing was not a prerequisite of proving improvement, fencing and occupation of the land were almost synonymous.

The enclosure movement that began in the Middle Ages was one of the most significant processes remodeling Tudor England and other parts of Europe. Enclosure signified the privatization of common lands that had been used publicly for livestock grazing and hay making, and sometimes to obtain wood. In England, riots and rebellions in the second quarter of the sixteenth century failed to stop the enclosures, and the displaced poor increasingly flocked to urban areas looking for work. But little work was available for the multitudes. Fear of overpopulation swept England. Young, restless, underemployed males made up the bulk of those available for service overseas. Ralegh would draft these men to serve in Ireland, sometimes placing them directly under his leadership, and recruited from their ranks servants and tenants for his colonies, soldiers, laborers, and sailors to crew his ships that explored, pirated, traded, and conveyed people to his colonies. The English elite believed that only overseas activities could ameliorate the grave social problem of the poor masses.

The English eyed Ireland as a potential solution to the overpopulation issue. It offered plenty of fertile land for agriculture, great forests of much-needed wood, and rivers full of fish. Many English, including Ralegh's elder half brothers, participated in schemes to gain control of Irish lands. This desire for land overlapped with the Tudors' quest to remake Ireland politically, civilly, legally, and economically. They meant to turn Ireland into another England.

The rationalization of English rule in Ireland—Tudor centralization of English authority in the province of Munster, the southern counties of Ireland—precipitated the First Desmond War in 1569.[5] Elizabeth earlier had attempted to wrest military and police authority away from the Anglo-Irish lords, whose substantial private forces limited English influence on Irish society, particularly by eliminating "coign and livery," a system by which lesser men were required to support the earls' private armies.[6]

Lord Deputy of Ireland Sir Henry Sidney intended his reforms to reduce the warfare and to transfer the obedience and allegiance of the people from their lords to the Crown. The people would be relieved of the arbitrary seizure of their goods and forced maintenance of their lord's soldiers with housing and food and instead would pay set amounts to the English government, which would provide them protection and services. Sidney might have succeeded, but Queen Elizabeth interfered by backing one group of Anglo-Irish (the Ormonds) against another (the Desmonds), precipitating the civil war in southern Ireland. This war set the stage for colonization in the region by the English and brought about the rise to national prominence of several of Walter Ralegh's kin, most importantly his elder half brother Humphrey Gilbert.

Gilbert, asserting dubious claims based on grants allegedly made four hundred years earlier by the original Anglo-Norman invaders, threatened or confiscated lands in the southwest. The Desmonds gained support from these families in the southwest, whose lands had been taken by the English. These attempted land grabs were English assaults on Anglo-Irish and Irish, but the swelling divide in Munster was more complicated. The Anglo-Norman Ormonds supported the English in order to strengthen themselves against the Anglo-Norman

Desmonds, but many of the Desmonds' Irish and Anglo-Irish vassals and tenants, as well as the townspeople of Cork, Waterford, Youghal, and other southeastern towns, also supported the English reforms. The people of the coastal towns traditionally supported the English because they benefited from trade privileges granted by English monarchs. Vassals of the Desmonds saw the English as a way to escape the Desmond yoke; freeholders and tenants saw a secure future for their property through a more equitable taxation system to replace the onerous coign and livery.[7]

While James Fitzmaurice Fitzgerald, a prominent Desmond, sought military aid from the Spanish, the English petitioned the English Privy Council and Lord Deputy Sidney for grants of land in Munster, guessing that rebellion was on the horizon and the rebels' land would be fair game.[8] The Privy Council interviewed unnamed gentlemen about the proposal and received offers from volunteers to fight in exchange for becoming beneficiaries of grants of land confiscated from those who rebelled—rebels lost their land to the Crown when attainted for treason. Though it might seem odd that English petitioned for attainted estates in the expectation that treason would be committed, the Earl of Desmond, the largest landholding Desmond, in fact, signed over his estates to other family members *in case* he rebelled. The documents would be produced only if the rebellion failed and his lands were attainted. It was common practice in Ireland to sign over lands to others in case the signee later became a rebel. In the Desmond Wars, many Anglo-Irish were declared rebels multiple times, so it was not so strange for English to volunteer military service in exchange for lands expected to be available from those attainted for treason.

The outbreak of the First Desmond War did not lead to a land rush of English moving to Ireland because the rebels first had to be defeated. To achieve this end, in September 1569, Humphrey Gilbert undertook for Queen Elizabeth a war of unrestrained terror in Munster—for which he was knighted by Lord Deputy Sidney. In little over a month, thirty castles surrendered to Gilbert. Some of these "castles" were stone tower houses that included a protective wall; others were not stone fortifications. The word *castle* simply designated some kind of fortification. Gilbert's method was to demand the surrender of a castle and, if refused, the defenders were hung, drawn, and quartered. According to Thomas Churchyard, a man of great military experience in Ireland who published *A Generall Rehearsall of Warres* (1579), heads were displayed at Gilbert's camp each night "so that none could come into his Tente for any cause, but commonly he muste passé through a lane of heddes, which he used *ad terroram"*—to terrorize. This brought "greate terror to the people, when thei saw the heddes of theyre dedde fathers, brothers, children, kinsfolke and freends, lye on the grounde before their faces."[9] Most of the rebel leaders submitted soon afterward, but James Fitzmaurice Fitzgerald refused, and the conflict dragged into 1573, when Fitzmaurice received a pardon.

Though Humphrey Gilbert and his friends received no lands to settle in Ireland, his spectacular efficiency impressed Queen Elizabeth and paved the way for him, and then his younger brother Walter Ralegh, to play the lead role in English overseas expansion.

Still a third overseas project shaped Ralegh's and England's view of overseas activities: Spain's successful empire in America. Spanish conquests had gained the Spaniards access to America's riches, notably gold and silver. The English hoped to share in the bounty. Only five years after Christopher Columbus first sailed to America, John Cabot, a Venetian sailor in the employ of Henry VII, sailed out of Bristol, England, for North America. Cabot's success locating new lands across the Atlantic ignited English interest in exploring potential routes through or around North America to the Pacific and Asia. Asia possessed wonderful things that Europeans coveted: silk, gemstones, and an array of spices used in medicines, cosmetics, food preparation, painting and dyeing, and as cleansers. If Asia could not thus be reached, then perhaps newly discovered America would contain some or all of these valuable commodities.[10] In the coming decades, the English occasionally suggested exploring farther west and north for a passage to Asia, and Henry VIII authorized at least three voyages, including one in 1527 led by John Rut, laden with trade goods for China. Poor success led to decades of relative inactivity, except for the English joining other European fishermen to exploit the Newfoundland fisheries.[11] Until the 1550s, the English had a limited presence in the western Atlantic.

In the decade of Ralegh's birth, the global setting for English overseas colonization was generated by the 1550 collapse of the Antwerp market, particularly as an outlet for English wool and woolens. This spurred the search for new markets overseas. The hope of establishing a trade route to Asia, especially one that went northeast because of England's need for trees for ships' masts and for hemp and naval stores, occupied the minds of many. Although they could not reach China by sea by this route—ice blocked the way—they did establish an important trade with Russia.

During the reign of Mary I, an important institution emerged to promote, conduct, and oversee English interests abroad: the joint stock company (the forerunner of the modern corporation). By 1555, a group of English merchants had banded together and received a royal charter as the Muscovy Company. The company enjoyed a monopoly of English trade rights with Russia, over the Northeast Passage from Europe to Asia, and over a prospective Northwest Passage to Asia.[12] This joint stock company became the model for future English overseas trading and colonizing ventures. In the sixteenth and early seventeenth centuries, these included the Levant Company (with rights to Turkey and the eastern Mediterranean), the East India Company (India), the London Company (Virginia), and the Massachusetts Bay Company (Massachusetts). The companies competed with court favorites, individuals and groups of individuals who received patents containing rights and privileges abroad. Thus, there were two models in England for overseas expansion: companies and individuals. Humphrey Gilbert and Ralegh would pursue colonization as individuals, with patent rights granted by the queen.

When Ralegh was in his teens, Gilbert and others challenged the Muscovy Company's rights to the northwest through three major overseas projects that overlapped at the end of the 1570s: to discover a Northwest Passage to Asia through or around America; to challenge Spain in the Americas by pirating treasure at sea and on land, including building bases and settlements in the Caribbean or on the nearby American mainland; and to colonize lands on the northwest Atlantic coast, which seemed the least attractive option.[13]

Though Gilbert articulated to the queen the desirability of pursuing all three endeavors, hoping she would choose him to lead the English adventurers, she appointed Martin Frobisher and Francis Drake to search for new routes to Asia and attack the Spanish in America, respectively. Both had enormous impact on English overseas expansion in the coming decades. Drake set a course that tempted a generation of Englishmen; plundering the Iberians (Spanish and Portuguese) provided the quickest way to wealth. Frobisher's expedition taught the English what not to do: although he was supposed to find a passage to Asia, his investors sidetracked him to search for gold, which spiraled into a national embarrassment that lost the investors their money and left the rich hesitant to invest in long-term overseas projects.

Gilbert had wanted to search for the Northwest Passage, but the Muscovy Company denied him the right to sail except as a company employee. When the Muscovy Company later refused Frobisher the right to sail, the queen granted license to Frobisher. By late July 1576, Frobisher had crossed the Atlantic Ocean to Baffin Bay near Greenland, where he and his men discovered a black stone that they stored as a memento of their journey but that ultimately stimulated one of the great fiascos of English overseas expansion.

The expedition unwound. Ice floes blocked the way forward; temperatures dropped though it was the middle of August. Before departing Greenland, the English encountered Inuits. They exchanged presents, and the two parties interacted with amity. But for unknown reasons, local people seized a small boat the English had brought along for exploring shallow waters and captured five Englishmen—never to be seen again by their fellows. With only thirteen men, no boat to go ashore, and a foot of snow on the ship's deck, Frobisher captured an Inuit and sailed for home.[14] In London, his expedition party received a hero's welcome—they had been thought dead, but they brought back the Inuit, proof that England had crossed the Atlantic and made landfall.

Though the expedition had accomplished virtually nothing, and the ailing Inuit soon died, the black rock Frobisher brought home led to new developments. Despite an array of assayers declaring the rock worthless, a Venetian goldsmith claimed it contained gold.[15] The queen and several of her ministers, excited at the prospect of gold, sent another expedition to retrieve more of the valuable ore. Separately, the queen granted the rights to colonize in America to Humphrey Gilbert, thus confining the Frobisher expedition to collecting ore—the queen did not want them to stray from making her money. On the other hand, the grant to Gilbert might not have been considered that important. To most English, the idea of settling land in America paled in comparison to looking for the Northwest Passage or discovering gold and silver.

Frobisher departed in May 1577. As became usual for English overseas fleets, captains impressed criminals for service. Miners and gentlemen composed the rest of the crew of 150 or so who sailed on the *Ayde* and at least four others of the queen's ships. Because he was instructed to return with more Inuits, one of Frobisher's first acts upon landing on Greater Island was to grab two Native men, who wrested free and sank an arrow into his buttocks.[16] English reinforcements recaptured one of the men and later subdued additional Inuits.

Despite it being mid-July, ice impeded mobility, though the English collected much black ore. English-Inuit hostilities continued as word spread of the interlopers' arrival. The painter John White, whom Ralegh later sent to Virginia to record Indian life, painted the skirmish at "Bloody Point," depicting Inuits on a cliff firing arrows onto an English ship, and the English returning fire with their guns. Typical of White's paintings, nothing was sensationalized. The battle is not even the dominant motif of the painting, ceding prominence to an Inuit in a kayak that takes up the width of the picture, serenely paddling in the foreground of the battle. The "fact" of the battle was less important than portraying the people in the context of the landscape, a stark, treeless terrain, with ice in the water and Inuits smartly clothed in parkas.

The expedition officially claimed the land for the queen and then sailed home, carrying three captives and a two-hundred-ton pile of ore. The unfortunate Inuits died soon after arrival in England, though not before one of them, Kalicho, demonstrated his kayaking and hunting skills in the River Avon. The Russians, Spanish, and French eyed the activities of the English on Greenland with suspicion. But there was no gold. The queen, her Privy Councilors, and other investors grew frustrated. The queen allowed three competing groups to attempt to extract gold from the black stone, which tripled the Crown's investment with the cost of constructing a different furnace for each group. Despite these setbacks, a third voyage was made to obtain more rock. But this expedition, too, was a complete bust.

The lesson learned by the queen, her councilors and their wives (many of whom had invested in the enterprise), and others of the propertied classes: be circumspect in investing in English activities across the Atlantic; investing in trade and plundering the Spanish of their New World possessions were much safer bets than finding gold in North America. The English remained interested in discovering a Northwest Passage and in settling the lands in the north but also peculiarly ignorant of how difficult it would be to colonize the cold terrain and sail through a Northwest Passage.

They did look in other directions. Some wished to discover southern routes to Asia. The Devonshire men from South West England, often called the Westcountry men—Drake, Gilbert, Ralegh, and their relations and friends—all looked to follow the Spanish to more temperate climates in the Americas. The Devonshire men sought to increase the English presence in South America, partly to establish a base from

3. Skirmish at Bloody Point

which to plunder the Spanish. John Hawkins and William Hawkins sailed frequently to Spanish American ports, and Richard Grenville, Ralegh's cousin, sailed around the Caribbean and developed interest in colonizing Florida.

Drake had as much experience as any Englishman in sailing American waters. He had first sailed to the Americas as a young man in the early 1560s with his elder second cousin John Hawkins; he was included in the 1568 expedition that fought the Spanish at San Juan de Ulúa in Mexico, where the English commander abandoned over a hundred men, who were ultimately punished by the Inquisition. By the early 1570s, Drake had become a practiced raider of ships and towns in Spanish America, well on his way to becoming England's most famous pirate. On Drake's early forays, the lack of a safe haven created logistical problems and extended the time and danger of plundering. On one foray in 1573, in the company of French pirates and *Cimarrones*—African slaves who had run away from the Spanish and whom Drake allied with—Drake captured an immense treasure of gold and silver from a mule train near Nombre de Dios in modern-day Panama.[17] He and his men could not remove the stores of riches, so they buried much of it, which a Spanish squadron largely recovered. This experience made it clear that a permanent English presence in the Americas would be most useful for pirating Spanish America.

Grenville led the way in pushing for English exploration around the equator, but the timing was not right in the mid-1570s, when Elizabeth sought to maintain good relations with Spain. She frequently steered new courses with Spain in response to the vicissitudes of foreign policy. In 1577, however, as relations deteriorated Elizabeth was more open to challenging the Spanish, and she approved Drake exploring the Pacific side of the Americas after first sailing through the Straits of Magellan—a Southwest Passage to Asia. The queen licensed Drake to trade in places not controlled by any European prince,[18] which allowed her to disavow any untoward activities on his part. He also was supposed to return the way he went.

The 1577 voyage turned out to be Drake's most famous. With five ships (and several pinnaces carried by the ships), he embarked on a three-year journey (1577–1580). He conducted reconnaissance of the Pacific Coast, plundered Chile and Peru, and reached at least as far north as California. Drake captured Spanish and Portuguese ships, held captives for ransom, then decided against returning through the treacherous Straits of Magellan, and instead sailed west across the

Pacific, circumnavigating the globe.[19] Having brought with him a quartet of musicians, Drake, who often sang with the band, conducted the first world tour by a musical group. He returned to England a national hero in September 1580, having demonstrated the profitability and utility of combining exploration with trade and piracy. In addition to American booty, he brought home trade goods from Asia. Investors rejoiced at an estimated 4,700 percent return on their investment. While Drake was away, the English had continued to pursue their interests in North America, but his success showed what the English could accomplish overseas, and not just in the Atlantic but around the globe.

Drake's adventures pointed the way for England to obtain wealth through a combination of plunder, exploration, and trade. Frobisher's expedition deterred the English from seeking gold through mining. Ralegh's education in overseas expansion developed not only from the example of Drake, a man he later partnered with in challenging Spain's New World empire, but also from that of his elder half brother Humphrey Gilbert, who theorized, proposed, and promoted multiple overseas activities and also gave Ralegh a prominent place in his enterprise. To obtain a position of prominence to expand the queen's interests and domain abroad, Humphrey Gilbert had to prove he was worthy. He would do so by offering the queen a vision of how England could challenge Spain and take its place as a maritime power.

CHAPTER 2

Annoying the King of Spain

Blueprints, Legalities, and Baby Steps

Ralegh likely would not have become a colonizer without his brother Humphrey Gilbert. Gilbert played a huge role in defining for Queen Elizabeth the overseas activities that England should undertake and rationalizing their importance. Gilbert took Ralegh under his wing and educated him for a life of service to the queen, while instilling in him the importance of England becoming a maritime power. More than anyone else, Gilbert also pursued actual English settlement of lands in America. In many ways, Gilbert provided a model for Ralegh as a courtier, imperialist, and servant of the queen.

Gilbert was born in the mid to late 1530s, likely in 1537. His (and Walter's) mother was niece to Katherine "Kat" Ashley (or Astley), Queen Elizabeth's much-beloved governess.[1] Gilbert attended Eton College before spending some time at Oxford, and his connection with Ashley paved the way for his joining the queen's household when he was about seventeen years old—about the time Walter was born. Gilbert subsequently could be found at the Middle Temple Court of Law in London, presumably studying law, before he undertook military service in France in aid of French Protestants, receiving a wound during the ill-fated Newhaven (Le Havre) expedition. His commander, the Earl of Warwick, told the queen, "Surely, there is not a vallyanter man that lyveth; and so hath his dedes well shewyd it now at this time."[2] As noted earlier, Gilbert spent time in the Irish service, first under Sidney in Ulster, and then in the First Desmond War, where he displayed brutal efficiency subduing rebels. In Gilbert, we find the combination of elements that Elizabeth and many other elite Elizabethans—women and men—found so attractive. Educated and articulate, he exhibited bravery to the point of recklessness and possessed an inquisitive nature and adept social graces.

Gilbert's mysticism might also have endeared him to the queen. Elizabeth and her favorite, the Earl of Leicester, both relied heavily on astrology and patronized the services of the famed magus Dr. John Dee. The Gilbert brothers and Ralegh became close associates of Dee, all sharing mystical interest in overseas expansion. They believed that discoveries in America, particularly through the Northwest Passage, could directly lead to the end of the world and the return of Christ. Gilbert recorded his mystical visions in early 1567 and wrote a book of magic about his contacting spirits.[3]

Both Gilbert and Dee came to be much trusted by the queen. Dee received the task of drawing up the queen's legal rights to colonize in America. Gilbert won the honor to colonize. Both understood that English expansion to America depended on it being a paying proposition, but their interest and vision continued to be shaped by the spiritual belief that New World discovery would draw Christians closer to God. Ralegh inherited from Gilbert this worldview, which they combined with a Humanist method of rational application to achieve one's goals. They both thought and planned much about overseas activities, and they deeply respected scientific inquiry, with the belief that science would not only enlarge human understanding of the physical world but also increase spiritual awareness.

Gilbert expressed his intellectual vision for English overseas expansion in 1566 when he wrote for Elizabeth "A discourse of a discoverie for a new passage to Cataia." This lengthy treatise argued for a Northwest Passage to Asia, which he volunteered to discover for England.[4] The tract won the support of the queen's chief minister, William Cecil, Lord Burghley. In exchange for discovering the passage, Gilbert sought monopoly rights over the trade route for himself and his brothers John and Adrian, but, as noted above, the Muscovy Company possessed the rights and would let Gilbert sail only as a company employee. Gilbert refused. Subsequently, while stationed in Ireland, he concocted schemes to colonize there.

At first Gilbert hoped for land in Ulster for himself and his Devonshire associates. But his attention turned from the north to the south, to Munster province, as a more feasible place for settlement. Offshore fishing provided much of the attraction of southeast Ireland, which Spanish and Basque fishermen exploited. But Gilbert and his Devonshire neighbors also wanted to plant settlers to cultivate the land—in the place of the Irish. By the time the project received approval from the English government, the First Desmond War had broken out and both warfare and Gilbert's responsibilities as military governor put the plans on hold.[5] It would be many years before the queen approved settlement of the Munster Plantation, and it would be Ralegh, not Gilbert, who played the lead role. But Gilbert's service to the queen and his articulation of the imperatives of colonization paved the way for Ralegh's rise.

After Sidney knighted him on New Year's Day 1569/70, Gilbert departed Ireland claiming problems with his eyes. Once his eyes improved, he continued to provide military service to the queen, wherever required—in the Netherlands, France, and Ireland—which kept him in the Crown's good graces. He also served on many commissions in England in the mid-1570s, accumulated a substantial estate, and found time to design an institution of higher learning—an academy—which he hoped the queen would finance. This academy, Gilbert believed, would promote English knowledge and expertise about the world and dramatically improve the nation's statecraft.

Gilbert's inspiration likely came from Portugal's and Spain's long experience training their navigators in maritime affairs.[6] England's knowledge of the seas lagged considerably. Crossing the Atlantic posed an array of problems, not the least of which was returning to a place previously reached. Charts and instruments of navigation, as well as mariners skilled in the use of both, were necessary for transoceania enterprise. John Dee helped English explorers by collecting the maps and charts he gathered through his extensive ties with publishers, scientists, and an array of intellectuals throughout Europe. Mariners, including the Gilbert brothers and Ralegh, made good use of Dee's personal library. Gilbert sought to systematize the collecting and archiving of knowledge, intending to institutionalize the training of men in the arts of navigation. He detailed the need to provide a broad education for a large class of men to assist the queen in ruling an England that would increasingly engage in overseas activities. He foresaw England becoming a global power and recommended the kinds of knowledge and training that bureaucrats would need to administer the nation's far-flung interests.

Gilbert designed his proposed academy to educate young men in London, especially the "youth of Nobility and Gentlemen" of England. The academy would provide a more practical and well-rounded education than Oxford or Cambridge. Gilbert stressed language instruction—a necessity for greater English interaction in Europe. The classics, Greek, Hebrew, and Latin would still be taught, but modern French, Italian, Spanish, and High Dutch (German) also would be offered. Gilbert also emphasized students strengthening their English language skills, by having an "Orator" to "practize his schollers," so they would be capable of giving advice to the queen on matters of "war and state."[7]

Preparation for public service would include the study of both civil and common law, because students ultimately would become justices of the peace, sheriffs, and attorneys. They also would receive instruction in military affairs. Bridging the civic and military responsibilities, and among the highest paid professors, was the "Reader of Morall Philosophie" (£100 per year), who would teach both civil and martial policies. The former made up a sort of comparative civics. The latter would comparatively analyze English and foreign armed forces, their arming, training, and usage.

A mathematician would prepare students in cosmography and astronomy—the arts necessary for navigation. He would instruct in the use of navigation instruments and, by using ship models, teach the parts of a ship, its rigging, furnishing, and the "perfect arte of a Shipwright." This instruction would be complemented by a cartographer to teach the drawing of maps and sea charts, the "rules of proportion . . . perspective," and measurement.

Gilbert proposed special arrangements be made for the study of the arts of alchemy, representing the latest developments in what today we call chemistry, that is to say, the discovery of the physical properties of matter, in order, through manipulation and combination, to create new substances. Many of England's leading mathematicians and scientists believed that Oxford and Cambridge had no interest in, and in fact bore hostility toward, fostering new discoveries of the physical world and, in confining themselves to the study of math and science of the ancient world, cocooned themselves in the belief that there was nothing new to learn except for what might irreligiously impose on God's domain. Gilbert's academy included the new math and science and called for legal protection of practitioners and collection and promotion of their findings. The academy would employ a Doctor of Physic to teach medicine and surgery, the latter essential since the only other place to learn was "in a Barbers shoppe." This physician and the natural philosopher would both be exempt from prosecution under the "Statute of the 5th of Henry the 4th, touching multiplicacion." This law prohibited alchemy that would increase the supply of gold and silver, which could presumably ruin England's currency. Although it was not repealed until 1689, alchemy seems not to have been punished, with but one prosecution for the crime during the reign of Edward VI, and its practice was authorized by monarchs. Yet Gilbert was certainly aware of the act, calling for suspension of prosecution at the academy so that experiments could be conducted publicly. Gilbert thought it necessary for the physician and natural philosopher, "by the fire and otherwise, to search and try out the secrets of Nature as many waies as they possiblie may." Free of government opposition, Gilbert expected the physician and the natural philosopher not only to conduct experiments to uncover the secrets of the material world but also to report their findings yearly and then archive their reports for their successors.

Gilbert hoped his academy would instill "glory" in "your majesty [that] shall make your sellfe second to no Prince living." Her praises would be sung in other lands. When her people went abroad, the "English gentleman" would be celebrated as "eyther a Souldiour, a Philosophor, or a gallant Cowrtier." But why did the queen need to extend her domain outside of England? Glbert addressed this central issue only in passing. Almost as a throwaway, and unelaborated upon, Gilbert provided two words to explain the imperative of Englishmen going abroad: the English inhabited a "frozen island." This phrase almost appears comical, but English who promoted overseas expansion typically emphasized England's barren environment. Anyone at Elizabeth's court who read Gilbert's proposal for the academy understood that England was a "frozen island." The English believed their homeland lacking in the natural resources available in warmer climes. Increasingly shut out of European markets, and barred by the Spanish from trading with Spain's American colonies, frustrated English perceived the nation's future lay overseas, where they would find the resources necessary to survive and prosper in a Europe increasingly dominated by Spain.

Elizabeth did not build the academy.[8] But Gilbert's dream articulated a vision of England on the precipice of overseas expansion and growing involvement in Europe. His plan reflected the Renaissance ideal of the scholarly man of action whose physical prowess was an extension of civic virtue and learning. The ideal gentlemen could be relied upon by his monarch to administer and adjudicate the law in the counties, lead men into battle, cut a polite figure at court, conduct errands abroad, advise his social betters, including the queen, and perhaps undertake or lead maritime enterprise. Gilbert's younger half brother Walter Ralegh epitomized this ideal.

Ralegh followed in Gilbert's footsteps and then walked far beyond them. Both matriculated briefly at Oxford, attained martial skills as young men in France, and promoted study of the practical arts in London. They both cultivated the character of the soldier/scholar/civic leader who devoted his career to service for the monarch (while lining his pockets with rewards). They both appreciated, more than most, the growing importance of England asserting itself overseas for economic and strategic purposes, and that the English had to sharpen their skills in foreign languages and navigation, and in their ability to explore the seas, open new markets, and find new places to "plant" people outside of this "frozen island." Ralegh excelled at the arts Gilbert prescribed for the queen's courtiers. He mastered oratory and the language arts. He compiled his own great library and became expert in civic policy and military strategy. Ralegh promoted English interests at home and abroad, advised the queen and her ministers, and did their bidding in a variety of ways and through numerous appointments. Like his elder brothers, Ralegh studied alchemy and became expert in the laboratory, analyzing the properties of physical substances and creating new substances, such as medicines. Ralegh came to epitomize the Renaissance man of late Tudor England. While Ralegh pursued his education through deep study and on the battlefields in France, his elder half brother Humphrey Gilbert continued to serve the queen while trying to convince her to allow him to pursue his and her interests overseas.

—

GILBERT CONSTRUCTED the earliest and most overt, if not the most extravagant, statement of Elizabethan militancy against Spain in overseas expansion. In 1577, while Frobisher sought the Northwest Passage to Asia, and Drake sailed to the Pacific, Gilbert proposed taking English overseas activities to a new level by colonizing lands outside of Europe. Gilbert not only helped define methods and goals overseas, but he served as a model for Ralegh. Gilbert's interest lay in establishing new colonies but also in replacing the Spanish in their American domain. He submitted a paper to the queen, "A Discourse on how hir Majestie may annoy the K: of Spayne," which proposed numerous ways to reduce the power of King Philip II (and other Europeans).

Gilbert volunteered to go to Newfoundland to seize the fisheries and burn or confiscate the ships there belonging to Spain, France, and Portugal. He naively blustered that "their shipping being once spoyled, it is likely that they will never be recovered to the like number and strength."[9] (Ralegh did not inherit this bluster.) Gilbert predicted disastrous results for England's competitors: foreign princes will lose "great revenues" by their exclusion from the fisheries, and their people must "endure great famine."[10] Here we see a military policy soon implemented in Ireland: creating famine to defeat one's enemies. Gilbert might not have been the first to recommend this policy to the queen, but many of his proposals were adopted in the coming decade: creating famine was used by the English in the Second Desmond War soon after Gilbert's recommendation to employ the tactic against Spain. Gilbert justified the policy against Spain, even though the two countries were not at war, "as [it is] lawfull in christen pollicie, to prevent a mischief" beforehand, instead of waiting to seek revenge after the mischief is done, "especiallie seing that god him selfe is a party in the common quarrelles now a foote."[11]

The conquest of Newfoundland should be followed by an assault "to disposses" Philip II of the West Indies—not just to remove the Spanish "but also to possesse for ever" the spoils of gold and silver mines, the rich soils, and all the trade. This would "bringeth a most happy conclusion" by making the queen's enemies poor and herself rich. England must go on the offensive to defend Elizabeth's realm. They must destroy enemy shipping to protect England "from all forraine perills."[12] This simple, brash policy became central to England in the coming decades, especially promoted by both the queen and Ralegh. The destruction of enemy shipping was viewed as the best method to protect the realm. Ralegh would deem this superior to building fortifications. He would also devote much of his career to dispossessing Spain of the West Indies, pursuing gold and silver, and seeking out the rich soils and trade of America that Humphrey said England should pursue.

The same day that Gilbert delivered this tract he submitted another with more detail on the strategy to be followed against Spain.[13] After describing Spanish treatment of the English as no better than "a Turke or Sarasen," Gilbert recommended wielding force against the King of Spain so he "knowe[s] that any kinde of peace shalbe better for him then warres with England." Gilbert proposed an attack on the Spanish treasure fleet and the ships of Spanish subjects,[14] followed by the conquest of Hispaniola and Cuba to obtain gold and sugar. He also recommended a strategy that Drake used in Central America—alliance with the slaves and ex-slaves of the Spanish. Gilbert noted that on Hispaniola there lived "a great number of Negros . . . that some tyme were slaves and have ronn away from theire Masters, and do dwell in many places of the Iland and have wives and children and be valiaunt men and theise will gladly receave ayde and libertie, and so they may be brought to do great service." What better allies than those liberated from oppression?

Gilbert's and Drake's willingness to countenance alliance with ex-slaves of the Spanish shows how the English viewed Africans at the time. Africans *could* be slaves, yet the English did not consider that all Africans should be slaves, nor that *only* Africans should be slaves. In the sixteenth century, slavery was yet to be confined to particular groups in the Western world, as there were tens of thousands of Europeans enslaved in North Africa and in Ottoman Asia, Turks enslaved by Europeans, and so on. Gilbert and Drake had no need to justify alliance with Africans, because skin color was not considered by the English as a badge of status. Skin color and perceived cultural differences could be sources of prejudice—Queen Elizabeth tried to bar Africans from England in the 1590s—but racist ideologies that designated whole people to one or another legal status, as free or unfree, had yet to form. Class, according to blood, remained the most significant divisor in Europe. As far as entire groups of people were concerned, in 1570s England, what mattered was that the *enemy of my enemy is my friend*, especially if they were, in Gilbert's words, "valiaunt men."[15]

In 1577, Elizabeth was not ready for war with Spain, but she was intrigued by Gilbert's arguments for English colonization of America in places where the Spanish had not settled. She had concerns about the legalities, however. If she planted new colonies, extending her sovereignty to new lands, she wanted her possessions to be on secure legal grounds for acceptance by other monarchs. Did she have the right to extend her sovereignty to the Americas, which, soon after Columbus had returned from there, the pope had granted to King Ferdinand to missionize the Natives?

Most generations of historians have assumed that the Protestant Elizabeth did not feel bound by papal judgments. But England had implicitly accepted the pope's decision for decades. Historian Ken Macmillan recently has shown that John Dee, whom Elizabeth employed to investigate her rights in America, carefully constructed legal arguments that did not impinge on whether the pope possessed the right to issue the papal bull that divided between Spain and Portugal the right to missionize in America and Asia. Dee told Elizabeth that she and England held an array of claims to North America that preceded the pope's decision and Columbus's sailing. Elizabeth's grandfather and father had acted on these claims by sending explorers to North America to places that the Spanish never visited and certainly had not secured for themselves. These claims, Dee believed, could attain international recognition.[16] But there was another reason for England to not explicitly argue against a papal bull: the queen did not want to alienate English Catholics, whom she expected to play a significant role as investors, sailors, and colonists.

John Dee was the right man for Elizabeth and her chief advisors to turn to about the legalities of overseas expansion. He had studied cartography and geography at the University of Louvain with two of Europe's foremost experts, Gerhard Mercator and Gemma Frisius. Today Dee is mostly remembered as a magus and astrologer, but he likely was England's most knowledgeable individual about world cartography. Sea captains, including Ralegh and members of Ralegh's family, consulted Dee for his knowledge of sea routes and geography, and he deciphered omens to suggest when they should sail.[17] Dee drew on the stars, crystals, and other talismans for answers but also his magnificent library. For additional assistance, he employed a full-time scryer, Edward Kelly, who mediated Dee's conversations with angels. Ultimately, Dee received a large grant of America from Humphrey Gilbert and even named a river in North America after himself.[18]

In 1577 and 1578, Elizabeth employed Dee to draw up several papers on English rights to colonize, explore, and establish trade routes to Asia via North America. In late November 1577, Dee had three meetings with the queen and her secretary, Francis Walsingham, to discuss his findings. These meetings and his papers played a significant role in gaining Elizabeth's support for English overseas activities.[19] The legal arguments Dee put forth balanced discovery with possession. Discovery gave legal rights to a monarch whose explorers had reached a land before the explorers of other monarchs. Failure to follow up discovery with occupation, however, passed legal rights to another monarch who permanently colonized a new land. The English returned to this argument time and again: to the English, claims must be secured by usage, and they held this view toward their own colonists in Ireland

and America, who could lose their claims if they did not actually effect occupation.

Dee did not address the rights of Natives living on the land. He likely assumed that the Native peoples possessed natural rights to their lands, and their leaders would become vassals of a greater monarch, Elizabeth. Native chieftains would share vassalage status with those English who received patents from her.[20] People could not be dispossessed of their lands, but particular monarchs—the few—held sovereignty over the lands of lesser kings.[21] Ralegh would propose this model to Queen Elizabeth in his plans for colonizing South America: rather than conquering Indians, he adamantly recommended that Elizabeth pursue a course of alliance and noninterference with indigenous polities that would accept her sovereignty and protection.

Dee undermined Spain's and Portugal's claims to the Americas outside of places of actual settlement. Columbus's discoveries were inconsequential because Columbus had landed nowhere near the North Atlantic lands reached by the Cabots as representatives of the Tudor monarchy. And according to Dee, King Arthur had conquered Iceland, Greenland, and many of the islands north of mainland Europe and along the northern reaches of North America long before Columbus. After Arthur, Elizabeth's claims were reinforced by others who sailed to these lands from Britain, including Madog, a Welsh prince whose story we learn more about in Part Two. Dee cited the more contemporary explorations of Frobisher and Stephen Borough as further confirmation of Elizabeth's claims. Dee urged Elizabeth to actively sponsor English expansion into these lands before the Spanish tried to make good their claim through occupation.[22] She assented by granting to Humphrey Gilbert a patent to colonize North America.

Gilbert likely knew for some time of the queen's impending grant and had been readying his fleet for a few months. He received the patent in June 1578 and tried to sail in September and October, but not until mid-November did the winds prove favorable to escape English shores. Though Gilbert's patent gave him six years to permanently establish a colony, the enterprise was already off to an inauspicious start.

The difficulty of the winds was only part of Gilbert's problem. A dispute with Sir Henry Knollys, whose father was treasurer of the Royal Household, rent the fleet in two. Gilbert commanded seven ships, and Knollys had three. Knollys apparently thought the purpose of the expedition was to pirate the King of Spain's ships, whereas Gilbert intended to colonize. Knollys can hardly be blamed for his mistake, because

Gilbert had promoted attacking Spanish positions and ships in his papers on annoying the King of Spain, and Knollys might have thought that colonization was simply a smokescreen to hide the expedition's true intent. Knollys seems to have used the promise of booty to enlist men, and he recruited the famed pirate John Callis to captain one of his ships. Knollys might have thought himself immune to prosecution because of his father's position in the queen's household, and he apparently suffered no legal problems for the piracy.

The English felt persecuted by the Spanish and Portuguese, believing it unfair that the Iberians claimed much of the world as their exclusive domain to colonize and trade. But the English seized any ships they could. English government records of the 1570s and 1580s are replete with foreigners' complaints of English piracy, particularly by the men of the South West—from Devonshire and Cornwall. Contrary to popular belief, these men were not privateers; they carried no letter of marque (license) from the government to seize ships of wartime enemies—England was not at war. Even when they did obtain license, the English tended to take whatever ship they could regardless of who sailed it.

Little is known of Gilbert's fleet after its November 1578 departure. He had enough provisions for a year but seems to have been away for only six months. He sailed to Ireland to obtain more supplies, departed Ireland, then returned. What he did next is unknown, but, apparently, he never sailed for America. Carew Ralegh, Walter's older brother, who captained the *Hope of Greenway* for Gilbert, also did not get far and returned with his leaky ship to England soon after departure. Walter Ralegh, in command of the *Falcon*, a royal ship, had the most eventful voyage.

The *Falcon* and likely another ship were the only ships in Gilbert's expedition actually to sail for America. According to one account, Ralegh wanted "to doo somewhat worthie honor."[23] He made it as far as the Cape Verde Islands off of West Africa. Apparently running short of supplies, he and the other ship headed home, faced down storms, and encountered some form of naval opposition that led to a loss of men before limping into Plymouth six months later. The derring-do of Ralegh contributed to his reputation as a man of action. Given the fact that none of the other leaders in Gilbert's expedition made it far from British shores, it seemed something of an accomplishment.

CHAPTER 3

Ralegh and the
Second Desmond War

Though Gilbert planned to depart again for America even before Ralegh had returned, the queen's Privy Council postponed
their excursion. At the end of May, the Privy Council wrote Sir
John Gilbert and "required [him] frendlie to advise" his brothers Humphrey and Walter not to sail. They or members of their "companie"
had recently taken all the oranges and lemons off a Spanish ship anchored in "her majesties streames at Walfled Bay within the Castell,"[1]
and the council demanded the return of the bark and the fruit or full
compensation. It was one thing to abscond with a foreign vessel at sea
and quite another when it was under Her Majesty's protection in port.
Just in case Humphrey and Walter did not follow their brother John's
"frendlie" advice, the Privy Council ordered the sheriff and other Devonshire officials, including the vice admiral and justices of the peace,
to prevent anyone from sailing, even if they had put in bonds, but
particularly Humphrey and Walter, who should be brought to land if
already on their ships in harbor.[2] By mid-July, the pillaged ship was "recovered and restored" to its owner. The guilty parties were members
"of the companie of Sir Humffrey Gilberte," but he was not held responsible. The perpetrators were too poor to compensate the Spaniard
the £100 value of the fruit, so the council ordered that the people of
Devon had to provide him three "quarters," that is three-quarters of a
ton of grain.[3]

By the time the Spanish owner was granted compensation Gilbert was gone. The government might have been willing to tax the locals for the stolen citrus because they needed Humphrey and his ships. Word arrived in England of a flotilla of soldiers from the Continent sailing for Ireland, and the government charged Gilbert with preventing its landing. He missed the flotilla and instead raided the Spanish coast at Galicia before sailing to Ireland. He captured a variety of foreign prizes. When his service ended in the autumn, the government recalled him to England. He left his ships on the west coast of Ireland. Some of his men stole his ships.

Gilbert would not sail again for America until 1583. For three and a half years, English resources that might have gone to overseas expeditions to America had to be devoted to Ireland—the pope's decision to become militarily involved in Irish affairs deterred the English from America; in the coming decade American colonization would be frequently sidetracked by the same three things: events in Ireland, relations with Spain, and the English propensity to go plundering at sea.

The extended postponement of Gilbert's expedition to America proved a boon for Ralegh. He received a military appointment in Ireland, which propelled forward his education, skill development, and career. In Ireland, he learned how to command men, and he displayed bravery and acumen in difficult situations that brought him notoriety at court. He also studied the landscape and its people so that when he was granted a huge portion to colonize, he displayed extraordinary vision for what it would take to succeed. The few years he spent in Ireland as a young man in his mid-twenties provided Ralegh a foundation of imperial and colonial expertise that made him a trusted voice on overseas affairs.

—

AFTER THE EARL OF DESMOND returned to Ireland in 1573, a period of fighting led to the earl giving up, receiving pardon from the queen, and taking on the task of securing peace in Munster province by the late summer of 1574. The events that followed ultimately prepared the way for English colonization of southern Ireland.

Within a year and a half, relations again deteriorated as some Anglo-Irish and Irish complained about the English land tax, known as the cess, which they believed was set inordinately high. The Desmonds had lost their rights to coign and livery and still wanted to find ways to collect monies to support their private armies. Without coign and livery, many of the gallowglass and kerne were unemployed and roaming the countryside. These soldiers were supposed to register with the government and take up farming. Many refused, and English authorities captured and executed more than four hundred in the late 1570s.[4] When some of the Desmonds decided to once again take up arms, they had a ready body to support them—the alienated professional soldiers who had once served in the private armies of Anglo-Irish and Irish lords. In July 1579, the Earl of Desmond's cousin, James Fitzmaurice Fitzgerald, after having made his way through France to Rome, convinced the pope to help the Desmonds. Fitzmaurice returned to Ireland, gathered allies, and fought both English and Irish who opposed him. In September 1580, the pope's six ships arrived and fortified Dingle harbor at Smerwick (Dún An Óir), in County Kerry.[5] While English forces laid waste to Desmond lands and castles in the southeast, the six hundred Italian, Spanish, and Basque troops sent by the pope dug in, leading the English to siege their fortifications.

Francis Walsingham, who held much responsibility for Irish military affairs, sent Ralegh to Ireland as a captain in the midst of the Second Desmond War. This was probably Ralegh's first appointment of significant military authority on land—and it provided him intimate familiarity with the precise landscape he later colonized in Ireland. His initial attainment of renown at the English court owed much to his service as a captain in Ireland.

The captains held an extremely important position in England's administration and securing of its interests. They worked on the ground in a variety of locales daily interacting with Irish and Anglo-Irish at all levels of society. Indeed, the captains usually were the highest-ranking officers responsible for directing the soldiers, securing law and order, and protecting English settlers and interests. The lord deputy moved the captains and their companies around Ireland as needed. Captains typically occupied a castle or coastal fort, conducted patrols, and captured and delivered suspected rebels to the lord deputy or provincial governors. They had at their disposal both horsemen and footmen, but the former allowed them to travel far and wide, depending on the government's needs. The captains were responsible for feeding, paying, and otherwise directing their men and submitted the troops' pay and expense forms to members of the English Privy Council or their appointees, not to the lord deputy.[6]

The oldest extant letter of Ralegh's was written from Cork to Lord Burghley, the chief officer in Elizabeth's government. It documented and explained the pay and expenses for his men on their voyage from England to the Isle of Wight to Ireland.[7] As he reported to the Privy Council and, particularly, to Sir Francis Walsingham, who dispensed patronage and directed the captains' activities, Ralegh had developed a clear sense of how the English government operated in Ireland and also the breadth of relations between the Irish, Anglo-Irish, and the colonial administration and power.[8] Ralegh also saw how his own service and his assessment of colonialism could open doors for him at the English court.

Superlative service as a captain in Ireland could lead to knighthood. Though the ranks of English captains were filled with men now lost in the obscurity of history, a fair number found good service a stepping stone to other appointments. Ralph Lane served as Ralegh's governor in America after being a captain in Ireland. Lane then returned to Ireland as a captain and was knighted. Richard Bingham, a relation of Ralegh's from Dorset, had extensive military service for over twenty years before becoming a captain in Ireland. On land and sea, he saw action in many parts of Europe and in the Mediterranean, occasionally conducting informal diplomatic negotiations. At age fifty, older than most of those sent as captains to Ireland, the already-pensioned soldier served at the siege of Smerwick, and then combatted pirates before receiving appointment as governor of Connacht, Ireland, in 1584, which led to his knighthood. For Bingham, his actions at Smerwick against the papal troops probably played a significant role in his assumption of greater positions of authority.

Less than two months after their arrival, in early November 1580, the papal troops at Smerwick surrendered to Arthur Grey, Lord Deputy of Ireland. All defenders, save for a handful of "gentlemen," were killed by sword. Legend has it that Grey offered terms to the defenders and then treacherously disregarded his promise. "Grey's faith" in Ireland represents broken promises. It also has come to symbolize the violence of English colonialism in Elizabethan Ireland—and Ralegh's association with that violence. Ironically, most of the violence at Smerwick was directed against non-Irish, and, in all probability, Ralegh was not at Smerwick.

Grey's account of what happened at Smerwick states that when he met with an Italian and a Spanish leader of the forces, they admitted they had not been sent by the King of Spain but by the pope. Grey asserted, in that case, their "unjust desperate and wicked actions" served "one that neither from God nor man could claim any princely power or empire . . . the right Anti-Christ."[9] Grey's secretary, Edmund Spenser, who was with him at Smerwick, eighteen years later defended Grey against rumors that he had promised or even given hope of terms. Spenser echoed Grey's assertion that these were not prisoners of war since they had no commission from any prince, which made them "onley adventurers that came to seeke fortune abroad."[10] The papal troops had arrived to serve with the Desmonds and their allies, according to Grey, who "were no lawfull enemies; but rebels and traytors," which made the interlopers "rogues and runnegates [renegades]." To make "terms with such rascals" was to dishonor the queen.[11] The legal and moral issue: even if the pope was a legitimate monarch, these men arrived to assist rebels against their sovereign. Rebels required no better treatment than death.

After the papal troops laid down their arms, and the enemy leaders joined Grey, he recounted, "I put in certain bands who straight fell to execution. There were 600 slain."[12] (Grey never mentioned in his report that there were Irish men and women inside the fort. An unknown writer to Secretary Walsingham confided that the Irish were hung.[13]) Many years later, after Elizabeth's death, commentators averred that she was much distressed by the massacre at Smerwick, but this is patently false. Elizabeth sent her "great thanks and commendations" to Grey, telling him that his performance was "greately to our lyking." If anything, she criticized his *sparing* of the expedition's leaders: "a principall should receave punishment before an accessary, which would have served for a terror to such as may be hereafter drawen to be executioners of so wicked an enterprise." Because they had been spared, she rebuked Grey for not sending them to London: they should have "ben reserved for os [us] to have extended towards them eyther Justice or mercy, as to os should have ben founde best."[14]

Since at least the 1840s in Ireland, Ralegh not only has been associated with the massacre at Smerwick but viewed as its instigator.[15] Yet Ralegh, as noted above, in all likelihood, was not at Smerwick. The two captains who led the massacre were two of his cousins. One was Edward Denny, whose mother and Ralegh's mother were sisters. Denny also was first cousin on his father's side to Francis Walsingham—Elizabeth's spymaster—who operated one of the most effective intelligence-gathering rings in Europe. Like Ralegh, Denny only recently had arrived in Ireland. Soon after landing, Denny wrote to Walsingham of the Irish, "The people are such, as Satan himself cannot exceed in subtlety, treachery, and cruelty." Denny held out little hope for obtaining honor in Ireland: "this kind of service is so groundless, so devoid of reputation . . . [it] happens in bogs, glens, and woods as in my opinion it might better fit mastiffs than brave gentlemen that desire to win honour."[16] Denny's prejudice against the Irish did not necessarily lead him to massacre Spanish, Italian, and Basques at Smerwick, though his zealousness to serve Grey, whom he adored, likely played a role. Killing six hundred foreign renegades who fortified themselves on the queen's land was deemed honorable because he performed this service for the queen.

The other captain who shared responsibility for the massacre was another Ralegh cousin, the aforementioned Richard Bingham. Bingham provides the most detailed eyewitness accounts of the massacre. In a letter to Ralph Lane, Bingham claimed that as they collected the prisoners, some of the English seamen joined them and initiated the violence—both sailors and soldiers "having possessed the place fell to revellinge, and spoiling, and withall to killinge, in which they never ceased, while there lived one."[17] Bingham never mentions Ralegh in his letter to Lane, nor in another he wrote of the massacre to Walsingham. Neither Bingham nor Denny nor Grey mentions Ralegh as being at Smerwick in any stage of the months-long siege or at the slaughter. Grey lavished praise for the massacre on Denny and Bingham. Nor was Ralegh included on a map of the English captains commanding the ships at Smerwick that prevented the defenders' escape by sea.[18] Bingham had no reason to exclude Ralegh, who would have received praise from the queen and Privy Council for his participation—unless he was not actually there.

After the massacre, Ralegh met up with Bingham and traveled with him to London, where Bingham went to deliver his report on Smerwick in person. Ralegh could have asked Bingham on their journey to include him in his letters, but such a bold lie would have risked Bingham's reputation. This was one "glorious" victory that Ralegh would receive no credit for at court. Some have assumed that Ralegh later received his extraordinary land grants in Ireland as a reward for leading the massacre—the queen's grant to Ralegh states that he was rewarded for his service in Ireland, but this was a common statement in grants to soldiers who saw duty there. A fabrication that appeared in an 1841 article in *The Scenery Antiquities of Ireland* (and that has been frequently cited by others) claims that a judge at Ralegh's treason trial in 1603 queried him about his behavior at Smerwick and that Ralegh responded that he was merely obeying orders[19]—I have yet to see this query and response in any of the various transcripts of the trial. It would have been an odd query to make, full of irony, at a trial where Ralegh was accused of treason in league with the Spanish to have a hostile judge ask him why he cold-bloodedly murdered the people with whom he was in cahoots.[20]

Ralegh also did not include the months of the siege in his pay records, which end in September, two months before the massacre, and do not pick up till well afterward. We can assume that Ralegh was on leave during the massacre.[21] Grey had assigned Ralegh to maintain order in County Cork, where Ralegh's cousin Richard Grenville previously had been sheriff. Unlike Denny and Bingham, the recently arrived Ralegh had no military experience leading men on land. He had commanded a ship for his brother on the voyage to America in 1578, and he had military experience as a young man in France, but not a command. I suspect that Grey was nervous about the inexperienced Ralegh, but he sized up his strengths. Ralegh was brash and brave, and like the other captains, he was out to prove himself—but his assignment for the next few years largely amounted to maintaining the queen's interests on a swathe of land along the east coast of Ireland that extended thirty miles from Cork to Youghal and inland for about twenty-five miles. This was no easy task because this territory lay in the cauldron that boiled over in both Desmond Wars. The task required someone who was energetic, diplomatic, resourceful, and intelligent and who could think on his feet (or on his horse) and act independently. This was not an assignment for either Bingham or Denny, whose military experience as campaigners made them more suited for the siege at Smerwick.

The main near-contemporary historical source responsible for placing Ralegh at Smerwick, written six years after the event, was by John Hooker, who has Ralegh directing the slaughter. Yet this account was constructed to *praise* Ralegh's service in Ireland. Hooker's placement of Ralegh at Smerwick was part of a detailed program to build Ralegh's credentials as a man worthy of being the queen's favorite. Another English source placing Ralegh at Smerwick was William Camden, who wrote in his *Annales* that Ralegh was one of the captains at Smerwick, but Camden did not pen this work until many years later when Ralegh was in prison for treason, at a time when England was at peace with Spain. One of the main purposes of Camden's history is to glorify both Elizabeth and her successor, King James. Though Camden did not blame Ralegh for the massacre, more important was his (falsely) relating how

Elizabeth detested what was done at Smerwick, an important view to push as King James wanted to maintain the peace England had finally made with Spain—better to blame the queen's soldiers (including the traitor Ralegh) for what happened to Spanish soldiers under the pope than to blame the queen, the king's kinswoman.[22]

If Ralegh had been at Smerwick, he likely would have participated in the violence. As a young captain—he was six to eight years younger than Denny and about twenty-five years younger than Bingham—he would have followed his elder cousins' lead. He understood that violence against Europeans under particular conditions was applauded by the queen and her government. He certainly supported Gilbert's earlier violence in the First Desmond War, as shortly after Smerwick he recommended to Walsingham his brother's reappointment to command in Ireland—an appointment that he thought eschewed not because of Gilbert's violence in the field, which had proved so successful, but because of his inability to control his violence in peace time. Later in his career, Ralegh theoretically approved of the use of assassination during the Nine Years' War.

In his own actions, however, we see little of the personal violence of his brother Humphrey and many of his peers. As a captain, Ralegh was a fearless leader of men. His bravery in war will be frequently remarked upon from his service in Ireland, Spain, South America, and the islands of the Atlantic. During his service in Ireland, and as a sea captain and buccaneer, an overseas colonizer, and holder of numerous offices that gave him all kinds of power over men, there is not a single instance of Ralegh brutalizing anyone—an exceptional record indeed. He engaged in fisticuffs with his peers, for which Elizabeth tossed the combatants into jail on a few occasions, but personal combat is quite different from lining the pathway to one's tent with heads and slaughtering civilians, renegades, or anyone else, as practiced by Humphrey Gilbert. Ralegh later oversaw the execution of Spanish in Trinidad as punishment or revenge for what the troops had done to his men and to local Indians. In the course of his life, Ralegh's methods of leadership revolved around his ability to work with diverse peoples. He was much more mediator than dictator or sadist. When he could, he worked to reduce and eliminate persecution and repression.

There were no diplomatic repercussions for Smerwick. Although some nineteenth- and early twentieth-century writers exclaimed a diplomatic outcry throughout Europe about the massacre, there was none. No complaint was made by the Spanish, with whom Elizabeth was officially at peace, or by the pope.[23] The queen did not have to defend what happened because the victims had not been sent by Philip II of Spain, for if the Spanish had invaded Ireland it would have been an act of war. The pope could make no complaint—his predecessor ten years before had issued a papal bull declaring Elizabeth a heretic and threatening excommunication of anyone who obeyed her. He could hardly complain about what happened to the troops he sent to invade Elizabeth's domain. As Elizabeth noted in her letter to Grey, the point of the massacre had been made—those who dared assist her rebellious subjects could expect the same treatment. There was, in Elizabeth's eyes, little difference in hanging Irish rebels or foreign brigands. Treason and invasion by interlopers were dealt with quickly and bloodily.

The Second Desmond War prepared the way for the "modern" English colonization of Ireland that placed English in large numbers outside the Pale, where most English in Ireland had lived over the previous four hundred years. The war began in 1579, before the massacre at Smerwick: Sir John of Desmond, brother of the Earl of Desmond, murdered his English friend Henry Davels, constable of Dungarvan, as he lay in bed. The act symbolized the break of the Anglo-Irish Desmonds with England. But not all Desmonds broke with the English. Nor did English Catholics feel an affinity for Irish Catholics.[24] The Desmonds and their vassals changed sides so often that their ideology, if they had one, was to maintain their lands and power as best they could against all threats.

Much of the war can be characterized as a dispute among the Anglo-Irish nobility, with local Irish supporting one or the other side. In late November 1579, anti-English Desmonds sacked and plundered Youghal, home of many pro-English Irish and Anglo-Irish. The English response was horrific. The newly appointed general, the Anglo-Irish Earl of Ormond, ancient enemy of the Desmonds, supported by Deputy Lord Grey, executed hundreds of alleged traitors. They then devastated the Desmond lands, destroying everything of value, particularly laying waste the crops in the fields. Ormond, representing his own and English interests, intended to starve the rebels into submission. The resulting famine struck rebels and innocent alike.

In an effort to end the rebellion, the queen issued pardons. Concerned with costs, she also reduced the army and removed Ormond as general, but this had the consequence of extending the war for another two years, exacerbating the effects on the populace of the earlier scorched-earth tactics. Many thousands died in both town and countryside. In Cork City, an Englishman reported that twenty to seventy people died every day.[25] Ralegh's friend and ally, the Anglo-Irish Desmond leader John Fitzedmund Fitzgerald of Cloyne, claimed to have lost over 90 percent of the people on his estates located between Cork and Youghal. In the postscript of a letter to the Earl of Leicester, Ralegh lobbied for assistance: "I am bold being bound by very conscience to commend unto your honors consideration the pitifull estate of John Fittes Edmondes of Cloyne, a gentleman and the only man untucht and proved tru to the Queen bothe in this and the last rebellion."[26]

The ties between a Desmond leader like Fitzedmund of Cloyne and the English show how erroneous it is to classify the Second Desmond War as a dispute between English and Irish or even English versus Desmonds. The Irish situation was much splintered, with varying groups and individuals of diverse interests, and those interests moved portions of families to one side or the other. Fitzedmund of Cloyne was unusual in always seeming to take the English side in war, but his primary goal was to maintain his lands, and his secondary goal was to retain other lands in Ireland in Desmond hands. It helped the rebels to have family members both for and against the English. The English goal was to bring order out of seeming chaos by finding ways to make leaders and the common people commit their loyalty to the queen. That was Ralegh's task as a captain in Ireland.

In the midst of the famine, from 1581 to 1583, Ralegh earned fame for his service in Ireland—for derring-do, mediation, and his reports on the situation to the English government. Ralegh learned the landscape extremely well, engaged the populace in a multitude of ways, and flourished as a soldier. It was then he established his friendship with the aforementioned Fitzedmund of Cloyne. Lord Deputy Grey sent Ralegh to court to report on Irish affairs, where he gained the attention of the queen. In the coming years, her government consulted Ralegh on a multitude of Irish matters and viewed him as one of England's foremost experts on Ireland. But it was his heroism in Ireland that initially brought him accolades and jealousy at the queen's court.

Ralegh noted his heroics in two letters he wrote from Ireland to Walsingham in February 1580/81, though he offered few specifics. Ralegh's letters reveal a youthful man of action out to prove himself worthy of his appointment as a captain in service to the queen. In 1581, the English hoped to rein in Anglo-Irish and Irish leaders in Munster province. It was an activist policy: accept English authority or be declared

an outlaw or traitor. The English sought to win over the leading vassals below the two great leaders, the earls of Desmond and Ormond,
particularly Desmond, to deny them a base to buttress their military
power against the queen and each other.[27] Ralegh's letter to Walsingham, written in response to one from the secretary, reported that the
next generation of sons of the second tier of nobility—Barry, Roche,
Condon, and others—all former rebels—were well inclined to Elizabeth and England. But their power must be feared because together
they had greater strength than the top tier of nobility. Ralegh noted
his "hard escape" from John Fitzedmund Fitzgerald, the Seneschal of
Imokilly (and not to be confused with Ralegh's friend of the same exact name, who was of Cloyne and succeeded his cousin to the title
of Seneschal after the former's death in 1589). It is almost odd that
Ralegh offered no details of the "hard escape" because the seneschal
was a renowned soldier. But the story made the rounds at the English
court. Instead of telling his story to Walsingham, Ralegh reported the
poor condition of other English companies in Ireland in terms of the
scarcity of soldiers and supplies: English policy in Munster would fail
without more support.

The next day, Ralegh again wrote to Walsingham: Dave Barry had
burned his own castles so the English could not use them and had
gone into rebellion. Ralegh desired one of the castles along with its
adjoining island for his own use, to provide "a safty for all passing-
ers betwen Corke and Youghall." But he needed General Ormond's
approval. Ralegh astutely noted an additional political problem. If he
occupied the castle, then it might be said "that ther takinge therof
was the hasteninge of Barries rebellion." This type of foresight illustrates Ralegh's acute awareness of how the colonizer's actions would
be perceived by the indigenous in a colonial situation. It did not stop
Ralegh from pursuing the property, but as a later colonizer of Ireland,
Ralegh saw nuance in local situations. Ormond refused Ralegh's request, so he went without the property. Ralegh railed against Ormond's
competency and the difficulty of having him as General of Munster
when there was an "incomperable hatred" between his family and the
Desmonds. Since Ormond's appointment as general two years before,
there were "a thowsand traytors more then ther were the first day." In
other words, the queen's favoring of one Anglo-Irish lord over another
had led to the alienation of so many Irish. Ralegh recommended appointing an Englishman to the post as general: his own brother Sir
Humphrey Gilbert, who had "ended a rebellion not miche inferior to

this, in t[w]o monethes!" No one was "more fered then he is amonge the Irishe nation." All of the traitors "would cum in hyre, and yeld them selves to the Queens mercy, were it but knowen that he were cum amonge them. The end shall prove this to be trew."[28]

Why had the English government not turned to Gilbert when he had performed so successfully in the First Desmond War? Ralegh claimed that his brother's recent behavior "in peace" had left his former "good service forgotten and hold hyme from the preferm[ent] he is worthy of." Gilbert's career had been tarnished since his successful subduing of rebels in 1569: a failed military campaign in the Netherlands, the intended expedition to North America that never crossed the ocean, and then the bungled assignment to prevent the landing of papal troops. When Gilbert finally arrived in Cobh, Ireland, he unmercifully beat a member of the local gentry and killed a local merchant— this violence "in peace" is likely what Ralegh referred to as spurring the government's lack of interest in appointing Gilbert general.[29]

The war wound down without Gilbert's assistance. In 1583, Ralegh's career as a captain in Ireland ended with his return to England. With Gilbert unwanted in Ireland, Ralegh joined him on his second attempted expedition to America. In Ireland, the Earl of Ormond was reappointed General of Munster and helped end the war. With so much of the native population decimated by starvation and disease, and many of the survivors having fled, the path was cleared for English colonization not only of Munster but also of America.

⁓

PART TWO

Catholics,
Morris Dancers, and Genocide

How to Colonize America

CHAPTER 4

"a man noted of
not good happ by sea"

*Humphrey Gilbert
Prepares to Colonize America*

With the end of the Second Desmond War, Elizabeth delayed colonization of Munster province in Ireland. She required an array of conditions be met and careful planning before she would distribute land. Who would lose their land to English colonists? What tracts did they own? What rules would govern the Munster Plantation? The planning, more detailed than any Tudor government project of the second half of the sixteenth century, took years.[1] Yet she demanded no advanced planning for America. Proprietary colonies, under Gilbert's patent and later under Ralegh's, were owned by individuals or groups, and the proprietors bore responsibility for designing, overseeing, and protecting their colony.

Humphrey Gilbert wrote much on the desirability of colonizing, yet gave no idea of what his colony should look like. His patent made clear that conquest of a Spanish colony was out of the question; he bore license only to build new colonies. We can assume from Frobisher's folly, which he had lightly invested in, that Gilbert did not expect to find gold, but he likely hoped for other valuable metals. Indeed, Gilbert had invested heavily in a scheme to turn iron into copper, and during the course of his second expedition to America he thought silver would solve the problem of future funding by attracting investment, particularly from the queen. Whether silver was the end or the means of Gilbert's hopes is unknown—perhaps it was both. Silver offered one way to maintain colonies, because one of a colony's purposes was to create wealth. Of course, there were other reasons to colonize, but most English understood that colonies could survive only if financially viable. Gilbert intended a broad exploration of the North Atlantic with multiple stops, likely to plant multiple colonies. He also set his sights on areas close to the Spanish, perhaps uninhabited islands in the Caribbean. All this activity required investors and colonists, and so he drew up detailed plans to attract both.

But Gilbert could not prepare for all contingencies. A good deal of faith was involved in sailing to places unknown (or little known). Weather could affect any expedition—good winds or storms, extremes of cold and heat. And then there was the human element. For instance, why should sailors sign on for a colonizing expedition when there were other opportunities at sea—namely, piracy? This basic question greatly influenced many early colonizing expeditions: Sailors had little interest in working with colonizers. Often, they had to be forced to sail. Gilbert not only lacked sailors but also possessed poor leadership skills at sea. Despite all his planning and his experience commanding on land and sea, there was an element of naivete in his character. His shock that Knollys went pirating on the first expedition would be matched on the second: unruly and mutinous sailors played a key role in sabotaging his efforts.

Gilbert's naivete extended to Native peoples. Gilbert hoped to establish good relations with America's indigenous peoples by amusing them. He brought toys, fripperies, and performers to entertain the Indians and his men. These included Morris dancers, hobby horses, and musicians "to delight the Savage people, whom we intended to winne by all faire meanes possible. And to that end we were indifferently furnished of all petty haberdasherie wares to barter with those simple people." Morris dancing had been popular in England since the fifteenth century and often was accompanied by hobby horses—people dressed in horse costumes.

There is no record of Gilbert's men encountering a single Native in America. Gilbert seems to have given little thought to the Native people beyond classifying them as of the common sort, like the bulk of his men. Recall that he had written in his early proposals for overseas expansion that the English would ally with the African enemies of the

Spanish. As with many other Elizabethans, class designated by blood was far more important than skin color or any alleged ethnicity.

Gilbert combined a complex array of characteristics. Intellectually broad and charismatic, he displayed a good bit of open-mindedness and religious tolerance, evident from his plans to create refuges for Catholic colonists in America and his willingness to ally with the slaves of the Spanish. On the other hand, one of his business partners described him as self-contradictory and a show-off with a profusion of vanity.[2] There was darkness in Gilbert as well. His violent nature revealed itself in Ireland in times of both war and peace.

Ralegh learned many things from Gilbert but followed a different course as a colonizer. He planned more meticulously, focused on settling different areas, and paid far more attention to the sailors and to the Native peoples. The same proved true of his relations with the Irish. Ralegh had a remarkable record of cooperation with the Irish. For a man who became the subject of more envy than any other Englishman, he was remarkably well liked by the diverse peoples with whom he worked.

—

DURING RALEGH'S CAPTAINCY in Ireland, Gilbert faced a shortage of funds to return to America to fulfill the terms of his patent. The theft of his ships in Ireland might have played some role in his financial downturn, and he complained about receiving inadequate compensation for his Crown service in Ireland in 1579. To raise money, Gilbert sold John Dee his rights in the far north above Newfoundland. Dee later partnered with Humphrey's and Walter's brother Adrian Gilbert to explore the area, but Dee and Adrian neither established a colony nor found a Northwest Passage.

By 1581, Humphrey Gilbert, hoping to establish a colony of English Catholics in America, turned to them for funding. He had to start permanent settlements by 1584 or risk losing his patent. Wherever he founded a colony, he would own all land within six hundred miles not already possessed by a Christian.[3] If he could disperse the settlements he started, all the better, for it would enlarge his claims.

Gilbert granted eight and a half million acres in America to English Catholics, along with nearby islands.[4] By the middle of 1582, the Catholics were active in their preparations; Richard Hakluyt's *Diverse Voyages* in late 1582 or early 1583 references Gilbert on several occasions as having his new colony under way—though he actually had yet to depart.[5]

The English government approved of the planting of English Catholics in America. Relations between Protestants and Catholics in England had been growing worse. John Foxe's *Book of Martyrs and the Elected Nation* had presented Protestant England with an anti-Catholic ideology and sense of national purpose in awareness of the threat of Catholicism.[6] The papal bull of 1570 had excused English Catholics from obeying Elizabeth, while English laws laid the groundwork for a new era of punitive legislation against the practice of Catholicism in England. Even though Elizabeth distrusted Protestant radicalism as much as Catholicism, Radical Protestant elements succeeded in convincing the government to create a system of fines against Catholics, buttressed in the Act of 1581—just as Gilbert was attempting to colonize. This legislation dramatically increased the fines for recusancy (refusal to attend the church services of the Church of England) to £20 per month and declared that anyone who tried to convert or recruit someone to Catholicism, "with the intention of withdrawing one's obedience from the queen," could be charged with treason.[7] The government hoped that English Catholic colonization in America would extend the English realm while reducing the "problem" of Catholicism in England. The government expected Catholics to pay any fines they owed before they left on "the nexte viaige for conquest" or to enter bonds for later payment. Then they could leave in good standing and freely return to England.[8]

The Spanish, alarmed at the threat English Catholics in America posed to Spanish settlements, urged English Catholics not to migrate.[9] When English Catholics began backing away from colonization, the English government offered to release Catholic prisoners (and other incentives) to convince them to invest in, and migrate to, America. But no separate Catholic expedition emerged until the settlement of Maryland in 1634.

In early 1583, Gilbert was about ready to sail when the queen stopped him. According to Gilbert, she "hath wish my stay att home . . . as a man noted of not good happ by sea." His "happ," his luck or fortune, may have referred to the failure of his expedition to America in 1578 and his inability to prevent the papal troops from landing in Ireland. Rumors of Gilbert's lack of competency at sea were rife.[10] He pleaded his case to Walsingham: in the "first enterprise I returned with great losse" because he would not "suffer any of my companye to doe any thinge contrarye to my worde given to her majestie and your self" (unlike Knollys and others who went pirating). Gilbert also offered excuses as to why he had not yet left English shores, mostly blaming the winds. He begged to be allowed to depart because he had invested so much money, and he resented the implication that his maritime skills were wanting or that he was physically not up to the task. His twenty-eight years of service for the queen should have counted for something. He did not wish to stay at home "idle . . . to beg my bredd with my wife and children, especially since I have her majesties graunte and lycense under the great seale of Englande for my departure, withoute the which I would not have spent a penny in this action."[11]

Five weeks later, Elizabeth relented. Whatever the reason for her change of mind, she did so with fanfare, giving Ralegh a present to deliver to Humphrey, "a token from her Majesty[,] an ancor guyded by a Lady as yow See." The queen wished Gilbert "great good hap and safety to your Ship as if hersealf were ther in person desireing yow to have care of yoursealf." As a further sign of her affection, she commanded Humphrey to leave his "picture" with Ralegh, who would send it to her. Ralegh, it should be noted, in a display of his own affection, when writing of the queen's change of heart, signed his letter to Humphrey, "Your trew Brother, W. Rauley."[12]

The Spanish ambassador to England, Don Bernadino de Mendoza, was furious. Mendoza knew that the English government planned to settle English Catholics in America.[13] The Spanish rejected all English claims to colonize in North America. Whether he succeeded in hiring an English spy to accompany the expedition, as he had with the voyage of 1578, is unknown.[14] But Mendoza was active. He organized the campaign in England to convince Catholics not to go to America, using secret priests to inform the people that it was a trick to get them to reveal themselves to the government. Mendoza threatened: if English Catholics went to Florida, "they would immediately have their throats cut," as the Spanish had done to the hundreds of French who settled Florida with Jean Ribaut.[15] Mendoza's threats worked, to an extent. He reported to Philip II that some English Catholics withdrew from the expedition, though others refused, claiming that Florida (meaning the Atlantic coast of the future United States) was "discovered by the French," not the Spanish, and that because Catholics in the New World like Cortés had made conquests independent of the Spanish Crown, so could they.

Dozens of individuals called "merchant adventurers" invested in Gilbert's enterprise. Many invested from £5 to £20 worth of commodities or money. Drapers, beer brewers, iron mongers, mercers, and bakers joined earls and knights as investors or joined the expedition. Many yeomen put in less money and received trade privileges.[16] When it finally left England, the expedition did not want for anything.

Gilbert was desperate for sailors. There was, it should be noted, little to no difference between Elizabethan pirate crews and nonpirate crews—the distinction seems to have been the purpose of the voyage, though a pirate ship could quickly become a mercantile ship and switch back to a pirate ship if the opportunities presented themselves. Gilbert had captured one of his ships, the Swallow, from the pirate John Callis, his nemesis from the 1578 expedition. Gilbert likely told the Swallow's crew that if they acquiesced to sail with him, he would not prosecute them for piracy. The Swallow's crew resented impressment for the voyage to Newfoundland because the opportunity for pirating riches would be limited. On a pirate or a fishing vessel, they received a portion of the profits; as sailors with Gilbert, they received a wage, which they could supplement by taking a prize along the way.

A second ship, the ten-ton Squirrel, was small but deemed necessary for reconnaissance along the American coast. It was captained by William Andrew and had as its master William Cade, both of whom became colonists of Walter Ralegh in Ireland. A third ship, the Golden Hinde, named for Drake's ship that circumnavigated the globe, was also small in size at forty tons and had Edward Hayes as captain and owner. On the fourth ship, the 120-ton Delight, Gilbert sailed to America with its captain and part owner, William Winter, whose father of the same name was one of Elizabeth's advisors. Richard Clarke mastered the ship. (Both Winter and Clarke had a fallout with Gilbert on the journey, and the Delight did not survive the voyage.) The fifth ship, the Bark Ralegh, belonged to Walter Ralegh, vice admiral of the expedition. This was Ralegh's investment in the voyage, the huge sum of £2,000 in the form of the ship and its "furniture," or its supplies.[17] The Bark Ralegh was by far the largest ship of the expedition, with a capacity five times that of the forty-ton ships. It carried most of the provisions for the extended voyage. Michael Butler, the ship's captain, likely was the same "M. Butler" who later became a Ralegh colonist in Ireland.[18] The ship's master was Robert Davis of Bristol, likely the same Robert Davis who later sailed with Ralegh to Guiana in 1595. (Captain Hayes might also have sailed with Ralegh to Guiana.)

The fleet set sail June 11, 1583. Yet none of the huge grants Gilbert had made to sundry individuals led to permanent settlements, and none of these people, as far as we know, ultimately sailed for America. Gilbert had to alter the plans for his enterprise to have even a chance of success. He knew of a New World locale where he would find a number of Europeans he hoped to turn into permanent settlers so he could quickly claim the region as a colony for himself. Instead of sailing south toward temperate Florida, he opted to go north to Newfoundland, only 2,100 miles from England. Gilbert intended to claim Newfoundland and gain control of the world's greatest fisheries—which he had proposed six years earlier in "A Discourse on how hir Majestie may annoy the K: of Spain." Then, as he had formulated in "A Discourse," he would sail south and plant another colony. But he had to get to Newfoundland while the fishermen were there, for they would be gone as soon as the cold winter hinted of setting in.

Two days later, the *Bark Ralegh* turned back. One sailor later claimed that the voyage was aborted because of a lack of victuals, but it is hardly credible that Ralegh discovered such a shortage two days after departure.[19] Gilbert, without knowledge of the situation, suspected the crew had forced the turnaround and hoped that his brother Walter would "make them an example of all Knaves."[20] Hayes later thought the ship turned around because of an unidentified "contagious sicknesse" that had struck much of the crew, including the captain, but not Ralegh. This explanation also seems suspect because none of the sailors on the other ships experienced the illness and it is unlikely it had spread in two days on a single vessel.

The most likely explanation: the impressed men forced Ralegh to turn back. It is difficult to believe that Ralegh would have abandoned his brother unless forced by dire circumstances—like the overwhelming threat of mutiny. Without the *Bark Ralegh* and its supplies, Gilbert's remaining four ships continued on. They had enough food to reach Newfoundland, where they could expect to obtain fish from the fishermen.

On the seven-week Atlantic crossing, the *Golden Hinde* and the *Delight* got separated from the *Squirrel* and the *Swallow*, which reached Newfoundland first. By the time the *Golden Hinde* and *Delight* found the *Swallow*, the pirate-manned vessel already had pirated a French ship, taking the fishermen's catch and clothing, and much of their gear. The crew tortured the fishermen to get what they could, probably hoping for hidden silver or gold, before releasing their ship.

Gilbert's three ships then found the *Squirrel* nearby at St. Johns Bay, anchored just outside the harbor. The English "merchants," that is, the fishing fleet, had barred the *Squirrel*'s entry to harbor. Gilbert's ships "made readie our fights" to force their way in. A "fight" is the defensive shield Renaissance-era ships placed on their decks and fired from behind. Even the tiny *Squirrel* carried one. The harbor held thirty-six ships of sundry nations. Gilbert "dispatched a boat" to make known his "interest," that he bore "Commission from her Majestie for his voyage." (Why the *Squirrel* initially was barred is unknown—perhaps a tax or entry fee of some sort was placed on boats by those already in harbor.) Much to Gilbert's embarrassment, his own ship ran aground on a rock. When the English fishing boats learned of his commission, they towed him into harbor.

No European power owned the Newfoundland fisheries, which were chiefly fished by French, Portuguese, English, and Spanish from various sites on the great island. Once on shore, Gilbert informed the ship captains that he claimed St. Johns for Queen Elizabeth and then performed the requisite ceremonies to confirm her sovereignty. He affixed the Arms of England, engraved in lead, "upon a pillar of wood" and claimed all land (for himself) within two hundred leagues, per his patent. Hayes stated that all accepted the queen's claim. They had no choice. The English fishermen had to accede because of Gilbert's commission, and the non-English likely nodded approval because of Gilbert's firepower and the possibility that the English fishermen would support Gilbert in a gun battle. The fishing vessels were no match for Gilbert's heavily armed ships, but the fishermen might not have been too shaken by Gilbert's claims because, after his departure, there is no indication that anyone accepted Elizabeth's sovereignty over Newfoundland. But while there, he taxed all the ships—after all, he needed to resupply his own since Ralegh's had not made it to Newfoundland.

To fulfill the terms of his patent, Gilbert needed settlers. This likely was his real reason for going to Newfoundland. The captains of the fishing boats, he hoped, would count as permanent settlers even though they were there only a small portion of the year. He offered plots for the owners to "dresse and to drie their fish."[21] This way, they would not have to scurry each year to obtain a proper spot, and Gilbert could create a stable society with land ownership, where he received rents and services for himself and his heirs. With one permanent settlement, he could claim all of Newfoundland, because his two hundred leagues of control from the settlement would include the entire island. Gilbert made the grants of land, but the papers apparently never reached England.

While some of his men collected the taxes, others repaired the expedition's ships or gathered information on the land and its commodities, consulting those fishermen "who had longest frequented" the island. Hayes and Gilbert perceived the land as beautiful and abundant. Stephen Parmenius, however, said in a letter to Richard Hakluyt that he could see nothing but "desolation." When Hakluyt published Parmenius's account, he conveniently translated the Latin description as "wilderness" instead of "desolation." The great propagandist for English colonization of America could not abide portraying the land as desolate.[22]

As the season waned, Gilbert wished to explore the Atlantic coast to the south, but many of his men preferred to go home. With Gilbert intending to look for future places to plant settlements, and not to pursue prizes at sea, many chose to go home. Some ran to the woods to await Gilbert's departure and then hitch a ride home on a fishing boat. Others stole from Gilbert's ships or from the fishermen, even capturing fishing boats and "setting the poore men on shore."[23] Many sailors were sick. Gilbert sent the *Swallow* home with the ill and others who wished to join them—but the pirates had to stay. The captain of the *Delight*, William Winter, who also was part owner of the ship, chose to go home without his ship. Captain Andrewes of the *Squirrel* also likely went home. These men may have feared Gilbert's leadership, or else they saw no hope for profit.

Maurice Browne, captain of the *Swallow*, stayed with the expedition and became captain of the *Delight*, taking on the *Swallow*'s pirate crew as well. Gilbert moved to the *Squirrel*, this "Frigate being most convenient to discover upon the coast, and to search into every harbor, or creeke, which a great ship could not doe." Hayes remained in control of his own ship, the *Golden Hinde*. The three ships departed St. John's on August 20. Nine days later, two ship's masters, Richard Clarke, formerly of the *Delight*, and William Cox of the *Golden Hinde*, argued with Gilbert about which way to sail. When Gilbert's decision carried the day, disaster ensued: the *Delight* struck ground and sank.[24] Sixteen men escaped the *Delight* on a pinnace, with around half surviving; they were picked up by a Basque fishing vessel, made their way to France, and arrived in England at the end of the year.

With the *Delight*'s demise, many of those on the *Golden Hinde* and the *Squirrel* "lost courage dayly," and, with the growing cold and loss of supplies from the *Delight*, they wished to go home. Those in the *Squirrel* suffered from lack of clothes and food. "They made signes of their distresse" to their fellows on the *Golden Hinde*, "pointing to their mouthes, and to their clothes thinned and ragged." Their distress spread to the *Golden Hinde*, and the men asked Gilbert to return to England. Hayes reported that Gilbert agreed, though against Hayes's wishes. Gilbert promised Hayes they would return in the spring. Two days after the loss of the *Delight*, the two ships set course for England. Nine or ten days later, the *Squirrel* sank, and Gilbert died. England's first attempt to colonize America came to an end without planting a single colony.

—

ALL WE KNOW about the last days of Gilbert and how he met his end comes from the pen of Edward Hayes. This account went unpublished until six years after the expedition, in 1589.[25] Hayes claims to have witnessed the sinking of the *Delight* in broad daylight, though no one on the other two ships saw sixteen men escape on a pinnace. He likewise claims not only to have seen Gilbert's ship, the *Squirrel*, go down but also to have witnessed Gilbert's death and to know the precise moment it happened—even though all of it occurred at night. It is hard to take Hayes's claims seriously.

His account is dramatic, full of omens. Hayes gave a Christian interpretation to all deaths, presenting them as just punishments from God. According to Hayes, the sailors on the *Delight* were killed by God for their piracy. The ship captain who died with them, Maurice Browne, Hayes described as a good man, "vertuous, honest, and discrete," but his fatal shortcoming was his inability to prevent his men from piracy. So, God had him die.[26] Hayes's arrogance is in identifying exactly which sin God punished each man for with death.

Hayes portrays Gilbert, in the last days of his life, as a man who at root was a good Christian, but there were troubling signs of something amiss. Gilbert gave in too easily to the men's demands to go home. Hayes described Gilbert's reason as "compassion," which Hayes found "unexpected" and unwelcome. Then the ships encountered a sea lion, which Hayes describes at some length because virtually all thought it an ill omen. The animal had ugly teeth, "glaring eies . . . a horrible voice, roaring or bellowing as doeth a lion." Incredibly, according to Hayes, Gilbert interpreted the encounter as a good omen. Hayes, painting a picture of a delusional Gilbert, sees what is ahead, whereas

Gilbert does not. Another omen appeared when the wind almost "swa-lowed up" the *Squirrel*. Two days later, Gilbert stepped on a nail and had to board the *Golden Hinde* for the surgeon to treat him. Then comes the most important line in Hayes's lengthy tract. After stating that the two men comforted one another "with hope of hard-successe to be all past, and of the good to come," they added a sign to help them keep their ships from losing one another: "So agreeing to cary our lights always by night, that we might keepe together."

The inclusion of eleven orders in Hayes's tract is suspicious. It is rare that an account of an early modern expedition would include the admiral's orders to his ships—the information is irrelevant to readers who wish to know of their adventure and what they found. Another oddity, the very first order was to keep a light burning at night, as if Gilbert unconsciously foreshadowed the events of his own death, for when Gilbert's ship's light did go out, Hayes declared Gilbert dead!

As the weather turned bad on the return voyage, Hayes entreated Gilbert to stay aboard the *Golden Hinde* "for his security." Gilbert re-turned to the *Squirrel*. Hayes saw danger, Gilbert did not. Another omen appeared: "Immediately after followed a sharpe storme." The storm passed. "Prayesed be God." (God will act in his own time.)

When the weather improved, "The Generall came aboord the Hind againe, to make merrie together with the Captaine, Master, and com-pany." In the 1580s, the term "make merrie" refers to eating with oth-ers with good cheer. Gilbert arrived in the morning and did not leave until evening. Gilbert and Hayes talked of a great many things. Hayes expressed confusion and surprise hearing Gilbert's lamentations. He understood Gilbert ruing "greatly the losse of his great ship, more of the men," but Hayes could not fathom why Gilbert regretted even more the loss of "his books and notes, and what els I know not." Even more startling, he found Gilbert "out of measure grieved" for "some matter of more importance then his books, which I could not draw from him." Hayes wondered whether Gilbert pined for a piece of lost silver ore. The "remembrance touched him so deepe" that he could not "containe himselfe," so "he beat his [cabin] boy in great rage." Before the *Delight* had sunk, he had sent the boy "to fetch certaine things," particularly the silver ore, and the boy had failed to do so.

Hayes includes these details for a reason. In part, it is likely that he reminds readers of the silver ore because he wants to convince the government to allow and support his quest to lead an expedition to Newfoundland to secure the land that Gilbert had claimed for the queen but that no one had actually occupied. With no permanent English settlement, Elizabeth's claim to sovereignty was dubious by her own (and Dee's) definition. Hayes followed this story with affirmation that before Gilbert died, he had become "wholly fixed upon the New found land." On his return to America, Gilbert intended to go north and to send Hayes to the south. The present expedition "had wonne [Gilbert's] heart from the South, and that he was now become a Northerne man altogether."

Though the expedition seemed an unmitigated failure, in Hayes's telling Gilbert repeatedly, confidently stated that the expedition had been a great success, alongside affirmations that there was silver to be found. Hayes includes these details because he had no physical evidence, and he needed investors for his next voyage to Newfoundland. To explain what had gone wrong with the quest, he painted a picture of Gilbert losing his mind. Death grew ever closer, but the "vehement perswasion and intreatie of his friends" could not "divert" Gilbert from his "willful resolution" of sailing in the *Squirrel*. It was, after all, "God's ordinance upon him." He suggested that the *Squirrel* was "overcharged upon their decks, with fights [defensive shields], nettings, and small artillerie, too cumbersome for so small a boate, that was to passe through the Ocean sea at the seasone of the yere," with "foule weather" imminent. Gilbert responded that he would not abandon the men on the *Squirrel* for the greater security of the *Golden Hinde*. Hayes thought Gilbert's reason was vanity: the "hard reports given of him [Gilbert], that he was afraid of the sea," led to his rash decision to tough out the rough crossing on the *Squirrel*.

A thousand miles from home, the seas grew "terrible," "breaking short and high Pyramid wise." As is usual in accounts of ships that sink in storms (or nearly so), Hayes reports that the experienced sailors "never saw more outrageous Seas." Hayes recounts more bad omens— they saw "an apparition of a little fire" in the night sky, "which seamen doe call Castor and Pollux . . . which they take an evill signe of more tempest: the same is usual in stormes." Some sailors interpreted Saint Elmo's fire as a good omen, but Hayes knew that it was bad. The next day, Gilbert's "Frigat was neere cast away, oppressed by waves, yet at that time recovered." We, the readers, know Gilbert is to die, but Hayes's narrative insists that Gilbert, too, recognized death's imminence. The omens mark man's fate. Hayes's narrative of deception, in reaching toward its climax, skillfully reveals Gilbert accepting his fate—so must we. The storm ended, the men "giving foorth signes of joy," while Gilbert sat on deck reading a book! As the *Golden Hinde* drew near, Gilbert "cried out unto us (so oft as we did approach within hearing)[,] We are as neere to heaven by sea as by land." "Reiterating the same speech," Hayes tells us, was "well beseeming a souldier, resolute in Jesus Christ."

That night, about midnight, the *Squirrel*'s lights "suddenly" went out, "as it were in a moment, we lost the sight," and the watch cried out, "the Generall was cast away, which was too true. For in that moment, the Frigat was devoured and swallowed up of the Sea." The surviving ship "looked out all that night, and ever after until we arrived upon the coast of England." But why would they have to look for Gilbert if they were sure that the sea devoured him?

The *Golden Hinde* reached Falmouth, England, twelve days later, on September 22, and then went to Dartmouth to ask if there was news of the frigate. Hayes reported to John Gilbert "of our hard successe." Hayes asked John if he wanted to interview the men, but he said he was satisfied with the captain's report. Because the sailors needed money to make their way home, Hayes sailed the ship farther east to get most of the men closer to their homes, and they were dispersed without being interviewed.

Hayes's account of Humphrey Gilbert's demise is defensive in nature: he constructed it to counter claims that Gilbert had been murdered. There was no reason for Hayes to include information about dispersing the men without anyone interviewing them or to assure readers that he had a legal right to do so, unless during the six years preceding publication of the account rumors had arisen that Sir Humphrey reached his death at the hands of man rather than nature. There are other peculiarities as well, particularly the fact that Hayes twice mentions that a light on the general's ship signified whether he lived or died, thus steering readers away from any other explanation. Also in the narrative, there is no struggle between the *Squirrel* (and its men) and the sea—the ship was "devoured and swallowed" by the sea in a gulp. If it was swallowed—and did not slowly sink—there must have been a storm, and so the watch would never have seen the ship go down at midnight.[27] The greatest peculiarity of all: nowhere does Hayes state how many other men were lost, nor does he name a single lost man besides Gilbert. In contrast, when the *Delight* sinks, Hayes notes the captain's demise and provides the names of several others, and a few survivors, and estimates the dead at "almost a hundred soules." Hayes does not identify the dead captain and master of the *Squirrel* at the time it went down or who took over the positions when the previous captain and master went to other ships. This is most unusual because Hayes ordinarily relates the names of the chief officers for each ship on the expedition. Gilbert was "General" of the entire expedition and neither a captain nor a master. He needed someone to navigate the ship, especially while he allegedly ignored his surroundings to read a book and pronounce repeatedly on his fate.

Hayes moralizes on the nameless crew of the *Delight* suffering shipwreck and death, but not on that of the *Squirrel*—perhaps because none of the *Squirrel*'s crew had died. Instead, he relates only the reason for Humphrey's death, which provides a moral lesson: Gilbert was "honest and godly" and intended colonization as a "service of God, and Christian piety" to bring the heathen to Christ. His faults comprised "temeritie and presumption." But God was displeased with his poor preparation. Gilbert was right to trust in God but wrong "not to entertaine every person and meanes whatsoever, to furnish out this expedition." Gilbert's fatal flaw had been excluding investors who could have better outfitted the expedition, though we know it was well supplied. Hayes uses this argument only to attract investors for his own search for silver in Newfoundland—and to show he would not waste the investors' funds.

What role did Gilbert's violent disposition play in his death? Hayes makes but one reference to Gilbert's aggression: the beating of the cabin boy. Hayes could be expected not to mention those Gilbert had executed in the First Desmond War—that would be something an Englishman would praise.[28] But another aspect of Gilbert's violent nature extended beyond those he killed in war and in peace. Gilbert liked boys. Early in his career, Sir Thomas Smith and William Medley, his partners in an alchemical project to turn iron into copper, each reported separately to the government that when Gilbert was in a temper, he took boys to "soothe" his spirit. This behavior in the field by a war commander was tolerated so long as he lined the path to his tent with heads, and there was little chance of Gilbert being charged with a crime against a servant boy.[29]

On board the *Squirrel*, circumstances differed. For most of the expedition, Gilbert sailed on the larger ships and had privacy. On the tiny *Squirrel*, which he did not sail on till departure from Newfoundland, there was no privacy. Hayes felt he could not omit from his report that Gilbert had mercilessly beat his "boy" for a "wrong" the boy had done days before. And Hayes noted the beating as quite odd because of its timing and that the alleged wrong committed bothered Gilbert so much more than the more substantial problems the expedition faced. Those who knew of Gilbert's propensity for boys, however, understood why Hayes related such a story.

Together, these clues seem to suggest that members of the *Squirrel's* crew had had enough of Gilbert. One, two, or more of the *Squirrel's* crew could have tossed Gilbert into the sea and no one would have been the wiser. Did they then sink the ship afterward or let it go freely? Did the *Squirrel's* crew, whose deaths were never reported, sail away? Or, after Gilbert had been "lost" at sea, did the *Squirrel's* small crew come aboard the *Golden Hinde*? Who on the *Golden Hinde* could have gainsaid in print what had happened? Elites in a position to have their voices heard had sailed home on the *Swallow*. The men who witnessed events were dispersed before being interviewed. Rumors must have followed Gilbert's death for Hayes to provide the details in his tract that would counter suspicions that Gilbert's death was a crime and not the result of a storm. Hayes's peculiar failure to mention the names of the deceased navigator and captain of the *Squirrel* is not so strange if they were still alive.

None of Humphrey's siblings raised a fuss. They might have wanted the story hushed because Humphrey's behavior could reflect poorly on them. Perhaps they were reconciled with losing their brother, especially if this walking time bomb had indeed lost his hold on reality, as Hayes portrays he had in his final days.

Humphrey's death opened opportunities for others to go to America. George Peckham, to whom Humphrey had granted land, immediately sought financing and recruited colonists. He did so without delay because Gilbert's grant was soon to expire: Humphrey's claim to Newfoundland might not have counted to Elizabeth because permanent buildings had not been constructed with year-round habitation. If Peckham were to quickly plant a colony, then Humphrey's brother John, his main heir, would hold patent to North America.

George Peckham, colonizing under Gilbert's patent, was the first Elizabethan to make a public appeal through the printing press to colonize America.[30] He offered a chilling prospectus.

CHAPTER 5

The Case for Genocide

George Peckham Visualizes Colonization

N
ews of Gilbert's death could not have arrived in England before the end of September 1583. Within a few days, George Peckham was already working on sending another expedition to colonize America. This can be viewed as further evidence that Hayes *knew* Gilbert was actually dead—if Gilbert's ship had been blown away by a storm, it could have shown up weeks or months later, like the survivors of the *Delight*, and then Peckham's preparation for an expedition without Gilbert would have looked odd. But Peckham was sure Gilbert was dead and moved quickly to make use of whatever grant Gilbert had made to him before Gilbert's patent expired.

By the second week of November, to gain support for his colony, Peckham published a tract, *A True Reporte, Of the late discoveries, and possession, taken in the right of the Crowne of Englande, of the New-found Landes: By that valiaunt and worthye Gentleman, Sir Humfrey Gilbert Knight.*[1] The first published account under Elizabeth to promote English colonization of America, the book's title announces that the queen had claimed sovereignty over Newfoundland—English colonization of America seemingly had begun.

Despite the title, the work relates little about the Gilbert expedition. Peckham rushed his book into print to convince English to finish what Gilbert had started, and not to let the colonial enterprise in America die. Peckham needed investors and colonists, and intended to draw on the same group of investors as Gilbert had. He copied Gilbert's system of land distribution and trade privileges to be exchanged for investment and provided an "Assurance" to those who had previously invested in Gilbert's expeditions that they would still get their rewards. He placed a chart at the end of the book detailing the benefits to be accrued from varying levels of investment.

Peckham may have emphasized the continuity of his prospectus with Gilbert's because he was well known by those at court to be a Catholic and wanted to assure everyone that this was not a Catholic enterprise. For several years, Peckham had been the central figure in the quest to establish a Catholic colony within Gilbert's patent. He had been one of the lobbyists to the queen to grant the patent to Gilbert. Gilbert thought enough of Peckham that he wrote him from Newfoundland about the expedition. Elizabeth and her government had no problem with Peckham leading English Catholics to the New World. He had ably served the queen as Sheriff of Nottingham, received knighthood in 1570, but then was confined to prison after providing sanctuary for priests in 1580. The year after publication of *A True Reporte*, in 1584, Peckham was returned to prison for breaking the law in his religious practice.[2]

Still, in 1583, having a Catholic in charge of English colonization might have been a bit much for some Protestant investors and prospective colonists. To assuage such doubts, Peckham recruited ten men to compose commendatory poems to open his book and praise the proposed enterprise. These men form a Who's Who of Elizabethan maritime celebrities: Francis Drake, Martin Frobisher, and John Hawkins, and also lesser-known worthies, such as Ralegh's cousin Richard Bingham, and sea captains John Chester, Anthony Parkhurst, and Arthur Hawkins. The other commenders included Sir William Pelham, known as a promoter of colonization, poet Mathew Royden, who had strong connections at Oxford and among the poets and well-to-do young gentlemen of London, and London merchant John Ashley, an associate of Richard Hakluyt. The varied emphases of the poems intimate that Peckham recommended subject matter to most of them so that different aspects of colonization would be covered, which was particularly important because Peckham's tract was more narrowly conceived than the aggregate of poems in promoting colonization.

The most striking theme in the poems is the death knell for an England where the people do not go abroad. Pelham's relatively long opening poem beckons the English to become like their neighbors and seek their fortune overseas instead of staying "pent at home, like sluggards we remaine." Several poets offered dire predictions that England could not maintain its population, so some must depart for distant shores. Colonization served God's purpose, according to John Hawkins, but the imperative was to "finde a soil where room inough, and perfect doth abounde." Much of Hawkins's poem equates England to ancient civilizations that colonized: Rome, Athens, Argos, and Troy. But none of these needed space like

> England where no roome remains, her dwellers to bestow,
> But shuffled in such pinching bondes, that very breath dooth lacke:
> And for the want of place they craule one on anothers backe.

Hawkins's vivid image of an England so crowded that "they craule one on anothers backe" would have resonated with many. Although England's population was only about three and a half million, many were dispossessed poor, particularly in London and the sea coast towns. Though the poverty had many sources, access to land played a significant role. The enclosure movement had removed much acreage from planting and usage by the common people, as land increasingly was turned to sheep for wool production. Rather than resulting in employment growth to produce finished woolens, the wool was sent abroad, particularly to the Low Countries, where it was dyed and processed. Discovering profitable commodities abroad, a place to ship the hungry could help the English break out of their doldrums by following the *only* foreseeable path to a glorious future: colonization of new lands.

All of the imperatives presented by the commendatory poets provide the context for Ralegh's colonization of America. Bingham's poem echoes Pelham's in pointing out how foreign neighbors (Spain and Portugal) reaped the rewards of colonization, "while sleeping we remaine." He, too, emphasized England's need for productive soil, which will return "treble gaine" (with English labor) "and make your names renouned another day." Bingham, like Pelham, also used the word "sluggards" to describe English who "lye at home." Colonization would elevate peoples' character by providing them the opportunity to labor. Drake simplified the issue: "The path to Fame, the proofe of zeale, and way to purchase golde" lay in traversing the seas.

The need for rich soils and land laden with natural resources, the opportunities for trade and to do service for God, monarch, and country, the attainment of fame and fortune, and the redemption of individuals all became standard English tropes for undertaking colonization.

Given that Peckham spent so little time on these important issues in his writing, it is questionable whether any of his versifiers actually read his work. He wrote his tract in five weeks and would not have had time to make handwritten copies to distribute to each, who would then have had little time to compose their poems. None likely knew what Peckham had to say or even cared. They had an idea of what they needed to provide for him: a strong recommendation that English get off their duff and follow Peckham to America to make their fortune, save England from overpopulation, and do service for God and Queen.

Through the centuries, numerous promotional tracts would be published to lure investors and colonists to America. In contrast to some of the seminal works to come, the first published promotional tract for English colonialism in America had relatively little lasting influence.[3] Peckham did not attract sufficient funds or adventurers despite his august commenders reciting a litany of reasons to participate in his enterprise. Even so, the treatise warrants a much closer look, for it reveals an English conceptualization of colonization of America before the English had colonized.

—

PECKHAM'S PURPOSE, in large measure, was to assert England's *right* to colonize in the New World. At first glance, this might seem odd; subsequent promoters rarely, if ever, addressed the issue of English rights, which were assumed. Prospective colonists cared about expected benefits, not their right to be in America and to own American land. Certainly, Gilbert assumed Elizabeth's and therefore his own right, and Dee had assured the English government (and Peckham) that Elizabeth had the right to colonize in the New World. Peckham, however, felt it necessary to visit the issue in a public forum and address new issues that had recently arisen concerning the rights of the English in America. What about the Native peoples' rights? Peckham's views of indigenous peoples, and their place in colonization and empire, were far different from those of Ralegh. In fact, Ralegh, over the course of his career, sharply countered these views.

Peckham sought to resolve two sources of problems of colonization. One was the hoped-for Catholic settlers. Peckham countered the Spanish pressure on Catholics to refrain from joining any English New World project by assuring English Catholics that Elizabeth's claim rested on "auncient right and interest . . . descended from the blood royall" of the Welsh Prince Madog ab Owain Gwynedd, who left Wales in 1170 and planted colonies in North America. According to legend, unrecorded until the fifteenth century, Madog, or Madoc, and other Welsh had migrated to America and intermarried with Native Americans. By the mid-sixteenth century, the legend had become the basis for Elizabeth's claims to the New World. Dee learned the story from the Welshman David Powel, who passed it on to Elizabeth. Peckham popularized the story by publishing it in his *True Reporte*. It remained popular into the nineteenth century; Lewis and Clark investigated whether any Welsh Indians existed on their cross-country journey, and Brigham Young hoped to discover which tribe comprised the Welsh Indians. Peckham's purpose was merely to parade the "truth" that Welsh ancestors of Elizabeth had been to America more than three hundred years before Columbus.

With Elizabeth holding claim to America through Madog's twelfth-century journey, there was another *right* that Peckham felt compelled to address. In great detail, Peckham assessed the rights of America's Native inhabitants to their land. Future promoters generally saw no need to discuss Native rights. The injustice was palpable, but there could be no colonies if Native peoples' "sovereignty" was accepted—land would then have to be extracted by conquest. Most English preferred to see themselves as the anti-Spanish, who would not use conquest to obtain sovereignty in America.[4] The English understood that Indians had their own "kings" and entitlement to their lands, but in English minds these lesser kings should cede sovereignty to the greater English monarch, much in the same way that, as Dee related, many European kings owed fealty to King Arthur, who held sovereignty over their lands.[5] Ralegh would be in line with Peckham on this point—that Native peoples should voluntarily enter the English Empire, from which they would receive benefits and protection.

It is difficult to say what is more fascinating about Peckham's discussion of Indian land rights—the arguments he used to extinguish those rights; the revelation that some of his contemporaries believed in the precedence of Indian rights over England's; or that both of these views emerged prior to English colonization of America. The English considered Native rights before a single colonist landed in America, and enough people had suggested there was a problem in taking Indian land so that Peckham felt he had to address the issue. In response, Peckham presented a detailed case by which violence could be used to transfer sovereignty from Indians to English: if Indians did not acquiesce to English domination, then England had the moral right to conquer.[6] This is where Ralegh's viewed diverged; Ralegh opposed conquest. Yet establishing the rationale for conquest formed the gist of Peckham's book. It was an argument that Ralegh opposed and for which he ultimately offered detailed alternative arguments to Queen Elizabeth.

Peckham's first chapter pretends to provide the "Argument of the Book" but instead recites what Gilbert accomplished—the confirmation of English sovereignty over Newfoundland—and the need for the English to finish what Gilbert started in terms of actual colonization. Then, before reciting Elizabeth's rights via Madog in the third chapter, the second chapter proclaims that it will "sheweth that it is lawful and necessary to trafficke with the Savages. And to plant in their Countries. And [this chapter will] devideth planting into two sortes." The "two sortes" are the crux of Peckham's argument. The first required but one sentence: "when Christians by the good likeing and willing assent of the Savages are admitted by them to quiet possession" of land. The second "sorte" received about three thousand words of explication: "when Christians being unjustly repulsed," they can "attaine and maintaine the right for which they doo come."

Peckham posited that the "savages may not justly impugn and forbidde" the English from entering their countries, "in respect of the mutuall society and fellowship betweene man and man prescribed by the Lawe of Nations." Since the time of Noah, "all men have agreed, that no violence should be offered to Ambassadours." The sea and havens "should be common." If the Indians refused to treat with the English, and barred them from their ports, it indicated that they were not "men" but savages. Almost as a non-sequitur, but ominously, Peckham asserts that those "taken in warre, should be servants or slaves." This would be the fate of those who would drive "Strangers [i.e., the English] . . . from the place or Countrey whereunto they doo come." These strangers, earlier referred to as ambassadors, were but English traders, yet Peckham elevated their status because they carried credentials from the queen to settle in America. All English traders and colonists, as long as they were given right by the queen, could not, according to Peckham, be denied the right to trade in America. The Indians could not turn away the English: both "Christians and Infidels" had agreed "beyond the memory of man" that people can carry their commodities to trade to other people's lands. Nor could they deny the English their right to settle because the English queen had granted her people permission.

Peckham's right of all people to trade where they chose reflects English resentment at being locked out of trade in parts of Europe by the Hanse, and in America by the Spanish, notwithstanding the fact that English laws were in place restricting foreigners from trading in England. Though Peckham suggested that the English should use "fayre speeches, and every other good means of perswasion to seeke or take away all occasions of offence," he did not suggest that they should be peaceful traders. Ideally, the English should convince the Natives that the English had come "for theyr good, and to no other ende, but to dwell peaceably amongst them," to trade, and "without molesting or greeving them [in] any way." The English should win Native hearts by giving them presents, beads and bells, bracelets and chains, "our prittie merchaundizes and trifles." This "will induce theyr Barbarous natures to a likeing and mutual society with us." Even so, they should enter the Natives' land well-armed and ready for a fight.

As did other Europeans, notably the Spanish, Peckham divided the Indians between "Savages" and "Canniballs." He promised that the English would defend the Natives from their "blood sucking neighbours, the Canniballes, wherby infinite number of their lives shalbe preserved." If, afterward, the savages used "violence in either repelling the Christians from theyr Portes and safe Landinges or in withstanding them afterwards to enjoye the rights for which both painfully and lawfully they have adventured themselves thether," then the Christians could "pursue revenge with force." To secure themselves, the Christians would build forts in the New World, and if the Savages attacked them, then the English may issue out and "take possession of theyr Townes, Cities, or Villages."

But Peckham makes clear that the English had the right to eliminate the Natives no matter how they responded. He chillingly recites examples from the Old Testament in which the Hebrews burned cities and destroyed all the inhabitants. Even those who forestalled their deaths by sending "Ambassadors unto Josua"—the Gebionites—though spared, still had to become "drudges to hewe wood and to carie water, and other necessaries for his people." Peckham explains: "Thus beganne this valiaunt Captaine his conquest, which he pursued and never left till he had subdued all the Hethites, Amorites, Cananities, Pheresites, Hevites, and Jebusites, with all their Princes and Kings, being thirtie and one in number, and divers other straunge Nations besides, whose lands and dominions, he wholly devided among Gods people." When Josua died, "Juda continued his work . . . and utterlie vanquished many Gentiles, Idolaters, adversaries to the children of Israel." And Gideon followed Juda, who "delivered the children of Israel from the hands of the multitude of the fierce Madianites . . . whose lands he caused Gods people to possesse and inherite." The English, God's people, had the right to dispossess, enslave, and kill those who were not God's people.

The Old Testament provided Peckham with biblical precedence for the "truth" of God's approval of his people smiting enemies and taking their land. The New Testament, according to Peckham, then beckoned the apostles to "dispense themselves to sundrie partes of the world, to the preaching of the Gospell" that "our savior Jesus Christ had suffered his passion." But the apostles had not reached all places and all peoples. Peckham called on bits of post–New Testament history to tell the stories of great men who went to distant lands like India, and "even unto this our native Countrie of England," and to "the rude and cruell Nation of the Scithians . . . and the remote Ethiopians." These great men employed themselves "in conquering the Gentiles to the knowledge of the holie Gospel, utterlie subverting the prophane Temples and abominable Idolatry." Peckham provided a list of "the woorthy lives of sundrie Emperors" who built by conquest of idolatrous peoples, and in his own time, Spain and Portugal have inherited this spirit. Peckham admits that some believe "this maner of planting the Christian Fath . . . to be scarce lawfull," but they are ignorant of the historical precedents Peckham cited. "Thus have I (as I trust) proved that we may justly trade and traffique with the Savages, and lawfullie plant and inhabite theyr Countries."

Few subsequent English writers so explicitly stated the justification and process for dispossession, enslavement, and genocide, but the thread remained implicit in so much of Anglo and Anglo-American history. The Natives must allow English traders and settlers, and if they displayed any hostility, God would bless the violence against them.

Still, Peckham did want the Natives to trade with the English, for the English economy needed new markets. Once the Natives had "but a little taste of civillitie, [they] will take mervailous delight in any garment be it never so simple: As a shirt, a blewe, yellow, redde, or green Cotton cassocke, a Capp or such like, and will take incredible paynes for such a trifle." Peckham assures readers that this trade would create great employment opportunities for a broad range of English workmen. Our "Townes and Villages," so many "nowe are utterlye decayed and ruinated," the people without work since raw wool was shipped overseas without English workers finishing it—these people would prosper once again when England created a market among America's Native peoples. This trade "shall be unto the Savages themselves verie beneficiall and gainefull." They would "bless the howre" that the English "enterprise was undertaken."

Trade would facilitate conversion. The English would bring the Indians "from falsehood to the truth . . . from the devil to Christ, from hell to Heaven." If this were all the Natives received for "the commodities they can yield us . . . they were more then [sic] fully recompenced." Some may object, Peckham averred, "that the Gospel must be freely preached," but "the workmen" must make their living. Plus, the English would teach the Indians how to more profitably use the land, "to understand how the tenth part of their land may be so manured and emploied . . . [to] yield more commodities to the necessary use of mans life." How could Indians possibly have just cause for complaint after receiving these gifts? In an important aside, repeated by generations of Christians to justify dispossession before, during, and after it occurred, Peckham added, "in my private opinion I doo verily think that God did create lande, to the end that it shold by Culture and husbandrie, yield things necessary for mans lyfe." The Indians were not making full use of God's gift. They lived in abundance, but did not see how much richer they could be. Apparently, these sober advantages of civility were not gift enough, because Peckham concludes with a climax of blood and sadism: "Lastly," he promises, the English would save the Indians' "poor innocent children . . . from the bloody knife of the sacrificer, a most horrible and detestable custome in the sight of God and man, now and ever heertofore used amongst them." If the Indians did not learn their lessons, then losing their land, liberty, and lives would be justified.

Peckham might be forgiven his ignorance of Native societies. He had no accurate notion of Native civilizations' accomplishments in the mechanical arts or of their mastery of food production. His conception of Natives sacrificing their children was entirely misconstrued by overextending isolated stories, mostly exaggerated. Nor did he see any irony in his suggestion that the English would protect the savages from sacrificing their children but kill them if they refused this protection. According to Peckham, Indians had no right to reject the arrival of a well-armed contingent sent by his queen. One wonders what the English would have thought of a few hundred Iroquois suddenly appearing in England demanding to trade and to settle.

Peckham used Christianity to provide justification and moral certainty that the English had both the right and the imperative to colonize, and that they could perpetrate mass murder in God's name. Hakluyt republished Peckham's tract and voiced support for the notion that Indians must accept Peckham's terms. He inserted marginalia approving its sentiment, that the English had the right to colonize in exchange for the offer of Christianity: "The bargaine can not be unjust where both parties are gainers." Peckham had tapped into the zeitgeist of colonialism: elimination of the "other"—if not literally through enslavement, forced removal, or murder, then figuratively by erasing their culture through religious conversion and "civilization."

We would be mistaken to think this was the only view the English held about colonization of Native lands. Peckham's tract makes clear that some English questioned their right to colonize, not just because of Iberian claims but also because of the rights possessed by the Native peoples. Nor did all English (or European) colonizers take such a militant view of colonization. Some believed that America's peoples had much to offer the world, and not just commodities and labor but knowledge about the physical and spiritual worlds.

One of these was Walter Ralegh. He and many of his associates held starkly different views of America's Native peoples and of empire building. And with Peckham's failure to colonize in the wake of Gilbert's death, Gilbert's patent lapsed. Humphrey's brother Adrian, along with John Dee and John Davis, petitioned to take over Humphrey's patent, but the queen rewarded her favorite, Walter Ralegh, with a new patent to colonize America.

—

For colonization to succeed, the English required investors, sailors, and colonists. All were difficult to come by. The English intended to turn the New World into a haven for English Catholics as a way to solve multiple problems: rid England of religious dissidents, obtain investors, and alleviate overcrowding by moving surplus populations of the unemployed overseas to become useful. English Catholic interest wavered, however, and George Peckham failed to make a go of things. Instead of moving to America, English Catholics began moving to Ireland when Munster opened for English colonial settlement in the late 1580s and early 1590s. Upheaval in Ireland later steered English Catholics to return to England, and again to seek New World settlement in the early 1630s.

Humphrey Gilbert had supported Catholic settlement not only because he was desperate to fulfill the terms of his patent but also because Catholics were his friends and relations. The Protestant-Catholic divide drew legal lines in England, but it did not erase the kinship and friendships that transcended religion. Religious prejudice throughout Western Europe led to violence, but personal ties, and even opportunities for collaboration in colonization, crossed the religious divide. As a colonizer, Walter Ralegh included Catholics among his colonists, and in Ireland he worked not only to end religious persecution but also to place Catholic holy sites into Catholic hands.

As evident from Peckham's tract, where the Native peoples fit into colonial schemes was problematic. Not only did religion serve as a potential and actual divisor, but so, too, did culture and the Natives' possession of land and resources that the colonizer desired. Natives possessed rights to their land, which led English like Peckham to conjure ways to extinguish those rights. Culture and cultural difference infused how the English thought about colonizing. On the one hand, their own religious culture pushed evangelism: convert the heathen. On the other hand, Native Americans often were labeled irredeemable and therefore could be dispossessed of their land, forced to labor, and killed. Gilbert, like Drake and Ralegh, lacked religious militancy—these men saw nothing amiss in working with Catholics or Native Americans or Africans. (Although they despised the pope and the King of Spain.) In Gilbert's mind, the Native peoples of America were akin to English commoners—light amusements like Morris dancing and hobby horses would earn their affections.

Ralegh differed from his brother Humphrey in numerous ways. Ralegh's imperiousness emerged when he contended with elites he despised. He generally developed favorable relations with his fellow commoners, even those considered vastly socially inferior. After gaining the queen's favor, Ralegh became the highest royal official in the counties of Devon and Cornwall. He periodically drafted men for military service in Ireland. There is no record of complaint and rarely much difficulty on his part supplying the ranks.[7] He generally did quite well winning men's loyalty. When given charge of the valuable stannaries that produced tin, the tin workers were happy with his leadership because he worked to improve wages and living conditions. Otherwise, he seems to have respected them enough to leave them to their business.

As a military man in Ireland, he took care of those in his charge. Men who sailed or otherwise worked for him often engaged with him in multiple enterprises. His personal bravery contributed to his men's loyalty. Perhaps the men appreciated that he was one of them—a commoner. If he had acted haughty to them, as he did to peers he disliked, he probably would have had fewer followers despite the queen's support. And when the queen did punish him, as when she had him thrown in the Tower of London, Robert Cecil recorded that the sailors gave him rousing cheers upon his release.

As for relations with Native peoples, Ralegh held unusual and "enlightened" ideas. He was an individual who appreciated Native peoples on multiple levels and for diverse reasons and purposes. In Ireland and in the Americas, Ralegh displayed a spiritual, intellectual, and temperamental tolerance and goodwill to Native peoples. And in all these capacities, he displayed growth over time. But even as a young man he took opportunities to act on his beliefs in regard to combining the interests of the colonizer (himself) with those of Native peoples (American Indian and Irish).

Ultimately, Ralegh vigorously countered Peckham's arguments that the Bible countenanced genocide against American Indians, and he opposed enslavement and removal. He came to believe that American Indians were specially blessed by God. He also worked to end persecution of the Irish (and also of the Brownists—the Pilgrims in England). Further down the road, he proposed a radical partnership between England and America's Native peoples. In 1584, these ideas were germinating as he took steps to become a colonizer, which depended on his place at court and the personal favors he hoped for from Queen Elizabeth.

PART THREE

—

"especiall grace, certeyne science and meere mocyon"

*Mysticism and the Empress
of English Colonialism*

CHAPTER 6

The Courtier

I n March 1584, Queen Elizabeth granted Walter Ralegh a patent to found and possess a colony in America. After stating her titles and offering her greeting, the patent describes Elizabeth's wonderful power: "Knowe yee that of our especiall grace, certeyne science and meere mocyon [motion], We have gyven and graunted . . . to our trusty and welbeloved servaunte Walter Raleighe Esquirer."[1] In the phrasing "especiall grace, certeyne science and meere mocyon," the queen affirms the centrality of her role in the colonizing enterprise.[2] She is the source of all favor and possesses mystical endowment. By "especiall grace," that is to say, her special favor, which she received from God, she granted Ralegh the patent entitling him to colonize in America. Science, or *sience* in the Anglo-Norman, which came to England through the French *cience*, refers to the state or fact of knowing. According to the *Oxford English Dictionary* (*OED*), in the word's sixteenth-century usage, this knowledge is neither opinion nor belief, but infallible truth. Science in the sixteenth century denoted knowledge as an attribute of God, as opposed to truth attained through reason and proof, as many would define it today. Coupling "certeyne" with "science" redundantly eliminates any ambiguity about Elizabeth's knowledge coming from God.[3] Likewise, in her phrase "meere mocyon," *mere* meant "pure" in Elizabethan England, and *mocyon*, according to the *OED*, meant a "prompting or impulse originating from God." Thus, the action of issuing the patent to Ralegh was a pure impulse originating from God through His anointed ruler. Historian Patricia Seed notes that the English were "unique" in Europe in holding "the idea that royal authority derives from God and comes to the crown by grace."[4] Cynically, we can read the entire statement as a boilerplate expression of the monarch's favor, judgment, and God-ordained power, but it held immutable truth to sixteenth-century English readers. As she was chosen by God to be queen, Elizabeth's actions expressed His will. When she granted favors to her servants, these, too, originated from God.

God gave Ralegh the right to colonize—it was God's will spoken through the queen. Elizabeth bridged the holy and the mundane. She was a vessel of God for His people. For God, she stood as head of the English Church. For God, she held sovereignty over England. Any colonies that her "trusty" servant established would be held and enjoyed by Ralegh, but she maintained sovereignty over them, and God maintained sovereignty over all. All Elizabeth's actions God directed and blessed.[5]

The mystical association of Elizabeth with colonialism ran deeply through English society, promoted and articulated by many, but the patent also encompassed Elizabeth's own assertion of rights, which she expressed by spelling out the practical operation of her colony. Elizabeth made clear that Parliament had no say in her overseas domain. She barred Parliament from making any statute or law that interfered with Ralegh's colonizing or his traveling back and forth between England and his colony. The patent's privileges and restrictions defined the parameters of Ralegh's power in his colony, and by doing so asserted Elizabeth's monarchical power against Parliament. She granted Ralegh and his heirs all the "right, royalties, franchises, and jurisdictions" on both land and enjoining seas of his colony, reserving to the Crown one-fifth of all gold and silver. He could expel anyone who attempted settlement within two hundred leagues (600 miles) of his patent if they were not there prior to his colony. Ralegh possessed full civil and judicial "power and authority to correct, punish, pardon, govern, and rule," in all "causes capital, or criminal, or civil, both marine and other," and not just over his settlers but over anyone within two hundred leagues. Moreover, he could establish any government, as long as its "statutes lawes, and ordinaunces may be as neere as conveniently they may be, agreable to the forme" of the same in England, and not against the "trewe Christian faithe, now professed in the Churche of England." In other words, Ralegh's colony should be similar to England, but not a facsimile. He could skirt Parliament's power—they had no say in Ralegh's colony—but not the queen's power, and the Church of England, her church, would be the religion of the land.

Elizabeth left it to her advisors, instead of Parliament, to oversee Ralegh's colony. The patent provided that Elizabeth's and her heirs' councilors could license Ralegh and his heirs to "embark and transport out of our Realm" people and goods "for the better relief" and support of the colony. Again, she asserted, Parliament could enact no "acte, statute, lawe, or other thing to the contrary." Nor could Ralegh buck her interests. If he robbed by "sea or land" any Christian prince in amity with her, Ralegh or his heirs had to "make full restitucion and satisfaccion of all such injuries done." Otherwise, he would lose the queen's "allegiaunce and proteccion."

She placed another restriction on Ralegh's treatment of colonists. The patent provided that anyone born in England, Ireland, or other lands "within our allegiaunces" and permitted by Ralegh to live within his patent would "have and enjoy all the pryvyledges of free Denizens and persons natyve of England . . . as yf they were borne and personally resiante [resident] within our said Realm of England." These rights, held by her subjects, were rights that neither a colony's proprietor, Parliament, nor the monarch could disregard—Elizabeth proclaimed these rights were carried from one of her dominions to another. The colonists' possession of all the rights of Englishmen, combined with the denial of any parliamentary power over the colony, almost two hundred years later provided the historical evidence for John Adams, who had studied the early patents, to assert that Parliament's taxation of American colonists was unprecedented and a new invention that went against the charter rights of colonies and the colonists' rights as Englishmen.[6]

We explore Parliament's response to Ralegh's patent in Part Four, but here we focus on the multifaceted central role of Elizabeth to the overseas enterprise. She alone could authorize English overseas expansion. For instance, in 1584, just as Elizabeth permitted Ralegh to colonize in America, she prohibited colonization in Ireland. She chose who could colonize: her courtiers were the ones most likely to be rewarded, first Gilbert and then Ralegh, and in the coming years she granted significant portions of Ireland to Ralegh and other courtiers. These courtiers were preeminent at Elizabeth's court—they largely defined court life and how Elizabeth and her reign were understood throughout the realm. Indeed, they created a cult around Elizabeth, one that not only included overseas expansion but that also made empire building a goal of her reign. The courtiers endowed Elizabeth with otherworldly attributes that merged with the mystical Christian philosophy of Hermeticism and the queen's self-conception of possessing "ceretyne science and meere motion." English colonialism emerged from an ectoplasm of ideas that the "empress" Elizabeth was destined to lead a universal monarchy that would expand into America.

An empress is never ordinary, but to command a universal monarchy bespeaks an extraordinary individual, and Elizabeth fit that role, too: she was proclaimed a goddess, and not just any goddess but one who combined the attributes of multiple goddesses. In one poem—a poem turned into a popular song in the 1580s or 1590s—by the third line, Ralegh had declared her to encompass five goddesses, Cynthia, Phoebe, Flora, Diana, and Aurora.[7] Others poets identified additional goddesses that the queen resembled or encompassed, but no one played as important a role in defining Elizabeth as multiple goddesses—or as the particular goddesses that became foundational for portraying the queen—as Ralegh, the great beneficiary of her "especiall grace" in America. Yet even a monarch as impressive as Elizabeth faced worldly difficulties in ruling England, which provided crucial context for colonization.

—

THE MID-1580s were a dangerous time for England. Ever since Elizabeth's father Henry VIII divorced his queen, Catherine of Aragon, daughter of Spain's Ferdinand of Aragon and Isabella of Castile, and removed England from the Catholic Church, relations with Spain had deteriorated, though they temporarily improved when Catherine's Catholic daughter Mary assumed the English throne in 1553 and married Spain's Philip II. But upon Mary's death, her Protestant sister Elizabeth had ascended to the throne. Spain retained hope of restoring England to the Catholic Church and reined in some of its hostility to England's Protestant monarch because of complications in Europe. The spread of Protestantism threatened Spanish interests around the Continent. Spain feared Elizabeth would support German, French, and Dutch Protestants. The Dutch Revolt had been an attempt to free the Netherlands from Philip II; if France became Protestant, it likely would ally with England. Protestantism thus threatened the core of Philip II's power, his position in Europe as the richest, most powerful monarch whose influence could be felt (and was feared) most everywhere.

Ralegh's career as a colonizer, politician, and soldier was shaped by decades of Spanish-English hostility. His hostile feelings were based in neither religion nor personal beliefs, though occasionally he railed against Spain's mistreatment of Native peoples. In the mid-1580s, just as Ralegh became a colonizer, Spain threatened to conquer England and kill the queen. American gold and silver funded the Spanish war machine. Ralegh, like Drake, Grenville, and others, intended to siphon off Spanish wealth through piracy. He also hoped that the creation of American colonies would generate permanent sources of wealth to help England compete against Spain.

Occasionally, intimating that her religious beliefs were not far from theirs, Elizabeth teased the Spanish with hope that she would return England to Catholicism. She could be as cunning as any monarch. Her religious sensibilities tilted toward high church ritual, but she understood that she had to steer her church through political minefields at home and abroad.

Her tacit and financial support of European Protestants intermittently drew her closer to France. The killing of French Protestants in the Saint Bartholomew Day's Massacre (1573) soured relations, but England and France seemingly needed one another to ally against Spain. Elizabeth flirted with the idea of marrying the French king's brother, François, Duke of Alençon, at a time when she could no longer bear children, a measure that could have brought France and England closer together without actually uniting the crowns. Ralegh, who had fought in France as a young man, was assigned to entertain the young duke, and the queen and Alençon appeared to have gotten along quite well. The duke's Catholicism was opposed in England, and when John Stubbs wrote a pamphlet in 1579 against the proposed marriage, Stubbs, his printer, and the publisher were all tried and convicted of sedition. The printer was pardoned, but Elizabeth had to be convinced not to have the other two executed. Instead, she had their right hands cut off. Elizabeth did not like her authority questioned. But she did not marry Alençon.

Elizabeth conducted foreign policy in consultation with her advisors. Her most important advisors in the 1570s and 1580s were William Cecil, Lord Burghley, who served her for forty years; Francis Walsingham, the queen's "principal secretary"; and her childhood friend, Robert Dudley, whom she made the first Earl of Leicester. All three were members of the queen's formal advisory board, the Privy Council. This council oversaw much of the day-to-day operation of foreign and domestic policy. In her predecessors' reigns, the number of councilors could reach as high as fifty. At the beginning of Elizabeth's reign, the council numbered just under twenty, a membership that steadily declined as she refused to replace those who died. The council thus became more exclusive, manageable, and focused to her interests.

Ralegh learned from all three men. From Burghley, he learned a circumspect foreign policy, much in league with the queen, to resist sending large armies to the European continent. From Walsingham, Ralegh learned geopolitics and perhaps the appreciation of how expanding trade to new markets would strengthen England at home. From Leicester, Ralegh took lessons in how to court the queen—how to be a dashing courtier. Interestingly, historians see Ralegh as a protégé of one or another of these men; someone had to guide him through the vicissitudes of the English court after Humphrey Gilbert died. Instead, it is more apt not to label Ralegh as a member of any faction; he did not follow anyone's lead. Once he had the queen's favor, he avoided factionalism and focused on overseas expansion and securing a political base in South West England. Elizabeth directly provided him with the patronage he needed.

Whatever the political sensibilities of those who served the queen, politics revolved around patronage. All hoped to earn the queen's favor. She personally distributed patronage, much of it to Burghley and Walsingham, to maintain support. She also personally rewarded favorites with the wardships of orphans, the "farm" privileges over various customs taxes and licenses, and an array of monopolistic rights.

With so much power, Elizabeth exasperated the men who served her. Some of this aggravation arose as a by-product of forceful individuals having to contend with an equally forceful monarch. Gender differences also played a role: the men had to take orders from a woman, and they questioned her qualifications to make decisions in such affairs as warfare and diplomacy, which they deemed incomprehensible to women. Commanders in the field chafed under her authority, frequently disregarding her orders.

Elizabeth avoided war when she could—not because of the violence but because of the monetary costs: it irked her to no end how little control she wielded over her commanders' spending. To rein in expenses, she preferred short-term drafts for service in Ireland to subdue rebellion. When pressed, she employed mercenaries on the Continent, particularly to support her French or Dutch allies. Mercenaries cost more than English troops, but they were "deniable" and gave her diplomatic flexibility.[8] She hated committing herself to irrevocable decisions in grave matters of state, particularly in foreign policy, and on questions regarding her imprisoned cousin, Mary, Queen of

Scots. At times she forestalled commitment by making promises to all, and breaking them as she may. Some of this behavior may have been planned, but it seems that Elizabeth often truly was frightened of setting herself (and England) on an unalterable course, thus her hesitations, quick changes of mind, and refusal to be pinned to one policy. With mercenary armies often fulfilling her commitments, she could deny to foreign ambassadors that involvement existed, though she and they knew it a lie. Even as she funded troops in the Netherlands and the Germanies to resist Spain, she looked the Spanish ambassador in the eye and said she knew nothing of the matter. He might have protested, or not; at times it was convenient for them both to leave the reality unstated.

Her hesitancy to commit to policies contributed to her propensity for supporting piracy. She could unofficially wage war at sea. It was much less costly than sending armies to Europe, less risky politically, and held greater potential for profits. Elizabeth thus gave great backing to the Devonshire men—Ralegh, Drake, Grenville, Hawkins, and numerous others—because they brought her wealth and served her political interests. Doing the queen's business while lining their pockets with other countries' treasure, they were less concerned with the queen's inconstant policies on the European continent. English pirates were like mercenaries at sea: their battles with enemy ships or ports were regularly discountenanced. And usually Elizabeth did not have to pay them. Her brother-in-law, Philip II, let her get away with piracy, even though Spain was the chief target, because he was preoccupied with resuming control over the Low Countries and could not send England and France into each other's arms. The loss of merchant ships was unfortunate, but Philip did not have to personally bear the costs. And considering the vast wealth Spain wrested from its empire, what the English pirates took seemed comparatively small. Though Drake was the most feared of all in Spain, Ralegh also earned a reputation as one of Spain's chief foes: a colonizer, buccaneer, organizer of pirating expeditions, soldier, and overall buttress of Elizabeth's power against Spain.

—

PERHAPS IT SEEMED like Elizabeth inhabited a man's world, but she really lived surrounded by a large number of women. Twenty-two females, sixteen of whom were paid, saw to the queen's daily needs.[9] These women were nobility or gentry. The paid servants were handsomely remunerated with a salary and coverage of all their expenses at court, including expensive clothing. They helped Elizabeth dress, over-saw her bodily functions, carried her personal effects, and amused her with games, conversation, and music. Also keeping the queen's company were a few "friends" and the wives of courtiers and other gentle-men, who helped entertain important visiting personages.

The woman Elizabeth associated with most intimately in child-hood from the age of three onward was Ralegh's great aunt Kat Ashley, who served first as nurse and later as governess to the future queen. Throughout her service, Ashley slept with Elizabeth and acted as her confidante, which sometimes got Ashley into trouble. She was con-fined to the Tower of London for suggesting to Elizabeth that she marry Thomas Seymour. Ashley also was imprisoned during Mary's reign for her religious views and later for possession of illegal religious tracts. Even when Elizabeth as queen appointed Ashley chief gentlewoman of the Privy Chamber, Ashley was confined to her room for pushing Eliz-abeth to marry Prince Erik of Sweden.[10]

It was not unusual for those wishing to have a voice at court to lobby the queen's women, or the courtiers, with substantial sums of money and jewels. The women could bend her ear for any number of purposes, and the queen used them in kind, too, to pass her ideas to their husbands or other men. Though Elizabeth developed good rela-tions with most of those who served her, she was a demanding task-master, especially as she grew older, and especially owing to problems in Ireland that led her to be harsher "toward her women."[11] Altogether, the queen and her ladies-in-waiting had immense impact on Ralegh's life: Ashley's prominence ensured that first Humphrey and then Walter had opportunity to prove their value to the queen; the queen herself became the fount for Ralegh's rise as one of the foremost men in En-gland; one of Elizabeth's ladies became his wife.

Elizabeth liked her younger men, handsome, martial, and urbane. Ralegh embodied these traits and an array of other qualities. The queen was learned, enjoyed conversation, and dabbled in poetry, both as poet and translator. Ralegh was extremely well read, analytical, and also ar-tistic. He composed poetry, played the lute, and sang and possessed a keen aesthetic sensibility that made him a master of fashion, from the placing of jewels on his shoes to the popularizing of broad lace collars for men. Elizabeth especially appreciated his intellectual prowess. A quick wit marked an individual's competitive advantage. Elizabethans enjoyed word play and oral sparring; they invented infinite ways to curse and demean in both jest and battle. In the same era, Shakespeare deployed a prolific array of puns to audiences that understood and appreciated them as ways to express irony. Ralegh possessed this wit, and it raised him above other men in the queen's estimation.

By securing the queen's affections, Ralegh attracted men to his train—a Renaissance-era term for a group of people moving together in line behind a single individual. Without prejudice of ethnicity or religion, he let individuals' talents recommend them. For example, he employed a Jewish assayer for his colony in America. His personal secretary was a "good Catholic."[12] When Ralegh arrived at court, he associated with many Catholics despite substantial intolerance of Catholicism in English society.[13] He developed lifelong friendships with American Indians. His intellectual and religious propensities always steered him toward religious tolerance and a spirituality that could be characterized as universalism. As did other Protestants, he likely considered the pope a great enemy of England because of the papal threat to Queen Elizabeth of 1570. But he had little or no contempt for Catholic spirituality, and he supported Catholics in a variety of ways in Ireland.[14] Despite his hostility toward Spain, he befriended Spanish people and admired Spanish accomplishments, particularly in building colonies. He possessed no ideology except service to the queen.

Ralegh owed his meteoric rise to Queen Elizabeth. She provided gifts and income to make him wealthy, appointed him to offices, and elevated his status to national fame. In return, he entertained her. She found him philosophical and spiritual, articulate and energetic. Earning her favor also earned him much envy: he became the most hated man in England while he was also much admired. His enemies charged him with atheism, yet in his later years, and after his death, he was revered for his religiosity. One of his books would be reviled for centuries as a pack of lies, another viewed for over a century as one of the greatest histories written by an Englishman. Indeed, he gained renown for having incredibly broad intellectual interests combined with an ability to actively engage in an array of activities, epitomizing the ideal of the Renaissance man. Ralegh possessed so many talents that he would have been a success without the queen's love and patronage; with her support, he emerged as one of England's brightest stars.

RALEGH FIRST CAUGHT Elizabeth's attention when Lord Deputy Grey sent him to court to report on Irish affairs. That he was Humphrey Gilbert's younger brother and the stories of his bravery in Ireland also garnered attention. Elizabeth could see for herself his charm and charisma. Whereas most people at court could only interact with the queen in her Presence Chamber, as a courtier, Ralegh gained access to the queen's Privy Chamber, where he enjoyed private conversations with her. Others allowed in the Privy Chamber included members of the Privy Council, also considered courtiers, and elites who held court positions that involved waiting on the queen, such as the Lord Chamberlain, the Vice Chamberlain, and the Captain of the Guard. The queen's cupbearers and servers, physicians, and various ladies-in-waiting and miscellaneous invited gentlemen also had access. Elizabeth alone decided who could attend her at court and who could be a courtier. No one became a member of the Privy Council without being known to the queen. No one below gentry became a courtier. Elizabeth eschewed "mingling with her subjects," particularly the "lower sort."[15]

The court comprised fifteen hundred to seventeen hundred people, including nearly a hundred peers, top government officials, and the queen's body servants. A relatively small number of courtiers and a great variety of hangers-on numbered to about five hundred; approximately a thousand workers supported the rest by providing food and services.[16] A place at court signified membership in the nation's inner circle or connection to someone in that circle, with the potential for assignment to valued offices and pecuniary rewards. It could also be costly—not all of the nobility and gentry wished to attend because they had to support their servants or they desired not to be absent from their own estates. For much of the gentry, however, there was no more important place to be. People attended court hoping to obtain licenses, special privileges, contracts, and pensions.

The search for money and favors was the sport of all courts, but according to one Spaniard, it reached its epitome in England. No less an authority than Spain's most successful money-grubbing courtier, Ruy Gómez de Silva, expressed astonishment at the jockeying among nobles and courtiers he witnessed during his visit to England when Philip II married Elizabeth's sister Mary. De Silva believed that the impoverishment of the English nobility (who were poor compared to the Spanish) created this situation. With his usual flair for the dramatic, de Silva sarcastically reported to a correspondent, "Upon my faith, even though interest is a powerful motive in all lands, it is nowhere in the world stronger than here, where nothing is done well except with cash in hand. We [the Spanish] have all brought with us so little money that, if they tumble to the fact, I do not know if we will escape alive; at the very least, we will be without honor, since in their disappointment they will flay us mercilessly."[17]

Most gentry and peers hoped for an invitation to court. Anyone, including high nobility, who wished to wield (or protect their) political power or obtain royal favors needed to be at court to further their interests and maintain their networks. Those assigned diplomatic tasks abroad—even brief tours—often viewed these absences as threatening rather than enhancing their position, fearing that as soon as they left court, their enemies would lay siege to available rewards. Not infrequently their assessment was correct. Those wishing to make money abroad—the merchant adventurers looking for licenses and privileges in Asia or monopoly control over newly discovered trade routes,[18] the buccaneers seeking leave to conduct marauding expeditions in the Americas and Africa, the prospective colonizers hoping for large estates in Ireland—all required court connections.

The merchant adventurer, buccaneer, and colonizer could be one and the same person. Sometimes he received license to pursue one venture and sometimes another, but often he combined opportunities to his own best advantage. If a man received privileges abroad, he could even hire others to exploit his licenses, though the Devonshire men tended to personally see their projects to fruition. Perhaps it was their distance from London and close connection to maritime activities. They went to sea seeking fame and fortune and won Elizabeth's support and admiration.[19] They sacrificed political power with their absence from court, though they retained influence in their home counties and a voice in foreign affairs, particularly regarding Spain and the Spanish Empire. Most of the Devonshire men were gentry and received knighthood for their service. Humphrey Gilbert, Francis Drake, Bernard Drake, John Hawkins, Richard Grenville, and Walter Ralegh, among others, took to the sea to pursue their ends, maintained their political power in South West England, and advised the queen and Privy Council on foreign and domestic affairs, but the nature of their work kept them from participating in the day-to-day operations of the Privy Council. In return for good service and a courtly manner, the Devonshire men became her chief men of the sea and received privileges to open trade routes, colonize, and lead expeditions against the Spanish; their numerous appointments and allowances enabled them to grow wealthier and dispense patronage in their home counties.

Elizabeth appreciated explorers and buccaneers. They made money for her; their courage and panache were bonuses. There were numerous ways to impress the queen. Good looks, charm, style, and wit provided a promising start. A refined jousting performance at the annual Accession Day tilts was another way to earn favor.[20] Ralegh and his fellow seamen did not have to joust[21]—they proved themselves at sea with their own special brand of courage. Profits also turned the queen's head, especially when their realization involved derring-do. Later in her life, when Ralegh and the Earl of Essex performed a great feat of daring in an attack on Cádiz, Spain, Elizabeth was not so impressed: they did not return with profits. But by then, she generally was much less enamored with male bravery. In her younger days, she appreciated both, as long as they led to tangible results.

As historian Joan Thirsk noted, the early colonizing enterprises, whether in Ireland or the New World, were undertaken by courtiers.[22] Anyone who wished to receive overseas privileges had to be personally known to the queen and to have provided successful service. Drake's success at sea was so extraordinary that the queen allowed him to stay away from court for long periods. On land, he avoided court, favoring his home in Devonshire instead. When he did appear, Elizabeth would disappear for hours with him. They gave each other precious jewels, and he accepted important assignments and privileges from her. Drake supported colonization and worked closely with the colonizers, but he had little personal interest in planting overseas colonies. He preferred exploring, trading, and marauding for personal profit and for the queen.

Those knights and peers of the realm who wished to serve the queen abroad without sailing the oceans tended to seek plaudits through army service in France or the Low Countries or through assignment to Ireland. Ireland offered less chance for glory than the Continent but more opportunities for wealth through colonizing enterprises or seizure of rebel estates. Ireland attracted men who hoped to improve their ties with England's leaders, because competent service opened further opportunities for advancement. The queen and her government valued those who could serve in Ireland and who were flexible and skilled enough to also serve at sea—like Humphrey Gilbert and Walter Ralegh. Such men need not have possessed navigational skills to command troops or a supply unit in Ireland or to conduct reconnaissance along the coast of Spain, but they needed enough skills to strategize when trouble arose and to know how to command seamen.

Courtiers with licenses for opportunities at home and abroad attracted investors and men willing to serve under their command. With significant patronage, they attracted great numbers to their under-

takings. Those who received permanent appointments to high political office or high appointments at court could create a faction, or at
least become a locus of influence. Ralegh's selection as Captain of
the Guard in 1586 or 1587—the date is disputed—afforded him an unusual amount of access to the queen that further buttressed his influence.[23] It also made him personally responsible for the queen's safety,
because he chose the men to fill vacancies in the guard. But even before receiving this signal appointment, Elizabeth granted him income-
producing privileges, and the Privy Council awarded him government
contracts. Ralegh held a monopoly over the issuance of retail wine licenses in all of England and command over the stannaries in Cornwall
that produced tin. As lieutenant governor of Cornwall and Devon, he
was responsible for raising men for military service and for supplying
troops, which gave him much opportunity for purchasing from farmers
and other suppliers. These rewards and offices allowed him to employ
many and to gather individuals into a following.

Courtiers interacted with the queen at innumerable social gath-
erings, large and small, and helped shape the court's social life and
politics by constructing and directing activities, from banquets and
dances to elaborate pageants and theatrical performances in London
and around the country during the queen's summer tours. To a significant extent, they were showmen. They used performances to promote
political policies.[24] The private side to their relations with the queen
involved intimate conversations and flirtations, when Elizabeth play-
acted at romance and sought advice and confided thoughts she would
not or could not confide in her ladies-in-waiting. Not all such affairs
were entirely private, and they, too, were used to make political statements and show favor. To whom did the queen bestow a dance or a
poem? To whom did she refuse the same?

Words carried much power at court, and good conversation was
expected of most courtiers. The ancient Greeks emphasized conversation as an art—Plato taught that conversation was essential for civility, a legacy embraced by educated Elizabethans. Rules of etiquette
offered guidelines for conversations between equals and for exchanges
between individuals of different social statuses, ages, and genders.
Courtiers especially had to master the etiquette of interaction with
the sovereign, which occurred across a vast social divide. In history
courtiers have been viewed as fawning individuals, in essence, liars,
preoccupied with complimenting their monarch and other social betters while sugar-coating their superiors' faults. Deference, indeed, was

crucial for negotiating distinctions of status and birth, but the manuals on civility emphasized the importance of honesty in conversation—though not an honesty that would insult.

Civil conversation, if used properly, enabled an individual to demonstrate prowess and assert power. The new civility downplayed deference to emphasize the substance of conversation—honesty.[25] Some, perhaps many, members of the nobility resented the new conversational form, particularly what they perceived as its lack of deference. It was especially irksome to nobility unskilled in the conversational arts, embarrassed by their own shortcomings. They viewed the speech and conversation of the courtier as "art" in a derogatory sense—as the manipulation of words for self-aggrandizement; a courtier's "honesty" was a pocketful of lies to a flustered noble demanding deference to their blood. This assessment was correct: courtiers did use "honesty" to elevate their status by demeaning others. But the courtiers, some of whom were of noble blood, were not attempting to overthrow the hierarchy from which they stood to benefit; instead, they were jockeying for position. Nevertheless, there simmered pervasive challenges to the status of blood in Elizabethan England. A wealthy merchant class and landed gentry sought to increase their social status and political power by asserting themselves in private rooms and on the public stage. Ralegh mastered the art of conversation, of courtship, and he was neither a revolutionary nor a merchant, but represented to bluer bloods the upstart climbing over their backs, all the way to the queen's favor.

Courtship of a monarch was not new to Elizabethan England, nor peculiar to England. Even a male monarch was to be courted by those seeking favors. Courtship revealed the nodes of power: factions formed around the competing networks of influence, with patronage and favors distributed on multiple levels, but particularly from the Crown to courtiers, who then patronized less-well-connected individuals. Elizabeth manipulated the factions to her own ends, wooing one, then another, and playing them against one another.

Courtiers understood they must properly court Elizabeth to obtain her ear. They learned courtship from observation and personal instruction, but books assisted them as well. The major manual for courtier behavior in Elizabethan England was Castiglione's *The Book of the Courtier*. Published in Italy in 1528 and translated by Sir Thomas Hoby into an English edition in 1561, it reached a wide readership in England among the educated classes. The much-admired Sir Philip Sidney apparently carried a copy of the book in his pocket when he traveled abroad.[26] It was extremely popular at the universities as a "conversational treatise,"[27] and one scholar of Tudor education concluded that the book became "almost a second bible for English gentlemen."[28] Although Castiglione's book treated a wide range of relationships, the most important was the courtier's with the sovereign. If the sovereign was male, the courtier kept the prince company, shared his recreations, assisted in his obligations, and proffered advice. He served as a model for the ruler's own proper behavior. As Castiglione noted, the courtier should help his sovereign become "moste wise, moste continent, moste temperate, moste manlye," which included cultivating the sovereign's physical capacities: rivalry in the hunt and in athletic competitions improved the prince's skills.[29]

The problem with Castiglione's book and other contemporary prescriptions for courtier behavior and civil conversation was that the English sovereign was not a man. Elizabeth desired her courtiers to treat her amorously.[30] She was, however, no ordinary woman to woo: courtship, at most, could have but a vague undertone of sexuality. The courtier was to address Elizabeth's beauty, express admiration for her many fine parts, and exclaim adoration for her above all others, but there could be no implication of a sexual conclusion to the flirtation. The model for this form of courtship is found in the medieval Arthurian romances still popular in Western Europe during the Renaissance. In this literature, a knight devoted himself in service to an unobtainable woman, often one who was married. Sexual tension existed but could not be consummated. If it did, disaster befell the couple.[31] The Arthurian romances took on new life in Elizabeth's reign, in poetry and prose, with the moral remaining the same: consummation led to disaster. When marriage was possible, consummation could be a legitimate end, and marriage was celebrated for its virtues but treated in the literature as dull and inconsequential. Unobtainable love remained a staple in Elizabethan literature because it titillated while stretching the boundaries of propriety for those hemmed in by social and legal strictures.

Playacting and role-playing (often as lovers) were common at court. Although they could act the role of a character, people frequently played themselves but enhanced their role in ever larger, more creative, and expensive ways. The most prominent way to bring attention to oneself was through dress. Appropriate cloth and tailoring were expensive. The queen made gifts of cloth to members of the court for special occasions, and an active used clothing market filled the needs of many.[32] The Earl of Oxford upped the ante by introducing decorated

4. Nicholas Hilliard miniature of Ralegh, circa 1585. © National Portrait Gallery, London

gloves and "other such fripperies at court," which won Elizabeth's approval.[33] Ralegh popularized huge frilly collars—ruffs—that set off one's head as no style before or since.[34] They might be described as creating a vision of a "head on a plate."

Women had begun wearing these outlandish ruffs mid-century, but Ralegh made them into a man's ornament as well. He could hardly have found another style so self-celebratory. He also bedecked himself in jeweled shoes and jeweled ornaments on his clothing, an earring (suitable for a man of the sea), and colorful, well-cut clothes that set off his long lines and trimness. Ralegh's dress alienated the jealous, who had difficulty keeping up with him. He could afford the ostentations because Elizabeth gave him precious stones and other gifts to maintain his dress and lifestyle.

Ralegh's courtship of the queen, though central to their relationship, involved much more than looking the part of a dashing courtier, treating her amorously, and producing an array of entertainments. The courtiers defined for the court and the nation how to think of the queen. They did much of this through poetry. Ralegh led the way in using verse not only to secure the queen's favor, and to create the images by which the country should view her, but also to promote England building an empire.

CHAPTER 7

The Cult of Elizabeth

C ourtship revolved around words—spoken, sung, and written. The courtly literature expounded on the dangers of women succumbing to flattery and then seduction. Hostility toward Ralegh undoubtedly reflected the belief that his use of words turned the queen's head. Ralegh's broad Devonshire accent was thought to have won Elizabeth with its charm, and if few could compete with the sound of his voice, even fewer could compete with his mastery and use of vocabulary. He also enlarged the scope of how a courtier might use words. It is probable that Ralegh introduced to court the singing of one's own poetry, which others then imitated, and he accompanied his singing with the lute, an instrument Elizabeth also played.[1]

Courtship was not frowned upon by all, and if some could only emphasize its lasciviousness and insincerity, others depicted courtship in moral terms. They emphasized the positive aspects of the courtier's service, the purity of the good knight, the deserved adulation of women (particularly Elizabeth), and the mutual obligations and affections created between men and women. Those viewing courtship, hearing its tale in song, or reading about it could judge for themselves the sincerity of the participants, the propriety of their behavior, and the morality of the relationship. Those who wooed the queen did not perceive Her Majesty as cheapened—she was a woman, and it was considered proper to court her as one should court any great lady—with one important difference: Elizabeth was a goddess.

Other women could be compared to goddesses (particularly through metaphors), but around Elizabeth an entire cult formed that treated her as possessing qualities of the divine. Elizabeth was the perfect woman. If her propensity to lie was clear to many, it could be dismissed, as was her inconstancy, as the inscrutable character of a divinity. It is doubtful whether members of the court believed her immortal or perfection itself, but many suspended logic and worshipped her as divine and the sole possessor of perfection. Many viewed her contradictorily as being all too human, yet above and apart from the masses, and that it would be the height of disrespect to attempt to resolve the difference.

—

A SIGNAL WAY for some courtiers to convey their love and adulation was through poetry—at which Ralegh excelled. Ralegh's love poetry came at a time when poetry was just gaining legitimacy in England as an accepted and worthwhile expression of self and a form of art. Love poetry had been considered trifling. Some opposed poetry when it was not written for moral ends. Before the 1570s, courtiers occasionally wrote and even performed poetry for the queen that often was in Latin and addressed Humanist concerns. Elizabeth, herself, translated poetry throughout her reign. England lagged behind the Continent by a half century in the secularization of poetry.

Poems by more than thirty courtiers during Elizabeth's reign have survived, and many other courtiers were known to have written for the queen. Additionally, numerous men who were not courtiers wrote poetry for and about the queen. Some of these attended court but did not enjoy courtier status; others, such as Edmund Spenser, became famous out-of-court poets. Composition of love poetry for the queen began in the early 1570s with the work of Sir Edward Dyer and the Earl of Oxford. Oxford, in particular, introduced a diversity of subject matter, "varied analyses of the lover's state," and, as an earl, "lent respectability even to so trivial a pursuit as the writing of love poetry."[2] In their poetry, the queen "has devastated her admirers . . . whom are overwhelmed with passion." But she remains utterly blameless.[3]

Toward the end of the 1570s, Philip Sidney "initiated a wholesale transformation of English poetry."[4] In addition to constructing pastoral entertainments, employing fictional motifs to present the drama of "lifelike love affair[s]," Sidney imbued his poetry with a sensuousness about real women at court.[5] Raised by intellectually accomplished women who were fine poets themselves, Sidney was the first English poet to treat women in a multidimensional fashion.[6] According to the great scholar of Elizabethan courtier poetry, Steven W. May, "Sidney wrote the first English sonnet sequence, introduced a multiplicity of new forms, and among his many fictions popularized a genteel pastoralism that merged with Spenser's humbler strain to foster a rich progeny in the decades ahead." Sidney's status as a "model courtier and national hero"—he was a renowned soldier and the son of a much-respected Lord Deputy of Ireland—dignified poetry as an "aristocratic pastime" and a "worthwhile art form."[7]

Though Sidney's pastoral verse influenced poetry outside of court, courtier poets took their cues from elsewhere. Ralegh's cousin Anthony Gorges produced innumerable love poems, and many translations from the French that were "admiring and celebratory" of women and devoid of complaints.[8] Gorges, Ralegh, and Spenser seem to all have read each other's work. But whereas Gorges wrote largely for himself, and Spenser wrote as a professional for whom poetry could lead to social rise with fame and fortune, Ralegh's concern at this stage of his life was to impress the queen. His success became the model for other courtiers. According to May, Ralegh's poems directly addressed the queen with a "multitude of styles and fictions richer in their variety and concentrations than anything undertaken by previous courtiers."[9] Belphoebe, Diana, and Cynthia—goddesses—were among the chief characters he used to represent Elizabeth, and then they were adapted by other poets. Ralegh's poetry not only praised Elizabeth but also made statements, sometimes public statements, about their relationship—a tact later adopted by the Earl of Essex in his relationship with Elizabeth. A talented poet in her own right, Elizabeth versified in response to Ralegh's poems, and these, too, became public statements expressing her view of her courtier.[10]

England's first national poet, Spenser, was the poet most directly influenced by Ralegh. Spenser hoped to become a courtier, and ultimately received a pension from the queen, but he never achieved courtier status. Ralegh was Spenser's patron, and he helped him achieve fame by bringing him to court and promoting his work. Spenser's magnum opus, *The Faerie Queene*, was inspired by Ralegh's poetry in celebration of Elizabeth. *The Faerie Queene* was the greatest work of English poetry since Chaucer's *Canterbury Tales*—and it remains the longest poem in the English language. This multivolume work published over several years created Arthurian romances that heavily drew on the literature and motifs of the ancient world, particularly the Greeks, with Elizabeth in various guises, including in a central relationship with Ralegh. The style and genius of the poetry were all Spenser, but he included two of Ralegh's poems about Elizabeth to illustrate the sources for his own articulation of the goddess queen. Spenser also provided an introduction to the work that comprised a (now famous) letter to Ralegh to explain why he wrote *The Faerie Queene* and what he hoped to accomplish.

Unlike Spenser, Ralegh did not intend most of his poetry for publication. Ralegh wrote for a select audience: the queen and members of the court. His poems mostly circulated in manuscript form, though his first published poem dates from 1576.[11] About fifty extant poems can reasonably be attributed to Ralegh, and many others of greater uncertainty.[12] After Elizabeth's death, a public hungry for Ralegh's words led to publication of several of his poems and numerous others under his name, which he may or may not have written.

Despite limited publication in his lifetime, Raleigh's poetry, in general, was a great success inasmuch as it brought him attention, positive and negative, from important personages. Many wrote poems in response to his, extending or challenging his sentiments. Poetry aided Ralegh's rise and attainment of power and influence at court. His work stood out from most of his peers', appealing to those who celebrated the Cult of the Virgin Queen, but he also composed a range that extended from the political to the religious and philosophical. Ralegh's poetry, along with his later prose, made him one of the best-read authors of seventeenth-century England. His views of politics, religion, and history became popular among the Puritans, in particular, and the English, in general, and it was not uncommon for authors and publishers to add to the canon by attributing tracts to Ralegh to buttress the authority of their ideas. Even John Milton published a two-hundred-page piece under Ralegh's name in 1658, of which Ralegh's authorship is dubious, but it expressed political ideas that Milton wanted to promote.[13] Though I address particular poems in the course of this book, here I discuss what it meant for a courtier to produce poetry.

Ralegh was not the only courtier to turn from the "manly arts" of the sea to poetry. Drake, Frobisher, Hawkins, and Gorges all tried their hand at versifying. To add poetry to one's repertoire displayed one's adoration for the queen in a highly acceptable, sensual way. The courtiers were a rough-and-tumble bunch. Dueling and fisticuffs, though disapproved of by the queen, were not uncommon. Ralegh and others learned that love poems tempered their rougher side in Elizabeth's eyes. It helped that Elizabeth was vain and welcomed these gifts, but she also was intellectually precocious, certainly the mental superior of most of her courtiers—she could not be presented with any old poem but only those that displayed cleverness.

In the 1980s and 1990s, a group of scholars called the New Historicists criticized Ralegh's poetry. They interpreted Ralegh's life and poetry (as well as the lives and poetry of his peers) as entirely utilitarian: they claimed Ralegh's every move, including his poetry writing, was for no other purpose than self-promotion. According to this understanding, Ralegh's success as a poet arose because he figured out better than most how to use verse to further his career. In Stephen Greenblatt's terms, Ralegh excelled in the art of self-fashioning. According to the New Historicists, it is improbable at best and mostly irrelevant whether he experienced personal pleasure in the act of creation or believed what he wrote. Instead, they view Ralegh's poetry as they do his dress, conversation, and other aspects of his life: everything he did was the outgrowth of a premeditated design to obtain the queen's favor to increase his personal power.

There is truth in this assessment. Ralegh looked after his own interests and was exceptionally gifted at self-promotion. However, Ralegh's motives were not monocausal. He cared about ideas and people: he was not the English Machiavelli, with his eyes unerringly on the goal of attainment of power, though he did read Machiavelli, which shaped his view of politics.[14] Ralegh's success as a courtier derived, somewhat, from his self-fashioning. He possessed an artistic bent, creating an image of himself that was physically dynamic, offensive to the envious, pleasing to the queen, and mimicked by others. His poetry can be viewed in a similar light, though those contemporaries who gainsaid his poetical skills did so less for what he had to say and more because they disapproved of what they believed were his ulterior motives. Yet much of Ralegh's poetry was not of the fawning courtier. His poems about death were heartfelt. His greatest work, *Oceans to Cynthia*, though designed to obtain the good graces of the queen, included passionate and impolitic ranting that arose from deep within him. Ralegh possessed a healthy dose of cynicism, evinced in his best-known poem, "The Lie," an unrelenting attack upon contemporary institutions and their representatives.[15]

The prolific scholar of Tudor England A. L. Rowse believes that Elizabethans lacked nuance and the modern sense of irony;[16] "The Lie," indeed, lacks nuance. The Elizabethans tended to the dramatic, even to hysterics. Elizabethan music, dance, theater, and other cultural expressions—though not Shakespeare's plays (and those of a few others, as well as Sidney's and Spenser's poetry)—were embarrassments to later centuries. Shakespeare is excused his Elizabethan nature, in that his main characters are destined to die in most tragedies, hardly a nuanced strategy, and his comedies are full of impossible coincidences. And yet, within these Elizabethan parameters, Shakespeare found enormous space for nuance.

The Elizabethans wore their hearts on their sleeves, along with jewels on their shoes and their heads on plates of lace. They heartily expressed themselves and were not embarrassed by emotional displays. But within the effusiveness, there is nuance galore. Rowse apparently equates nuance with quietude. A loud fanfare to celebrate martial exploits lacks nuance, but we do better to look toward the Elizabethan musical genius John Dowland than horns blaring military music. The queen's musician produced (arguably) the world's most melancholic music, including the masterpiece *Lachrymae Tears*. Each of that piece's seven movements might be viewed as overbearing in their expression of deepest melancholy. Melancholy, itself, can be thought of as antithetical to nuance since the sadness is so profound. But melancholy in Dowland's hands is incredibly nuanced—and influenced by the mysticism of Hermeticism.[17] Slight alterations from one movement to the next express nuanced distinctions in the depths and shades of sadness, all of which completely wash over the listener.

It would be unfair to accuse Ralegh of lacking self-awareness, especially because "The Lie" epitomized self-awareness—the poem mocks himself. Ralegh's self-fashioning constituted conscious acts of self-creation. His broad range of writing, though (partly) the product of self-fashioning, exhibits an individual living the examined life. Ralegh and his peers sought to understand the universe and man's place in it; they thought deeply about themselves, their societies, God and spirituality, the nature of matter, the meaning of death, the past and the future, and how the individual related to all things. Their concern with the self is astonishing in its breadth. From their relationship to God, to the contemplation of the relationship of the physical to the spiritual, their reflective nature is evinced in the melancholy that overhung all, a recognition (and result) of the difficulty of reconciling the irreconcilable. This generation, more than so many others, felt compelled to live what they thought—to "do" and to "be"; they so tried to connect their ideas to lived existence.

Ralegh, Sidney, Spenser, Gilbert, and so many others who wrestled with the deepest questions about the human condition—most all of them mystics in trying to understand the unseen universe—believed in the mutability of the spiritual with the material world and struggled with the shape of their own spiritual condition in their physical body. They went out into the world to accomplish an array of achievements, to fashion a world that reflected their innermost thoughts. The Arthurian tales they revered praised noble deeds. Soldiering constituted a noble profession, with the learned and virtuous general the highest ideal. One hundred fifty years later, when James Oglethorpe, member of Parliament and the chief colonizer of Georgia, who personally directed the utopian experiment to connect his own ideals into a living reality, looked for someone to whom to compare Frederick the Great, in terms of combining physical and intellectual accomplishments, he thought of Sir Walter Ralegh. In Ralegh's own time, when Shakespeare's Hamlet asks, "To be or not to be," the question is resoundingly answered "to be" by a generation of Elizabethan adventurers, whose sense of limitation, however, manifested in a self-awareness that they might not be up to the task. Despite their bravado and courage, they heard whispers from their inner selves "not to be." But brave on they did. Drake, Grenville, and Hawkins, like Gilbert, died at sea; Frobisher died from wounds attained during a siege. Ralegh, the only long-lived one of the lot, died as bravely as any of them.

We should not make the same mistake of Ralegh that the envious made—to think that the quest for fame, wealth, and power governed his every move and whim. He certainly reached for the stars. His abilities and accomplishments were widely recognized in his own time and through the centuries. Ralegh contemplated the meaning of life in philosophical, political, social, and spiritual terms. If he wrote about love to impress his queen and peers and bested his competitors by winning the queen's approbation, as well as securing a large cadre of friends and admirers (not to mention an enviable estate), he truly adored his queen. He loved her as a goddess; he believed in the images of the cult he helped perpetuate. Fortune made her queen, of that there was no gainsaying. And his fortune depended on her. She had no peer in England as the fount of favors. When her prospects for marriage came to naught and Leicester failed her—abandoning her—by remarrying, she had hopes of growing old with Ralegh. They could talk of love and innocently flirt, and nothing would come of it but devotion.

Ralegh worshipped Elizabeth as a goddess because she was one. Elizabeth held the power of life and death over her minions. She could bestow riches or misery on anyone in her realm. She healed the sick through her touch, her blessing, her very presence in a room.[18] When

Marcus Gheeraerts the Younger painted the "Ditchley Portrait" of the queen for Sir Henry Lee, the queen stands atop a map of England. She is the sun—a common motif to represent Elizabeth—who controls England and all its inhabitants.[19]

The faults Elizabeth possessed were seen by those who worshipped her as inconsequential, beyond questioning. Goddesses are, after all, temperamental. She presided over all worldly affairs and spiritual, too, as head of the English church. To not have the goddess shine her light upon you, to not be in her favor, was to suffer, as Ralegh would suffer when she later exiled him from court. If Elizabeth had not been queen, Ralegh and his fellow courtiers would not have adored her as a goddess. But she was queen, and no ordinary monarch. Leicester could not see Elizabeth as a goddess—he had known her too long, since childhood. Burghley, too. Ralegh was a newcomer in her life. His worship was contagious. His success at winning hearts—her heart— undoubtedly inspired others to imitate him. He became the courtier *par excellence* by knowing exactly how to worship his sovereign, which she further prompted by her acceptance of this worship. He succeeded because she did not disdain or lose interest in him: adoration alone was not enough; otherwise, she would have grown bored with it and him. Ralegh possessed so many fine parts, physically and intellectually, that he was a man worth being worshipped by.

Elizabeth achieved the status of goddess in part by (allegedly and probably) remaining a virgin. If she had not been a virgin, *everyone* would have known because privacy was in short supply at court, even in the queen's rooms, and tongues would have wagged. The queen always slept with a woman in her bedchamber.[20] Foreigners, particularly the Spanish, spread rumors of the queen's promiscuity, but these did not and do not hold. Regardless of whether she was a virgin, Protestant English believed she was and made her a substitute for the Virgin Mary. In late medieval Europe, the cult of the Virgin Mary had elevated worship of the Virgin above that of Christ. Mary was the approachable mediator between the individual and Christ. But Protestants did away with the worship of the holy mother as idolatrous and destroyed much of the precious iconography that represented her. The Virgin Mary, of all the saints, was by far the most significant subject of adoration to

---

5. The "Ditchley" portrait of Queen Elizabeth I by Marcus Gheeraerts the Younger, circa 1592. © National Portrait Gallery, London

fall under Protestant attack. But to remove her as a figure for adoration was not to remove the need of people to adore. Elizabeth ruled an earthly domain and thus qualified as an object of adoration that was not irreligious. Religious associations and connotations were made because she ruled God's church and her virginity permitted parallels with the Virgin Mary to be drawn. Historian Carol Levin observed, "Elizabeth and her Councillors deliberately appropriated the symbolism and prestige of the suppressed Marian cult in order to foster the cult of the Virgin Queen. This proved a valuable resource for Elizabeth in dealing with the political problems of her regime."[21]

Elizabeth's "visitations" around England possessed a quasi-religious aura, with recognition by all classes of the queen as similar to the Virgin Mary. The day of her accession to the throne and her birthday were both celebrated as holy days. Catholics were especially offended that the religious celebration of Elizabeth's birthday fell "coincidentally, [on] the eve of the feast of the nativity of the Blessed Virgin Mary. Catholics such as Edward Rishton complained that English Protestants . . . 'show the greater Contempt for our Blessed lady'" by solemnly celebrating Elizabeth's birthday and downplaying Mary. But as Levin points out, Protestants thought the sharing of Elizabeth's birthday with "the nativity of the Virgin Mary" was "more than simply coincidence; they considered it a divine omen."[22] About Elizabeth's death, Roy Strong notes the "posthumous praise rarely suggests the death of a human at all." For example, one "revealing tribute" in verse asserted that Elizabeth had taken her place in heaven second only to Christ's mother:

She was and is, what can there more be said,
In earth the first, in heaven the second maid.[23]

The worship of Elizabeth rationalized fidelity to the queen while reinforcing the people's identity with her and the England she ruled. This only increased as the very life of the nation appeared threatened, its religion under attack and future prospects ostensibly limited and declining. Melancholy was the song of the Elizabethan soul, even as they swore not to succumb. In worship of the queen, both she and the minions felt exaltation. All could unite to serve and bask in her glow. But a goddess cannot be confined to any plane. Her reach extended to both a universal and heavenly place. Ralegh wove a cult around Elizabeth, and others joined in spinning the weft and warp. They envisioned the queen as empress of a universal monarchy.

The Cult of Elizabeth was indeed a cult, with rituals, worship, and even a priesthood of sorts—the courtiers. And though it was playful, the pomp and celebrations were meant to bring joy and happiness to the adherents *and* to the subject of their affections, it lay grounded in multiple realities even as its belief system remained mystical. The reality: Elizabeth was an extraordinary queen of legion talents and powers; her court worshipped her. The adulations parsed her otherworldly qualities. Some may have thought these expressions mere kowtowing at worse and metaphors at best, but determining their substance was presumptuous. Who deigns to doubt that a goddess is a goddess? Certainly, there was no profit in doing so.

The key to understanding the Renaissance, especially in England, is to see no war between reason and mysticism and to perceive the former as the method expected to reveal the truth of the latter. It was plain that Elizabeth was a goddess. The poet articulated that truth. Today, poetry is often treated as a form of fiction, but many educated Elizabethans deemed it the highest expression of truth. Those who worshipped Elizabeth recounted in verse the many ways she displayed her goddess qualities; only comparison to multiple goddesses could do her justice. One goddess in particular was selected by some, especially those interested in colonialism, to represent the queen: Astraea. To unravel how Elizabeth as Astraea had bearing on English overseas activities, we need to look more closely at the relationship between reason and mysticism.

The new Renaissance scientists did not doubt the existence of God, let alone God's power. They were confident that humans could discover the physical nature of the world God had created. Sixteenth-century religious critics of the new science found it presumptuous and dangerous for humans to claim they could know God better by understanding the physical properties of His Creation; God required faith, not understanding.

Many Renaissance intellectuals who hoped to uncover God's truths in the unseen world through scientific inquiry into the physical world subscribed to the religious philosophy of Hermeticism.[24] Hermeticism grew out of sacred texts ascribed to Hermes Trismegistus, believed to pre-date the New Testament. They gained increasing currency in the fifteenth century, and reached their apogee of influence in the sixteenth century. They speak of a single universal religion while presenting the potential of man to manipulate nature, such as through alchemy. To transform matter through alchemy required a laboratory in which physical materials were combined, often subject to an element of ignition such as fire. Ultimately, alchemy gave birth to chemistry: experiments were recorded, and mathematics played an increasing role in calculating the properties of substances. The purpose of the manipulation often was materialistic: some hoped to create gold or silver; others hoped to extend the physical life of humans through cordials. But the Hermeticists' ultimate goal remained uncovering the secrets of nature to bring man closer to the divine, which, some thought, might initiate the millennium. Hence, the study of science was a divine calling.

In his later years, Ralegh provided England with a Hermeticist's view of history. His magnum opus explained God's relationship to man and suggested that man's highest calling was the study of physical matter. As a young man, Ralegh was thoroughly acquainted with Hermetic teachings through his older brothers. He conducted all sorts of laboratory experiments that ultimately brought him international fame, and he surrounded himself with Hermeticists who pursued a "natural philosophy" that perceived America as occupying a central role in the redemption of not only Europe but all humankind.

Drawing inspiration from Hermes's texts, and particularly from texts penned in early modern Europe by followers of Hermes, the belief arose in England and elsewhere that Queen Elizabeth had been chosen to effect the reunification of Christianity. Elizabeth would be empress of a universal monarchy. The concept of the universal monarch dated to Constantine, was inherited by Charlemagne, and in the sixteenth century was resurrected by Charles V, the Holy Roman Emperor.[25] The great historian of universal monarchy and Hermeticism, Francis Yates, details how the concept of Elizabeth as the universal monarch infused English society and received support abroad. The universal monarch was an imperial monarch, that is, their rule extended beyond national boundaries to encompass something much greater. John Dee, according to historian Glyn Parry, "tutored Elizabeth in these magical imperial mysteries."[26] Hermeticists thought of Elizabeth as not merely an English monarch but also a divine ruler above other kings and queens. They so successfully transmitted these ideas that no one living in Tudor England, Yates asserts, could escape the imperial theme of the era.[27] In art, poetry, plays, and innumerable public celebrations, Elizabeth was portrayed as not just a queen but also an empress. Her reign would initiate a Golden Age, if not through her own actions, then through the actions of her knights, whose bravery and virtuous lives led them to fight for the good and true. The Italian monk Giordano Bruno gave Elizabeth the name Astraea—Virgin of the Golden Age—meaning she was the greatest monarch, who would rule over "some new world." She was, he gushed, "One in whose presence the mystic truth unveils itself."[28]

Bruno was a renowned mathematician, astrologer, and Hermeticist who traveled widely in Europe and lived in the French embassy in England from 1583 to 1585, just as Ralegh prepared to colonize America. Bruno's cosmographical views were considered radical. He followed Copernicus in believing that the earth revolved around the sun, and he went even further in theorizing the infinite nature of the universe and that stars were in fact suns around which unseen planets revolved and perhaps supported life. Bruno's associates in England included John Dee and Dee's Hermeticist friends, namely, Ralegh, Thomas Hariot, and Sir Philip Sydney, the Earl of Leicester's son-in-law, all of whom gave Bruno access to the highest levels of the English court. While in England, Bruno published many tracts promoting the Cult of Elizabeth and her destiny as empress of a universal empire, a view likely inspired by Dee. Bruno asserted, "Her title and royal dignity is inferior to no other monarch in the world; . . . [she] would bring far horizons within her girdle . . . to include not only Britain and Ireland but some new world, as vast as the universal frame, where her all-powerful hand should have full scope to raise a united monarchy."[29] Bruno was executed in 1600 by the Inquisition in Rome on an array of charges, including his holding numerous heretical beliefs and practicing magic. Ironically, today he is mostly remembered as a martyr for science, yet his mysticism lay at the foundation of his thinking and might have been seen as the greater threat by the Inquisition.

Hermeticism attracted both Catholics and Protestants, intellectuals who believed that the impeding millennium made the biases of Christian sectarianism irrelevant.[30] (Dee himself had been a Catholic priest before he converted to Protestantism. Ralegh later condemned religious differences among Christians as ridiculous and respected and celebrated non-Christians for their religiosity.) Many Hermeticists held faith that belief in God and God's powers transcended anything as slight as the form of church and Christ worship. The Hermeticists welcomed overseas exploration and colonization as a means by which Christians would be introduced to other cultures and religions that would reveal their secrets about God.

Elizabeth was the best hope to lead the way, according to the Hermeticists. As head of the church and a monarch, she could protect Christians from ecclesiastical and secular evils. God had chosen her through her descent from King Arthur. It seemed both logical and mystical for Elizabeth to be the one to guide England's imperial destiny in the Golden Age.[31] The perceived role of Elizabeth as defender of persecuted Christians enlarged after England defeated the Spanish Armada in 1588. For instance, Yates found an obscure Italian who dedicated a book to Elizabeth, hoping that she would bring peace to Europe and freedom from tyranny; many Italians hoped for liberation from Spain.[32] Yates also discovered a German taken with England's victory over the Spanish Armada, betokening Elizabeth as standing for "some universal solution of religious problems which were circulating below the surface in sixteenth-century Europe."[33]

Dee's work is replete with references to Elizabeth as an imperial ruler. In his *General and Rare Memorials* (1577), he called her "the pilot of the 'Imperial Ship.'"[34] He was not the only one. Sir John Davis of Hereford composed for the Cult of Elizabeth a series of twenty-six poems titled *Hymnes to Astraea*, the Virgin Justice.[35] Spenser's *Faerie Queene*, dedicated to Elizabeth as "most high Mightie and Magnificent *Empresse*," revolved around the concept of Elizabeth as the "imperial virgin." Merlin himself allegedly had prophesied "a line of kings and 'sacred emperors' culminating in the royal virgin Elizabeth."[36] Spenser's hope for the Golden Age, and Elizabeth's representation of Astraea, is articulated in the *Faerie Queene's* fifth book:

> For during Saturnes ancient reigne it's sayd,
> That all the world with goodness did abound:
> And loved virtue, no man was affrayd
> Of force, ne fraud in wight [no unfortunate person] was to be found:
> No warre was known, no dreadful trumpets sound,
> Peace universall rayn'd mongst men and beasts,
> And all things freely grew out of the ground:
> Justice sate high ador'd with solemn feasts,
> And to all people did divide her dred beheasts.
> Most sacred virtue she of all the rest,
> Resembling God in his imperiall might;
> Whose soveraine powre is herein most exprest,
> That both to good and bad he dealeth right,
> And all his works with Justice hath bedight [adorned].

God had chosen Elizabeth to be the imperial queen, to bring justice to His people:

> *Dread Souverayne Goddesse, thou doest highest sit*
> *In seate of judgement, in the' Almighties stead,*
> *And with magnificke might and wondrous wit*
> *Doest to thy people righteous doome aread [decree].*[37]

Elizabethan art also portrayed the imperial theme inclusive of America. For example, in the Sieve Portrait of Elizabeth located in Sienna, Italy, on a beautiful globe behind her left shoulder Europe is covered in darkness, except for the British Isles. The globe and the ships moving west to America represent England's future.[38] By 1581, Dee wrote a book, since lost, that by its title implies England's interest in converting Native Americans.[39] The imperial theme, expressed in poetry in and out of court, in pageantry, in legal documents, and in a variety of published tracts and private letters, gave English overseas expansion divine purpose, undertaken by a divinely chosen monarch, a goddess, who would initiate the Golden Age.

———

IN 1584, ELIZABETH was just past fifty years of age. More than ever, it seemed important to worship the Virgin Queen, to sing the heart's phrases of adulation and awe for the great goddess Elizabeth. Her errant knights went to sea to herald the Golden Age, to accomplish great deeds in her name, to lift England out of the doldrums. Economic malaise and overpopulation required new lands and natural resources to meet the shortcomings of this "frozen island." The threat of Spain grew stronger, but so, too, did English confidence in challenging the most powerful monarch in Europe. Drake's ease in raiding Spanish American towns and the capture of Iberian ships fed English militancy. Elizabeth passed Ralegh the standard to extend her sovereignty to America.

For Ralegh, the Golden Age meant building an empire that would provide England the means to solve its economic and demographic problems. His part encompassed challenging Spain by siphoning off its American wealth and, even more importantly, establishing colonies for English settlers. New World settlement would relieve England of overpopulation and provide new markets for English goods: both colonists and Natives would purchase English products. And the New

World offered commodities that England lacked, such as trees and fish, and plants for use in medicines, perhaps spices as well. Ralegh expected—hoped—that colonization would be conducted on pacific terms. Soldiers would be sent and a fort built to defend the English from hostilities, particularly from the Spanish, but he expected his people to get along with the Indians. He was not sending conquistadors to take control of the land and enslave the Native people. The Golden Age that Ralegh envisioned comprised a partnership between English and American Indians. In all of Ralegh's attempts to colonize, he promoted good relations with Native peoples. Ralegh's Hermeticism led him to welcome the forthcoming encounters with America's Natives. There was so much he wanted to learn from and about them. It took some time for Ralegh to articulate these ideals in his writing, but in his actions his possession of an incredible degree of religious and ethnic tolerance is evident.

Elizabeth's reign initiated no Golden Age to protect Christians and unify Christianity, but she did live in a Golden Age of sorts. She surrounded herself with a large and talented group of courtiers, the most impressive generation of monarchical advisors in English history. Burghley and Walsingham were extremely competent, if not brilliant in politics, as was Burghley's son, Robert Cecil. The English bureaucracy worked well on a variety of levels, particularly in developing the navy, and conducted an elite level of detailed planning, which, however, often fell short in execution. The Elizabethans understood that they had to plan for the future, but it took trial and error to find the proper means to administer policies.

The cult Ralegh helped create lasted for nearly twenty years after she granted him a patent to colonize America, but it could not survive Elizabeth's death. Another cult, related to the Cult of Elizabeth, was in the womb as Ralegh colonized: the cult of nationalism, which became the cult that ultimately defined the English imperial expression.

There developed no unifying religion in England, nor, after Elizabeth, a monarch around whom a cult could be formed (unlike in France). In England, unlike in Spain and France, the national legislature gained an unusual degree of power and influence. Parliament's challenge to monarchy in the seventeenth century produced a stalemate of sorts, with one or the other alternately gaining the upper hand: the king was beheaded and Parliament ruled supreme, but then the pendulum swung again as Cromwell took power and again with the restoration of the monarchy and again with the Glorious Revolution, a continual balancing of power between monarch and Parliament that stabilized in the eighteenth century. With neither monarch nor Parliament powerful enough to hold the reins of power without the other, the nation itself became the cult worshipped and enlarged. This allowed all to mutually support imperial expansion, all to worship at the same altar. Otherwise, the English Empire would have disintegrated, the victim of centuries-long power struggles between sovereign and legislature. Instead, all actors mutually supported the cult of the nation's empire: the subservience of nonwhites, the preeminence of the mother country over its colonies, the exclusion of Scots from benefiting from the empire until the Act of Union (1707) and the creation of the United Kingdom (a new nation to worship), and the imperial flexibility of assimilating non-British Europeans and Protestants not of the Church of England into the empire. Scots, Germans, Huguenots, Swiss, and other Europeans learned that the British Empire could be a beautiful thing for them because it offered citizenship and materialistic opportunity, as well as religious tolerance. Exclusions were based on race, and non-Protestants were not always allowed, but the English Empire welcomed many who wished to join the imperial cult.

PART FOUR

"The land itself would wage war on them"

The Roanoke Adventure

CHAPTER 8

Planting a New World Colony

I n 1584, Walter Ralegh embarked on an unparalleled decade of overseas expansion. He attempted to colonize on three continents: Europe, North America, and South America. His fame today as a colonizer largely owes to his being the first Englishman to plant a colony on the lands of the future United States. Few are aware of his search for El Dorado in South America. Fewer know of his role as a colonizer of Ireland. Taken together, Ralegh's simultaneous efforts to colonize on three continents elucidate the possibilities, and many of the parameters, of English colonization in the early modern era. They show what the English thought they could accomplish and how their material efforts matched or failed to match their expectations.

In the 1580s, most English likely did not know what to make of the North American endeavor. It made more sense to move colonists overseas to Ireland, where people from England had migrated for hundreds of years. The New World, in the minds of many English, was the domain of Spanish conquistadores. The famed Spanish conquests of Mexico and Peru, yielding lands and peoples rich with precious metals, provided one model for English colonizing in America. Some English migrated to Ralegh's colony in North America in hopes of obtaining gold and silver, or even copper, but neither Ralegh nor most of his investors expected to find precious metals there. If this wealth appeared, they would rejoice, but they had no viable reports of American Indians along the Atlantic coasts possessing precious metals. The Spanish conquistadores had explored the lower Southeast (and Southwest) of the future United States in the previous seven decades and found none, though the existence of pearls had been documented along the coast of the Gulf of Mexico, and the Spanish maintained hope of discovering great mines of silver in New Mexico.

Ralegh and his propagandists promoted a far different form of colonization for North America than the one they believed the Spanish practiced. Ralegh intended to transport large numbers of English to produce, gather, or trade for valuable commodities. This strategy of colonization in North America was not predicated on the employment of Indian labor in the mines, on public works projects, or on agricultural estates to support the wealthy, the church, and the state. Though the English eventually enslaved tens of thousands of Native peoples, they did not plan on using Native labor and did not do so during Elizabeth's reign.

Ralegh's propagandist Richard Hakluyt (the Younger) correctly perceived and defined the future of English colonization: the movement overseas of poor and other unwanted Europeans to become producers of raw materials and consumers of finished English goods.[1] Historians often credit Hakluyt with designing this model, forgetting that Ralegh and Gilbert, who both engaged in schemes to colonize in Ireland, North America, and elsewhere, explicitly planned to move English to new lands to produce and gather commodities.

In a state paper, Hakluyt details why the queen should support Ralegh's efforts to expand her realm overseas. This "Discourse of Western Planting" offers five main reasons for England to colonize in America:[2] (1) using it as an opportunity to bring Christ to the Natives; (2) expanding trade (which suffered at the hands of the Spanish) by obtaining valuable commodities unavailable in England; (3) providing new markets for English goods; (4) providing employment for the idle poor who would gather and process commodities (which already had been noted in the queen's patent to Ralegh); and (5) providing England with land for overseas naval bases.

Hakluyt's "Discourse" neatly identified the raison d'être for English colonization in the coming centuries. Although conversion of Natives mostly remained an afterthought, it continued to provide moral justification for English expansion: the charter for every English colony in America included conversion of the Natives as a reason for the colony's existence. Establishing naval or privateering bases evolved into ports to maintain the overseas fleet for what became the world's most powerful navy and for merchant ships intent on obtaining commodities and dominating markets. Colonies for centuries provided the means for

England to rid itself of the "idle poor" and, Hakluyt could have added, religious and political dissenters and criminals, who would become New World producers and consumers of English goods.

Ralegh understood these reasons and more to build overseas colonies. He brought to the task the recognition that it would take much planning and a good deal of patience to succeed. He set in motion the building of an English Empire.

PLANTING A COLONY in the New World three thousand miles from England required a great amount of preparation. Decisions had to be made about where to go and who to send. Ralegh determined not to return to the north—Newfoundland posed too many problems. A more temperate climate made colonizing more feasible. The English had little knowledge of the Atlantic coast between Newfoundland and the Florida peninsula. They were ignorant of not only the natural resources but also the tides and currents for this crossing. Ralegh needed to rely on people who could investigate, assess, and help him figure out where and how to settle. As would become typical of his career, Ralegh employed talented individuals to advise and work for him. His most important employee, who played a critical role with his American colony and became a lifelong friend and associate, was Thomas Hariot, the most original and important English mathematician and scientist of his era.

Hariot graduated Oxford in 1580 with a bachelor's degree, and apparently he was introduced to Ralegh by Richard Hakluyt.[3] Hariot studied at Oxford with Thomas Allen, one of England's foremost mathematicians and students of mysticism. Modern students of the history of science tend to view Hariot's interest in natural philosophy, particularly its mystical elements, as incongruous for a great scientist; likewise, they ignore the mysticism of other leading scientists of the early modern era. Hariot likely developed his interest in natural philosophy under Allen. They shared beliefs in what they wanted to learn about the mysteries of the universe and the necessity of using mathematics and laboratory experiments to make new discoveries. Allen, Hariot, and Ralegh all later moved to Ralegh's lands in Ireland, where they pursued their mutual interests in the natural philosophy of Hermeticism.

Hariot was in his early twenties when he moved in with Ralegh into Durham House, the great house on the Strand in London that dated to the mid-fourteenth century. Alternately a palace of bishops and princes, Henry VIII had given it to Elizabeth. Elizabeth's sister, Queen Mary, confiscated the house, but Elizabeth took it back when she became queen. She granted it to Ralegh in 1583, and it became his chief residence. Situated on the Strand at arguably the best location in London, Durham House gardens extended to the Thames and it was convenient to most everything of importance in London. Ralegh turned the house into an intellectual center, attracting poets, playwrights, natural philosophers, and other thinkers. The socializing included playing cards, drinking, and, a few years later, smoking tobacco, which Ralegh and Hariot grew famous for and likely inspired others to take up. At Durham House, Hariot tutored Ralegh in science. Ralegh educated Hariot as well. Hariot, it is believed, came from a humble family in the vicinity of Oxford and would have benefited from introduction to Ralegh's large and diverse social circle. Ralegh put to use Hariot's incredible array of talents and even some that were mundane: Hariot assisted Ralegh with his accounts and sundry business and legal matters, and he kept many of Ralegh's papers, which he burned after Ralegh's death.

Hariot formed an important bridge between medieval algebra and Newton and Descartes. He made significant contributions to mathematics in regard to the use of zero, binominal and quadratic equations, and creation of mathematical symbols. Hariot delved into optics, built the largest telescope in England, and preceded Galileo in the use of a telescope to draw the moon. His work on refractions stunned and upset Kepler and connected to his speculations on the atom—the most important theorization on the atom produced between the time of Aristotle and that of Newton. He pursued his work on astronomy and refraction in large measure to improve navigation, and he educated Ralegh's mariners before their voyages to America. On his own journey to America, Hariot experimented and tested his theories. His interest in understanding the physical character of the universe was fueled by the desire to uncover the unseen, hence, his interest in the atom, the face of the moon, and distant galaxies. The creation of instruments to analyze the heavens and to sail ships had practical application, but it possessed spiritual components. Some have dismissed Hariot's spirituality, accusing him of atheism, but atheism in the Renaissance did not refer to lack of a belief in God but to unorthodox spiritual beliefs. Hariot's sustained interest in natural philosophy illustrates his propensity to the mystical—he frequently wrote in the margins of books on natural philosophy, but we also must consider his mentorship by Allen, and the fact that the two most important patrons in his life both combined the practice of science with mystical pursuits: Walter Ralegh and the Wizard Earl, Henry Percy, 9th Earl of Northumberland.

Ralegh needed Hariot's help to get his colonists to America. Hariot's analytical skills and practical nature were useful in amassing and improving Ralegh's colonizing fleet. He compiled notes on ropes, cables, and masts and compared foreign to English ships. In 1583, he helped Ralegh with the design of the *Bark Ralegh*, used for the second Gilbert expedition and then for Ralegh's expedition to America. The *Bark Ralegh* was a two-hundred-ton ship reputed to be the best and most technologically advanced in England. (Ralegh eventually sold the ship to the queen, and it remained in use well into the seventeenth century.) Hariot's concern with ship construction extended from speed to steering and cargo storage, and he, too, was not shy about consulting experts, including the foremost shipwrights in England, to compare their ideas on producing the best ships. His comprehensive notes also covered aspects of fleet operation such as the organization of the men into their watches and the share each mariner would receive if a prize was taken. But what Ralegh especially needed Hariot for was navigation.

Navigating ships to the New World was a tricky business. In the first half of the sixteenth century, English mariners lagged behind their Spanish and Portuguese counterparts. English sailing was largely confined to the English Channel, the coasts of the British Isles, and the Mediterranean, with the exception of the fishermen who went to the North Atlantic fisheries and a few English, like the Hawkins, father and sons, who sailed to Africa. Francis Drake, Stephen Borough, and John Davis, all from Devon and all associates of Ralegh, had sailed American waters but were unfamiliar with the region Ralegh intended to colonize. In general, the English lacked maps and basic navigational skills for overseas routes. It took centuries for some problems to be solved, such as devising adequate methods to determine longitude, but even latitude was a problem. Observations of the sun and the pole star were necessary for determining latitude, which was Hariot's greatest contribution to the sailing portion of the American voyages. (Hariot also produced a practical solution to the Mercator problem, the difficulty of creating a map by which ships could follow a compass course.)[4]

Early modern Europeans relied on dead reckoning and the magnetic compass to sail ships and plum lines to measure depth, and they kept track of their position with the assistance of an hourglass. Ralegh directed Hariot to educate the mariners in navigation. Hariot penned the *Arctican*, since lost, as a navigation manual for explorers headed to America. A decade later, as his patron prepared to sail for South America, Hariot delivered six lectures for Ralegh and his navigators that simplified the *Arctican*. An expert on Elizabethan navigation compared Hariot's lectures to concurrent navigation manuals and describes "Hariot's pedagogical style . . . [as] truly a model of pragmatic clarity and conciseness." Hariot explained how to use the cross-staff and to easily correct the errors resulting from not locating the instrument at the exact center of the eye. He also told the mariners to disregard the problem of refraction, though he studied the problem intensively and made some of his greatest scientific contributions in refraction theory. And he instructed the mariners to disregard the problem of the parallax of the sun's altitude because the impact was small.[5]

Hariot eschewed giving navigators the theories behind his mathematics and navigation—they probably would not, and had no need to, understand them. Creating usable, easy-to-comprehend charts to effect successful navigation was what counted. One of his greatest contributions was the creation of a flow chart—in fact, he may have created the *first* flow chart—of the step-by-step procedure for determining latitude.[6] As the navigator moved along the chart, if certain conditions did not apply, then another pathway appeared until he found the appropriate line to follow.

After the initial voyages to America, Hariot continued to devote much energy and effort to the mathematics and science of navigation, not only preparing Ralegh for his expeditions to South America but also over several decades creating "great tables of meridional parts calculated (in effect) as logarithmic tangents," for which he "had to call into existence a whole new range of mathematical techniques, such as the conformality of stereographic projections, the rectification and quad nature of the logarithmic or equiangular spiral, the exponential series, and the derivation and use of interpolation formulae."[7] Hariot's calculations, charts, instruments, *and* refinement of instruments were as practical and useful as those produced by anyone in the sixteenth century. His willingness to share his findings through public lectures, tutoring, correspondence, and informal exchanges spread this knowledge to English navigators, which elevated their navigational skills to, and sometimes surpassed, the level of other European maritime nations within a decade of the first English sailing to Roanoke.[8] Ralegh's efforts to colonize in the Americas, if nothing else, helped advance English navigational knowledge so the nation could compete effectively with Spain and Portugal overseas.

—

ONLY ONE MONTH after receiving his patent to colonize in North America, in April 1584, Ralegh dispatched two barks across the Atlantic on a reconnaissance voyage. Philip Amadas, a nineteen-year-old member of Ralegh's household from Plimouth, commanded the *Bark Ralegh*, and Arthur Barlowe, a soldier who likely served under Ralegh in Ireland, commanded the other. The journey took ten weeks. For three and a half weeks, they sailed to the Canaries, off the northwest coast of Africa. They spent an additional month sailing to and through the West Indies, during which time they discovered they had tacked too far to the southeast. From Puerto Rico they entered the Bahamas but were forced to sail northward. The error offered valuable information, shortening the length of future voyages. After twelve days in the islands, they proceeded to the Atlantic coast of North America, reaching the Carolinas on July 2 and spending eleven days slowly heading northward at a rate of about ten miles a day. Though southerly winds impeded their progress, it is likely they traveled slowly in hopes of finding the best place to settle the future colony.

On July 13, 1584, they found a river to land on the North Carolina banks at Hatteras. They claimed the territory for Queen Elizabeth, "according to the ceremonies used in such enterprises." Since the only other "such enterprises" was Gilbert's venture at Newfoundland, we can assume that Ralegh instructed his men to use the same ceremonies employed by his half brother. There, Gilbert "(after the custom of England)" cut a "turffe"—a piece of sod, to symbolize possession of the land—and a "rod" (or stick) to represent the queen's authority and placed "the English arms, engraved on lead affixed to a pillar erected in the place."[9]

Barlowe, who penned the expedition's official account, effusively claimed that despite the sea overflowing the land, everywhere "we founde such plentie . . . in all places . . . on the sande, and on the greene soile on the hills, as in the plaines, as well on every little shrubbe, as also climbing towardes the toppes of the high Cedars."[10] Such abundance, he enjoined, could not be found anywhere in Europe: it "were incredible to be written." Barlowe can be forgiven his exuberance—the abundance of the New World had become an expected trope among those who crossed the Atlantic, and even more among some who had never been. Barlowe wrote what potential investors in New World projects wanted to hear. The bounty of trees and animal life symbolized the edenic character of the Carolina coast, perhaps nowhere more so than in the great stands of forest. Much of England lay deforested. Ships and masts required lumber, as did naval stores, house construction, and furniture. Ralegh's appreciation of the economic value of trees would become apparent later in Ireland, where he established a massive lumber operation. But most English did not intend to colonize America for trees but envisioned finding silver or gold or a new and easy passage to Asia. Ralegh had to redirect English attention by identifying a range of potential commodities to attract investors.

Barlowe's and Amadas's selection of Roanoke Island to establish camp probably arose from several factors. Their ships had protection from the sea on the mainland side of the island, and they needed to stay close to and guard their ships, their lifeline. The river also provided some protection from potential enemies on the mainland. Over the next few years, this and subsequent English parties explored the mainland and along the coast to find a better place for permanent settlement. Roanoke Island could never support a substantial colony. When Ralegh's propagandists praised the bounty of the land, they meant the mainland, not the island to which they kept returning, which was only supposed to be a beachhead for the colony. To plant a colony on the mainland, the English first needed to ingratiate themselves with an array of Native peoples, who otherwise could block their settlement. Even settlement on the island required Native approval. The English could not attempt conquest, which would be too costly, and go against the grain of what they hoped to avoid—colonization in the perceived Spanish manner: the killing and enslaving of Native peoples. Ralegh intended a pacific settlement, his people befriending Indians.[11] Prospects looked quite promising when the Indians of Roanoke Island put on a special welcome.

On the third day of Barlowe's and Amadas's first visit, the New World came to the English. Three Roanoke Indians rowed their small boat to the mainland side of the island. One disembarked and walked along the land looking out to where the English anchored. The English rowed ashore to meet him. The English could not understand what the man said, but all expressed amity and the English invited the Indian aboard, where he received a hat and shirt, among other things, and tasted their wine and meat, "which he liked very well." After visiting both barks, he returned to his boat and began fishing in sight of the English. In but thirty minutes he had filled his boat and signified to the English that each of their barks should enjoy half of his catch. He then departed.

This first encounter boded well for the English. They had entered others' land and freely offered gifts. The Indian responded in kind. So many first encounters in the New World ended otherwise. Armed Europeans were invaders when landing on American shores. Many did not care to consider that they had no right to enter these lands without negotiating their presence. Fortunately for the English, the Roanoke Indians did not know the English had already claimed sovereignty in the queen's name, because Barlowe and Amadas had not prosecuted her claim in a threatening manner. Nor did the English appear as invaders after booty. To the contrary, they appeared as traders with goods to exchange.

The brother of the king of the Roanoke Indians, Granganimeo, arrived the following day with forty or fifty men. Barlowe noted that the Indians ignored the fact that the English were armed. Undoubtedly, the Natives knew the English posed a military threat, and Barlowe recognized that the English must be on their guard, but the Roanoke Indians impressed him with their civility, orderliness, and ceremonies of welcome. Barlowe presumed that the Indians communicated that their people and the English were as one. Other Europeans venturing into North America made the same, perhaps willful, mistake, failing to realize or accept that ceremonies of welcome augmenting the exchange of goods did not mean permanent alliance, let alone subservience. Indians usually expected proof, not ceremonies, to establish firm bonds, such as fighting alongside one another against enemies.[12]

The English likely were not the first Europeans the Roanoke Indians encountered, or at least had knowledge of, because shipwrecked Spanish occasionally washed ashore. Barlowe learned that twenty years earlier the Roanoke Indians had found a Spanish shipwreck or part of a shipwreck with no survivors, so they had a bit of familiarity with European material culture. Sixteen years earlier, the Roanoke might also have encountered the Jesuit expedition that established a mission on the Chesapeake to the north in 1570 and that was destroyed by Indians the following year or subsequent Spanish expeditions meant to resupply the Jesuits and then to punish the Indians who had killed the missionaries.[13] Even if they had not met the Europeans who traversed the waters of their territory, the Roanoke Indians would have known of them through the trade they conducted with other Indians.

Cognizant of the diplomatic value of the English presents, the king's brother received them gratefully. But when the English distributed some goods to four of his leading men, Granganimeo gathered them up for himself, letting the English know that all diplomacy must pass through him. The English immediately grasped that the Roanoke society was hierarchical. Barlowe made no mention of the Indians giving the English any gifts, so we may assume that the previous day's bounty of fish sufficed.

The Indians' acceptance of English gifts marked a prelude to trade. They returned the next day with pelts to exchange for English goods. The English revealed the extent of the merchandise they had brought and let Granganimeo take that which he most valued, "a bright tinne dishe," in which he bore a hole to hang it from his neck. The English received twenty animal skins for the dish and an additional fifty for a copper kettle, showing the great profit to be made from trade with the Natives. The Roanoke men also desired hatchets, axes, knives, and swords, but the English refused; they did not want to part with all they had brought just yet. They expected the Indians to have more to trade, further riches that could be obtained in future exchanges for these wares. The Roanoke must have been satisfied with the strangers' intentions, because a few days later Granganimeo brought his wife and children and other women Barlowe described as of "the better sorte," basing his assessment on their adornment of fancy jewelry, especially copper pendants "hanging in every eare." The common people then arrived, bringing much to trade, especially leather, shells, and "divers kindes of dies very excellent." When Granganimeo was present, no one could trade but him or other elites, whose status was signified by the "red pieces of copper on their heads, like himself."

Over the next two months, the expedition accomplished what it set out to do: reconnaissance. The English studied the local inhabitants and the terrain. The Natives showed themselves helpful, friendly, and civil. Granganimeo sent meat every day to the English, as well as fruits and vegetables, particularly maize (corn). When the English showed up at the Roanokes' town with no Roanoke men present, the women stripped the English and washed their clothes. With no women in the English party, the Roanoke women must have recognized the visitors' need to have females provide particular kinds of labor. When two

Roanoke men returned from hunting and discovered the English feted by the women in their town, tension arose and the English almost grabbed their weapons. Granganimeo's wife took away the Roanoke men's bows and arrows and broke them. At nightfall the English returned to their ships, perhaps to avoid offending the men, but certainly out of fear of being attacked in their sleep. Despite these precautions, Barlowe asserted they had nothing to fear.

Barlowe's report on the colony gave no indication that the Roanoke would oppose an English settlement.[14] He wrote, "Wee found the people most gentle, loving, and faithfull, void of all guile, and treason, and such as lived after the manner of the golden age," the great era of peace and prosperity of the ancient world, which Ralegh, Bruno, and others hoped Elizabeth would restore. Barlowe depicted the Natives as honorable people among whom the English could easily live and whose virtues would redound to the newcomers.

Despite this edenic portrayal, Barlowe admitted numerous Indian towns along the coast engaged in "bloodie" warfare with one another. Many of "the people are marvelously wasted, and in some places, the Countrey left desolate."[15] Was this assessment accurate or a way for Barlowe to imply there would be space for English settlement amid what otherwise could be viewed as a teeming Native population? Barlowe made sure to note that the English need not fear these wars, for Indian arms were inferior. "When we discharged any peece, were it but a harquebush, they would tremble thereat for very fear." The Indians' wooden weapons and breastplates posed no threat to properly armed and armored Englishmen.

Barlowe closed his report for Ralegh by announcing their justification for returning to England. They had conducted the reconnaissance expected of them and, more specifically, "taken in possession by us, to her Majesties use, and so to yours, by her Majesties grant," this country, which Barlowe certified by having ten of the leading men, including himself, attest so there could be no doubt that Ralegh was fulfilling the terms of his patent, which still required permanent settlement.

One final sentence, which did not appear in the first publication of Barlowe's account printed in Richard Hakluyt's *Principal Navigations* (1589) but likely was in the original manuscript presented to Ralegh, referred to two Indians the English brought home to England. These Indians had been mentioned earlier in the manuscript as a source that Ralegh had consulted on Indian society, particularly on social divisions. The excluded sentence, which closed Barlowe's manuscript, stated, "We brought home also two of the Savages being lustie men, whose names were Wanchese and Manteo." There could be any number of reasons for the initial exclusion of the sentence, but most likely it seemed a frivolous addendum after the more important certification by the English, which immediately preceded it in the document, that the land had been properly claimed for the queen and Ralegh. After all, the Indians already had been cited, though not named, and the 1600 edition of *Principal Navigations* merely righted the record by including the missing sentence. But the final sentence reinforces the earlier attribution of an important source of information for English reconnaissance. Barlowe had done little, if any, exploring of the mainland, and language difficulties precluded the gathering of much information on Indian towns, warfare, and culture. How could Barlowe have learned about the Spanish shipwreck, for instance, or of the wars between Indians without someone to relate the information in English? Manteo and Wanchese must have been the source. They began learning English on the voyage home, and then in England spent much time with Thomas Hariot, who quickly gained a degree of fluency in their language and instructed them in English. Hariot even created a unique syllabary to record their language. Manteo and Wanchese provided Barlowe important details about Indian culture, town locations, and history. For instance, Barlowe noted the existence of Indian peoples far inland, correctly recording the name of an Indian leader (Menatonon) Ralegh's next expedition would meet. Without Manteo and Wanchese as sources, Barlowe's reconnaissance would have been sorely lacking and certainly abbreviated.

Ralegh almost certainly had urged his men to return with Indians, in all likelihood with the Indians' permission. Manteo and Wanchese might have volunteered to go at the behest of their chiefs, to whom the English posed the request. The English promised to return the following year.[16] The Indians likely thought the reason for the English departure was to obtain more goods to trade. In retrospect, bringing Manteo and Wanchese to England was the great accomplishment of the first Roanoke expedition. In England, their arrival disproved naysayers and demonstrated that Ralegh's people actually reached America.

Ralegh used his Indian guests to great advantage. He paraded the pair around London, initially in their Native dress and subsequently in European clothing and shoes. A German visiting London, Lupold van Weld, stated that no one could understand the Indians, but he might not have been aware of those English who had conversed with the Indians, either on board the ship or, like Hariot, in Ralegh's household. A Spaniard who met Manteo and Wanchese on their return to America reported that they spoke English. He also noted that the Indians were tall and well taken care of by the English.[17] Wanchese and Manteo had immediate impact on English perceptions of Roanoke. A bill in Parliament referred to the "great comodities" of America "revealed & made knowen unto us" by Ralegh's Indians. One observer later bristled at the exaggerations. After the completion of the next major expedition to Roanoke, he "complained that the expedition would have been more successful 'yf the Report had beene true which was geven out by'" Ralegh's Indians.[18]

Discussion of what the first expedition found, and what Manteo and Wanchese claimed to exist in America, occurred in December 1584, when a bill was brought before the House of Commons to confirm the queen's patent to Ralegh. Historian David Beers Quinn notes that it is unclear why Ralegh introduced this bill because it added no rights.[19] America was not part of England, so Parliament had no power there. Only a monarch could obtain or claim sovereignty in America. Ralegh likely thought that putting Parliament on record confirming the queen's patent would gain broader support for the enterprise from both private and government sources, in effect turning Ralegh's colony into a national enterprise. The bill did not presume on the queen's right to grant the patent but was "An acte for the confermacion of the Quenes majesties Lettres Patentes graunted to Walter Ralegh Esquire Touchinge the discoverie and Inhabitinge of certeyn Foreyne Landes & Cuntries."[20]

The act advertised the propagation of "trewe religion" as one of the colony's goals, as well as increased trade and employment to benefit the queen's "lovinge subjectes as otherwise shulde spende there time in Idellnes to the great prejudice of the Common Welthe." In Ralegh's colony, these people would "be trayned in vertuous and Commodyous Labor." The act referred to the completed voyage by Barlowe and how, through the "charge[,] Labor and procurement of the said Walter Rawleigh a Land called Wyngandacoia" was discovered uninhabited "by anye Christian Prince or Christian people."[21] The importance of the expedition returning with Manteo and Wanchese was noted by reference to "some of the people born in those parts brought home into this realm of England." The success of the voyage was confirmed by the "singular great commodities of that Land [which] are revealed and made known unto us which discovery hath been heretofore attempted by diverse persons and never brought to any such perfection."[22]

Ralegh thus had accomplished what no Englishman had done before: laid a physical foundation for a colony in the New World. His men had visited the land, discovered its economic potential, and returned with friendly Natives. (Frobisher had done similarly in Labrador, but that was not intended to be a colony but was a search for a passage to Asia and then a place to locate and bring back gold.)

The House of Commons took up confirmation of the queen's patent. Parliamentary bills required three readings before passage, and the first took place on December 14. In the afternoon, after the second reading, it was "committed unto Mr. Vice-Chamberlain [Sir Christopher Hatton], Mr. Secretary [Sir Francis Walsingham], Sir Philip Sidney, Sir Francis Drake, Sir Richard Greenfield, Sir William Courtney, Sir William Mohun and others."[23] It is unknown who the "others" might have been, but Walsingham and Sydney were actively interested in overseas expansion, and the others named, except Hatton, came from South West England. Quinn believes that the unidentified "others" also referred to members from the South West, the backbone of Ralegh's colonization efforts.

Shortly afterward, "The Committees [sic] for Mr. Rawleighs Bill were appointed to meet presently in the Committee-Chamber of this House." Two days later, the bill "was brought in by the Committees not altered in any word." A motion was made to engross the bill, which "after some Arguments" was ordered done. Two objections then arose concerning the "lybertye gyven to him [Ralegh] to take anye person with him which ys willinge to goe" and the fact that Ralegh could take with him from England anything without export license.[24] On Friday the eighteenth, the bill received its third reading, and "after many Arguments and a Proviso added unto it, passed upon the Question." The proviso added that no one in prison for debt or "any other cause whatsoever or the wife, ward, or apprentice of any other person or persons" could "depart this Realm" for Ralegh's colony without their husband's or master's permission.

Members of the Commons thus had some very good reason to balk at confirming the queen's patent. No one questioned her right to grant the patent, only that Ralegh could not disregard English laws as those laws applied in England.[25] The proviso made specific objections to

Ralegh removing from England debtors in prison or any other prisoners and dependents by contract: wives, wards, and apprentices. Why
had Elizabeth allowed Ralegh to interfere with domestic hierarchical
relations, that is, husbands and wives, masters and dependents? She
might have granted Ralegh this widespread right of removal because
she thought of it as a form of impressment, whereby authorities legally
drafted men into army and naval service regardless of the wishes of
these men's masters. Colonization had become important enough to
Elizabeth that she was willing to have her people drafted into service
as colonists, allowing Ralegh to abscond with England's dependents.
In confirming Ralegh's patent with a proviso, the Commons parried the
queen's assertion that she could override English masters' rights over
their dependents. The decision to send these people had to be made
by English authorities, local or parliamentary.

In granting Ralegh license to remove debtors and dependents,
Elizabeth had signaled that she understood Ralegh's colony as a place
to send the poor. But it was not envisioned as a project of exile and
abandonment. On her own, Elizabeth declared in Ralegh's patent the
important precedent that her subjects would maintain their rights as
English citizens if they removed to her overseas possessions: colonists
would not be legally inferior to those who remained in the mother
country; colonial proprietors could not disregard their colonists' rights
as English people. Ralegh controlled the political and economic life of
the colony, but the guarantee of individuals' rights ensured the new society would be akin to England.

By the end of the Commons debate, Ralegh undoubtedly had
agreed to the Common's restrictions. As a new member of Parliament,
he was sensitive to assertions of Parliament's privileges and preroga-
tives.[26] His interest in presenting the bill was to curry favor from the
Commons. But this had been an important discussion. No one could
foresee that *many* colonies lay in England's future, but with the queen's
desire to build an empire, the Commons recognized that precedents
were being set. Members of Parliament were conscious of their rights
and suspicious of monarchical attempts to curtail their power and role
in legislating. From their perspective, it was essential not to back down
on the supremacy of parliamentary law within England, an item con-
tested by Tudor monarchs and challenged by their Stuart successors
as well.[27] In the event, Ralegh's bill passed the Commons but failed in
the House of Lords for reasons unknown.[28] Perhaps the lords felt that a

parliamentary act confirming the queen's patent was redundant, which it was, because patents for overseas colonies were outside of parliamentary jurisdiction and solely within the monarch's purview.

Whatever the reason for failure, the bill succeeded in other ways. It advertised the accomplishments and purposes of Ralegh's proposed colony to a wide swath of influential and important Englishmen. It made clear Ralegh's rise to prominence not only in the queen's estimation but also among members of the House of Commons. The half brother of the deceased Gilbert had become the most important member of the family, including the vast cousinry. Passage in Commons illustrated strong support for overseas expansion among English gentlemen, the merchant class, the seagoing adventurers, and even some of the military leadership. But would the nobility support expansion of the realm under a commoner? It must have been unsettling to see so much hoopla devoted to colonization. Spanish upstarts like Cortés and Pizarro had amassed uncalculated riches in America. If Ralegh succeeded in doing the same, then jealousy of this commoner could reach dangerous proportions.

Nevertheless, Elizabeth made clear that Ralegh had her full support. From his monopoly over licenses to serve wine (1583) to his exclusive right to colonize America, Ralegh had become the queen's well-rewarded favorite. A few months later, she selected Ralegh to oversee the stannaries in South West England responsible for tin production. A few weeks after Ralegh's bill failed in the House of Lords, Elizabeth knighted her favorite.[29]

CHAPTER 9

Summer of Discontent

E ven before the first expedition had sailed for America in April
1584, Ralegh was preparing a second. To demonstrate economic
viability, he needed to find a place with resources that could
be shipped to England. Discovering such a place would take time, so
there was an expectation that trade with the local Natives would fill
some of the gaps in subsistence and marketable commodities. Ralegh
would do his part by periodically sending supply ships, and eventually
permanent colonists.

Most of the men on the second expedition would be engaged in
security. The Spanish were a particular concern because English settlement on Spanish-claimed land in America was unprecedented. The
Spanish might react as they did in Florida, where they put hundreds
of French colonists to death in 1565. There was also the case of almost
a hundred English captured by the Spanish in Mexico: after the Battle of San Juan de Ulúa (1568), John Hawkins had to abandon many
of his men. They dispersed into the countryside before being rounded
up five years later and delivered to the Inquisition. Very few survived
their sentences.

With the men selected, the expedition was nearly ready; however, the queen barred Ralegh from sailing with it. His older cousin,
Sir Richard Grenville, would take his place and lead seven ships from
Plymouth, England. Today, Grenville retains fame for his oceangoing
exploits, but at the time he commanded the expedition to Roanoke,
there is no record of him having performed military service at sea. However, seafaring was a family legacy. His father captained Henry VIII's

flagship, *Mary Rose*, which sank off Portsmouth in 1545—to the horror of the court, which had gathered to send it off on its maiden voyage. The ship's remains can be seen today at the eponymous museum in Portsmouth. Of the vast Ralegh cousinry, Grenville was among the wealthiest, having outlived his brothers and inherited his father's landed estate. Wealth and family name led to his election to Parliament, even before he achieved his majority. A man of great pride, he killed Robert Bannister "in an effray," for which he received pardon.[1] He also developed resentment toward his cousin Francis Drake and, at Roanoke, toward Ralph Lane, who served as colonel in charge of military affairs and held command after Grenville left. Nevertheless, Grenville faithfully served his cousin Walter, and they developed an excellent partnership in private and public affairs, becoming the two most important political leaders of South West England. In April 1585, he set out for the newly named Virginia, an appellation Ralegh had bestowed in honor of the Virgin Queen. This expedition tested the character of the English in their ability to get along with the Natives over time.

—

THE FIRST SHIPS of the second expedition arrived at Roanoke in early June 1585, and Grenville arrived on the nineteenth. The expedition remained almost a year. Ralegh's expectations of his leaders seem clear: build a fort and housing, explore the mainland and the coast, secure Indian friendships and alliances, and plant crops.

Even before the expedition had departed England, Ralegh was preparing still more ships to bring supplies. He was uncertain about who he should send as settlers. Should he send miners, farmers, viticulturists, or other kinds of skilled and semiskilled laborers? Of the 107 men on the first ships of the second expedition, 13 were listed as "Master" and one as "Captain." These would not be expected to perform manual labor. Some of the masters likely paid their way to America as "adventurers." They ventured their capital and their lives in hopes of making a fortune, probably dreaming they would find some commodity they could bring back to England. Another group comprised a mix of soldiers and skilled and unskilled laborers whose work was necessary to support the settlement. The skilled would have included smiths, carpenters, a gunsmith, baker, brewer, and cook. Ralegh also appears to have provided a shoemaker and a basket maker.[2] He employed Joachim Gans, a Jew from Prague, to assay metals and sent

Thomas Hariot and the painter John White to amass a great variety of information about America.

The English sent word to the great chief Wingina, whom the English labeled a king, of their arrival and dispatched Manteo with several men to the mainland, possibly to the Indian town of Secota, and others to the town of Croatan, where the earlier-arriving English were discovered. On July 11, while many remained behind to repair the *Tyger*, Grenville led an expedition carrying eight days of provisions across Pamlico Sound with the probable intent of visiting the local Indians and seeing the mainland. Many of the leading men accompanied the general, including Lane, Amadas, Hariot, and White. They visited three Indian communities, the town of Pomeioc, the village of Aquascogoc, and the town of Secota, remaining but a day at each, indicating they wished to make a quick survey of these nearby towns and the landscape. White produced pictures of two of the towns, the Indians, and the lay of the land. Upon returning to their ships, the English realized that three days earlier one of the Indians at Aquascogoc had stolen a silver cup. Grenville sent Amadas across the sound to demand its return, "and not receiving it according to his [the chief's] promise, we burnt, and spoyled their corne, and Towne, all the people beeing fledd."[3]

It was a striking overreaction. Why did the English punish with impunity the theft of a silver cup? The violence likely had been ordered by Grenville, a violent man who believed humanity only obeyed authority because they feared punishment. This was how a captain commanded a ship, and an admiral commanded a fleet. But this was certainly not a diplomatic way to treat people you had just met. From the perspective of Grenville and Amadas, Indians had to learn not to trifle with the English. The English were unlikely to see themselves through the Indians' perspective: as interlopers who must negotiate their presence.

The draconian measures immediately created suspicion and hostility. None of the local Indians would have understood English retribution as warranted—a stolen cup was hardly worth the destruction of a village. From many American Indians' perspective, stealing from another group of people was a way to prove one's bravery and masculinity. The English should have responded by stealthily stealing something of theirs to display their manliness. Their violent overreaction informed all Indians of the region that the English were unlike any of the peoples they had yet known. Indians engaged in bitter warfare, but the quick escalation from theft to destruction of a village made English behavior inscrutable and dangerous.

Fortunately for the immediate prospects of the English, they had Manteo. Whereas Wanchese deserted the English upon arrival at Roanoke, becoming a foe of their settlement, Manteo remained a steadfast friend. He visited King Wingina's brother, Granganimeo, who apparently invited the English to settle near his village on the north side of Roanoke Island.[4] The English agreed, and Grenville overlooked Lane's construction of fortifications while exploring parties went farther north through Albemarle Sound. On one sortie, the English discovered enemies of Wingina, slew about twenty men, and on their return gave the female captives to their allies. Wingina would have been delighted with the captives but was more wary of this evidence of English military power.[5] Grenville sent his half brother John Arundel to England to report on the colony's progress and needs. The queen knighted Arundel, another signifier to the court of how much she valued the Virginia enterprise.[6]

Grenville stayed two months at Roanoke, long enough to see the fort completed. Having fallen out with Lane, he was probably happy to leave, but there was little need for him to stay. He had fulfilled his charge. He had established a settlement and would return home to report to Ralegh and obtain more men and supplies. On the way home, he captured a Spanish ship of at least three hundred tons—a richly laden ship. One Portuguese merchant claimed the *Santa Maria*'s cargo contained 40,000 ducats (£10,000) of gold, silver, and pearls and twice as much value in sugar, ginger, hides, and other commodities. Grenville denied the ship carried precious metals and listed the main commodities as sugar and ginger, and only half the value of what the Portuguese merchant claimed. Whether Grenville and his men pocketed much, the investors in the expedition turned a handsome profit.[7] The capture of the *Santa Maria* easily paid the cost of that year's Roanoke expedition plus profit.

There was more pirating to come. One of the ships that had carried men and supplies to Roanoke, the *Lion*, sailed to Newfoundland and met up with the *Golden Royal*, commanded by Bernard Drake.[8] Ralegh had intended to send Drake to Roanoke with supplies, but Elizabeth ordered Ralegh to dispatch him to Newfoundland to warn English fishermen not to take their catch to Spain, which had placed an embargo on English ships. Along the way, Drake captured a Portuguese "prize" ship with a valuable cargo, and at Newfoundland he took seventeen fishing vessels. When the *Golden Royal* joined forces with the *Lion*, they sailed to the Azores and captured three Portuguese ships from Brazil and a French ship from Africa. Ralegh's take from this haul helped fund the next expedition to Roanoke.[9]

In capturing the *Santa Maria* on his return to England, Grenville demonstrated that piracy could supply the wealth and some of the commodities Ralegh hoped to gain from a colony. Grenville proudly reported to Walsingham that the prize would be "sufficient to answer the charges of each adventurer" who invested in Ralegh's colony "with some gain."[10] In London, Henry Talbot, upon hearing of Grenville's prize, wrote that "this shippe, will make Sir Water Rauley a saver by his voyage." Talbot contrasted the declared riches of Roanoke, that is, the great "fertiletie of the soile, not to bee inferior to Englande," to the region's lack of gold and pearls. He opined, "The earth is good, but wantes both cattel, & manuringe, and therefore it is thought the voiage [the colonial enterprise] will have bad sowcccesse [success]."[11] To many English, a fertile country (albeit one that required cows) could hardly compete with one of barren soil that possessed precious metals.

Colonization was expensive, and the value of Iberian prizes could be extraordinary. The lure of piracy constantly threatened the prospects for permanent English colonies because colonization took much more effort, greater capital investment, and more people than snaring merchant ships at sea. Building a new society in America did not entice those who desired a quick return on investments. How long would it take for colonists to earn significant profits? Ten years? Twenty years? A generation or two? Only the young and desperate could have found this attractive. Men of substance and maturity, concerned for their family's and nation's future, might have seen long-term advantages in overseas colonies, but as the young and desperate preferred to take their chances on the high seas as pirates, the older men with capital preferred to invest in these same pirates.

Even Ralegh could not resist the temptation. As he readied a third expedition to Roanoke to plant permanent colonists, he and Francis Drake busily prepared a privateering expedition on a scale like no other to wrest the New World's riches from Spain. But as Ralegh set about realizing the grandiose scheme to singe the Spaniard's beard and secure his tiny colony in North Carolina, the second expedition at Roanoke was simultaneously hurtling toward disaster.

No records explicitly document what happened at the Roanoke colony after Grenville's departure in September 1585 until March 1586, when Lane's recording of spring and summer commences.[12] Lane noted no exploration was made to the south, but a party that likely included White and Hariot traveled northward. We can assume that during those five unrecorded months, White and Hariot busily amassed information about Roanoke and its environs, including the geographic detail they used to produce a superb map of the region.[13] The other men's activities are largely unknown. They must have spent some time obtaining maize from the Indians, perhaps through trade, but otherwise they did not stray far from Roanoke.[14]

By spring 1586, the colony was experiencing food shortages. Spring was a lean time for the Indians as well, because they had traded or shared much of their maize supply with the English and the new planting had only just begun to grow. Wracked by hunger in a strange land thousands of miles from kin, dependent on the goodwill of people whose culture appeared inscrutable, English nerves frayed, and the subsequent falling-out can be traced to English demands for sustenance. Manteo's intermittent presence eased some of the tension, for he could translate language and culture. And Manteo had friends willing to help the English. But Manteo likely spent most of his time with Hariot and White, who widely explored the mainland and required his diplomatic service.

While Hariot and White were away, most of the English hung around Roanoke Island hoping riches would magically appear. The men, to some extent, followed the orders and cues of their leader Lane. Lane admitted to difficulty controlling the men, but disrespect of his authority was not the primary problem. Lane and his men became increasingly suspicious of the Roanoke Indians, who responded in kind. Wanchese likely did not help matters, owing to his hostility toward the English. More palpable was Wingina's concern that the English were forging alliances with his enemies, which was true, as Lane worried over declining food supplies and spread his net further afield.

One prospective Native ally in particular fueled Lane's fears. For two days in late March, Lane kept prisoner a great chief named Menatonon, who commanded seven hundred fighting men in the province of Choanoke, about 130 miles northwest of Roanoke.[15] Lane thought Menatonon was "impotent in the lims, but otherwise for a Savage, a very grave and wise man . . . not onely of his owne Countrey . . . but also of his neighbours round about him as wel farre and neere, and of the commodities that eche Countrey yeeldeth." Lane claimed to have learned more about Virginia in his two days with Menatonon "then I had received by all the searches and salvages that before I or any of my companie had had conference with." This statement indicates just how little respect Lane had for the reams of information Hariot and White gathered about Indian life and culture. It also belittles Manteo's contribution.

After seven months in America, Lane finally had discovered a "savage" he found useful, one who spoke his political language. Menatonon explained the region's geopolitical configurations and spoke of avenues to quickly obtaining wealth. Lane's eyes grew wide at Menatonon's talk of pearls: big and small, black and white, of a great store in his country and in a neighbor's country. He gave Lane a rope of large black pearls. Lane ruefully recounted that if Ralegh's supply ship had arrived "before the end of April," Lane would have taken two hundred men "with the guides that Menatonon would have given" to that neighboring king's country to get his pearls. Lane would have secured that country with small forts built every "two dayes journey," with "a mayne fort" at the "Bay or Porte" of pearls. With so many valuable pearls within grasp, Lane felt he could do what he did best and secure a valuable commodity and the supply line for getting there and back.

But an army travels on its stomach and Lane needed food. Lane released Menatonon for a ransom, which included his son Skiko and enough victuals to carry Lane and his men to meet "another kinde of Savages, dwelling more to the Westwarde," likely the Tuscarora. Still the food shortages grew worse. And at a great assembly, Wingina, who changed his name to Pemisapan, urged Lane not to go, claiming that these distant Indians were allying with ones nearby to destroy the English and the Roanoke. Menatonon confided to Lane that there did exist a growing confederacy against the English, but that it was "wholly procured by Pemisapan himselfe."

In April, relations with the Roanoke improved, and not a moment too soon. Pemisapan had his men set up weirs to catch fish for the English, and his people "sowed a good quantitie of ground," which would suffice "to have fed our whole company (God blessing the growth) and that by the belly for a whole yere."[16] Pemisapan also gave the English a "certain plot of ground for ourselves to serve," an indication that the Roanoke had not ceded to the English all the land around their settlement—and that the English recognized Roanoke land ownership.

The English had to find enough food to last from April to July, when the maize would be harvested and a new supply ship was expected from England. But then "Ensenore our friend died," as did

Granganimeo, and Pemisapan turned to receiving counsel from the enemies of the English among his chief advisors. The Roanoke Indians' refusal to bring food indicated to Lane hostile intentions. Pemisapan planted no fields on the islands for the English. Tired of English pestering, the Roanoke Natives deserted them. The Powhatan repeated this same situation over twenty years later at Jamestown, abandoning the English in response to incessant demands for food.[17]

Food, then, was the crux of the problem. Lane asserted he had no seeds to plant.[18] Hunting offered no solution because game was scarce in spring and hunters risked attack. The men could line-fish, and some did, but the English needed weirs to catch enough to feed everyone. Lane rued that "wee had no weares for fishe, neither could our men skill of the making of them," but his account offered contradictions, because he later noted that if "our weares should fayle us (as often they did) wee might very well starve."[19] And later still, he believed that the Indians planned to rob the weirs "and also to cause them to be broken and once being broken never to be repayred againe by them."[20] Whatever the exact circumstances, and Lane's report equivocates, he knew the English could not feed themselves.

The English had impressed the Indians with their weapons, clothing, and sundry material possessions, but other things about them were baffling. The absence of English women to plant crops and gather foodstuffs must have seemed unnatural. Manteo would have allayed Indian confusion about the absence of English females at Roanoke at least to explain that females existed in England, but the fact remained that the English at Roanoke had no women to feed them. What kind of men were these to bring no women to cultivate and prepare food? Were they idiots?

The English were just as hard-pressed to understand the Roanoke Indians. Lane saw evil in the Indians' abandonment. Food shortages would force the English to disperse to seek "crabs and fish to live," leaving the colony vulnerable to attack.[21] Lane perceived Pemisapan conspired to prevent all Indians from trading "any victuals whatsoever" to the English. Lane followed the script that Pemisapan allegedly had written. He had no choice. He sent a company of twenty-one to Admirals Island to feed themselves and to keep watch for ships. He sent eleven others to another island to do the same. Additional parties moved to the mainland to live on oysters and casada.[22]

English inability to feed themselves, according to Lane, led the Indians to hold the English and their God in contempt. In his words, they "began to blaspheme, and flatly to say, that our Lord God was not God, since hee suffered us to sustaine much hunger, and also to be killed" by the Indians on the mainland.[23] Lane plotted with Skiko to discover Pemisapan's true intent. He had held on to Menatonon's son because he needed him—he needed a voice to counter Pemisapan's, a voice to explain what was going on around him. When Menatonon made an offer for his son's release, Lane refused. No amount of pearls could relieve English hunger, and Lane could not let Skiko go. With Manteo likely off with his own people or with Hariot and White collecting information about the Indians and the region, Skiko and Menatonon became Lane's lifeline.

Lane and Skiko concocted a ruse in which Skiko escaped only to be recaptured by Lane and put in leg irons. Lane threatened to cut off Skiko's head. He spared him at Pemisapan's request and released Skiko to him. Lane implies this was all carefully planned and "perswaded" Pemisapan that Skiko "was our enemy to the death." Pemisapan then *allegedly* confided to Skiko his plans against the English. Skiko slipped away to inform Lane of the conspiracy. Lane considered it possible that Skiko was playing him. Whether he knew the truth or not, and he likely did not know if a conspiracy actually existed, Lane felt it necessary to note in his report to Ralegh that "one of Pemisapans owne men" also revealed the plot against the English. Thus, Lane had two witnesses.

Believing that the Roanoke used copper to bribe other Indians to join them in an assault upon the English, Lane determined to strike first. Entering the Roanoke village under pretense that he had come to buy food and hire hunters for an expedition, Lane and his men opened fire at Pemisapan and some of his chief werowances. Pemisapan fled after suffering a shot in the buttocks. One of Lane's Irish "servants," Edward Nugent, the deputy provost, pursued the chief into the woods and returned with his head.[24]

Ralegh's ideal for colonization—living in harmony with the Native peoples—unraveled as quickly as the colony itself. Whether or not the Roanoke Indians actually had intended to attack the English, the fact that Lane saw fit to assault the people whose land he occupied gave the lie to English pretensions of a benevolent settlement. Dependent for food on the Roanoke, all Lane could conjure was to resort to force. He hoped that the surviving Roanoke would flee and allow the English to forge new alliances to obtain food, specifically with the Chowan and Weapemeoc, and he still had the alliance and help of Manteo and the Croatan. But it quickly became apparent that English settlement at Roanoke was untenable. Lane's killing of the Roanoke leadership, coming on the heels of the earlier destruction of the Aquascogoc village and the killing of some of Pemisapan's enemies, foreclosed the possibility of the colonists easily earning new allies.

Ralegh learned from this episode not to place a colonial settlement in the hands of someone like Ralph Lane, a soldier with no interest in working with Native peoples except if he could dictate the terms. With relations spoiled at Roanoke, the English would have to offer a great deal of trade goods and significant military aid to convince any Indian group in the area of the benefits of alliance. Why would the Natives choose to ally with an inscrutably violent people who did not possess the wherewithal to feed themselves? Fortunately for the English, a little over a week later Drake's armada arrived.

CHAPTER 10

Singeing the Spaniard's Beard

English ships often lurked off the Azores and Canary Islands, waiting for cargo-rich Iberian ships sailing along the African coast to or from Asia and America. Sometimes the pirates patrolled close to Spanish ports, but increasingly they infested Caribbean waters looking for stray ships on their way to Cuba or elsewhere or those separated from the Spanish convoys that guarded them on their way to Spain from America. English, Dutch, and French ships also preyed on fishing vessels returning from Newfoundland and small ships trading in the Mediterranean. And they preyed on each other. In the 1580s and 1590s, Ralegh supported and participated in these enterprises.

Three months after the second expedition's arrival at Roanoke, on September 14, 1585, Sir Francis Drake sailed to the Caribbean at the head of a twenty-nine-ship flotilla. Ralegh had placed the colonization of America on the backburner and helped organize a massive expedition led by Drake to wrest from Spain its wealth flowing in from the Indies and American mainland.

In intent, it was the most audacious plan yet by the English against Spanish America. Queen Elizabeth was throwing the gauntlet down at the King of Spain's feet. She had an excuse for setting loose the trusted Drake against the Spanish: Philip had seized English grain ships in Spain. But her proposed punishment hardly fit the crime. She intended to use Drake to bring Philip to his knees with a lightning-quick assault on Spanish America. Her commitment to war had grown clearer in August 1585, as Drake prepared his flotilla: England concluded the Treaty of Nonsuch, promising seven thousand soldiers to help protect the Dutch from the Spanish.

Many historians do not perceive a relationship between Drake's expedition and Ralegh's colony beyond the fact that Drake visited Roanoke on his return to England. But the two were nevertheless connected. We do not know who raised the idea to attack Spanish America, but Ralegh would have known of Humphrey's earlier plan, and it was Ralegh who convinced Elizabeth to employ Drake to lead the expedition.[1] Both men thought the best way to counter Spain was by sea, and Drake had set precedence for this expedition twelve years earlier when he sacked Spanish towns in the Americas in the early stages of his circumnavigation of the earth.

Ralegh was Drake's ally at court, his fellow West countryman, and a distant relative: one of Ralegh's grandfathers was John Drake, apparently a relation of Francis's. If nothing else, Drake's foray could assist Ralegh's colony by lighting numerous fires for Spain to extinguish before turning its attention to the small flames the English lit on Roanoke Island. Ralegh's colony was extremely vulnerable—the Spanish could eliminate it at any time. But a diversion of Spanish attention from Roanoke was not the only reason for Drake's flotilla, which would have been laughable—no one would risk war with Spain to protect a tiny outpost. And Drake's quest risked making Spain more inclined to destroy the colony. Undoubtedly, Roanoke was not the raison d'être for Drake's expedition, but it most likely was the germ that set Ralegh's mind in motion and spurred his support.

The expedition was grandiose on a level that only Drake and Ralegh could imagine. The plans represented Gilbert's defined methods and goals and Ralegh's strategic thinking, but the estimate of riches to be attained was likely the product of Drake's imagination inspired by his earlier ransacking of Spanish America. Elizabeth approved the plan and invested in the enterprise. She cared about the future of Roanoke, but not enough to help finance the colony beyond the lending of a ship for the first expedition. She increased her support by empowering and financing Drake's foray, which met Elizabeth's own needs to divert Philip's attention and resources from Europe *to* America, redirecting Spain's energies away from the Low Countries, England, and Ireland. England feared the Low Countries, or Ireland, would become a launching pad for a Spanish invasion of England. In fact, it became a principle of English/British foreign policy for the next 350 years that the Low Countries could not be controlled by any foreign power.

To Elizabeth, the beauty of Drake's voyage was that it could accomplish her goals while paying for itself. Unlike with the seven thousand soldiers she sent to the Netherlands, presumably the English government would not have to spend a farthing on Drake's expedition. If all went according to plan, the foray would generate spectacular treasure, enough to fund those exorbitantly expensive soldiers in the Low Countries and Ireland, enough, perhaps, to vastly improve England's military standing in Europe. Elizabeth intended to counter Spain's war machine by siphoning off its American treasures on a spectacular level.

———

THE QUEEN AND HER MINISTERS had been burned before. Their investment in Frobisher's mining of fool's gold at Baffin Island had come to nothing, and she would not repeat the folly. Wresting wealth from Spain was different: Drake was a proven commodity. His circumnavigation had yielded fantastic profits. According to famed economist John Maynard Keynes, the English foreign debt was paid off with the queen's share of the proceeds from Drake's circumnavigation with enough left over (£42,000) for her to capitalize the Levant Company.[2] This new foray promised even greater rewards.

Funding for the expedition ran to £40,000. Elizabeth provided half, including £10,000 in ready money and the other half the lease of the two most significant ships of the flotilla, the *Elizabeth Bonadventure* and the *Aid*, along with their ordnance, additional weaponry, munitions, and other supplies. In exchange, she would receive half the profits. It was a substantial investment on Elizabeth's part, but the estimated return was staggering.

The detailed blueprint for the expedition predicted a return of 4 million ducats—£1 million. The queen's expected share of close to a half million pounds sterling would be enough money to build and outfit a navy of a hundred 500-ton ships and still have half left over to fund several armies to fight on the continent of Europe. Not included in this estimate is the plan's supposition that Drake would capture two hundred ships off Honduras and his seizure of gold and silver ships.[3]

Drake planned to ravage the Canary Islands and the Cape Verde Islands and then to head to the West Indies to conquer Margarita before striking many of the principal Spanish possessions in the western Atlantic. His main objective: Santo Domingo, on the island of Hispaniola. Reputed to be an extremely wealthy city, it stood as the venerable symbol of Spanish power in the Indies. Drake then intended to sail to the Spanish Main to Rio de la Hacha on his way to seize the pearl fisheries, followed by a strike on Cartagena, in modern-day Colombia, where he expected to extract riches in the neighborhood of a million ducats. Then to Nombre de Dios in Panama to reunite with his old allies, the Cimarrons, the African runaways from Spanish slavery he had befriended a dozen years before. With five thousand Cimarrons and a thousand of his own men, he planned to make his way to the town of Panama, which "standeth upon the sea coast in the South Sea, and doth [receive] all the treasure that cometh by water from the new Kingdom of Peru, which may be taken without resistance." With his pinnaces, Drake intended to search "all the coast of the Honduras" to obtain supplies for the return voyage, along the way snaring, the report proclaimed, as many as two hundred Spanish frigates. And, for good measure, he would capture "many rich men, and ransom them for 100,000 ducats."

In none of this did Drake suggest establishing any permanent occupation. The foray to Central America was all about booty (and perhaps an empowerment of the Cimarrons in Panama), and it was the prequel to the grand event—the capture of Havana. Drake planned to "raze" Havana and, if possible, "leave a company of soldiers" to force the Spanish to find another place to send the flotas that guarded the treasure ships on their way to Spain. This would open a window of opportunity for the English to flood into the Indies and seize more Spanish treasure ships. If Havana was taken, then the Spanish settlements in Florida and South Carolina became indefensible. Roanoke would be secured and Ralegh could initiate a quick expansion of English colonies along the Atlantic coast.

In reality, Drake's flotilla visited nowhere near the number of places he intended, but it did do some damage. After a relatively uneventful voyage along the African coast, he headed for Santo Domingo, the first Spanish settlement in the New World. They arrived December 31, 1585. Only six months prior, Grenville had stopped there on his way to Roanoke, and the English and Spanish had shared food and wine and conducted trade. Drake's armada, hopeful of a half million ducats in booty, broke bread with the Spanish, but only *after* he had subdued them.[4]

The Spanish believed Santo Domingo to be utterly secure from invaders. The city boasted the strongest fortress in the Indies. By sea, ships had to enter the Ozama River to approach the city, where the presumably impregnable fortress guarded entry. But the Spanish had farmed out the fort's defense, and the warden maintained only a skel-

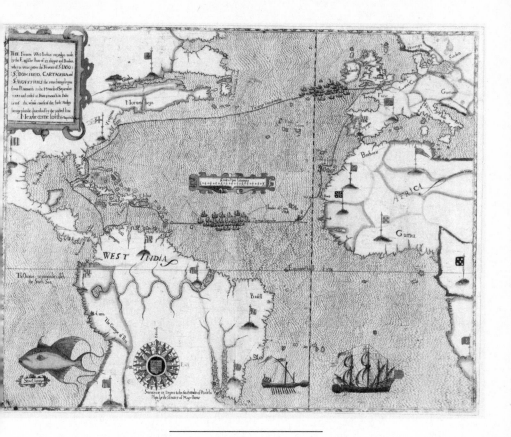

6. Drake's foray through the West Indies

eton crew. The two galleys ordinarily stationed at Santo Domingo for extra protection could not perform their duties, as one was recently shipwrecked and the other was unseaworthy.[5] Not that it mattered. Instead of attacking by sea, Drake landed nearly a thousand men west of the city. The unaware Spanish not only failed to keep watch of the coast but also had no pickets to warn of an overland advance.

Shortly after dawn, the English entered the city and Drake let loose his ships' cannon. The victory was as easy as it was quick. The Spanish might still consider Drake a pirate, but with nearly thirty sails before Santo Domingo, he was now a pirate in command of a huge war fleet, an English war fleet making a heavy-handed assertion of Tudor power in the Spanish domain.

Ralegh's planting of Englishmen at Roanoke suddenly looked different. Perhaps the English were not just playing at New World colonization after all. They could mount a flotilla and use it effectively in

America. English seafarers had proven their skills pirating and raiding, but this latest was on a new scale and with a new purpose. The queen and her servants had launched a large military expedition by sea against a bastion of Spanish power.

As it turned out, the city was not nearly as wealthy as expected. The population was in decline and much of the housing had turned to rubble.[6] Still, Santo Domingo boasted rich monasteries and many beautiful homes, which bore the furnishings of elite families. Drake demanded one million ducats to spare the city. Upon realizing that the residents did not have that kind of money, he reduced his asking price by 90 percent. The citizenry balked and Drake ordered selective destruction of portions of the city in a game of chicken with the city fathers. They finally reached agreement on 25,000 ducats, about £6,000, 2.5 percent of Drake's initial demand. The English also took slaves from the inhabitants—Native American, African, and galley slaves. After one month's stay in Santo Domingo, the flotilla set sail for Cartagena, both a more formidable opponent and more important administrative locale.

Cartagena's keepers received word of Drake's armada sailing in the Caribbean but did not know of Santo Domingo's conquest until the day he arrived. They readied their defenses. Women and children, as well as valuables, were removed to the countryside. As at Santo Domingo, Drake ordered a nighttime landing of a thousand men. Spanish sentries reported no activities. When the English encountered the Spanish land forces, mostly civilians, instead of each side fighting, both raced to the city. Losses were minimal as the English entered Cartagena and most of the Spanish kept running, heading to the countryside to reunite with their families. The commander at Cartagena, Don Pedro Vigne y Manrique, was later court-martialed and sentenced to death for his failure to defend Cartagena.[7]

Again, the English found little plunder. There was mainly heavier merchandise that the Spanish could not quickly remove, such as oil and wine. Drake negotiated with the city's bishop to spare Cartagena's destruction. When the bishop halted negotiations, Drake threatened to burn the town, and by way of example he destroyed a few houses of the rich. Cartagena's city fathers reopened negotiations, and the two sides settled on a ransom of 107,000 ducats' worth of bullion, a far better haul than at Santo Domingo, but nowhere near what the English expected. As he had done years earlier, Drake also demanded ransoms for captured individuals.[8] He took Cartagena's artillery. And slaves.

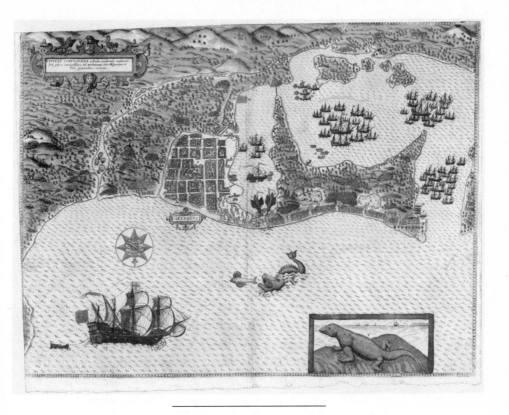

7. Drake's fleet at Cartagena

Cartagena turned out to be the expedition's high-water mark. With about 20 percent of his men ill, Drake opted against meeting up with the Cimarrons and by-passed Mexico to sail to western Cuba to take on drinking water, but could find none. The English sailed past Havana—it looked too formidable to attack—and landed at Matanzas, east of Havana, where they found water.[9] After consulting with his captains about the decision not to attack Havana, the fleet hovered near the city, hoping to capture ships laden with riches, but got nothing. They then headed to Roanoke Island by sailing north along the Florida coast.

This route was most unpromising for booty. A Lieutenant Crofts believed Drake's decision to sail for Virginia resulted after "an assembly of the captains" conducted near Santa Elena (Parris Island, South Carolina).[10] But Drake must have determined to go to Roanoke much earlier, for he had no other reason to sail along the Florida coast.[11] There was no opportunity to obtain Spanish riches or do any damage, other than to help Ralegh's colony by eliminating St. Augustine and Santa Elena. The Spanish maintained these settlements only to keep foreign powers from occupying them, where they could then threaten Spanish holdings and trade routes.[12] Ralegh had invested in Drake's adventure to the amount of £400, and Drake supported Ralegh's challenge to Spain in building a New World colony. Drake saw its long-term value as a base for English ships seeking refreshment on their Atlantic voyages.

Drake's flotilla reached St. Augustine in early June 1586. The city sits on the Matanzas River, protected by the sea; to reach it, they had to pass St. John's fort, only recently constructed. Massive tree trunks made the fort seem formidable. The English placed four ordnance across the river from the fort and let loose a barrage of cannon. The Spanish fled to the countryside because the fort was indefensible. The mount had not been finished, and there were over 250 women and children hiding in the bush. If the garrison were defeated, one Spaniard later claimed, their dependents "would certainly have perished at the hands of the Indians, as was obvious."[13]

Small European settlements on the mainland Atlantic coast depended on the Native peoples living in the environs for food and protection from hostile inland peoples. In return, they received trade goods and military alliance. The Indians could easily have destroyed St. Augustine, even after the fort was completed, by siege or burning. The fort was built to protect the town from European invasion by sea. Less than a cannon shot from the town was a village of Catholic Indians considered by the Spanish to be close allies.[14] They were expected to conduct reconnaissance and protect the Spanish from hostile Indians.

The arrival of the English, however, revealed the limits of accommodation between Spanish and Indians. The Spanish tried to raise a party of Indians to reconnoiter and conduct a raid against the invaders. Much to Spanish disappointment, their Indian interpreter could recruit only ten men. The fact that the Spanish were still relying on an interpreter *twenty years* after settlement reveals the degree to which Indians and Spanish lived a segregated existence. When the Spanish abandoned the fort, the Indians "sacked this city and stole everything there was in the houses." Their actions "inferred the evil intention they entertained."[15] This behavior confirmed for the Spanish that they could not trust the local Indians: accommodation and friendship were two different things.

Spanish accounts of the English invasion fail to mention that the English marched into St. Augustine carrying a red flag, a warning that no quarter would be given. Spanish officials did not want to appear as cowards by admitting this in their explanation for St. Augustine's abandonment without a fight. Drake had not unraveled the red flag elsewhere, and did so here as revenge for the Spanish massacre of Protestant French in Florida that gave birth to St. Augustine. The town sat on the Matanzas River—*Matanzas* is the Spanish plural for "slaughter"—so named by the Spanish for the two slaughters of the French near St. Augustine in 1565. Drake would not punish all Spanish for the sins of Pedro Menéndez de Avilés, who had ordered the massacres, but he aimed to punish any Spanish associated with this bloody place.

Given the abandonment of the fort, there were no Spanish to kill, but the English found other ways to take revenge. Over the course of the week they spent at St. Augustine, they destroyed everything that demonstrated a Spanish presence: orchards, fields, gardens, and every building. This was not just revenge but meant as help for Ralegh's Roanoke establishment by eliminating the closest bastion of Spanish power. The English also confiscated the artillery and munitions and added to their booty the governor's strongbox, which contained the garrison's pay, 6,000 ducats. But Drake left untouched the adjoining Indians' fields and villages. Drake likely believed that all Indians resented the yoke of Spanish dominance and it was better not to alienate people who could become future allies when they could make Spanish rebuilding more difficult. The Spanish confirmed that the English studiously left the Indians' village alone, and had "sent persons . . . to flatter these natives."[16]

The Spanish of St. Augustine lost nearly everything. One Spanish witness rued how the city had been "well populated, comfortable, fruitful and abounding in many things." After Drake's raid, "Everybody was left naked, stripped of everything, in the open country, and without recourse."[17] Juan de Posada reached St. Augustine from Cuba soon after Drake's departure and saved the Spanish settlers. He brought men and supplies, averring in a letter to the Spanish Crown that if he had been but two weeks later the Indians would have killed everyone. European-Indian accommodation had its limits.[18]

The townsman's claim that St. Augustine was a flourishing community demands a bit more investigation. Taking the deponent at his word, the garrison had carved out a "comfortable" existence; the large number of women and children evinces that this was no mere frontier outpost but one transitioning into a mature and stable community. Yet the view from Havana, which administered St. Augustine, was quite different. Immediately after Drake's arrival at St. Augustine, officials in Havana called for Florida's abandonment. Some of this might have been jealousy, because they preferred the Crown spend money on Cuba rather than Florida. Alonso Suarez de Toledo saw St. Augustine as a waste of resources. The comforts the townspeople enjoyed did not derive from the fruits of the land but from the Spanish treasury. Suarez employed "plain speaking" to Philip II, describing St. Augustine as "entirely unprofitable nor can it sustain its own population. Everything must be brought in from outside."[19]

Indeed, from 1564 to 1577, Florida consumed over a fifth of the Spanish Empire's outlay for defense of the Caribbean.[20] Suarez asserted that funds spent on Florida should be diverted to improving the harbor at Havana and supporting galleons to protect the sea route. Occupying Florida was unnecessary because Florida's coast from Cape Canaveral to St. Augustine was so dangerous that a base there offered little to a prospective enemy. More importantly, Suarez could not believe that any other European nation could establish a permanent base. The Spanish possessed an array of settlements to support St. Augustine. "Santo Domingo," he said, "Puerto Rico, Cuba, Yucatan and New Spain." Yet "the garrison of Florida has nevertheless suffered actual hunger." If Spain could barely keep St. Augustine fed, "what would happen to foreigners there who must bring their subsistence from a great distance to an inhospitable coast? The land itself would wage war on them!"[21] Hence, the Spanish need worry little about Roanoke—the English had no places nearby to support it, any settlement would be indefensible, and the coastland was inhospitable. What Suarez might have specified, if he had known, because it seems as true for St. Augustine as it did for Roanoke: Europeans could not count on Indians to feed them, and the local Natives could prove untrustworthy and dangerous.

Suarez was right that the English could not support themselves at Roanoke. They needed to go farther north to Chesapeake Bay. The North Carolina coastal region was ill-suited for the kind of profit-making activities that the English envisioned in the sixteenth century. Of even greater import: the English did not know how to colonize, how to get along with America's Native peoples. Individuals like Hariot and White understood the necessity of accommodation, but Grenville and Lane did not. One misguided or ignorant leader could ruin the prospects for a colony.

With his numbers much reduced by illness, Drake departed St. Augustine. He was off to Roanoke, with a stop at Santa Elena, a small Spanish outpost. Arriving at Santa Elena, unsure of the shoals and lacking a pilot, he decided against disembarking and continued north along the coast. Spotting an English bonfire, he reached Roanoke on June 9, 1586. The colony was in disarray. Lane had poisoned relations with the assault on Pemisapan and his people. The English badly needed food and a new place to live. Drake offered Lane "victuals, ammunition and clothing, but also of barkes, pinnaces and boates," and to carry away the "weake" and "unfit," and replace them with others.[22] Drake and Lane agreed the colony should abandon Roanoke and resettle at Chesapeake Bay, a more fruitful location and one where the English had yet to alienate the Native people. If they ran out of provisions at the new settlement—Drake could only leave them enough to last until August—Lane and his men would head home in the vessels Drake provided.

A great storm struck the coast and altered plans. One ship, the *Francis*, with many English intended for the Chesapeake already on board, headed out to sea and continued to England. Many of Drake's ships broke anchor and also headed out to sea. Lane had a change of heart and decided to leave with Drake. The colonists on shore had to quickly pack and just as quickly have their possessions put aboard the remaining ships. Showing little care for the colonists' belongings, some of Drake's sailors tossed the chests into the sea. Whether they did so to prevent their ships from being overburdened or simply to escape the coast as soon as possible or out of spite for reasons unknown, much of Hariot's and White's work was lost. Manteo and another Indian, Towaye, chose to join the English; they were of great help to Hariot, filling in the gaps of lost information about the land and the people.[23]

According to Richard Hakluyt, immediately after the colony's departure, a supply ship arrived at Roanoke, turned around, and went home to England.[24] A month to six weeks after the colony's abandonment, Grenville also arrived at Roanoke with supplies and colonists, maybe one or two hundred, indicating that Ralegh planned a rapid expansion, though he likely had already decided to move the colony to the Chesapeake according to Grenville's recommendation. Grenville unsuccessfully searched the environs for the colony and for Indian towns and found only three Indians, two of whom escaped. The one who remained spoke some English and told Grenville that the colonists had departed. He joined Grenville and returned to England, where he was christened and renamed Ralegh, and where he remained with Grenville until his death in 1589.

Ralegh prepared another expedition for Virginia, one intended to fulfill the charge in his patent to establish permanent settlements. Despite the miserable end of the Lane expedition, he avidly publicized English success in America as if they had not experienced disaster.

In England, a member of the Privy Council asserted that Drake's expedition was not "so good successe as was hoped for."[25] This assessment likely referred to the small amount of booty, but there were also questions about its strategic accomplishments. Though Drake had largely destroyed St. Augustine, the English had not removed and replaced the Spanish anywhere. But from Drake's foray the English learned that the locales they attacked had little inherent economic value except as part of a Spanish network. Santo Domingo had fallen into insignificance, and Cartagena gained much of its importance later. Their value in 1586 lay in their connection to other places that produced valuable natural resources. Even if the English could have maintained permanent control over most any of the Spanish coastal towns in the Americas, the riches of the Spanish Empire would have been funneled to other entrepôts.

Of course, there was one spot Drake had considered occupying, and perhaps the English should have taken it while they had the chance: Havana. Havana's conquest would have been worthwhile because of its value for interrupting trade routes. An English Havana would be a permanent thorn in the Spanish Empire, a threat to Mexico and much of the West Indies and Central America. Spain would have had to pull out all stops to reconquer it. No spot was better located in the Caribbean for strategic purposes: ships had to pass Cuba on their return to Europe. Cuba had the added advantage of possessing rich agricultural lands that made the island valuable regardless of its strategic importance. Still, the English were not ready to commit to such a grand scale of colonization. The occupation of Roanoke Island was quaint in comparison.

The reality was that the English lacked capital, skills, and supportive colonies to take and hold any Spanish colony. Elizabeth and her advisors considered the expense too great. Ralegh and his investors had to bear the costs of Roanoke. The "big" money went to pirating, and to the trade companies, where risks could be widely shared and the returns more immediate. The queen put her money into the Drake expedition because she trusted Drake to earn a profit, and if he had gathered even a quarter of the projected booty, it could have funded more expeditions, perhaps ones solely or almost wholly undertaken for strategic purposes. But that had not occurred.

The "assets" of Drake's foray were variously estimated by official committees at approximately £64,000 to £70,000.[26] Rumors were rife that Drake and others pocketed substantial amounts of jewels and other precious items because certainly the Spanish estimated the booty as much higher. However, the commission sent by the government to assess the flotilla's take was adamant as to the correctness of Drake's accounting. Much worth noting, during Drake's foray, Grenville, sailing for Ralegh, independently captured a single Spanish ship near Bermuda. The haul was estimated at 120,000 ducats—more than *half* the take of Drake's entire flotilla. In other words, capturing two Spanish or Portuguese prizes could have yielded as much as the entire West Indies expedition, and with far fewer expenditures on food and wages. On Drake's foray, seamen wages reduced the assets by more than one-fourth because they were entitled to one-third of the booty. The shareholders, including Ralegh and the queen, all lost one-fourth of their investment, as each pound returned only fifteen shillings, though the queen's loss was less because the two valuable ships she provided were both returned to her.

Despite the financial losses, the voyage had its successes. The capture of so much ordnance was not to be sneered at. One account stated that 240 cannons were taken, most of them brass.[27] The Spanish not only had to replace these but also had to figure out how to defend all the places Drake attacked and even those he had not: they expected the English to return. Drake's raid forced the Spanish to divert much-needed resources to the Americas.[28] Santo Domingo and Cartagena were rebuilt and refortified, the latter receiving the great city wall it became known for, and much was spent on securing Havana, St. Augustine, Puerto Rico, and various locales in Central America. King Philip also sent ships to hunt the English corsairs and to protect the ports and shipping lanes. Historian Irene A. Wright notes, "Spanish [financial] credit was completely shattered" by Drake's raid.[29]

Spain no longer seemed invincible. This last point was more important in England than elsewhere, at least in terms of patriotism and national confidence. John Hooker recorded in his commonplace book that Drake's return from the Indies "with great ryches and honor . . . inflamed the whole countrie with a desyre to adventure unto the seas yn hope of the like good successe . . . a greate number prepared shipps

marynors & soylders & travelled every place at the seas where any prof-
fitte might be had." Hooker rued that many were "undonne" by these
adventures,[30] but he captured the spirit that prevailed among many
young men in England that fortunes could be made pilfering Spanish treasure, that honor and glory could be accrued by singeing the
Spaniard's beard: patriotism, assaulting the Spanish, and expectations
of great personal gain became a triad of English overseas expansion
for 250 years. More immediately, Hooker noted that some of the English intended to go to the West Indies, some to "wyndganne do Coye"
(Roanoke), and others sought a "waye to China by the northe pole"—
the Northwest Passage. Hooker thus reflected the English perception
of the purposes of overseas expansion: to loot the Spanish, to colonize,
and to seek out the riches of Asia.[31] Pursuit of these dreams involved
great physical risks, not just to individuals but to the nation.

After Drake's voyage, there was no going back in challenging Spain.
Philip would not allow it. He viewed crushing England as necessary to
protect the Spanish Empire and eliminate the foremost protectors of
the Protestant heresy in Western Europe, who supported the Dutch
rebels.

Was Drake's voyage worth Philip's wrath? The economic returns
said no, though the cost to the English government was insignificant.
Given English support of the Dutch rebels, Spain was bound to increase hostilities against England. Drake's foray likely was the straw
that broke the camel's back: Spain prepared a mighty armada to conquer England. Elizabeth took preemptive action and ordered Drake
to attack Spain. His assault on Cádiz (and elsewhere in Iberia) in
the spring of 1587 led to the destruction and capture of over a hundred ships, enough to forestall for a year Spain's attempt to conquer
England.

The emergence of a great military contest between England and
Spain steered attention away from the mystery of Drake's foray: the
fate of the American Indian and African slaves Drake had confiscated
from the Spanish, particularly at Santo Domingo and Cartagena. They
were not included in the lists of the expedition's assets.[32] The slaves
comprised two groups: galley slaves and predial slaves, those owned
by individuals or attached to estates. The galley slaves included Turks,
French, German, and probably other Europeans and Moors; the latter comprised Africans and American Indians. There is record of the
French and Germans receiving their release and attempting to return home.[33] It is also likely that the Turks were released and received

passage on an English ship.[34] The Ottomans were at war with Spain, and Drake rarely missed a chance to cultivate alliances with Spain's enemies, as he had done with the Cimarrons in Central America and the Indians at St. Augustine.

During Drake's foray, Spanish observers expressed surprise that Drake carried away so many slaves. One wealthy individual of Cartagena held for ransom claimed that he had to turn over four of his "best slaves" to pay his own ransom. Then Drake allegedly said he could ransom these slaves, but it does not seem to have occurred, because in the next sentence the Spaniard noted that Drake "carried off 50 slaves from this city."[35] Suarez reported Drake taking "300 Indians from Cartagena, mostly women, 200 negroes, Turks and Moors, who do menial service." Suarez was surprised because Drake "carries them along though they are not useful in his country."[36] David Beers Quinn proposes that perhaps Drake intended to use them "as reinforcement for his now depleted manpower."

Certainly, Drake had space for the newcomers in his fleet because so many English had died of illness along the way, and many of the Turks and Moors were of use for their seafaring skills. The Indian and African slaves were another matter. Spanish observers (and Quinn) thought it likely that Drake intended to leave them at Roanoke to build the colony.[37] Diego Fernandez de Quiñones reported to King Philip that Pedro Menéndez Márquez "writes me that he took the depositions of three negroes who speak Spanish and remained behind when the corsair [Drake] left [St. Augustine]. They say he meant to leave all the negroes he had in a fort and settlement established at Jancan [Roanoke] by the English who went there a year ago. There he intended to leave the 250 blacks and all the small craft he had."[38]

There is no way of knowing for sure what Drake envisioned, but his alliance with the Cimarrons provided a template. He likely thought that those he liberated would gladly work with the English to build Roanoke and defend it against Spain. Pedro de Arana also thought Drake intended to construct a settlement on the coast, as he had everything necessary, including "negro labourers who in his country are free."[39] Gabriel de Luxan and Quiñones earlier had noted to the king that Drake intended "to make a settlement at some point on the Florida coast so situated as to serve as a base from which to over-run all the Indies and attack the fleets. He has taken with him everything required, by land or sea, to establish a settlement, including even negroes which he seized at Santo Domingo and Cartagena."[40] But when

Drake arrived at Roanoke, there was no mention in the records of him offering to leave the Africans and Indians. In fact, there's no mention of the Africans and Indians at all.

What happened to this, the first and largest of the lost colonies associated with Roanoke? There is barely a mention in the historical record. Those celebrating Ralegh's later "Lost Colony" often do not like this earlier colony to be mentioned. The historian Quinn was one of the few who thought that "the Indians and negroes may well be reckoned a 'lost colony.'"[41] The later "lost" colony comprised "white" settlers and the first English child born in the future United States—Virginia Dare. That colony also included seventeen "white" women. The celebration of Roanoke always has been a celebration of whiteness. The hundreds of Indian and African women and men of the earlier lost English colony have been shunted off into nonexistence. Perhaps the Indians and Africans were sold, but the only places Drake could have sold them were in Spanish colonies, and under the circumstances, it is extremely unlikely that any Spanish allowed English ships into port to make a sale at that moment in time. If they had done so, it would have been widely reported and considered treasonous. It is also clear these people were not brought to England, where if they had arrived *as slaves* they would have been listed as assets of the expedition. Their presence in England would have been widely discussed, eliciting commentary from any number of observers. The Indians would have been shown off, and the Africans, too, as exotica. The arrival of hundreds of Africans and Indians in 1586 would have been the talk of the court. We must consider other alternatives.

Could the Africans and Indians have been left at Roanoke to fend for themselves? Grenville, who arrived soon after Drake's departure, made no mention of them, nor did John White when he returned to Roanoke the following year, so if they had been left, they did not remain on the Outer Banks of North Carolina. Some have postulated that the Indians and Africans became the progenitors of the Melungeons of North Carolina, but Melungeon DNA shows only small traces of Native American ancestry, and around three-fourths of the slaves Drake freed likely were American Indian.

The most likely possibility: when Drake's ships began shifting colonists from Roanoke to the Chesapeake, the Indians and Africans were dropped off at the Chesapeake settlement or somewhere along the way. The ex-slaves could have found refuge in the enormous Dismal Swamp on the North Carolina–Virginia border, where they may even have become progenitors of the later African-Indian maroon communities that lived there from the seventeenth through early nineteenth centuries. No other alternative seems likely.

—

As ENGLAND AND SPAIN geared up for war, Ralegh pushed forward with his plans to colonize Virginia. His star was in the ascendant. The queen's granting of multiple rewards to Ralegh left no doubt that he had become her favorite. As a close personal advisor, he had her ear. Her other leading men consulted Ralegh on policy in Ireland, and he played the lead role in organizing the southwest counties' contributions to the defense of the realm against an impending Spanish invasion. Moreover, it became clear that Ralegh would be assigned a prominent position in the planting of a colony in Ireland. Under his own initiative, and with government help, he also set in motion long-term preparations to colonize in South America.

In the summer of 1586, when Richard Grenville arrived at Roanoke Island to find the colony deserted, he took his three ships through the Azores hoping to capture a richly laden Iberian ship, as he had done the previous year after delivering the second expedition to Roanoke. He captured a ship with few commodities. Grenville's men broke the captive sailors' fingers to get them to reveal their hidden silver or money. Apparently, they gained nothing from the cruelty. One Spanish gentleman promised the English supplies if they would release the ship. The Portuguese navigator confided to the English that this Spaniard was of great importance—he was worth more than any supplies he promised. The English released the crew except for the Spanish gentleman, the Portuguese navigator, and two others. This episode at sea opened another course of colonization for Ralegh and England. Ralegh was bitten by the gold bug and turned his eyes to South America and the search for El Dorado.

Today El Dorado is thought of as a "lost city of gold," but in the sixteenth century, it seems first to have referred to a rich ruler who dressed in gold dust. He and his people possessed so much of it that he could cover himself each day in a blanket of gold. In related legends, El Dorado also referred to a great lake, country, or empire. El Dorado filled men's imaginations with incredible riches. Whoever discovered El Dorado would be as famous and wealthy as Cortés and Pizarro.

The gentleman captive of Richard Grenville was Pedro Sarmiento de Gamboa. Today Sarmiento is largely known for his book, *The*

History of the Incas, which went unpublished for centuries. In his lifetime, Sarmiento was much relied upon as a naval commander, navigator, mapmaker, and colonizer. In the 1570s, stationed in Peru, the viceroy sent him to capture Drake on his return through the Straits of Magellan, which Drake avoided by circumnavigating the globe. Assigned to secure the dangerous straits, on three expeditions Sarmiento surveyed them at great peril and led colonists to establish settlements in the area.

Grenville took Sarmiento to England, where he was poorly treated for a few weeks and then brought to court and presented to Ralegh. Ralegh and Sarmiento became fast friends. They shared interests in navigation, science, Native peoples, colonization, and Hermeticism. In common, both men had to be protected for their beliefs. Ralegh (and Hariot) periodically were called before magistrates for their unorthodox utterings and suspected heresies, with the government coming to their aid to obtain their release. In Peru, the Inquisition believed that Sarmiento's study of astronomy involved necromancy—communication with the dead—for which he was banished, but the viceroy prevented execution of the sentence. In 1575, a viceroy again prevented his banishment and Sarmiento returned to his service for the monarch.[42] The Inquisition's accusations against Sarmiento included his possession of magic rings and magic ink; if a woman received a letter from someone who had used the ink, then she could not resist the letter writer. Evidence demonstrating Sarmiento's Hermeticism includes the allegations that he followed the precepts of Moses, the most important biblical figure to the Hermeticists; that his rings were engraved with Chaldean characters (typically used as Hermetic symbols); and that he was one of the founders of the Fraternity of the Rose Cross, a proto-Rosicrucian organization that emerged out of Hermeticism.[43]

Trusted by their monarchs, intellectually precocious men of action, and sharing interests in America, America's Natives, and magic—Sarmiento could not have found a better captor than Ralegh. England and Spain were not officially at war, but Drake's foray was just completed when Sarmiento arrived in England. John Hawkins was about to leave with a fleet of four thousand men to pursue Spanish prey. Ralegh received Sarmiento as an honored guest, much to the dismay of Don Antonio, the Portuguese Pretender to Portugal's throne, who resided in England when not in France. It is not clear why Don Antonio grew enraged at Ralegh's treatment of Sarmiento, though it is notable that the ship's navigator who had revealed to the English Sarmiento's identity also was Portuguese. Elizabeth appeased Don Antonio by ordering Sarmiento to prison, but Ralegh intervened, so she released him to Ralegh. The enraged Don Antonio plotted Sarmiento's assassination, but another Portuguese man warned him of the plot. International politics was a dangerous business.

Sarmiento and Ralegh conversed in Latin about their mutual interests. Over a quarter century later, Ralegh recalled their conversations with amusement in his book *History of the World*, particularly a story Sarmiento had told him about mapping the Straits of Magellan. Sarmiento related other stories that piqued Ralegh's imagination, stories of El Dorado, whose riches exceeded those of Mexico and Peru. These stories completely won Ralegh over to the quest for El Dorado. An appreciative Ralegh gave Sarmiento a "special house" to use in England and a Spanish-speaking gentleman to "attend. . . . and keep guard over him."

Having gained Ralegh's trust, Sarmiento drew interest from others at court, including Elizabeth, and he obtained an audience with the queen. For two and a half hours he and Elizabeth conversed in Latin, and they were joined by Burghley, Lord Admiral Charles Howard, and others. The queen had a mission for the Spanish guest. Sarmiento received a "passport" for Spain that allowed him to return to England "if it should be necessary." Ralegh borrowed a "thousand *escudos* in pieces and pearls" to give Sarmiento for his voyage and service.[44] Sarmiento was to deliver a "letter of Peace" to King Philip from Elizabeth.[45] This letter presumably conveyed Elizabeth's wishes to repair relations with Philip. Sarmiento departed London in October 1586 for Calais, traveled to Paris, and on his way south through France was captured by Huguenots who detained him until 1589—after war officially had begun between England and Spain. It is doubtful that the delivery of a letter from Elizabeth could have prevented war with Spain in 1588. Philip would have seen the letter for what it was: an attempt by the queen to forestall hostilities and confuse the situation.

Overlooked by historians is Ralegh's grateful payment to Sarmiento likely for the tales he told and assistance he gave to Ralegh regarding El Dorado. Sarmiento's stories presented a four-decade-long Spanish quest to find El Dorado.[46] Ralegh appreciated the magnitude of the quest and its potential payoff. A little over a month after Sarmiento's departure, before Ralegh had sent the third major expedition to Roanoke, Ralegh sent four English boys to France for transport to South America, to pave the way for his search for El Dorado. He sent the boys to learn the Native languages so that when he arrived to search for El Dorado he would have translators.

Members of the English government wrote "many letters" to the admiral of France to convey the boys to Trinidad and to modern-day Venezuela.[47] The letters likely originated with Ralegh and Lord Admiral Howard, the chief admiral of England, because both had entertained Sarmiento and were considered by the admiral of France as influential and important correspondents at the very highest level of the English government. England and France often cooperated where Spain, the common enemy, was concerned, and it was to Spain's claimed domain that Ralegh wished the boys transported. The reasons why the English wished to go through the French are not spelled out but likely owed to fear of a Spanish invasion of England, which compelled the English to keep their own ships at home. Ralegh sent to France an Italian captain who knew where to take the boys in Trinidad and to the mainland. It is this captain's identity that likely earned Sarmiento the rich reward from Ralegh. This unnamed Italian had sailed for King Philip of Spain and at various times had settled and traded at Trinidad, then "had gone over to Don Antonio with the greater part of his men," and joined the Pretender in England. Sarmiento must have seen the Italian captain, who was quickly ready to sail.

The French provided one of their own captains, Jean Retud, with the task of taking the party to Trinidad. The Italian not only knew how to get there but also was familiar with the Indians of Trinidad and those near the mouth of the Orinoco River on the mainland across from Trinidad. This was the latest place from which the Spanish tried to access El Dorado, so Sarmiento had provided Ralegh with more than legends, but insider information. Ralegh provided the Italian with a "cargo of axes, knives, jews' harps," beads, and cloth to give to the varyious Native groups that would host the children. The Italian left two of the boys with Indians at Trinidad, then took a brigantine and soldiers up the Orinoco to scout for a possible place for Ralegh to settle and to drop off the other two boys with local Natives.[48]

Eight years would pass before Ralegh arrived at Trinidad to search for El Dorado. The demands on Ralegh's time grew legion. The threat of Spain hung like the sword of Damocles over England, and Ralegh spent much of the next fifteen years countering Spanish power, including defending England from invasion, participating in military expeditions, and colonizing Ireland, an island that became a Crown imperative to protect from Spanish occupation. Every step of the way, Ralegh had to consider Elizabeth's needs. His relationship with the queen remained paramount to his fortune. Yet the energetic Ralegh consistently stamped his personality on each of his enterprises. And regardless of the numerous demands upon him, he found time to promote his American colony in useful and far-reaching ways.

PART FIVE

—

"a brave new world,
That has such people in't"

Roanoke as Cultural Production

CHAPTER 11

A Briefe and True Report

L ane's abandonment of Roanoke and the disappointing return of the one to two hundred colonists Ralegh sent with Grenville's relief expedition did not deter Ralegh from preparing yet another expedition. The colony required a new leader, and Ralegh's choice was nothing less than remarkable. Lane's poisoning of relations with the Indians led Ralegh to select the painter John White to govern the colony. Neither a soldier nor a gentleman of apparent substance, White did not possess the military or political experience requisite for administrators of colonies. To provide the trappings of authority, Ralegh had a coat of arms created for the painter and a seal made for the city White should establish in Virginia, to be named Ralegh.[1] What White lacked in political experience he could make up for with his broad and relatively deep knowledge of American Indians.

The selection of White signifies Ralegh's full recognition that Virginia should not have been a military enterprise. The colonists were to be armed and capable of defending themselves, but Ralegh was intent on altering the tenor of the colony. Who better than White to do so? He was unusually interested in understanding Native peoples and their cultures, and he knew as much about Virginia as any Englishman, save perhaps for Thomas Hariot.

Ralegh and White recruited colonists, including White's pregnant daughter and her husband. Many were farmers who could carve out a subsistence for themselves so as to not rely so heavily on Ralegh's financial support. Ralegh had not abandoned the idea of commercial development for his colony, but he recognized that food producers would provide stability and permanence.

John White, Manteo, and around 120 colonists sailed for Virginia on the *Lion* in May 1587. Their journey was fraught with dangers and ultimately resulted in the failure of Ralegh to establish the first permanent English colony in America.

———

THE VOYAGE got off to an unpromising start. Simon Fernandes, the *Lion*'s master, continually disregarded White's title as captain and made the decisions.[2] This undermined White's standing with the colonists from the beginning.

After arrival at Roanoke, Fernandes refused to take the colonists to the Chesapeake Bay. At the Chesapeake, they were supposed to meet Sir George Carey, a noted privateer who perhaps carried additional supplies, but the primary purpose of Carey's voyage does not seem to have been to aid the colony.[3] Still, his going to the Chesapeake confirms Ralegh's intention was to have the colony planted on the mainland to the north, not on Roanoke Island. Ralegh apparently planned to leave Manteo at Roanoke, gather intelligence from a garrison left by Grenville, and have Fernandes take the colonists to Chesapeake Bay. Whether the garrison was intended to accompany the colonists or stay at Roanoke is unknown.[4] The English likely meant to retain Roanoke as an armed haven for their ships. Whatever the ultimate goal, upon reaching the Chesapeake Bay, Carey found no English and sailed away.

At Roanoke, Grenville's garrison was gone. Manteo led a party of English to Croatan to find his people and to learn what happened to Grenville's men. Nervous about English intentions, the Croatan fled. The English reassured the Croatan that they wished "to renew the olde love, that was between us." The Croatan returned but warned the English not to take their food because they had little to spare, even as they "feasted" the English with what they had. The Croatan expressed perturbance at English inability to distinguish them from other Indians: the previous year, one Croatan man had been "lamed" when Lane's men confused him for one of Wingina's men. The Croatan requested a token or badge to ensure that a mistake would not recur.

The next day they held a conference. The Croatan, as allies of the English, agreed to "certifie the people" of Secota, Aquascogoc, and Pomeioc as allies or enemies. All would be forgiven and forgotten on both sides if friendship was given. As the Croatan negotiated with the neighboring people, they learned what happened to Grenville's garrison. Thirty men of Secota, Aquascogoc, and Dasamongwepeuk had attacked the garrison, killing two men. The others fled to their boat and "departed." (The garrison was never heard from again. Indeed, they comprise the second set of "lost colonists," after the Africans and Indians brought by Drake.)

The Croatan attempt to make an alliance with the local Indians failed. Seeking vengeance on those who had destroyed the garrison, the English mistakenly attacked the Croatan, killing one. Though aggrieved, Manteo reassured the English that it was his own people's fault for being in an abandoned village of the enemy and not warning the English. Four days later, Manteo was christened "by the commandement of Sir Walter Ralegh . . . and called Lord thereof, and of Dasmongueponke, in reward of his faithful service." Performing the ceremony in Virginia rather than in England might have been done to inspire other Indians to convert, but more likely the purpose was to display to local Natives the English seal of approval on Manteo, who not only had symbolically become English but also likely was intended to command the garrison after the colonists' departure.

Five days later, John White's daughter Eleanor gave birth to Virginia Dare, named for the colony. Virginia was the first English child born in America. Another English child was born shortly thereafter.

Fernandes was anxious to leave, probably to go pirating, and he refused to carry the colonists to the Chesapeake. The colonists entreated White to return with Fernandes to report their situation to Ralegh in person. White refused. It would be a "great discredite" for him to leave. He feared the slander that would arise in England, where people would say "he went to Virginia, . . . [but] never meant to stay himselfe." Moreover, the colony likely would move to the Chesapeake on its own or with the help of another ship, and he expected the colonists would pilfer his belongings, as had occurred earlier when he was gone from Roanoke for just three days. The colonists offered him a bond for his goods and begged him to go. He assented and the ships sailed the next morning. Three weeks later, on September 17, the two boats separated. The larger went pirating, while White on the small "Fly" boat with fifteen men, only five of whom were healthy enough to work, set course for England. The return took seven weeks.

Three weeks later, Richard Hakluyt published a translation of René de Laudonnière's history of the French colony in Florida with a

dedication to Ralegh. Hakluyt suggested that America would be easier to colonize than Ireland: "one hundred men will doe more nowe
among the naked and unarmed people in Virginea, then one thousande
were able then to doe in Irelande against that armed and warrelike
nation." With his eye on the "idle" poor of England, many of whom
were ex-soldiers who had served in the Low Countries, and Dutch
refugees from there, he declared that the nation could "spare tenne
thousand able men" and not miss them. "I see no fitter place to employ
[them] . . . then in the inward parts . . . of Virginea against such stub-
born Savages as shall refuse obedience to her Majestie."[5]

It was a dubious proposal. Ten thousand men could not be induced
by any means to go to Virginia to cultivate the land. The young preferred their chances at sea pirating, where the potential returns were
so much greater—the English pirated an estimated thousand Spanish
and Portuguese ships from 1585 to 1603.[6] Those who chose to farm
preferred Ireland. Very few wished to colonize America. Those who
could sponsor ten thousand colonists—the queen or a consortium of
the rich—also had no reason to pursue colonization of Virginia. Only
the lure of precious metals could spark an appropriate level of investment, and without a proper lure, large numbers of Tudor English were
not ready to commit to settling colonies in America.

And whatever chance Ralegh's colony had for success was doomed
by Fernandes leaving the colonists at Roanoke Island. The island was
ill-suited for significant agricultural development and extractive industries. The English could not move to the North Carolina mainland because most of the Indians were hostile to the English because of their
history of violence. The colonists were trapped on an island with danger all around.

While the White-led colony supposedly was building a settlement
on Chesapeake Bay, Ralegh turned to promoting his colonial enterprise
in America by way of publishing. He began by prompting the publication of materials his employees generated on English accomplishments
in America. The subsequent documentation, both written and picto-
rial, reveals much about the expectations and hopes of Ralegh (and
other English) for America. This promotion turned out to be one of the
most important legacies of Roanoke in terms of how Europeans understood American Indians. The illustrations prepared by White formed
the basis for published illustrations of Native Americans for centuries, particularly in the English-speaking world. The texts, written by
Hariot, influenced subsequent English colonizers and promoters and

became foundational for outlining what the English should expect in the New World. This cultural production also reveals the infusion of Hermeticism into Ralegh's and his men's characterization of America.

There existed several forms of media for disseminating information and representations of Ralegh's Virginia. Besides his advertisement to Parliament, he could publish texts and engrave pictures, create theatrical performances, and use word of mouth to tell the story of America. The stage, indeed, soon became an important medium for portraying the New World, most importantly in the early seventeenth century with Shakespeare's *The Tempest*. Ralegh could have designed and performed an entertainment for the queen and court. Oppositional voices envious of the queen's favorite derided Virginia, some positing his ships never reached the New World. More troublesome were veterans of the Lane expedition, who caviled against America's potential.

Ralegh wanted to create a record of what his colony had accomplished and its great potential moving forward. He assigned Hariot to pen an account of Virginia. It was privately published, then republished by Richard Hakluyt alongside other accounts of Virginia, as part of his multivolume compendium of English overseas activities. Hakluyt's volumes of *Principal Navigations, Voiages, Traffiques and Discoueries of the English Nation* became the literary foundation for English overseas expansion. But Hariot's writings and White's paintings of Virginia found a different venue that allowed them to quickly reach a wide audience: they were combined into a single volume that enjoyed immense success and a lasting legacy. Ralegh arranged for the talented Flemish engraver and publisher Theodor de Bry to publish it. De Bry engraved White's paintings and expertly designed a volume for them and Hariot's writings.[7] De Bry's artistic and marketing skills spread knowledge of Ralegh's colony throughout Europe. Much of what these men generated served ulterior purposes: to promote Ralegh's colony and English accomplishments and to make money for de Bry.

To promote Virginia's economic potential, Hariot penned *A Briefe and True Report of the New Found Land of Virginia* (1589).[8] Historians generally date the work to 1588, but Hariot dated the volume February 1588/89 in the later edition published by de Bry, which means it was published after the New Year in 1589.[9] This distinction is important because it supports centuries of rumor that Hariot revised and finished the text while living with Ralegh in Ireland. This allowed Ralegh to influence the shaping of the manuscript in terms of subject matter and purpose.

Hariot's stated reason for writing was to counter the "slaunderous and shamefull speeches bruited abroad by many" who had been on the earlier voyages. Hariot claimed that some had been at Roanoke for a year yet did not know what to make of their experience, and thus spouted absurdities. These men had not seen the countryside because they spent almost all their time on Roanoke Island, or were only "after golde and silver," and when that "was not so soone found . . . had little or no care of any other thing but to pamper their bellies." Those who had "a nice bringing up, only in cities or townes" and who had not "seene the world before" thought the place "miserable" because it had no "English cities, nor such faire houses, nor . . . their old accustomed daintie food, nor any soft beds of downe or fethers." In contrast, Hariot had "beene in the discoverie" of the larger region, and his special charge "in dealing with the naturall inhabitantes" allowed him to have "seene and knowne more then the ordinarie."

As far as the public was concerned, Ralegh had accomplished little. He sent men and supplies to Virginia and then the men returned. None were richer but those who captured Iberian ships en route. Hariot characterized the brevity of the earlier voyages as "onelie for supply and transportation," while his own voyage had conducted reconnaissance for an entire year to lay the groundwork for permanent colonization. Hariot's expedition's manifest accomplishments in identifying valuable commodities led to Ralegh's "replanting this last yeere a new colonie." Hariot devoted the bulk of the *Briefe* to describing these commodities.

Published accounts of overseas adventures had a ready market in Europe. Exploration and travel narratives ordinarily depicted overseas monsters, cities of gold, and stories of incredible humans and their bizarre cultures—a genre that Ralegh tapped in the 1590s in a book about the Empire of Guiana. Hariot eschewed titillating readers with his adventures or with the absurd. He complemented his descriptive and analytical narrative of the landscape with stories of Native culture, some from his own observations and others that Indians told him. The English intelligentsia, and many of the middle class, welcomed the information Hariot provided about the natural world of America.[10]

A market for overseas cartography proliferated, reflecting the growing European interest in distant lands, and the maps often included representations of tropical flora, monsters, strange animals, and humans, combining European curiosity for the geographically distant with the terrifying and fantastic. Hariot's and White's maps of Ralegh's

Virginia limited the superfluities. For one map, White painted numerous whales, including fierce ones spouting through their blowholes. De Bry's engraving of the map eliminated the whales in favor of more ships and a single sea monster. Likewise, Hariot's discussion of the land and its commodities tended to the pragmatic, such as which plants colonists could make use of in Virginia and which they could export to England. For potential investors and colonists, a sober rendering held greater value than the fantastic stories published by other overseas travelers.

Hariot divided commodities into three types: "Merchantable," "victuall and sustenance," and "other." The first "Merchantable" commodity he discussed, silk grass, was not actually a potential commodity. It held significance to Hariot as an indicator that silkworms would thrive in Virginia. Silk was in great demand in Europe, an insatiable market. The return on silk could make the entire Ralegh colony worthwhile: many future English colonizers of America would pursue production, importing both silkworms and experts to oversee the crop. Despite repeated efforts, none of the North American colonies made a success of silk.

Hariot highlighted other valuable commodities that could turn profits. Several were necessary for shipping, such as hemp, pitch, tar, turpentine, and rosin (a resin made from turpentine); others possessed alleged medicinal properties, such as wapeih and sassafras. Hariot also reported the existence of a huge vein of alum, which Europeans imported from Asia for use in dying woolens. (The mineralogist at Roanoke was wrong about the presence of alum.) Additionally, Hariot extolled the existence of cedar trees (actually juniper) for furniture; grapes for wine; walnuts for pressing into oil; animal skins and furs; and iron. Though the Roanoke colonists had not discovered veins of copper, the Indians' adornment of copper jewelry evinced its availability, which hearsay placed at about 150 miles away. Almost in passing, Hariot mentioned that silver might be near the veins of copper, but he did not emphasize this.[11] Hariot also advertised the potential for pearls, though admitted he had yet to find desirable ones.[12] And even if Virginia had nothing of marketable value, Hariot believed the English could introduce other crops besides silk, including an array of plants for manufacturing drugs and dyes (especially woad, which produced a blue color), and exotic and profitable food crops, such as sugarcane and citrus fruits.

Of all the aforementioned commodities, over a century and a half later North Carolina's great stands of pine proved the most valuable.

Indigo, rather than woad, became an important crop in the Carolinas for production of blue dye. Sugar, indeed, became a massively important crop in New World colonization, but it could not be profitably produced in the English mainland colonies. Hariot misread the importance of the land's latitudinal location: Europeans assumed that lands on the same latitude could produce the same commodities. The same mistake applied to citrus; yearly frost at Roanoke precluded the profitable production of oranges and lemons. In fact, most of the other commodities suggested by Hariot proved untenable on the islands and mainland of North Carolina. Iron mining to the north in Virginia did take on great importance in the mid-eighteenth century. Animal skins also provided income for Europeans, as they did for Indians, but there were much better areas for hunting and trapping than in North Carolina and Virginia. What Hariot did not state but what he and Ralegh presumed was that the permanent colony would not be planted at Roanoke but on the Chesapeake, over a hundred miles to the north, which indeed possessed much more promise for economic development. Virginia, too, had an abundance of trees and possessed rich agricultural land with better, safer, and easier access to the sea via rivers that penetrated the mainland, allowing oceangoing ships to travel upriver for one hundred miles.

The later colony in Jamestown tried silk, viniculture, and a variety of other enterprises that Hariot suggested. These all failed, giving way to tobacco, which would define the colony and dominate its economic development. Hariot did note tobacco as a potential commodity of value, one with many medicinal qualities.[13] He reported that tobacco accompanied Indian ceremonies and celebrations, and that it was given as an offering to the gods. The English in Virginia copied the Indians and would "suck it after their manner, as also since our returne." Since bringing it to England, they had "found manie rare and wonderful experiments of the vertues thereof; of which the relation woulde require a volume by itself: the use of it by so manie of late, men & women of great calling as else, and some learned Physicians also." Ralegh's own smoking of tobacco quickly spread its usage through court and contributed to its spread through Europe.[14] But it would be over thirty years before English settlers produced tobacco for a profit in Virginia.

Ralegh did not need every project to succeed in Virginia; one or two would suffice, as tobacco later proved. What laid the foundation for success Hariot had identified: the abundance of food and trees.

Readily available food allowed for great demographic growth and reduced a colony's dependence on imports. Trees could always be turned into lumber for export, to supply wood-short areas of the Atlantic World, and the Eastern woodlands provided a plentitude of trees. This gave planters and farmers economic flexibility when downturns occurred in world markets for the staples they produced. Tobacco, for instance, experienced much market volatility; so falling back on food and tree harvesting saved them during declines. Colonists from New England to Georgia engaged in logging for lumber and ship construction and for profitable industries such as stave-making, barrels, furniture, and local construction.

But food remained the key. The foundation for Virginia's long-term success, as it had been for the Native peoples, lay in rich soils and appropriate climate for production of the region's staff of life: maize. From Virginia southward, three crops of maize could be produced each year. White grasped the importance and produced a detailed illustration of the maize fields that yielded a staggered crop. If the first crop failed, another two could be grown the same year, which guarded against lean times. Additionally, Hariot pointed out, peas, beans, a variety of gourds and pumpkins, roots, fruits, fish, and birds all were there for the taking, gathering, or cultivating. Most of these could be combined with maize for nutritionally rich dishes. Maize provided over half the calories consumed by American Indians in the South.[15] The region was built on food abundance, which allowed a large portion of the labor force to work in nonsubsistence activities. Roanoke suffered food shortages under Lane partly because of their island location and partly because the men had not planted maize. Likewise, in a better location on the mainland, the Jamestown colonists later starved, but not because the environment was difficult but because the colonists refused to work to feed themselves.[16] At both Roanoke and Jamestown, English depended on supplies from England and hoped and expected the Natives to feed them.

One would not know from reading Hariot's *Briefe* of the food shortage and utter disaster that marked the end of the Lane expedition. Hariot reported that problems with the Indians existed and that both sides were at fault, but he provided no account of the reasons for the dispute or the actual assault and killing of Pemisapan. He did not want to frighten prospective settlers and investors. Instead, for readers curious about the Native peoples, Hariot offered the first English ethnography of American Indians.[17] He had visited Native communities and witnessed daily life and ceremonies. He assessed Native use of the environment and gathered information about folkways and cosmology. Hariot's narrative was written to promote Ralegh's colony. Despite his agenda, Hariot provides a wealth of valuable information on the Roanoke-area Indians and of the prospects for England's future as colonizers.

Hariot's stated purpose was to "speak a word or two of the naturall inhabitants, their natures and maners . . . that you may know, how that they in respect of troubling our inhabiting and planting, are not to be feared; but that they shall have cause both to feare and love us, that shall inhabite with them."[18] Historians and literary critics often quote this statement as Hariot announcing England's incipient dominance over Indians and the landscape. But I do not believe that was Hariot's intent. He attempted to allay prospective colonists' and investors' fears of Indians, which initiated a common trope for those writing about Indians in colonial America.[19] Most Europeans would not migrate if they thought the Indians dangerous. Hariot emphasized the Indians' humanity, highlighting cultural attributes deemed worthy of admiration.[20] Disputes with Indians could be avoided, these promoters of colonization noted, if Europeans treated Indians with justice. Hariot alludes to English treatment of Indians at Roanoke in only a few places, most notably in a passage on English brutality, but the gist of Hariot's writing, overlooked by generations of historians, is to show that Indians and English could live *together*.

This was Ralegh's intent. Subsequent promoters of English colonization might have supported harmonious relations between Indians and English but gave no suggestion that they should be near neighbors, and often there was an implicit idea that the Indians would disappear. Hariot, however, foresaw English colonists living among or very close to their Native hosts. It is worth repeating his phrase, they "shall inhabite with them." Hariot never even hinted that English colonization was predicated upon conquest. Hariot, Ralegh, and (I presume) other English could not conceive of a colony in America without Indians. The Indians were as much a part of the landscape as the trees. Hariot even prefaces his discussion "of the nature and manners of *the people*" with an account of native tree species and other "commodities for building."

Hariot would not have presented this perspective of colonization without Ralegh's direction—it was his colony, and Hariot was his employee. At Roanoke, though Ralegh made no explicit statements about the Native peoples, it is clear from his actions that he intended a peaceful colony for both Indians and Europeans.

To allay European fear of Indians, Hariot blended discussion of Native attributes with derision of their military capabilities vis-á-vis the English. Indians possessed no metal armor, only wooden bows and arrows, and "targets [shields] made of barks, and some armours made of stickes wickered together with thread." The Indians lacked "edge tooles or weapons of yron or steele to offend us." The "greatest" Indian society they found was "but eighteene townes . . . [of] seven or eight hundred fighting men at the most." The latter must certainly have seemed a potential threat, but Hariot discounted Native warfare. He correctly noted the Indian manner of fighting as surprise attacks at the "dawning of the day, or moone light, or els by ambushes, or some suttle devises." Natives did not harness their forces like the Europeans: "Set battels are very rare, except it fall out where there are many trees," which the Indians use to defend themselves, "after the deliverie of every arrow, in leaping behind some or other." The Europeans would have the advantage against the Indians "In so many manner of waies, as by our discipline, our strange weapons . . . especially by ordinance [sic] great and small . . . by the experience we have had." But nowhere did Hariot imply that conquest should come to pass.

Living in harmony would result from Indian desire to access English power and material things. Indian intelligence, according to Hariot, would lead them to see that friendship with the English was in their own best interest. Indians had neither "tooles, nor any such craftes, sciences and artes as wee, yet in those thinges they doe, they shewe excellencie of wit." For the moment, naivete led Indians to "esteeme our trifles before thinges of greater value." But as Indians recognized the superiority of English "knowledges and craftes . . . they shoulde desire our friendship & love, and have the greater respect for pleasing and obeying us." Hariot expressed a common European trope about indigenous peoples: Indian cognizance of their own inferiority would make them compliant. Hariot's assertion of eventual Indian submission implies that the Indians had *yet* to please and obey the English or display adequate friendship and love. Hariot's readers might have attributed this refusal to the Indians' savagery or heathenism, but Hariot blamed the English for failing to provide "good government." Without traditional English institutions, the colony could succumb to anarchy or chaos. Only when the English established a permanent society could the normal modes for regulating human behavior be put in place. These institutions would also pave the way for Indian uplift, as they "may in short time be brought to civilitie, and the imbracing of true religion."

Hariot, like Ralegh, was brought before the authorities for his unorthodox religious beliefs and appears to be reciting a trope when he said the Natives can be brought to "true religion." The predominant European view was that Indians lacked a spiritual system that could be termed religion; they possessed inchoate superstitions. A second view: Indians worshipped the Devil, which provided justification for Europeans killing and enslaving them.[21] Hariot, like Ralegh, was neither so simple-minded nor dismissive of Indian religiosity. He perceived that Indians possessed a system of beliefs, rituals, and practices that were not Devil-inspired, "although it be farre from the truth." Hariot's view, shared by some Catholic missionaries, was that converting Indians to Christianity involved substituting one religion for another—an easier task than missionizing among people who had no conception of religion.[22] Hariot discussed Indian religiosity at length, noting their belief in multiple gods, but "one onely chiefe and great God." (Ralegh later made this same argument in defending heathens as pious people.) Hariot even alluded to an Indian story similar to that of Adam, though the Indians claimed that woman was created first, by which "one of the goddes conceived and brought foorth children: And in such sort they say they had their beginning."

Hariot was impressed that the Indians built "houses appropriate or temples" for their gods. They gave gods human shape by sculpting idols. They "woorship, praie, sing, and make manie times offerings unto them." Even more significant for evincing Indian spirituality, to which Hariot devoted detailed discussion, were Indian concepts of eternity and immortality, providing certain evidence (to him) that Indians could easily grasp Christian concepts. Religion provided Indians a moral compass. Hariot explained that Indians believed that if they lived properly, they would go to heaven; if not, then "to a great pitte or hole" analogous to hell, "there to burne continually: the place they call *Popogusso*." The Indians even told Hariot of the recent resurrection of two men.

Recording and repeating Indian stories is different from understanding their cosmological significance. If anyone in England was prepared to do both it was Hariot, given his interests in cosmology, his skills of observation, and his understanding, however rudimentary, of

Native language. Despite these advantages, the task was difficult. Hariot cannot be blamed for this; later Europeans who spent *years* living with Indians, and who possessed a high degree of language fluency, failed to comprehend Indian spirituality in holistic fashion. They could identify forms and practices and record stories, but linking all together into a cosmological whole eluded them. To facilitate his understanding, Hariot established a "special familiarity with some of their priestes," by which he claimed to have learned the "summe of their religion." This "summe" identified gods, the afterlife, and religious stories, the central religious categories to a Christian, but the latter assumed that other religions' concepts of God, the afterlife, and their religious stories must all be false. Conversion to Christianity, Hariot perceived, would occur naturally as exposure to the English undermined Indian "traditions and stories" and gave them "no small admiration of ours." Indian myths must fall beneath the weight of the Christian Bible.[23]

Language difficulties, Hariot warned, would impede conversion, but if words could not show Christian truth, English material culture would convince Indians of English superiority and the authority of their religion. Hariot presented a long list of things that English displayed to Indians that incited awe, including a variety of instruments, from "sea compasses" to a "perspective glass"—an early telescope—to guns and fireworks, "bookes, writing and reading, spring clocks that seem to goe of themselves, and manie other things . . . [that] so farre exceeded their capacities to comprehend the reason and meanes how they should be made and done, that they thought they were rather the works of gods then of men, or at the leastwise they had bin given and taught us of the gods."[24] The Indians, Hariot reasoned, made a direct connection between European objects and European enjoyment of spiritual favor. Hariot offered as evidence the Indians' reception of the Christian Bible, which they came to believe (by English prompting) was the source of English power. The Indians would "be glad to touch it, to embrace it, to kisse it, to hold it to their brests and heades, and stroke over all their bodie with it." To Indians and English alike, *things* possessed spiritual power. Despite the Reformation's attack on the notion of the spiritual power of objects, and the Protestant destruction of Catholic iconography, many sixteenth-century Englishmen retained their "superstitious" beliefs.[25] Protestants continued to pursue talismans for their magical properties, such as protection from illness and evil spirits or the promise of good fortune.[26] People of all classes accumulated gems and crystals as portals between the seen and unseen.

The Bible itself not only was considered an otherworldly creation of God but also was imbued with clues to the secrets of the universe.

Hariot likely did not invent his report of Indians physically embracing the Bible as a repository of special powers. Why did Roanoke-area Indians, and other Native peoples, caress the Bible? And did it signify that they wanted to exchange their "superstitions" for Christianity? It is extremely unlikely that Indians intended to discard their religion, even when undertaking Christian conversion. Native converts throughout the Americas usually grafted Christianity onto their cosmology as a means to enlarge their spirituality. The main benefit to many, whether at Roanoke or elsewhere in the Americas, was hoped-for assistance against ill health. Throughout the world, humans perceived a direct correlation between health and religious beliefs and practices. They appealed to gods, priests, and other otherworldly intermediaries for cures.[27] They understood the cause of misfortune as the machinations of evil people and spirits or their own spiritual shortcomings.[28] Many believed in the power of charms and prayers to protect from malfeasance. Hariot asserted that the main reason Indians desired access to Christian power was to heal the sick.[29] Wingina and other Indians often joined the English in prayer and the singing of psalms in hopes of gaining favor from the forces of the Christians' religion. When Wingina twice fell sick, he "sent for some of us to praie" so that the Christian God would heal him or allow him to live with him after death. (During drought, as well, the Indians asked the English to pray to their God for help.) The Indians feared, according to Hariot, that their succumbing to illness occurred from "offending" the English.

Hariot's discussion of Indian health leads to one of the *Briefe*'s most notable passages: the high mortality experienced in Indian villages that the English had visited. Hariot wrote that this phenomenon occurred only at towns that opposed the English, which the English had taken no revenge upon "because wee sought by all meanes possible to win them by gentlenesse." Within a few days of English "departure from everie such town, the people began to die very fast, and many in short space." Hariot does not identify the illness but only says that the Indians "neither knew what it was, nor how to cure it," and they had experienced nothing like it since "time out of minde." Hariot confirms how quickly Indians could succumb to illnesses carried by the Europeans for which they possessed no antibodies.

Why did the illness strike only those who had used "subtle device" against the English? Perhaps the offending villages were not previously exposed to the English on their first trip to Virginia. But I wonder whether Hariot actually read the evidence backward and assumed that villages that succumbed to illness must have offended the English. It is possible, given the course of events that Hariot recorded, that the Indians really did believe the English God punished them for offending the English. Hariot asserted that Wingina was convinced that the Christian God could and did slay the Christians' enemies. And that Indian enemies pursued friendship with the English to avoid the casting of illness upon them. When Indians recovered from the illness, they attributed that, too, to the Christian God, who rewarded their professions of friendship to His people. "This marvelous accident in all the countrie wrought so strange opinions of us, that some people could not tel whether to think us gods or men, and the rather because that [in] all the space of their sicknesse, there was no man of ours knowne to die, or that was specially sicke: they noted also that we had no women amongst us, neither that we did care for any of theirs."

The strange, mystical character of the English launched much speculation. Some Indians believed that the English "were not borne of women, and therefore not mortall, but that wee were men of an old generation many yeeres past then risen againe to immortalite." Others prophesied that the English, of whom more would soon arrive, would kill more Indians in the manner "already done" by disease and "take their places." The English ability to assault their enemies without weapons led to a host of opinions about English motivations for coming to Roanoke. An eclipse of the sun just before the English arrival and sighting of a comet "a few daies before the beginning of the said sickness" also were interpreted as bad omens and God's favor of the English. Hariot asserted that the Indians' many "opinions" tying their illness to displeasing the English, becoming friends with the English to end their illness, and subsequently believing in the power of the Christian God to kill and to cure were all signs that the Indians "may be brought through discreet dealing and governement to the imbracing of the trueth, and consequently to honour, obey, feare and love us." Hariot's use of the terminology "honour, obey, feare and love us," though interpreted by some as announcing impending conquest, I interpret as the vow of marriage between two peoples. The Natives, like America, to use Hakluyt's words, were to be a bride to Ralegh and, through him, the English.[30]

There would be no marriage. But there was a clumsy courtship. Hariot fills in what Lane had failed to mention: Wingina's interest in the English provided the potential for close relations, if not a merging of societies. Wingina desired access to the Christian power to heal. He likely desired access to English power for other purposes as well, such as military alliance and trade goods and new knowledge. But neither Indian nor European could understand the other, though they tried, physically and symbolically, to incorporate each other into their societies and cosmologies.[31] These fantasies were doomed. Indian myths about English immortality could not survive. English technology did not save English from hunger. English malevolence evinced their spiritual power as evil. English killed Indians over trite matters. Hariot blamed both the English and the Indians for the turn of events: "some of our company towardes the end of the yeare shewed themselves too fierce, in slaying some of the people." The English should have forborne the causes, Hariot thought. They "might easily" have done so, though the English, he said—perhaps he had to say—had been justified. Although Indians had altered their opinions of the English, Hariot asserted (in order not to scare away prospective colonists) that the English had nothing to fear. Nonetheless, he called for due consideration to avoid future conflict. The Indians had shown their malleability in adjusting to the English: the English had to do the same by using their power wisely.

Hariot's "Conclusion" for the *Briefe* reaffirms the great advantage of colonizing Virginia. The English should settle on the mainland rather than on the islands, for "we found the soyle to bee fatter, the trees greater . . . the grounde more firme . . . finer grasse, and as good as ever we saw any in England; . . . more plentie of their fruites, more abundance of beastes; the more inhabited with people, and of greater pollicie & larger dominions, with greater townes and houses." All this land lay unclaimed by any Christian prince and it "cannot but yeeld many kinds of excellent commodities, which we in our discoverie have not yet seene."

Virginia had an excellent climate with wholesome air—very important for avoiding illness. Hariot informed readers that only 4 of 108 English had died during the year in Virginia (and these had arrived sick), a remarkable record, particularly in light of the want of clothes and victuals.[32] A colony only needed supplies for one year before it could feed itself after clearing land and planting crops and learning "the taking of beastes, fishe, and fowle" (another indication that the English lacked skills that the Native people possessed in abundance). Hariot praised Ralegh for his liberality in granting large portions of land: "the least that hee hath graunted hath been five hundred acres to a man onely for the adventure of his person."[33] Hariot closed his account by promising a future "chronicle" to divulge "what els concerneth the nature and manners of the inhabitants of *Virginia,*" the multiple voyages to the colony, Ralegh's role in colonizing, and so on.

The *Briefe* was first published privately in England in February 1588/89, then republished by Hakluyt in his *Principal Navigations* (1589). Hakluyt, with Ralegh's permission, arranged to have the Flemish engraver de Bry publish Hariot's *Briefe* in Germany, in a large volume, which would include engravings of White's drawings of Roanoke accompanied by Hariot's captions. Both de Bry and Ralegh expected fame from the endeavor, and Hariot, too, viewed the publication by de Bry as a point of pride.[34] Hariot's *Briefe*, in its new context as part of a larger illustrated volume on English colonization of Virginia, appeared less as a propaganda tract and more as a fount of information about American Indians, the land, and the initial English accomplishments.[35] But it is White's paintings paired with Hariot's captions that mark the greater significance of English accomplishment.[36] The English's intimate knowledge of Indians, their physicality, folkways, religion, and culture, offers a stunning portrait of America that contrasts with the portrait associated with the "black legend" of Spain, which characterized the Spanish as a nation of ruthless conquerors lacking in all sympathy for Indians, and by extension Protestants, as confirmed by their cold-blooded killing of hundreds of French Protestants in Florida in 1565, the subject of de Bry's second volume, and by the ongoing Spanish attempt to crush the Dutch Revolt.[37] The Virginia volume produced by de Bry implicitly depicts the English as the anti-Spanish.[38] It should also be seen as an expression of the religious philosophy of Hermeticism, wherein curiosity about, and study of, the Native people lead to greater knowledge of God's Creation. Hermeticism provided White, Hariot, de Bry, and Ralegh with the intellectual context for producing the most important ethnography of American Indians in the future United States until the invention of the camera.

CHAPTER 12

Publicizing Ralegh's Virginia

T heodor de Bry arrived in London sometime around 1585–1586, his skills as an engraver in great demand. Born in Liege, from which he was banished for his Protestantism, de Bry carried his formidable skills many places before settling in Frankfurt after leaving London in 1588 or early 1589. In London, his engraving for the title page of *The Mariners Mirrour* (1588), was, according to Peter Stallybrass, an historian of printed texts, "as sophisticated as anything that had been printed in London up to that point."[1] De Bry also produced dozens of engravings to mark the death and funeral procession of Sir Philip Sidney, the most "celebrated" funeral of 1580s England.[2] In England, de Bry met Richard Hakluyt, and likely through him met Ralegh, Hariot, White, and the French painter of the ill-fated French colony in Florida, Jacques Le Moyne. De Bry agreed to republish Hariot's *Briefe*, to which he would add his own engravings of White's paintings of Virginia. The resulting thirty-five-centimeters-tall—over thirteen inches—eighty-two-page volume was a landmark publication in four languages, Latin, German, French, and English. Hakluyt translated Hariot's captions for White's paintings from Latin into English, and other English associates of de Bry in Frankfurt, where de Bry returned when he engraved and published the Virginia volume, assisted him by translating the English texts into the other languages. It is usually assumed that the English and French volumes did not sell well because the subsequent de Bry volumes, a compendium of European overseas activities, only appeared in Latin and German, but a falling-out between de Bry and Ralegh might have led de Bry to forgo the English market.[3] (One of de Bry's associates, James Garet, thought Ralegh would be upset, if not irate, when he learned that de Bry did not dedicate the non-English volumes to him.[4])

Nonetheless, the Virginia volume was a success and led de Bry and his sons to publish thirteen more volumes on the Americas and thirteen on Asia over a period of forty-four years. They published additional volumes in abridged formats. The collection retained its fame for centuries, the engravings copied again and again by engravers to represent Indians in dozens of books.[5] It is rare for images to retain their popularity for over two hundred years—a tribute to how powerfully these sixteenth-century depictions of Native Americans tapped into the zeitgeist of Europeans. While serving his country in France after the American Revolution, Thomas Jefferson purchased a copy each of the America and Asia series, which he later donated as part of the foundation for the Library of Congress.[6] In this regard, we can say that de Bry's volumes both reflected and substantiated images foundational to the formation of American society.

The Virginia volume provided an ethnography of American Indians unlike any yet published. Earlier books had explored Native American life, and in sympathetic fashion, but Hariot and White offered a striking intimacy.[7] De Bry's engravings were far superior to most of the previously published woodcut illustrations of America's Native peoples.[8] De Bry engraved copper plates, which were more difficult to carve, less forgiving of mistakes, and more expensive to print but which allowed for sharper lines and more defined print than woodblocks. White's portraits of individual Indians also displayed individuality, and though the engravings were not identical to the paintings, they clearly took their cue from White's conceptualization. All Indians were not the same. Compare de Bry's treatment of Indians from White with his engravings of Jacques Le Moyne's paintings of Florida Indians, which were published in the second volume of the America series. White's Natives retain an individuality lacking in Le Moyne's. The engravings of White's Indians were copied far more than the engravings of Le Moyne's, though Le Moyne's scenes of activities gained great currency through the centuries, particularly in the twentieth century because of their dramatic renderings of battles, torture, and deathways.[9]

Although the French colony was settled over twenty years prior to Roanoke, de Bry published the Virginia volume first, likely owing to an agreement between him and Ralegh in exchange for lending White's paintings to the engraver. From Ralegh's (and maybe de Bry's) point of view, it also was more pressing to publicize an active English colony than to recall a defunct French colony. Ralegh wanted to assert his rights and Elizabeth's sovereignty over Virginia. The Virginia volume publicized throughout Europe Ralegh's and England's accomplishments in America. But what Ralegh's peers in Europe could also see was a view of America that presented the Natives as people worth knowing, people who possessed a culture that Europeans should engage. The absence of Europeans in White's pictures thrust readers into Native life. Ralegh's colonization appears benign, the Europeans drawn into Native communities rather than arriving as conquerors. The perspective must have alienated enough of de Bry's readers that his subsequent volumes transformed the Natives into devils both sadistic and savage. In contrast, Ralegh had twice lived with Manteo, and he knew other Native peoples, whom he valued as friends and companions. Ralegh desired the Virginia volume to make a statement about English colonization, where the Natives were shown living and flourishing without Europeans. He had already begun formulating ideas of empire in which the Natives and the English accommodated to one another and where Natives maintained their culture.

—

De Bry's investment in the volume was driven by his intent to grow his publishing business, but it also allowed him to expand his artistry in depicting the exotic non-European world to Europeans. He recognized the existence of a public hungry for information, particularly visual images, of the New World, Africa, and Asia. Travel accounts of foreign lands had been popular for over a century, though heavily illustrated volumes were rare, and the artistry of the engravings generally was primitive in comparison to de Bry's.[10] De Bry took the initiative of adapting White's paintings to market conditions.[11] Although the content of the book largely owes to White, Hariot, and Ralegh, to whom de Bry gives credit,[12] at various points de Bry proudly claims the finished product as his own, warns others against plagiarism, and inscribes his initials on his engravings to remind readers of his contribution as engraver and publisher.[13] Literary scholar Shannon Miller notes de Bry's frontispiece is unprecedented in publishing because it asserts his "financial investment in the book" and that the engravings, production, and publication are products of his skills and effort.[14]

De Bry skillfully reproduced White's artistry when he chose to, but he also altered or "improved" many pictures. He repeatedly sought to

Americanize White's portraits by placing them into a Virginia context: he grafted White's studies of individuals onto White's separately drawn landscapes. He also added many trees to scenes of Indian activities to reflect Hariot's account in the *Briefe* of bountiful forests. The added birds, fish, and deer highlight Virginia as a land of plenty. The gratuitous additions of landscape sometimes distorted Indian life. In *Their Manner of Prainge with Rattels abowt Fyer*, White's painting shows Indians celebrating a great feat, but de Bry's addition of Indians fishing in the background diminishes the celebration as a communal activity that *all* participated in. White himself created composite scenes, but he resisted adding superfluities or unnecessary dramatics or contexts that could lure the viewer away from the essential nature of the scene or individual.[15]

De Bry's most obvious alteration of White's paintings lay in his Europeanizing of Indian bodies, adding muscle to arms and legs in the classical Greek style.[16] Despite the attempt to make Indian bodies more familiar to Europeans, the result is that they appear more exotic than in White's originals. De Bry's addition of back views of people in some of the portraits turns Indians into subjects for judgment, as objects for a voyeuristic viewing of Indians as "others." White's more intimate view of individuals shorn of landscape (except for small bits of the earth on which they stand), and in color denied to the engraver, provides warmth: females, in particular, are portrayed sympathetically as genuine and friendly. White includes details of their clothing, jewelry, tattoos, and body painting. Breasts are revealed. Yet the drawings do not titillate. De Bry's renderings, however, occasionally emphasize female sexuality; the women are alluring.

One of the starkest transformations occurs in de Bry's engraving of a man and woman eating. The couple sit on the ground at opposite sides of a large round platter. In White's painting, the Indians' knees are drawn close to the body in an awkward pose from a European perspective. While they eat, the man watches his wife, who looks dreamily to the side, perhaps with a slight smile. De Bry's engraving moves the woman's knees away from her body, which would have made it more difficult for her to reach for food. Her legs are positioned for sexual intercourse.

As Miller points out, it is de Bry's transformation of the woman's face, however, that most signifies the sexualized nature of the engraving. He shifts the woman's eyes to engage the viewer. Her lips part, also signifying her attention is directed to the viewer, not to her repast or to her husband. Miller believes the woman "seems to invite a male viewer not only to the meal, but to the fruitfulness that the land has to offer. She, like the land, invites colonizing."[17]

Miller and other literary scholars have analyzed the sixteenth-century published tracts on colonization and found that English males described the New World and its peoples in gendered language.[18] Male fantasies of domination over women become the metaphors for Eu-

8. John White drawing of *Theire sitting at meate*

9. Theodor de Bry engraving of *Theire sitting at meate*

ropean male domination over the land and Indians. Miller provides a nuanced analysis of the evolution of English gendered interpretations of the New World, from the attempts of Gilbert to colonize Newfoundland to Ralegh's Virginia. Even before Ralegh undertook his Virginia enterprise, Miller shows an America identified in England as a "weak woman" in possession of gold, defiled by the Spanish, and beckoning the English across the Atlantic. In contrast, England's own barrenness is reflected in Queen Elizabeth's and England's infertility: the English must seek succor elsewhere for the sake of their future—the pliable woman/land of the New World awaits.[19]

Miller identified a subtle shift of English interest from Newfoundland to Roanoke. Language and purpose changed. "Virginia, in part infused with the characteristics of the English queen for whom the colony was named, becomes a virgin land. . . . Virginia, a chaste woman, is a viable economic investment."[20] Hakluyt's dedication to Ralegh of his translation of Peter Martyr's *Decades* (1587) turns Virginia into Ralegh's wife. Hakluyt tells Ralegh Elizabeth has "given" Virginia to "you to be your bride."

> *If you persevere only a little longer in your constancy, your bride will shortly bring forth new and most abundant offspring, such as will delight you and yours, and cover with disgrace and shame those who have so often dared rashly and impudently to charge her with barrenness. For who has the just title to attach such a stigma to your Elizabeth's Virginia, when no one has yet probed the depths of her hidden resources and wealth, or her beauty hitherto concealed from our sight.*[21]

The metaphors of a "fertile" New World, of "virgin land," and of "probing" the wilderness became standard in English and later Anglo-American descriptions of the American landscape.[22] It is no surprise that the beauty of the land is equated with women's fertility or that male sexual fantasies were placed on Indian women and their land. However, the blending of worries over the queen's and England's barrenness is historically specific to the moment in time when England first attempted overseas expansion to America. Colonization could not provide an heir for Elizabeth, but it could provide economic relief and allay the malaise that seemed to blanket the nation's future prospects.

The language of male domination over women and the projection of male fantasies of domination in colonization equate the two. Miller shows that the conceptualization is not static. I would add that it is not the whole story: not all English males held these fantasies. White's paintings and de Bry's engravings of White's paintings illuminate two very different views of colonization. In sexualizing the Natives, de Bry hoped to sell his book in Europe. Perhaps he expected his reinterpretation of White was the best way to depict Virginia to a variety of males; the way he altered the drawings evinces the self-consciousness of his efforts, and these alterations were made without Ralegh's or White's knowledge. White's original drawings indicate that he was *not* enveloped in gendered fantasies. This is significant because it shows that not all English were engaged in male fantasies of domination in colonization—a simple point overlooked in much of the gendered analysis of the period that assumes all English (and European) males shared these same fantasies—and that European males could produce depictions of indigenous peoples without fantasizing domination. White attempted to understand Indians on their own terms.

Moreover, the colonizers held a multiplicity of motivations and perspectives. Ralegh sent Hariot to collect information that would aid him in understanding the land and attract investors; Hariot did Ralegh's bidding in producing the propaganda tract *A Briefe and True Report*. Yet in Hariot's captions that accompanied White's drawings, reproduced in de Bry's Virginia volume, the propaganda elements are subdued. The keen observer of nature and people remained focused on limiting himself to empirical explanations of what White painted. Colonization as both sexual fantasy and extension of male dominance over females could never suffice as the entire story.

Ralegh employed White and Hariot because of their excellent skills observing and recording the kind of valuable, realistic, and sober information he needed for his colony to succeed. Ralegh was a practical man, and in colonizing Virginia there is no evidence of his propagating male fantasies, as he later did in his book on Guiana. The sexualization of the people and places of Virginia in de Bry's work is all the engraver's, and not Ralegh's, White's, or Hariot's. Why did Ralegh, Hariot, and White not sexualize women? Perhaps it did not occur to them. Perhaps, too, the three men were so enveloped in the Cult of Elizabeth that they dared not sexualize the females of Virginia, the place named in honor of the queen's virginity. If de Bry saw virgin land as a place requiring fertilization, Hariot and White saw a New World that sufficed for European needs without improvement. Yes, the English could introduce new crops like silk, but Hariot's *Briefe* never mentions manuring or building fences to improve the land, which would stamp an Englishness upon it as was so typical in Ireland, recommended by Lane and Grenville for Virginia, and later central in the colonization of New England. The drive to dominate America is peculiarly muted in the cultural production of Roanoke generated by Ralegh, Hariot, and White.

If White's drawings are an indication of Ralegh's purpose, and they must be because Ralegh arranged for their publication, his approach to the Indians reflected respect and curiosity. Ralegh intended his colony to thrive through good relations with the Indians, who would desire English goods and trade, and all would live together in harmony. Ralegh's selection of John White to lead the *permanent* settlement of Virginia with the 1587 expedition evinces Ralegh's desire for harmonious relations to avoid the military character of the Lane expedition. Ralegh had learned that a military establishment could not help but alienate Indians. In choosing White as governor, Ralegh opted for the painter who appreciated the Indians' differences from the English, and who did not view difference as a threat, a large contrast with Grenville and Lane, veterans of the Desmond Wars, who thought diplomacy with Natives best effected by intimidation.

Little is known of John White outside of his activities working for Ralegh in both America and Ireland. He was a trained limner—a skilled painter, as evident in his paintings of the Frobisher expedition with his wonderful portraits of an Inuit man and an Inuit woman carrying her child inside the hood of her parka.[23] White's extraordinary skill combining realism with a lack of judgment of Indians likely caught Ralegh's attention. Given that relations between Inuits and English were violent, it would have been easy for White to demonize his subjects. Recall how in his picture of Inuits firing arrows at the English, he shows another Inuit calmly paddling his kayak in the foreground. Ralegh likely could find no one better suited for his needs, a person enthusiastic about encountering New World peoples and who would not exaggerate their character.

White titled his illustrations of Virginia for Ralegh,

The pictures of sondry things collected and counterfeited
according to the truth in the voyage made by Sr Walter Raleigh
   knight,
for the discovery of La Virginea. In the 27th yeare of the most happie
   reigne of our Soveraigne lady Queene Elizabeth. And in the yeare
   of or Lorde God. 1585.

By "counterfeited," White meant simulated, that he tried to accurately capture Indian life with his images.[24] White purposefully avoided distorting Indian physicality and culture, not even to romanticize it. Objectivity was unobtainable—observers can never be entirely separated from their observations—but White and Hariot consciously strived not to exaggerate or alter Indian life as they saw it. The Indians, we can assume, would have chosen different aspects of themselves to portray in words and pictures. They would have been able to provide much deeper explanations of their culture and reveal things that White and Hariot could not have perceived, but they would have selectively hidden what they did not want to share. They would have taken for granted ubiquitous aspects of their culture, while emphasizing other aspects that held significance for them. And their depictions would have varied depending on which Indian produced the text and pictures—a werowance would emphasize different aspects of life than would a warrior or child or elite female. In some ways, White and Hariot might have been able to provide clearer views of the surface of these societies. Without the deep cultural knowledge the Indians possessed, White's and Hariot's *different subjectivity* had advantages. As outsiders, the two Englishmen captured portions of Indian life that the Indians likely would have thought too banal to share with others, such as cooking, planting fields, building canoes, and carrying small children. But ordinary activities were of great interest to Europeans. White's pictures confirmed that no matter how odd, exotic, or fantastic these Indians appeared, they were members of the human family.

White and Hariot provided a standard of mediation that other English and Anglo-Americans did not match for hundreds of years. No one subsequently produced such nuanced portraits of Indians and their lives. No one displayed Indian life in so many daily contexts. Migrants and visitors to America generated meaningful written accounts of Native life, but not until the age of photography in the mid-nineteenth century were sustained visual studies made of the Indians north of Mexico. De Bry's future engravings of the Americas' Native peoples devolved into portraying Indians as diabolical, as monsters bereft of individuality and humanity. Europeans painted Indians; portraits exist, including fascinating examples of Indians in scenes.[25] Still, White stands out for his holistic and intimate depictions. His portraits are character studies of types: chiefs, religious men, mothers, children, the elderly.[26] Similarly, he captures activities as a "type" practiced by Indians of the region, while carefully distinguishing entire communities from one another, showing the physical differences of their towns and the variance in tattoos and hairstyles.

Seventy-seven of White's original pictures have survived, as have some copies and engravings of missing originals. White produced on the journey to Virginia pictures of fish, shellfish, insects, fruits, and birds, as well as the coast of Dominica and two views of a fortified encampment at Puerto Rico. Also surviving are drawings White likely made on the initial visit to the mainland towns of Pomeioc and Secota soon after English arrival at Roanoke, though White's and Hariot's details imply multiple visits to these towns.[27] White later hued his drawings with watercolors, perhaps after his return to England.

White's portraits provide intimate studies of Indian bodies: their dress, markings, hairstyles, and the objects of importance that they touch; but, like the towns, no background is provided. The starkness of White's landscapes belies the lush environment described by Hariot in his *Briefe*. Unwilling to distract the viewer from his subject, White mostly eschews artistic flair that would bring attention to himself. He certainly possessed the capability of adding expertly rendered flourishes, as demonstrated in his depiction of smoke, but in his paintings of American Indians he consistently recorded the patterns of life and the people while subduing his ego and without passing judgment. Ralegh needed to know who these people were and how they lived; he did not require White to interpret cultural meaning, though Hariot and White could explain to him what the pictures did or did not make readily evident.

When White was meticulous, it was purpose-driven. He recorded an array of Indian tattoos and their placement on Indian bodies.[28] The tattoos display individuals' town identity. Women's tattoos varied by town as well and by placement. The women of Pomeioc, for instance, tattooed a wide band with long spokes around their upper arms. White also carefully recorded distinct hairstyles, which varied from one town to the next. Distinctions in personal appearance thus varied by town, gender, occupation, and social status. Religious men possessed their own unique hairstyles: the priest bore a raised portion of hair at the front of the forehead cross-wise, almost from ear to ear, and in *The Flyer*, a conjuror wears a black bird on the right side of his head and has no crest like the priest's. One of the most useful aspects of White's ethnography is his capture of body movements that seem disconsonant with European body movements. For instance, in *The Wyfe of an*

10. John White drawing of a Pomeioc woman and child titled *The wife of an Herowan of Pomeiooc*

Herowan of Pomeiooc, he shows how a mother carried her young child over her shoulder with one leg hooked through her arm. In one of his most ingenious compositions, of Indians dancing, White portrays an array of individual movements to help the viewer gain a sense of the dance's fluidity. Dancing, walking, sitting, and standing all caught White's attention.

Without Hariot's accompanying captions for de Bry's engravings, Indian poses would have seemed awkward, inexplicable to European eyes. The captions generally range from three hundred to five hundred words each, some longer. De Bry usually placed the text on the page facing the engraving. Hariot's captions explained and enlarged on White's drawings, retaining their focus on the scene rather than connecting the information to the larger purposes of colonization. Scholars rarely comment on Hariot's captions and thus miss how they and the *Briefe* were produced for different purposes.[29]

Like White's paintings, the captions generally are matter-of-fact presentations of Indians, their daily activities, and their cultural practices, provided without political commentary and shorn of patronization and romanticization.[30] Hariot's captions affirm the engravings' "truth," while suggesting that Indian "difference" is not to be feared but, indeed, it should be studied. An intellectual fearlessness in Hariot's and White's approaches reflects Ralegh's own fearlessness toward difference. Hariot and White were unafraid of not knowing the answers, that their lack of definitive knowledge would make them or the Indians look bad. They opened a door for Europeans to learn more, to find out why Indians lived as they did and how they *flourished* on their own without European mediation. It is clear in Hariot's and White's work that the Indians have no need for the English despite the general European view that Europeans could teach Indians so many things to make their lives better. Hariot and White knew firsthand how the English starved at Roanoke, and though the Indians also went hungry, they saw Indian ingenuity keep Indians from needing the Europeans' material assistance. Ralegh carried this idea to South America, where he witnessed Natives living in abundance, and then recommended to the queen they leave the Natives alone to pursue their material lives as they always had done, except for teaching them particular skills so they could defend themselves from the Spanish.

White's most striking pictures were of Indian activities, and it is these, in their totality, that display the wholeness of Indian societies, their rich diversity, and their self-sufficiency. His detailed and beautiful depiction of the town of Secota includes not only trees but also three types of planted fields, "Their rype corne," "Their greene corne," and "Corne newly sprong," evidence of the Indians making great use of the land's fecundity.

The painting provides a composite of village activities, such as Indians dancing around poles, a couple "sitting at meate," and "The Howse wherein the Tombe of their Herounds standeth." White created separate and more detailed drawings of these scenes that show Natives at "solemne prayers" and "solemne feastes." By noting the prayers and the feasts are solemn, Hariot eliminated the savage label of Peckham and others. Hariot, White, and de Bry shared interest in portraying the Roanoke-area Indians in a nuanced manner, as multidimensional people. Whereas Hariot's *Briefe* delved into Indian cosmology, White's illustrations and Hariot's captions depicted the physical nature of

11. John White untitled drawing of a Native dance

everyday life. More-difficult-to-explain Native Indian activities were addressed in a sensitive manner without condemnation.[31]

Hariot and White easily could have interpreted what they witnessed with horror. Instead, by humanizing the people, they implicitly presented Ralegh's colony as the anti-Spanish: as good Europeans not out to exploit, enslave, and kill Indians. Many English thought that their form of colonization would differ: they would embrace the heathen to convert them to true Christianity.[32] English views of Spain's inhumanity toward America's Native peoples had been made explicit through the steady stream of propaganda generated by the Dutch, who were engaged in a liberation movement from Spanish dominance.[33] The Protestant Crusade against Catholicism lasted centuries, buttressed by this "Black Legend." In the 1580s, English colonizers perceived that Native people would join them in alliance against the Spanish. White's drawings, popularized by de Bry's engravings, could be made to speak for a Protestant perspective of English appreciation for Indian humanity and ingenuity; the Indians' land is bountiful, an Eden that would support Indians and English, not a place to ravage and steal Indian bodies and possessions.

12. John White
untitled drawing
of the town of
Secota

Ralegh's infant English colony seemingly had passed the Spanish in its embrace of the New World by the intimacy of the portraiture.[34] The volume could establish Ralegh's reputation in Europe as the humane English colonizer whose people produced this splendid intellectual and artistic production, symbolizing English moral superiority. By depicting Indians as different but by withholding the judgment that difference made them inferior or diabolical, the Virginia volume made a powerful political statement about Ralegh's motives and intentions in the New World. The English come off as idealists, Humanists, and good Christians—the violence that actually occurred between English and Natives remained muted in this published record. The de Bry volume neither illustrated the violence nor recounted the many skirmishes.

The question remains: From where did this intellectual and temperamental openness arise? The same source that posited that Elizabeth would be empress of a universal monarchy that would re-form the world. The Hermetic perspective tied the Virginia volume together. Ralegh, Hariot, White, and de Bry all subscribed to the religious philosophy of Hermeticism. Planted throughout the de Bry volume on Virginia were symbols and information that Hermeticists would readily recognize as signifying the relationship between American Indians and God. In effect, these were affirmations that the Indians possessed a special relationship to the divine.

CHAPTER 13

Fire and Smoke

The Hermeticists' Indians

The general public probably did not know much about the status of Ralegh's colony. Many were aware ships kept departing for Virginia. Yet the discontented returned unimpressed with Virginia's prospects, and rumors abounded that precious metals were nowhere to be found.

The propaganda—the documentation generated by Hariot, White, de Bry, and Hakluyt—however, was designed to tell a different story. Hariot's *Briefe* highlighted a Virginia that would produce a plentitude of valuable commodities. De Bry's engravings of White's pictures, placed alongside Hariot's captions, presented a story of Virginia's fascinating Native peoples. The volume in toto confirmed for England and the rest of Europe a fait accompli: Ralegh had built a colony in America, one that would challenge Spain. The colony would produce profits, and the English would live in harmony with the Natives. Hakluyt heaped effusive praise on Ralegh, declaring the courtier on a level with Vasco da Gama, the famed Portuguese explorer of the East Indies. For a 1586 French publication of René de Laudonnière's account of the French colony in Florida, Hakluyt offered a Latin verse in praise of Ralegh as England's greatest explorer, despite the fact that Ralegh had never been to Virginia.

The Portuguese subdued the tracts of China
And the stout Spaniard the fields of Mexico:
Florida once yielded to the noble French:
Virginia now to thy scepter, Elizabeth!
The illustrious race of Portugal celebrates its Gama,
And the land of Spain boasts its Cortes,
France gives the palm to Laudonnière and brave Ribault,
But we, noble Ralegh, assign first place to thee.[1]

The next year Hakluyt penned a lengthy dedication to Ralegh of Peter Martyr's *Decades* (Paris, 1587), which praised Ralegh's accomplishments in America, suggesting he stood on the precipice of even greater deeds. The Martyr volume was a most appropriate place to signify and contextualize England's entry into New World colonization. The Italian chronicled the first decades of Spanish exploration and conquest in the New World up until 1525, and was considered by many to be its most important historian. The time had come, according to Hakluyt, for England to pick up the mantle of Sebastian Cabot who, "in the year 1496," accompanied by "three hundred Englishmen, he, first of all Christian people, discovered the whole tract of land which stretches from the North Pole to the latitude of the Pillars of Hercules." Unfortunately, to England's great loss, Cabot went to work for Spain: "How great a disaster the defection of so great a man from our country."[2] The unfulfilled task of New World exploration these many years later, "reserved" by "divine Providence," now fell to Ralegh. And who better for Hakluyt to dedicate these chronicles of Martyr to than Ralegh, who already had "spent nearly 100,000 ducats in equipping . . . new fleets for the establishment of a third colony to open up countries before unknown and inaccessible." Ralegh had devoted "every care, every thought, and endeavor" toward seeking out "new kingdoms over land and sea." He had promoted "the navigator's art" and "the mathematical sciences" by maintaining in his household Thomas Hariot, learning from Hariot these "noble sciences," and together teaching Ralegh's "sea-captains, of whom there are not a few, [how they] might link theory with practice, not without almost incredible results." Hakluyt urged Ralegh to build a larger fleet, for Virginia was just the beginning. Ralegh must "Reveal to us the courts of China and the unknown straits which still lie hid: throw back the portals which have been closed since the world's beginning at the dawn of time." Of this unseen universe, "There yet remain for you new lands, ample realms, unknown peoples; they wait yet, I say to be discovered and subdued, quickly and easily, under the happy auspices of your arms and enterprise, and the scepter of our most serene Queen Elizabeth, Empress—as even the Spaniard himself admits—of the Ocean."[3]

Hakluyt considerably added to the propaganda promoting Virginia by his publication of *The Principall Navigations* (1589), which included an array of accounts documenting the history of English overseas expansion "Round About the Whole Globe of the Earth," extending from the ancient world to the present day. De Bry's volume of Virginia, however, published in 1590, had much greater immediate reach in Europe, being published in four languages and sold at the major book fairs. The book not only implicitly portrayed the English as humane colonizers but also encoded Hermetic messages to the intelligentsia of Europe. The text, and particularly de Bry's engravings of White's paintings, assured readers that God had blessed the Natives. America beckoned Europeans, according to the Hermeticists, not for purposes of conquest, but to bear witness to God's work firsthand.

—

TODAY, AS THROUGH THE CENTURIES, Ralegh is famous for smoking tobacco. It is curious that White's paintings and de Bry's engravings of Virginia exclude tobacco smoking. The Indians used tobacco at most social and diplomatic occasions. De Bry's later volume on Florida Indians features examples of Indian smoking. Hariot discussed tobacco in his *Briefe*. The celebrations White painted surely included smoking, yet he excluded it. It is possible that White did not like tobacco and thus omitted this ubiquitous facet of daily life. Perhaps White did not want tobacco smoke to interfere with the Hermetic messages he sent in his portrayal of another kind of smoke. Smoke, indeed, was critical to White's depiction of Indians—the smoke produced by wood fires, not tobacco.

No other element of the natural world so connected Indian life and culture in White's and de Bry's illustrations than fire and smoke. Hariot frequently referred to, and characterized, fires, whether or not they were central to the illustration. For the picture of the town of Secota, he explained, "This people therefore voyde of all covetousnes lyve cherfullye and att their harts ease. Butt they solemnise their feasts in the nigt, and therefore they keepe verye great fyres to avoyde darkenes, ant [and] to testifie their Joye." Fire was as requisite for a celebration

The Seething of in Potts

their meate. of earth.

13. John White drawing of *The Seething of their meate in Potts of earth*

as it was for most daily activities.[4] Few of White's depictions of Indian life lack fire. Besides the portraits of individuals, from which he excluded fire as he did other external matter, fire is absent only from the painting of a couple eating and of an Indian dance.

White and Hariot connected fire in daily life to Indian ingenuity.[5] For his painting of an Indian cooking over a fire, White drew a huge earthen pot, maybe three feet tall and half as wide, of which Hariot assures us "Their woemen know how to make earthen vessells with special Cunninge and that so large and fine, that our potters with lhoye [throw] wheles [wheels] can make noe better." These pots can be moved "from place to place as easelye as we can doe our brassen kettles." Although Hariot says, "They have set them uppon an heape of erthe to stay them from fallinge," and "one of them taketh great care that the fyre burne equallye Rounde abowt," White's rendition fails to match the text.

In White's painting, there is no heap of earth, and the huge pot, only loosely secured by the kindling burning underneath and around it, mysteriously does not tumble. Hariot also duly notes Indian care for another fire for cooking in his caption for White's *The Broyling of Their*

Fish over the Flame of Fier. This time White's painting better matches Hariot's caption, which notes for the engraving that "they make a fyre underneathe to broile . . . not after the manner of the people of Florida," who used a small fire to slowly smoke the fish. Again, Hariot saw fit to comment on Indian control of their fires: "They take good heede that they [the fish] bee not burntt." At first glance, it seems odd that Hariot comments on Indian control of fires: of course the Indians would not let their food burn. But fire's association with the devil made it imperative for Hariot and White to place Indian fires in a positive light.

Indian skill with fire also was noted for the illustration *The Manner of Makinge Their Boates*, which Hariot gushed "is verye wonderfull." The Indians employed fire to both fell the trees and hollow the logs. They burned the bottom of the tree until "yt is almost burnt thorough, and readye to fall they make a new fyre, which they suffer to burne until the tree fall of yt owne accord." After "burninge of the top, and

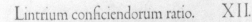

14. Theodor de Bry engraving of *The manner of makinge their boates*

15. John White
drawing of *The
manner of theire
fishing*

bowghs," they place the tree on forked posts "at suche a reasonable heighte as they may handsomlye work upon yt."[6]

Removing the bark with shells, the Indians would then fire the inside of the log and scrape off the loosened wood, a process repeated over and over until the boat was complete. Thus, even without "Instruments of yron, or other like unto ours, yet they knowe howe to make them [boats] as handsomelye, to saile whear they liste in their Rivers, and to fishe with all, as ours." Hariot concluded, "This god indueth thise savage people with sufficient reason to make thinges necessarie to serve their turnes."

The English found equally impressive the many ingenious ways the Indians snared fish. White created a composite painting of multiple methods, from the use of spears and nets to expertly crafted weirs. (Recall, too, Barlowe and Lane spoke at length about fishing and English inability to imitate the Indians.) Dominating the painting's foreground is an Indian canoe (nearly the width of the picture) full of fish. (Recall, too, when the first Indian encountered the English at Roanoke, he went off and quickly caught a huge number of fish to present to the English.) Hariot's caption for the engraving explains the composite scene, as with the making of weirs by "settinge opp reedes or twigges in the water, which they soe plant one within a nother, that they growe still narrower, and narrower. . . . Ther was never seene amonge us soe cunninge a way to take fish." But most startling: in the center of the canoe two Indians feed a fire! The reason is unexplained in both the painting and Hariot's narrative for the de Bry engraving, but it depicts Indians fishing at night: the fire illuminates sleeping fish that could be speared and netted. Viewers would have marveled that the boat did not sink from the fire.

Fire also played a role in Indian celebrations, though Hariot made few comments about the function, except to note the importance. For an untitled White painting, titled for the engraving *Their Manner of Praing with Rattels abowt t[h]e Fyre*, Hariot stated that to celebrate when "they have escaped any great danger by sea or lande, or be returned from the warr in token of Joye they make a great fyer." Around the fire they sit with rattles and sing and "make merrie." Here is a rare instance when Hariot directly inserted himself into Indian activities as not just an observer but as one who has been "amonge them" during the festivities. Hariot could provide no interpretation of the celebration beyond "it is a strange custom, and worth the observation." He perceived no religious connotations to the celebration, for he employed the word *solemn* to identify Indian activities infused with spirituality. Unable or unwilling to label a celebration that today we might identify as a bonfire party, White and Hariot limited themselves to reporting what they had seen, refraining from inferences.

White did paint a dance without a fire. As Hariot informs the reader, dances ordinarily occurred after sunset to avoid the heat, and fires provided necessary light. But this "solemn feast" brought together Indians of neighboring towns during the day, "every man attyred in the most strange fashion."[7] Around a circle were placed wooden posts taller than the dancers, at the top of which were carved faces like nuns "covered with theyr vayles." (In all likelihood it was a harvest celebration.) At the completion of the dances, all went to "make merrye," by which he referred specifically twice in the text to eating. To the present day, this Green Corn festival is celebrated by Southern Indians. The absence of fire in the illustration may be explained by this being a daytime celebration, but fire also would have interfered with the dance, for there are dancers in the middle of the circle where a fire would normally be located. The elaborate dance and its appendages, that is, the carved heads on posts, the painter's depiction of the dance's unusual steps, and the dancers' dress elevate the celebration to its own unique category of Indianness. But how would Europeans interpret these cultural differences?

Indian dances could be viewed by Europeans as heathen or diabolical. White's paintings and Hariot's descriptions bring order to the celebration to steer Europeans away from drawing negative conclusions. This must have been the most difficult painting for White to execute because he details the Indians' choreography (see illustration 11 in Chapter 12). He slows the dance to view it more carefully. In the middle "Three of the fayrest Virgins" embrace while turning in a circular manner. The three stabilize the painting with their fluid and harmonious movement, in contrast to those on the outer ring, whose dance steps would appear jarring to Europeans. Holding rattles, spears, and large sprigs, and "beeing sett in order" around the outer circle, the Indians "dance, singe, and use the strangest gestures that they can possiblye devise." Unable to explain the dance, White ingeniously records an array of poses that transform what otherwise could be viewed as chaos into a structured event.

What White and Hariot could not explain, they recorded. The new science of the late sixteenth century, later termed Baconianism, grounded the scientific method in the collection of evidence. Without a method, Hariot and White confined themselves to information on the Indian dances. They understood dancing, but Indian styles varied so greatly from the familiar that they did not know what to make of them.

The use of fire was similar—the Indians, like the Europeans, used fire for cooking and warmth, but they also used fire in different ways that the Europeans had not seen before. The Indians impressed the English with how they used fire to remove trees, hollow out logs, and fish from their boats at night. Whereas Europeans associated uncontrolled fire with the Devil and the fires of Hell, Hermeticists deeply associated the controlled fire with God: Fire symbolized God's presence and power. God destroyed Sodom and Gomorrah with fire. Of greatest importance to the Hermeticists was Moses's conversation with God at the Burning Bush—the seminal moment in Hermetic lore, the foundation of Ralegh's religious philosophy. God's earlier presence in the life of man was not discounted, from Adam and Eve to the near sacrifice of Isaac by Abraham, to the flooding of the world, and so on. Ralegh discussed all these in his last book, *The History of the World*.

To Hermeticists, Moses's relationship with God differed from all others'. The Hermeticists identified Moses as the original "juggler" or magician, through whom God displayed His power to transform one substance into another, and then whom God made the vessel for His power: Moses's staff became a snake, he turned water into blood, and he parted the Red Sea for the exodus from Egypt. The Hermeticists saw themselves as the inheritors of Moses. Magicians, Ralegh later wrote, were the most pious of men. Like the three magi who visited baby Jesus, the magician devoted himself to studying the divine. The Burning Bush, the only fire that gave off no smoke and whose transformation established God's presence to speak directly to Moses, represented God's willingness to communicate with man, to bring selected humans—magicians—closer to Him.

Magicians used fire for alchemy. Ralegh and his brothers Humphrey and Adrian practiced alchemy. In the proper hands, fire could be used as a catalyst to effect the transformation of one substance into another, thereby uncovering secrets of the universe, the identity and nature of the secret properties God bestowed on material things. Indian use of fire in so many clever ways—to transform trees into boats, attract fish at night, to preserve fish for lean times—these were all acts of alchemy and provided evidence of God's blessings upon them.

The Hermeticist White thus overemphasized, undoubtedly at the direction of Ralegh, fire and smoke in his paintings, which became even more exaggerated in de Bry's engravings. Virtually every fire in the engravings is larger and more dramatic than in the original painting, with huge clouds of billowing smoke.[8] De Bry's rendition of the fire broiling fish is a fire that in reality would have destroyed the fish and the wooden apparatus holding the fish. The Indians sitting around the fire with their rattles would likewise have been burned to cinders if de Bry's engraving was true to life. The lack of realism is reinforced by the relatively few logs creating huge amounts of flame and smoke. De Bry's large fires essentially blaze out of control as if to demonstrate how the Indians harnessed nature—fire—for their use but lacked the civility to temper its usage. The exaggerated fires clash with Hariot's text for the engravings, which repeatedly notes the care Indians take to control their fires. Although de Bry's engravings did not depict the over-large fires doing damage, they depict activities on the verge of disaster. De Bry's exaggeration of fire implicitly shows that the Indians' savagery remained close to the surface of their lives. God endowed them with the gift of knowledge to use fire in numerous productive ways, but the fires, like the Indians, could easily burn out of control.

The billowing smoke in White's and de Bry's illustrations of Indian life represents the unrepresentable: God.[9] De Bry engraved and published three Hermetic books in the 1590s. His sons followed their father's path and turned the family firm into Europe's leading publisher of alchemical texts in the seventeenth century.[10] De Bry's Hermeticism is evident throughout the Virginia volume. His exaggeration of fire and smoke explicitly represent God endowing Indians with His power. Savages benefit from God's blessings, even when they have not been exposed to Christ, much like the ancient Hebrews.[11] De Bry's most significant Hermetic addition to the volume is an engraving of Adam and Eve.[12]

To modern minds, the engraving appears incongruous in a book on American Indians, so much so that many of the modern reproductions

16. De Bry
untitled engraving
of Adam and Eve

17. Engraving of
Noah after landfall,
from the de Bry
volume on Florida

of de Bry's engravings of Virginia exclude the Adam and Eve image as irrelevant. On the surface, the engraving is a simple statement that Indians live in a Garden of Eden. The picture might also imply Indian innocence. A man in the background with a skin covering his nakedness hoes the earth. This man likely represents the arrival of Europeans to America and their working of the blessed land. The European regains virtue through rural pursuits in America. But what of the Indians? There is a snake curling its way into the center of the picture. Does the snake represent that the Indians are about to lose their innocence, their privilege of living a blessed life without need for Christ?

De Bry's introductory engraving to the second volume on America, the one on the French colony in Florida,[13] confirms his Hermetic conceptualization of American Indians. Even more than the Adam and Eve image, this one is almost always excluded from modern volumes reproducing de Bry's engravings of Le Moyne's paintings.[14] This engraving, too, appears at first glance to have nothing to do with American Indians: it depicts Noah having led the animals off the ark.

In the right foreground, Noah makes a sacrifice on an altar and a cloud of smoke billows up to the sky, where יהוה, the Hebrew spelling of Yahweh, the unpronounceable four-letter name of God, is written.[15] De Bry's engraving is especially appropriate for a volume on American Indians when we recall that Noah is pre-Abrahamic: he was not a Jew, yet he converses with God, does God's bidding, and sacrifices him. The Indians, too, according to Hermetic thinking, were in touch with God, who provided for them before their exposure to Judeo-Christian religion. In *The Jewish Alchemists: A History and Source Book*, Raphael Patai notes that the Hermeticists believed "Noah saved this secret lore [Hermeticism] from being lost in the Great Flood," then it passed through one of his sons, and eventually to Hermes Trismegistus, and from Hermes to the Hermeticists of the Renaissance.[16]

American Indian descent led Christians to question whether Indians were prelapsarian—of the time before the fall of man.[17] If American Indians existed in the time of Noah, wherein all humanity was killed by the flood save for Noah and his family, then the Bible was wrong that all had died.[18] How and when did Indians arrive in America?[19] In Christian tradition, the peoples of Europe, Africa, and Asia descended from each of Noah's three sons, Shem, Ham, and Jaspheth. So, from whom did American Indians descend? Barlowe's account for Ralegh of the first Roanoke expedition suggested that the Indians lived in prelapsarian conditions, because their lives evinced "the earth bringeth foorth all things in aboundance, as in the first creation, without toil or labour." Hakluyt excised this sentence in the second edition of his *Principal Navigations* (1598).[20] That Barlowe stated it and Hakluyt printed it in 1589 but deleted it from the next edition at least implies that in the 1580s both thought it possible that Indians lived in a sinless state before exposure to true Christianity or at least that their sins, their heathenism, did not mean that God had forsaken them. The excision by Hakluyt and de Bry's placement of the Noah engraving in the Florida volume indicate that Hakluyt and de Bry no longer saw the Indians as prelapsarian. This "correction" probably resulted from criticism from other Christians.

De Bry's engraving of Noah implies that the Indians, like the rest of humanity, descended from Noah's loins through his sons. If the image of Noah was not enough to proclaim de Bry's new stance, then the Latin text accompanying the engraving made his view explicit. De Bry unequivocally stated that the Indians descended from one of the sons of Ham. It had become a Christian tradition to associate Africans with one of these sons, Canaan.[21] In the book of Genesis, Ham looked upon his father's nakedness, and when Noah learned this, he cursed Ham's son Canaan to become a servant of servants unto his brethren. Though no mention is made of skin color or slavery, early modern Euro-Christians used this passage to justify enslavement of Africans. De Bry separated the Indians of Florida, and by implication all American Indians, from Africans by not naming the son of Ham from whom they descended. Association with Ham, however, implied a lesser status. De Bry noted in the Florida volume that the Indians, whose physicality he highly praised as great, strong, bold, and agile, were "nonetheless dissimulators and untrustworthy." Skin color separated them from the Africans, for the Indians' "ghostly and dirty colors" came from the oils they used to protect their flesh from the sun, for when they were "newly born" they were "quite white."[22]

It is most interesting that de Bry labeled Indians dissimulators, when it was he who intended to mislead. Although in the Florida volume he stressed that Indians had not been blessed by God and did not live in an edenic state of innocence, he still tied them to Noah and the transmission of mystical knowledge. The engraving proclaims the Hermetic message of Noah igniting a fire, which turns to smoke, which leads to God. De Bry appeased the censors and the censorious by his written text, eliminating Indian association with a prelapsarian Eden, placing them within biblical tradition, identifying their character flaws, and explicitly stating that they required salvation. And yet, this engraving that opens the volume on Florida maintains the Indian connection to the divine, as the billowing smoke at Noah's altar leads to God, and the Indians remain conveyers of Noah's mystical knowledge.

The publication of the de Bry volume on Virginia was a special moment in time, when a significant portion of English were prepared to engage and study Native Americans, hoping to enlarge their own vision of the world and obtain greater knowledge of God's Creation. There were no "grotesques" in Ralegh's Virginia. The only reference to the Devil occurred in Hariot's caption for the engraving of the juggler or conjuror.[23] But no similar reference was made to Indian priests. The Flyer (the original term White used), or juggler or conjuror, represented an individual who consulted omens about when to undertake battle and who possessed other secrets and charms to be employed for reasons of health. These men "be verye familiar with devils, of whome they enquier what their enemys doe, or other suche thinges." It is possible that de Bry added this statement about devils to the text, as he added other statements to Hariot's captions, but Hermeticists generally would have agreed that both black and white magic existed, and they would have assumed that some Indian conjurors practiced black magic, just as some Europeans practiced the black arts. Yet the downplaying of the association of Natives with black magic might also have been at Ralegh's suggestion, because he made no mention of such an association in his own later ethnography of Native peoples, and in another book he dismissed much of black magic as being merely the performance of tricks.

The function of the priests in the Virginia volume differed from that of the conjurors. The priests' main task, at least according to White's pictures, was to oversee the charnel house that contained the bones of the dead and the statue of the God Kiwasa. The priests' function was to ensure proper ritual in respect of the dead. Priests possessed magical skills; Hariot described priests for de Bry's engraving of a priest as "notable enchaunters," but he made no reference to the magic they performed. Instead, in the same sentence where he labels priests enchanters, he immediately follows with noting they enjoy hunting ducks, swans, and other fowl. The priest is thus displayed as a typical Indian, albeit "well stricken in years, and as yt seemeth of more experience then the common sorte." In contrast to the conjuror, who potentially engaged the forces of the Devil, the priest represented Indian morality, civility, and belief in the afterlife.

Having connected Indians to innocence using the engraving of Adam and Eve in the Garden of Eden, and then having emphasized the blessings they received from God, who endowed them with the means to flourish despite their ignorance of Christ, what remained for White, Hariot, and de Bry to show was how Indians fit into the postbiblical family of humanity. Fire and billowing smoke assured Hermeticists that Indians held connection to God. For most readers, White's—de Bry's—humanizing of the Natives by sympathetic depictions of their bodies and activities provided reassurance of the Indians' common humanity. (In later volumes, by contrast, de Bry added tails to Indians to evince their diabolism.) Hariot, White, and de Bry created "living" Indians tied to a specific locale, Ralegh's Virginia, and possessed of positive social qualities. Indians farmed and fished as communities, commemorated important occasions, cared for their children, and respected elderly people.

INDIAN OWNERSHIP OF IDOLS, however, was problematic. More than any other aspect of Indian culture, the possession of idols signaled a difference from Europeans. Differences in Indian dress, dance, food-ways, and housing could be attributed to the variances of environment and history.[24] But idols and multiple Gods were viewed as antithetical to the Christian belief system.

The Virginia volume took pains to portray Native worship as the result of ignorance that merely required rectification. Hariot notes that, in addition to the God Kiwasa, the Indians had two, sometimes three idols "but never above" in their temples; the last phrase is meant to downplay their importance, as if to say an entire community was not full of idols. Hariot tried to elicit sympathy for the Indians in their ignorance: "Thes poore soules have none other knowledge of god although I thinke them verye Desirous to know the truthe."[25] Why does he think so? When the Europeans kneeled to pray, "they went abowt to imitate us, and when they saw we moved our lipps, they also dyd the like." Hariot could not know that this scene would be repeated across the Americas when Indians encountered Europeans doing strange things, like praying—Indians mimicked European behaviors; European observers noted through the colonial era that mimicry provided a chief form of humor for Indians. Whether Hariot recognized the Indians' comedy in mimicry or not, he would not dare say to European readers that Indians mocked Christianity. Instead, he asserted this behavior as indicating the likelihood that they would become Christians, as he piously intoned, "God of his mercie grant them this grace."

De Bry, toward the end of the volume, turns readers' attention from Kiwasa to the corpses he guards as a way to display the Natives' piety. In front of a charnel house burns a small fire that, if nothing else, implicitly shows that the living actively tend to the dead. A priest, who "hath his lodginge" under the scaffold, "Mumbleth his prayers nighte and day, and hath charge of the corpses." Hariot observes, "Thes poore souls are thus instructed by nature to reverence their princes even after their death."

Respect for one's betters required neither fear, nor force, nor Christianity—it was deemed as natural a state among the Indians as were the distinctions between classes in England, which Europeans viewed as God-ordained. Indians were not untamable savages (wild men), because they lived in a social order in which they respected their betters and tended to them even after death.

18. John White
untitled drawing
of an ancient
Pictish man

To assess the ability of Indians to assimilate to English culture, White created what amounted to a comparative ethnography that extended to contemporary people of other parts of the world.[26] He painted a Turkish man with a sword and two Turkish women covering their faces with two different hijabs. He produced two paintings of Florida Indians, a man and a woman, which he based on paintings by Le Moyne. Additional studies, no longer extant, but for which we have seventeenth-century copies, include five pictures of Brazilian Indians and portraits of the Doge of Genoa, a Roman soldier, and a medieval European man. De Bry chose not to engrave any of White's contemporary comparisons, but he eagerly engraved and published some of White's representations of ancient inhabitants of the British Isles.

Ralegh provided de Bry with five of White's portraits of Picts and ancient Britons. De Bry states on the cover page of this closing section of the Virginia volume that White "assured" him that he found these "Figures . . . in a oolled [old] English cronicle." They "showe how that

19. John White
untitled drawing
of an ancient
Pictish woman

the Inhabitants of the great Bretannie have bin in times past as sauvage as those of Virginia."[27]

White's colorful and dramatic renderings equate the ancient inhabitants of Britain with the Indians of Virginia in several ways. Two men, perhaps meant to be Picts, are entirely covered with body art. One man's body bears dramatic depictions of animals—griffins, lions, snakes, and an owl.

He wields a shield in one hand and a decapitated, blood-dripping head in the other, and his sword hangs behind him. The other man bears no animal images but has designs on his body from head to toe. A woman also is covered head to toe with detailed and complex body art, including stars, half moons, and sunbeams, suggesting her lack of Christianity and worship of nature. She, too, wields weaponry: a sword and three spears.

Not only are all three of these adults naked, but both males' genitalia are prominently displayed.[28] The message is clear: the ancient

Britons were similar to the Virginia Indians. They painted their bodies, engaged in savage wars, and had no shame in their nakedness. Yet not all ancient Britons were alike. When de Bry engraved the man holding the decapitated head and the woman, they were identified as Picts, ancestors of the people of Scotland.[29] Two additional portraits, also unidentified by White, were engraved by de Bry as neighbors to the Picts. In both White's paintings and de Bry's engravings of the two, the male and female have no body paint. Perhaps the message was that not all the inhabitants of the British Isles were from Scotland or as savage. Both of these figures have their genitalia covered.[30] Although the woman wields sword and spear, she appears somewhat domesticated. It is quite possible that White meant to show the evolution of the ancient Britons, and de Bry shifted the story to make them contemporaries.

De Bry may have had little guidance on what to do with these pictures. He understood the gist of White's message—to compare Indians with other peoples in other places and times—but he was given no captions to explain the pictures. Hariot did not write captions for these engravings; they were probably written by one of de Bry's English associates, who apparently was so unfamiliar with the Picts that he stated they were the ancient inhabitants of England rather than Scotland. The captions are puerile and merely recite what is readily apparent in the engraving, offering no additional context or information of substance. As in the engravings of Virginia, de Bry added background to specifically locate the subject with a place. Anachronistic depictions of ships, castles, and villages confirm that Picts and ancient Britons were Europeans. The gist of the argument is reinforced, whether White meant the ancient Britons to have derived from the Picts or to have been their contemporaries: we Europeans have evolved from savagery, and so, too, can the American Indians.

IN SHAKESPEARE'S *The Tempest*, written about 1610 or 1611, Miranda exclaims:

Oh Wonder!
How many goodly creatures are there here!
How beauteous mankind is! O brave new world,
That has such people in't![31]

The irony in Miranda's exclamation was not the discovery of New World peoples but of encountering Europeans on this island besides herself and her father. She was filled with joy, but her father, Prospero, knew better. He had suffered in Europe and found refuge on this unnamed island. Now he had used magic to bring these Europeans here, intending to punish them for having wronged him years earlier.

In *The Tempest*, Shakespeare addressed European anxiety about the New World and skewered its delusions. Shakespeare saw through the charade of a malevolent New World inhabited by the Devil's minions. The Europeans were morally no better or worse whether they lived in Europe or the New World. And in the New World, the Europeans could be as malevolent as Caliban, the half-human, half-monster who lives on the island where the play takes place. Shakespeare also understood that Europe had succumbed to exoticism of America. In Act 2, when the Italian jester Trinculo first sees Caliban, he states that were he

> *in England now, as he once was, and had but this fish painted,*
> *not a holiday fool there but would give a piece of silver:*
> *there would this monster make a man;*
> *any strange beast there makes a man:*
> *when they will not give a doit to relieve a lame beggar,*
> *they will lay out ten to see a dead Indian.*[32]

The audience would have immediately picked up Shakespeare's reference to the peculiar English view of Indians (in a play about Italians)—a moment to inspire self-reflection: Why are the English so curious about Indians that they would pay a fair amount to see a dead one rather than a small coin to help an invalid.

As the English had worried for centuries over the degeneration of their people in Ireland, so, too, did they worry about the same process occurring in America. The Hermeticists countered this perspective and nowhere more effectively than in de Bry's Virginia volume. The book stamped a Hermetic view upon the Indians as peoples blessed by God. The Natives' primitive culture did not make them inferior to Christians in terms of morality, ingenuity, or relation to the divine, a perception of heathen peoples that Ralegh expanded upon later. The Virginia volume of Hariot's texts, alongside de Bry's engravings of White's paintings, boosted advertisement through Europe of Ralegh and English accomplishments in America. The brilliance of the propaganda lay in implying how spiritually advanced and moral were the English colonizers, who embraced America's peoples to enlarge the body of Christ and to gain greater knowledge of God's Creation, a noble enterprise of redemptive qualities for both Natives and English. Each would gain new knowledge and draw closer to God's design.

Hakluyt, however, was worried. In his dedication to Ralegh of Martyr's *Decades*, he felt it necessary to "exhort" and "admonish" Ralegh to stay the course. God had presented Ralegh the opportunity to colonize Virginia and "new kingdoms over land and sea." Despite Ralegh's assurance in a recent letter, in which he "freely swore that no terrors, no personal losses or misfortunes could or would tear you from the sweet embraces of your own Virginia, that fairest of nymphs," Hakluyt had reason to doubt Ralegh's "constancy." Much was at stake: "the salvation of countless souls," an "imperishable monument of your name and fame" that future ages "will never obliterate." Hakluyt provides no cause to doubt Ralegh's wavering except by reference to the "foolish drones" who "treacherously published ill reports" about Virginia.[33] But we can assume that Hakluyt's concern lay with Ralegh's plan to move to, and colonize, Ireland.

It would have been inappropriate for Hakluyt to criticize in print the queen's plans to settle the province of Munster with English colonists or Ralegh's role as the most significant planter of Irish land. A rueful Hakluyt wrote to Ralegh from Paris before publishing the dedication, which he had sent to him earlier, perhaps for vetting, "I heare nothinge from you of the acceptation of my dedication of that noble historie of the eight decades of Peter Martyr, which wil cost mee fortie french crownes, and five monethes travayle [labor]." To provide an excuse for again writing, Hakluyt claimed he wanted to learn whether "her majestie have of late advanced" you, for "I wold be gladde to be acquainted with your title, and if there be any thinge else that you wold have mentioned in the epistle dedicatorie, you shal doe wel to let mee understand of yt betymes."[34] We do not know whether Ralegh replied, but we do know he was busy planning colonization of Ireland. How mundane colonization of Ireland must have seemed to Hakluyt when Ralegh had the chance not only to colonize America but also to open English trade with China. The romance, the imperative, the regeneration of individuals and the nation, the creation of a universal monarchy that would augment a new Golden Age to benefit the entire world, the fulfillment of spiritual and material needs by crossing oceans to colonize continents—all these awaited Ralegh's lead.

The English gave a lot of thought to colonizing Ireland, much more than they gave to America. For one thing, Ireland was familiar, practically next door, and the English were much less sure of what to expect of America. Second, a lot more was at stake in immediately colonizing the Emerald Isle, whereas America represented a long-term solution to English problems of overpopulation and lack of natural resources; Ireland related to their survival over the next few years. The circumstances of colonizing Ireland required a different application of English energy, planning, and conceptualization than did the colonizing of America, though both projects emerged from the same imperative of countering Spanish wealth and power. In Ireland, England hoped to harness Irish resources, but it also had to keep Spain out of Ireland.

By 1586, in the aftermath of Drake's foray through the West Indies, the English knew that war was imminent and that Spain intended to invade and conquer England, perhaps by first conquering part of Ireland. To forestall invasion, in April 1587, the queen sent Drake on a raid of the Iberian coast to destroy Spanish and Portuguese shipping. Over one hundred ships were sunk or captured, with the *pièce de résistance* the taking of the *São Filipe* near the Azores— its cargo assessed at over £100,000. The English had no doubt that the Spanish would rebuild the fleet to attempt to conquer England, so Elizabeth and her councilors pushed ahead with the colonization of southeast Ireland to prevent Spanish occupation that would allow Spain to launch an invasion of England from so close a location. While John White led Ralegh's colonists to Virginia, and Spain prepared to invade England, Sir Walter Ralegh undertook the colonization of the Munster Plantation.

PART SIX

Fictions of Colonization

"Re-peopling" Munster

CHAPTER 14

Planning the Munster Plantation

I n the aftermath of the Second Desmond War, the queen's Privy Council prepared England's first modern scheme of colonization.[1] Unlike the Virginia colony, a proprietary colony that lay almost entirely in the hands of Ralegh, the Munster Plantation was a royal colony established and directed by the monarch. Elizabeth held the power of sovereignty, which gave her the right to confiscate the lands of those who rebelled against her. When noble landowners of Munster committed treason, many people of their clan lost their land. Only those who possessed enough status within a clan to claim ownership through earlier (written) conveyances by the clan leader held onto their land.

The transition from Anglo-Irish and Irish ownership and occupancy to English ownership and occupancy was riddled with fictions. To begin: Elizabeth operated under an illusion that the Irish no longer existed on the lands the English intended to settle. She believed that most Munster Irish had died or abandoned the region during the Second Desmond War. Her government's planning excluded Irish who might wish to live in the colony: no English could employ Irish. This was done to achieve the centuries-old goal of keeping English and Irish physically separated so that English would not become culturally Irish.

The illusory disappearance of Irish in Munster was matched by a series of additional fictions of colonialism. Colonization is a physical process that involves movement of people and transfer of land ownership, but it is also an ethereal process—a set of ideas that the colonizer employs to justify the alterations. In the English colonization of Munster, fiction was piled upon fiction. Not only were the Irish not gone, they had great difficulty identifying the land of traitors. Only the Irish really knew what a tract encompassed, and they generally were unwilling to help the English sort things out. The queen added problems by often changing her mind as to who should lose their land. She granted lands to English, who later learned that the previous landowner had regained their rights to their tracts. The confusion over land—who owned it, where it was located, and how it could be conveyed—was beyond English capabilities to settle according to their own "rational" system of colonization. They responded by creating the fictions that would define the Munster Plantation.

—

EVEN BEFORE RALEGH sent the first expedition to Roanoke, English were champing at the bit to join in the "repeopling" of Munster after the Second Desmond War. The Privy Council collected data, formulated and reformulated plans, and yet, still, in 1585, the queen had "given deaf ears to business." Although the Privy Council began advertising their proposal "for the Re-peopling of Munster," Elizabeth refused to issue grants before a survey of the attainted lands—the tracts seized from traitors—was complete.[2] To replace the Anglo-Irish and Irish traitors, the Privy Council hoped to attract English of credit and character, particularly "the younger sons or brothers of gentlemen, and of the abler sort of yeomen."[3] This included the same two socioeconomic groups that, two decades later, the London Company wished to settle at Jamestown. A third group comprised agricultural laborers, to be drawn from the English working poor, and to be recruited by the most substantial migrants, the "Undertakers," who received the largest plots of land. Because the character of the "meaner sort," the laborers, was of little consequence to the queen and Privy Council, they were barely mentioned in the Privy Council plans for the Munster Plantation, except in terms of the number needed and their duties. The Privy Council assumed that the English would direct the energies of labor to good production; lack of direction would lead to failure.

Many of the elite and yeomanry were "second sons," who could not inherit their father's landed estate in England, which went to the eldest male because of the laws of primogeniture and entail. Ordinarily, the younger sons of gentlemen filled positions in England as clergymen, military officers, lawyers, and merchants. But many eschewed the professions and desired landed estates: Ireland rather than America beckoned in the mid-1580s.

Unlike Ralegh's Virginia, a speculative enterprise on a largely unknown continent, Ireland seemed more of an extension of England. Virginia was exotic, distant, and unknown. In the 1580s, given the choice, many men of substance, and the poorer sort, too, chose Ireland over Roanoke. (Many would choose northern Ireland over America in the seventeenth century as well.) Munster had the advantage of offering fertile land propinquous to the Irish Sea and English markets. Prospective settlers were assured, even though mistakenly, that the Irish had abandoned their lands, and there were no dangerous Indians to contend with, as there were in Virginia. As a colonial enterprise, America was experimental, whereas English had migrated to the Emerald Isle for hundreds of years. The circumstances had changed in that the Munster Plantation was supposed to involve intensive colonization on a grand scale outside the Pale. If the adventure failed, they could return to England. In the event, the Munster Plantation did not draw the large numbers of migrants that the English government expected. Hopes in the first decade of colonization ranged from an ideal population of roughly eleven to twenty-five thousand English settlers, but reached only about four thousand by 1598.[4]

Elizabeth colonized Munster with the seignory system based on a medieval model. Over seventy years after the establishment of Munster Plantation, the proprietors of the Carolina colony would use the same land system, including the granting of baronies of twelve thousand acres. We often forget that colonies in Ireland and America were largely designed to replicate medieval society, albeit with a Humanist sensibility of improvement.

Thirty-five of eighty-five petitioners received grants from the queen of up to twelve thousand acres each, though most received far less and Ralegh received far more. The recipients were called Undertakers. The largest grants were referred to as seignories and were designed to create lords of the manors with considerable legal power over tenants but much less power over those who held their land in fee simple, the highest form of ownership. Most settlers in Munster received their land from the Undertakers, to whom they owed rents and service, depending on the terms of the agreement. Colonists were expected to assume the same socioeconomic status they held in England. Tenants in England would become tenants in Ireland. Those of higher status would negotiate freeholds. Substantial tenants held their land for their life-time, and when they died, the parcel passed to the next heir. There was also a copyhold for life in which the tenant held the parcel for their lifetime, with two recipients held in reserve for after their death, a son and a grandson. After the third inheritor, the parcel would return to the lord of the manor. Lower-level tenants were termed cottagers and held their land on a yearly basis. They lacked the security of multiple-lifetime leases for their families, but they also possessed mobility, allow-ing them to obtain better yearly arrangements. The shortness of their leases made them much less likely to improve building structures.

The Undertakers like Ralegh recruited the substantial colonists, and lessees were responsible for bringing their own laborers, but the English government assisted in the endeavor by offering its own in-ducements to prospective settlers. Planters received relief from taxes owed to the queen.[5] They also were excused from paying duties on goods transported from England to Ireland for five years.[6] They re-ceived various customs privileges to any country in "amity with Her Highness."[7] Moreover, when it was reported that freight charges were inordinately high for the colonists coming out of England, the Privy Council regulated these in the migrants' favor.[8] Colonists were also promised some respite from military service, including the guaran-tee they could not be forced to leave the province of Munster except in cases of foreign invasion, when they would receive pay from the queen.[9] With colonists expected to provide military service for only brief terms, essentially in their own communities, the queen promised to provide garrisons to defend the settlers, with captains who "shall be sympathetic with this plantation."[10]

Ralegh was responsible for recruitment of male colonists for his seignories. (The men were expected to bring their families.) An expe-rienced recruiter, he had filled drafts for military service in Ireland. He raised troops from his home county of Devon, but bore even more responsibility for the neighboring county of Cornwall, where he was appointed by the queen as lord lieutenant. Recruits from South West England generally served in the southeast of Ireland, and, even be-fore colonization of Munster, there was some expectation or hope that those who served would re-up for continued service or remain in Ire-land as settlers. A significant number of Ralegh's colonists were former soldiers who were settled together. The Privy Council hoped to group colonists together from their home parishes because they would better "cohabit" if drawn from the same shire or county or, even better, from the same "neighbourhood, familiarity, or alliance among themselves." The "men-servants" and "maid-servants," the Privy Council directed, should also be brought from home so as not to lead the planters to employ Irish in these positions.[11] Ralegh made grants to men from London and elsewhere in England, but most of his colonists were from the South West, many of whom he knew through military service, pirating, and the Roanoke enterprise.

Government planning for Munster included detailed estimates for expenses to be borne by the colonists. The Privy Council wanted to make sure that settlers understood what lay before them, because earlier grantees of land in other parts of Ireland often never took up their claim or abandoned the effort after a brief attempt. Undertakers who failed to sufficiently settle their Munster seignories would have their land revert to the Crown. Significant outlays of money were expected for the first year of settlement, offset by the prospect of obtaining productive land at little or no cost. A gentleman needed £275 for the first year, a farmer (yeoman) £70, a copyholder £28 12s. 8d., and a cottager £6 4s. 8d. Considering that a skilled laborer in England earned about £15 yearly, start-up costs were high for those who did not come from wealthy landed or mercantile families. Even the potential cottager could have trouble because the amount needed approached a half year's earned income in England.[12] Those who migrated without capital became farm laborers, lured by the prospect of steady employment in a rising place.

The Privy Council's estimates of capitalization costs came from Ralegh's cousin George Carew. Out of many cousins, Ralegh might have been closest with Carew. They shared a love of history, colonization, and service to the queen. Carew's knowledge and skills were much appreciated by the monarch and Privy Council. They relied on him for decades for his knowledge of Irish affairs, and he received government appointments as President of Munster, Master of Ordnance, and was raised to the nobility by King James I, becoming a baron and then an earl. In 1585, while Ralegh planned Roanoke, Carew presented the Privy Council with the blueprint for necessary planter expenses for their Munster estates. These figures covered the costs of human labor, animals, and planting, defining what settlers should bring or could expect to receive from their employers. The Munster Plantation was intended to be an agricultural enterprise that invested heavily in livestock that could be exported to England. The small farmers would provide crops to support their larger neighbors. Though sheep were emphasized, the English government hoped the colonists would continue the Irish tradition of shipping cowhides to England—which had fallen to insignificance with the Second Desmond War.

Ralegh's elder half brother Adrian Gilbert, who became a colonist in Ireland, provided Ralegh a variety of supplies to take to Munster. Since Ralegh did not intend to personally operate agricultural units, these were likely for him to sell to his farmers or tenants. The items included ten cows and a bull (valued at £36 13s.), eight oxen (£40), ironsmith tools (£30), and "special fruit" trees (£8 6s. 5d.).[13] We will return to the special fruit trees and to nonagricultural labor as well, but it is worth noting here that in the Privy Council's plans for the Munster Plantation almost no thought was given to nontraditional agriculture and to nonagricultural production. Unlike Virginia, which could supply crops not produced in England, Ireland's economy was expected to imitate England's.

The largest seignories, consisting of 12,000 acres, were intended to support ninety-two families, not including the Undertaker. Twelve families privileged with grants of 300 or 400 acres would be joined by 42 copyholders of only 100 acres each and "inferior tenants in smaller lots on which at least 36 families must be settled."[14] Since these 36 families were apportioned in total 1,500 acres, the inferior sort would receive on average 40 acres, a tenth of what a yeoman received, but an amount deemed the minimum necessary for supporting a family. (The 40-acre minimum likewise was often thought the necessary minimum in colonial America.) The number of 92 families actually understates the whole: The 12 largest farmers and freeholders were expected to employ 36 adults and 24 children. The Undertaker himself was to retain for his own use 2,100 acres (17.5 percent of a full seignory)—the demesne, which comprised his castle and surrounding lands. He was expected to employ 10 adults and 2 children, hardly enough to cultivate the land and care for the livestock on such a large agricultural unit. Perhaps the Privy Council expected the Undertakers to draw on the labor of their tenants to supplement those devoted to the demesne. In Ralegh's case, he did not show any intent to develop his multiple demesnes—he had several because of the extraordinary size of the grant he received from the queen—and instead he leased or otherwise conveyed the rights to others to farm his principal tracts. All told, each full seignory was expected to have a population of around 230 adults plus children. Very few Undertakers—a little over a dozen—received a full seignory. And of those, Ralegh was one of the few to quickly send over settlers. But he had the skills to recruit and colonize, and the government expected him to lead the way.

The Munster Plantation, generally, could not be peopled until surveyors identified the parcels of land that reverted to the queen for granting to the English. To this end, the queen sent surveyors to Ireland to document the areas in rebellion during the Desmond Wars, which included land in counties Limerick, Tipperary, Waterford, Cork, Kerry, Dublin, and Kilkenny. She charged the surveyors with recording all ploughlands of those attainted with rebellion. In the medieval era, a ploughland sometimes signified the amount of land an ox or team of oxen could till over a certain period of time, but there really was no standard size or agreement on the character of a ploughland. A rough estimate is 80 to 150 cultivable acres. In Ireland, virtually all agricultural estates were named and contained a varying number of ploughlands, ordinarily one to three, though the largest estates contained a dozen or more. The surveyors' task was to identify the names of estates and the number of associated ploughlands, and who owned the estate at the time of the Desmond Rebellions—the queen needed to know precisely which lands she possessed from the rebels. Only two of the surveys survived into the twentieth century, the Peyton (1584–1586) and Desmond (1586). Housed in the Irish Public Record Office, most were destroyed by fire during the Irish Civil War in 1922, but a detailed copy of the Peyton survived and a portion of the Desmond. The Peyton Survey covered Great and Small Limerick, while the Desmond covered Limerick, Kerry, Cork, Waterford, Tipperary, Dublin, and Kilkenny.[15] Work on the Desmond Survey, which included the lands granted to Ralegh, began in August 1584 and was completed in October 1586. (In other words, the survey took place at the precise time Ralegh sent his three expeditions to America to assess the landscape and prepare for colonization.) Over a hundred people joined the initial surveying party on its trek through Munster. No doubt many were scouting out potential ploughlands to claim. The English government covered the cost of the party, an expensive proposition, but they much wanted substantial English to put in claims. Ralegh did not join the survey party. He did not need to because he already knew precisely which tracts he wanted. The queen's favorite had no worry about competitors, and he began sending colonists to his seignories even before Elizabeth had granted him the land.[16]

One of the biggest problems the surveyors faced was identifying the tracts, which almost always had Gaelic names. These names dated back many hundreds of years, and most survive to the present day, though some tracts have since been divided.[17] With so many locals fled or dead from the Desmond Wars, the surveyors claimed they were hard-pressed to find people to help them identify the tracts and their owners at the time of rebellion; perhaps the locals just hid from the surveyors. Only in parts of Limerick did the surveyors have a guide to provide this crucial assistance. Despite English intent to bring order and efficiency to this epic colonization scheme that transferred ownership of a huge part of Ireland from one group of people to another, the process was messy and took decades to complete.

The English system required a proper paper trail designating who owned specific plots of land. Finding the names of tracts proved a problem, as did the contours of each. The Irish system was based on the name of a tract, whereas the English system was predicated on exact measurements, or at least identification of landmarks to distinguish one tract from the next. But the surveyors of Munster could not depict the tracts in a meaningful English fashion; they had neither the time to define nor the time to measure the parcels of land. Instead, they resorted to the Gaelic names, whose boundaries were defined by tradition, and, hopefully for the English, buttressed by the contours of the land. The surveyors made wild guesses as to how many acres each tract possessed; it is clear that they did not examine each tract's boundaries. Colonization was constructed upon fictions, and nowhere is this more apparent than in the creation of new land systems.

The English government accepted the imperfect nature of the surveys and proceeded anyway. They expected future surveyors to make more perfect renderings of the ploughlands.[18] Contrary to the historiography, which accepts English claims that their system of landholding and grants was precise so that the number of acres listed in a tract was generally, perhaps universally, perceived as a "truth," the English had almost no concern with how much acreage an individual actually received because no one knew! Measuring the parcels was impossible, and no one could be sure whether parcels granted were correctly identified and where their borders were located. The great irony is not that the Privy Council fell short in its plan to totally make over Munster into an English land system that granted titles to measured or otherwise well-defined parcels but that the English retained the ancient Irish system for defining units of land by the Gaelic names of amorphously designated ploughlands. And the ploughlands indeed were amorphous. The surveyors found them overgrown and indeterminate.[19]

In other words, the colonization of Munster saw the replacement of the Irish system . . . with the Irish system. The English liked to think they were modernizing Ireland, rationalizing its land system, but, if anything, the tracts were less well defined. Moreover, multiple claimants to the same pieces of land frequently occurred because the surveys were so bad and the queen often changed her mind, giving tracts she had granted to English back to the Anglo-Irish or Irish owners. The English often simply refused to comply.

Tradition—Irish tradition—had to be relied on through the years to determine the boundary between one ploughland and the next, and even one large estate and the next. Probably, English grantees, unsure what they actually possessed, invented claims to their vaguely defined tracts. What a tract ultimately comprised was left to tradition. Local juries of English, Irish, and Anglo-Irish determined the contours of tracts in disputes, and they relied on hearsay and traditional knowledge, keeping alive the Gaelic names and the old way of life that was no longer supposed to have relevance. Even today, over four hundred years later, many of the original tract names survive in Ireland.

English colonialism sat upon concepts of land ownership and usage that amounted to legal fictions insomuch as the English could not meet their own terms, and they denied the colonized people their land rights for not meeting those same terms, rules, and concepts. For instance, the English often denied Irish and Anglo-Irish their rights to land in Munster by saying that all the tracts belonged to attainted estates and not to these "lesser" individuals who lived on and farmed the tracts. These people had to produce legal documents proving ownership, which they usually could not, so their land was taken from them. The lands of the attainted nobility also were confiscated, though the English did not necessarily have proper paper descriptions of the tracts, and much of the land might indeed have been granted to Irish and Anglo-Irish by the lords, as the occupants claimed. So, the English confiscated tracts defined by oral tradition and refused claims of others based on oral tradition. Then they relied on oral tradition to define the land and to settle disputes.

Ralegh understood the problem of identifiable tracts, hence his desire to have all his many parcels contiguous so borders between tracts would not be as important. The queen expressly granted the Undertakers *all land between tracts in their seignories*, which helped them circumvent the problem of ill-defined parcels. If a grantee owned contiguous estates, he could define the boundaries of each. Thomas

Hariot was certainly aware of the problem of tracts not being mea-sured—when he redid surveyor Arthur Robyns's map of Ralegh's In-chiquin tract, which included Hariot's parcels, he included a depiction of a drafting compass alongside a table for measuring the tracts. If no one else cared about precision, or had the means to be precise in mea-suring the tracts, Hariot certainly did. Hariot's papers include scraps showing the method and mathematics he used for figuring out the size of an island Ralegh granted him in the Blackwater River, and we might assume that he and White provided similar descriptions of the land for the incoming colonists, who then had their leases signed by Ralegh.[20]

Arthur Robyns's official surveys of Ralegh's land were among the last he made, but they likely are indicative of all his surveying work in some regard. Most tracts were left unidentified on the surviving maps, though Robyns listed many in the cartouche with inclusion of their ploughlands. The only tracts Robyns actually outlined on the map of the northern portion of Ralegh's seignories, showing their approximate location, were those that Anglo-Irish claimed. In other words, he noted the location only of tracts Ralegh might *not* be granted. (In the event, Ralegh received these too.) The written grants by the queen to Ralegh provide an even fuller list of tracts but no real descriptions as to their exact location. The listing was more complete than Robyns's maps, for Ralegh himself identified every possible named estate and ploughland he could claim as existing in the contours of his seignories, attempting to leave virtually nothing to chance, so that no one could later put in a claim to a parcel in the midst of the others. That he largely accom-plished his goal is rather remarkable, displaying his ability to get locals to help him identify the approximately 150 Gaelic-named tracts. Locals likely helped him render the Gaelic names phonetically in English, to add clarity to the legal documents that gave him ownership.

Fortunately for Ralegh, Thomas Hariot was expert in producing the kinds of documents that Ralegh used to buttress his claims. Maps were one form of documentation, like the grants, that created illu-sions of reality that could be employed to assure others of the facts. In the coming years, mapmakers produced maps of Ireland, colorful and majestic, often of Munster, with the names of the Undertakers, like Ralegh, sketched in to show their domains and English success.[21] Whether the Undertakers' names were placed in the correct locations or they actually had settled their lands with any success was hardly a consideration. Production of these maps substituted for a reality that the Privy Council and other English wanted to believe: that Ireland could be made over by willing the transformation into existence.

Robyns's and Hariot's maps were less dreamy because they homed in on portions of the Ralegh seignories, not only labeling potential Anglo-Irish landowners within his domain but also those on his borders, further evidence, supported by reams of documents, that many Anglo-Irish retained their lands in Munster despite the queen's belief that they were all gone. Desmonds, Roches, and Condons all held sizable chunks of land and were Ralegh's neighbors. These maps, unlike those published for popular consumption, had a more practical purpose: to represent the landscape for purposes of receiving grants from the queen (the northern maps) and to detail what he had received on the portions of the Inchiquin barony and the location of Molana Abbey and adjacent tracts (the southern map). Hariot's representation of the Inchiquin barony was more detailed than Robyn's mapping of the northern portion of Ralegh's grant. Hariot included marshes, waterways, and significant manor houses and castles. Ralegh required his own maps to illustrate the queen's written grants of land—evidence in case there were later disputes.

Ralegh received the tracts he wanted and could use them as he pleased. As the queen's favorite, he likely was the only grantee who had no restrictions placed on his use of the land. His economic plan for his seignories is discussed in greater detail below, but in brief outline: the Inchiquin barony would be used for agricultural production. This area offered easy access to Youghal, Cork City, and the Atlantic Ocean via the Irish Sea. With Youghal and Cork so close, and the land not quite as good as that to the north, I suspect that the farmers were expected to produce market vegetables for the urban population. In contrast, Ralegh's lands on the northern reaches of his seignories along the Bride and Blackwater Rivers, which also easily connected to the Atlantic through Youghal, had even better soils for pasturage and farming and contained massive stands of trees. The northern portion also lay close to other English seignories, and Irish neighbors who could be drawn on for trade and labor (despite the queen's restrictions). Ralegh intended these lands to be the engine for not just his seignories' economic development but the entire region to the west and northwest. It should also be noted that the Knockmealdown Mountains framed his seignories on the northeast, providing a modicum of defense from attack in case of rebellion in the north. Ralegh's intent was to control the entire contiguous area from the mountains to the coast. His connection to the queen gave him first choice of lands in the Munster Plantation, and even though Elizabeth delayed issuing grants until the surveys were complete, and Ralegh's lands were among the last surveyed, that did not prevent him and other favorites from preparing settlement on the tracts she had promised.

Sealed grants from the queen and surveys and maps of the land by the queen's surveyors did not create an entirely new reality of land ownership in Munster. Despite the ostensible sanctity of a sealed grant from the queen, many of the new owners found that they might not in fact own the tracts they were granted and had settled. English officials in Ireland, including the lord deputy, tried to settle overlapping claims of English claimants, but the loser in a dispute often petitioned for redress from the Privy Council.[22] One notable case of this sort, and by no means the only one, involved Patrick Condon, Ralegh's neighbor in County Cork. Condon had been a rebel in the First Desmond War, then changed sides in the Second. Ralegh once considered him a threat to the English, but not a great one, and Condon had proved his loyalty to the English government and had his name removed from the attainted list—an action strongly opposed by the Irish Parliament. English administrators in Ireland lobbied the Privy Council for Condon's re-attaintment, providing documentation that he had led the sacking of Youghal in 1582/83, an act, they argued, for which he should never be forgiven.[23] But Elizabeth had a long history of pardoning elites who later proved their loyalty, and Condon gained a strong supporter in Ralegh.

Condon was supposed to have all his lands restored, but much remained in the hands of Arthur Hyde, who held positions in the English government in Ireland. Despite the Privy Council's almost unfailing support for Condon against its own appointees in Ireland, Condon did not receive all his lands in his lifetime—a story we return to in pages to come. Still, Anglo-Irish of substance like Condon were extremely important to the Privy Council, which saw elites as necessary for ensuring the good governance of the common folk. If the Irish remained at peace, then the cost of administering Ireland would be drastically reduced. Although Irish were banned from working for English on the Munster Plantation, they could legally work on land leased from Irish or Anglo-Irish who had retained their lands, such as Patrick Condon and Lord Roche. Without this outlet to earn their subsistence, it was assumed they would rebel. Better to have the loyal Anglo-Irish elite maintain order among the "meaner sort" than to have these people illicitly working for the English or becoming rebels. Nonetheless, historian Michael MacCarthy-Morrogh estimates that by "1611 about one-third of the whole plantation area [of Munster] had been returned to local inhabitants."[24]

In those cases where the queen supported the claims of rebels restored to favor, the English government had great difficulty forcing compliance by their administrators in Ireland. Tension characterized the relationships between the English government and its administrators in Ireland, particularly with the lord deputy. The latter and his minions commonly disregarded orders, especially where the attainment and incarceration of Irish were concerned. The detainment of one complainant, Maurice Fitz-Gerald, for eight months against the home government's intentions was indicative of the leverage Her Majesty's administrators possessed. England had difficulty recruiting top men for service in Ireland—a seemingly thankless job—and allowed them to get away with murder, literally, when men died in prison despite the home government's orders for their release.[25] If the queen punished her appointees, she risked alienating others from taking their places.

The lord deputy, the president of Munster, and others received much instruction and cajoling from Queen Elizabeth to both help the Undertakers and to ensure justice for loyal Anglo-Irish and Irish. As the planters began arriving in Ireland, the Privy Council sent letters to chief officials in Ireland and Munster province. The queen thanked the latter for helping the "Undertakers and their associates," but with subtle sarcasm she "required them to continue the like dysposicion and favour towardes them as they had begonn."[26] Some of the tensions with the Undertakers stemmed from the privileged position they enjoyed in receiving their grants and choosing their land. The Crown's appointees often competed with the Undertakers for tracts. Lord Deputy John Perrot, for instance, the highest English official in Ireland, complained about Ralegh obtaining more than the maximum one seignory. Ralegh and Perrot had a history of hostility. Both were confined to Fleet Prison in early 1580 for attempting to duel. (Ralegh would again be confined a few months later for another fray.)[27] Ralegh scorned Perrot's "impertinent objections" to his receiving a grant of three and a half seignories. If Perrot thought his status as lord deputy would carry weight with the queen, he was mistaken. Lord Burghley advised Perrot to keep his thoughts to himself, because Ralegh "is able to do you more harm in one hour than we are all able to do you good in a year." Perrot was not one to hold his tongue and complained to Walsingham of the queen revoking a patent to his son in favor of Ralegh. Perrot would be disappointed with the outcome.[28]

Perrot's complaint about Ralegh getting more than the maximum allotment of land arose because his own family had been victimized. English jealousies were compounded by the commoner Ralegh receiving so many favors from the queen. The court operated on patronage, as did courts and governments throughout Europe. If there was a difference in England, it was the burgeoning opposition to the granting of monopolies, which came under attack in Parliament in the 1590s. (Ralegh had incited envy when he was granted the monopoly for issuing licenses to sell wine in 1583.) Trade monopolies especially raised envy. There was growing opposition to the privileges granted to companies and individuals trading overseas. Little argument could be made against the queen's granting of Virginia to Ralegh because the Crown, not England, possessed sovereignty in overseas lands. But Perrot and others had cause for complaint against Ralegh's privileged position as the queen's favorite in Ireland because the Munster Plantation was presented by the Privy Council as a "project" of the English nation— all were invited to join as colonists in a rationalized transformation of southern Ireland.

Unlike the sporadic and haphazard planting of the past, the seignories were laid out in a rational (if fictional) manner with rules and regulations, limits and encouragements, privileges and responsibilities defined for all. Just as monopolies became antithetical to the rationalization of government under way in 1590s England, and in subsequent centuries, the privileging of favorites like Ralegh undermined England's plan to transform Ireland, at least in terms of morale. It revealed hypocrisy and weakness in English government designs to create a society based on (English) law and fairness. Potential long-term adverse effects were not seen. Ralegh received so much land and land so advantageously placed, and with special privileges, that he had the potential to dominate the region as his predecessors the Desmonds had done. That Ralegh failed to do so is a story that future chapters relate, but his successor, Richard Boyle, succeeded, rising to become the Earl of Cork, the richest man in Ireland. He would dominate the region in ways not envisioned by the queen and Privy Council when they created the Munster Plantation.[29]

In the Undertakers, the Privy Council hoped to create a class of land barons that would oversee the orderly remaking of Ireland in England's image. It was probably thought that a few men like Ralegh and

Sir Christopher Hatton, another of the queen's favorites, should rise to the top of Ireland's landed class as men deserving of the highest status, hence their land grants extending beyond the specified limit of one seignory. Over the centuries, England had both feared and supported the great families of Ireland that fought with one another in endemic wars while also administering Ireland for the English monarchs. Ireland still possessed high nobility at the time of the settlement of the Munster Plantation. The "flight of the earls" that occurred at the end of Elizabeth's reign had yet to take place, when much of the remaining elite Irish leadership, particularly from the north, fled to the European continent. The Crown looked to the elite to maintain order in society but also worried those same elites might challenge the Crown's authority or fight one another. The law bound all to good behavior, though privilege existed within the legal system, stemming from blood or influence. The queen and Privy Council wanted all to live by laws, rules, and regulations, but they were happy to operate in gray areas because they believed that societal success depended on talented individuals like Ralegh, who transcended categories of blood because of the special favor of the queen and his own talents. Nonetheless, as Ralegh took on a greater and more public role, concerns about the quality of his blood had to be allayed.

CHAPTER 15

Bloodlines

Captain Ralegh and the Desmonds

As Ralegh grew in prominence, it behooved the government to show publicly that Ralegh deserved the queen's favor and the multiple command appointments he received. John Hooker, who might have been a relation of Ralegh, was called on to recount Ralegh's life for a new edition of Holinshed's *Chronicles*. This popular history of England, Scotland, and Ireland was first published in 1577. Hooker was added to the team of authors who wrote the second edition of *Chronicles*, published in 1587. Although not all Elizabethans accepted the scholarship unquestioned, the second edition was highly influential, inspiring Shakespeare's *Macbeth* and *King Lear* and providing standard reading and reference for educated English well into the next century.

Hooker's assignment for the three-volume work was Ireland, where he had spent time during the First Desmond War. He provided details of both Desmond Wars and their causes. He dedicates his contribution on Ireland to Ralegh, who by 1585 had become one of the most important Englishmen to have served in the wars and who was one of the queen's great favorites, as evidenced by his patent to colonize in America. It is possible that Hooker intended the dedication as a gift to Ralegh for previous patronage or, more usual with such dedications, in hope of receiving patronage. After the book's publication, Ralegh made Hooker steward of his estate at Bradninch. (He already held appointment as coroner of Exeter.)

Yet, judging from the manner in which Hooker details both Ralegh's military career and his family history, it is likely that someone else urged Hooker to write about Ralegh. Hooker's rhetoric displays a twofold purpose: he justifies the queen's selection of Ralegh as her favorite, demonstrating whereby people owed him obedience; yet he constantly reminds Ralegh that he must live up to his responsibilities. It is unlikely that Ralegh was enthralled by these reminders or the descriptions of the shortcomings of his ancestors that led to the decline of his family. Lord Burghley was the most likely source for Hooker's literary strategies, because he was the one most concerned with reassuring the English that Ralegh deserved the appointments and rewards he received from the queen.

What makes Hooker's stories even more fascinating is how they couple the failures of Ralegh's ancestors with the degeneration of the Desmonds in Ireland. After centuries of honorable service to the monarch, the Ralegh family, of noble blood, had gone bad—just as the Desmonds had in the 1560s. Ralegh, however, was restoring honor to his house. His story showed that those of noble blood can ultimately achieve redemption.

—

HOOKER PROBABLY RECEIVED the stories he tells of Ralegh's heroism from the courtier, either in person or more likely by written account. Given my belief that Burghley was behind Hooker's popularizing of Ralegh's story, I envision the elder statesman directing Ralegh to write an account of his heroics in Ireland for Hooker to use. Hooker depicted a resourceful and brave Captain Ralegh. In one telling incident, determined to seize Lord David Roche, Ralegh headed late in the evening for the man's castle, Ballie in Harsh, twenty miles from Cork, along the way outwitting an army eight times the size of his forces, then outmaneuvering another group five times the number of his men, before talking his way inside Roche's castle. After delivering "some speeches," and by "devises and meanes, that little by little, and by some and some," he finagled passage through an iron gate and gained entry for "all his men." Lord Roche then entertained Ralegh's men with dinner before Ralegh told him why he had come: "that he and his wife were accused to be traitors," and that he was commissioned to take them to Cork. A fearful Roche agreed to go. In the dead of night, through hostile territory, Ralegh and his men safely escorted their captives to Cork, where Ralegh met "with no little admiration that he had escaped so dangerous a journie, being verelie supposed . . . that he could never have escaped." An important postscript to the story relates that Roche "did so well answer himself, that in the end he was acquited, and taken for a true and a good subject," both then and in the future, "with three of his sons . . . [subsequently] killed by the enemie in hir majesties service."[1]

Whatever the truth of the details of the story, the implication was that Ralegh's ability to avoid hostilities in the capture and delivery of Roche, who was inclined to the English, prevented what could have been an unfortunate break between the English and this Anglo-Irish leader and his people. Indeed, Ralegh had argued in letters to the government that success in Munster hinged on the English establishing their authority to end the constant wavering of local leaders.[2] Violence could have toppled good intentions on both sides. Ralegh's skills and steadfastness of purpose had secured to the English a valuable Munster aristocrat.

Before returning to Hooker's depictions of Ralegh, we should take a closer look at Lord Roche, because he and his family represented those at the top of the second tier of elite landholders, just below the Desmonds and Ormonds in Munster. The Roches were an ancient Anglo-Norman family associated with the lands around Fermoy on the Blackwater River to the west of Lismore Castle. They also frequently filled the office of mayor of Cork City in the Elizabethan era, with at least six different Roches serving. Their "ancient" enemies included the Condons and other elite families with whom they variously intermarried and allied with or against, including the Barrys, the Fitzgibbons, and the Desmonds. In all these families, individual members variously sided with and against the English in the Desmond Wars.

Despite David Roche's marriage to the Earl of Desmond's daughter (and his son's marriage to the earl's niece), he sided with the English against James Fitzmaurice in the Second Desmond War. As noted above, he lost three sons fighting for the English. Yet he and his kin had to receive many pardons from Elizabeth in the 1570s and 1580s. Roche chafed at paying taxes to the Crown and insisted that he had the right to tax his own subjects. Negotiating his loyalty to the Crown was tricky business because disputes with his neighbors persisted regardless of the Desmond Wars. Local disputes entwined with disputes over Crown authority. One lord could attack another in the queen's name, even when the dispute had little or nothing to do with the queen, hence some of the reason for the issuance of multiple pardons to the members of the second-tier families. Of course, some actually "required" pardon because of direct opposition to the queen, but Elizabeth could not imagine a society without its natural-born leaders— she feared leaving the Irish to their own devices without aristocrats to maintain order.

In Lord Roche's case, the family seems generally to have been supportive of the queen, faring well in the Desmond Wars until the Condons, as the conflict wound down, dealt a near devastating military blow that forced Roche to scramble for mercenaries to replace his dead and injured kin and forces. He and his Desmond wife, who were accused of treason by other family members, were again pardoned but died in 1583. Despite their loyalty to the Crown, the new Lord Roche, Maurice, would have to fight to retain his lands from those who thought they should go to the queen as reparations for his father's alleged treasons. The New English remained immensely discontented with the queen's repeated issuance of pardons.

Another of Hooker's stories relates the tale of Ralegh fighting great odds to save his "man," Henry Moyle, which included Ralegh having his horse shot from beneath him while crossing a river, then refusing to abandon his soldier, facing down the enemy, and escaping with his man to safety. The story is likely true in capturing the spirit of events— the escapade in some fashion had occurred. Ralegh and Moyle developed a lifelong relationship, and Moyle became one of Ralegh's key colonists and lieutenants in Ireland. He provided distinguished service to the queen and accepted military appointments wherever he was needed.[3]

Hooker used Ralegh's career as a captain in Ireland to show him as a leader of men who commanded respect from English, Irish, and Anglo-Irish. In one episode, one of Ralegh's men, an Irishman named Patrick Fagen, saved his captain's life. Yet, rather than giving credit to Fagen, Hooker ascribes the credit to Ralegh's "servant," meaning one of his soldiers, "Nicholas Wright a Yorkshire man," who "willed and called to an Irishman there, whose name was Patrike Fagaw [sic], that he should looke to his capteine," while Wright took on six of the enemy and slew one. At Wright's direction, Fagaw rescued Ralegh, just as an "Irish gentleman" arrived, James Fitzrichard, "with his kerne [soldiers] to the rescue of the captain." Fitzrichard's men were slain "and himselfe in danger," when Ralegh beckoned Wright, the overzealous hero eagerly pursuing a party of the enemy and not noticing Fitzrichard's peril: "Wright, if thou be a man, charge above hand & save the gentleman.

Who at his maister's commandment pressed into the middle of the enemies, and slew one of them, and so saved the gentleman."[4]

Fitzrichard, along with his son James Fitz John, both of whom
were Geraldines (the family that included the Desmonds), years later
around 1609 leased the tract Garran from Sir John Fitzgerald. Fitzgerald also had control of Castle Myles, which had been Ralegh's land.[5]
Their stories are further reminders that not all of the Desmonds opposed the queen and that some received portions of the land that
Ralegh was granted by the queen; in some ways Ralegh replaced the
Earl of Desmond as the great landholder of the area, with second-tier
vassals below him, but the big differences lay in the decline of the
warring between vassals and that Ralegh made no attempt to claim
coign and livery. I do not mean to imply that all Irish and Anglo-Irish
preferred Ralegh's overlordship to the Earl of Desmond's, but that
some did, and that some Desmonds allied with the queen, and later
with Ralegh.

Whatever the truth of the story of Fagen and Wright saving Ralegh,
as with other stories in the *Chronicles*, the importance of blood—of
one's class—is of utmost importance. A man must do his duty by his
betters and at their direction. To Hooker, men and women of good blood
can go awry, and then they are all the more dangerous because they can
lead the common folk astray. Commoners, the elite believed, generally
did not possess the ingenuity *not* to follow their betters who had turned
bad. It was as if the common folk were perceived as lacking a moral
compass and thus required direction from the elite. The stout-hearted
Nicholas Wright had to be directed by Ralegh to return to save the gentleman Fitzrichard, just as Wright had to instruct his lesser, Fagen, to
save his master Ralegh. Of course, a larger message in Hooker's stories
concerns Ralegh himself, to whom Hooker in his dedication "wisheth
a long, happie, and a prosperous life, with the increase of honour."
Wright, Fitzrichard, and Fagen all came to Ralegh's aid because he, as
their superior, deserved saving. Ralegh saved his man Moyle at the river
because the "great" bear responsibility for dependents, though no one
would have blamed Ralegh if he had left him. But lesser men had to be
reminded of their duties. That Wright and Fagen stood by their captain
reflects as much on Ralegh as it does on his men: they were well trained
to their duty and saved him because he was worth saving.

Having illustrated Ralegh's fine character and ability to lead, Hooker
informed the English that Ralegh's bloodlines made him worthy of

being followed. Without these bloodlines Ralegh could not possibly deserve standing so high in the queen's estimation.

Ralegh's bloodlines and the story of Ireland in the Desmond Wars held almost equal weight in the lessons Hooker imparted to readers. The Desmond Wars and Irish history served as rationale for Elizabethan colonization of Ireland. To illustrate the proper hierarchy necessary for the peaceful and prosperous functioning of society, Hooker cited Anglo-Irish, like Fitzrichard, and Irish like Fagen, as participants in English colonization who proved their civility in helping their betters. Loyalty to Ralegh was an act of obedience and loyalty to the queen, the ultimate authority under God. But Hooker had to contend with public opinion among many English elites who thought Ralegh unworthy of his station. This sentiment could undermine Elizabeth's authority or, at least, confidence in her judgment. To Ralegh's soldiers, Ralegh had to be respected as a captain in service to the queen, but he also earned respect through his leadership skills and personal character. When Hooker published his work in 1587, Ralegh held an array of appointments that required obedience from the queen's subjects. Gilbert had similarly enjoyed the queen's favor but had earned the right through his renowned military accomplishments. But Gilbert had not stimulated the queen's romantic interest on the scale that Ralegh did, nor was he rewarded with so many financial plums and high offices. This highly public favoritism seemed an ostensible overstepping of bounds that was not faced by the queen's later favorite, Robert Devereux, because he was an earl and thus possessed blood worthy of the queen's affections and rewards.

With many at court and out of court jealous of the commoner who enjoyed the queen's great support, Hooker offered readers a mini-biography of nearly four thousand words as part of the dedication of his portion of the *Chronicles* to Ralegh. It began with genealogy because a man's story begins with his blood. Ralegh's blood justified the queen bestowing her favor upon him and made possible his completing tasks for the queen and providing leadership over others. At the time when Hooker was writing, Ralegh was the single most important symbol of England's intent to colonize: he had the monopoly on Virginia, and it already was known he would play a chief role in the "planting" of Ireland. If the symbol of colonization was tarnished, how many English would participate in these enterprises? What respect could America or Ireland achieve if led by a man of inferior blood?

Hooker preceded Ralegh's genealogy with one for the Geraldines (the Desmonds), the traitorous family held responsible for the Desmond Wars, descended from Norman nobility, and all "honourable in blood." This is the family whose lands Ralegh would occupy in Ireland. Hooker follows the Geraldine line in Ireland for centuries: "they continued verie honourable, dutifull, & faithfull subjects, for the course of sundrie hundreds of yeares: untill that this brainesick and breakedanse Girald of Desmond, and his brethren, allies, and complictors, forgetting the honour of his house, and forsaking their faith, dutie and alegiance, did break into treasons,"[6] The "brainesick and breakedanse" reach an unhappy end: the earl had his head cut off and "set upon London bridge"; his brother "was hanged as a theefe, quartered as a traitor, and his head and quarters dispersed and set upon the gates and wals of the citie of Corke." Another Desmond had "his head cut off and set upon the castle of Dublin, and his bodie hanged by the heeles at Corke." His son was "disinherited" and placed in the Tower of London; his "wife destituted of all honour and livings, leadeth a dolefull & a miserable life. His capteines, soldiers, and men of warre, put all for the most part to the swoord." Of the common people, those not killed in the war mostly perished from famine. There was "nothing" on Desmond land "to be seene but miserie and desolation."[7]

All these consequences, Hooker assured his readers, were "A notable and rare example of Gods just judgment and severe punishment, upon all such as doo resist and rebell against the higher powers and his annointed." The Desmonds' rebellion against their anointed ruler Elizabeth "is accounted [by God] the greatest [offense] . . . and in the highest degree." Hooker concludes, "For as it is written, Who resisteth against the higher power, resisteth against Gods ordinances, and he shall receive judgement. And the Lord shall root him from out of the face of the earth that shall blaspheme his gods, and curseth the prince of the people." On the other hand, the Lord smiled on His "people" who "live in all subjection, humbleness, and obedience." As an example, "hir majesties good subjects dwelling within the English pale" enjoyed God's "manifold blessings . . . they sow and till the land, and doo reape the fruits." In case readers did not fully understand his point, Hooker reiterated it is "woorthie to be thoroughlie observed . . . God's just judgement against the rebels and traitors, . . . [contrasts with his] mercie and love towards the obedient and dutifull subject."[8]

The Desmonds' mistake was in not following the virtues of their ancestors. Hooker reminds Ralegh that it is "the examples of our ancestors, and the actions of our forefathers" that should guide him "in civill government or in martiall affaires . . . [just as] they drew from the examples of their ancestors before them." Hooker asks Ralegh's pardon for digressing to speak "of your selfe and of your ancestors," but "as I am somewhat acquainted in their descents, let me make bold with you to laie the same down before you." He recounts Ralegh's genealogy, shining light on ancestors "of great honour & nobilitie . . . with the degree of knighthood." Ralegh's male ancestors descended from royalty, Henry I, "And in like maner by your mother you maie be derived out of the same house." Their example must guide Ralegh: "These all were men of great honour and nobilitie, and whose ventures are highlie recorded . . . in the chronicles of England; some greatlie commended for their wisdomes and deepe judgements in matters of counsell, some likewise much praised for their prowesse & valiantness in martiall affaires, and manie of them honored for both."[9]

But something had gone wrong. Over generations, Ralegh's ancestors degenerated, as "the honour became to be of worship," "untill by little and little the honor and estimation of your noble and worthie ancestors seemed at length to be buried in oblivion . . . utterlie forgotten as though it had never beene." But "it pleased God to raise" your name "as it were from the dead . . . and brought you into the good favour of your prince, who hath pleased to reward and honour in you the approved faithfull service of your late ancestors and kindered deceased." Ralegh's ancestors, according to Hooker, had become too full of themselves, forgetting the qualities that made them honorable, but the queen recognized that the essence of their good qualities had survived in his blood.

To avoid his ancestors' fate, Ralegh must always remember his responsibilities. We are "not borne to ourselves alone" in this world, Hooker reminded Ralegh; we owe service to others. The "prince, the countrie, the parents, freends, wives, children and familie," all "claime" an interest in us, and "we must be beneficial" to them, "otherwise we doo degenerate from that communitie and societie." Hooker lectured Ralegh on the need to continue to work hard. He recounts from Ralegh's life those events that prepared him for the service he now performed, his "yeares at Oxford," his spending "a good part of your youth in the warres and martiall services" in France so he could better "serve your prince and commonweale." Then he learned maritime affairs by sailing the seas with brother Sir Humphrey to discover new countries from which they would have obtained "infinit commodities" if a "dangerous sea fight" had not ensued, wherein Ralegh escaped the fate of many others, including Humphrey, who perished at sea. (Hooker conflated the voyages of 1578 and 1583, evincing that Ralegh did not check the stories Hooker wrote of him.) This "was a matter sufficient to have discouraged a man of a right good stomach and value from anie" further sea adventures, yet you "did not give over" and continued to serve your country, making "a plantation of the people of your owne English nation in Virginia, the first English colonie that ever was there planted, to the no little derogation of the glory of the Spaniards." Virginia brought honor to his prince and "benefit" to the "common wealth." The "lost" Natives were to be brought to "the knowledge of the gospel, and a true christian religion." Could there be "a more acceptable service before God?" The Natives can be transformed from their "savage life to a civill governement, neither of which the Spaniards in their conquests have performed." To Virginia, England would send its "frutelesse and idle people" to obtain "infinit commodities."

Here, Hooker's account grows hyperbolic. He affirms that Ralegh's work has been no less difficult than Caesar's! He proceeds in this vein, extolling Ralegh's talents and accomplishments, which would continue to grow because he has "indured so manie crosses," envy, and misfortunes, yet has persevered with God's blessing, and the blessing of the queen, who has "laid upon you the charge of a governement in your owne countrie, where you are to command manie people by your honourable office of the stannerie, and where you are both a judge and chancellor." Nonetheless, Hooker lectures Ralegh to remember that no matter his pedigree from "noble ancestors," and God's blessing of him "with knowledge in learning," he must remain "virtuous, just & good." God has been careful to "restore the house of your decaied forefathers to their ancient honor and nobilitie, which in this later age hath beene obscured." Hooker says: Do not stray from virtue—"be bold and valiant for the defense of your countrie." Follow your ancestors' "steps and examples."[10]

Hooker's elegy was designed to reassure England of the courtier's pedigree and his virtue in God's eyes. The queen's appointment of Ralegh to command men and render judgment in their disputes confirmed her confidence in him. His many accomplishments, especially in Virginia, would redound to the glory of England and the benefit of its people. But more important than Ralegh's story was Hooker's contribution to the story of England in Ireland, for the English government was undertaking a program of colonization alongside of which Virginia paled in comparison. Hooker recited England's history in Ireland to show how the past led to this seminal moment in time. The Desmond Wars of the previous two decades had only recently ended, preparing the way for the next stage of history of England in Ireland. Ralegh's service in the Desmond Wars, a story of immense bravery, when good Irish served English, as Fagan saved his master, coupled with Hooker's dedication of his history of Ireland to Ralegh, evinced for readers what brave English can accomplish among a savage people when those of good blood do their duty and their inferiors heed their charge to obey. The good, wise, and courageous soldier, servant of the queen, Ralegh had proved his worth as a soldier in Ireland and deserved his patent for Virginia and all other offices bestowed upon him. The queen now bid Ralegh lead the way in colonizing Ireland.

CHAPTER 16

Ralegh in Youghal

I n 1587–1588, under the looming threat of invasion by the Spanish Armada, Elizabeth barred all ships from sailing to America, including a relief expedition of seven or eight vessels that Ralegh had prepared and that was to be led by Richard Grenville. Ralegh received permission to send ships only if Drake did not need them all for defense of the realm. Historians have blamed Ralegh for abandoning Roanoke, but, indeed, he sent two ships to the colony: a twenty-five-ton ship to carry John White and a handful of new colonists, and a thirty-ton, likely an escort to convey supplies before going pirating. They left in late April 1588 and immediately went pirating, capturing a Scottish and a Breton ship, taking their cargo, then releasing the men and the ships. The two English vessels then sailed to Madeira, where a French ship chased White's and boarded it. Many died, but White survived. The ship and men were released and sailed home. Ralegh's other ship went home as well, so neither made it to Roanoke, through no fault of Ralegh.

When Ralegh moved to Ireland, he needed someone to look after Virginia. He created a company of sorts composed of nineteen associates who received privileges in Virginia in exchange for administering the colony. But after eighteen months, Ralegh returned to England only to find that nothing had been done and no expedition prepared to relieve and develop Virginia. Ralegh organized a relief expedition, though the queen again barred ships sailing to America with the expectation that Spain would send another armada against England. Ralegh again received special permission for two ships to carry White, new settlers, and supplies. But, though the captains agreed to take White, they refused to take the settlers, perhaps because they intended to go pirating and did not want women and children on board. Departing Plymouth March 20, 1590, they carried cannon to reinforce the colony or, even more likely, the fort at Roanoke, which would be turned into a base for giving succor to English pirates. They presumably would remove the Roanoke colonists to the Chesapeake.

On the way to America, the ships went pirating but nevertheless reached Cape Lookout, North Carolina, in early August. Because of a variety of difficulties, it took another two weeks to reach Roanoke Island. They found no one there. Perhaps one group of colonists had gone to the Chesapeake, while another went to live with the Croatan. It was clear that one or both groups departed hurriedly. They had buried some of their property but only superficially. Indians had dug up the chests and emptied them. The English did not look for the colonists or seek out their Croatan allies. One of the two ships, the *Moonlight*, headed home because many of the men were sick. The other, the *Hopewell*, sailed toward Trinidad to winter, presumably to return to Roanoke in spring. Instead, it, too, sailed for England. Ralegh's colonists never were heard from again. When Jamestown, Virginia, was settled by English in 1607, the colonists heard from local Indians that there had been English living in the area with Indians until the year before, when they were killed.

Ralegh was in the city of Youghal (pronounced "yawl"), three thousand miles from Roanoke. As for other English, Roanoke was only a dream to Ralegh, an abstraction in his mind. But his mental images were more vivid and diverse than most others'. He had White's watercolors. He had Hariot with him. Wanchese and Manteo had lived with him as well. American Indians remained important to him through his life. He developed personal relations with many, and even penned an important ethnography on the Natives of Guiana. Further down the road, at the nadir of his existence in the Tower of London, American Indians kept him company. But at Youghal, the practical aspect of "knowing" Indians was foremost. Although they were in Ireland to colonize, Ralegh and Hariot must have spent much time discussing Virginia, even comparing the two colonizing enterprises in America and Ireland. How could they not? Each involved similar processes and plans: moving people, relations with the Natives, assessing the landscape, and prospects for profitable enterprises. Their eyes were on the future even as they were ignorant of Roanoke's present.

Neither Ralegh nor Hariot, as they smoked in the gardens of Myrtle Grove, Ralegh's new home in Ireland, and prepared propaganda to promote Virginia, knew the fate of Roanoke. While in Ireland, Hariot likely penned and revised his famous tract on Virginia, *A Briefe and True Report*, and he likely took this time to compose and revise the text that accompanied de Bry's engravings of White's paintings. If the propaganda Ralegh generated about America bore fruit, he could obtain more investors and press forward. But for the moment, there was no money to be made at Roanoke save through the pirating that accompanied the resupply expeditions. When Ralegh thought about what actually was happening in Virginia, he probably figured his settlers were in the process of undertaking the mundane tasks, clearing land and sowing seeds, building shelters, and (hopefully) creating harmonious relations with the Indians. The small colony would need time before it could reap financial rewards. To fulfill the terms of his patent, he merely had to effect permanent settlement—and that was under way. Sending more colonists to speed up the process was problematic because Ralegh needed colonists in Ireland. And he needed them immediately. Other Undertakers required the same. The queen and Privy Council indicated they wanted a quick planting by threatening to take away unsettled grants. There could be no hiding of success or failure— everyone would know how Ralegh fared. He not only had the largest area to colonize but the most important, the heart of Desmond land.

It was hoped Ralegh would turn his seignories into the most loyal and productive English plantation. Who better for the queen to choose for the task than the experienced colonizer of Virginia and expert on Ireland who understood the people, physical environment, and political situation in both large and small terms. If he succeeded, others could follow his model, and more English would have a mind to emigrate. The queen and Privy Council had many problems to deal with at once, the threat of Spain, religious troubles in England, and the issue of succession among them. Ireland, too, was a large problem. Many English expected an imminent Spanish invasion of Ireland; Ireland remained a drain on the treasury. If Ralegh and the other Undertakers could quickly plant settlers, it would add to Elizabeth's authority in England, and she would become known as the monarch who had tamed wild Ireland and secured England's backdoor. If Ireland could be made to pay, or at least not lose, England money, then it would be a great accomplishment indeed.

Ralegh's plate was full, hence he did not send White to Roanoke until 1589 to learn the fate of his colony. Maybe Ralegh was short of cash—after all, he was spending what he had on Ireland and doing so without investors, making expensive alterations to Myrtle Grove and probably shouldering a host of expenses to assist the settlers on his seignories. Of course, he needed a fine house to proclaim his greatness to all, to show that he was lord of an estate that should be envied in both England and Ireland. He held a vast domain: Elizabeth had granted him an area of approximately 237 square miles. It was much smaller than what he would possess in Virginia if he fulfilled the terms of his New World patent. But the Irish land was much more valuable, and so much easier to develop.

Virginia mostly existed in the English imagination as part of the unseen universe, whereas Ireland was more easily grasped. Many English knew Ireland. The landscape, real and imagined, was closer to England's than America's. An Irish estate did not carry the caché of a similarly sized estate in England, but in some ways it could be better. The land was fertile and possessed impressive natural resources, as did America's, but its reality was more readily perceived and exploited because it was so close to England. The speed with which Ralegh could reach London from Youghal was roughly analogous to the time it took someone from northern England to reach London, though depending on winds and currents, it could be much quicker or slower. There were negatives from an English perspective: Ireland was inhabited by Irish and settlement might be dangerous, but Ralegh believed, as did other Undertakers, that they would transform the landscape, wrest its riches, and through the planting of English turn Ireland into an extension of England.

—

FROM MYRTLE GROVE, Sir Walter Ralegh held a commanding view over the city of Youghal. Ralegh radically altered the architecture of the structure constructed around 1550, "perhaps even reversing the face of the building." Like other English in Munster, he took an old house and put a new face on it, apparently adding ashlar masonry, gables, chimneys, and moldings and redoing or adding doorways and "multiple-light windows."[1] The Blackwater River flowed in front of him, the port but a five-minute walk downhill. The sea lay about a mile to the east. Myrtle Grove stands very close to St. Mary's Church. The original

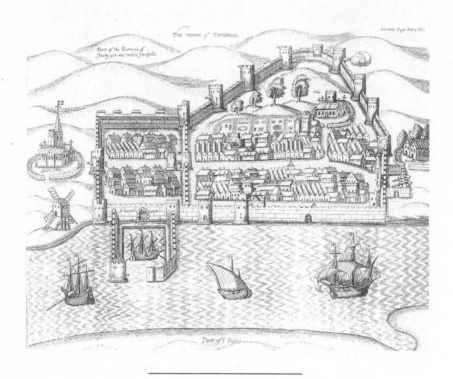

20. Town of Youghal

home, indeed, was likely associated with the church as the warden's home. The thirteenth-century St. Mary's, which still holds services in the twenty-first century, had been taken over by Protestants during the Reformation. On the south side lay St. Mary's College and Gardens. Above the college and gardens and wrapping around the west and north sides of Myrtle Grove were the town walls, most of which, like the house, church, college, and gardens, survive in the present day. From this majestic spot, Ralegh could spy ships entering the port from the wider world. The heart of his domain lay north along the Blackwater and along the Bride River that fed into the Blackwater. Across the bay before him, he had a beautiful view east of the river, an area he would try to gain control of in the coming years. Behind his home, he could ascend to the top of the steep hill and look over his lands, which extended many miles westward toward Cork City. Although not a member of the nobility, Ralegh had a large domain to lord over, prime lands that once belonged to the fifteen earls of Desmond.

Ralegh had never visited his Virginia colony, but at Myrtle Grove he intended to personally oversee the initial settlement of his seignories. Just as he had sent Thomas Hariot and John White to Virginia to record the fauna and flora and report on the people and the economic possibilities, he had brought Hariot and White to Ireland. In Ireland, he did not need them to assess the people, and he knew the landscape better than they. But they provided valuable service mapping and contributing to the legal documents conveying land to the colonists.

Youghal was an excellent choice for Ralegh to situate himself. Besides its ideal location as his seignories' hub close to the ocean, the port is largely protected from Atlantic storms. The town today is an attractive coastal community worthy of a holiday, but for hundreds of years it had been a center of activity that placed it on par with Waterford and Cork, and, in some ways, it was superior. For centuries, Youghal had been a beehive of Christian activity and piety, perhaps more than anywhere else in Ireland. The oldest Christian church in Ireland, now long gone, dated to the fifth century. At an unknown point in the distant past, a small Augustinian church was built near the sea and associated with Saint Coran's Holy Well. Just north of town, on the Blackwater River, lay Molana Abbey, founded in the sixth century on a small island off the west bank. By the end of the eighth century, Vikings had raided the interior, then they settled and built Youghal in the ninth century. Shortly after the Anglo-Norman conquest, Robert Fitzstephen received a charter from King John and rebuilt the Viking town. His half brother, Maurice Fitzgerald, the progenitor of the earls of Desmond, inherited Youghal from his brother and, beginning with him, the Desmonds, Youghal, and Christian institutions became thoroughly enmeshed for the next 350 years. The Desmonds sponsored the building of Ireland's first Franciscan monastery and a Dominican monastery, adjacent to and outside the town walls on the south and north sides.[2] Knights Templar followed by constructing Templemichael, with a preceptor overlooking Molana Abbey and additional buildings at nearby Rincrew overlooking Youghal from the north.

Youghal was a destination for pilgrims to visit Saint Coran's Holy Well, Molana Abbey, and the Franciscan monastery, which housed the small ivory carving "Our Lady of the Graces," with which several miracles were associated.[3] (The carving is currently housed at the Franciscan monastery in Cork City.) When Templemichael went into decline with England's suppression of the Knights Templar in the early fourteenth century, the site was granted to their rivals, the Knights of Saint John, though it is unclear whether the order used the buildings and lands. This transference seems to have had little impact on the vitality of the other religious institutions in the area. In the mid-fifteenth century, the 7th Earl of Desmond, Thomas Fitzgerald, established Saint Mary's Collegiate Church to train seminarians, by which time the nunneries associated with the Franciscans and Dominicans also seem to have been established. The erection of the Collegiate Church may have been directly related to scandals that rocked Molana Abbey in the 1450s. After the abbot, John McInery, was removed on various charges of malfeasance, the pope granted indulgences in 1462 to pilgrims who helped repair the abbey. The Fitzgeralds might have played a role behind the scenes in restoring the abbey's reputation, for in that same year Thomas, who was appointed Lord Deputy of Ireland, succeeded not only in having Youghal granted privileges as a royal port and two years later establishing the college but also in having the pope appoint his illegitimate relative (maybe a half brother) prior of Molana.[4]

All in all, the Fitzgeralds through the centuries turned Youghal into a center of Christianity, attracting monastic orders, pilgrims, papal support, seminary students, nuns, and royal favor. Religious institutions stretched in a line from the Irish Sea through Youghal along the west side of the Blackwater River for several miles. Of course, it did not hurt that Fitzgerald, in 1462, had also defeated the rival Ormonds at the Battle of Pilltown (also on Ralegh's future lands) in the only battle of the Wars of the Roses fought in Ireland. (Desmond was a Yorkist, Ormond a Lancasterian.) However, in 1466 Desmond was charged with treason and beheaded. His son and successor was short-lived, dying at age twenty-eight, murdered, perhaps at his own brother's bequest. The brother succeeded him and became the 9th Earl of Desmond.

Despite the instability at the top, and the frequent threats posed by the neighboring Ormonds, Youghal flourished until its sacking in the Second Desmond War. The Desmonds effectively destroyed the monasteries they had built and sponsored: they had no reason to leave them to the Protestants. Today, as noted above, the church and the collegiate seminary, as well as Ralegh's house and Saint Coran's Holy Well, survive, and the ruins of Molana, Templemichael, Rincrew, and the Dominican Abbey (now a cemetery) can still be visited. The Franciscan monastery has disappeared under newer construction.

Though Youghal lost its importance as a center for Christianity in the mid-sixteenth century, its economic future looked most promising.

Located forty miles southwest of the port city of Waterford, and thirty miles northeast of the port city of Cork, Youghal remains today, as it was in the late sixteenth century, a much smaller city than Waterford. (Cork and Youghal had roughly the same population in the late sixteenth century.) In Ralegh's time, Youghal's imports paled in comparison to Waterford's, as the latter's ancient status as a royal port with monopoly privileges over the importation of wine into Ireland gave it a leg up on competitors. But Youghal led both Waterford and Cork in exports owing to its rich agricultural lands, the abundance of fish in the Blackwater, and, during Ralegh's time and well into the seventeenth century, other natural resources of the hinterland.

Ralegh's seignories prompted the city's rebirth and economic growth in the 1590s. Youghal's golden age as an economic hub came in the seventeenth century, when the port's trade increased so much that it became second in Ireland to Dublin.[5] Ralegh did not own the town's land, but Youghal depended on him for defense and, more importantly, the economic activity he both initiated and controlled. In the 1590s, virtually all goods shipped out of Youghal were produced on Ralegh's lands. For those who lived farther afield, if they did not use the port at Cork, they required Ralegh's permission to use the Blackwater River to reach Youghal, though there is no evidence that he tried to collect tolls. Ralegh became Youghal's mayor for two years, 1588 and 1589, and the city's denizens must have been pleased to have the queen's favorite so close at hand. In 1589, many in Youghal, Catholic and Protestant alike, might have thought the city's economic future secured. In the aftermath of the desolation of the Desmond Wars, new people were arriving from England who would produce goods to be shipped through Youghal, and the newcomers required goods and services. With Ralegh's connections at court, Youghal could expect special privileges and opportunities that only a man of his station could provide.

Most of Ralegh's colonists likely arrived at Youghal, so he would have met or welcomed many of them; in fact, he knew most of them. Some would have traveled west for up to ten miles onto the barony of Inchiquin. This is where many of the former soldiers were settled under the leadership of Ralegh's comrade in arms, Henry Moyle. The veterans likely were grouped together to provide a militia for defense of Youghal and to fulfill Elizabeth's charge to settle people together who possessed strong ties with one another. Just outside of Youghal to the north, Ralegh planted a small enclave of friends and relations from Devon who were Catholic. These men were granted large portions of land and were expected to attract their own settlers, presumably other English Catholics. Farther north along the Blackwater River for ten miles and more, and along the Bride River that feeds into the Blackwater, Ralegh planted numerous settlers of various standing and skills: tenants, freeholders, many nonagricultural laborers, and even merchants, in what became the most densely settled area of colonists on Ralegh's seignories.

Ralegh had broad plans for developing his colony. These were based on a sound assessment of available resources and reflected the same grandiose yet practical interests he displayed with the colonization of Virginia. He promoted the production of glass, iron, and lumber, expansion of the fisheries, and linkage of his seignories to world markets extending from Youghal to the Canary Islands, Seville, Amsterdam, London, and other ports in England, including distant Yorkshire. This was a far cry from the region's previous trading partners, which basically consisted of Bristol and some Spanish ports. Basque fishermen had long fished off of Youghal, but their trade with the port was limited. French trade in the region, largely wine, went to Waterford. From the time of Ralegh and extending through his successor Richard Boyle in the seventeenth century, Youghal was a "colonial" port in the mercantilist sense of the term, exporting from its environs raw materials in exchange for manufactured goods. Iron, fish, and lumber, for instance, made up the basis for colonial production in Munster (and elsewhere in Ireland) as they would later in seventeenth-century New England.[6] Local production of glass on Ralegh's seignories was later mimicked by glass production at Jamestown and elsewhere. (Glass was expensive and difficult to ship; hence, colonials in the early stages of colonization produced it themselves if they could.)

Ralegh's lands in Munster were mostly located in the counties of Waterford and Cork. In effect, his seignories straddled the border of the two. He was intimately familiar with these lands from the days of his military service, having spent a winter at Lismore Castle on the northern reaches and at Cork City on the southwestern border. Based on this experience, when requesting land from the queen, he knew exactly what he wanted. He claimed virtually all land within the estuary of the Blackwater for about fifteen miles north and west of Youghal. The river turns almost due west about fifteen miles inland, and he claimed lands mostly on the south but also the north side of the river. Only a few estates in this area remained out of Ralegh's hands, and to extend his reach he convinced the Bishop of Cashel to permanently lease him the valuable Lismore estates, which expanded his holdings along the Blackwater so that he ultimately controlled the river itself. Ralegh also leased or purchased estates from Anglo-Irish on both sides of the river and had rights through the Lismore lease to the rents and entitlements of more distant tracts.

All in all, Ralegh made a highly rational decision to control a single geographic area that was well connected by its waterways to Atlantic markets and that had a modicum of protection geographically. For instance, with most of his lands on the south and west sides of the Blackwater, potential enemies had to cross the Knockmealdown Mountains to reach him. They also would have to cross the Blackwater at its few fordable areas because in general the river was difficult to cross and there were no bridges. His seignories were by no means impregnable—and they would be heavily raided in the 1590s—but the region was more easily defended than many others. With high points along the river on both sides, there were several sites where tower houses commanded river traffic.

At Myrtle Grove, Ralegh undertook agricultural experimentation that had a huge impact on the course of Irish history. In all likelihood, he and Hariot introduced the New World strain of potato that became the staple of the Irish diet. Other strains of the potato from Spanish America might have been introduced previously, but it was the North American strain that became popular. There's no definitive evidence that Ralegh was responsible for the potato's introduction, but the circumstantial evidence is mighty strong. Hariot was responsible for documenting New World agriculture and for considering the possibilities of a variety of crops. Who else but Hariot would have carried potatoes from Roanoke to England and then to Ireland?

Other circumstantial evidence that Ralegh and Hariot introduced the North American potato: Munster, in general, and the counties of Waterford and Cork, in particular, became the first centers of Irish potato production, and the lands abutting the county line were Ralegh's. It is likely that Ralegh recommended the crop to his settlers. Also, centuries of rumor posit that Ralegh or Hariot first planted the crop at Myrtle Grove. Given Ralegh's and Hariot's bent for experimentation, especially as Hariot was spending his time at Youghal writing about agricultural endeavors in Virginia, planting a trial crop that they could keep their eye on is a logical deduction. As discussed in Part Eight, Ralegh was preoccupied with finding numerous ways to make colonization work in Ireland. Introducing the potato fits this larger pattern.

The practicality of the potato was nowhere more evident than in Munster. One of the main strategies the English used against the Anglo-Irish and Irish in the Desmond Wars, which was used again in the Nine Years' War (1594–1603), was destroying food crops in the fields to starve the rebels into submission. Fields of wheat and oats, familiar crops, were easy to identify and burn. However much the Irish came to enjoy the potato for the ways it enhanced their diet, the potato's popularity was likely prompted by the security it provided for poor and rich alike. The potato grows underground, does not require particularly good soil, but does require much water—of which Ireland has no shortage. Fields of potatoes were much less easy to identify, and mature potato vines reach about two feet tall, can be planted in fields or tucked in obscure places, and it would have been near impossible for troops to dig up and completely destroy the crop; burning left the potatoes undisturbed belowground. Potatoes are also a much better dietary staple than wheat, providing more protein, minerals, and vitamins, including vitamin C. Humans can survive on a diet composed almost entirely of potatoes, which cannot be said of other grains and vegetables, or of most any other food source. The potato was thus more reliable than any other crop in terms of its nutritional value and its resistance to human attempts to destroy it. The terrible and unfortunate irony is that war and famine spurred its adoption, and overreliance on the potato then contributed to the great famine of the nineteenth century, the result of a blight that decimated the crop.

Ralegh's own experimentation with food production is evident in the expensive fruit trees he planted at Myrtle Grove; documented evidence shows that Ralegh's half brother Adrian sent these to him for planting in Ireland. (The fruit trees on the grounds of Myrtle Grove are presumed to be those same trees or their descendants.) Allegedly, and widely believed, Ralegh introduced the first cherry trees to Ireland by planting some at Affane, which he brought from the Canary Islands, and these were the progenitors of the famed "Affane cherry" of the nineteenth century.[7]

Rebuilding Myrtle Grove, experimenting with plants, overseeing colonization, and discussing with Hariot his writing on Virginia were but part of a cosmopolitanism that Ralegh helped reintroduce to Youghal and the surrounding area. Before the Desmond Wars, Youghal had indeed been connected to the Continent, as Ireland itself had been for centuries, both through an array of religious institutions and as a port city that attracted a fair number of Europeans to trade. Urban diversity led to an unusual degree of tolerance. This tolerance was evident in the 1550s when Youghal selected William Moses Annyas Eanes, a Portuguese Jew, as mayor. This was remarkable, to say the least, because Christians throughout Western Europe viewed Jews with great suspicion, if not hostility. (Very few Jews lived in England at this time, because they had been barred since 1290.) Francis Eanes, a likely descendant of William, served three terms as mayor, including as late as 1581 in the midst of the Second Desmond War.

The urbanity of Youghal, made manifest by visits from poet Edmund Spenser, would have been attractive to Ralegh; Ralegh apparently paid return visits to Spenser at his plantation, Kilcolman. Allegedly, Spenser wrote portions of *The Faerie Queene*, an epic of Arthurian tales prefaced with a famous letter to Ralegh wherein Spenser explains his purpose and expresses gratitude, from "Spenser's Window" at Myrtle Grove. We know for certain that Spenser was inspired by Ralegh's poetry, particularly his depiction of Elizabeth in various forms as the moon goddess, Diana, or Cynthia, which Ralegh had popularized and Spenser employed to great effect in *The Faerie Queene*. Spenser was on the verge of recognition as one of England's greatest poets. Ironically, he earned this fame mostly for poetry he wrote while living in Ireland. Ralegh played no small role in bringing Spenser to the attention of the queen and court, and he helped procure for Spenser a yearly £50 pension from Elizabeth.

The Faerie Queene was published in two parts, the first three books appearing in 1590, and the next four in 1596. It is the longest poem in the English language. Undoubtedly, Spenser and Ralegh discussed the work in 1588 and 1589. The poem uses Ralegh as inspiration for the character of Timias, and Queen Elizabeth as the subject of Timias's love, Belphoebe. (She was represented by other characters as well.)

For centuries, this massive work has been the subject of literary criticism, and Spenser's allusions have been deconstructed for clues as to the poet's conceptualization of the English court, Christianity, pastoralism, colonialism, empire, and so forth. Book V, in particular, has stood in for Spenser's envisioning of Ireland. And well it might— the poet's use of nouns clearly denoting Ireland has led generations of scholars to see it as political in nature. To C. S. Lewis, who adored most of *The Faerie Queene*, Book V was an embarrassment, its allegories too stark and political in depicting Ireland. Subsequent generations have echoed Lewis's opinion, while analyzing who represented who, and what represented what, in Anglo-Irish history. One problem that exists with these analyses is the way they are informed by later developments in Irish history, and by their reading of Spenser's *A View of the State of Ireland*, a prose work that proposes how England *should* colonize Ireland.

Teleologically, centuries of colonialism in Ireland are read backward, and the violence of Book V becomes predictor, if not justification, for what is to come. Spenser represents, from this perspective, a radical Protestantism devoted to the destruction of the Catholic Church and Irish culture, a fantasy played out in his poetry. There are manifest problems with this approach to understanding *The Faerie Queene*. In fact, *all* the books of *The Faerie Queene* use violence as a literary engine. Violence is part and parcel of Arthurian tales. It is also dubious to label Spenser a "Radical Protestant" when his Catholic sensibilities are paramount throughout *The Faerie Queene*. If we refrain from reading the later bloody history of England in Ireland into Spenser's poetry and, as has become de rigueur in some circles, all English colonialism as a product of *The Faerie Queene*, then it might look and read differently.

Whatever Spenser felt about Ireland, the Irish, and England's future in Ireland, *The Faerie Queene* was a work of fiction, and a fantasy. Even as characters were sometimes drawn from real people, the characters remain fictional. Spenser scholars rightfully chafe at the notion that Timias, based on Ralegh, was actually created to be the embodiment of the man, or that Belphoebe was a realistic rendering of Elizabeth. The characters are types, ornately drawn, to fill the poet's needs. Real people provide the clay, not stone, from which Spenser sculpted. His characters can be seen as ideals for people to emulate or disdain, and sometimes, perhaps, ideals for the real counterpart to live up to, but they were not meant as exact representations of the individuals on whom they drew. As Spenser informed Ralegh in his prefatory letter for *The Faerie Queene*, "The generall end therefore of all the booke is to fashion a gentleman or noble person in vertuous and gentle discipline."

Spenser, like Ralegh, was not a Radical Protestant.[8] The term *Radical Protestant* is often used to denote those who pushed Elizabeth to militarily support European Protestants against Spain. Most English Protestants, however, opposed Spain for its threat to Elizabeth and England, and because Spain represented the interests of the pope. One did not have to be a Radical Protestant to view the pope as evil. He wanted to destroy English Protestantism, and that was enough to make him the enemy of all Protestants. With or without the pope,

Catholicism still represented false Christianity to the Radical Protestants. The latter believed that the priesthood stood in the way of
individuals forging a personal relationship with God. The Catholic
Church's emphasis on the saints and the Virgin Mary as intercessors
between men and God also stood in the way of individuals' direct relationship with God. Radical Protestants wanted to eliminate mediation, hence the English law providing that each church must place
the Bible in a place of easy access to all members of the community.[9] They wished to replace Catholic "superstition"—magical relics,
contemplation of images, and prayers to saints and the Virgin—with
individual knowledge of the Bible, which each must read and contemplate themselves.

Elizabeth's church, however, maintained the mass, though brought
to the people by its performance in English and use of the *Book of
Common Prayer*. Her church did not discard all material representations of God, as communicants could still drink Christ's blood. The
radicals, on the other hand, sought a return to "primitive" Christianity, shorn of this materialization of God. The ideal place of worship
was simple and plain, without adornment. They wished to entirely end
the priesthood. They sought a transformation in English religious life,
practice, and belief.

Hermeticism was not Radical Protestantism. Hermeticists like
Ralegh, Hariot, and Spenser emphasized the common ties among all
Christians and sought reunification of Christianity and the second
coming of Christ. Hermeticism appealed to Catholic and Protestant
alike because of its belief in the sacredness and efficacy of holy things.
To Hermeticists, holy things were more powerful than words, because
substances were imbued with the divine. Drawing on the Jewish Kabbalah, Hermeticists believed words themselves, like letters and numbers, could possess divine power. The Protestant Hermeticists did not
reject the Catholic Church because of idolatry but because of its elevating of human remains, like the bones of saints, into a special extension of divinity. The Hermeticists believed that all matter was infused
by the divine.[10] Edmund Spenser, as a Hermeticist, was no Radical
Protestant. In Book V of *The Faerie Queene*, idols and temples are destroyed, which some scholars interpret as emblematic of his personal
war on the idolatry of the Catholic Church. But in *The Faerie Queene*,
some idols, temples, and even paintings are depicted as holy, and characters are to meditate on these things as a Catholic would.[11]

We must be careful in subscribing the author's beliefs to his fictional work. What we see in *The Faerie Queene*, if nothing more, is Spenser's utter familiarity with Hermetic symbols and philosophy. But it must be added that a Radical Protestant would not have used these expressions of divinity in materiality, let alone in an approving manner, as the sentiment itself would have been viewed as diabolical. It is a reminder that men like Spenser and Ralegh could hate the Catholic Church and the pope, but not necessarily be anti-Catholic in terms of theology and Catholic people.

The Protestants Ralegh, Spenser, and Dee, like their Protestant Hermetic contemporaries, not only retained Catholic veneration of material objects but also focused their spiritual philosophy upon them. Dee, who had been a Catholic priest, was obsessed with the powers that could be wrought from things, believed in meditating upon them (like many good Catholics), and saw the transformation of substances—alchemy—as key to man's relationship with the divine. The Protestant side of Dee believed that the powers of the divine were not available to all, only to the chosen few, and he wished to keep sacred magic out of the hands of those destined for hell. This exclusivity is not seen in Ralegh or Spenser or most Hermeticists. It would be easy to discount Spenser's Catholic associations in *The Faerie Queene* if, like C. S. Lewis in his assessment of Spenser, we conclude that "all allegories whatever are likely to seem Catholic to the general reader"; Catholic allegories are what Spenser had to work with. But the tropes Spenser used are the same Hermetic Catholic tropes employed by Dee, from the statuary and temples of ancient Egypt, to the Cult of the Virgin Mary/Queen Elizabeth, to the depictions of the efficacy of priestly practices, to the sanctity of art and dream visions, and even to the bugbear of Protestantism, the veneration of saints.[12]

The iconography that Dee, Ralegh, and Spenser shared is Hermetic: the moon, silver, and burning fire form the triad of Hermetic representation of the goddess/Virgin Mary, divine metal, and engine of mutability. All play prominent roles in Book V of *The Faerie Queene*, which was published within two years of the Spanish Armada's attempt against England. At the height of anti-Spanish, antipapal sentiment in England, Spenser penned a work that made overt expressions of Catholic religiosity.

For Ralegh, things had meaning, even holiness, as did places. Ralegh's respect for the sacredness of particular material matter is made evident by his treatment of holy sites near Youghal. He placed his friend and fellow Hermeticist Thomas Hariot at Molana Abbey. Just outside Youghal, Ralegh settled Hariot's mentor in mysticism, mathematics, and science, the Catholic Thomas Allen. At Molana and at Ralegh's home, and probably at nearby Templemichael and Rincrew, the local Hermeticists met. To the present day, local folk believe that the ruined abbey had been a site for strange goings-on. Spenser surely knew the abbey, even naming one of his characters Molanna in *The Faerie Queene*. Ralegh placed English Catholics at these holy sites and abutting them, evincing his concern for their preservation and maintenance and keeping them out of the hands of those who might do otherwise.

—

PLANNING THE MUNSTER PLANTATION was the greatest bureaucratic project of Elizabethan England. Years of thought and effort went into defining what would occur in the overseas Irish colony. Elizabeth and her government, however, had little idea of how to bring these plans to fruition. Surveying the land, Elizabethans believed, would rationalize ownership and disbursement of tracts much as the Domesday Book had done after the Norman Invasion of England in 1066. The various "surveys," in effect, would do the same: document the lands of traitors that would be given to English colonists. But the data presented in the extant surveys are virtually all the result of guesswork. Elizabeth's government did not invest enough money, nor have the time to properly survey Munster. Just listing and naming the estates was a herculean task. And unlike the Normans, who claimed ownership of 95 percent of the land, Elizabeth was concerned with distinguishing the tracts of faithful Irish and Anglo-Irish from those of the unfaithful, who would lose their land. She tried to bring fairness to the process through the creation of commissions, but the scales of justice tilted in favor of English colonists—until they tilted away, and then went back and forth for decades. Elizabeth hoped for justice but lacked the will and power to enforce her directives in the Munster Plantation.

The rule of law depended on who administered it. That law and authority, according to Elizabeth and her advisors, depended on blood and selection by the queen. Elizabeth selected Ralegh as her most significant colonizer. He had to plant his seignories within the parameters her Privy Council drew up for the Munster Plantation. Being the man he was, Ralegh employed his own surveyor, Thomas Hariot, and his illustrator John White to bring clarity to his estates.[13] He knew he had to rationalize his ownership and that it was up to him to make his seignories a success. But why should people follow and obey this commoner who invited so much envy? Ralegh's blood was so tainted that John Hooker had to be employed to fictionalize an account of Ralegh's ancestors that would justify his authority over large numbers of people in England and Ireland.

Granted, Ralegh showing up in Youghal to direct his plantation in the midst of Munster's devastation after the war was a statement by the queen about the seriousness of the project. Ralegh's plans were ambitious and carefully thought out, and he chose competent assistants who grasped his vision. His familiarity with the land and his tolerance of diverse peoples eased the task, but it still required much effort. His Hermeticism reflected his openness and respect for others and their religion and spirituality, so Youghal was the ideal place for him with its numerous holy sites and impressive cosmopolitan history. He also had with him some of England's most impressive intellectual figures: Hariot, Spenser, and Thomas Allen.

In Hariot, Ralegh could ask for no better companion. Whereas Spenser complemented Ralegh's artistic side, shared his obsession with court, poetically and philosophically enlarged on the Cult of Elizabeth, and contemplated the future of Ireland, Hariot tutored Ralegh in science, kept his accounts, and explored the meaning of the universe with him. (They were also smoking and drinking buddies.) All three thought much about, and participated in, English overseas expansion. There is no evidence that Hariot shared Ralegh's and Spenser's belief that Elizabeth was destined to lead a great English empire because Hariot wrote no state papers, as fellow Hermeticist John Dee had done, though he did pen *A Briefe* and the captions for de Bry's engravings of White's paintings. We do not know what Hariot thought of the Irish or the empire or much of anything about politics because he carefully avoided them. This correspondent of Kepler had his eye on the stars, the universe, and man's place in the cosmos. But his interests were dangerous to himself. In the 1590s, he was accused of atheism, like Ralegh, and brought before the authorities in England, where the new science was perceived as a heretical attempt to disavow revealed knowledge or, worse, as black magic attempting to discover and exploit God's Creation in league with the Devil. These fears about Hariot had yet to fully erupt, but Dee's library was burned by a mob in 1589 (years earlier Dee had been arrested for "calculating"). Ireland—the Munster Plantation—might have been a safer place for Hariot than England;

that his Hermetic mentor Thomas Allen, a professor at Oxford, followed him there gives credence to this view. Youghal and its environs
were not just a plantation for colonial development but also a spiritual
center for Hermeticists and a place to escape religious persecution in
England.

Fear of Spain and England's persecution of Catholics heightened
anxieties and emphasized national security. In the midst of settlement
of the Munster Plantation, England prepared for war with Spain. Ralegh was responsible for defending the realm in England and was
charged with helping to secure Ireland. Munster had to be colonized
without delay. Ralegh threw himself into the task, even as he continued to pursue his other interests, such as planting at Myrtle Grove,
hobnobbing with Spenser about poetry, the court, and Ireland, and
consulting with Hariot about his manuscripts on Virginia. Ralegh also
found time to fornicate with the daughter of one of his settlers, which
produced a child, about which little is known. Colonialism involved an
array of fictions, but the child was real, and unrecognized by Ralegh
until the next decade.

More immediate to Ralegh, in August 1588, was the Spanish Armada
of three hundred ships sailing to conquer England. Responsible for the
coastal defense of Cornwall and Devon, Ralegh likely left the immediate supervision of security to Grenville, and as Captain of the Guard
reported to court to defend the queen. With the armada's destruction,
Ralegh returned to Youghal to continue colonization.[14]

Ralegh's plans for his seignories involved much forethought. Colonists could not be settled in a haphazard manner. Because he employed
agents to assist him, it is sometimes insinuated in the historiography
that Ralegh played little direct role in establishing his Munster Plantation. This could not be further from the truth. Ralegh not only had
intimate knowledge of his colonists but also formulated comprehensive plans covering what he wanted to do with particular areas of his
seignories. Colonists were assigned tracts according to their skills and
roles on his plantation. But as much as Ralegh shaped his plantation,
others also played a huge role in shaping it: English officials in Ireland, competitors of various stripes, and local Anglo-Irish and Irish all
created their own realities and fictions to counter those of Ralegh and
Elizabeth.

PART SEVEN

Our right existed as long as
"the memory of man runneth"

*Settlement and Resistance on the
Ralegh Seignories*

CHAPTER 17

Preparing the Plantation

Establishing Authority

I n his New World patent, Ralegh possessed the rights to create any society he wished with virtually no restrictions. In Ireland, by contrast, his colony and colonists were subject to the queen and her Privy Council and to the laws of the Irish Parliament. Nonetheless, Ralegh held significant powers over his Irish seignories as a great landowner. He distributed tracts as he wished, as freeholds, leases, or in virtually any other form akin to those used in England under the common law. Local administration of his plantation followed the medieval practice of baronies, which included establishing local juries to settle disputes, while county government, through the office of the sheriff and the presentments of juries, enforced laws against his colonists. As in Virginia, Ralegh had to fulfill one particular term of his patent or face reversion of the land to the queen: he had to plant settlers.

Ralegh recruited colonists by offering them land or employment. Those migrating for land received acreage and terms reflecting their social status in England. Tracts varied from fifty to a few thousand acres, with leases ranging in length from one year to three lifetimes to four thousand years, with a privileged few receiving freeholds that provided great flexibility in holding or conveying their grants to others. The more substantial colonists were expected to bring laborers with them to work the land, but Ralegh also lured English laborers for work in rural industries.

Ralegh's plantation could succeed only if he established authority over his seignories. Cognizant that the safety and prosperity of his colony depended on relations with Irish and Anglo-Irish, Ralegh took measures to halt the persecution that persisted since the end of the Desmond Wars. This began by assigning Henry Moyle to the position of sheriff and charging him with ending the persecution. Also exemplifying Ralegh's method as a colonizer—to create an inclusive plantation—he worked with local Anglo-Irish and Irish in a variety of enterprises, foreseeing that the impact of his economic activities could extend far and wide. Despite his efforts to soothe relations between the English and the locals, Ralegh faced determined resistance that was so subtle he never realized he was being tricked out of profits from a substantial portion of his seignories by Anglo-Irish, Irish, and his own English settlers. Facing multiple challenges to his authority, Ralegh sometimes won, and sometimes lost, but overall laid a foundation for the success of the Munster Plantation.

—

BY GRANT RALEGH WAS ENTITLED to 42,000 acres of land. Most historians repeat this figure, though his entitlement, what he could and did legally claim, was closer to 150,000 acres. Ploughlands varied in size, but the surveyors made clear, and the queen later confirmed in her patents, that only arable land was included in the estimation for purposes of granting acreage—"meadow pasture, woods, bogs, mountains, or waste," much of them attached to the ploughlands, were not counted in allotments and were retained by the Undertaker. Land transformed into arable land was then subject to taxation.[1] Thus, Ralegh's three and a half seignories included an estimated 42,000 acres of arable land, but the additional untillable land almost quadrupled the size of his grant to an area of roughly 237 square miles. Considering that the woods would be quickly and profitably exploited, the additional acreage was a boon to Ralegh's fortune.

Ralegh broke up many of his properties by granting individuals the demesne (the lands that the former castle owner cultivated) and by lopping off and granting to others additional ploughlands associated with an estate. Ralegh attracted men of substance to his seignories, but he did not expect any to be grandees who could bring the twenty or thirty families necessary to work huge estates. In effect, there was no second-tier aristocracy on Ralegh's lands as there was with the Anglo-Irish and Irish elite.

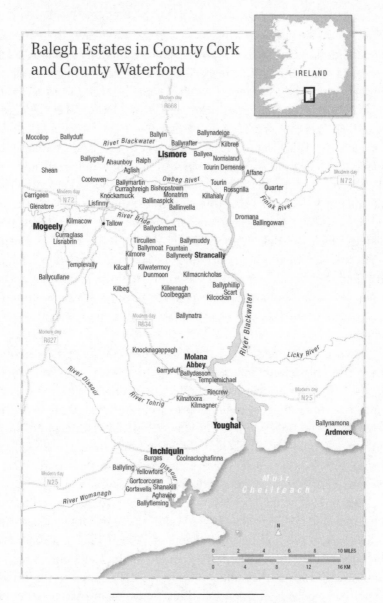

21. Ralegh estates in County Cork and County Waterford

Until his seignories were populated with sufficient numbers of agricultural laborers (or workers in industries), Ralegh did not expect to
develop new population centers beyond one particular area, Mogeely,
along the Bride River. He did gain control of Thickpenny's Town, along
the Blackwater several miles north of Youghal. This was not part of

Ralegh's original grant because it was leased by Anne Thickpenny, the widow of an Englishman who frequently supplied English troops with food. Anne shared her husband's business skills and acted as a land agent for others, including overseeing the leasing of Lismore Castle, through which Thickpenny's Town had some legal connection (though Lismore was about ten miles upriver). Despite its moniker, Thickpenny's Town was more of a hamlet than a town. It was located at a key point on the Blackwater River, below where the Bride entered, and there were substantial estates nearby from which Robert Thickpenny likely purchased the victuals he supplied to the troops. Via a grant from the queen, Ralegh obtained this land from Anne, along with the former Dominican Priory next to his home in Youghal, which Thickpenny also held by lease. Ralegh undoubtedly obtained Thickpenny's Town to make sure an outsider was not the go-between for his lands along the river and the outside world. He leased much of the surrounding tracts to his friends and relations and seems to have paid little attention to this section of the Blackwater, expecting these men to develop the area on their own.

A few other parcels in the northeast corner of Ralegh's seignories, where the Blackwater makes its sharp turn west, remained in the hands of Irish and Anglo-Irish who fought against the Desmonds, but Ralegh obtained most of their lands as well. Although there is no indication in the records that he intimidated these landholders into parting with their parcels, in all likelihood he pressured them to sell and take up lands on the east side of the river, where he also made purchases. In the nineteenth century, one member of the Croker family, for instance, recalled how "The lands of Affane are said to have been given by Garrett Fitzgerald for a breakfast to Sir Walter Raleigh."[2] It behooved these individuals to sell and become clients of Ralegh so as not to alienate the queen's favorite, to whom they could look for help and protection, and through Ralegh they obtained a strong connection to the English court. The east side of the river, where these Anglo-Irish resettled, indeed became much more developed in the early seventeenth century. Ralegh's power in the region affected *all* landowners on both sides of the Blackwater because he *owned* a large stretch of the river.

In official documents the queen designated Ralegh Admiral of the Blackwater River. *Admiral* in the sixteenth century, as it does today, referred to someone who commanded a fleet, but its usage here is closer to its original connotation in Arabic, which remained relevant in early modern England, as a governor of a territory.[3] Because Ralegh governed the river, he could prevent use of the waterway—a degree of ownership that became a key fact of investigation almost three hundred years later during a parliamentary inquiry into fishing rights on the Blackwater. Parliament determined that Elizabeth's grants to Ralegh gave him exclusive ownership of the river, including the very ground on which the river flowed, for about twenty miles. It is worth reiterating: the acres of ploughlands made up only a part of Ralegh's grants; he owned everything else around, within, and between the ploughlands. If Ralegh wished, he could have prevented other landowners' sale of produce at Youghal, for many had no other way to get to market by water or by land except through his domain.

Ralegh also held military power over his lands. Although the lord deputy commanded English troops in Ireland, it was Ralegh's recruits from Cornwall and Devon who filled the companies assigned to the region, and the documents refer to their captains as "his men." The military companies were placed in Ireland to protect the English colonists from the Irish, but they could also maintain the Undertakers' authority among their lessees. For instance, in the early seventeenth century, when Ralegh still owned his colony but had not stepped foot in it for over a decade, the Archbishop of Cashel, who had leased a portion of Lismore from Ralegh (after Ralegh leased it from him), complained of "Ralegh's man," a Captain Nuse, as having beaten him "like a dog" and burned his home.[4] In his complaint, the near eighty-year-old archbishop recounted how Nuse (and presumably his men) attacked him with pikes and halberds and shot bullets at him. Under other circumstances, the archbishop claimed, he would have given Nuse "his deserts," but instead he had to "bear injury rather than to use just revenge." Whatever the facts of the assault, it is clear that the archbishop knew Nuse was Ralegh's man, and he expressly asked the Privy Council to notify Ralegh of what the captain had done to him.[5] At least in Ralegh's case, military companies clearly were an extension of his authority.

Ralegh also placed soldiers on his lands as colonists. One was Henry Moyle, who headed his own company on the Inchiquin barony. Moyle not only had served under Ralegh as a soldier in Ireland but also had captained ships at sea. He sailed with Frobisher in 1578 and later, in 1595, commanded one of the queen's pinnaces in Ireland.[6] In 1596, he joined Ralegh in the English assault on Cádiz, Spain, in which he captained a ship. Still later, he was back in Ireland serving as a captain on land into the early seventeenth century. Ralegh created a position for him analogous to his own as Lord Warden of the Stannaries in Cornwall, where, in addition to Ralegh's operation of the tin mines, he held both military and judicial powers. As Lord Warden in Ireland, Moyle was in effect Ralegh's deputy in charge of military and judicial affairs on Ralegh's seignories. But to provide Moyle more substantial power, to reinforce his authority on the seignories, and to augment his influence in the surrounding areas, Ralegh sought Moyle's appointment by the queen as Sheriff of County Cork, a position of much judicial authority. From a political standpoint, Moyle was an excellent choice for the role. Like Ralegh, he was a cousin of Sir George Carew, who had great influence with the Privy Council as an expert on Irish affairs.[7] Moyle worked with Ralegh on the settlement of the Desmond lands *before* Ralegh officially received his seignories. Ralegh was sure which lands he would receive and prepared for colonization by seeking to alter the political landscape of County Cork. He determined to remove the old guard, those standing in the way of restoring amity with Irish and Anglo-Irish. Although much of the Desmond lands were deserted, a significant number of Irish and Anglo-Irish remained in the towns along the coast, and there were refugees in the countryside. At the end of the Desmond Wars, the Irish or Anglo-Irish James Myagh (also referred to as James Meade, James Meaghe, James McKedaugh O'More, and James Mc Cedaugh M'More, as well as several other variants) needed to be shoved aside.[8]

Moyle was appointed Sheriff of County Cork in place of Myagh in July 1586, but the path to power was not a smooth one.[9] The council and Lord President of Munster, John Norreys, rejected Moyle's appointment. Myagh remained another year as sheriff, while accusing Moyle of conferring "with the notorious traitors and rebels whom I have apprehended and brought to Cork with great danger of my life." The prisoners were arraigned and then condemned on charges of treason, but Moyle stepped in and promised to "stay their executions and procure their pardon at his own charges."[10] The Second Desmond War had been over for *three* years, but Myagh was still hunting, incarcerating, and executing alleged rebels and their families and friends. Local government officials like Myagh felt empowered to disregard the English Privy Council because the queen's top appointees in Ireland, like the recently knighted Sir John Norreys, and a succession of other Lords Deputy, also ignored many of the directives of the Privy Council without facing adverse consequences. This was not because the Privy Council was unaware—they kept a close eye on Irish affairs—but they lacked the will to force compliance with their directives.[11]

Moyle obtained the prisoners' release. Myagh saw nothing wrong in his own actions, admitting to his severity in punishing the prisoners, who by his account had not been rebels but people who had associated with or given succor to rebels. He marched off to Dublin to complain to the lord deputy and council. This time Dublin refused to support him, so Myagh went to London to ask the Privy Council for a pension to retire. Refused, he returned to Cork with an appointment as a justice rather than as sheriff. The Privy Council apparently had mixed feelings about Myagh. He had been promised a grant of land next to Ralegh's seignory, but the council withdrew the promise in favor of Arthur Hyde. Myagh's son John, a student at the Middle Temple in London, also petitioned Lord Burghley for a grant in Cork, and he, too, was denied.

A clue to Myagh's and his son's character can be gleaned from a letter the elder John wrote to Walsingham thanking him for a favor shown his son in London, "who is envied and maligned by his own countrymen students there for his virtue."[12] This virtue might refer to a rigidity that isolated the son as an outsider at the inn of law, a rigidity he apparently inherited from his father. The father was an impractical choice as sheriff in Cork when the Desmond Wars ended, and the new regime needed to pave the way for reconciliation, peace, and settlement of Munster by the New English. Myagh still had his value, however, in rendering judgment on the criminals brought before him by the new sheriff, Henry Moyle. And that was the point: the sheriff was the most important officer in the county, certainly where crime was concerned. The sheriff determined whether a crime had been committed, and whether an alleged perpetrator should be brought to justice, though a grand jury could do the same. A man like Myagh could sustain a reign of terror; a man like Moyle could end one.

By November 1588, the Privy Council was considering removing Myagh from his position as second justice in Munster, and the chief justice and attorney general were already making recommendations for his replacement.[13] Myagh was attainted for treason and lost his castle and the town of Nyvas, which included five ploughlands—a substantial estate. We might surmise that the lack of rewards and support from the Crown had sent him into rebellion, but his crimes against the queen were not considered severe enough to land him in prison, though he was detained indefinitely in England.[14] It was typical in Tudor and Stuart England to detain in England Irish and Anglo-Irish deemed politically dangerous, sometimes in prison and sometimes not, to prevent them from "mischief" upon returning home. By 1592, Myagh alleged he had fallen into great poverty, as the "unlawful devices of my enemies procured your honor [Lord Burghley] to take me to be an ill member of the commonweal of my country, and one that did benefit myself by extortion and other unlawful means." Myagh denied all charges and prayed for some compensation for victuals he had once supplied to the troops so he would have money to return to the land of his birth, Ireland, to die. Burghley refused the request and referred it to the queen, whose disposition is unknown.[15]

The new sheriff of Cork, Moyle, did not receive his grant from Ralegh until the summer of 1589, but he was already inhabiting the land, as reported on Ralegh's census of May 1589. The lands Ralegh granted to Moyle had belonged to the Seneschal of Imokilly, John Fitzedmund Fitzgerald, cousin (and neighbor) of Ralegh's friend of the same name, John Fitzedmund Fitzgerald of Cloyne. The former, along with another neighbor, Patrick Condon, had been removed from the list of the attainted in the autumn of 1588. Fitzgerald, intermittently admired by the English for his courage and strategy, had been one of the most significant rebel leaders in Munster. Pardoned in 1575, he took up arms again in 1579 and in February 1581 had almost captured Ralegh in the Second Desmond War.[16] After his mother was executed by the Anglo-Irish Thomas Butler, Earl of Ormond, in 1583, and as the Desmond Wars wound down, Fitzgerald sought pardon from the queen.

The Privy Council informed the government in Ireland of the imminent pardon of Fitzgerald, held prisoner in Dublin Castle, and to expect him to file suit for the return of his land. He might, they suggested, have to receive compensatory grants elsewhere.[17] But the administration in Dublin was loath to release him and ignored the Privy Council orders.[18] In the meantime, the Privy Council decided to completely restore Fitzgerald's lands and compensate the Undertakers elsewhere. The Dublin government still had not released Fitzgerald when he died in Dublin Castle in late February.[19] Though there is no suggestion in the surviving records that he was murdered, the new lord deputy, Sir William Fitzwilliam, may have been culpable. Fitzwilliam's refusal to release Fitzgerald, he stated, resulted from his need to draw up exact terms of the pardon.[20] The queen had not requested the lord deputy to provide any "terms," yet another in a long line of examples of Lords Deputy doing as they pleased. Fitzwilliam's stalling could have arisen from the obsessive fear of a second Spanish Armada, this one to land in Ireland, in which the influential Fitzgerald might have led his followers into supporting the Spanish. But Fitzwilliam might also have hoped to figure out a way to prevent the restoration of Fitzgerald's lands.[21] (Ralegh's portion of the seneschal's lands was one of the last portions he received.) Killing Fitzgerald would not have altered restoration of the tracts because they would have gone to his heir. An even more likely reason for the refusal to release him was the disdain so many New English in Ireland held for the Desmond rebels and the queen's pardons.

Pardoning traitors occurred so often, and with so many receiving multiple pardons, that the New English believed it made a mockery of law and order. Ralegh was one of the few New English to have suggested to the Privy Council a policy of pardoning during the Second Desmond War.[22] Elizabeth needed her appointees to oversee the Munster Plantation, but she could not leave the Anglo-Irish and Irish irreconcilable to the new regime.

With Fitzgerald's death, his restored lands passed to his one-and-a-half-year-old son, Edmund, which meant that they also passed into wardship. Wardships were a common way for English to gain income from the estates of orphans. The monarch controlled wardships and granted them to others as a form of patronage. A Court of Wards and Livery operated to regulate wardships, but their patent unfairness—outsiders got to enjoy the orphans' estates until the children reached their majority—made them very unpopular and led to their disbandonment in the seventeenth century.[23] The queen granted Edward's wardship to Ralegh, who in turn granted it to Moyle. Moyle thus controlled the estate's income until Edward came of age at twenty-one years old. Unfortunately for Moyle, the grant to Ralegh was never affixed with the "great" seal, and years later, while Moyle was employed in the queen's service, an Englishman named Newman, who had been poking among the records in Dublin, saw the oversight and put in a claim for the wardship, which the Dublin government in the queen's name granted. Moyle petitioned the Privy Council for redress, and the queen ordered the Dublin government to convince Newman to rescind his claim. She promised to find Newman another wardship, and Moyle had his wardship of Edmund restored.[24] The queen was never happy when her servants were taken advantage of while doing her service, but she nonetheless promised Newman another reward despite the fact that he had known precisely what he was doing. Elizabeth understood human nature—at least the greed that drove men. As for young

Edmund, he received the estate upon coming of age and lived in the castle until 1647, when it was destroyed during the English Civil War.

Moyle's story illustrates how Ralegh, in Ireland as in Virginia, carefully prepared for colonization. He had his man made sheriff to ease relations with the Irish. Just as he appointed John White to succeed Ralph Lane as governor of Virginia, he worked to rid County Cork of scoundrels in power like Myagh, whose personal hatreds and vendettas led him to persecute, torture, and execute the innocent. Ralegh placing his soldiers under the competent and sympathetic Moyle on the Inchiquin barony was a wise move. Obtaining rewards for Moyle, like the wardship, and plots of land for the soldiers, helped ensure loyalty. Moyle handsomely paid back his superiors by filling a variety of military appointments for the queen.

But the high-and-mighty Ralegh, as smart and savvy as the best of them, could be outwitted. On his seignories, he fell victim to a ruse so well executed that throughout his life he had no inkling that he had been tricked—nor did millions of people in subsequent generations who believed the story of the Countess of Desmond.

CHAPTER 18

Resistance to Plantation

R alegh focused on settling colonists in three areas of his seignories: along the Bride River below Lismore, along the west
bank of the Blackwater River by Molana Abbey just north of
Youghal, and along the seacoast southwest of Youghal on the old Inchiquin barony. After Ralegh arrived in Youghal in 1588, he discovered
a problem with Inchiquin. These prized lands had a prior claim upon
them that could forestall his control of the barony. The Countess of
Desmond claimed dowager rights to the castle and its demesne, which
included a great number of ploughlands on this, the most significant
Desmond estate in the region.

The story of the Countess of Desmond is a beloved one even today. Her fame owes to her alleged accomplishments, including the
extraordinary length of her life, and to Ralegh telling her story, which
convinced others of its truth and importance. But the even greater
significance of the story of the Countess of Desmond is that it reveals
how some Anglo-Irish and Irish resisted colonialism by Ralegh. Taking
up arms against the colonizer was not a choice in the 1580s (though
it became one in the 1590s). Instead, people used stealth and their
knowledge of the law and the colonizers to create their own fictions
under colonialism.

THERE WERE, IN THE 1580s, two women alleged to be the Countess
of Desmond. One was Eleanor, née Butler, the widow of Gerald Fitzgerald, 15th Earl of Desmond. Eleanor was an influential woman whom

Queen Elizabeth had unsuccessfully tried to lure into convincing her husband to turn himself in during the Second Desmond War. Ralegh (correctly) believed that parlays with her were useless.[1] Although Eleanor lost all from the rebellion, Elizabeth ultimately granted her a pension and she lived well into the reign of Charles I. Unfortunately, Eleanor has been confused with another Countess of Desmond, who, if she existed, might have been named Katherine. The latter became known because Ralegh told a story that spread through Europe: that the countess was extraordinarily ancient. After her death, many believed that she had lived to the ripe old age of 140. To this day, stories of the long-lived Countess of Desmond continue to be told in Ireland and around the world.

Many myths were associated with the countess: The ancient dowager loved to climb trees, and died after a fall from a cherry or apple tree. She traveled to England from Ireland at well over a hundred years of age (to see the queen or king) and after crossing into England pulled her daughter in a cart all the way to London—a myth actually told about Eleanor, who did visit the English court, but the story was transposed into one about Katherine. Another story, and a quite popular one, was that the countess danced with Richard III at his wedding in 1472, about 117 years before Ralegh met her. Another: she grew so old that she developed a second set of teeth, a story sometimes embellished to include a third set of teeth. Though Ralegh did not create these stories, it is his relation of the countess's ancient age that stands at the root of the tales.

Almost all those who generated the mythical stories about the countess were English—and none ever met her except Ralegh. Ralegh's cousin George Carew, obsessively interested in all things Irish and who built a fantastic archive documenting Ireland, drew a genealogy of the countess after her death, though one that was not at all clear about where she fit into the Desmond family. No one seemed to know which Earl of Desmond the countess had married. Fascination with the countess persisted through the centuries. In the seventeenth century came most of the myths. By the eighteenth century, her stories were standard fare; Horace Walpole used the countess as a source in his book *Historic Doubts in the Life and Reign of King Richard* (1768) and creatively extended her longevity to 162 years. In the mid-nineteenth century, the countess gained even greater fame as many essays and books were published to prove how old she was when she died. Their stories and her story are important to our story of Ralegh and English colonization in

Ireland. The real story is an elaborate and important ruse that tricked Ralegh out of fully benefiting from some of the lands the queen had granted him.

The ruse was first spotted by a "Miss Hickson," who also published under the names Mary Hickson and Mary Agnes Hickson. She was a tenacious researcher and prolific writer of Irish history. She reported her findings in an extended essay, "The Old Countess of Desmond: A New Solution to an Old Puzzle," published in four parts in the 1881 editions of the periodical *The Reliquary: Quarterly Archaeological Journal and Review*. This essay came on the heels of much other nineteenth-century work investigating the veracity of stories about the countess. Hickson, from Tralee in County Kerry, was the daughter of a minister in the Church of Ireland. As a historian, her contemporaries sometimes disagreed with her conclusions—she was somewhat forceful, if not "over the top," in her judgments of people and events—but there is no gainsaying her unusually sharp ability to analyze primary sources. One journal editor who published a Hickson essay, while applauding her research saw the need to "emphatically dissociate himself" from her conclusions on the character of both Lord Grey (of Smerwick infamy) and Queen Elizabeth.[2] Hickson liked to provoke. She was flustered by the mythologizing of history, and in particular thought the Irish nationalist, anti-English sentiment of Victorian Ireland presented a skewered history of the Irish past. She saw colonial Irish history as characterized by bloodletting, but on *all* sides, and noted this violent history was not peculiar to Ireland, but in the character of European history.

Hickson fearlessly studied controversial subjects, transcribing and publishing documents other historians thought best left unpublished.[3] At a time of rising Irish Catholic nationalism and religious tension throughout Ireland, it was impolitic—to some—to recall the massacres of Protestants by Catholics during what is often seen as the bloodiest period of Irish history, the 1640s, particularly when so many Catholics suffered and lost their land as a result of the violence. In Victorian Ireland, the massacres of Protestants had been mythologized as never having occurred, but Hickson included numerous depositions and other evidence showing that they had.

When Hickson turned her attention to the Countess of Desmond, there was relatively little at stake politically, and as noted above, she was following on the heels of other scholars who had been analyzing the evidence and who had proven that the countess could not have lived to 140 years of age, and that she likely was in her late eighties or early nineties when Ralegh met her; thus, she died at around a hundred years old. Hickson went well beyond these scholars in deconstructing the story of the countess by systematically examining an array of archival sources and, among other things, showing that Ralegh was the *only* eyewitness to have affirmed the countess's existence. Englishman offers readers the stories of her teeth growing back and of her walking five miles daily to market, never intimated that he actually met the countess, who was thought to have died thirteen years before he wrote in 1617. (Hickson postulates that she died well before 1604, but I take this up below.) Even Carew, who wrote the murky genealogy, was in Ireland from 1588 to 1592, and served as president of Munster in 1600, when the countess presumably lived, never met her, nor quoted anyone who had, nor referred to her in any of his voluminous posts except to report her death, which, I suspect, he might have learned after making an inquiry about her. No report exists of her funeral or burial. Carew relied on his cousin Ralegh's say-so that she was a real person.

It is only from Ralegh that we have any knowledge of the countess's existence. He spread her story through the English court, mentioning the problem her jointure posed to him in a note to the Privy Council.[4] No Irish mentioned her until years after her death, and only in the context of repeating or building on the stories that English who had never met her spread. Ralegh's remarks in his book *History of the World* (1614) confirmed for history the countess's authenticity: "I myself knew the old countess of Desmond, of Inchiquin, in Munster, who lived in the yeare 1589, and many yeares since, who was marryed in Edward the Fourths time, and held her Joynture from all the Earles of Desmond since then, and that this is true all the Noblemen and Gentlemen of Munster can witness."[5] The context for this passage was Ralegh's discussion of the longevity of biblical patriarchs. The last part, the reference to witnesses, was a flourish of the pen, Hickson noted. Edward IV died in 1483—if Munster folk could testify to the countess's existence over a hundred years later, then there were *dozens* of well-born people over 110 years of age in the 1580s or over 140 in 1612.

Hickson and other nineteenth-century researchers proved that the countess could not have married any of the Desmond earls of the late fifteenth or early sixteenth centuries. Key evidence was also provided from the fact that no contemporary Irish chroniclers of the Geraldines—one of the two most important families of southern Ireland—ever mentioned the countess. In other words, the Irish did not know of her existence, which would be highly unlikely for a countess on the Inchiquin estate. Before Ralegh met her, no one at the English court mentioned her, and it was common in Tudor England for members of the leading Anglo-Irish families to visit the English court.

The authority that Robert Sidney, the 2nd Earl of Leicester, cited in the confused and whimsical story he recorded in 1636 or 1640 of the ancient countess traveling to the English court to petition Elizabeth, toting her aged "decrepit" daughter "in a little carte," was told to him years earlier by "Mr. Harriott."[6] What amuses me about this story is that Hariot lived with Ralegh in 1589 in Youghal and never mentioned that he had met the countess, who lived at Inchiquin several miles away and allegedly walked to Youghal every day. To walk daily to Youghal, she would have taken the Cork Road and passed within feet of Ralegh's house at Myrtle Grove, where Ralegh and Hariot surely would have waved at her or maybe even offered her tea. But Ralegh, too, never mentioned the countess walking to Youghal. As already noted, the story of the countess's trip to the English court was about Eleanor, not Katherine, and it was to the court of James I, not Elizabeth, when Katherine would have been dead.[7] Hariot was having a laugh at Leicester's expense and surely would have told him personal stories of the countess if he had indeed met her. That he said nothing beyond the far-fetched story of a different countess toting her aged daughter to court in a cart adds more credence to the idea that the countess probably did not exist in 1589, let alone 1604.

If the countess did exist, according to Hickson, Katherine was likely the second wife of Thomas, the 12th Earl of Desmond, who died in 1534.[8] That would place her birth in the late fifteenth century, which would put her between ninety and a hundred years old when Ralegh allegedly met her in 1589.

Yet the fact that no one in Ireland recorded the existence of the countess before Ralegh is almost certain proof that she was a fictional character. How could an aged countess, residing at Inchiquin, no less, have escaped comment for a hundred years by not appearing in any letters, genealogies, memoirs, or court records? Two Desmond Wars were fought on and around her estate, and no one mentioned her even in passing.

Hickson documents the ruse by which Ralegh was fooled from taking control of Inchiquin, which the countess claimed by dower rights.

The chief conspirator, Hickson speculates, was John Fitzedmund Fitzgerald of Cloyne, Ralegh's friend, and a staunch ally of the English. Fitzedmund's importance in this episode lay in the 150-year quest of his branch of the Fitzgerald family to attain and maintain control over the See (Church) lands of Cloyne against adjacent lands, including Inchiquin.[9] Over the previous twenty years, and well into the next century, he steadily wrested away the lands of the neighboring Carew family, which included Ballymartyr (now Castlemartyr) and numerous other tracts that abutted Inchiquin and Cloyne. He also had obtained Cloyne's See lands in 1575 for £40 and an annual rent of £5—lands that brought him much profit in leases until the Second Desmond War reduced the local population dramatically.[10] Fitzedmund kept increasing his holdings and, despite his loyalty to the English Crown, he maintained good relations with the Desmonds and the Irish who opposed the English.

A common practice among the Anglo-Irish was to sign their lands over to others so that if a rebellion against the English failed and they were convicted of treason, their lands would not be forfeited to the Crown. These documents often were created years before an actual rebellion occurred, the papers held in reserve and only presented if necessary, showing that the great land barons recognized that rebellion was always a possibility—or that they might be accused of rebellion by their Anglo-Irish enemies. This situation created much confusion in Munster province over which lands were actually attainted after the Second Desmond War, because many landholders claimed that the Earl of Desmond or another attainted rebel had conveyed their lands to them before committing treason, and in some cases this probably was true.

The Irish Parliament tried to circumvent the transfer of lands by rebels before they committed rebellion, in "An Act to make void certain fraudulent conveyances made by the late rebels in Ireland."[11] In Parliament, John Fitzedmund Fitzgerald of Cloyne spoke against the act and admitted that he was one of three men to whom the Earl of Desmond, several years before the rebellion, had signed over his lands, which should later revert to the earl's son. The Irish Parliament, which was meeting for the purpose of attainting the land of the earl and his followers, suddenly had the rug pulled out from beneath them—there was little land to be gained from the earl's attainder. This would effectively have reduced, if not prevented, the English plantation in Munster: there would be hardly any lands for the queen to grant if the attainted earl, before committing treason, had signed them over to Fitzedmund et al. for the earl's son.

Then Sir Henry Wallop, the vice treasurer of Ireland, produced another document, drawn two months before the first in 1574, whereby the earl and others, including John Fitzedmund Fitzgerald of Cloyne, bound themselves together against the queen, even by force of arms, if the English made any attempt to reduce the earl's lands. With proof that the earl had conveyed his lands after signing a document that planned treason against the queen, the later conveyance became null and void. The Parliament asserted the queen's rights to the earl's lands and colonization proceeded apace.

Though embarrassed by the revelation, Fitzedmund seems not to have been harmed in the least. Everyone knew of the practice of signing over lands in case of attainment for treason. The English continued to speak about Fitzedmund in positive terms—these kinds of shenanigans were expected in the preservation of family land. Fitzedmund's support of the earl and his son's claims to the lands likely held him in good stead with the late earl's supporters. Inchiquin itself had once been "part of the See lands of Cloyne," according to Hickson, and these former church lands were the basis of Fitzedmund's wealth.[12] Now it was supposed to be a jewel in Ralegh's seignories. Hickson speculates that in league with Fitzedmund were Roger Skiddy, the former bishop of Cloyne, and John Synnott, both of whom had been witnesses to the earl's conveyance of his lands to Fitzedmund and the others in 1574. In 1575, the countess allegedly had conveyed her rights to the castle and lands of Inchiquin to the Earl of Desmond, who then conveyed the same to Maurice Shehan and David Roche for the use of John Synnott rent-free for thirty-one years.[13] Synnott's claim was rejected in 1588, when virtually every other claim by Anglo-Irish and Irish was rejected, but this was not the end of the matter.[14]

Hickson argues that the legal machinations of Synnott, Skiddy, Shehan, and Fitzedmund over the Inchiquin estate, which the Countess of Desmond claimed by dower rights, led to the rebirth of a likely deceased countess in the late 1580s. I believe the countess never existed. After they had failed to preserve the Desmond lands in 1586, the conspirators saw a way to keep the Inchiquin manor and associated lands from the English for a period of years. Synnott enrolled a conveyance by the Countess of Inchiquin to the earl, which was unsigned but which bore her alleged seal. It likely was a forgery made in 1586 or 1587, not in 1575, as noted above, because the countess did not exist.

This conveyance, allegedly in 1575, was not accepted by the Irish Parliament in 1588. The earl's conveyance of Inchiquin to Synnott, also properly sealed, was also unsigned. In all likelihood, the nonexistent countess was invented because she would have an indelible claim to the Inchiquin estate during her lifetime—her dower rights were unaffected by the 15th Earl's treason—for she allegedly had been married to a previous, albeit unnamed, earl.[15] As long as the countess was kept alive, the lands would remain out of Ralegh's control.

Fitzedmund was not the only one who thought of dower rights as trumping attaintment for treason. The English commissioners in Ireland overseeing the survey of attainted estates wrote to Elizabeth of the problem of jointures, the dower rights of women: Anglo-Irish knew that dower rights protected a woman's land from her husband's treason.[16] The queen could not let noblewomen be denied their legal rights; the whole English system of land ownership rested on legalities protecting land ownership that had to be maintained. In the case of the Countess of Desmond, the Anglo-Irish and Irish fraudulently used the English system against the English, but they would have viewed the confiscation of rebel estates as unjust.

No one after the commission's rejection of Synnott's claim to possess land conveyed by the countess challenged the countess's claim because instead of appealing to another commission, her claim was made personally to Ralegh. He traveled to Inchiquin in 1588 or 1589, where he met someone dressed as an elderly countess. Ralegh accepted that there was nothing he could do about the lands until she died. He "owned" Inchiquin, but during her lifetime the countess occupied the manor and controlled the demesne. Locals occupied many of the tracts, and Ralegh leased out others, but the countess controlled the rent. Ralegh was restricted in how much he could charge. He played a waiting game: he created leases providing that as soon as the countess died the rent would double.

If the English lessees learned of the fraud, they had no reason to tell Ralegh because then their rents would rise. Of those who leased large portions, Robert Reve and his wife were connected by marriage to locals, though he either never took up his lease or did not stay long. Possibly, he knew of the fraud and did not want to get into trouble with Ralegh if the latter found out, but more likely his absence was because he had inherited two manors in Suffolk and decided to seek his fortune there. Thomas Allen, Hariot's Catholic friend and mentor from Oxford, received with a partner the valuable White's Island, across a small river from Inchiquin, and he, too, did not stay very long. Robert Sawle received from Ralegh most of Reve's lease a few years later. He hailed from an Anglo-Irish Catholic family with close ties to the Desmonds, so he, too, would have no reason to tell Ralegh of the fraud for his rates would double.

Ralegh himself went to England and did not return to Ireland until long after the alleged countess was dead and he had long divested himself of his Irish lands to Richard Boyle. In fact, the countess was said to have died in 1604, shortly after Ralegh sold his seignories to Boyle. When Boyle took control of Ralegh's seignories, he never mentioned in his voluminous diaries that detailed his economic transactions and social activities on a day-by-day basis that he had any problem with the rents of Inchiquin, or that he was waiting for the countess to die, or that she had died, or even that he had met her! Boyle visited all of his lands and would have discovered the ruse if he had not already known of it, for he was connected to the Desmonds through marriage. He made no mention of the countess, in all likelihood because she never existed.

As for the local Irish and Anglo-Irish tenants on the Inchiquin lands, they certainly knew their rights and can be seen as coconspirators in and beneficiaries of the ruse. Ralegh was convicted of treason in 1603. Despite his earlier sale of the land to Boyle, when King James I considered confiscating Ralegh's lands in Ireland from him, an inquisition followed by an inspection was made. The County Cork jury collected information on the manor and barony of Inchiquin. The lessees were thus able to place on a legal document for the king their claim to "a certain Common of Estovers," held by all tenants, "whether they held the land for a term of years" or a "term of life or lives." The lessees asserted this right as existing since the time "to which the memory of man runneth." *Estovers* refers to the rights of tenants to take wood from the landlord's estate to repair their homes, for tools, and so on. In this case, Inchiquin's people added that they possessed the right to take wood for their fires and that the woods of Ballyglassin was the precise place allotted to them. These rights, hence, preceded Ralegh's ownership and continued during and beyond.

They asserted that the rents they paid on the Inchiquin lands also were traditional. One lessee stated his rent was yearly payment to the lord "issuing out of and from the towns and lands of Tupples and Moneloghan [Moanlahan] . . . one pair of Yellow Spurs."[17] Other yearly rents for tracts included such insubstantial amounts as 8 p.; 20 p.; 1 s.;

2 s.; and so on. More common were rents ranging from 8 s. to £1, but there was an exception at the other end of the scale. The lessee of Garryvoe was charged £7. This tract, however, included the castle and lands of the Anglo-Norman Carew family, the estates of whom Fitzedmund of Cloyne had been steadily whittling away by taking mortgages on their land and then refusing to allow the family to redeem their parcels.[18] Hence, there was one local family that did not benefit from the ruse and that paid a higher rate.

Fitzedmund's probable authorship of the ruse reflected his lifelong ability to maintain the support of the common people, many of whom had family living on his adjacent lands. I would add that he might have hoped to ultimately gain control of these lands from Ralegh, but the opportunity did not arise. On the other hand, the whole episode illustrates the ability of the local people in league with traditional local leaders to resist English colonialism. The jury's inquisition and inspection made clear that the occupiers of the Inchiquin lands expected their rights and rents to be maintained *after* Ralegh's ownership. Whether the land reverted to the king or went to the new purchaser, Richard Boyle, the people maintained their rights to the woods at Ballyglassin and expected their traditional rent payments to continue.

It should also be considered that some of the tenants had not actually occupied the lands under the Desmonds and that they fabricated the low rents they paid on Ralegh's land. According to Ralegh, Fitzedmund lost 90 percent of his tenants to war and famine during the Desmond Wars. His lands bordered Inchiquin on the southwest. Would not most of the neighboring Inchiquin tenants have died as well? It seems quite likely that surviving Irish tenants displaced from Ralegh's non-Inchiquin lands simply moved to Inchiquin and posed as long-term tenants—perhaps Fitzedmund invited them to do so. For centuries, Irish and Anglo-Irish clans had moved families from one tract to another. The resistance to Munster Plantation was broad: many people were a party to the ruse and benefited by it. In the midst of the rapid transfer of land from Desmonds to Ralegh, local Irish carved out a place for themselves to continue their lives on their clan's ancient lands. Fitzedmund, celebrated by the English for how very English he appeared, understood the niceties of the legalities of English land ownership, enough to be a ringleader with the 15th Earl in trying to secure Desmond lands for the earl's son, then in presenting the case to the Irish Parliament, and finally by seeing that dower rights would forestall Ralegh's control of Inchiquin. The ruse worked because the people went along with it, and Ralegh had no doubts. He certainly would not question the dower rights of a countess.

One question that remains: Why did subsequent generations believe the story of the Countess of Desmond living to 140 years of age? Even today her tale remains popular and her face is known throughout Ireland by the many inauthentic paintings believed to be of her. Continued interest in the far-fetched story of the countess reflects people's own hopes for longevity. The myths about the countess all assert her physical fitness: climbing trees, the daily five-mile walks to Youghal (and home, too!), pulling her aged daughter in a cart to London. The stories had just enough feasibility to keep them alive. When Ralegh told fantastic stories in his book about South American Indians, many were skeptical. The stories were too fantastic, the context too strange, and the people too exotic to readers. Readers attributed Ralegh telling such stories to his ego. Yet, as scandalous and offensive as contemporaries and later generations found the stories Ralegh told of Indians, he was highly respected for his later writings on history, politics, and other subjects that readers could relate to and understand. Moreover, his book *The History of the World*, in which he related the story of the countess, was greatly celebrated as the wisdom of a national hero.

Ultimately, the story of the Countess of Desmond survived because people wished it to be true. Some museums in Ireland persist in relating as true the story of the Countess of Desmond alongside artifacts claimed to be her possessions. But maybe the most important reason she is so revered is that she is seen as an aged widow who survived decades of hard times in Ireland because of her strength of character. It is as if she stands in for the noble character of all Irish women who have suffered but prevailed. As one Irish woman barked to a friend of mine when presented with evidence that the countess never existed, "They said the same thing about Jesus."

CHAPTER 19

Ralegh's Colonists

The only inhabitants of Ralegh's seignories who generally are remembered today are Ralegh and the Countess of Desmond. Of those, one probably remained in Ireland no longer than eighteen months (though he later returned when he no longer owned his seignories) and the other did not exist. Some might know of Thomas Hariot, and a few are aware of John White. Yet figuring out who comprised the colonists is important for exploring what Ralegh intended for his Munster Plantation.

For Ralegh, colonization was a personal endeavor. He knew many of his settlers—those he gave grants of land to had some kind of connection to him. He likely knew what to expect from them, and they from him. In contrast, he would have known much less about those who toiled for his lessees or in the extractive industries established on his land. He had neither the power nor the means to micromanage the grantees, but it is clear that he carefully decided where individuals should be settled, and he created infrastructure to facilitate their success.

—

ONE DOCUMENT that provides important clues as to whom Ralegh granted and leased tracts is a census Ralegh compiled for the Privy Council in early 1589.[1] This census does not provide a complete portrait of his colonists but includes only 154 of the settlers who arrived the first year, and it excludes laborers who worked for those who received land. To supplement the census, Ralegh's conveyances of land in various forms to freeholders and substantial lessees are available, though these exclude many of the later-arriving poorer folks who rented small parcels for which no contract was drawn. There is a surviving rent book from the period of Ralegh's ownership, but damage has rendered much of it unreadable. Other clues about the colonists can be attained from the papers of Richard Boyle, who purchased a substantial portion of Ralegh's seignories in the seventeenth century and kept detailed diaries that include entries on some of Ralegh's settlers and their children and grandchildren. Another large group, for whom there is virtually no information, comprised the hundreds of workers employed in extractive industries. Thus, Ralegh's census, and those completed by other Undertakers, cannot provide anything near a full portrait of the New English colonists because so many arrived after the census was taken and the poorer folk and family dependents were excluded. But it is a starting point for analyzing the colony's initial settlement.

The census resulted from a series of questions posed by the Privy Council to all Undertakers. Ralegh provides among the most detailed of all replies, probably to show the Privy Council that he took seriously his planting of Munster. It may seem a small point, but it is not, that Ralegh could provide first and last names for most of the adult males. For army and naval officers, he substituted their rank for their first name; the Privy Council knew exactly to whom he referred when he listed Lieutenant Davis or Captain Maries because most, if not all, of the lieutenants and captains in Ireland received appointment from the Privy Council. Of males, only one adult, John the Armourer, has no last name on the census, and neither does "Owen the boy." Wives and children were left unidentified on the census, but whether an adult male brought a family or not was noted.[2] Besides the armorer, Ralegh's early settlers included a clerk, a baker, a smith, and five merchants.

Four of the five merchants settled at Mogeely, the focal point of the plantation, on the northwest reaches of his lands on the Bride River, below Lismore. (Note here that Ralegh's Mogeely [Gaelic for "flood-plain"] is not to be confused with the modern Mogeely, a name derived from Imokilly, located about twelve miles to the southwest just above Castlemartyr.) Historians mistakenly assume Ralegh most valued Inchiquin and Lismore on his seignories, the former because of its prominence to the Desmonds, the latter because it was a regional center before the Desmond Wars and then regained importance in the seventeenth century. From the Middle Ages, Lismore held the largest market fairs in the area. But no market fairs were held for decades because of the Desmond Wars, and Lismore's market potential was made moot for Ralegh because it was in the hands of the Archbishop of Cashel, so Ralegh could not restore it to its former significance—at least not until he gained control of it, and even then Mogeely remained the focal point of his seignories in terms of economic development and population.

Under Ralegh, Mogeely became the commercial and industrial center of the region. The nearby rebuilt town of Tallow experienced a significant rebirth in the 1590s as well. As today, farmers in the area could access needed services at Tallow, such as shoemaking and blacksmithing, and they could purchase from a variety of shops. But Mogeely became the economic powerhouse of Ralegh's Munster Plantation, hence the settlement of so many merchants at Mogeely and the lightning-quick establishment of several economic enterprises. Mogeely merchants engaged in larger commercial transactions over a much broader terrain that extended well beyond Ralegh's seignories. From Mogeely, merchants disseminated goods to the Irish living to the west and north of Ralegh's holdings in exchange for their cattle and crops. These merchants also supplied goods to the hundreds of workers Ralegh sent to Mogeely. Elsewhere on his seignories, Ralegh had little concern for the buying, selling, and production of commodities, as those residing on the southern portions of Ralegh's lands could access Youghal for their market needs.

Nearly a sixth of the men listed on Ralegh's census were labeled *esquire* (5) or *gentleman* (19). *Esquire* generally referred to the eldest sons of knights or the eldest sons of the younger sons of nobility, and *gentlemen* designated those more distantly removed from nobility and knights. One gentleman on the census was also listed as a smith, perhaps a goldsmith or a silversmith. Three were captains, who probably hailed from prominent families. None of the gentlemen were included among Ralegh's list of copyholders and cottagers settled in County Waterford, which is to be expected. None of the copyholders or cottagers received named ploughlands (also called carucates), because their portions were too small, whereas the esquires and gentlemen received specifically named estates or ploughlands that once had belonged to larger estates. The largest settlement belonged to Henry Moyle, who was denoted as occupying land "Upon the Barony of Inchequiyn." There he settled with "his own company daily attendant upon him."[3] Moyle divided many of the ploughlands among his men, and the Privy Council would have appreciated that Ralegh looked after security by installing a police and military force of former soldiers turned colonists under Moyle that could be quickly gathered for service in Youghal or Cork City and assist Moyle in his duties as sheriff. This allowed the company of men sent by the queen to defend colonists stationed near Mogeely, fifteen miles due north of Inchiquin, where greater threats existed because of the heavy concentration of Irish to the north and west.

Before their arrival in Ireland, Ralegh's settlers were connected to him in a variety of ways, primarily through Devon. Familial ties bound Ralegh to many of the leading families, which had intermarried through the centuries. He also held close ties with families below the gentry. As Lord Warden of the Stannaries, he knew many of the working men in both Devon and Cornwall. His position as the queen's Captain of the Guard further connected him with families at various levels, from whom he chose guardsmen. As Lord Lieutenant of Cornwall since 1585, Ralegh bore responsibilities for raising men to fight in Ireland and for defense of the realm wherever needed. Hooker noted that the office bestowed judicial duties on Ralegh, though it is unclear in what legal matters the lord lieutenant held jurisdiction, because the office had no function in the operation of local government. The Privy Council occasionally referred judicial disputes to Ralegh, both in Cornwall and (later) in Jersey, where he became governor, so he seems to have functioned as an arbiter for disputes that came under the Privy Council's jurisdiction, making recommendations to them when he could not settle a dispute himself. As Lord Lieutenant and Vice Admiral of Devon and Cornwall, Ralegh was further linked to families of all levels in South West England. Ralegh bore responsibility for inspection of the coastal forts in the region and for occasionally fulfilling those forts' supply needs. He sometimes held responsibility for purchasing food for army recruits as well. Many Devon and Cornwall farmers thus benefited from Ralegh's patronage for feeding the military, which also aided his recruitment of colonists.

One sailor and soldier who migrated with Ralegh to Ireland was a Captain Fulford, who settled with Henry Moyle at Ballymartyr. Fulford was almost certainly Andrew Fulford, who captained Ralegh's ship *Job* from 1585 to 1586 at Roanoke. Earlier he had served with Ralegh in Ireland and was with him when he captured Lord Roche at Roche's castle. Seafarers Robert and John Mawle or Maule also settled on Ralegh's land. Robert became one of Ralegh's two main agents in Ireland, handling his business arrangements when Ralegh was unavailable. He had studied law in London at the Middle Temple, as did a handful of Ralegh's other men. Robert settled at Ballantray, on the Blackwater River, while John settled upriver on the Bride. Both having been subscribers to Gilbert's 1583 expedition evinces their interest in overseas colonization. Another seafaring associate who settled on Ralegh's seignories was William Andrewes, one of the five esquires listed on the census. Andrewes also had sailed on the 1583 Gilbert expedition in command of the *Squirrel*. The *Squirrel's* master under Andrews was "one Cade," most likely William Cade, yet another Ralegh colonist.

It is impossible to identify all of the settlers listed on the 1589 census. Many were relatively poor and left little trace in England or Ireland. And with the Nine Years' War (1594–1603), many moved to the coastal towns or returned to England and later were replaced by new settlers. The difficulty of identifying individuals is compounded by the ubiquity of many names. Still, a fair number of the 154 named males enter the historical record. One of the more unusually named settlers, which makes him easier to trace, was Hugh Graterix, whom Ralegh listed among the copyholders and cottagers of County Waterford. Graterix colonized with his family and likely was the father or uncle to William Greatrakes, who held minor offices in Munster beginning about 1593. William rose quickly by marrying into the family of Richard Croker in 1591. (Croker was another of Ralegh's settlers, though not listed on the census, and he had been a comrade in arms in Ireland.) William Greatrakes's son, also named William, later identified himself as a gentleman from Devon when he attended Oxford in 1619. Not only had the family risen and the younger William proven himself to possess many fine attributes, but notably he identified himself at school by his heritage in England rather than his place of birth in Ireland. A year later, however, he entered the Inner Temple to study law and seems to have had his identity placed upon him—he was listed among the students as the son of William Greatrakes of Aughmore in Ireland.[4] (Aughmore was a part of Ralegh's seignories on the east side of the Blackwater.). William's son, Valentine, born in 1628 on Ralegh's former seignories, later achieved fame in England as a faith healer known for his laying on of hands.[5] King Charles II invited him to Whitehall to perform—the family certainly had risen from its humble origins as lower-stratum colonists on Ralegh's seignories. At some point family members returned to spelling their last name in a way closer to that used by Ralegh on his census: Greatorex.

Another unusually named colonist listed among Ralegh's copyholders and cottagers barely enters the historical record except for inclusion on Ralegh's census and Ralegh's irate mentioning of him in a letter.[6] Without the census and the letter, we would have no knowledge of Nabugodonizer [Nebuchadnezzar] Jewell. Jewell spread rumors of Ralegh having fathered a child by Anne Goold in Ireland. Despite Ralegh's adamant denials, the child likely was his and probably was conceived at the time Ralegh compiled his census. He left the child £331 in his will of 1597, though his admission to being her father was half-hearted: he referred to her then as "my Reputed Daughter."[7] Six years later, however, in 1603, while imprisoned in the Tower of London and even more unsure of his future, Ralegh urged his wife to "Be Charitable to her, and teach thy son to love her for his father's sake." He admitted in the same letter that he had "given nothing" to his daughter, who at this time would have been around fourteen years old. Why Ralegh had been so penurious is impossible to say, because illegitimate children were common among the elite, many doing quite well in society, and this particular child was conceived when Ralegh was single and before he courted his future wife. As for Jewell, like Ralegh's child, his fate is unknown.[8]

Some of Ralegh's colonists were Irish who served in the English army. These include Patrick Fagen (or Fagan), Conogh Fagen, Cayheir MacDonogh, Manus Mac Sheeth, and others who received land alongside English colonists. Patrick Fagen, recall, was the Irishman who saved Ralegh in an episode recounted by Hooker. Personal connections between English and Irish, as between Ralegh and Fagen, trumped the Privy Council's and queen's instructions that no Irish be settled on the seignories. Eight months after Ralegh's census, Fagen was in Lisbon on an errand for Robert Coppinger of County Cork (the Coppingers were also Irish associates of Ralegh). Fagen accompanied Henry Skiddy, a factor in the wine trade from Lisbon to London. They likely went on Ralegh's behalf, because Ralegh was actively engaged in trying to bring more wine into England.

The Coppingers' connections with Ralegh, and the rewards they received from him, are even more revealing than the Fagen connection of the ability of Irish and English to mesh their interests and families on the Ralegh seignories. Walter Coppinger, like Fagen, emerged as an ally of Ralegh after performing singular acts of service to save English during the Desmond Wars. The Coppingers were longtime denizens of the land of Ralegh's seignories in the area of Mogeely and also across the Blackwater River where modern-day Coppinger is located. Ralegh had a special relationship with the Coppingers. Soon after receiving his seignories, he leased, what was in right, though not under English law, the Coppingers's own land, Lisnabrin, to them for four thousand years at an annual rate of four pence per acre.[9] Conveying the land in terms of a ridiculously long lease rather than a freehold grant had its advantages for the Coppingers. As a freehold, Coppinger would have owed service, including military service, to Ralegh or his heirs. But a lease did not carry the same responsibilities, and the four pence per acre yearly rent ensured that no one could complain that the Coppingers were not paying tax on their parcels.

Undoubtedly, Ralegh knew the Coppingers from when he spent the winter at Lismore Castle in 1581, but they already had proven their character after a battle that had destroyed Tallow during the Second Desmond War. Walter Coppinger went to the battlefield to tend the wounded and took home Ralegh's man Hugh Croker from Devon and nursed him back to health. After the war, Hugh and Richard Croker settled on Ralegh's Irish land and married into the Coppinger family. Hugh named one of his children Wat, which was Ralegh's nickname, and Richard was presented with a gold watch from Ralegh that remained with the family at least into the early twentieth century. The Coppingers and Crokers became intimately connected with the Boyles, and they continued to rise among the leading families in the area.[10] In other words, some of Ralegh's settlers and local Irish were extremely well placed on Ralegh's lands to increase their estates, intermarry, and form a local elite.

English Catholics made up another significant group of Ralegh's colonists. At least two of the four esquires that I can identify on Ralegh's 1589 census were Catholic; I cannot identify the religion of one esquire, William Andrewes. Ralegh granted Thomas Allen (esquire) and William Badby (gentleman) White's Island and four ploughlands—a large grant. In the early seventeenth century, Englishmen Fynes Moryson claimed that relatively few English Protestants took up the Undertakers' land, which led them to sell to "English Papists." The latter, he noted, tended to be the "most turbulent, and so being daily troubled and questioned by the English Magistrate, were like to give the most money for the Irish land."[11] Ralegh settled Catholics from the start. It is doubtful that he charged them higher rents or made them unfavorable deals, because he had personal ties with those who migrated and gave them large estates. One Catholic family from Devon with whom Ralegh had strong ties was the Floyers. John Floyer captained a ship for Ralegh in 1592. Anthony Floyer received the land at Templemichael, adjacent to Molana Abbey. Anthony was suspected of illegal activities in France and was highly suspicious because of his association with recusants. He was tried in England for allowing a priest to christen his children, but the charges "were dropped when the witness withdrew his statement."[12] Floyer was joined at Templemichael by other Catholics. Hariot eventually conveyed his rights to Molana to Anthony's brother William in 1597, thereby ensuring that both holy sites remained in Catholic hands.

Next to Templemichael and conjoined with it in Ralegh's census is Castle Myles, where another Devonshire Catholic, Anthony Carew, received land. The Raleghs were related to the Carews (both Catholic and Protestant), and one of Ralegh's sons would later be named Carew. Although Ralegh's census lists Anthony Carew (gentleman) as living at Castle Myles, it is more likely to have been Ralegh's cousin Henry Carew. This Henry's son, also named Henry, was quite a firebrand and frequently in trouble with the law in England for impolitic speech and recusancy. At one point, his father had to post £1,000 in securities for young Henry's release, which was obtained only after Ralegh wrote a letter in favor of the boy.[13] Both the Floyers and Carews returned to England from Ireland during the Nine Years' War.[14]

One English Catholic with whom Ralegh clashed but who was not one of his colonists, and who in fact competed for his lands, was Sir William Stanley. Born in 1548, Stanley had served England with valor as a young man in the Netherlands in the late 1560s and then in Ireland beginning around 1570. By 1579, he had been promoted to captain and knighted at Waterford, and he served in many posts throughout Ireland. In 1583, when Ralegh left Ireland to join Gilbert in colonizing America, Stanley replaced Ralegh as commander of the garrison at Lismore. Stanley participated in many battles throughout his career—he seems to have been sent to every hot spot where his military skills were needed. He excelled in battle, on retreat, and as an administrator. Allegedly, he was a terror in Ireland in the mold of Humphrey Gilbert: the Catholic Stanley bragged that he had hanged over three thousand Irish rebels.

Despite the applause for his military service emanating from the English court, and his administration of the English government at Munster during Sir John Norreys's absence, Stanley did not receive a seignory in Ireland, though it is unclear whether he actually applied for one. (He might have been forewarned that he would not be a recipient and should not apply.) Stanley was interested in New World colonization: in 1582–1583, he was projected as a potential leader of an expedition to colonize English Catholics on Gilbert's patent.[15] He also held interest in Irish land, as he rented Lismore Castle from Anne Thickpenny from 1584 to 1586, leaving his family there when he took assignment under the Earl of Leicester to fight the Spanish in the Netherlands. We can assume that Stanley would have loved a grant of the lands bordering Lismore, which eventually went to Ralegh.[16] Stanley captured the city of Deventer (Netherlands) in 1586, which he commanded with mostly Irish troops, but then he surrendered the city to the Spanish in January 1587: he had gone over to the Spanish side.

When and why Stanley decided to defect is unknown. His brother was a Jesuit and appears to have had some influence with him, but his longtime stellar service for the queen implies that some event dramatically altered his perspective. His exclusion from rewards in Ireland could have played a role. Elizabeth had considered Stanley for high appointment, perhaps as Lord Deputy of Ireland, and it did not hurt Stanley's prospects that Elizabeth's childhood friend, Leicester, was one of his strongest supporters.[17] Stanley's military reputation was immense; after he changed sides, English administrators in Ireland (for years) feared him leading an army of Spanish to conquer Ireland. With so much support for Stanley at court, it is hard to see why he would have gone over to the Spanish without doing so because of being refused lands in Ireland and because of his resentment of religious prejudice. He would not have left his wife and children at Lismore if he had not expected to return. Up until the surrender of Deventer in 1587, Stanley's service was of the highest order of loyalty, so something happened to suddenly lead him to change sides.

At the time of Stanley's treason in 1586, Ralegh had reserved for himself the lands that abutted Lismore. Ralegh could not purchase Lismore since it was held by the Archbishop of Cashel until 1589, long after Stanley's treason. But Stanley likely wanted the adjoining land and would have expected also to receive the castle because it was common for English captains to obtain an Irish estate through occupation followed by a grant from the queen. Stanley had probably left his family at Lismore during his service in the Netherlands because he expected to return to Ireland in an important administrative capacity. Lismore Castle and the surrounding lands were the most desirable location in the region for an important man; he might have hoped to restore it as a regional center. Stanley leaving his family there was like putting in a claim to the castle and abutting lands. But the queen gave the lands to Ralegh. After committing treason, the resentful Stanley described Ralegh as "the blacke man." Of the queen's infatuation with Ralegh, he vulgarly observed, "when the blacke man is owt of hir Maties [Majesty's] sight, she is not well plesed, who puttith all men in dispayer in his absens. The Service the blacke man hath done hit is no marvayle of his recompence."[18]

When Stanley committed treason, his family was still at Lismore. Ralegh tried to wrest it from them. At first, the Privy Council ordered the seizure of all Lady Stanley's property but then reversed course and did not remove her from Lismore.[19] Ralegh eventually won the prize, obtaining a lease for a hundred years from the Archbishop of Cashel. When complaint was made against Ralegh in 1590 by Lady Stanley's representatives, the queen put the kibosh on any suits filed against her "servant" Ralegh by the "traitor's wife."[20] Lady Stanley joined her husband in exile.

—

THE QUEEN'S CHOICE of Ralegh to receive the largest portion of land reflected not only his status as her favorite but also his perceived abilities to succeed as a colonizer. Ralegh moved to Ireland, knew all of his adult male landholding colonists by name, and took extraordinary measures to improve relations with local Irish and Anglo-Irish by placing his right-hand man Moyle as Sheriff of County Cork, situating Catholic settlers at Catholic holy sites, and including Irish and Anglo-Irish in the colonial economy he developed on his seignories. He also placed four of his five merchants in an unusual place: inland on the northwest edge of his holdings, where they could conduct trade with the Irish and supply the hundreds of workers he would send to labor in extractive and manufacturing industries. Ralegh had grand plans for rural economic development and commerce that would incorporate his seignories into a vast network of international trade. Almost overnight, he connected his plantation to the Canary Islands off the coast of Africa, to Spain, the Netherlands, northern England, and London. Just as the Virginia colony disappeared, though few knew of its fate, and the public was fed de Bry's publication heralding Ralegh's New World colony, Ralegh's other colony, his Irish colony, emerged with great prospects for success.

PART EIGHT

~

Colonization as an
Economic Enterprise

CHAPTER 20

The Plantation Economy

O ne of the settlers who lived on Ralegh's land, John White, left little trace of his life in Ireland beyond an outstanding artifact: the Mogeely Estate map, now considered a national treasure as the oldest detailed estate map in Ireland. White and Hariot worked together on this beautiful map in 1598.[1] Hariot provided the acreage of the numerous portions listed in the cartouche and likely helped White scale the various sites.[2] White colorfully rendered the buildings, land, and fencing. The map is worthy of intensive study, requiring a magnifying glass to pick up nuance in the detail. It highlights how quickly—in ten years—the English had developed the area. Historians long have viewed the map as an exaggeration, an ideal of what the English intended to accomplish, but written documents and recent archaeological study confirm Mogeely's economic vibrancy and development. One archaeologist notes that the White "map is reliable as it depicts Elizabethan field systems along with settlement forms and patterns."[3] Numerous sizable tracts of land at Mogeely had been enclosed in the English manner, and the buildings displayed on the map actually existed. The map depicts thirty-four parcels of land totaling a bit more than 1,135 acres. These parcels include a restored "oulde Orchard" and a new orchard, six islands, two garden plots, fourteen enclosed agricultural areas, and several fields, as well as the castle, the "Courte and Wasteland," the dock and river banks on the Bride River, a rabbit warren, and two parcels appended to Mogeely by Ralegh. Unidentified in the map's legend but included on the map's borders are the Mogeely woods and other tracts belonging to the Ralegh seignories:

Kilcoran, Curryglass, and "Guy Towses land." The castle occupied less than an acre of land. Keeping in mind that *castle* referred to a fortified location, not necessarily a single building, Mogeely's castle could hold many hundreds of men.[4] Almost half of the total land at Mogeely was enclosed, providing protection to thousands of head of livestock.

As early as 1586, tenants were required to live close to the castle: "no tenant belonging to the lands of Mogeely shall henceforth dwell abroad . . . in woods, bogs, glens and other remote places . . . but shall presently resort and dwell within the town or depart from those lands."[5] The English were extremely nervous about Irish roaming, hence this order that they must live in the town or leave. What is significant about this notation in the official records is that Ralegh had not actually been granted any of his land yet.

Who were these tenants? Who was their landlord? As with other lands on the Ralegh seignories, it seems Ralegh had organized and begun settling the area well before he received his grants. The initial

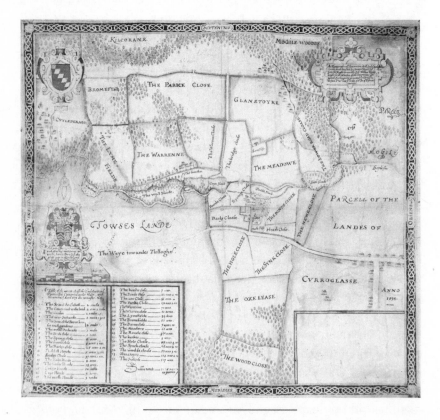

22. John White estate map of Mogeely, 1598

tenants probably were Irish who had worked the lands before the Desmond Wars, and they may have attracted other displaced Irish. Ralegh's friend and neighbor of Mogeely, Walter Coppinger, may even have placed tenants there.

Once Ralegh colonized Mogeely, many Irish remained in the area working on nearby lands. They retained close connections with Mogeely through trade, and probably through the exchange of labor. Some may also have become tenants of Ralegh's lessees. If the local Irish were distrustful of Ralegh, Mogeely's neighbors to the east, the Coppingers, could have smoothed relations between them and the English; Patrick Condon, to the west of Mogeely, probably did the same, because Ralegh, Condon, and the Coppingers all worked together on a variety of matters. Other than the soldiers who settled with Moyle, Mogeely likely was the first place Ralegh sent English colonists. They would have found many of the fields already cleared and planted by the aforementioned Irish tenants, hence, the quickness with which the colonists could enclose the land and erect buildings.

Mogeely's houses were constructed in the style of housing in Somerset and Devon, where most of the English at Mogeely hailed from, a style later common in parts of early Virginia. English styling and materials reflected English choices. Houses flanked roads in diverse nucleated settlements much like in later New England, with individual lots around forty-five feet wide. The settlement pattern of the residences and the enclosing and naming of the fields reflected not only English choices but transformation of the landscape to English ownership, further signifying, at least to themselves, that by their "improvement" they possessed full rights to the land. Civilization, the English would have congratulated themselves, had replaced barbarism. But if the English marked the land in an English manner, Irish markings remained as well: White's map depicts small enclaves of Irish houses. Ralegh's intent, as at Roanoke, was that colonists should live in harmony with the Native people. In the 1590s, the relationship revolved around mutual economic and defensive support. In the Nine Years' War, Mogeely defended Irish locals from raiders, while local Irish provided the English with intelligence about the enemy.[6]

Irish brought their livestock and crops to Mogeely to feed the local workers, and they received goods in exchange. Mogeely became *the* marketplace in the region because farm products were transported easily by boat or overland to Youghal or Cork. But Mogeely itself produced a variety of items for local trade and the international market economy. A mill at Mogeely cut lumber that went into the building of local houses and a church. Glass and pottery were produced at Mogeely, as was iron. Weirs at Mogeely, constructed with local lumber, provided plenty of fish to complement the people's diet and for sale elsewhere.

However much English colonization arose from fear of Spanish dominance of the Emerald Isle, the English goal was to transform Ireland into a stable, productive, tax-generating colony. The expense of administrating Ireland demanded income, and the drive for revenue stood at the root of the Desmond Wars. Productive settlements would lead to English population growth and to colonists paying rents to Undertakers, who, in turn, paid rents to the Crown.

In less than a decade, Mogeely became a flourishing enclave, a great success story of English colonialism: colonists lived in relative harmony with the Irish, extractive industries boomed, and local manufacturing fulfilled some local needs while providing items for export. Ralegh created this success at Mogeely and elsewhere on his lands in Ireland because of his huge vision for his plantation's economic development. He sought to fit Ireland not only into England's economy but also into an Atlantic economy that extended from Europe to Africa. Trade would be the lifeblood of the empire, and Ralegh illustrated this by creating new Atlantic trade routes from Ireland to Africa to England. He recognized, as few others did, that precious metals were unnecessary for colonial success; instead, wood could be the most important staple colonized lands provided to the English Empire, establishing a pattern followed by virtually all future English colonies on the Atlantic: logging of trees to make lumber for ships, housing, furniture, and other goods. Ralegh's vision of colonizing took in an array of economic enterprises that involved hundreds of people. His vision of empire extended in multiple directions that encompassed multiple purposes, but he always understood that success depended on food for sustenance and profits for maintenance of colonies.

—

ON ARRIVAL IN MUNSTER, many English colonists encountered Irish ploughlands that were heavily overgrown owing to abandonment over the previous twenty years, but clearing out the thickets of brush, though labor intensive, yielded great results. Munster soils were rich and well watered, with manuring less important than in many other areas of Ireland, especially because wheat had scarcely been planted over the previous two decades. The planters' main tasks on arrival were to employ laborers to clear and seed the land, and to construct housing. As long as the planters had labor and did not have to face external threats, the work could proceed relatively quickly, given that the Undertakers and other men of substance (supposedly) brought food and other supplies to last at least a year.

Most colonists did not have as much labor at their disposal as those at Mogeely did or that Moyle enjoyed with his ex-soldiers, but as in later New England, the New English colonists of Munster were intent on making their colony look like Old England, and they likely fenced their ploughlands whenever downtime was available. They did much of their fencing with stone and hedgerows, which today separate estates on Ralegh's former seignories between the Blackwater and Bride Rivers. What is today considered a typical and beautiful characteristic of the Irish countryside began as a Tudor transformation of the landscape.

Additional economic activities on the seignories were left to the discretion of the Undertakers. For a colonizer like Ralegh, who understood colonization of the New World as a path to extract, cultivate, and process commodities for the English (and European) market, it was natural for him to perceive Ireland in similar terms. It would not be surprising if Ralegh was the one who convinced the queen in 1589 to allow the Undertakers to export commodities from Ireland for fourteen years without custom duties.[7] He was not the only Undertaker to enlarge the economy of his seignories beyond agricultural production, but he was unusual in promoting a diversity of enterprises. Ireland had a wealth of resources that could fill English needs and those of other markets.

Ralegh selected the location of his seignories in large measure because of the area's superior potential for agricultural production: fertile lands were the most important factor for attracting colonists. But the vast array of possible nonagricultural commodities is probably what led Ralegh to claim such a large allotment, and in particular the landscape between the Bride and Blackwater Rivers: great strands of trees, incredibly rich fishing, bountiful veins of iron, and many, if not all, of the ingredients necessary for glass production could be found there. Fishing involved continuance of an activity ancient to the region; iron extraction comprised reviving a long-dormant industry; glass production introduced a new enterprise; lumber, which drew the most interest from Ralegh, was not only necessary for producing iron and glass and useful for the main forms of fishing practiced on the rivers but also key for connecting Ralegh's seignories to the burgeoning trade networks of the Atlantic.

Commercial fishing had been conducted on the Blackwater River (and other rivers in Ireland) for hundreds of years. We know through import records that in the early sixteenth century over 50 percent of Irish exports to Bristol (likely the lead port for Irish goods in England) comprised fish, a figure that actually had declined from the late fifteenth century, when fish totaled 78 percent of exports to Bristol.[8] The decline in fish as a percentage of exports continued as agricultural exports from Ireland gained prominence, but how much fish was exported does not appear to have declined in real terms. The growth of lumber and iron exports from Ireland contributed to the relative decline of fish in the seventeenth century, which was compounded by the English increasingly obtaining cod and other fish from the North Atlantic. Nevertheless, fishing in Ireland, especially for salmon, remained substantial, especially in the southeast of Ireland in Waterford, Cork, and the counties to the southwest.

Mostly non-Irish, especially Spanish and Basques, fished offshore from Munster, whereas the Irish focused on the rivers. The Munster Blackwater River boasted one of the best salmon runs in all of Europe.[9] The river held numerous other types of fish, especially pike, but salmon and eel were the species most noted in commercial records. In the seventeenth century, other species were introduced by Ralegh's successor, Richard Boyle, but salmon remained the most important commercial fish in the Blackwater for hundreds of years.

There are (and were) well over a dozen ways to snare salmon, many of which were practiced in the sixteenth century. Noncommercial fishermen used rod and line, though an ancient and more popular method was spearfishing. As among the Algonquin Indians documented by John White at Roanoke, night fishing was also popular. Both American Indian and Irish fisherman used a bright light to attract fish, then threw a spear with a rope attached to the end to pull the fish in. In the early seventeenth century, this method was outlawed in Ireland, except for use by English soldiers.[10]

Commercial fishing for salmon in Ralegh's time and after usually was done with weirs and nets (before the fish reached the weirs); weirs were the most common method at key locations on the Blackwater and Bride Rivers. The weirs were made of either wattle and stakes, or wood, or some combination, and required much maintenance. Fish swimming upriver swam into a V-shaped apparatus, though some weirs were designed to snare fish returning to sea. The Irish employed weirs as early as the fourteenth century, and they were widely used on the Blackwater in the sixteenth century when Ralegh received his seignories.

The Blackwater weirs, unusual in not extending across the entire river where they would hinder passing boats and ships, appear to always have been located adjacent to land because this was the easiest way to maintain them.[11] Two of the most important historic sites on the Blackwater River likely owed their existence to the salmon run: Ralegh's Lismore Castle and Hariot's Molana Abbey were the two best places for snaring salmon. Lismore, by far, was the premier locale for salmon on the Blackwater, if not in all of Ireland. The weirs were situated across the river from the castle. Salmon was so plentiful for so many centuries, we can assume that it was the dietary staple that sustained significant population growth and the popularity of regional fairs at Lismore. Much closer to the sea, sixth-century Molana Abbey sits on an island in the Blackwater just offshore at a particularly wide bend in the river, which reduces the current. Enough salmon hugged the island shore on their swim upriver to convince the abbey's builders that it was an excellent location to obtain a great supply of fish. The monks could walk just outside the abbey walls to snare enough to carry them through to the next season—salmon are easily preserved by drying and smoking. For centuries after the abbey stood in ruins, whoever owned the land or leased the rights to fish at Molana continued to snare salmon in weirs.

Ralegh's grants from the queen, which he supplemented through his permanent lease of the lands of Lismore, provided him a monopoly over fifteen miles of the Blackwater River and its fish, extending from above Lismore all the way to Molana Abbey. Conflicts over fishing rights in the Blackwater between locals and the river's owners have existed from at least the time of Ralegh's possession until the present day. In the nineteenth century, the British Parliament (on a few occasions) determined that exclusive rights to the river's fish from Molana Abbey to Lismore date to Ralegh's grants from Queen Elizabeth and his lease of Lismore Castle and lands. Richard Boyle later purchased those rights, which have passed through the centuries to subsequent owners. Parliament urged in the nineteenth century that locals be permitted to continue to fish for their own personal use, per traditional practice, but commercial fishing lay monopolized in private hands.[12]

Today, the Duke of Devonshire, who owns Lismore, retains exclusive rights to Blackwater River fishing, much to the dismay of many locals.

The Lismore fisheries had been controlled by the See of Lismore from at least the early thirteenth century until Ralegh gained control in 1589.[13] Before Ralegh obtained the fisheries, the bishop of Lismore leased them out and received in exchange, besides the yearly rent, the "fourth fish"—25 percent of the catch. After conveyance of Lismore to Ralegh, the bishop continued to receive the fourth fish. (He also received £13 6 s. 8 d. per year for the entirety of the Lismore property.) The fourth fish was worth about £80 in 1637, which, if typical, meant that the Lismore catch brought in £320 per year to its lessee minus the bishop's portion and the church tithe.[14]

Ralegh farmed out his fishing rights through leases—his father had done the same in Devon.[15] Lessees received rights to exclusively fish a particular location, and they usually did not possess rights to the adjacent land beyond a small spot to service their weirs. (Molana Abbey was an exception because Ralegh granted Thomas Hariot the Abbey, its land, and the valuable fishery.) Ralegh leased the Lismore fishery to Robert Carew of Exeter. The lease stipulated that Carew's sons, Roger and William, would receive the lease on their father's death for the duration of their lives.[16] Carew's lease included the "weirs, hooks and other engines [fishing equipment] and devices." In exchange, within three years he had to build "a new marine house, [and] a sluice or flood gate for 12 foot boats to pass with lumber, wood, and other necessaries." Ralegh's stipulation of improvements on the river at Lismore benefited his other operations by facilitating the shipping of staves and other goods through this narrow portion of the river. Carew's yearly rent of £20 sterling—the highest amount paid for fishing rights on the Blackwater and likely in all of Ireland—illustrates the immense value of this locale for salmon fishing.[17]

Ralegh placed only one significant restriction on Carew in the lease, one that might surprise modern readers: the practice of conservation. Carew could catch only 100 salmon per year. This might seem hardly worth taking on such an expensive lease until one realizes that each of the salmon Carew kept apparently weighed 100 pounds or more, a size unknown today. If the average fish taken weighed 100 pounds and Carew took 100 each year (the smaller ones were let go for future harvesting), that's 10,000 pounds of fish.[18] With the bishop receiving a quarter of the take, Carew could still clear 7,750 pounds of fish (not including the tithe). Excluding the tithe, Carew paid approximately £1 per 375 pounds of fish, or if the fish averaged a low of 50 pounds each, then he paid £1 per 250 pounds of fish; effectively, Carew paid to Ralegh 1 p. for the right to 2½ pounds of salmon. Another way to consider the value of the Lismore fishery: its £20 annual rent plus the fourth fish was more than five times the value of the leases of Lismore's land, which included five large tracts of over a hundred acres each, plus the lands Ralegh leased to Lismore's provost and burgesses.

Not only were the smaller fish left to return each year at a larger size, but Ralegh's lease to Carew included a hefty fine of £4 for every salmon taken beyond the first one hundred. Ralegh had no compelling reason to maintain the one-hundred-fish limit besides conservation, but it is likely the policy was in place before Ralegh obtained control of the fishery. Although the historian of Irish fishing, Arthur Went, did not notice the conservation techniques practiced at Lismore under Ralegh, nor the huge cost of the fishery to Carew, he saw the result three hundred years later: "great abundance of fish is still taken daily and exported" from the Blackwater, and the proprietors still practice conservation, releasing many of the smaller fish, a tribute to foresight and tradition.[19]

There were and would develop numerous other weirs downriver and a few upriver as far as Mallow, and later even farther west, but Lismore remained the key spot for centuries.[20] Ralegh possessed most of the other sites for capturing salmon along both the Blackwater and the Bride, essentially giving him a monopoly on Ireland's richest salmon run.

Ralegh possessed a salmon weir at Lysfinny on the Bride, one at Ballynatray (then called Ballynetra) near Molana Abbey, two salmon and two eel weirs on the Blackwater at Conhie, one at Ballyecallagh on the Blackwater, which was part of Stroncally, and three other salmon weirs at Chanon's Mill near Ballynatray. Additionally, Mogeely had at least one salmon weir.[21] Ralegh included in his sale of Molana Abbey to Hariot "two ruinous salmon and eel weirs" on the Blackwater.[22] At least one of these weirs, as with numerous others aforementioned, were repaired and remained functional for centuries.

On Ralegh's estate of Curryglass, adjacent to the south side of Mogeely, was the location of Ireland's first glasshouse. Sometime after the Second Desmond War, Richard Spert wrote a paper on Ireland, asserting "there is in sundry places of the country great store of fern with fuel sufficient where glass houses may be set up for the making of case glass or any sort of glass."[23] By 1588, the glasshouse at Curryglass produced both window and drinking glass, though most of what was exported was window glass.[24] George Longe took over the glass-works and exported mostly window glass from "Youghal and Waterford to Bristol in the early 1590s."[25] The glasshouse was located at Curry-glass because it was close to the raw materials. Glass requires "sand silica and ash with limestone inclusions" and clay that could be turned into crucibles during the firing process.[26] Also essential was a ready and huge supply of wood—two cords per day were needed. According to Joe Nunan, "Beech was the preferred wood for glass production as it contained manganese, a natural decolorizer. However, as it was not a native species," cobalt was "imported from mainland Europe" and when added to the process gave the glass its blue hue.[27] The Curry-glass glasshouse lasted quite a long time; Richard Boyle later bought it and in 1614 leased it to Walter Coppinger.[28] Ralegh's relationship to the glassworks is unknown, besides its location on his land alongside other manufacturing operations. Its importance to the larger economy appears limited compared to other commodities produced at Mogeely, but it did fill local needs and provide yet another export.

Another goal of Ralegh was to mine and forge iron ore. England had plenty of iron but lacked the wood necessary for forging, and the devastation of war had limited the availability of labor for large-scale production in Ireland. With a ban on employing Irish on the seignories, the English imported their own labor. Ireland suffered shortages of mined iron, along with wheat, victuals, and cloth, in the late sixteenth century and relied on French imports for iron, with smaller amounts coming from the Spanish. There is no doubt that Ralegh knew he was sitting on a rich vein. *Curraglass*, which means "the morass of the red rivulet," refers to the stream at neighboring Lisnabrin (another Ralegh tract), which turned red from the iron. Iron had been forged there since at least the Middle Ages, though perhaps not in the sixteenth century. Forgepool was another of Ralegh's parcels in the same Tal-low–Mogeely corridor along the Bride River by Curryglass and Lisna-brin. Ralegh may even have invented the name Forgepool (not knowing the Gaelic name) to signify the place where iron could be forged. Ra-legh's expertise with metals derived in part from his appointment as Lord Warden of the Stannaries overseeing tin production.[29] The mine-workers provided the bulk of tin in England in the Tudor period and throughout much of human history, because the mines in Cornwall and Devon operated from the Stone Age until the early twenty-first century. As with the salmon fisheries, Ralegh encouraged others to un-dertake the iron mining on his land. Thomas Norreys, who served as a captain in the Desmond Wars and became an Undertaker to the west of Ralegh in Mallow, leased land from Ralegh to establish next to Mogeely an ironworks with Ireland's first blast furnace. Ralegh might have forestalled establishing his own operation until he saw how Norreys fared;[30] in the meantime, he provided Norreys not only the mine but also the requisite fuel.

The market for iron was immense and could support multiple operations, but the main reason, I believe, Ralegh opted to first exploit lumber was because he was less interested in filling the demands of the Irish market and more interested in the opportunity to engage in international trade.[31] Lumber and iron both typified colonial enterprise in the coming centuries. In mainland North America, from Maine to Georgia, the *first* enterprise ordinarily undertaken by colonists was the felling of trees for barrels, planks, masts, and roof shakes. Ralegh's intent for Munster lumber was quite focused. Although the Mogeely operation provided lumber for his settlers and planks for ships, Ralegh's main interest lay in the manufacture of huge pipe staves that each held about 125 gallons of wine, for transporting that valuable commodity from overseas producers to markets.[32]

Wine was one of the chief imports into England, and demand was constant.[33] Ralegh wished to manufacture pipe staves, supply them to producers, and fill them with wine, apparently leaving a portion of these enormous wooden casks with wine producers as payment for the wine. Traditionally, the French satiated English thirst with wines from Gascony and Bordeaux, but the Wars of Religion in France hindered trade, particularly with the assassination of the Duke of Guise in 1588. The simultaneous war between Spain and England precluded the latter obtaining large imports from another traditional supplier, Spain, so Ralegh turned his attention to the Canary Islands off of Africa. Although a Spanish domain, Ralegh received permission from the Privy Council to ship pipe staves to the Canaries for wine. The islands welcomed English traders, who noted how well they were treated there. The islands needed casks to ship wine, and the English liked to drink their sweet Malvasia. The wine made for happy English, and the tax on wine imports filled the queen's coffers and those of her favorites who held related monopolies, including Ralegh.

Recall that Ralegh held the monopoly on licenses for serving wine in English taverns and other public houses. Thus, the more he kept the grapes flowing, the more licenses he could issue. Ralegh had agents keep track of unlicensed establishments; it is clear from the wide range of documents in English archives related to Ralegh's licensing that he invested much energy into this important source of personal income. Indeed, it might have been his most important source of regular income. The English were a nation of wine drinkers—beer was an everyday quaff of low alcohol content consumed at breakfast and lunch, whereas wine was the beverage of choice in many taverns and private homes for those desiring something stronger.

Ralegh organized pipe stave production on his lands, and from 1589 to 1593 he and his partners sent thirteen ships loaded with 384,000 staves out of Ireland—enough to ship forty-eight million gallons of wine. (Ralegh miscalculated his own figures in stating he shipped 340,000 staves.) Almost all were bound for the Canary Islands off the northwest coast of Africa. Each stave measured about five feet in length. In 1650, pipe staves sold for £20 sterling per thousand in the Canary Islands,[34] which translates to Ralegh's operation in its first five years producing £7,680 worth of staves, and then obtaining additional income from the wine transported to England in them. Ralegh's partners included Henry Pyne, who commanded the lumber operation at Mogeely that produced the staves, Edward Dodge, and a Dutchman, Veronio Martens. The last named provided the connections for including Amsterdam in the stave–wine network of trade—in fact, the very first ship the partners used to transport staves hailed from Amsterdam. Martens also may have sailed on several of the voyages. He was with the cargo on a trip that began in Flushing, included the purchase of a ship at Plymouth that then conveyed the staves to the Canaries from Ireland, and then was scheduled for a return to London but was forced to land at Middlesbrough in Yorkshire, which became a repeat destination for the partnership's future deliveries of wine.

The export of staves became a matter of concern for the queen and Privy Council when Ireland's lord deputy, Sir William Fitzwilliam, accused the partners of sending their ships to Seville. The direct trade with Seville provided the Spanish with pipe staves, and return voyages from the islands that included a stopover in Seville may have occurred because the islanders could not provide enough wine to fill the staves and more could be had in Spain. The English government had been unconcerned about the purchase of Spanish wine during wartime but became alarmed that Ralegh's planks could be used in Spanish ship construction. Following Fitzwilliam's recommendation, the queen barred the export of staves.

Fitzwilliam resented Ralegh's favored treatment at court and in Ireland. It is not entirely clear why he disliked Ralegh, beyond considering Ralegh an upstart, but Fitzwilliam by personality and viewpoint was quite the opposite of Ralegh in terms of plans for Ireland. Fitzwilliam had served as Lord Deputy of Ireland from 1571 to 1575 and then returned to England, where he supervised the execution of Mary, Queen of Scots. In 1588, he returned as Lord Deputy of Ireland, where he opposed Ralegh's policies of accommodation to Irish interests and was imperious and combative with people from all walks of life. Tense relations between him and Ralegh first arose in late December 1589. Ralegh, then in England, had received news from Ireland that his enemies thought he was no longer in the queen's good graces and that he had been forced to leave court. "If in Irland," Ralegh spat to his cousin George Carew, "they thincke that I am not worth the respectinge they shall mich deceve them sealves." He haughtily confided, "I am in place to be beleved not inferior to any man to plesure or displesure the greatest. . . . I can anger the best of them." Ralegh warned Fitzwilliam through Carew that if the lord deputy did not stand by him, as Ralegh had stood by the lord deputy, "be it att is may." Ralegh measured himself against Fitzwilliam and found the latter lacking: Ralegh had more honorable offices and "also by that nireness to Her Majestye which still I injoy." Ralegh said he was "willinge to continew towards hyme all frindly offices," but expected the same from Fitzwilliam toward Ralegh and his friends.[35] Fitzwilliam did not accept the olive branch.

By mid-July 1591, Ralegh was winning the battle with Fitzwilliam. Carew wrote the lord deputy to reassure him of the queen's approbation for his services in Ireland, but her approval was countered by her wondering why he needed so many soldiers in a period of quiet. She also questioned his policies, particularly in matters of religion: Why did the lord deputy unnecessarily rile up the Irish? No connection was made by Carew between Ralegh and these criticisms, though everyone knew that Ralegh advised the queen and Privy Council on Ireland. (And, indeed, Ralegh opposed the persecution of Catholics and often supported the reduction of men in peacetime.) Carew also reassured Fitzwilliam on a more personal matter—that the queen did not believe the slanders Ralegh had written to Lord Burghley about the lord deputy and his wife.[36] The dispute between Ralegh and Fitzwilliam was not over, particularly in regard to Ralegh's international lumber operations. Ralegh's prospects in Ireland and elsewhere became increasingly entwined with affairs at court as he became a target of envy and jealousy, particularly because he was on his way to becoming the single most important man in government.

With Elizabeth's court the ostensible center of the universe, it is understandable that gossip, slander, and fawning were the preoccupations of many hoping to attain awards and appointments. Ralegh's advantage was that he could turn gossip into slander by depositing it in the ear of Burghley or any of a number of high officers in the queen's government. He certainly knew what it was like to be on the other end of gossip; the rumor mill churned grist that the Earl of Essex, a new favorite of the queen, had bested Ralegh in the queen's affections. Other men had more power than Ralegh and Essex, such as Burghley and Walsingham, directing government policy and decision making under the queen. Walsingham, however, died in April 1590, and Burghley was seventy years old. It was clear that a new man or men would emerge in their places to hold the reins of government under the queen.

The court's minions hoped to tie themselves to either Essex or Ralegh. Essex, the earl, was the more logical choice. He had youth, charm, and the queen's affection. But Ralegh was the proven commodity. His seignories in Ireland were a success, settling not only agriculturalists but hundreds of workers in manufacturing; the stannaries Ralegh directed in England produced tin, and the workers were happy; Ralegh was respected by both the military men (Drake and Lord Charles Howard who commanded the navy) and the leading intellectuals and his fellow courtiers. His Lord Lieutenancy was a success, and he could be relied upon for recruitment of men for service by land and sea. Ralegh displayed acumen in diplomacy and was as informed of worldly affairs and events as were few men in England. He continued to be responsible for the queen's personal protection as Captain of the Guard. A few historians have noted that Ralegh likely would have become Burghley's successor as the most important person in the English government under Elizabeth—if not for the events that were about to unfold.

CHAPTER 21

Of Friendship, Marriage, and Goddesses

I n the late 1580s and early 1590s, the queen's favorites, Ralegh and Essex, sometimes had an uneasy relationship, but it was not fraught with the hostility and intense competitiveness that contemporaries thought and that later generations have repeated. Gossip is gossip, and its generators spread tales they hope are true: a common refrain was that Essex had replaced Ralegh as the queen's favorite.

It is clear that at the beginning of her infatuation with Essex Ralegh indeed felt hurt. Around the time that Ralegh began colonizing Roanoke, if not before, he penned the poem "Fortune Hathe Taken Away My Love." The tables had turned on Ralegh—he no longer was the young favorite replacing older men but was becoming an older favorite. With the emergence of Essex, Ralegh directly addressed the queen with his concerns and his melancholy.

fortune hathe taken away my love
my lyves joy and my soules heaven above
fortune hathe taken thee away my princes
my worldes joy and my true fantasies misteris
fortune hathe taken thee away from mee
fortune hathe taken all by takinge thee
deade to all joyes I onely lyve to woe
So ys fortune become my fantasies foe

Fortune, in all likelihood, specifically referenced Essex, giving the poem a double meaning. Ralegh rued that fortune had defeated virtue and that the queen had failed to rectify the injustice: "So blinde a goddes did never vertue right." Self-righteously, Ralegh closed with a reminder that his love and virtue remained:

> *but love farewell: thoughe fortune conquer thee*
> *no fortune base nor frayle shall alter mee.*[1]

The poem became popular at court. It is likely that Ralegh read it to others and distributed copies before its printing in George Puttenham's *The Arte of English Poesie* (1589) along with Elizabeth's poetic, playful, if condescending response meant to reassure her favorite that he had not lost his place. Quite likely Elizabeth also meant her poem as a statement to others that Ralegh remained in her favor.

Elizabeth begins her poem with two playful nicknames for Ralegh— Pug and Wat (a diminutive of Walter), setting a light tone to dissipate Ralegh's despair.[2]

> *Ah silly pugge werte thou so afraid,*
> *mourne not (my Wat) nor be thou so dismayd*
> *it passeth fickle fortunes powere and skill,*
> *to force my harte to thinke thee any ill.*

She complemented Ralegh's claim that fortune will not alter him with her own that "so blinde a Witche" will not

> *conquere me. No no my pugge....*
> *fortune I knowe sometimes doth conquere kinges*
> *and rules and raignes on earth and earthly thinges*

But Elizabeth avers, in her, too, virtue will hold sway. Though she chose Ralegh by fortune, fortune will not alter her choice. She tells him, put away the tears and fears, his dead joys and woe:

> *Revive againe and live without all dreade,*
> *the less afraid the better thou shalt spede.*

Elizabeth, Ralegh, and Essex had their spats. They possessed huge egos that easily bruised, but there was little if any of the outright hostility that gossipers hoped for among the three in the late 1580s. Essex was about fifteen years Ralegh's junior and over thirty years younger than the queen. She was enamored with Essex, but she found Ralegh stimulating as an intellectual and a courtier. He had proven himself as a man of a multitude of parts in service to the queen and realm, for which he continued to be amply rewarded.

Essex soon learned the queen's wrath. In 1590, he secretly married the widow of the much-revered soldier and poet Sir Philip Sidney, daughter of the recently deceased Walsingham. Essex returned to court, but the queen's hostility induced him to go abroad. He went to France in command of English troops, hoping to retake Rouen. The expedition was a disaster and he was ordered home.[3] Essex regained the queen's good graces. His followers were elated—Ralegh will be vanquished! But in real life there was not much competition between them.

The fifteen-year age gap helped allay differences. Their interests barely overlapped: Ralegh's lay in colonizing America and Ireland, in pirating, developing his estates, administering the queen's affairs in South West England, and obtaining any plums that he could; Essex looked toward martial exploits, with few of the bourgeois interests of Ralegh in trade and commerce. Essex's pursuits were those of the landed elite, the pastimes of the nobility. He was smart and appeared to others as a man among men. With the queen having no children to whom people could flock as a future locus of power, they were left with Essex.

If Essex and Ralegh competed at all, it was for what the queen could offer or a great assignment of power that included patronage they could distribute and their own chance to earn immense plaudits. While Ralegh colonized Ireland, there was little of importance on the horizon beyond prospective military expeditions against Spain. Ralegh was Captain of the Guard; Essex was Master of the Horse. Ralegh held the monopoly on retail wine licenses; Essex held the monopoly on importation of sweet wines. Ralegh's importation of sweet wines from the Canaries increased Essex's income—an area of mutual co-operation that historians have overlooked. These monopolies signified the queen's identification of Ralegh and Essex as her favorites. (When the queen later punished Essex for his insubordination, she took the wine monopoly away from him.) Essex was uninterested in Virginia; Ralegh would not have volunteered to go to France to retake Rouen. Other plums, such as estates and offices, they might have competed for, but not enough to hurt their relationship. The queen's favor was of the utmost importance to each, and both eyed a future where Burghley was gone and they might attain greater influence over the government. Ralegh had the advantage over Essex of greater understanding of government, administration, and policy. His growing list of offices displayed the queen's confidence in him. Essex had no interest in the day-to-day details of government that a Burghley or a Ralegh could muster, but Essex could hold an executive function and play a leading role in foreign policy.

Ralegh's more immediate competition was Robert Cecil, Burghley's son, whom the father was grooming as his successor. Cecil was a master of detail and administration—much more than Ralegh. Ralegh could be viewed as somewhat halfway between Cecil and Essex in terms of skills for running the government under Elizabeth if given the chance. Akin to Essex, Ralegh could operate outside the halls of government as a military leader and a leader of men. Cecil could never lead troops, nor go to any trouble spot and lead others to solve a problem. Scoliosis and his hunched back limited his political work outside of administration. He excelled in his knowledge of the inner workings of government, whereas Ralegh excelled in the arena of strategy, working with a diverse array of people, and seeing the larger world beyond England.

The best evidence backing up the argument that competition between Ralegh and Essex was inconsequential to both men in the early 1590s is a particular fact that denotes not suspicion but immense trust between the two. This was an event that was part of a larger affair that altered Ralegh's life in just so many ways, ultimately influencing the development of his Munster Plantation and spurring him to push forward with colonization on another continent, South America.

RALEGH WAS IN ENGLAND in 1591, and at some point he fell in love with one of the queen's ladies-in-waiting, Elizabeth "Bess" Throckmorton, the daughter of Nicholas Throckmorton, a much-respected former diplomat to France. By late July, Bess was pregnant. In mid-November, the couple secretly married. The child, Damerei, was delivered at the end of March. Less than a fortnight later, the Earl of Essex stood as godfather at the baby's very private christening. The affair, pregnancy, marriage, birth, and christening all were kept secret from the queen.

Why had Essex served as godfather for Ralegh's child? Perhaps it was payback for a favor. Ralegh might have run interference with the queen for Essex for his marriage. The facts are this: Ralegh and his in-laws trusted Essex enough for him to not only witness the christening but also play a lead role. Secondly, Ralegh trusted Essex to be his son's godfather and Essex accepted the responsibility. Whatever the nature of the competition between them for the queen's favor, they obviously saw eye-to-eye on some things and had bonds between them that others did not see. This relationship contrasts with that between Ralegh and Robert Cecil, whom historians consider as Ralegh's political ally and friend. Indeed, their ties grew closer in the 1590s, but Ralegh lied to Cecil about his marriage, flat-out denying its existence.[4] One explanation for this: he knew Cecil would not keep the secret from his father, Lord Burghley, and the queen. Ralegh trusted Essex to keep his secrets.

It seems that Ralegh had no actual plan of when to tell the queen about his marriage. Bess had been on leave from service when she gave birth, so the queen did not know of the pregnancy. She returned to her duties as a lady-in-waiting, and the child died shortly thereafter. There was no good time to tell the queen about the marriage and it is unclear when she learned of it. But learn of it she did.

By early June 1592, Ralegh appears to have been held under house arrest at his Durham House residence by his cousin George Carew. Bess was confined under house arrest at different quarters. In late June, the final papers were drawn for the queen's gift of Sherborne Castle and associated lands to Ralegh. Ralegh had received many plums in terms of lands and houses, but Sherborne held great personal meaning for him. It provided him the estate of a great country squire in his native Devon. Ralegh held not only the chief office in the region as lord lieutenant but also the physical trappings that reflected his position as the most important man in the South West. Elizabeth finagled to obtain the estate for him from its owner, who received a bishopric in exchange. Ralegh would pay slightly over £200 yearly to the bishop, an enormous sum, indicating the value of the estate.[5]

Why did Elizabeth not withhold Sherborne from Ralegh when he was under house arrest? My guess: the queen did not know Ralegh had married the previous November. He was under house arrest for getting Elizabeth's lady-in-waiting pregnant. It was one thing for Ralegh to have sexual relations with one of Elizabeth's maids, and quite another to have married her. House arrest was appropriate punishment for despoiling the queen's maid. Barred from seeing the queen, whom he one day espied from the tower of Durham House, Ralegh took up a dagger against his keeper George Carew, who pulled out one of his own, Ralegh's cousin Arthur Gorges reported. Gorges tried to separate them and wound up with hurt knuckles, which put an end to the fight. Perhaps Ralegh's panic at Durham House reflected his realization that he was in for a mighty fall. He must have known that Elizabeth would soon learn the worst—that he had married. Maybe this last bit of information was kept from her until the final papers for Sherborne were confirmed.

By late July, the queen had learned all and placed the couple in separate quarters in the Tower of London.[6] As far as Elizabeth was concerned, what Ralegh and Bess had done was unconscionable. The queen's lady-in-waiting could not marry without the queen's permission. These women, who dressed and undressed the queen, who waited on the monarch during her most intimate moments, had sworn an oath to serve. Obviously, the couple believed that Elizabeth would not have granted them permission to marry. Elizabeth could be quite generous about the marital desires of her ladies but at other times was small-minded and mean. Bess's crime was twofold: she married without permission, and she humiliated the queen by keeping secret her affair, pregnancy, and marriage. She had stolen the queen's much-loved Ralegh. Elizabeth never forgave Bess.

In the queen's mind, the marriage put the lie to Ralegh's years of courtship. Elizabeth had doted on Essex, was infatuated with him, but Ralegh's professed love had held constant for twelve years. Elizabeth could probably tolerate Ralegh's sexual escapades as long as they were discreet, did not involve one of her ladies-in-waiting, and held no emotional attachment. Elizabeth was both goddess and companion: she and Ralegh each knew where the lines were in their relationship. Then he willfully disregarded the rules and, like a coward, kept secret the pregnancy with an off-limits woman. In the midst of all, he was supposed to sail on an expedition for plunder, which would have given him an opportunity to flee before the queen learned of the marriage. But she prevented him going at the last minute, professing she had been without him long enough while he was in Ireland. At some time, he would have to face the music. Though Ralegh probably knew this would not end well, there really was no way for him to comprehend the oblivion that awaited.

With his back against the wall, Ralegh's letters become whiny and graceless while these same circumstances ignited an unusually high level of poignancy in his poetry. Extant are wonderful examples, especially from his later life: Ralegh's meditations on death and his cynicism about life and society reveal a mature thinker and able wordsmith. But none of these compare to a poem he composed during his confinement in the Tower for marrying the queen's lady-in-waiting. The poem erupts from a well of despair, with little self-censorship of his feelings about Elizabeth and their relationship.

He penned his masterpiece, "The 21th and Last Booke of the Ocean to Scinthia," probably shortly after composing another, "My Boddy in the Walls Captived," in which he compared his physical captivity to his memory of Elizabeth. The latter was "so delightfull,"

> *loves fire and bewtys light I then had store,*
> *butt now closs keipt, as captives wounted are*
> *that food, that heat, that light I finde no more,*
> *Dyspaire bolts up my dores, and I alone*
> *speake to dead walls, butt thos heare not my mone.*[7]

The above appears a trial run for expressing his despair, but it lacked the scorching fire of "The 21th and Last Booke of the Ocean to Scinthia."[8] ("Ocean" referred to Ralegh; "Scinthia," to Elizabeth.) This poem expresses Ralegh's grief at losing Elizabeth's love. For more than five hundred lines, Ralegh spews bitterness: the loss of Elizabeth's love is too much to bear—she, not he, is at fault! Many who have read the poem find it beguiling that Ralegh never mentions his wife or that the love of his wife cannot suffice for replacing the queen's lost love, hence he must have been insincere: an actor composing his own lines who must not love his wife or is disingenuous in his declarations of love for the queen. Yet Ralegh's poem is not disingenuous. These were two different loves, of a wife and of a goddess. Ralegh saw no incongruity in worshipping the goddess and marrying the mortal; the poem unflinchingly pleads his case that his love for the queen, Cynthia, is true.

Elizabeth idolized love: she was nourished by the love of her subjects and the adoring love of her courtiers; these had to suffice in place of the physical intimacy denied her by her position as the Virgin Queen. Elizabeth understood Ralegh's love in classic courtier terms of a great lady and her knight—a love that could never be consummated, an impossible love of adoration, a pure love unsullied by physical fulfillment. Ralegh was *her* knight and should have devoted his life to her as Captain of the Guard, her personal protector.

His marriage proved false his love. If she was his goddess, why did he require another love? The old friend, "lover," with whom she had shared heart and mind, as much as she could, had betrayed her by marrying her servant. It fell to Ralegh to convince Elizabeth that his love was true, that his marriage had not diminished his special love for her. We cannot discount Ralegh's ulterior motive for authoring the poem: he desperately hoped to return to the queen's good graces; that, too, fueled the fire. Cynically, we can say that Ralegh's impassioned plea through courtier poetry, a poetry that Elizabeth loved, was merely the act of a cunning man. But his declarations of love are accompanied by so much venom that it is his disillusion that stands out utmost. The world that the courtier created was a charade. And yet, the monarch held power over life and death; she could make dreams come true or inflict interminable pain. Religion demands faith and the suspension of logic, and the Cult of the Virgin Queen required the courtier to see and present Elizabeth as a woman unlike all others, with rituals of worship to acclaim and affirm her unique and special qualities. Ralegh's heartfelt epic iterates, as we would expect, his worship and love for Elizabeth. How he misses her terribly. But he berates Elizabeth for not seeing or understanding the depths of his feelings for her. The goddess has no right to be jealous.

The poem begins "Sufficeth it to yow my joyes interred." With his unhappiness owing entirely to the queen, he laments his emptiness.

> If to the livinge weare my muse adressed,
> or did my minde her own spirrit still inhold,
> weare not my livinge passion so repressed,
> as to the dead, the dead did thes unfold,
> sume sweeter wordes, sume more becumming vers,
> should wittness my myshapp in hygher kynd.
> but my loves wounds, my fancy in the hearse,
> the Idea but restinge, or a wasted minde,
> the blossumes fallen the sapp gon from the tree.
> the broken monuments of my great desires,
> from thes so lost what many th'affections bee,
> what heat in Cynders of extinguisht fiers?

Ralegh's happiness lies completely in Elizabeth's hands: "Shee gave, shee tooke, shee wounded, she appeased." He recalls for her how he went

To seeke new worlds, for golde, for prayse, for glory,
to try desire, to try love severed farr
when I was gonn shee sent her memory
more stronge then weare tenthowsand shipps of warr
to call me back, to leve great honors thought

Ralegh recounts his grief in enthralling detail. It is as if his body has been "violently slayne"; he is as the cold winter earth without "her life gevinge soonn," a whole forest deserted by its stream; he is left with but a "withered minde, widdow of all the joyes it once possest." Bitterly, he turns his rage upon her—*he* is the wronged party—her withdrawal of love is the real betrayal, not his error. He falls into pathos:

Twelve years intire I wasted in this warr
twelve yeares of my most happy younger dayes,
butt I in them, and they now wasted ar
of all which past the sorrow only stayes,

The loss of Elizabeth's love has led him to distraction, mourning, loneliness, emptiness.

Therefore all liveless, and all healplesse bounde
my fayntinge spirritts sunck, and hart apalde
my joyes and hopes lay bleedinge on the ground

Elizabeth remains a goddess to Ralegh, alternatively referred to as Cynthia, Diana, and Belphoebe. As with other goddesses, she is perfection itself but possesses one character fault: cruelty. Just as she cannot forgive his one error, he cannot forgive her cruelty, her inability to forgive. He vows to forget her love and to only remember what she has become:

Bellphebes course is now observde no more
   . . .
the sythes, the grones of all our past desires
ar cleane outworne, as things that never weare . . .

and

a Queen shee was to mee, no more Belphebe
a Lion then, no more a milke white Dove,

a prissoner in her brest I could not bee
shee did untye the gentell chaynes of love

Ralegh asserts that his error "never was forthought," perhaps mean-
ing that he did not think marriage would so alienate Elizabeth. Still,
Elizabeth should not interpret that his mistake was to love her less.
She had wronged him, left him with nothing but sorrow. Can she end
his pain? "Shee is gonn, Shee is lost, shee is found, shee is ever faire."
No, her love is gone: "my woe must ever last."[9]

Only Elizabeth can end his despair. In the final, brief Book 22,
"entreatinge of sorrow," he concludes,

knowinge shee cann renew, and cann create
green from the grounde, and floures, yeven out of stonn,
by vertu lastinge over tyme and date,
levinge us only woe, which like the moss,
havinge cumpassion of unburied bones,
cleaves to mischance, and unrepayred loss,
for tender stalkes.[10]

"The 21th and Last Book of Ocean to Scinthia" is one of the great
courtier poems of the age.[11] Ralegh's despair was a fount for his creative genius. It details Ralegh's feelings toward Elizabeth as a goddess, the courtier's passionate love and worship for his goddess, and
the depths of his despair at the withdrawal of her love, her cruelty. It
is unusual as a courtier poem in its harshness toward the object of his
adoration, though Spenser, too, wrote of the queen's cruelty to Ralegh.

The poem bridges the chasm between the fantasy world of the
court and courtship and the stark reality of prison. The unseen world
of fantasy, in which Elizabeth was a goddess and provided Ralegh rewards and offices, had been replaced by a fall from grace and physical
confinement. Poems of adoration provided a mode of worship, as did
courtier behavior in numerous social settings: music and dance, the
hunt, the special theatrical performances created for the queen. But
reality seeped in: courtiers like Ralegh undertook dangerous tasks for
their queen and received tangible rewards. Ralegh knew that death
could come at any moment, in service to the queen or otherwise. But
in reality, he did not expect her withdrawal of love. The bond was broken. The twelve-year courtship was over—unless his poem could bring
redress.

The great irony: Elizabeth probably never read the poem. She likely never knew it existed. Ralegh gave the poem to Robert Cecil with instructions that he should give it to Elizabeth if it would help him. Cecil thought better of doing so, and it lay undiscovered in his papers until 1860.

Poetry would not regain the queen's affections nor earn release from imprisonment. Ralegh needed to perform some office or substantial task, perhaps pay a hefty fine, to gain his freedom. Fortunately for him, something huge fell his way.

CHAPTER 22

A Courtier's Disgrace and the Shipping of Staves

In the wake of Ralegh's arrest, the plantation in Ireland suffered at the hands of one of his rivals. Lord Deputy Fitzwilliam used the opportunity to go after Ralegh on several fronts. Ralegh allegedly had failed to pay the queen £400 in fees owed her out of the rentals to his tenants. Fitzwilliam ordered the sheriff to confiscate all of Ralegh's tenants' cattle and gave Ralegh one day to make good on the debt or the cattle would be immediately auctioned. Ralegh could not possibly meet the deadline, being in England. He protested that payment to the queen was only 50 marks; the lord deputy apparently was unaware that Ralegh had negotiated a lower payment scale than the other Undertakers', or if Fitzwilliam knew, he refused to accept that Ralegh should enjoy such privileges.

That the matter was clearly personal between the men is made evident by Ralegh having been the *only* Undertaker to actually pay the fees. Following the lord deputy's orders, the sheriff "tooke away five hundred milch kine [cows] from the poor people. Sume had but two, and sume three, to releve their poore wives and children, and in a strange country newly sett downe to builde and plant." Ralegh complained to Cecil, "Your cussen the dotinge deputye hath dispeopled mee. . . . It is a sign how my disgraces have past the seas and have bynn highly cummended to that wise governoure, who hath used mee accordinglye." The letter matched sarcasm for the lord deputy with pathos at his own decline in fortune, but it opened with an assessment of the current situation in

Ireland. Ralegh predicted a rebellion fomenting in Ireland, for which the queen earlier had expressed scorn. Ralegh would not push the point because he did not want to be laughed at again, but he had more to say on the matter if Cecil was interested. Ralegh was right: the Nine Years' War in Ireland lay just ahead.[1]

Fitzwilliam and Ralegh also disputed tracts of land in County Waterford. In June 1590, the lord deputy and his council ordered the local authorities to support William Hetherington's possession of Kilbeg against Robert Maule, Ralegh's agent.[2] Hetherington apparently won the dispute because he still possessed the tract in 1604.[3] This tract near Ballyfinshog broke up Ralegh's lands. Fitzwilliam also lopped off valuable estates that Ralegh had obtained from the Lismore lease. These additional properties included Ardmore, on the Atlantic seacoast across the mouth of the Blackwater from Youghal. Fitzwilliam, Ralegh complained, "hath forcible thrust mee out of possession of a castell," to support the lord deputy's cousin Richard Wingfield's claim, and refused to allow Ralegh's attorney to make his case.[4] Wingfield transferred his claim to John Dowdall, a Devonshire man who had served in Ireland since at least 1569, when he commanded the garrison at Youghal. Ardmore became his home base, and for many years he bore responsibility for most of the nearby coastal fortifications in County Cork. He despised the Irish. He thought them "a nation bred idly and in looseness of life." He could not fathom why the Irish "hate to be governed by civil laws," as they attained peace and prosperity under English rule, "the like they never attained . . . these three hundred years."[5] Ralegh derided Dowdall's character and associated him with Fitzwilliam, asserting that the lord deputy was fleecing the queen for £1,200 to fund a band of worthless soldiers under "a base phello, O'Dodall"—an incendiary claim to make, because the queen believed the lord deputy was wasting her money in Ireland.[6]

Cecil sent a letter to Ireland to investigate the matter for Ralegh, but nothing seems to have been done. Ralegh was "ejected" from Ardmore by Dowdall in 1594, a legal action later claimed as "unknown" by a grand jury, which ten years later reported that they knew of no court that had issued the ejectment.[7] Despite the spurious legality of the ejectment, Ralegh would probably have had to use force to move Dowdall out of Ardmore, and Dowdall had his own men to support him.[8] Ralegh did not return to Ireland to push his claim.

Shortly after he entered the Tower, Ralegh received word that the expedition of plunder he had organized captured an enormous prize returning from the East Indies. The Portuguese carrack, *Madre de Dios*, had seven decks full of commodities and ranks among the greatest captures of treasure. The cargo's value was estimated at £500,000— roughly two and a half times the sum of English government expenses in an average year! This sixteen-hundred-ton ship carried five hundred tons of spices (not including pepper, hence the even more valuable spices by weight) and an incredible array of jewels, silks, gold, and silver. The spices, including cloves, nutmeg, and mace, were used not just for food but also for cosmetics, perfumes, medicines, cleansers, and myriad other purposes.

When news reached Amsterdam of the capture, Dutch traders flocked to England to purchase portions of the booty. After the ship docked in Dartmouth in early September, it immediately was looted by a large and dangerous mob, and more than two-thirds of the cargo was stolen. Ralegh was consulted in prison about the disposal of the spoils, including the queen's share. Elizabeth released Ralegh under escort to secure the remaining cargo and to sort things out, if not also to figure out where most of the stolen cargo went. As a key shareholder, he had an interest in getting back what had been taken. Upon reaching Dartmouth, Cecil recorded that the mariners exploded with joy at seeing Ralegh. Ralegh soberly went about his work, reminding all that he remained the queen's prisoner. The unpilfered portion of the goods was valued at £144,000. Men were sent through the towns to recover what they could, apparently enjoying limited success, perhaps because they kept all they recovered.

The queen disregarded Ralegh's figures on the investors' shares. The Earl of Cumberland and a group of London merchants came out handsomely. The largest group of investors, led by Ralegh, received a pittance, in effect losing money on the expedition. The queen took more than half the prize, £80,000, on an investment of less than £2,000.[9] According to Ralegh, this was the largest gift the queen ever received: a "ransom" for his freedom.

Before the end of the year, the queen also released Bess from the Tower. Elizabeth barred her from ever returning to court; Ralegh, too, was barred and would not return for another five years. Freedom from confinement made it easier for Ralegh to lobby for the reopening of his shipping of staves. This was key to the prosperity of Mogeely, and hence to his Munster Plantation, as well as to his own income from the monopoly he held on retail wine licenses.

By January 1592/93, the Privy Council, meeting at Hampton Court Palace, considered Ralegh's request to remove the "restraint." Ralegh was not the only one affected: according to Ralegh, the other Undertakers, on whose behalf he claimed to petition, also desired to ship "to the Islandes where the trade is free for her Majesty's subjectes and they kindelie used."[10] It is unknown how many Undertakers cut down trees and made staves, but at least one, Sir Henry Wallop, believed to have been one of the original designers of the Munster Plantation scheme, since 1586 had an operation to rival Ralegh's not far to the north of his.[11] In the spring of 1593, a few weeks after arresting Ralegh's man, Henry Pyne, for shipping staves, Lord Deputy Fitzwilliam almost sheepishly admitted that Wallop, who was the Lord Treasurer of Ireland responsible for administering the queen's money for the military, had "passed no less abundance of pipe staves out of Ireland than Mr. Pyne."[12] Wallop, too, shipped his staves to the Canaries and to France, though the fact that he later itemized the Madeira Islands first on a list of locations where the staves went makes me wonder whether he focused his efforts on the wine of the Portuguese Islands.

Ralegh reminded the Privy Council of the wine and other commodities that the staves brought into England and Ireland, and that Norway and the other northern countries already provided Spain with staves. Spain was not desperate for pipestaves and hogsheads—but the islands off of Africa needed what the Undertakers in Ireland could provide. The Privy Council approved Ralegh's request as it would provide employment for the English in Ireland, as long as planks and other timber for ship building were not transported. Wallop later asserted the overall value of the timber industry to the Irish economy, as it drew trade to the plantations, provided employment for many, and offered a "good example and help otherways of the Irish subjects, their neighbours."[13]

Before asking the queen to allow Ralegh to export staves, the Privy Council turned to Lord Treasurer Burghley to examine the matter—his support might be crucial to convince the queen. They deferred to Burghley because "your lordship is best acquainted with the cause of the restraint (growing as we remember upon suggestion from the lord deputy [Fitzwilliam])."[14] The council forwarded Ralegh's reasons, as well as their own, for lifting the restraint, and Burghley pored over the documents. He had to consider whether Ralegh and his partners indeed had sold timber to Spain and also the potential alienation of the lord deputy. Might he resign his position if he lost his dispute with Ralegh?

By March, Fitzwilliam had undertaken his own investigation into Pyne's activities. He found that Ralegh's operation felled trees on Patrick Condon's land, which Fitzwilliam opposed because he supported Arthur Hyde's claim to the very same land. The argument over stave production and export thus entwined in a dispute over land between the Anglo-Irish (Condon) who had been restored to their lands and the New English (Hyde) who opposed the pardons. Elizabeth's government, it is worth reiterating, supported the pardons against the New English and her English administrators in Ireland. In April, Fitzwilliam reported that a ship belonging to Ralegh and his partners "lately laden with pipe staves and plank had stolen away." He again arrested Pyne, who complained to Cecil that his confinement was without just cause. The lord deputy collected evidence against Pyne to forward to England. A Dutchman testified that Pyne was shipping planks, alongside staves and hogsheads, to Spain. Justice Jessua Smythe went to Mogeely to collect testimony and examined three Englishmen at Ralegh's Lisfinney estate who testified that Pyne told a messenger of Condon that he needed to "arm himself" with "as good men as Hyde" to win his land dispute. One of the Englishmen, Philip Tabbe, interviewed by Fitzwilliam's agents, alleged that Pyne "hoped to see the time when Hyde . . . should be hunted out of the country."[15]

Cecil jumped into the matter with his usual efficiency.[16] He conducted his own investigation on the quiet. Sir Robert Gardener reported to him from Dublin that as for the "examinations formerly taken against Mr Pine," and "now sent over by the Lord Deputy," he found "much malice with subornation and much more affirmed than proved."[17] Even from a distance of more than four hundred years, the testimony against Pyne looks sketchy, and one wonders that the lord deputy even bothered to forward it to the government. Most of it involved hearsay allegations that Pyne "was the only man who did receive and send intelligence between the fugitives beyond the seas, and the recusants in England and Ireland." I have found no evidence of Pyne's religious affiliation, but it was typical among late-sixteenth-century English conspiracy theorists to proclaim their enemies in league with Spanish Catholics. Fitzwilliam might even have put the witness up to the allegations, because he earlier had spurred the arrest of the previous lord deputy, John Perrot, for being in league with Philip II to overthrow Queen Elizabeth.[18] In the coming decade, Pyne's enemies in Ireland repeatedly accused him of giving succor to England's enemies. He was exonerated every time.[19]

In the following year, the queen's personal physician, Rodrigo Lopes, a Portuguese Jew who had converted to Protestantism, was hanged, drawn, and quartered for allegedly conspiring with the Spanish to poison the queen. The Earl of Essex had pushed for Lopes's death in a powerplay between his and Cecil's factions, and though few believed Lopes actually guilty, the charge of conspiring with the Spanish for the queen's death was enough to justify his conviction and punishment. The complete lack of evidence in the charges against Lopes and Pyne did not prevent those who knew better from stoking the embers of fear for political gain.

By May 1593, Ralegh was at Sherborne still stewing at his misfortune. Ireland remained on his mind. While under arrest, he had begged Cecil for news of Ireland, then offered Cecil advice on the placement of troops and pinnaces. As usual with Ralegh, his perspective focused on necessary details within the larger pattern. His strategy for Ireland, he instructed Cecil, must be seen in the context of the wars in France and the troubles in Scotland. And if he could, he put his own role or prospective role in the equation. In this case, he rued his recent difficulties from preventing his employing two or three bands of "Inglishe, well armed" to maintain English power in Ireland. Ralegh cautioned Cecil about the "endless" wars in France, which had led England to "forgett the defens next [to] the hart": Ireland. On the surface, Ireland hardly seemed worth the expense. The queen "shall fynde it no small dishonor to be vexed with so beggarly a nation, that have neather armes nor fortification." But England had to secure Ireland because of Spain, which used it "to inforce us to cast our eyes over our shoulders while thos before us strike us on the braynes."[20]

A month later Ralegh returned to Durham House in London to personally address Lord Burghley about the staves. Ralegh informed Burghley that owing to the restraint on his exporting to the islands, "a great quantitie of barrell and hogshead bords . . . will rott uppon the ground." He would also be forced to bring home the workers, who "are appointed to serve Her Majestie with their weapons uppon anie occasion, which will prove to be a great weakening of the province of Munster." Ralegh requested permission to export the boards into England, as they were needed in the West Country, and he would pay bonds to insure they would not be shipped elsewhere. Ralegh added a self-righteous postscript: for the production of casks in Ireland, he and his partners "shall rather deserve thankes, then that wee shall need to make any great sutes for it." He blamed Fitzwilliam for the situation and asked Burghley to order the lord deputy not to interfere with the shipments to England, and that Ralegh should have to answer only to Burghley.[21]

Although Ralegh could not return to court, two months later he could be found hunting in the royal forest of Gillingham near Dorset, to which the queen had appointed him ranger in 1584. Henry Pyne went in his stead to "sollicite . . . for a dissolution of the restraint procured by the Lord Deputies lettres" so that the partners could ship staves to the islands, not just England. Meanwhile, Ralegh lobbied Cecil and urged him to lobby the Lord Admiral, Charles Howard. In the postscript for this letter to Cecil, Ralegh displays an ease of interaction with Cecil, a man with whom he was on familiar terms and he viewed as something of a peer. Like Ralegh, Cecil was untitled, and though his father had been raised to the peerage, the family was of the gentry and wielded great political power. Ralegh asked Cecil to send him a new falcon for hunting, and in exchange he would send him a roan gelding. These kinds of exchanges and gifts characterized their relationship over the next decade.[22]

At the end of June 1593, the English government began to settle the dispute over the staves. The Undertakers could ship their staves and other lumber, but only to England. The Munster operations had to have approval of the vice president of Munster (Thomas Norreys, who owned the ironworks on Ralegh's land), while those outside of Munster had to seek the lord deputy's permission. Moreover, no trees could be taken from Patrick Condon's land because he was attainted and outlawed for treason—an odd stipulation because Condon had long been removed from the attainted list, a matter the English administration and Parliament in Ireland never accepted; soon the English government would again support Condon in his dispute with Hyde. The Lord Admiral, Charles Howard, received first crack at purchasing Irish lumber for the navy. Additionally, the Privy Council ordered the lord deputy to release the depositions he had collected about Pyne, a task "we require you in any case not to faile." The very same day the Privy Council also expressed disapproval to Fitzwilliam for interference with a jury about to render a verdict in a property dispute. The council told him that he probably had good cause to interfere but that he must allow the trial to proceed.[23]

Ralegh and Pyne were unsatisfied with the compromise that they could ship lumber only to England. Ralegh prepared a report for Burghley that Pyne had shipped staves and "no other commodities." He asserted that the Waterford merchants had long shipped "pipe staves to the King of Spain's countries without any restraint." The customs on wine brought into the queen's coffers by Ralegh's ships ranged from £300 to £700 per ship, and tended to the higher end, making a lucrative income for the queen. To answer an accusation that they were denuding the forest, Ralegh's partners asserted that not one in a hundred trees had been felled. Moreover, they already had invested £6,000 and had reaped a return of but £3,000. The work was backbreaking and expensive because the woods lay three miles from the river and the trees had to be moved by animals and on men's backs. Ralegh reminded Burghley that the queen had granted them "14 years free liberty for transporting any wares or commodities," which gave "encouragement" to take on this expensive investment. They employed over two hundred English, which improved the lives of the farmers with purchasers for their food. Months more would pass before a final decision was reached on the staves.

Pyne's appearance before the Privy Council proved a great success. By late November, the Privy Council had ordered the lord deputy to allow Pyne to ship pipe staves "to the Islandes, Burdeaux, etc."[24] Two months later, Fitzwilliam begged for his recall. He claimed illness and old age (he was 69), but it is not far-fetched to suppose that his loss in the Pyne case and the queen's criticisms had led him to believe it was time to resign.[25] A replacement arrived in August.[26]

With the Privy Council in full support of the timber operation, Henry Pyne expanded production and continued the economic and defensive improvements of Mogeely. He became a key figure in English colonization of the Munster Plantation. He and Ralegh would be at loggerheads over the profits in just a few years, and Pyne might have played a leading role in a fiasco that occurred when Ralegh attempted to establish his own ironworks next to Mogeely: the men were prevented from working and had to return to England, indicative of Ralegh's seeping loss of control over his Munster Plantation. Ralegh increasingly relied on others to handle his Irish affairs. In England, Ralegh remained engaged in Irish policy, and he wrote letters, particularly to Cecil, to support the suits of individual Irish.[27] Barred from court, he threw himself into developing his Sherborne estate until another colonial project excited his attention, one that he hoped would bring him the fame of Columbus and the riches of Cortés since he could no longer look to the queen for plums. Instead, Ralegh went in search of something much grander: the famed Lost City of Gold.

—

PART NINE

The Colonial Impulse

Search, Discovery, Redemption

CHAPTER 23

The Search for El Dorado

C olonialism requires an impulse.
A colonizer possesses a state of mind to leave their homeland for somewhere new.

Yet history and culture shape what the colonizer seeks, envisions, and acts on. Current events—the state of the colonizer's world—instill ideas about where to colonize, how to get there, and what they should find.

If history, culture, and current events are insufficient to stoke the colonial impulse, fictions and myths are constructed to explain what will be done and why their fellows should join them. Stories are created to convince the colonizer's sovereign authority to permit the colonial enterprise and explain how it will benefit them and their people—and the people to be encountered in new lands.

All of these ideas, intentions, hopes, and rationalizations are in turn modeled by what the colonizer thinks about the nature of society and how they might shape a new society in the colonized land. The colo-nizer not only designs a society for colonists but also casts their eyes on the home society. The intent of colonization is to improve one's life and the lives of people at home—and, quite often, the people whose lands are colonized.

Those intent on conquest are not colonizers. The death and de-struction they reap are deliberate; the exploitation of Native people is planned, as when Hernando de Soto brought chains to La Florida to secure and enslave the Native peoples.

Colonization can occur after conquest if the conquerors' monarch intervenes, declares sovereignty over the conquered territory, and reconstitutes the society of conquerors and conquered into a colonial society. But the English eschewed that model in America. In Ireland, England employed force to subdue rebellion, not to attain new territory but to "plant" lands that the Crown already possessed in the Munster Plantation. That force was just as violent as the force employed by the Conquistadors in America, but the native Irish were still citizens of the English monarch's empire, with legal rights to their lands. As we have seen, only the lands of traitors were confiscated for planting with English people, though the reality was that many Irish lost their lands because the English claimed those lands belonged to their lords who had committed treason and not to the families that farmed them. In northern Ireland, the force used at the end of the sixteenth century and through the seventeenth century even more clearly represented conquest because it was directed at peoples on lands that England claimed for hundreds of years but never really established a strong sovereignty over.

Colonization, as opposed to conquest, possesses a utopian element. The amassing of resources from colonial lands is driven by physical imperatives, but ideas shape the route to the outcome: a prosperous colonial society and mother country. Successful realization was envisioned as the creation of new overseas societies and the furtherance of prosperity at home. On a mundane level, those who emigrate to colonies—the colonists—often hope to get rich and return home with their riches, but the colonizers—those who own the colonies—think in terms of societal improvements. Many of the English colonies, for instance, were founded on utopian values. The colonizers believed that perfect, or at least perfected, societies could be constructed. From Plymouth to Massachusetts Bay, and from Carolina to Pennsylvania to Georgia, English colonizers thought their purpose was not just to improve their own lives but also to serve the interests of humanity. No colonizer thought, *Let us move to a new land to create a worse society than we have at home.* In contrast, those who remained at home usually believed that colonies could only become, at best, a poor facsimile of the mother country, but those engaged in the process of constructing colonies saw the process as redemptive for both Old and New Worlds.

The social, intellectual, political, and economic forces of colonialism ultimately required an impulse to set them in motion. For instance, the Spanish threat to overrun England led many English to believe that only through overseas expansion could they obtain the wherewithal to compete. England required gold or other precious metals, an array of commodities, and more land for a population that believed it did not have enough to survive. Another impulse, connected to fear of Spain but also a spiritual impulse, was the belief that Elizabeth should be empress of a universal empire that would save both Old and New Worlds from the papal anti-Christ and prepare the way for Christ's return and the impending end of the world, or, at the very least, bring on the return of Constantine's Golden Age. English melancholy sought both spiritual and physical nourishment. A spiritual emptiness and foreboding led English to seek succor in distant places. Capturing Iberian treasure ships returning from the East and West Indies or pursuing any number of adventures abroad, from locating new trade routes to new places to live, was more than mere distraction or simply a way to line one's pockets: the English sought enhancement of their well-being holistically, for themselves, for their queen and nation, and for Christendom.

For a man of non-noble blood like Ralegh, colonialism offered a wide range of solutions. Colonialism was a service provided for the queen and for England, an opportunity to amass wealth, status, and fame, and a chance to create new societies and remake old ones. For Ralegh, the mid to late 1580s colonialism, though not all-consuming, was a period of hyperactivity, when he undertook the planting of English in both Virginia and Ireland and prepared the way for a third adventure on a third continent. Recall: a germ of an idea entered his mind in the 1580s and gathered such force that he invested in its fruition financially, politically, and intellectually: the search for El Dorado. But he lacked the impulse to actually colonize this new land then; the time and circumstances did not arrive until the mid-1590s. Not only did Ralegh have to take care of his affairs in Virginia and Ireland, but also his ascent in the queen's affections led to the growth of his influence, which carried ever more demands on his time in England.

By 1594–1595, however, Virginia had become a distant memory. His Irish lands were developing without needing him to be on location, or so he thought. And then everything fell apart at court, and Ralegh was barred from performing some of his duties as Captain of the Guard. Fortunately for Ralegh, the queen did not take away the many perks he enjoyed, the sources of his wealth, such as his monopoly over wine licenses and his operation of the tin stannaries and his other positions of power in South West England.

Ralegh remained a powerful figure in England, and ending Ralegh's influence would have alienated the region's elite, so many of whom the queen relied on for their expertise at sea. Elizabeth did not like making irrevocable enemies. By opting not to remove the major sources of Ralegh's income, she was able to remain the wronged queen rather than the vengeful monarch. His followers understood her hurt and held no resentment of her, keeping them emotionally preoccupied with hoping he would regain her affection—every accomplishment or service he performed was reported to her.

But the mighty had fallen several notches on the social ladder. Ralegh no longer had the queen's ear—she refused to talk with him. He felt impelled to win back her heart. He still did the queen's business in Parliament, administered the southwest counties for her, and regularly conferred with her chief ministers on affairs of state and foreign policy. But he yearned to again stand by Elizabeth's side. That was the impulse for Ralegh to embark on yet another colonial enterprise, one so fantastic that if he succeeded, she must welcome him back. This impulse met all the prerequisites of colonialism in Tudor England. From Ralegh's perspective, it would challenge Spain, provide access to valuable commodities, offer new lands for settlement, and fulfill the quest to create a universal empire under Elizabeth—an imperial scheme that would benefit England and Europe, as well as millions of peoples of the Americas. Ralegh hoped to add to the queen's empire the world's richest, most magnificent empire of gold, diamonds, and other treasures: El Dorado.

THE SPANISH SEARCH for El Dorado dates to 1541, when Gonzalo Fernández de Oviedo told a story of El Dorado after interviewing Spaniards from Quito, Peru, in his book *Historia general y natural de las Indias* (Seville, 1535–1547). Oviedo warned readers that his story "was based on hearsay from Indian sources."[1] Still, he believed it was likely true.

Cieza de León, who actually visited Quito, also told the story in print. He reported that Gonzalo, younger brother of the famed conquistador of Peru, Francisco Pizarro, who went to Quito in 1541, where there were so many unemployed men, "youths or veterans," "became eager for the discovery of the valley of *El Dorado*."[2] Its presumed location: east of the mountains. An expedition that entered the lands of the Quijos Indians learned from them that farther on they would find a great valley "teeming with Indians who possess great riches, for they all wear gold ornaments." Everyone in Quito wanted to go.[3] A year later, Gonzalo wrote to the King of Spain that he would go "conquer and explore . . . Lake el Dorado," the first mention of a lake linked to the gold.[4]

The legend evolved to apply to other places, most notably to the lands of the Muisca in Colombia, but most Spaniards remained focused on the lands farther east. Other chroniclers and conquistadors followed in the sixteenth and seventeenth centuries in search of the great lake. Gold might have become associated with lakes because Native artifacts of gold occasionally were found in lakes (even to the present day), and some Indians held sacred ceremonies on rafts on lakes. John Hemming, the longtime director of the Royal Geographical Society who studied the origins of the legends, argues that the stories originated with the Spanish, not the Natives, upon their return to Quito from Bogotá. Many had seen gold dust in the region and had fought with Natives, who fiercely defended themselves, defeating Spanish expeditions. The Spanish assumed that to fight so fiercely, the Natives must have been defending gold. Hemming also claims that Pedro de Puelles, a Spanish conquistador, played an important role in promoting the legends by testifying to the existence of "'fine gold and gold dust from mines' of the upper Magdalena," a river in Colombia, "and he hinted that there was more to be found." Puelles's word carried weight because he was lieutenant governor of Quito in 1540 and then governor in 1544.[5]

Three Spanish expeditions went in search of El Dorado in 1541. They scoured the difficult terrain of "the eastern foothills of the Andes, 600 kilometres southwest of Bogotá," just north and south of the northwest border of Ecuador.[6] Repeated failures ultimately led to a shift in the expected location of El Dorado to the Orinoco River, perhaps at its source about a thousand kilometers east-northeast of Bogotá, or perhaps on the Amazon River east of Quito. Disaster followed disaster, and expeditions disintegrated. Royal prohibitions placed on conquistadors slowed the onslaught, but governors received permission to conquer regions, which allowed Diego Fernández de Serpa, in the context of establishing a settlement near the mouth of the Orinoco, to search in 1569–1570. His attempt ended in death at the hands of Natives.

Subsequent series of attempts were undertaken by Gonzalo Jiménez, who had played a lead role in the conquest of Muisca in Colombia decades earlier. Decades of searching for El Dorado only increased his obsession. Jiménez chose his niece's husband, Antonio de Berrío, as his successor to the governorship of El Dorado. Berrío received the income from Jiménez's vast estates in Colombia. Beginning in the early 1580s, Berrío searched for fifteen years from Bogotá across the northern reaches of South America to the Atlantic. Along the way he added—or collected—detail upon detail to the legend of El Dorado and its great lake Manoa. Berrío spent much of his time looking for an easy route to the Orinoco River. He learned that El Dorado was inhabited by Incas who fled Peru and who likely relocated in the north-central part of the continent. Initially, this meant traveling south from the Caribbean Sea to one of the many rivers that fed into the Orinoco. Finally, Berrío determined it would be best to search inward from the mouth of the Orinoco on the Atlantic. After squandering his seven daughters' dowries on his quest, his funds ran short. He settled at Trinidad, waiting for his lieutenant to return from Spain with more men and money to make another foray. He believed he was so close to finally locating El Dorado. But in April 1595, Sir Walter Ralegh arrived and took Berrío prisoner.

Ralegh's assault on the Spanish at Trinidad was a model of brutal efficiency. When he arrived with two ships, he dispatched a letter to Berrío demanding a meeting, claiming, according to Berrío, that what he had to discuss concerned "service to His Majesty King Philip." Ralegh enclosed a ring and icons of the Virgin and Saint Francis to represent that he did not oppose the Spaniards' religion. Berrío refused to meet but sent his nephew to deliver food to the English. Four days later, Ralegh and one hundred men attacked at dawn. They bound Berrío's nephew and the others who had escorted him and killed them by sword. Ralegh claimed this as revenge for the year before, when his Captain Jacob Whiddon had landed at Trinidad and received the promise of safety for his men to take on fresh water, only to see eight of his men killed. (Berrío had boasted of orchestrating their deaths.)[7]

Ralegh's other stated reasons for revenge are equally noteworthy. After the killing of Berrío's nephew, Indians joined Ralegh's men and together they captured Spanish soldiers, some of whom were killed. The Spanish had been in the process of building a city, St. Joseph, and, at the Indians' insistence, the English burned the city to the ground. Ralegh's revenge, he stated, resulted from his disgust that the Spanish at Trinidad had "made the ancient . . . Lordes of the country to be their slaves, that he kept them in chains" and tortured them. The chiefs he freed had been found "wasted with torments" and starvation.

Out of respect, he recorded and published the names of each: "*Wan-nawanare, Carroaori, Maquarima, Tarroopanama & Aterima.*"[8] Ralegh proudly wore the mantle of liberator of Indians during his search for El Dorado. Everywhere he traveled on the mainland he promised the Indians alliance against the Spanish and that he would free them from Spanish tyranny as he had done for the Indians of Trinidad.

At Trinidad, Ralegh brought to shore wine he previously had captured from a Portuguese ship. He liberally plied his Spanish prisoners to loosen their tongues. They spoke glowingly of El Dorado—though they had not seen it. Berrío did all he could to disabuse Ralegh of the notion that El Dorado could be quickly found. After all, Berrío had spent a dozen years searching.

It is easy today to mock those who searched for El Dorado at great expense of life and fortune as on a fool's errand, but as anthropologist Neil L. Whitehead points out, the Natives of northern South America really did have gold, which they skillfully worked into magnificent objects. The European searchers' mistake was in believing that the Natives had great caches of the precious metal that would satiate their quest for a golden city or lake.[9] The Europeans also erred in transposing the gold they found in Colombia as coming from an El Dorado to the east and south in the Orinoco and Amazon watersheds or in the uplands of Guiana, where there existed no great cities. In the late twentieth century, artifacts of gold were found near where Ralegh visited in Guiana, but through the centuries the scarcity of golden objects discovered archaeologically has called into question Ralegh's "truth" in reporting a significant "native metallurgical tradition in Guiana." Whitehead argues that overwhelming evidence shows that these items existed. Their absence from the archaeological record results from their being traded off to Europeans in exchange for European goods and from Europeans looting burial sites. An array of English and Spanish in the sixteenth and seventeenth centuries reported that the Orinoco Indians worked gold objects and traded them, so much so that they were "common."[10]

Historians' concern with the truth of Ralegh's stories has distracted them from comprehending his stories' significance. Everything Ralegh related is part of a story—or sequence of stories. Some, such as tales of El Dorado and of the gold he saw and held, had the "truth" of being part of decades of stories told and acted on by the Spanish; Ralegh almost surely reported faithfully the gold objects he saw among the

Indians as did so many other witnesses who reported the same. Once we accept the "truth" of Ralegh's vision—that there was gold—it is easier to understand how he and so many others believed that the stories of El Dorado were essentially true. Then we can unpack the stories Ralegh transmitted about El Dorado and his vision and plans to colonize South America for England.

CHAPTER 24

The Discovery of Guiana

O ver the next four weeks in spring 1595, Ralegh led an expedition up the Orinoco River in search of a civilization possessed of an incredible amount of gold. Leaving behind about a hundred men, he took with him another hundred on a barge he had fitted out at Trinidad. It had to carry the men and furniture, but not draw a lot of water.

Time was short. Berrío had claimed that Spanish troops were on their way to Trinidad. An even greater time pressure was the inevitable change in seasons—the English had arrived near the start of the rainy season. Tropical rains would inevitably overflow the rivers, making river travel difficult and exploration of the surrounding mainland nearly impossible. Fortunately for Ralegh, the heavy rains held off for a month. As with the first expedition he sent to Virginia a decade earlier, this one was intended to examine the lay of the land over a two- to three-month period, assess the area's prospects, establish friendly relations with the Natives, and calculate the men and equipment necessary for success.

With Hariot's work on Virginia as his model, Ralegh collected data on an extensive terrain: rivers, peoples, plants, minerals, crystals, animals, and so on. He garnered much information from Berrío, who had given him a list of the numerous rivers that fed into the Orinoco, but he personally traversed four hundred miles of the Orinoco, recorded distances from one tributary to the next, sampled a large swath of landscape, and provided names for groups of people with some indication of their relationship to others. Ralegh's account of the peoples and their locations was not always a model of clarity, but he mapped the Orinoco and collected evidence of the physical world that certified his ability to be an observant and curious traveler.

As could be expected of a Hermeticist, he was deeply interested in stones and gems that could be used in the laboratory and for healing. He and his men collected numerous samples for closer examination upon return to England. His discussion of spleen stones, for treatment of liver and spleen ailments, is the first recorded usage of the term in the English language, according to the *Oxford English Dictionary*. Ralegh carried a spleen stone till his death, which likely indicates he had a long-term chronic health problem that he thought the stone relieved. In addition to stones, Ralegh searched for evidence of gold and for trustworthy information about El Dorado. He assessed the geopolitical situation and looked to negotiate with the local peoples in a way that would fulfill their mutual needs. He warned his men against committing any injury upon the Natives, and before departing the area of each group, he publicly punished any of his men who had committed theft: the Indians were meant to know they would always receive justice from the English. Ralegh insisted that none of his men sexually abuse the Native women, that they should not behave like the Spanish, whose abuses were widely reported in the contemporary literature. When he finished his journey up the Orinoco, with panache worthy of Francis Drake, Ralegh returned to Trinidad and released his prisoner Antonio de Berrío. Of greatest substance for his own needs, Ralegh created a vision of the Orinoco region as the pathway to phenomenal wealth.

That pathway extended through difficult terrain but also through the lands of the Borderers, the people who inhabited the eastern border of the Empire of Guiana. Without their assistance, Ralegh learned, he could never reach the Empire of Guiana, what the Spanish called El Dorado. In Ralegh's relatively brief time of exploration, conducted under physically demanding circumstances, he formed positive relationships with the Borderers. He cultivated each group he encountered. Ralegh never reached the Empire of Guiana, but he forged ties with an important leader of the empire's Borderers: Topiawari. This ancient Indian leader became Ralegh's authority on the Empire of Guiana. Because Ralegh would not return to England having found great caches of gold, he had to buttress his own credibility with that of a special American Indian.

Ralegh needed an authority because his own was suspect. He had neither plumbed the depths of any gold mines nor seen for himself the world's richest city, Manoa. Lacking physical evidence, Ralegh referenced more than a half century of Spanish searching for El Dorado: surely, the world's greatest explorers, who had discovered and conquered the magnificent empires of Mexico and Peru, would not waste their time on the chimerical. The reports of a few Spanish witnesses, who allegedly had been to the golden city of Manoa, kept alive the Spanish search and convinced Ralegh of El Dorado's existence. The Borderers' donning of gold jewelry and their possession of gold plate confirmed for Ralegh the existence of great stores of gold.

When he returned to England, skeptics questioned where he had obtained the few bits of gold, stone, and jewels that he brought home—some claimed he never went to Guiana and had hidden in Cornwall the entire time! If only Ralegh had brought a load of plate and great numbers of Native gold icons to prove provenance, he would have had the evidence he needed. Otherwise, all was hearsay. On shaky ground, as he frequently did in life, Ralegh turned to words to rescue him. He wrote and published a book about his exploits: THE DISCOVERIE OF THE LARGE, RICH, AND BEWTIFVL EMPYRE OF GVIANA, WITH *a relation of the great and Golden Citie of Manoa (which the Spanyards call* El Dorado) *And of the Prouinces of Emeria, Arromaia, Amapaia, and other Countries, with their riuers, adioyning. Performed in the yeare 1595.*[1]

To separate his story from Spanish legends, Ralegh almost entirely discarded *El Dorado* from his lexicon and replaced it with "Empire of Guiana." An *empire* sounded more impressive than the vague *El Dorado*. Ralegh's book title even announced that the place called El Dorado by the Spanish was actually the golden city of Manoa, in the larger political entity, the Empire of Guiana. With a flourish of the pen, Ralegh had excised Spanish legends and replaced them with "real" places. His strategy was to transform his quest from the fantastic, moving past the long and spectacular series of failed Spanish enterprises to locate a legendary city of gold, into a realistic pursuit of the Empire of Guiana, the world's richest civilization.

—

INCREDIBLY, AN EXISTING DRAFT of the book shows the adjustments Ralegh made to the text after incorporating suggestions from Robert Cecil and Charles Howard.[2] Cecil was the queen's second most important minister after his father, Lord Burghley. He had taken over Francis Walsingham's duties as the queen's secretary after the latter's death in 1590 and was on the eve of his appointment as her secretary of state. Howard was Lord Admiral of the Navy since 1585, seeing England through the threat of the Spanish Armada and overseeing the development of the English navy. He served as lord admiral for thirty-four years. From Cecil and Howard, Ralegh received advice on his manuscript that had little to do with censorship and keeping government secrets about Guiana and more about helping Ralegh make an effective case to gain support for another expedition to locate the Empire of Guiana. They suggested highlighting Spanish authority about the existence of the mines and eliminating some, not all, of Ralegh's extraneous discussion of Indian cultures. The imperative for the book: Ralegh, Cecil, and Howard hoped it could convincingly make the case that vast profits awaited. Ralegh related his own tireless efforts in taking the "Discoverie" of Guiana as far as he had. Throughout the book, he touts his authority, his knowledge of Guiana and the Orinoco River Valley, and his friendship with the Natives who would guide and support the English in their quest to subdue the Empire of Guiana. Despite a reduced discussion of Indians in the published version, the Native peoples remain central to the story. Ralegh took unusual steps to buttress Native authority, because reliance on the word of Natives would not sit well with many English, who could not fathom how Indians, lacking the institutions and belief structure that the English associated with civilization, could be so wise and circumspect that Ralegh would follow their advice and guidance.

Ralegh formulated a strategy of telling incredibly exaggerated stories of Native Americans as a way to win the trust of English readers. He fed English prejudices about some Indians being physical oddities—almost beyond belief—which allowed him to raise others to being extremely wise. Ralegh had much experience using stories to convince others to suspend belief, as when he turned Elizabeth into multiple goddesses. Just as Elizabeth's roles as multiple goddesses buttressed her sovereign authority, Ralegh buttressed his own authority as expert on Guiana by relating wild tales. He turned himself into *the* expert on Indians by distinguishing the characteristics of one group of Natives from the next. He echoed European tropes of American Indian exoticism so that readers would believe him all the more when he offered an Indian's "factual" account of the Empire of Guiana.

Readers through the centuries have misconstrued Ralegh's *Discoverie* as a pack of lies designed merely to entertain. The most offended observation came from the philosopher and historian David Hume. In his six-volume *The History of England* (1778, Vol. 4), he described Ralegh's book as "full of the grossest and most palpable lies, that were ever attempted to be imposed on the credulity of man." Hume did not see how these lies—Ralegh's stories—had a purpose: to obtain support for a return to Guiana. Ralegh told tales of strange Indians, whom he admitted he had never met, insisting they must be true because so many Indian and Spanish witnesses had confirmed them. Similarly, what he had learned about the location and means to reach Guiana must be true because a most trustworthy Indian had said so, and the Spanish, too, were convinced of the empire's existence. Notably, Cecil and Howard did not recommend excising the fantastic tales. They must have understood Ralegh's strategy, for they instead focused on eliminating some of his asides and unnecessary elaborations about Indians. They recommended keeping the essentials of the most unlikely stories about exotic Indians, which could be contrasted with his sober accounts of the Empire of Guiana.

One of the two great fantasies Ralegh related was of the extraordinary Ewaipanoma—"a nation of people, whose heades appeare not above their shoulders, which though it may be thought a meere fable, yet for mine owne part I am resolved it is true, because every child in the provinces of *Arromaia* and *Canuri* affirme the same." These people without heads had their mouths "in the middle of their breasts," as was confirmed by Topiawari's son, whom Ralegh brought to England and who stated "that they are the most mightie men of all the lande."[3]

The other fantastic story, which Ralegh admits is a digression but cannot resist relating, is about the Amazons, a substantial tribe of warrior women. Ralegh did not invent the Amazons in South America. The Spanish had reported their presence as early as 1500 and named the great river after these mythical people. Yet Ralegh ignores the Spanish precedent for the stories and focuses on his own authority—those who live along the Orinoco, "the most ancient and best traveled" of the indigenous peoples—who told him about the women. Ralegh's discussion, however, is designed to place America's indigenous peoples into the flow of world history. As with his relation of the Ewaipanoma, his story of the Amazons is drawn from ancient mythologies that held wide

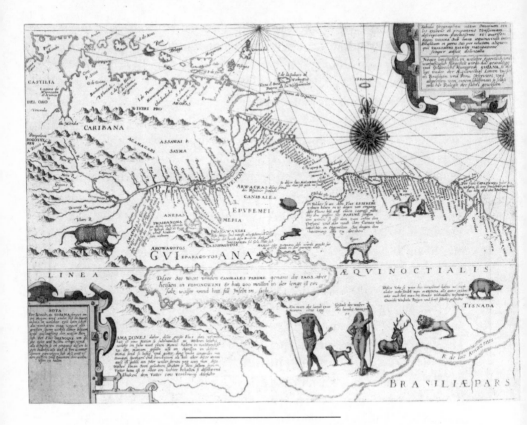

23. Jodocus Hondius map of Guiana with an Ewaipanoma and
an Amazon warrior, based on Ralegh's "Account of Guiana," 1599

currency in Europe: "The memories of the like women are very ancient
as well in *Africa* as in *Asia*."[4]

Ralegh's stories of the Amazons fed men's sexual fantasies. The
Amazons reversed gender roles, for they were mighty women warriors
who dominated men militarily and sexually. Once a year, Ralegh reports, the Amazon women chose men from among the neighboring
peoples for the purpose of sexual intercourse and to "feast, daunce,
& drinke." This lasts for one month. Notably, Ralegh uses no derisive
terms, such as *debauchery*, to refer to the month and its activities. If a
son is born, they give the child to the father, if "a daughter they nourish it, and reteine it."[5] Ralegh's expertise licenses him to claim that the
ancient writers were wrong and that Amazon women do not mutilate
their breasts, so they can, indeed, nourish their children. The women
also filled their sexual needs at other times of the year. Ralegh avers
that the Amazons "accompany"—a sixteenth-century euphemism for

fornicate with—their prisoners, "but in the end for certaine they put them to death: for they are said to be very cruell and bloodthirsty, especially to such as offer to invade their territories."[6] The Amazons, too, possessed much gold. But Ralegh does not recommend conquest.

Not till the end of the book does he hint at a future relationship between the English and the Amazons beyond military alliance. After the Empire of Guiana is subdued, then "those women shall heereby heare the name of a virgin [Elizabeth], which is not onely able to defend her owne territories and her neighbors, but also to invade and conquere so great Empyres and so farre removed."[7] Ralegh had moved from the titillation of women warriors sexually dominating men—females seeing to their own sexual needs before destroying the objects of their pleasure—to the Cult of the Virgin Queen, who's state of virginity was emblematic of her superiority and a marker of her as a great empress.

Ralegh's readers would have known little to nothing of the region's actual Natives because little information flowed to Europe about the Orinoco River Indians. His entire book can be interpreted by readers as fantasy—Ralegh's fantasy—but by placing these peoples in the ancient world, Ralegh's *Discoverie* gains authority. From a practical standpoint, the Amazons and the Ewaipanoma, Ralegh assures his readers, will make excellent allies and become sources of gold. Because he wants the English to ally with them, he does not deride the Amazons or the Ewaipanoma as monsters. Though playful, his tone is nevertheless sincere in relating how the English have no need to fear these Indians for their peculiar characteristics. The stories add levity to his narrative amid all the hardships he and his men survived in their travels and their failure to bring home gold. But they are more than distraction. These stories display to readers Ralegh's access to the exotic, as a man who knows the New World better than any other Englishman. Ralegh hoped to attain the fame and respect of Marco Polo and John Mandeville, great travelers whose storytelling about Asia was as important to their reputations as their adventures. In the book, Ralegh hoped to inspire others to join him on his adventure to America.

He uses his personal adventure to strengthen his credentials for making his case about Guiana. He had led Englishmen to Trinidad, defeated the Spanish and captured their leader, then entered the treacherous regions at the mouth of the Orinoco. He traversed four hundred miles of the interior, befriended Indians, conducted reconnaissance, and recorded his findings. He balanced and wove together entertaining stories of exotic Indians with his quest to locate the Empire of

Guiana. He attempts to impress upon the people of England that this is a God-ordained or blessed enterprise. As soon as he returned from Guiana, Ralegh made a show of attending church "daily to heare sermons, because he hath seen the wonders of the Lord in the deepe." This behavior, an observer noted, "'tis much comended and spoken of."[8]

The "action" in *Discoverie* takes place almost entirely along the Orinoco River. The plot is built around Ralegh's foray east to west up the river, identifying each of the dozens of rivers he passes, with occasional discussion of the peoples who lived north and south. Farther north, unseen, is the Caribbean Sea, bordered by Spanish outposts. Ralegh turns the Spanish into a specter haunting the Borderers, the Indians who inhabit the edge of the Empire of Guiana. The Borderers hate the Spanish, who have wronged them. (Of course, the Spanish also haunt the English, not only by the threat they pose to England's survival as a nation but also by their incredible success in the New World. Should not England share in the riches?) To the south of the Orinoco live the Amazons, and other mostly unnamed peoples, and impenetrable jungle. The Amazon River lay to the south about two hundred miles, connected to the Orinoco by the Casiquiare River. Ralegh had no reason to venture southward because the Empire of Guiana presumably was west. But the reality is that the land south of the Orinoco remains one of the most remote places on the earth into the twenty-first century. This area straddling the border of modern-day Venezuela and Brazil only recently has been developed, modernized, or whatever euphemism one wishes to employ to describe the entrance of machinery and capitalism to transform the landscape. It made sense to Ralegh that mythical peoples in world history inhabited these locales that known peoples had not visited.

The landscape Ralegh passes through is hot, dense, and foreboding. The English follow the rivers, mostly the Orinoco, though Ralegh sends parties out on a few of the tributaries to the Orinoco from the north. He and his men mostly travel by water, for there is little firm ground to walk on. He reassures readers that the reason the Spanish had failed for over a half century was because they could not find the way to Manoa. The rivers from their northern outposts led to the Orinoco, at which point those who sought Guiana had to travel west. But the Spanish, according to Ralegh, failed to use these routes or could not make their way west without the Borderers' help. The text does not make clear why the northern routes to the Orinoco are inconvenient—was it the jungle? Or were these routes only inconvenient to the English because the Spanish barred their way, and to the Spanish because the Borderers barred their way? The Empire of Guiana could not be easily approached from the west, from Colombia or Ecuador, which the Spanish occupied, because the Andes Mountains would have to be crossed. A southern approach was impossible because the Amazonian rain forest would have to be traversed. That left only an easterly approach from near the mouth of the Orinoco River—the route that Berrío had pursued; the route used by Ralegh, who hired a Native pilot to negotiate the river.

Ralegh hoped to find a way to bypass the river's mouth. He claimed to know an alternative and privately confirmed with the queen and her ministers that he knew exactly where this entrance lay of which the Spanish remained ignorant. But he worried about the existence of another entrance below the mouth, which the Spanish might locate. Upon his return to England, he sent his trusted friend Lawrence Kemys, who sailed with him to Guiana, to return to South America and conduct reconnaissance between the Amazon and Orinoco Rivers. Inspired by Ralegh's book, the Ley family also searched for this entry, as did sailors of other nations. Even if they had discovered this convenient route to the Orinoco, it was still five hundred or a thousand or more miles to reach where the Empire of Guiana was allegedly located. In essence, Ralegh's book is about his "Search" for the route to the empire and his assurance that with "Discoverie" the English could block others from using this same route.

The key to finding and controlling the exclusive route to Lake Manoa was to forge an alliance with the Borderers and then protect them from Spanish conquest. Ralegh repeatedly asserts that the Borderers were inveterate enemies of Spain and would welcome an alliance with the English to keep the Spanish out of the region. Even so, he admits that some Borderers associated with the Spanish, allowed them into their country, and that Don Juan, a nephew of Morequito, the former king of the Borderers, had been christened by the Spanish, who hoped to make him leader of the Borderers. Without alliance, the Empire of Guiana was inaccessible because the Borderers knew the only way there. Spanish failure owed to their inability to ally with the Borderers. The Borderers thus became Ralegh's authority for nearly everything of substance: they gave Ralegh news about the Spanish and the Empire of Guiana; they knew the way to Manoa; they provided the information about the Amazons and the Ewaipanoma; they possessed gold and knew where it came from. Treated fairly, and protected from the Spanish, Ralegh was sure the Borderers could be counted on as allies and friends.

To drive home his point, several times Ralegh recounts the killing of Morequito, the signal event that irredeemably alienated the Borderers from the Spanish. Ralegh has no fear that the Borderers will ever forgive the Spanish, only that the Spanish could conquer them. Morequito had allowed ten Spanish "and a Frier (which *Berreo* had sent to discouer *Manoa*) to travell through his countrey." On their return, "the people of *Morequito* set upon them, & slew them all but one that swam the river," and took 40,000 pesos worth of gold. In revenge for killing the friar and the ten Spanish, Berrío captured Morequito and executed him, and then the Spanish "spoiled his territorie, & tooke divers prisoners," including "the unckle of *Morequito* called *Topiawari*," who later was released. Ralegh's story sets up the new king, Topiawari, as the natural ally of the English because he is an "irrevocable" enemy of Spain.[9] Topiawari's people shared their leader's view of the Spanish because their land had been spoiled by them.[10] As Ralegh traveled along the Orinoco, he let each group of Borderers "know that we were enemies to the Spanyards," that the English queen would protect them, and that Ralegh would deliver the Indians from Spanish tyranny as he had done for the Native peoples of Trinidad. This brought the Indians joy, and they supplied the English with all sorts "of provisions to entertaine us."[11]

Ralegh's repetition of the story signifies the shaky ground on which he stood—he had no hard evidence of the existence of the Empire of Guiana or personal knowledge of how to get there. Instead, he forged a friendship and alliance with the Borderers' wise chief, Topiawari, who would support the English and lead them to Manoa, an opportunity the Spanish missed because of their cruelty. The gracious hospitality of the Borderers evinces their love for the English and imitates Cortés's success in Mexico, one of the best-known stories in Europe about America. Cortés had been expelled from Tenochtitlan, yet returned to conquer the Aztecs by allying with their Native enemies, who provided provisions and military assistance: they, too, were borderers. As in the story of Cortés, no matter how much against the odds the English operated in an inhospitable terrain, the Borderers could vastly improve these odds by providing material comfort, guidance, manpower, and supplies. To Ralegh, all hinged on this alliance, but the English had to return at the right time and with the right men and equipment.

Ralegh's most skillful act of storytelling is in recounting his relationship with Topiawari. Other indigenous people appear in *Discoverie* but are given no individuality. Topiawari grounds the book. From the fantastic—the Amazons and Ewaipanoma—to the drudgery of traveling up and down the Orinoco, from the useful, curious, and valuable—spleen stones, gemstones, and the abundance of food—to the goal of locating the Empire of Guiana, Ralegh flies with abandon through an exotic South American landscape. In contrast to this series of stories and adventures, Ralegh's conversations with Topiawari are "real" conversations.

The reader sits at the feet of Topiawari listening to him as Ralegh did. The New World gains meaning as a place of circumspect Natives. Ralegh's quest to locate the Empire of Guiana and to access its gold, jewels, and precious stones, his slogging adventure along the Orinoco, the specter he paints of Spanish evil and competition: none of these matter without Topiawari. Only Topiawari can lead the English to Guiana and its gold.

Few Europeans would have gone to the New World in the sixteenth century but for gold and silver. Barring the prospect of obtaining precious metals from Native peoples, English males preferred to pirate the precious metals from other Europeans at sea. Relatively few humble English sought land to farm in America until the seventeenth century, and, even then, English, like other Europeans in America, desired to produce commodities, particularly staple crops that could be exported at great profit, rather than to engage in subsistence agriculture. For most, moving to America was about obtaining wealth, not merely surviving. In the sixteenth century, gold and silver held pride of place as the lure of the Americas. The precious metals, as in Mexico and Peru, belonged to the Indians. They knew where the mines were located. Their artisans transformed silver and gold into precious objects. Europeans envisioned wresting away and melting down the wonderful pieces the indigenous peoples created with gold and silver, eradicating the Indians' possession by removing every mark of Native craftsmanship and spirituality. They also hoped to discover mines, but they would take whatever was readily available. Ralegh and the Hermeticists nonetheless appreciated Native culture and religiosity. Recall from the inventory of his possessions for his third imprisonment in the Tower of London he carried on his person "a Guiana idol of gold." Ralegh was bent on neither conquest nor removal of Guiana's indigenous peoples. He needed Topiawari. The English needed the Borderers.

Ralegh insinuates a partnership. His respect for Topiawari reflects the respect he wants the English to give to Indians because without Topiawari and his people, Ralegh and the English cannot succeed. Topiawari possesses the political authority on which Ralegh relies for answers and assistance. Berrío provided Ralegh with a Spanish authority on the truth of Guiana, but Berrío repeatedly had failed to reach the Empire of Guiana, and his killing of Morequito alienated the people he needed. The English, Ralegh urges, will not make the same mistakes as the Spanish because they will heed Native wisdom. Topiawari explains to Ralegh the exact situation by which he can succeed, but Ralegh must wait. At first, Ralegh's impatience to search led Topiawari to turn his back on him—Ralegh had to learn his lesson.

When Ralegh introduces us to Topiawari, he refers to him as the "old king" who had to rest after traveling to meet the English "at the port of *Morequito*." Ralegh already knew who he was: the uncle of the king killed by the Spanish. Ralegh told the new king why he was there, to defend the Indians from the Spanish, describing "her Majesties greatnes, her justice, her charitie to all oppressed nations," while proclaiming her many "beauties and vertues." Then Ralegh "began to sound the olde man as touching *Guiana*," inquiring about its condition, government, how well it was ruled, its size, who were its "friends or enimies . . . and finally of the distance," and how to get there. The king instead spoke of his own people's identity, that all the Borderers extending to the sea, including his own, were of Guiana, "but that they call themselves *Orenoqueponi*" because of the "great river." Ralegh asked him about the peoples on the other side of the Andes, and Topiawari issued a "great sigh," for he had lost his son in a battle there. Knowing that Ralegh was intent on exploring farther west toward Manoa, Topiawari left him to his own devices and returned to his own town twenty-eight miles distant. Just like that, Topiawari abandons Ralegh, telling him they would talk again on Ralegh's return. Ralegh "marvelled" at this old man, whom he estimated at 110 years of age, for his "gravity and judgement, and of so good discourse, that had no helpe of learning or breed."[12] Ralegh is not perturbed by this wise elderly man leaving, for at this point in his journey Ralegh was intent on ascending the Orinoco River in search of gold. He was not ready for the advice of the wise Native leader.

Ralegh sent out parties to look for guides, for Topiawari had offered none. Ralegh hoped to locate mines of silver and precious stones and to explore. He admits to finding the way difficult, that he had become "a very ill footeman." But his men urged him on, hoping to reach the "thunder of waters," a dozen or so waterfalls that lured them through a valley of incredible beauty. They reached a place where the stone beneath their feet "promised eyther golde or silver." They dug with their "daggers and fingers" to no avail. Ralegh later rued their lack of proper tools. He also later learned from a Spaniard that he had found "*El Madre del oro*," a great belowground gold mine. One of his men returned from exploring with stones like sapphires; the Orenokepone said they knew of a mountain of these "verye large peeces growing Diamond wise," but whether these were real sapphires, crystals, or fake diamonds, Ralegh did not know.[13]

The text is filled with stories like these. There are cannibals who sell women and speculation on whether the English could invade Peru—all chatty-like distractions to deter the reader from realizing that Ralegh's and his men's wanderings accomplished so little. But this was a fateful day for Ralegh, having found "El Madre del oro." Over the next twenty years, he formed in his mind the idea that he had located one of the world's greatest mines of gold. And more than twenty years later, he returned to South America intent on digging up this mine's secrets at last.

Torrential rains made the river increasingly dangerous. Sometimes it rained ten times in a day. The English retreated down the Orinoco. They had been a month from their ships. Though they used no labor to propel the barge and moved against the wind, the current carried them a hundred miles per day. On the return, Ralegh stopped to call for Topiawari because he wanted to take one of his people to England to learn the language. Topiawari met him with many people laden with provisions, "as if it had beene a great market or faire in England." Topiawari welcomed Ralegh because he had given up his quest upriver. With an interpreter, Ralegh conferred with Topiawari, who recounted the geopolitical situation of his people—a language Ralegh understood.

Ralegh asked the elderly leader "to instruct me what hee coulde, both of the passage into the golden partes of *Guiana*, and to the civill townes and apparrelled [militarily equipped] people of *Inga*," the emperor of Guiana. Pleased that Ralegh accepted that it was the wrong time of year to go forth, and that Ralegh did not have "sufficient numbers for such an enterprize," Topiawari "gave me this good counsell": Guiana would be difficult to subdue. If Ralegh had proceeded, the emperor would have killed them all. Instead, Ralegh must unite the emperor's enemies against him. Ralegh needed not only guides but also laborers to feed his army. The journey would be arduous and the English could not "indure the march in so great heate, and travell, unlesse the borderers" carried "their meate and furniture."[14] The Spanish had tried without the Borderers' assistance and made it four days distant to the town of the Epuremj, where the Indians of the emperor set the dry grass on fire and smothered them.[15]

Ralegh asked Topiawari whether he thought Ralegh had enough men to take the town of the Epuremj, which had defeated the Spanish with fire, because they were so close and had much gold, and whether he could procure guides and men to help. Topiawari said he would go if the rivers remained fordable, but Ralegh had to leave fifty soldiers to defend his people until Ralegh returned, and returned not just from taking the gold but from England. In other words, Ralegh cannot attack one town for its gold, inciting the emperor to revenge, and leave Topiawari defenseless to face the consequences. Ralegh tells his readers he did not have fifty good soldiers, for many of his men were laborers and rowers, nor did he have enough gunpowder, shot, and armor to leave with these men, who would not be able to resist a Spanish assault. Some of Ralegh's men volunteered to stay—Ralegh names them for his readers to show he had brave men who were committed to reaching the Empire of Guiana—but Ralegh did not let them stay, for they would perish, and he feared Berrío's claim that Spanish troops would soon arrive.

Ralegh could not put Topiawari in peril with the Spanish. Return next year, Topiawari promised, and he would bring together all the Borderers to serve the English, and the weather "woulde be more seasonable to travel." The Borderers, Topiawari added, did not care about gold. They wanted the return of their women seized by the Epuremj. The Epuremj themselves cared more about warring to obtain women than they did "eyther for gold or dominion." They wanted to produce children to increase their power on these dangerous frontiers. Ralegh agreed to forgo attacking the Epuremj and to return the next year. He justified his decision, that sacking one or two towns for six or seven thousand pounds worth of gold was not worth risking the millions they could obtain the following year, and all the "rich trade" England would gain from alliance with the Borderers. Ralegh expressed his every confidence in the willingness of the Borderers to help him on his return, a deal Topiawari sealed "freely," giving Ralegh "his onelie sonne to take with me into England." In exchange, Ralegh left with Topiawari two young men, Frances Sparrow who agreed to stay and was instructed to try to make his way to Manoa and, if possible, to go inside the city, and Ralegh's servant, *"Hugh Goodwin*, to learne the language."[16]

Leaving behind Sparrow and Godwyn should give us pause to ask what happened to the four boys Ralegh sent to Trinidad and Guiana eight years earlier. Ralegh makes no mention of the boys in his correspondence or in his published account of his journey. It is likely that he never saw them again.[17]

It might seem daft for Ralegh to have sent four boys to the South American jungle to be taken care of by Native people. Europeans understood that children learn foreign languages much more quickly than adults, and Ralegh was not bothered by the prospect of the boys becoming "savages" by living with Indians for an extended period—as others would have feared—for he had different views of Indians than most Europeans did. He held an unusual degree of respect for and openness toward Native peoples and cultures.

Upon returning to England, Ralegh was committed to following up his first expedition to Guiana. A flurry of letters Ralegh and his wife exchanged makes evident their anxiety about achieving support. Thomas Hariot joined in, putting his stamp of approval on Guiana's prospects in a letter to Robert Cecil, who supported the project with money but needed to convince the queen to back Ralegh, whom she had yet to entirely forgive. The queen always needed money, but even if she did not personally invest, her public support could rally investors. Hariot had no influence with the queen, but his continual assistance of Ralegh was invaluable, and his expertise as a scientist carried weight with English intellectuals.

Hariot helped Ralegh with his collections of materials about Guiana and likely by editing his writing. He did this as a friend and associate because he had otherwise found a new patron in the Wizard Earl, Henry Percy, Ninth Earl of Northumberland, a close friend of Ralegh and a fellow Hermeticist. With Ralegh's fall from the queen's favor, and his varied colonial and political projects, Hariot found Percy's support convenient. Percy provided Hariot with a handsome salary, a house, and facilities to pursue his experiments away from the public eye. Percy was renowned for his scientific interests and enjoyed much respect in government and intellectual circles. For the moment, at least, it was safer for Hariot to be under Percy's wing. The three, however, remained lifelong friends, as the many scattered records of their socializing, smoking, card playing, and trading of ingredients for laboratory testing testify. Even when the Crown withdrew its support from these men, they still had each other. Years later, Ralegh and Percy found themselves fellow prisoners in the Tower of London, where Hariot frequently visited them and they continued to smoke, play cards, and conduct scientific experiments as if little had changed.

It was one thing to pursue intellectual interests, and quite another to colonize. Elizabeth seemed generally uninterested in supporting the enterprise in South America. But if Ralegh could obtain financial support for Guiana without her, she likely would give her blessing. She had nothing to lose by adding Guiana to her empire, but she remained reticent about publicly supporting Ralegh's hopes for Guiana. Elizabeth's concern over the Spanish would soon lead her to agree to a direct assault on Spain, particularly its treasure fleets; this took precedence over Guiana. Even as Ralegh was drawn into this expedition against Spain, he drew up a confidential plan for Guiana that, I assume, alternately bemused, befuddled, confused, and intrigued the queen's councilors. The proposal Ralegh presented was focused, clear, and logical, but the perspective might have been beyond the councilors' complete understanding. On the other hand, maybe the queen's men understood Ralegh and his vision of empire, a Hermeticist's view, a religiously and culturally tolerant view, better than I give them credit for. But certainly, Ralegh's vision made little sense to historians of subsequent centuries, who lived during and after the Age of Empire, who knew of a British Empire on which the sun never set. The assumption has always been that Ralegh helped originate that empire by sending colonists to North America. He might have been a failed imperialist, but historians have thought he awaited the rest of England catching up to where he stood on the timeline of English imperial development, at least in terms of colonizing in North America.

But what if Ralegh's blueprint for empire was little like what ultimately developed? What if Ralegh envisioned an empire without conquest, where the Native peoples would be full partners in the colonial enterprise? The idea of an anti-imperial empire seems to make no sense—yet Ralegh proposed such an entity: a benevolent empire.

CHAPTER 25

The Benevolent Empire

At its root, colonialism is the movement of a group of people to new lands. If the lands are heavily populated, as in the case of Tenochtitlan, the Aztec capital, conquest must take place before colonization. If the newcomers are simply looking for wealth, as in the case of the conquistadors, then they might arrive looking for a fight and abuse the Native people until they get what they want. This was not an option in the initial English colonial forays in America—the newcomers may have arrived armed, but they lacked the military power to conquer Natives. They had to negotiate their presence.

Typically, they did not arrive as conquistadors. For the English, the true enemy was the Spanish, and the Native peoples were perceived as potential allies in that fight. Even though individuals like Grenville and Lane believed military power must be employed to obtain Native subservience, their actions ultimately made colonization at Roanoke untenable for the English. This manner of conquest was costly, difficult, and put new colonists at great risk.

New colonies depended on alliance and trade with local Natives to earn protection from more distant, politically hostile peoples. In subsequent generations, many English would initially display military power to impress the Natives and earn their respect, but they did not attempt conquest until they thought they had achieved secure permanent settlements. John Smith famously balanced negotiation and hubris with the Powhatan in Virginia; James Oglethorpe did the same with the Yamacraw and Creek in Georgia. William Penn and Roger Williams, on the other hand, took a different tack in establishing Pennsylvania and

Providence Plantations (Rhode Island), respectively, by showering Natives with presents in exchange for land and peaceful relations: these colonizers possessed a pacific disposition that promoted friendship as the means to coexistence. There were examples like the Carolina colony, where the settlers employed violence against local Native peoples almost from first settlement, but usually colonists waited until they had a modicum of security before turning to enslaving, swindling, attacking, and taking Natives' land.

Whatever tack they chose, the English had to make accommodations with the Native peoples to establish colonies. If they prematurely used force, as with the violence instigated by Lane at Roanoke, then the colony failed. Most European colonizers recognized that the exchange of presents and goods would pave the way for their settlement near indigenous peoples. In many places where Europeans settled, local Natives welcomed the outsiders because of the commodities they offered and for the potential of military alliance. In the case of the Empire of Guiana, on the surface there appeared to the English no alternative to violent conquest—empires were too strong to allow outsiders (i.e., the English) to settle without accepting subservience to the emperor. In Guiana, the English were not simply looking for land to colonize: they wanted the Indians' gold, hence the conquistador model seemed the only viable one to adopt. But Ralegh created a new model, a model that reflected the material, spiritual, and practical nexus of his worldview.

As did other Europeans, the materialistic Ralegh desired gold for the wealth and power it would bring. The spiritual Ralegh, however, understood indigenous peoples as humans blessed by God. They should not be abused, and their peaceful interactions with the Europeans would be mutually beneficial. The pragmatic Ralegh, the experienced colonizer, sought a peaceable way to obtain gold and alliance with the Natives, which would, he argued, fulfill the needs of both peoples. As in Ireland and at Roanoke, Ralegh conceived of colonization as an act of co-creation, of English and Natives working together.

———

RALEGH WAS NOT philosophically opposed to violence. But Spain remained an immediate threat to the very existence of England, and with that in mind, Ralegh never took his eye off Spain in New World colonization. The Hermeticists' universalism looked to bring people together but accepted that some institutions and individuals should be fought to the death. The Spanish threat could be overcome only by England obtaining great stores of wealth. Although they looked to the spiritual, the Hermeticists did not reject the material universe. If anything, they believed that the unseen universe could be accessed, and would be more deeply accessed, as they gained greater understanding of the physical domain.

The Hermeticists saw no need for or benefit from living a Spartan existence. They did not eschew material wealth—most of them were elites. They did not see the material and spiritual in opposition to one another but as separate realms of existence that could be transcended, one to the other, through portals. Gold held a special significance for potentially bridging the spiritual and material.[1] Gold could help access a portal, and Christians associated it with the divine. Of all substances, gold was the one that drew the most attention from scientists and elite artisans. In sixteenth-century Europe, whether people were spiritually or materially inclined, or both, most thought that gold was the most spectacular product of European entry into the Americas.

Many of the world's peoples recognized gold as possessing great inherent value, placing it as a substance above others. The Hermeticists, who desired gold, valued numerous objects: an array of crystals and stones that could be used in healing, to invoke good fortune, or to facilitate connections with otherworldly beings. The most valued material matter of all to the Hermeticists was the legendary philosopher's stone, believed to possess properties that enabled access to the divine, healing, and the transformation of material substances, such as turning lead into silver or gold. If one possessed actual caches of gold, then one did not need the elusive philosopher's stone: one would possess the wealth to purchase other precious stones that opened portals to the spiritual realm. Europeans expected gold to alter one's life from an existence of scarcity to one of abundance, both materially and spiritually.

Most of those who sought great quantities of gold likely had limited interest in the spiritual, but Ralegh recognized that gold was not an end in itself. Though he wished to maintain and increase his personal abundance, he also saw that gold could allow England to construct a mighty navy and hire troops to combat the Spanish. Gold presumably could, along with colonization, solve England's problems of limited land and natural resources. For Ralegh, personally, gold could earn the queen's forgiveness and secure his place as her most important subject. Gold, he knew, could not buy his way into heaven, but it could change the material world in positive ways. He perceived that only the hope for gold would entice England to ally with South America's Native peoples, and together they could remove Spain from the Americas, securing both the Natives' safety and the safety of England in Europe. Gold could bring prosperity to the English and to the peoples of the Americas.

It is easy to denigrate the love for gold as a pathology or an indicator of grave individual and social ills. Ralegh and other Europeans perceived gold as a panacea for the health, security, and happiness of individuals and nations. The early modern drive to accumulate massive amounts of gold reflected the instability and threats faced in Europe: only a large infusion of wealth, it was believed, could help overcome the massive problems society faced. In Spain's case, gold, silver, and colonialism could help repair the splintering of Christendom by giving that nation the military power to implement unity and conformity; in England's case, gold was necessary to withstand Spain's pretensions to crush Protestantism and install its tyrannical rule over Europe and the Americas. As Ralegh wrote and published *The Discoverie of Guiana*, England, France, and the Dutch Republic negotiated a Triple Alliance against Spain. All three believed their nations in dire peril—all hoped to obtain gold and to halt Spain's accumulations of the precious metal. English, French, and Dutch pirated Iberian ships to obtain gold and other treasure and to reduce Spanish wealth. Building overseas colonies and empires would be the next step after piracy to increase power and wealth while reducing that of Spain.

An empire would allow the English to funnel gold to themselves from its source. To control the sources of precious metals and gemstones, the English had to colonize new lands and concurrently enlist the help of Native peoples to achieve their ends. Just as every ounce of gold not in English possession could potentially wind up in Spanish coffers, Indians unallied with the English could help the Spanish against the English as allies or laborers. Ralegh wrote *Discoverie of Guiana* to enlist English to follow him to South America to obtain great amounts of gold, but he needed to explain more precisely for the queen and court why they must extend Elizabeth's realm to Guiana as a counterweight to Spain and how it should be done. The court likely had little interest in Ralegh's stories of Amazons and Ewaipanoma except for purposes of entertainment. They understood gold and feared Spain. Ralegh's *Discoverie* was too limited and diffuse for their needs. If the queen and her ministers were to build an empire, they required facts, plans, and vision—and Ralegh was ready to supply the government with what it needed.

In his paper, "Of the Voyage for Guiana," Ralegh composed one of the most remarkable documents of colonialism produced in Tudor England. It reveals how he, the English individual with the most experience colonizing and the one who had thought about colonizing in just so many ways, envisioned and rationalized England creating a benevolent empire in the New World—a partnership between English and Indians. Though this paper's existence is not unknown (it has been published several times as an appendix to republications of Ralegh's *Discoverie*), its content has been ignored through the centuries. Even those who republished it failed to understand it.[2]

The contents of "Of the Voyage for Guiana" provide a radical conception of empire and colonialism that did not fit with the common understanding of the British Empire. To both imperialists and anti-imperialists, Ralegh's proposal appears to reflect no recognizable reality. But when "Of the Voyage for Guiana" is contextualized in terms of Ralegh's career as a colonizer, it makes perfect sense. It reveals Ralegh's encapsulation of how England should build an empire, particularly addressing the relationship to be established with Native peoples. "Of the Voyage for Guiana" is a culmination of Ralegh's years of thinking about colonialism. He explains why England should not attempt to conquer the Empire of Guiana and should instead follow a different path than Spain in the New World. If he had explicitly presented these ideas in *Discoverie*, he risked alienating and confusing his audience. Ralegh's creation of a state paper for the eyes of the queen and her ministry, however, opened the possibility for shaping empire in a way that relatively few—only those who believed there was so much to be learned from Native peoples and that colonialism could create something greater for all—had envisioned.

Ralegh had to counter the English assumption that conquest was the only way to access Guiana's riches. He had to convince his readers of a new way of thinking. But first, as in *Discoverie*, he had to make perfectly clear the benefits of Guiana. He began in general terms with a trope: the moral imperative to bring Christianity to the Indians. This would end their idolatry and associated cultural practices, including "bloody sacrifices, ignoraunce, & incivility." Secondly, to free Indians "from [the] intollerable tirrany of the *Spaniards*." But why, specifically, Guiana? Guiana offered the queen the opportunity to enlarge her dominion with a place possessed of "pretious stones, gold, silver, pearle . . . [and an avenue to] many other Empyres," including Peru.[3] Thus, regardless of the profits to be accrued in Guiana, alliance between English and Guianans would immeasurably add to English security by forcing the Spanish to defend their colonies, reducing the probability of direct attacks on England.

Guiana offered additional "inducements."[4] The Borderers had agreed to submit to the queen's protection from both the Spanish and the emperor of Guiana, and in return would supply an abundance of food, a ready supply of horses, and both steel and copper, which would reduce English costs in South America. Secondly, as Ralegh noted in *Discoverie*, the English could easily fortify themselves along the Orinoco to keep the Spanish out of Guiana. In other words, once the English were in Guiana, the Spanish could not remove them. (In the history of colonialism, crowns fretted over extending their empire to distant lands that they might not be able to permanently control—it was humiliating to lose a portion of one's empire and called into question the monarch's competency and legitimacy to continue as a monarch.) Ralegh also referenced prophecies as an inducement for the English to go to Guiana. Prophecies had famously guided the Spanish in their conquests of Mexico and Peru. Ralegh stated that even if a prophecy was not to be believed, the Spanish were spooked by them, notably, that an Inga would return to reconquer Peru; that is, the Inga of Manoa, who was also referred to as the emperor of Guiana.

In case anyone doubted that the English could legally colonize Spanish-claimed lands, Ralegh reminded his readers that the Spanish did not have "just title" to lands in America. According to Ralegh, the pope had granted the Spanish and Portuguese the right to spread the gospel to the Indies, not to take Indian land. Their unauthorized and immoral conquest resulted in atrocities, Ralegh affirmed, that led to the deaths of twenty million American Indians, "reasonable creatures made to the Image of God." This sadism would lead God to "root out the *Spanish* nation from the world." The Indians are "as free by nature as any *Christian*," and they are akin to the English in possessing no other enemy than the Spanish, a people "abhorred by God, and man."[5] To Ralegh, the issue was not whether the English should go to Guiana and whether it would profit the queen, but how to subdue the Empire of Guiana. There were but two choices: they could expel the Inga of Manoa and have the Natives elect a new emperor, namely, Elizabeth; or, what Ralegh strongly recommended, they should draw the Inga into paying homage to the queen so that he would become her vassal. Ralegh admits that conquest would be more profitable, but he preferred the safer expedient of leaving Guiana as it was and giving it a place in Elizabeth's empire just like King Arthur held sovereignty over lesser kings. The Empire of Guiana would ally with the English under Elizabeth, and together they would take Peru from Spain, fulfilling the prophecy that the Inga would return to rule Peru. If, instead, the English were to attempt to conquer the Inga of Manoa, the Inga would invite the Spanish to help him ward off the English, and the Guianans would refuse to receive the gospel from the English.[6]

An empire without conquest was not simply a matter of practical strategy—it was a moral imperative. As Ralegh lays out, being Christian and English, it is "farr better" to join with allies "under the defence of the Almighty . . . then to purchase our securitye by assaulting Guiana." The English should not follow the "practises" of the Spanish "in the conquest of the Indies." Ralegh counters Spanish methods and the arguments of George Peckham (see Part Two) that both Old and New Testaments justified the dispossession, enslavement, and deaths of American Indians. Ralegh offers a biblically based argument "that no Christians may lawfully invade with hostility any heathenish people not under their allegiaunce, to kill, spoile, & conquer them, only upon pretence of their fidelity." Ralegh cites Old Testament examples to show that not only did heathens possess lands "by the gifte of God" but so, too, did "Idolaters, pagans, & godlesse persons." It would be unjust to deprive these peoples "of their goods, lands, libertyes, or lives."[7] "The good Kings of Israel or Juda" acted against the Idolaters only if the latter had wronged them, not because of their idolatry. Ralegh denies that God gave any Christians license to deprive non-Christians of their land, and he refutes Peckham's notion that the English were God's chosen people, inheritors of the privileged status of the Israelites. Christians, Ralegh reminds his readers, "are commaunded to doo good unto all men, & to have peace with all men; . . . to give none offence to one or other."

The Bible showed that Christians owed obedience to their non-Christian rulers. Christ instructed his "disciples to pay tribute to Caesar, an Infidell. . . . Therfor no Christian Prince under pretence of Christianity only, & of forcing men to receive the ghospell, or to renounce their impietyes," may invade "any free people not under their vassalage." Christ never bestowed that power on Christians, and he never exercised that power himself. Instead, the English must act according to "the lawe of nature & nations" that designated "priority of possession" for lands and goods "against all straungers." Ralegh warned against hypocrisy. We "hould it unreasonable that the Pope upon cullour of religion only . . . or that any Prince should therefor presume to intrude upon our dominions." Likewise, no Protestant may invade the lands of Papists, Muscovites, or Turks. And if any excommunicant or Mahomedan "or an alien Atheist" came to England, as long as they did not engage in "seducing our people" from their religion, they could not "be assaulted in goods or person."[8] No right existed to deny people of their lands or property on the basis of their religion or lack thereof.

Ralegh formulated a stunning elaboration on the limits of Christian rights abroad. After reminding the queen and her ministers that Christians have no right to conquer infidels on the grounds of their infidelity, he asserts that even after sending preachers to deliver the gospel, infidel refusal to accept or their "giving hard measure to the preachers" provides no grounds to "overrunn their countryes."[9] He cautions against sending preachers abroad unaccompanied by security forces because people are essentially blameless for attacking outsiders who come into their country to convert them from their religion. Ralegh makes it clear that although the English should convert the Indians to Christianity, he does not mean that ministers should be sent to them. Ralegh expects conversion to be a slow process that would occur after the Natives better knew the Christians; Natives would convert in their own time. In essence, Ralegh states what became English policy. The English government took little interest in conversion of Native American and African peoples until the eighteenth century, and even then left the task to nongovernmental organizations.

Ralegh saw himself as a proxy for doing the Crown's bidding in Guiana and that he would employ a moral and practical policy. To "advantage ourselves without conquest," he urges alliance with the Borderers, Epuremi, and Guianans and to unite them into a league against the Spanish (and their allies). Although the Borderers know that the Spanish are the enemy, Ralegh proposes a propaganda campaign to educate the Indians about the extent of Spanish cruelty, sending them books with illustrations of Spanish atrocities against Indians throughout the Americas. Once again, Ralegh displays his awareness of the importance of images, as he had shown in his personal dress and in having John White's illustrations engraved and published by Theodor de Bry. Ralegh proposed sending enough illustrations to Guiana that they could be passed by Native leaders to their vassals, and these should include rhetoric of the pope as "the great Inchantor or cousner [deceiver], & troubler of the world . . . who giveth his followers dispensacions to steale, robb, rebell & murther: & likewise pardoneth for mony whatsoever wronges or villanyes, are by them committed."[10]

An alliance with the Indians was necessary. To lay the groundwork, Ralegh recommended giving presents, as a sign of English wealth and generosity, and to display what the Indians can obtain from them through trade. Most importantly, the English must promise to protect the Indians from the Spanish. Ralegh recommended sending to the Indians maps depicting Drake's foray through the West Indies in 1585–1586, particularly his "exploits at Santo Domingo," to show examples of English victories against the Spanish, and other illustrations, including maps, that depicted English shires and London and the countries allied with England. These would confirm English power because the Indians had only the word of the English that they were a great people. The Indians already knew that the Spanish were powerful because they had seen manifestations of that power. But the Indians did not know the English. To show that the English were on a level with the Spanish, Ralegh suggested that they offer evidence to the Indians that the King of Spain had chosen among all the princesses of Europe to marry Elizabeth's older sister and predecessor, Mary.

Ralegh expected the Indians to renounce idolatry and to worship "the only true god." But then he steps back to cite biblical and historical examples as proof that alliance can be made between Christians and "Idolaters." The English do not have to wait for Indians to become Christians to ally. The Indians are "teachable & capable of all good learning" and will become good Christians, but there is no reason to be troubled by them not being Christian. It would be enough for the Inga of Manoa to surrender the ensign of his empire to Queen Elizabeth, who would return it to him, symbolizing that he has become a "cheife of the Crowne of *England*." Her Majesty would assign a lieutenant to direct Guianans in "their conclusions both of warr & peace"—the greater monarch retains a say over the foreign policy of the lesser monarchs. The Guianans would also provide "a great tribute" to the queen and her successors comprising the use of "some rich mines and rivers of gold, pearle, silver, rocks of pretious stones . . . with some large fruitfull countryes for the planting of her Colonyes."[11] Thus, Guiana would become a nation in Elizabeth's empire, but not necessarily an inferior one, though she would assign them a lieutenant to consult in their foreign affairs, but implicitly, there would be no interference with domestic matters. It is worth recalling that in Tudor England Elizabeth had asserted in her patents to Gilbert and Ralegh that Parliament had no power over the administration of her colonies.

To bind their peoples together, Ralegh recommends the Indians send "hostages" to England, who upon being civilized and converted would return home and "may be matched in marriage with English women."[12] Other Indians will then take their place in England, repeating the process. Marriage long had been used by most societies as a way to forge closer ties with other societies, and it was not unheard of for Europeans to promote marriages with non-Europeans. As early as the thirteenth century, the widely read and influential German Arthurian epic, *Parzival*, by Wolfram von Eschenbach, included positive depictions of intermarriages of European and African elites. In the early modern era, Portuguese elites had pursued marriages with African elites, and in the coming centuries European males frequently intermarried with Native women in the Americas.[13] But Ralegh's proposed offering of English females to Indian males seems unprecedented in the history of European colonialism in America.[14] These were not intended as royal marriages, but marriages of elites, and indicative of a more general policy of promoting intermarriage among Indians and English. Ralegh's proposal is another example of how American Indians and their skin color were not perceived as inherently inferior by the English in the sixteenth century.

Ralegh's intent to create a close partnership with the Indians is evident in other ways. He follows his recommendation on intermarriage with a sweeping proposal for the English to arm and train Indians in the European manner of war. England would offer to protect the Indians from the Spanish and "all other intruders" and help the Guianans recover Peru. But they also should teach them the "liberall arts of Civility," so they will "be comparable to any christian people," and instruct them in European military skills, such as the use of cavalry and the handling of weaponry. Moreover, England should send artisans to instruct the Indians in the making of armor and ordnance. This, Ralegh affirms, is his "principall scope whereunto in this Treatise," that the English are not to go into America like Spanish "conquerers against a naked unarmed people" but "must instruct the Indians in the use & skill of making Armour" so that Guianans, who already were skilled goldsmiths, would be able to not only defend themselves from the Spanish but also manufacture armor for themselves and the English. Ralegh proposed nothing less than elevating Guiana's military expertise to the level of the English, and not just as soldiers but as munitions experts. He insists that Indians could be trusted with the knowledge of manufacturing European weaponry. Their faithfulness was evinced by their loyalty to Cortés and other conquistadors. Considering how humbly they served "mercilesse Spaniards," how much more faithful the Indians would be to the English. Ralegh believed the Indians were a simple people without malice, who were peaceable, patient, and lacking in deviousness. If the English had any worry about Indian trustworthiness, they could withhold teaching them how to make "powder, or some other necessaryes," until they had fully proven their fidelity.[15] But as long as the English publicly punished their own soldiers and artisans who wronged the Indians in any way, Ralegh fully expected the Indians to remain faithful.

After again recounting Spanish atrocities, Ralegh concludes with the *pièce de résistance* of his proposal. Obtaining gold, colonizing in Guiana, allying with the Indians, arming them, teaching them how to make weapons and armor and to defend themselves against the Spanish—all these were but preface to Ralegh's grandiose plan: Elizabeth should send four to five hundred military men, including officers, gunners, armorers, "Casters of great Ordinance," who would lead the Indians against the Spanish Empire in America, in Peru, Mexico, Florida, and so on.[16] If nothing else, this all-out assault would bring safety to England and Guiana by forcing the Spanish to defend their far-flung empire. Ralegh cast the Indians as shock troops of the English Empire. Equity, justice, and intermarriage would secure the affections of Indians for the English. But the bonds of England's benevolent empire would be forged by force of arms. Indian military might would be cultivated and employed by the English to both groups' mutual benefit.

As Ralegh's hopes for Guiana and for building an empire without conquest reached a crescendo, duty called him in another direction. The battle with Spain remained at the forefront for Ralegh and for England. It was not yet to be fought in Guiana, but much closer to home in Spain and in the Atlantic. And Ralegh played a lead role.

CHAPTER 26

Wheel of Fortune

R alegh's life and career comprised a series of rises and falls.
     But the wheel of fortune spun more quickly than usual in the
     period between 1595 and 1597, for Ralegh and for England.
The prospects for incredible wealth and a powerful and extended empire appeared so suddenly in Guiana and might just as quickly have
disappeared. Good and bad fortune awaited in Ireland. Over all loomed
the specter of King Philip II of Spain, who threatened English sovereignty in Ireland and English prospects in Guiana, and who planned to
conquer England. The wheel dealt fortunes as much emotional as temperamental. Ralegh and his peers believed that England could turn the
corner and emerge from the miasma that clouded their future by eclips-
ing Spain on the high seas and in distant lands.

A publisher provided Ralegh posthumously with a motto (different
from his own): *Data Fata Sequutus*—"Fate Followed [Him]."[1] Ralegh
had reached incredible highs at court and had sunk to the depths of
despair with the loss of the queen's affections. In later years, too, he
rode the wheel of fortune round and round. He sometimes succumbed
to histrionics when all seemed lost, as when the queen withdrew her
affection, but most of the time he remained calm under pressure. In
his poetry, he addressed "fortune" in theoretical and philosophical
terms, but in 1595–1597, he grew frustrated with his fate—Guiana was
slipping away. Even so, new doors of opportunity opened for him: a
chance to earn an enduring reputation for military heroism and a return to the queen's good graces.

—

IN THE WINTER of 1595–1596, Ralegh awaited the impact his book on Guiana would make, hoping he could gain the support necessary for England to create a grand alliance with Native peoples in South America. Would the Spanish beat him to it? By mid-January, he received word from his brother John Gilbert that Spain had not sent military forces to secure Guiana against the English, though settlers were being encouraged to move there. The King of Spain had other ideas for his troops: to invade the Low Countries and England.[2] A month later, the English learned that two thousand Spanish settlers had been raised for Guiana.[3]

Ralegh grew despondent. In November, he wrote Robert Cecil from Sherborne "from this desolate place," referring to the state of his mind. He reported news of the Spanish sending a fleet of sixty ships to Ireland, but foremost in his mind was Guiana, "whether it pass for a history or a fable." And though it might seem that he is referring to the truth or illusion of a golden empire, and perhaps he intended a double meaning, what he primarily questioned was the reality of English settlement in Guiana. Other English had sailed for Guiana to preempt him. Ralegh worried that these interlopers would "sack" the Indians for their gold "rather" than win "the kings to Her Majesties service."[4] If they alienated the Borderers, he warned, Guiana would remain a fable for the English, for they would have no way to get there.

Two days later, Ralegh worried that Cecil might not believe him. He wrote Cecil again to remind him "that it is no dreame which I have reported of Guiana." Ralegh cited George Popham's "Relation" of Guiana, which comprised recent letters in which Popham, who had just been to Guiana, asserted there really was gold there. Ralegh iterated to Cecil for the queen's benefit, "I know that the like [fortune] was never offred to any Christien prince." He affirmed that the French and Spanish were in pursuit and if there was delay, "I conclude that wee ar curst of God." He beseeched Cecil: convince the queen so "that none be suffred to foyle the enterprize." The Borderers must be protected from those who would pilfer. Ralegh wished that he could be the one sent to direct English activities, "to govern that countrey which I have discovered and hope to conquer for the Queen without her cost." Undoubtedly, he used *conquer* here to assure Cecil that he would do what was necessary to extend the queen's sovereignty to Guiana, but this would not include sacking the Indians. There was so much at stake: large treasures befitting the queen and, though he did not again mention it, the proposed alliance with the Indians to employ against Spain, a relatively inexpensive way to wage war and bring King Philip to his knees.

Ralegh did not wait for fate to intervene. He continued to prepare for his return to Guiana and sent a "barke to the countrey to cumfort and assure the people" not to despair, "nor yeild to any . . . other nations."[5]

Ralegh also reported that Hariot had finished mapping the land (based upon Ralegh's drawings and data), and he again told Cecil, who having edited Ralegh's book on Guiana needed no reminding, that Guiana possessed many riches besides gold. There were diamonds, pearls, amethyst, and other precious stones. Ralegh emphasized the diamonds as greater than any found in the East Indies—the world's best. And if Cecil needed another reminder, Ralegh iterated that Spain's power rested on its gold from the Indies, because of which it threatened all Europe. English revenues could not maintain the fight against Spain.[6] They had to access the wealth of Guiana.

Two weeks passed. Ralegh again wrote Cecil, sending this letter "post hast[e]" with its time of arrival at each stop recorded—evidence of its urgency. Sent at one p.m., the letter took nineteen hours to reach Cecil, one horseman passing it to the next, with five stops before arrival in the suburbs of London. "I beseich yow lett us know whether wee shalbe travelers or tinkers, conquerors or crounes [imbeciles], for if the winter pass without making provision" there can be none collected in summer. Delay would mean "farewell, Guiana, forever. Then must I determyne to begg or run away, honor and gold and all good forever hopeless."[7]

Ralegh also sent a letter to Lord Admiral Charles Howard with news that the Spanish would soon send a fleet to pursue Francis Drake and John Hawkins. They were on the queen's business in the West Indies, attacking the Spanish and seeking to capture Spanish treasure. Ralegh suggested Howard send a couple of small ships to warn them.[8] Howard complied, but Hawkins had died of dysentery two weeks before, near Puerto Rico, which Drake unsuccessfully attacked. By the end of January, Drake, too, was dead, likely from dysentery. Ralegh reminded Howard that Guiana needed to be resolved, for if they did not gather victuals soon, the enterprise must be delayed another year.

That same month, Ralegh sent Lawrence Kemys, his second in command on the Guiana expedition, to explore the coast between the Amazon and Orinoco Rivers, in hopes of finding another route in—especially important if the Spanish reinforced Trinidad and found a way to close off the mouth of the Orinoco. Ralegh also wanted Kemys to assure the Indians that he would return. As a show of good faith, he sent home Topiawari's son.[9] In Guiana, Kemys did not find the two young men Ralegh had left with Topiawari. According to Ralegh's wife, Topiawari had died.[10] It is unknown when the English learned the fate of the two boys, but Hugh Goodwin, according to the Spanish, had been eaten by a wild animal, though the Indians might have told this to the Spanish to protect Goodwin. The other fellow, Francis Sparrow, or Sparry, was captured in March by the Spanish, probably right before Kemys reached Guiana. Sparrow spent at least seven years as a prisoner of the Spanish. Sent to Spain, he converted to Catholicism, married a Spanish woman, and at several points almost achieved release from prison in exchange for Spanish prisoners in England. But Sparrow had told the Spanish that he buried a great treasure in Guiana and they should send him to retrieve it. This forestalled the Spanish from making Sparrow a galley slave, though the king finally ordered him to the galleys but without demanding that he row. The sentence continued to be preempted. Sparrow's story of buried treasure was generally doubted, but it protected him from being sent to the galleys, and it also prevented his inclusion in a prisoner exchange. Imprisoned in Madrid, he was still alive in 1603 when the governor of the island of Margarita, then in Spain and about to return to his post, received permission to take Sparrow to America to retrieve the gold he had buried. It is unknown what happened to him thereafter.[11]

On Kemys's return to England at the end of June 1596, he prepared and published an account of his voyage. Echoing Ralegh, in a lengthy poem that sets off his account, he announces:

Riches, and Conquest, and Renowne I sing,
Riches with honour, Conquest without bloud;
Enough to seat the Monarchie of earth.
Guiana, whose rich feet are mines of golde,

. . .

To be her sister, and the daughter both
Of our most sacred Maide: whose barrennesse
Is the true fruite of vertue . . .

. . .

Then most admired Soveraigne, let your breath
Goe foorth upon the waters, and create
A golden worlde in this our iron age,
. . . [12]

Much like Ralegh, Kemys had little actual evidence of riches in Guiana. His main purpose was to counter criticism of Ralegh and the argument that Guiana was an imaginary place that Ralegh had invented. Kemys collected data on the rivers and peoples, which he turned over to Thomas Hariot for the map he was producing. Hariot reassured Cecil, "Although Cap[tain] Kemish be not come home rich yet he hath don the speciall thing which he was injoyned to do as the discovery of the coast betwixt the river of Amasones & orrinico." Hariot, probably with Kemys's urging, complained to Cecil that Kemys's ship's master had been "selling copies of his travelles & plottes [maps] of discoveryes." Cecil ordered the man's arrest and confiscation of his papers.[13]

Hariot and Ralegh's wife, Elizabeth, both had to look after Ralegh's interests in Guiana because Ralegh had departed England before Kemys's return. The wheel of fortune had carried Ralegh to Spain, where fame and glory awaited.

—

JUST AS RALEGH WAS RETURNING from South America in 1595, the Lord Admiral of the Navy had proposed the idea of attacking the Spanish Navy at the port of Cádiz and capturing the Spanish treasure fleet on its return from the West Indies. Intrigued by the project, the queen had sent word to the Netherlands to organize assistance, and a call for additional help went out as far as Denmark. The actual goals of the expedition were kept secret, and news spread out of England that the gathering of ships and supplies was in preparation for defense against an expected Spanish invasion. When the English and Dutch flotilla sailed in June 1596, very few of the ship captains knew the destination, as they received sealed instructions to be opened only if they became separated from the fleet.

Lord Admiral Howard personally commanded the naval operations, and the Earl of Essex received command over the army. The French loss of Calais to Spain in April 1596 weighed heavily on the allies' minds, because Spain had another place from which to launch an invasion of England or the Low Countries or advance into the heart of France. Elizabeth approved of the expedition because offensive operations against the Spanish fleet could set back Spanish capabilities for a year or more. As usual, Elizabeth looked to military operations that could, at a minimum, pay for themselves but that would hopefully reap great profits. In this case, profit would consist of the capture of the West Indies or East Indies (Portuguese) treasure fleets, or else the capture of Spanish warships and ordnance.

Elizabeth's instructions spelled out for her commanders what she wanted and what to avoid. She insisted that Lord Admiral Howard not risk her great warships. This, in effect, meant they should not fight at close quarters, which the hired ships should do instead. She also warned Howard and Essex against plundering Spanish towns. Elizabeth was rightly concerned that the men would be interested in sacking towns only to fill their pockets with booty, whereas she was interested with capturing treasure at sea, which was deemed much more valuable and to which the queen was entitled a large share. Everyone desired plunder.

In addition to the 6,772 sailors, the 150 English and Dutch ships carried over 6,000 men for army service. The latter were volunteers, and though they received wages, they signed up for the expedition with hopes for an opportunity to steal from the Iberians. Unlike the Dutch troops, who generally were well trained, the English volunteers had to be drilled for a month before departure.[14] Ralegh was late arriving at Plymouth to join the expedition because he had difficulty recruiting men and supplies, which made Essex nervous because Elizabeth at any time could cancel the expedition. But all was made ready. The fleet was divided into four squadrons, one each led by the lord admiral, Essex, Ralegh, and Lord Thomas Howard.

Elizabeth was concerned about how the rest of Europe would view an attack on Spain. To that end, Lord Burghley and Cecil wrote a "Declaration," to be signed by Lord Admiral Charles Howard and Essex and published in five languages: English, Spanish, French, Dutch, and Latin. The expedition's stated purpose was to defend Elizabeth's realm against the King of Spain, who planned to invade her again without just cause. She intended to have the declaration distributed in Spanish and Portuguese ports. She promised to punish any of her people who committed any offense against people who were not helping Spain, but those foreigners who helped Spain would not be protected.[15] The queen's wariness can also be seen in her instructions to Essex and Howard.[16] Under pain of death, no one was allowed to land in any country other than Spain without the generals' knowledge. She also insisted on twice-daily prayers, no religious disputes, and no swearing, gambling, or brawling. Though her instructions about sacking cities were not followed, remarkably, when the English took Cádiz, the women were left unharmed.[17]

Looming over the expedition was the queen's relationship with Essex, the twenty-nine-year-old earl who enjoyed the love of many in England. As a virile young man of impeccable lineage, he ostensibly complemented the queen's feminine rule with a dashing masculine presence. Cecil, Essex's chief rival in government, lacked martial ardor, while Ralegh lacked the blood of Essex, the civil power of Cecil, and the favor of the queen that he once enjoyed. But Ralegh could not be left out of an important role in the expedition. Drake and Hawkins were away—word of their deaths had not arrived in England. Lord Admiral Charles Howard had little actual experience at sea, and Essex was an army man. Lord Thomas Howard did have significant naval experience, though it was his fleet that barely escaped the Spanish Navy in 1591, when he was unable to protect his vice admiral Richard Grenville, who died in the encounter.[18] Ralegh was thus the most renowned man of the sea left of the Westcountry men. Given his influence among the sailors, captains, and navigators, and the confidence of the lord admiral and the queen, it was almost inevitable that he would play a lead role in the expedition.

Ralegh's participation in the expedition might also have been important because of the mounting tension between the queen and Essex. Essex repeatedly urged a more active English military presence in France to counter Spain, with himself leading the charge, but the queen remained both reticent and irresolute. Sometimes she said little, sometimes she hinted at supporting Essex's activist policy, but then she would go quiet once again. The Spanish threat against Calais had heightened this tension. He wished to provide decisive assistance to the Dutch to save the French town from the Spanish. By the time Elizabeth assented, the town of Calais, but not its citadel, had surrendered to the Spanish. Elizabeth agreed that Essex could take troops across the channel, but only if the King of France agreed that England would hold the town until the French were strong enough to maintain its defense. Henry IV of France refused. He worried that the English would keep Calais because it had been possessed by England for over two hundred years until France had finally taken it back in 1558. Elizabeth finally accepted Henry IV's terms, but she was too late. The citadel had fallen.

When Essex left court ten days later, relations between him and the queen were stone cold.[19] As was his wont, Essex imagined a conspiracy against him, which included Ralegh. Almost three weeks later, he received a letter from Elizabeth threatening to recall the leaders of the impending Cádiz expedition and substitute lesser men in their place or to cancel the expedition altogether. Essex had expended his own money on supplies and feared losing all; his investment could be recouped only with the capture of booty. He wrote Cecil in complaint: "We are either commanded unpossible things or held in irresolution."[20]

Meanwhile, Elizabeth was beginning to doubt the wisdom of risking half of her navy on offensive operations when the Spanish could land an armada in England or Ireland. She also worried about Essex's rashness and whether he and others might involve her in more than she bargained for militarily and diplomatically. Indeed, Essex made no secret about his desire to do something spectacular that she had not agreed to—he intended "to establish a base in some Spanish port" to effect a permanent blockade of Spain.[21] He also proposed taking towns in France and the Low Countries, which is likely the last thing she wanted to hear. She allowed the Cádiz expedition to proceed, and the leaders to retain their positions, likely with her advisors assuring her that the lord admiral, Ralegh, and others would rein in Essex. After all, the ships could sail nowhere without the lord admiral's permission.

The fleet departed June 1, 1596. On the way to the Spanish coast, a council of war was held aboard the *Ark Royal*, Ralegh's state-of-the-art ship designed by Hariot and sold to the queen. The council agreed to attack Cádiz, seize the warships in its harbor, and capture any merchant ships' cargo. Cádiz was Spain's main port for trade with the West Indies, so there was a good chance they could snare merchantmen loading or unloading. On June 11, they reconfirmed Cádiz as their destination, but because they had sailed distant from the coast so as not to be spotted, the fleet were unsure of their location in relation to the port. Fortunately, they captured three German boats that had just left Cádiz, which reported that no one there had any idea that the English were on their way and that fourteen merchant ships sat in the harbor full of goods destined for the Indies. Maybe ten or twelve Spanish warships were also there to provide escort to America. Both the English sailors on the expedition and the Spanish who caught wind of an English fleet having left England believed the destination to be either Lisbon or Calais. An Irish ship on its return to Waterford from Seville confirmed that the Spanish did not know the English were on their way and that there were over two dozen ships in harbor full of valuable goods. As the English fleet approached Cádiz, Ralegh took sixteen ships to the coast to scour for more Spanish ships so that they would not be bottled in from the rear.

The English had no real plan of what to do at Cádiz. Should they destroy the warships or capture them? What about the merchant ships? What should they assault first? While Ralegh was away, it was decided that Essex should storm the city and perhaps capture the merchantmen, while the lord admiral would attempt to block in the Spanish fleet and attack the warships if necessary. All understood that the queen wanted the ships laden with cargo to be captured intact—they could pay for the entire expedition with much left over as profit. Time seemed of the essence because the Spanish might burn the cargo ships to keep them out of English hands. Essex called for an immediate attack, but no one would go without a plan. A great wind arose, which should have forestalled disembarking the army, but Essex tried anyway until Ralegh arrived and insisted in front of all the generals that Essex desist. The earl and the lord admiral blamed each other for the position they were in. Howard had refused to risk the queen's ships, thus the decision to land the army. With all in seeming disarray, Ralegh stepped in with a new plan.

Instead of first landing an army to capture the city, he convinced Howard that they should use their ships to force their way into the harbor, but to do so without using the queen's great ships. And they should wait until the next morning. It was too late in the day, the men had to be organized, and they had to come up with a plan of action. They had yet to choose how to fight and who should lead, who would follow, and whether they should board the ships or fight them or otherwise. Essex was delighted that they would fight and agreed to wait till morning. Ralegh devised a plan of attack, which he submitted that evening to the lord admiral. They would use the queen's large ships' cannon to batter the great galleys from a distance, which would protect her ships and hopefully preoccupy the Spanish so they could not burn their own vessels. Meanwhile, the flyboats and other small vessels would approach the Spanish ships for boarding. They hoped to capture the Spanish galleys intact so the English could take their ordnance and recondition the ships for the queen's navy.

Ralegh placed himself in the starring role. The Lord Admiral and Essex would stay with the great ships while Ralegh led the charge. Over eighteen craft supported him. Facing fire from the ordnance on the curtain wall of the city's fortifications and from the galleys, Ralegh responded with trumpets blaring, "disdaining to shoot one piece at any one or all of those esteemed dreadful monsters." The ships that followed him "beat upon the galleys so thick as they soon betook them to their oars" to escape boarding. Ralegh set his eye on one ship, the royal warship *St. Philip*, for he was "resolved to be revenged for the *Revenge*." The *St. Philip* had been one of two ships that boarded Richard Grenville's *Revenge*, resulting in Grenville's death.[22]

The preliminary battle at Cádiz waged three hours when, despite orders not to board, Ralegh decided to do so, for his own ship was going to burn or sink. The earl and the lord admiral assented, and other ships jockeyed for position to board the enemy. When Ralegh's ship fell to third in line, he outmaneuvered those in front so he would have the glory of being first, placing his ship, he noted, to protect those behind him. The Spanish began burning their own warships; the men jumped into the water and drowned in large numbers. Ralegh claimed that the English saved many but that the Flemings employed "merciless slaughter" until Ralegh and the lord admiral beat them off. The fifty-five-ship Spanish Armada at Cádiz was badly defeated.

The English landed their army to subdue Cádiz. The townspeople locked the doors of the city to their soldiers who retreated to the suburbs. The English followed but found a way into the city, and hundreds poured in. Ralegh recalled, "I received a grievous blow in my leg, interlaced and deformed with splinters, in the fight." Some of his men carried him so he could see, but the pain was so great, as the English flooded into the city, that he grew afraid "to be shouldered in the press" and returned to the ships. There he found no one in charge, and few English otherwise, because the sailors followed the soldiers into the city, not wanting to miss out on the plunder. Ralegh later claimed that because of his leg he got no booty, only kind words and usage. He complained, "I have possession of nought but poverty and pain. If God had spared me that blow, I had possessed myself of some house."[23] Later, he admitted to commissioners investigating the expedition that he got £1,769 worth of plunder out of approximately £12,000 claimed by the expedition's leaders. There was so much more, but the soldiers and sailors did not admit to any plunder at all.

The next day, from aboard ship, Ralegh "sent" a request to the lord admiral and Essex, who had spent the evening in the town, to send a fleet to follow the Spanish ships bound for the Indies, "which were said to be worth twelve millions," but the "confusion" in town was so great he received no answer.[24] The merchants of Cádiz and Seville offered the English a bounty to spare the merchant fleet at Cádiz, but the following morning the Duke of Medina set fire to it and to most of the remaining ships of war and their cargoes. The English were able to salvage only two of the great galleys, including the *St. Philip*. The Flemings took much of the ships' ordnance, and the English took the ordnance of the city. The English also took a great many hostages in the hope of ransoms.

The burning of the merchant ships was a disaster for both the Spanish and the English. The merchant ships and their cargo were worth an estimated £3 million—almost $800 million in 2019 currency. This would have reimbursed the queen her £50,000 investment in the expedition with plenty of profit left over. The soldiers and sailors had no intention of relinquishing to the queen their booty from the sacking of Cádiz, and the hostages, by right, belonged to the officers. As the English pondered their next step, they sent a messenger to inform the queen of the taking of Cádiz, and another, Sir Edward Hoby, to Morocco in search of assistance, such as ships, victuals, and manpower.

The English and North Africans had been in contact for some time to work together against Spain. From the Moroccan perspective, Elizabeth was little more than a client monarch doing their bidding in exchange for assistance. They hoped that King Philip's preoccupation with England would give them the opportunity to retake Andalusia, to reverse the *Reconquista* that had pushed the Muslims out of Spain in the fifteenth century. The North Africans had been selling Elizabeth copper for her cannons, saltpeter for gunpowder, and other metals "not found in her lands." The payoff: an English fleet sent earlier against Lisbon allegedly had forced the Spanish to retreat "in humiliation." The Moroccans praised Elizabeth for her attacks on Cádiz, for "capturing and drowning" Philip's soldiers, and for "nearly cut[ting] him off from the bounty and imports of India."

A high-ranking official in Morocco noted Spanish fear "of the predator-like ships of the people of England." In the attack on Cádiz, the English had "deflowered and raped" the city. This official thought the English had fired the merchant ships—perhaps Hoby had chosen to impart this rather than the truth that the English had failed to prevent their destruction. Nonetheless, the Moroccans received a quite accurate account of the battle and sacking, colorfully rendered. They learned that Philip was so angry at the loss of the city that he refused to redeem the hostages. Philip felt disgraced because the fall of Cádiz had "demeaned his stature before rival kings. They now become desirous of his lands and opened their mouths from every side to devour him."[25]

At Cádiz, the English debated whether to keep the city. If they could hold Cádiz, it would become a permanent thorn in the side of the Spanish. Most of the high officers supported a permanent occupation. They decided to keep it if they had enough supplies to maintain a garrison of several thousand men for four months. Lord Thomas Howard and Ralegh would then go after the West Indies fleet headed to Spain. Essex said he would assent to leaving a permanent garrison only if he stayed as its head, which would force Elizabeth to reinforce them because she could not suffer the public outcry of abandoning the popular earl. The senior officers balked. They could not return to England having left Essex in Spain; without receiving the queen's permission to permanently secure Cádiz, she would resent them all. The senior officers understood the risk of forcing foreign policy on the queen, whereas Essex increasingly wanted to do just that. Many arguments were put forth to abandon Cádiz, including that they had no charge to hold it and that it would interfere with their instructions to do more damage on the Spanish coasts or islands and to capture the returning West Indies fleet. When the commissary general of the expedition reported that they did not have four months of supplies (which likely was untrue), the leadership saved face by abandoning their conquest.[26]

On July 4, 1596, the English departed the city with forty-two hostages. As they sailed away, they watched a quarter of the city burn from fires they had lit. At sea, a council of war met to discuss the next step. Essex desired to pursue the West Indies fleet. Again, a shortage of victuals was cited as reason not to pursue a course for the expedition.[27] William Monson, an officer on the expedition who later wrote an insider's history of the English navy, asserted that the sailors and soldiers wished to go home to enjoy their booty; they were satisfied with their haul.[28]

The leadership decided to sail along the Portuguese coast on the way home to see what damage could be done. They landed outside of Faro and then burned the town and some outlying villages. As historian R. B. Wernham observed, the operation was "pointless." The place had no wealth except for a library whose books were brought to England and given to the newly established Bodleian Library at Oxford University. The council of war decided against attacking similar unimportant locales that would bring no honor to the conquerors of Cádiz.[29] Moreover, it dawned on the English that they had attacked their Portuguese friends, many of whom chafed under Philip II of Spain. After deciding to sit outside Lisbon with hopes of catching the return of the Portuguese East Indies fleet, a strong wind drove them toward home, and despite hesitations and discussions along the way to change course, they sailed into England in early August to face an irate queen.

The men were rather full of themselves for having sacked Cádiz, but Elizabeth thought the expedition a missed opportunity, perhaps even a failure, and certainly one that disregarded her express orders. She had prohibited the plundering of Spanish cities and blamed Essex for disobeying her. She blamed Howard for not going after the West Indies fleet. She did not want to pay the wages of sailors or soldiers. She blamed Essex for not sending the soldiers home immediately after taking Cádiz when they would not be needed for the later naval operations. The failure to prevent the burning of the merchant fleet especially irked her—they could have secured those ships and their cargo if they had not sacked the city. She established a commission to search the ships for plunder and found little; the men had socked it away and had corrupted the commission with bribes; one of the commissioners was even sent to prison. Lord Burghley advised the queen against trying to recoup her losses by confiscating the hostages from the officers—not that it mattered; their ransoms went unpaid and they languished in prison for seven years, gaining their release only after Elizabeth died. The queen demanded her ships immediately return to sea to pursue the West Indies fleet. Ralegh's cousin Ferdinando Gorges promised to freshen the ships as quickly as possible.

Essex moved the troops from Plymouth to Portsmouth, hoping to take them across the Channel for an assault on Calais. Elizabeth refused, saying she would send the troops to the Netherlands and Ireland. She reneged on sending the troops to Ireland, but nevertheless refused them to Essex. The ships could not be reconditioned in time to go against the West Indies fleet. The queen's relationship with Essex, though not yet posing a threat to her crown, remained cold, and this made it easier for Howard and Ralegh to evade criticism. Nonetheless, everyone was barred from publishing accounts of the expedition (and thus defense of their actions) except for a single letter that gave a milquetoast account praising the leaders of the expedition. (Some of the participants sent their accounts abroad to be published.) Ralegh never published his account, though his grandson later did.

The English public seems to have been unaware of or unconcerned about what the expedition did not accomplish: the capture of the merchant fleet or the West Indies fleet. They thought Cádiz a smashing success that displayed English military power. The English had not only opened Spain's front door, they had walked in and set fire to the parlor. Drake's foray to the West Indies in 1585 had been a revelation of English skills at sea, and his destruction of much of the Spanish fleet at Cádiz in 1587 had put off the Spanish invasion of England until 1588. But recent attempts against Portugal had not fared so well, and the West Indies had seen no similar successes. Cádiz changed everything, for it showed that English naval power had indeed ascended on a trajectory to surpass Spain's.

Ralegh emerged as the hero of Cádiz. He received praise from all sides for having displayed his courage in battle and for the acumen of his directing Essex and Howard away from their plans to begin with a landed assault and to his own plan to board the ships that defended the city, which resulted in little loss of English life and ships. No one blamed Ralegh for the sacking or for the failure to secure the merchantmen. That had been the responsibility of Essex and Howard, respectively. The queen even talked to Ralegh at court, though she was not ready to restore him to his full duties as Captain of the Guard.

Despite the costs of the expedition to the queen, Cádiz was a great victory. Some historians view it as the greatest victory of the war with Spain that spanned from 1585 to 1603. The English had captured a famous and important Spanish port. King Philip was beside himself at the loss of his ships of war and the huge cargo intended for the Indies. In financial straits, and intent on sending an armada against England, he repudiated his debts so he could obtain revenue from his mortgaged lands. The conquest of Cádiz led to a general loss of Spanish confidence in their monarch, and many wanted to replace him on the throne with his son.[30] According to one of Essex's spies in Spain, "the fall of Cádiz almost maddened Spain into revolt."[31] The great novelist and poet Miguel de Cervantes, along with other poets, "satirized Medina and the shameful events at Cádiz." They "could not openly criticize Philip II. Therefore, they chose to concentrate their efforts on the immediate and most visible scapegoat."[32] According to one scholar, Cervantes's poem about the fall of Cádiz is "one of the great satiric sonnets of the Spanish Renaissance." At Philip's death in 1598, Cervantes penned and performed another brutal sonnet at the dead king's tomb.[33]

Philip became bent on revenge against England. Despite the loss of so many ships, he scurried to put together another armada to send against England. Twenty warships and additional vessels carrying troops sailed for England in October 1596. A storm destroyed most of the fleet. Philip then went about preparing another armada to go against England or to support a rebellion in Ireland.

Elizabeth countered by preparing her own armada. She was intent on capturing either the West Indies or East Indies treasure fleet. And she would allow Essex the chance to redeem himself, with Ralegh again joining him. The two had gotten along quite well on the Cádiz expedition. Ralegh's advice was well received by Essex, and the queen recognized Ralegh's value in both understanding naval matters and deflecting Essex's rashness. It also helped that Ralegh had great influence with the sailors and captains, while Essex carried influence with the army. As they prepared for the next stage in the war with Spain, however, the English had to contend with the outbreak of war in Ireland.

CHAPTER 27

Reincarnation

Ireland and the Course of Colonialism

I n 1595 and 1596, Ralegh began to lose sight of his colonial enterprise in Ireland. In England, he continued to be consulted on Irish affairs, and he promoted development of his lands on the Munster Plantation, but he did so from afar. The prospects for the Munster Plantation paled beside Guiana's in Ralegh's mind. Guiana could solve all of England's and Ralegh's problems: with the wealth of Guiana, England could defeat Spain and purchase what it needed to keep Ireland in line. But the queen's pragmatism trumped Ralegh's dreams. Direct and immediate action against Spain took precedence. Spanish threats against England and Ireland loomed as Philip II gathered ships and supplies for another armada. The massive preparations alerted everyone to Philip's intentions. The English did not know where Spain would strike, but they knew it was coming.

The deaths of Drake and Hawkins, and earlier of Grenville and Frobisher, left a vacuum in experienced leadership at sea. Ralegh's expertise in naval affairs was ever more needed. Charles Howard, Lord High Admiral of the Navy, frequently consulted Ralegh for advice and service. Ralegh's later writings on the sea showed him likely to be the foremost naval strategist in England. Centuries before Alfred Thayer Mahan published his highly influential book, *The Influence of Sea Power Upon History, 1680–1783*, Ralegh published his own macroanalysis, *A Discourse of the Invention of Ships, Anchors, Compass, &c.* Mahan's argument came right from Ralegh, who famously said in *Discourse*,

"For whosoever commands the sea commands the trade; whosoever commands the trade of the world commands the riches of the world, and consequently the world itself."[1] This became the creed of the British Empire.

Ralegh understood that the navy rather than the army and fortifications should be the buttress that protected England. Lord Admiral Howard called on Ralegh whenever England was threatened by sea. Howard understood how to administer the navy, and the importance of building the best ships, but he lacked Ralegh's larger vision and battle expertise at sea. And not that fortifications were unimportant—Ralegh oversaw the fortifications of the southwest coast of England and the Island of Jersey, which he worked diligently to improve. The close friendship Ralegh developed with Lord Henry Cobham might have arisen from the latter's responsibility for the Cinque Ports. Both men essentially held charge of the defense of the southern coast of England.

Ralegh was indispensable as long as Spain remained a threat. The queen was more difficult to charm than in times past and tired of the challenges to her judgment in military and foreign affairs, but she recognized Ralegh's value. As her relationship with Essex and his supporters deteriorated, a result of his pressuring her to allow him to direct diplomatic and military affairs, her relationship with Ralegh healed. Ralegh ached to resume full duties as Captain of the Guard. She was almost but not quite ready. He threatened to return to the plough, country life at Sherborne, but his services were required at court.[2]

Ralegh's value at court to the queen and her government was highlighted in 1595–1597 by the political factionalism that grew dangerous in England. Within the highest circle of government, Ralegh ran interference and mediated between Cecil and Essex. No one played a greater role in soothing relations between the two. Ralegh's success at getting Cecil and Essex to work together was celebrated, and the three formed something of a triumvirate. Ralegh's friend and relation Arthur Gorges later recalled, "For albeit the Earle had many doubts and jealousies buzd into his eares against" Ralegh, "yet I have often observed, that both in his greatest actions of service, and in his times of chiefest recreations, [Essex] would ever accept of his counsell and company, before many others that thought themselves more In his favour."[3]

With Ralegh's attention focused on naval affairs, the defense of the realm, and the competition between Cecil and Essex, he gave little thought to his lands in Ireland. Yet this was a critical moment for the Munster Plantation and for the course of colonialism in Ireland.

Despite the idealism of Ralegh and other Humanists and Hermeticists that colonialism would work for the benefit of all, there remained great discontent among the Irish and Anglo-Irish. Ralegh, Spenser, Elizabeth, and others in the English government hoped to save Munster province—in fact, all of Ireland—from rebellion. Whatever difficulties the English faced in Ireland, they were not short of ideas, and Spenser put forth the most powerful set to solve England's problems there. But as Spenser and Ralegh both knew and argued, it was the failure of men—their behavior, corruption, venality, and ill will—that got in the way of peaceful solutions that purported to bring justice and prosperity to all.

—

OVER THE YEARS, historians have criticized Ralegh for not following through on his colonial enterprises, as if he lacked skill and fortitude, but these critics do not see the careful attention he paid to most enterprises or how his attention was drawn in multiple directions. Ralegh's peers saw in him an effective, diligent individual of imagination and open-mindedness who could be relied upon to plan and complete government tasks and who provided valuable advice. If not for Ralegh's marriage, as numerous political historians have observed, Ralegh likely would have become the queen's first minister, overseeing foreign affairs. In criticizing Ralegh's colonization of Ireland, critics miss an essential fact: Ralegh's plantation was a model of success in fulfilling English goals.

Ralegh's Munster lands attracted significant numbers of English farmers and nonagricultural laborers. Mogeely was an economic powerhouse. But in the mid-1590s, Ralegh lost touch with the plantation. His patronage of iron production became something of an embarrassment (though his plantation as a whole remained a success). Probably within weeks of his publication of *Discoverie*, he had leased lands near Mogeely for iron mills to "George Goringe and Hebert Pelham, esquires." What occurred next illustrates Ralegh's disconnection from his lands.

When a "companie of workemen and servauntes" sent by Goring and Pelham arrived at Mogeely to build forges and smelt iron, Ralegh's own "tenauntes and borderers thereaboutes" opposed the newcomers with "obstinacie and forward dealinges." Moreover, allegedly, his agents in Ireland already had leased the land for the ironworks to other parties without his knowledge. The very day Ralegh sailed to Cádiz on the queen's business, the Privy Council investigated his plea for "re-dresse of the wronges" against Goring and Pelham. Part of the prob-lem related to a "like complaint" Ralegh filed simultaneously with the Privy Council against "Nathaniell Barter the elder, who entered into bonde of 1,000£ to Sir Walter Raleghe for performemance of certeine covenauntes" that he now "refuseth to do (without anie good grounde or color as is informed)." The Privy Council required the government in Ireland "to call the said Barter before you and to enjoyne him ether performe the covenauntes . . . as he ought" or bring him to us.[4] Barter likely had been contracted to oversee the building of the ironworks and had reneged; perhaps he was threatened by those at Mogeely engaged in competing operations. The opposition of Ralegh's "tenauntes" likely refers to those engaged in lumber (Henry Pyne and his workers), with "borderers thereaboutes" referring to workers at the adjacent ironworks run by Thomas Norreys and to the glassworks at Curryglass, both of which were on Ralegh's land.

The people of Curryglass had a reputation for being particularly contentious. One exasperated official in 1598 rued that conflict with the Irish in the Nine Years' War was not enough conflict for the English at Curryglass because they frequently jarred with, and sued, one an-other. The mayor of Cork cited the frequent lawsuits from Curryglass as indicative of people who "were so famous, they were never quiet, while they had a penny in their purses, but arresting and binding to the peace, that they were called the clampers of Curryglasse."[5] (*Clampers* is a derisive term referring to the poorness of their arguments.)

The glassworks, Pyne's lumber operations, and Norreys's forge all used up the woods around Mogeely. Workers had to go farther and far-ther afield to cut trees, and it was difficult and expensive to move the wood. Just two years later, in the midst of the Nine Years' War, sixteen of Pyne's woodsmen were killed while working in the woods by the men of Gerald FitzJames Fitzgerald who wanted to cut for themselves the very same trees.[6] Iron and glass all depended on huge amounts of wood for fuel, and the lumber operation could not exist without trees. Henry Pyne had made agreements with neighboring land owners, in-cluding Gerald FitzJames Fitzgerald and Patrick Condon, to harvest their trees. The new ironworks threatened the livelihood of the es-tablished operations because it would monopolize the trees on a large tract of land. The abject return to England of Goring's and Pelham's ironworkers illustrates Ralegh's ignorance of the economic activities in which he partnered on his land.

While Ralegh was absent from Ireland, Pyne insinuated himself into the corridors of English power. His entry owed to his representing Ralegh's interests. Earlier we saw how Ralegh and Pyne worked together to obtain the right to ship staves abroad in wartime. They apparently were the only ones permitted to do so, and the Lord Treasurer of Ireland, Henry Wallop, learned to his dismay that only Pyne received license to ship staves where he pleased.[7]

Pyne did not need high office in Ireland to earn favors from the home government. Pyne's appearances before the Privy Council, and his letters on Irish affairs, were much appreciated in London, even by the queen. The continual slanders against him by his enemies in Ireland were repeatedly rebuffed by the queen's ministers, who appreciated his strengthening the Munster Plantation and English interests like no one else. In Ralegh's name Pyne controlled significant parcels of land and labor. (Later they disputed how much independence of action Ralegh had allowed him and whether or not some of the parcels had been leased to Pyne for eighty-eight years.) Pyne epitomized the kind of man that the government originally had conceived of leading the Munster Plantation as an Undertaker. He developed the land, secured the plantation, led English settlers, and knew what he was talking about with Irish affairs because he had worked successfully with so many Irish.

With the Spanish threat hanging over England—rumors and expectations of Philip II preparing another armada for England or Ireland never entirely abated—alarm periodically arose about the shipping of planks from Ireland to Spain. The privileged Pyne, in particular, continued to ship lumber to foreign ports. Simultaneously, the Privy Council expressed concern about the denuding of Irish forests. Over the centuries the belief has taken hold that the English cut down the trees in Munster to eliminate hiding places for the Irish. Though there were proposals to create highways by cutting large swaths, as with the salmon fisheries, sixteenth-century English and Irish had a keen sense of preservation of resources for the future. In the case of the English, the trees held special importance. England largely had been deforested by the late Middle Ages. They required the strongest trees for ship masts and a ready supply of trees for ship planks; they also needed naval stores, such as tar and pitch produced from wood. England relied on the northern countries (modern-day Norway and Sweden) for much of their lumber for the navy. Later, with the colonization of America, they eliminated dependence on foreign sources. In North America, England gained access to the great white pine for ship masts—a tree reserved for the king. But before that discovery, English sensitivity to preserving the forests was acute. While much of the forests *would* be denuded in Munster, this largely took place under the Stuarts in the seventeenth century when trees were felled for a great expansion of iron production. England by then had the North American forests as surety for the future of the navy.

Conservation and military interests overlapped. William Waad received a patent from Queen Elizabeth to ensure that the pipe staves, planks, and other timber products produced in Ireland were not shipped to Spain and other enemies. By 1596, the Privy Council described the massive timber production in Munster as a "great havock . . . in diverse places of the woodes." From England, Waad could not possibly fulfill his charge to regulate forest usage, especially because he often was called upon by the government to perform extraordinary duties investigating conspiracies against the queen and undertaking special missions to foreign dignitaries and courts. He appointed Ralegh's man Pyne to carry on his work in Ireland. At first glance this seems an odd choice—the fox overseeing the chicken coop—but Pyne had his self-interest to guide him in supervising where timber was harvested and shipped. Who better than he, the foremost shipper of Irish timber to Spain, to know how to prevent that? The Privy Council exhorted Ireland's lord deputy and council to give Pyne every aid in ending the "great havock" and preventing the shipping of timber to England's enemies. Elizabeth expected to see the offenders punished and to recover one-half of their fines for herself, and she "require[d] your Lordship and the rest to give all aide and assistance unto the saide Henry Pyne."[8] Thus, Pyne and Ralegh could produce timber for foreign markets while preventing others from benefiting (and further denuding the forests).

A major reason Pyne remained high in the Privy Council's esteem was his success turning Mogeely into a fortified community using the hundreds of men that Ralegh had sent him. This alone made Ralegh's plantation a huge success, for these men required pay only if they actually were sent on military assignment. According to several observers, Pyne built the most significant fortress in the entire province of Munster. He also convinced local Irish to enter Mogeely's economic orbit. In the early years of the Nine Years' War, which broke out in northern Ireland in 1594, Mogeely played a key role in minimizing the impact of the rebels in portions of Counties Cork and Waterford. Mogeely and its satellite castle a mile or so away at Lysfinny stifled rebel attempts to capture livestock on Ralegh's seignories. Both fortifications sat on the Bride River and commanded roads north–south and east–west. The rebels apparently did not have boats to carry the livestock away on an alternative route, the Blackwater River, and even if they did, they would have had to pass strongholds on Ralegh's land, such as Stroncally Castle, to reach their base in the Drumfenning Woods to the west and north of Mogeely.

Pyne convinced many Irish to bring their cattle and crops to him, and he offered them ready money and security for themselves and their livestock. The rebels tried many ways to eliminate or capture Mogeely and Pyne. At the onset of the conflict, they left Mogeely alone because Pyne provided an avenue for the exchange of their goods with the Irish who traded with him and relied on Mogeely for protection of their property. However, the White Knight and others allegedly captured about £1,200 worth of English livestock in the vicinity of Mogeely, an attempt to starve the people out of their fortifications, and they killed fourteen soldiers "to terrify the rest, that they should yield the place." After a four-month siege, the attackers tried to breach Mogeely's walls with six hundred men, a battering ram, and ladders. Failing that, they captured Pyne's brother and threatened to hang him in front of the fortress, promising that everyone could leave with their property if they would only yield and that when the war ended they would return the castle in good condition. Pyne refused; the fate of his brother is unknown.[9] The effectiveness of armed settlers and colonist-built fortifications was not lost on the English. Colonialism could be effected without the monarch's soldiers, and, indeed, English monarchs disdained sending troops to colonies except when they were fighting their own imperial wars against foreign colonial powers.

The rebellion had dissipated in Munster province, though it was by no means over in northern Ireland. From his plantation Kilcolman, thirty miles from Mogeely, Ralegh's friend Edmund Spenser used this period of relative calm to finish writing his reflections on the failures of English colonialism in Ireland, *A View of the Present State of Ireland*. While Ralegh prescribed for the queen a "policy" of colonialism in South America based on coexistence, cooperation, and co-creation, Spenser detailed a policy for Ireland that also promoted coexistence and cooperation, but not co-creation. In Spenser's prescription, the English Crown would dictate the terms, but the goal was the same: both Irish and English should live and work together to mutually benefit from colonialism.

Could a single program of colonialism work in both Guiana and Ireland? In common, the areas to be colonized posed significant challenges. The Native peoples possessed great military power, the terrain posed immense difficulties for the English, and Spanish intervention was almost inevitable. From an English view, both Guiana and Ireland were inhabited by tribal peoples who lacked a recognizable system of laws and who did not share English religion. But there were differences. Ireland was a familiar place where English had been active for four hundred years; Guiana was completely new: the English had almost no experience with a rainforest environment, and Guiana's location thousands of miles from Europe meant cost and travel time increased exponentially.

Unlike the Spanish, the English could not draw on any colonies or outposts for assistance in Guiana. Ralegh made no complaints about the great distance to get there, and the lack of supporting bases, because he did not want to deter English interest. As for the environment, Ralegh did complain, but he likely believed that the English would adapt as the Spanish had. The spirit of adventure that led sixteenth-century Europeans to travel vast distances to exotic places in pursuit of wealth and fame evinces a fearlessness to engage the wider world.

But Ireland beckoned much closer to home. It did not possess great caches of gold, but it had impressive natural resources like trees, iron, and fish. Ireland seemed less of a risk than America because it was easier for a colonist to abandon. In 1596, English colonization of Ireland was in process, while colonization of the Americas remained a failure in Virginia and only a possibility in Guiana.

As the New English settled Munster, their relations with the Old English remained tense. The persistence of overlapping land claims fueled hard feelings, extended legal cases, and fomented sporadic violence. The Tudor government had to find a way to pacify all parties to create a prosperous and peaceful plantation. It needed to maintain the allegiance of the "loyal" Old English, who presumably could keep their Irish tenants peaceful and laboring. Simultaneously, the English government hoped that the New English, like Ralegh, would transform the lands of Old English traitors into prosperous farms using English laborers. The English intended to extend the program they had initiated in Munster to the north of Ireland, where many Irish leaders still owned the land but had gone into rebellion with the Nine Years' War. The English expected the Irish elite to accept English centralization, which would reduce the Irish leaders' power, particularly the power to tax. They required Irish leaders to accept English encroachment into their lives and to give up their old ways by adopting the English political economy. The Tudors wanted the Irish to give up being Irish.

Tudor fear of Irish culture was as great as ever. The English government tried to instill English legal and landholding practices and to make the Irish more beholden to the monarch than to their local lords. It sought to privatize land ownership, as in England, and to alter Irish family names to reduce people's sense of belonging to a sept or clan. No English yet proposed a like transformation of the Native peoples of America, but over the centuries the English colonies and then the United States attempted to implement the same policies that were tried in Ireland—entreating and extorting Natives to adopt the idea of private land ownership, the English system of land use, the English language and Anglicizing their names, and the transfer of their allegiances from their families and clans to the English monarch or president of the United States.

Ireland, not Guiana or Virginia, was England's preeminent, in fact only, colonial problem. And it was Ralegh's friend Edmund Spenser who provided the understanding of English colonialism that the English carried reflexively through the centuries—not just to Ireland but to most everywhere the English went.

—

WITH THE OUTBREAK of the Nine Years' War, Spenser addressed the problems of colonizing in a prose work that left little doubt of his thoughts and feelings. In about sixty-five thousand words, Spenser offers a controversial prescription for England to end several hundred years of futility integrating the Emerald Isle fully into the English monarch's empire. Written at the same time as Ralegh's *Discoverie* in 1595–1596, Spenser tried to publish it in 1598. Probably because of English government censorship in the midst of war with Ireland, the work remained unpublished until 1633. It articulates a Humanist view of colonization that assesses England's failures and proposes ideas for resolution. It does not represent how all Humanists (and Hermeticists) would have chosen to colonize Ireland, but it lays bare typical English views of the problems of colonizing and offers solutions that made sense to English colonists (and their descendants).

The Elizabethans identified all of the major issues about Native people that through the centuries haunted English colonizers, encapsulating them in the belief that non-English peoples were dangerous if they did not imitate the English in physical appearance and culture. Some characteristics could not be changed (or easily changed) such as skin, hair, and eye color, but these physical attributes were as irrelevant to Spenser as they were to Drake, Ralegh, and other, though not all, Elizabethans. (Elizabeth, herself, was highly prejudiced against Africans' skin color and tried to bar Africans from coming into England.) What mattered to Spenser, and to the Puritans in later New England, and to many white people in the United States to the present day, was how the descendants of Africans, Native Americans, Irish, Hispanics, and other non-Anglos dressed, wore their hair, and carried themselves. Spenser intuitively and analytically identifies this cultural "problem" of colonialism and describes what should be done about it.

Spenser presents his ideas in A View of the State of Ireland in the form of a dialogue between Eudox, an Englishman who poses questions, and Irenius, an Englishman of much experience in Ireland, who recites history and suggests remedies for England's Irish problem. A View is oft-cited, and frequently reviled, as a cold-blooded manifesto of colonial English racism. Modern sensibilities are perturbed by Spenser's call to alter Irish culture and by his plans to starve the recalcitrant into submission. But Spenser should be read carefully and contextualized properly to understand his vision for colonizing Ireland. He does not represent future colonizers or colonists who wished to remove, enslave, or kill Native peoples. He was an assimilationist, a Humanist who saw colonialism as an opportunity to create a new society. His ideals were utopian and meant to benefit all. But we must approach his design with caution. Despite the rationalism he employs to construct a benevolent colonialism, his argument is infused with, and sometimes overwhelmed by, his emotions and biases. The logic of Spenser's utopian ideals epitomizes the colonizers' good intentions toward the colonized, but the deep-seated prejudice against the Natives' culture repeatedly undermines those "good" intentions.

Ralegh differed from Spenser on the issue of cultural differences. With his ease interacting with the Irish and Native Americans, he likely failed to grasp why his fellow English had so much trouble with cultural difference. He spent a great deal of time with American Indians in England, continuing the tradition started at Roanoke of bringing home American Natives. In Ralegh's later years, Natives were his constant companions. In contrast, Spenser developed no close relations with American Indians. His sole concern was the Irish, with whom he had lived for many years. As an intellectual, Spenser appreciated Irish culture, and like Ralegh, he did not assert English cultural superiority over the colonized. In the book, Irenius reminds Eudox that "it is certaine, that Ireland hath the use of letters very anciently, and long before England." Irenius informs Eudox that on their arrival in Ireland, the English were "very rude and barbarous . . . it is but even the other day since England grew civill."[10] Spenser's sympathy for Irish culture might have radiated from his celebration of pastoralism in his poetry—of the virtues of living a simple life devoid of the corruptions of contemporary society in England. Nonetheless, Spenser avers, there can be only one culture in a society, so the Irish must adopt the culture of the English. Then a fair and just society can be built for all.

Spenser's *A View* states what the English should do, how they should do it, and why. *A View* offers a step-by-step process for turning a recalcitrant Native people—the Irish—into a population satisfied with English rule. It also addresses what needs to be done to prevent English abuse of the Irish. Modern scholarly excision of Spenser from his historical context has obscured his progressive views of the Irish situation, which, if nothing else, were more sympathetic than the views held by most English. It is worth iterating: for so many European colonizers, the colonized were to be removed, killed, or placed into subservient positions as laborers. Spenser instead articulates a colonialism in which the Natives are a reflection of oneself. His concept of elevating and assimilating Native people is racist because he wants to alter the culture of the colonized, but his goal is to create a nonracialized society, where all are culturally alike and positioned to enjoy together the benefits of society. Cultural conformity, Spenser believed, was necessary for creating peace and prosperity in a society of diverse peoples.

Cultural conformity did not mean the alteration of Irish religion. Like Ralegh, Spenser avidly opposed forcing Natives to give up their religion.[11] He calls for a policy of religious tolerance and rebukes those who would use "terrour and sharpe penalties" against Irish Catholics; religion should be "rather delivered and intimated with mildnesse and gentlenesse."[12]

Spenser even more adamantly opposes forcing the English legal system on the Irish. For hundreds of years the English tried to impose legislative and common law in Ireland and failed—why should they expect this to change? Ireland must be completely made over before English laws could have a good effect. Spenser blames the corruption of the English for perverting the law in Ireland, and he defends the continued use of Irish Brehon law, which, although imperfect, proved effective because it enjoyed the people's respect. Spenser calls for the adaptation of laws to Irish needs and that new laws should not be rammed down Irish throats. "For lawes ought to be fashioned unto the manners and conditions of the people, to whom they are meant, and not to be imposed upon them according to the simple rule of right."[13] Spenser has Irenius advise "moderation" in "tempering, and managing, this stubborne nation of the Irish to bring them from their delight of licentious barbarisme unto the love of goodnes and civilite."

Spenser's solution to transform the Irish from barbarianism to civility is through force of arms. Modern critics of Spenser's colonization plans decry their predication on brute force, that the Irish were not consulted on their futures, and the colonizers' rationale: they were "civilizing" the inhabitants, a belief that was used at numerous times and places to justify dominating the Natives and disinheriting rightful owners of their land. Spenser, however, opposes taking land from the Irish. He foresees Irish imitating English as productive tillers of the soil. Irish agriculturalists would be transformed into English-style farmers. This could occur only if the Irish ended their ancient manner of keeping cattle, which involved roaming from place to place.[14] "Civilizing" the Irish was not a question of law but of instilling new work habits to be practiced in communities fashioned after the English style.

The English considered the Irish "freedom" to roam their greatest cultural ill. Freedom, to many English elites, was an undesirable state, for it meant independence from the ties that bound individuals to a community. Irish roaming and freedom were nearly synonymous and implied disregard for laws and a lack of obedience to superiors. Englishmen understood that people possessed rights and liberties that varied by one's place in the social order; freedom, on the other hand, led to anarchy because it placed the individual's needs above the community and social order. Spenser's condemnation of the freedom of mobility became a hallmark of the criticism the English later made of American Indians. Particularly in New England, the English practiced a policy of containment of Natives because their freedom to roam was considered a military threat. The Puritans of New England also feared their people might abandon their communities to live free like the Indians. Spenser believed this roaming led Irish to lives of crime. Those who roamed stole from those who planted. England could create a functional civil society in Ireland only if property crime was reduced. Thieves abounded in Irish woods and mountains and found refuge in the boolys, the roaming cattle grazers. Whether people were English, Irish, or American Indian, Englishmen like Spenser wanted common folk to live in one place in close proximity to neighbors, who joined together to protect property and enforce proper moral behavior.

Spenser puts little faith in law compelling men to behave, and more in an entwined hierarchy; laws without good governance were meaningless. On the local level, "an English man, or an Irish man of speciall assurance," would provide leadership under an alderman, who would be "an English man of speciall regard." For this model, Spenser looked to the past, to village life in the Middle Ages in England, where a "hundred did containe an hundredth villages."[15] These were organized with a hierarchy of responsibility that bound all. Every year the people would assemble before the justices of the peace to survey "what change hath happened since the yeare before; and, the defects to supplie, of young plants late growne up"—how were the young folks maturing?—"so as pledges may bee taken for them, and they put into order of some tything"—groups of ten men responsible for each other's good behavior—with "bookes made thereof accordingly."[16] Spenser devotes many pages of *A View* to outlining this ordering of society on the local level because this would be the foundation of good order in Ireland.

To end hostilities between Irish and English, Spenser urges "Intermingling." As with Ralegh's view of Indians and English coinhabiting, Spenser believed that if Irish and English lived as neighbors in the same communities, they would form a "union of manners, and conformity of mindes . . . to be one people, and to put away the dislikefull conceipt both of the one, and the other." "[D]ayly conversation" would "bring them . . . unto better liking of each other" and make them less apt to harm one another.[17] Intermingling is one of the most radical suggestions Spenser offers for Ireland's future. The plantation scheme of the 1580s under Elizabeth had been designed for areas bereft of Irish population and with Irish barred from living with, and working for, the English. The New English would not succumb to Irish culture and language because the septs would be broken and a new order established. Spenser, too, called for forbidding the *O*'s and *Mac*s in Irish names as part of the process of breaking the septs.[18]

Spenser adamantly opposes those who argued for Irish removal. He affirms, "Ireland is full of her owne nation, that ought not to be rooted out." His faith in the ability of the Irish to adapt to the English colonizers is presented in a rising crescendo of Irish potential. In the new intermingled communities, leaders are English, but the Irish should hold positions of responsibility.[19] For instance, the tithes for the church should be collected by "an Irish man," and Irish should be permitted to become Anglican priests, and eventually bishops.[20] The groundwork for the cultural transformation of the Irish (and the Anglo-Irish) lay in educating Irish children in grammar and the sciences, while adult males would learn civility by laboring on English-style farms.[21] Many Irish would rise economically by obtaining freeholds and learning trades. English-style labor would keep the Irish from rebelling. But the roaming must end. The Irish can maintain livestock but must "keep a plough going." Countries that live on cattle are the most "barbarous and uncivll, and also greatly given to warre."[22]

Everyone must speak English. Irenius was particularly vexed by the English in Ireland speaking Irish, for "it is unnaturall that any people should love anothers language more then [sic] their owne." According to Spenser, intermarriage and the use of wet nurses were to blame. The child learned from the Irish mother/wet nurse the Irish tongue first. English became their second language, and Irish remained for them more natural and carried with it "manners and conditions." The problem became that "the speach being Irish, the heart must needes bee Irish: for out of the abundance of the heart, the tongue speaketh." Irenius believed intermarriage "perillous." Ancient history had shown that "worthy issue" could come from such unions, but the "evils" were "infinite"—the children would be "framed and fashioned" by their mothers to her Irish culture.[23] To feel allegiance to English monarchs, a child's first language must be English. Spenser does not say explicitly but implies that if everyone spoke English, then the intermarriage that followed would not pose a problem.

Before the intermingled communities of colonizer and colonized could create a new Ireland, England had to end the Nine Years' War. Spenser's plan to do so comprised the most controversial part of his work. His solution begins with the use of force. "Reformation must now bee the strength of a greater power," so the Irish cannot "cast away the English subjection." The "sword," Irenius confirms, will be the engine for change—but he quickly clarifies, "I did not meane the cutting off all that nation with the sword . . . but by the sword I meane the royall power of the Prince." The prince must end the rebellion and use troops to "bring in all that rebellious route [armed assemblies] and loose people"—the "wandring companies [that] doe keepe the woods, spoyling the good subjects."[24]

Spenser calls for reform of the military, particularly of the captains, and recommends that only those who served in Ireland, at least at the level of lieutenant, should be appointed because men transferred from service on the Continent were ignorant of the Irish people and places. But his most notable recommendation is his strategy for ending the war in but eighteen months. Spenser suggests distributing the soldiers into garrison governments. Instead of pursuing the enemy, place the troops in key positions in every county, with food and other supplies for half a year, and then campaign in winter, driving the enemy "from one side to another, and tennis him amongst" the garrisons. The enemy would have no time to pasture their cattle. They would have to eat their livestock or starve the following summer from lack of milk and crops. The garrisons would keep the enemy out of villages so they could not sell their spoils or receive succor. This strategy, it should be noted, was employed shortly thereafter by Lord Mountjoy to great effect to help end the Nine Years' War.

Spenser did not invent this strategy but based it on Lord Grey's policies in effect during the Desmond Wars, from which Spenser also took his view of a surrender policy. Once a garrison was well established, a proclamation would be issued offering the people but twenty days to submit, "principalls and ringleaders" excepted. Out of pity, the garrisons must accept these common people, who would not ordinarily rebel, "but are by force drawne by the grand rebells into their action, and carryed away with the violence of the streame, else they should be sure to loose all that they have, and perhaps their lives too." The gentlemen who surrender should also be received (as long as they bring their cattle), but they must be sent off to another part of the island so that they do not later "releive their friends" or provide news of the garrison to the enemy.[25]

Eudox approves of Irenius's policy to provide "no compassion" for those who "will follow the course of their owne folly" coupled with mercy for those who submit. But how, he asks, will the war conclude in such a short time? Irenius's response provides a haunting picture of what happened in the Desmond Wars, which Spenser and Ralegh both witnessed. "The end will (I assure me) bee very short . . . although there should none of them fall by the sword, nor bee slaine by the souldiour." Unable to manure their fields, nor pasture their cattle, "they would quickly consume themselves, and devoure one another." He continues:

The proofe whereof, I saw sufficiently exampled in these late war-res of Mounster; for not withstanding that the same was a most rich and plentifull countrey full of corne and cattle . . . yet ere one yeare and a halfe they were brought to such wretchednesse, as that any stony heart would have rued the same. Out of every corner of the woods and glynnes they came creeping forth upon their hands, for their legges could not beare them; they looked like anatomies of death, they spake like ghosts crying out of their graves; they did eate the dead carrions, happy where they could finde them, yea, and one another soone after, insomuch as the very carcasses they spared not to scrape out of their graves; and, if they found a plot of water-cresses or shamrocks, there they flocked as to a feast for the time, yet not able long to continue therewithal; that in short space there were none almost left, and a most populous and plentifull countrey suddainely left voyde of man and beast; yet sure in all that warre, there perished not many by the sword, but all by the extremitie of famine, which they themselves had wrought.[26]

Those who refused to submit, according to Spenser, had brought the terrible famine on themselves. These Irish, Eudox protests, are the subjects of Her Majesty. She "being by nature full of mercy and clem-ency . . . will not endure to heare such tragedies made of her poore people and subjects." Will Elizabeth not prevent this policy from be-ing used again? After all, Grey had employed it and was declared by many "a bloodie man . . . [who] had wasted and consumed all" so that a general pardon was declared by the queen. Irenius rues the calumny heaped on Grey, for he was a "gentle, affable, loving, and temperate" man who did not delight in blood, but did what must be done. Grey's policy was to punish "heades and principalls" of the rebellion and to reclaim "all the meaner sort."[27]

Spenser, speaking through Irenius, asserts that the queen must em-ploy his famine policy. English troops would never be able to root out the rebellion by following the rebels through difficult terrain. More-over, there was the prohibitive cost of financing the troops with no end in sight. England must draw a line: those who submit will be pro-tected, those who refuse will die by starvation.

Spenser's chilling solutions to the problem of Ireland epitomized the Humanist modernizer. Sixteenth-century Humanism never in-cluded pacifism as one of its precepts, but certainly there was the sen-timent to use war only to achieve rational ends, such as defense of one's country. The state's use of violence in Ireland was not a story of conquest to Spenser. The conquest, imperfect as it was, had taken place hundreds of years before under Henry II. For Spenser, this was a story of subduing rebellion and then remaking society through colonization and cultural transformation. Labor, education, and order would comprise the pillars of the new society. Intermingling the colonizer with the colonized would provide the Irish with the example of civility and inspire the English to retain their own civility. Peace, harmony, prosperity, and security were the rewards for those who productively labored and abided by the law.[28]

Spenser's and Ralegh's ideal was to create "just" societies where England colonized. Both identified corruption as the greatest threat. Corruption in the English administration of Ireland undermined all attempts to create a just society. Every level of society and bureaucracy, Spenser argues, required reform. In the book, he rails against English judges and juries, soldiers and landowners, calling for one of the most prominent figures in England to be appointed to live full-time in Ireland to overlook the administration of the island and assigning colonels of the highest integrity to oversee the captains and the military establishment. "The chiefest helpe for prevention" of corruption "must be the care of the coronell that hath the government of all his garrison."[29] But beneath the administrators, the system of everyone living together, intermingling, and examining their neighbors' conduct would work, he thought, to minimize the corruption of humans and their institutions. The state and church could not effectively enforce morality and conformity—but people could be induced to behave by living in close-knit communities where malfeasance was easily detected. This was a Humanist solution: most people would succumb to corruption without a well-ordered society to ensure vigilance.

Spenser and Ralegh shared this cynicism about people and their institutions. Whether Ralegh shared Spenser's confidence that an orderly society could or should be created is unknown, but his skepticism is apparent. He and Spenser both affirmed the pastoral virtues of country life over the corruptions of the court and its personages. Humanist modernizers recommended a return to rustic simplicity, to basic virtues shorn of the unnecessary and corrupting influences of society that spread vice. For example, the negative influences of court, a necessary evil, could be mitigated by returning to one's country estate. Spenser and Ralegh had even traveled to court together from Ireland to procure what they needed, then returned to Ireland. In later years, when he was exiled from court or grew tired of court life, Ralegh took sanctuary at his Sherborne estate in England. It seems hypocritical of Spenser and Ralegh to criticize court when both benefited from the court hierarchy. Spenser received a pension from the queen—but he doubted the virtue of her appointees. Ralegh owed his monopolies, political appointments, and patents to colonize in America and Ireland to his position at court—yet that did not stop him from penning one of the most brilliantly cynical poems of the English Renaissance that describes society's institutions and the people who corruptly use them for their own ends. This poem, "The Lie," Ralegh wrote at the time of his exile from court, as he prepared his trip to Guiana.

The modus operandi of "The Lie" is Ralegh sending his soul on an errand to give the lie—to rip away the veil—to expose hypocrisy and decay. He begins with the large picture, wishing to "give the world the lie," and creatively moves through the most powerful institutions. The court glows, but the source is burning rotten wood; the church "shows what's good, and doth no good." Rulers are not governed by their inner selves but by external forces. The wealthy and high-born care only for themselves and not for those who deserve and require care and guidance. As Ralegh shifts the poem to human traits, he universalizes his sentiments, from elites to all people. Virtues are empty. Zeal lacks devotion; love is only lust. Everything is transitory: time is only motion; "Tell flesh it is but dust." Wit and wisdom come under attack, as do traits that many viewed as benign, or good, such as nature and justice. Not even the poet's pastoralism is immune to criticism: faith "fled the city," but even in the country it "erreth." Much of "The Lie" implicitly mocks Ralegh's own good fortune in the world, as when he laments that "virtue least preferreth"—one's value in society proceeds from the favor received and not from anything internal to the individual. Ralegh ends the poem as it began, noting the weakness, physically and spiritually, of the body, a theme he explores in other poems; only the soul is immortal. In a melodramatic close, Ralegh admits that as the author of "The Lie," he is no less worthy of stabbing than everyone else, but his soul will live on:

> Go soul the body's guest
> Upon a thankless errand,
> Fear not to touch the best
> the truth shall be thy warrant;
> Go since I needs must die,

and give the world the lie.
Say to the Court it glows,
and shines like rotten wood,
Say to the Church it shows
what's good, and doth no good.
If Church and Court reply,
then give them both the lie.
Tell Potentates they live
acting by others' action,
Not loved unless they give,
not strong but by affection.
If Potentates reply,
give Potentates the lie.
Tell men of high condition,
that manage the estate,
Their purpose is ambition,
their practice only hate:
And if they once reply,
then give them all the lie.
Tell them that brave it most,
They beg for more by spending,
Who, in their greatest cost,
Seek nothing but commending.
And if they make reply,
Then give them all the lie.
Tell zeal it wants devotion
tell love it is but lust
Tell time it metes but motion,
tell flesh it is but dust.
And wish them not reply
for they must give the lie.
Tell age it daily wasteth,
tell honor how it alters.
Tell beauty how she blasteth,
tell favor how it falters
And as they shall reply,
Give everyone the lie.
Tell fortune of her blindness,
tell nature of decay,
Tell friendship of unkindness,

tell justice of delay.
And if they will reply,
then give them all the lie.
Tell arts they have no soundness,
but vary by esteeming,
Tell schools they want profoundness
and stand too much on seeming.
If arts and schools reply,
give arts and schools the lie.
Tell faith its fled the City,
tell how the country erreth,
Tell manhood shake off pity,
tell virtue least preferreth
And if they do reply
spare not to give the lie.
So when thou hast as I
commanded thee, done blabbing,
although to give the lie,
deserves no less than stabbing,
Stab at thee he that will,
No stab thy soul can kill.[30]

The cynicism of "The Lie" is in calling to task all people for their hypocrisy, venality, and mortality. Virtue was a façade. Yet the poet, Ralegh, was an idealist. In him and other Elizabethans, cynicism gave way to hope, melancholy gave way to elation. One moment the English knew only foreboding, and then the pendulum swung to effusions of a glorious future. Fear of the Spanish colossus funneled into schemes to reduce King Philip's empire, discover lost cities of gold, and dream of building a universal empire that would restore the Golden Age of Constantine.

But so much was illusory. There was no El Dorado or Empire of Guiana. Elizabeth never commanded a universal empire. Reincarnation might occur as England established one colony after another, each unique and yet all characterized by sensibilities and patterns that existed from the Age of Elizabeth—and even before, some dating back hundreds of years into Ireland, and even earlier to the Norman Conquest of England. The medieval world became the early modern world became the modern world.

PART TEN

"The arte of Magicke is the arte of worshipping God"

Colonialism as a History of the World and Universe

CHAPTER 28

Treasons

The last years of Ralegh's life were full of adventures, though not all of them welcome. He sailed to distant shores and explored the world and the universe in multiple ways. Though his explorations often occurred under unfortunate circumstances, he nonetheless ascended to great heights. As throughout his adulthood, royalty remained central to his life's course, offering him a wide array of awards and punishments, from the opportunity to amass wealth and influence to being flung into the abyss. Meanwhile, the last years of Elizabeth's reign saw the continued reduction of the Spanish threat but also the near collapse of her rule in Ireland. The most severe domestic challenge she ever faced derived from the Earl of Essex, the consequences of which influenced Ralegh's standing in the next regime.

By any measure, they were extraordinary decades. The wheel of fortune spun Ralegh from being the most despised man in England to the most revered. He earned renown that lasted long after his death, with fame in England that somewhat exceeded Shakespeare's into the second half of the seventeenth century. Some of that fame resulted from what Ralegh represented and how he faced misfortune. Despite being subject to the vagaries of monarchical whim and self-interest, and to a course of events that proceeded beyond his control, Ralegh made the very best of difficult situations by what he did, said, and wrote. Integration of his interests in America and colonization, the unseen and physical manifestations of the material world, monarchy and statecraft, all merged in incredibly productive ways.

—

In 1596–1598, PHILIP of Spain sought revenge any way he could. He considered landing in Ireland to stir an Irish rebellion and to avenge England's support of Dutch rebels against Spain. If weather prevented an Irish landing, the Spanish might land across from Ireland at Milford Haven in Wales, where they thought they could find Spanish sympathizers and together attempt to overthrow Elizabeth. Growing impatient with these preparations, Philip turned his attention to an assault on England via Calais. The queen's advisors conferred about the expected invasion, and Ralegh thought there was little to worry about: Philip generally took a long time to amass his naval forces, and his resources were spread so thinly that he could not form an armada on the scale of the great armada of 1588.

England would take the offensive. After the queen responded positively to proposals for an attack, Cecil, Ralegh, and Essex met and worked out the details. The three concluded a "treaty of peace" to work together. This gave Ralegh the contract to provide the expedition with three months' victuals for six thousand men at 9 p. each per day, totaling £3,000 per week for six weeks. The food supplies would be stored in three locations: Winchester House (owned by an associate of Essex), Ralegh's Durham House on the Strand in London, and at Bridewell Palace, which Cecil oversaw. Though this partition could be seen as a way to allow each the opportunity to skim, perhaps it left each responsible for preventing skimming. Ralegh's enemies thought he would make a fortune off the contract. He, of course, stated that he would be a "looser" but that "few are of that opinion besides hymselfe."[1] As in times past, the expedition was intended to go to Spain to destroy ships and supplies, then to sea to search for the treasure fleet.

Essex commanded, supported by Ralegh and Thomas Howard; Lord Admiral Charles Howard chose to remain in England, as did Cecil. The English armada would carry both navy and army personnel. Just before departure in June 1597, Ralegh was restored to full duties as Captain of the Guard: he reattained privileged access to the queen.

The expedition's first destination was the harbor of Ferrol in Galicia, Spain. A violent storm forced half of the ships to return to England, the others dispersed, and some eventually reached Spain. In these reduced circumstances, the commanders sent home most of the soldiers, allowing some to return to duty in the Low Countries. The remaining ships and sailors went to Coruña, about twelve nautical miles from where the Spanish Armada lay moored in port. The Spaniards did not take the bait to meet the English at sea and the English could not risk entering the harbor at Ferrol. They needed to go elsewhere to do damage to the Spanish.

Receiving intelligence from a privateer that the Spanish would sail for the Azores to guard the returning treasure fleet, Ralegh and Essex sailed to capture the treasure fleet before the Spanish escort arrived from Ferrol. They planned to meet at the island of Flores, and on arrival they learned their information was false—neither treasure fleet nor Spanish naval fleet was on its way. Half of the English fleet was directed to Graciosa, and others to St. Michael and Pico in the Azores, in part to seek out stray treasure ships. Essex sent Ralegh to the island of Fayal, where he would join him for an attack on the island. William Monson, one of the captains, later wrote, "Here grew great questions and heart-burnings [bitterness] against Sir Walter Ralegh."[2]

Ralegh waited. Each day he held a council of war. On the fifth day, he landed to obtain water. The Spanish, five hundred strong, taunted the English to attack. Ralegh complied, and the Spanish abandoned the town. Essex arrived and seemed happy with the result, but his supporters intimated that Ralegh should not have attacked without Essex's permission. They baited Essex, suggesting that Ralegh just wanted all the credit for himself. Ralegh defended himself as a principal commander with the right to initiate an assault. Ralegh's and Essex's squadrons might have come to blows, but Lord Thomas Howard convinced Ralegh to apologize. At some point during the dispute, Essex had "cashiered" Ralegh's officers, and with Ralegh's apology they were restored to their positions. No mention of the dispute was made in the "Official Relation" of the expedition, and neither did the Spanish accounts make mention of what happened between Ralegh and Essex, but they did express amazement that the town and churches were not destroyed and that the women were protected from abuse.[3]

The expedition returned to England in late July 1597. Once again, Essex had failed to capture the treasure fleet. When his squadron arrived, he was immediately sent to Falmouth to guard the coast against a Spanish invasion. But a storm deterred the Spanish from reaching their destination. This was Philip's last attempt to invade England and get his revenge. He died in autumn 1598.

Yet Elizabeth stewed. She was quite unhappy with the outcome of the expedition. She blamed Essex for failing to accomplish anything of importance. For his part, Ralegh thought that they had accomplished a fair amount: England had been defended and most of the expenses were borne by Philip, who had to send troops and supplies to various locations to ward off the English fleet, which took pressure off of the Dutch and the French. From a personal standpoint, the expedition further restored Ralegh to the queen's good graces. Upset with Essex's treatment of Ralegh, she increasingly relied on Ralegh and Cecil. She grew so exasperated with Essex that on one occasion, when he turned his back on her, a serious violation of propriety, she boxed his ears. She would give Essex one more chance to prove himself. She ordered him to Ireland to put an end to the Nine Years' War by defeating the rebels in the north.

CENTERED IN THE NORTH since its outbreak in 1594, the Nine Years' War spread to Munster province in 1598. In October, an anonymous writer noted that the English lands along the Blackwater, particularly on Ralegh's seignories, had been abandoned by the settlers. "All the English of the seignory of Sir Walter Ralegh, viz., John Harris, William Andrews, with others ran away."[4] Some of Ralegh's tenants and others did flee, but many remained behind, including Henry Pyne, who provided a refuge. But the poorly defended inland town of Tallow, which held sixty householders and their families, was burned to the ground, returning it to the state of ruin it was in when Ralegh had resettled it. Many of the survivors did not return to England. Those who did not move to Mogeely went to Youghal, Cork, and other fortified coastal communities.

The queen was irate with Sir Thomas Norris, Lord President of Munster, who was supposed to crush the rebellion. Cecil informed Norris, "It hath not been a little grievous to Her Majesty to find that Province under your charge so much wasted by the rebels." The Privy Council promised to send supplies so he could suppress the revolt and reminded Norris that the key was to divide the Irish—"to sever them"—and then offer them pardon.[5] "You know the nature of the Irish, how easily they are divided."

A week later, a much-disturbed Elizabeth wrote directly to Norris to express her displeasure. "How strange," she said, that "a revolt has happened in our Province of Munster." Although Norris had predicted this, she scolded him for not nipping it in the bud, "when the first traitor grew to head with a ragged number of rogues and boys you might better have resisted than you did, especially considering the many defensible houses and castles possessed by the undertakers," who received no support from him. She gave Norris personal "Directions" on how to proceed: He should seek out "certain persons, either out in rebellion or suspected, who might be used as good instruments against the capital rebels." She named in particular three—the White Knight, "who should be assured that no extreme or injurious course will be taken against him, but that his complaints will be graciously heard and considered"; Donogh McCormack, who would be pardoned and his country guaranteed to him if he repented; and Patrick Condon, "to be promised a gracious end of the suit between him and Hyde." Once again, the queen's letter makes clear that she understood the tribulations faced by clan leaders from the Undertakers infringing on and having been granted their land, and once again she promises to make amends as long as they remained loyal or returned to loyalty.[6] The continued inability of the English government to ensure justice for Irish and Anglo-Irish shows the lack of will and ability that defined colonialism not only in Ireland but also later colonialism in America. Ordinarily, colonists and local colonial officials were at fault for the injustices inflicted on Native peoples, which the home government refused to prevent, rein in, and rectify.

English defeat in Ulster at the Battle of the Yellow Ford, in April 1598, forced Elizabeth to take action, though it was difficult to find an agreeable leader for an expedition to Ireland. Rumors arose that Ralegh was first offered the position of Lord Deputy of Ireland, but he had no interest in going. His interests lay in England at court, where he again stood in the queen's good graces, hoping to obtain more offices and to be raised to the peerage. After many months, Essex agreed to head an army if he received appointment as Lord Lieutenant of Ireland, which he obtained at the end of December. He arrived in Ireland in early April at the head of the largest English army in the Age of Elizabeth—16,000 footmen and 1,300 horsemen.[7] Instead of going to northern Ireland, as expected by the English government, Essex went to Munster, to the lands of Ralegh and his neighbors. Essex hoped to pursue and defeat the White Knight, who had fought on the English side in the early stages of the war but whose loyalty was repeatedly questioned, as was that of his ally Condon, Ralegh's neighbor who supplied trees for the lumber operation. The English government trusted the White Knight enough that he had been made Moyle's successor as Sheriff of County Cork in 1596. They understood that he, like Condon, needed to have his lands restored, but the White Knight's enemies had the ear of Essex and steered the general against him. When the White Knight destroyed his own castle and hid in the countryside, Essex was forced to look elsewhere for someone to attack.

Norris urged Essex to attack Conna, a castle near Mogeely of the Sugán Earl, an ally of Hugh O'Neill from Ulster. Essex needed beef and munitions, which were sent to him via the Blackwater River through Ralegh's lands to Fermoy. On June 13, the English marched for Fermoy. The army headed west, spending the night between Conna and Mogeely, "a castle which H. Pine holds of Sir Walter Rawleighe."[8] Essex met Pyne at Mogeely but did not tarry, and the next day led his troops toward Affane on Ralegh's land, through "a great pass by Lysfynnen, where the rebels threatened to take their leave of us, and to leave in our army some impression of their valor; but we saw not a man of them." Essex "had secretly placed 400 men in the bawn" (a defensive wall that circles an Irish tower house), hoping to surprise the rebels if they followed, but to no avail. At Affane, half the army forded the Blackwater at night—this could be done only for about an hour twice a day at low water—and the rest of the army followed the next morning.

After all these maneuvers, this crossing effectively ended Essex's campaign in the region. He had done little more than march through Ralegh's lands. He conferred with Norris about how many troops to leave to man the garrisons and recommended burning and spoiling anything that could not be protected by the garrisons to starve the rebels into submission. Essex departed for Waterford, which he soon left for Leinster and then Dublin. He remained in Ireland for three more months before returning to England against the queen's orders.

Before departing Waterford, Essex apparently had arranged a cease-fire in Munster, which the rebels disregarded by laying an ambush for Pyne when he went to resupply Lysfinny.[9] The ambush failed, but the rebels declared that anyone selling food to Mogeely would suffer pain of death. They cut down thousands of trees to create a five-mile-long fence, warning Pyne's men not to cross it. One of the Desmond leaders, John McRedmond, again offered to end the ambushes outside Mogeely if Pyne would cease supplying Lysfinny, "nor draw drafts upon them," referring to his enrolling local Irish in Mogeely's defense. In exchange he promised to warn Pyne "when any foreign forces should come into the country," which likely referred to Tyrone's men in the north of Ireland as well as the Spanish, who the English feared would assist the rebels. Pyne again refused and the rebel leaders plotted his assassination. An old soldier recently returned from Spain examined Pyne's fortifications at Mogeely and confirmed that they must starve the people out or use ordnance to win the day. Without cannon, the rebels captured Mogeely's livestock, attempted to prevent the farmers from planting their crops, and intimidated Irish from selling their food to Mogeely.

The rebels apparently failed. Norris reported that "Mogeely is in all respects better provided than any other castle in Ireland (kept for Her Majesty)." It could lodge over three hundred men and enjoyed a location that enabled it to protect the coastal settlements by bordering on hostile inland areas: it "may be the bridle and key of most of them." In sixteenth-century usage, *bridle* referred to a fortress that checks the enemy, so Ralegh's Mogeely provided a restraint on the rebels, keeping them from assaulting other areas.

Pyne was one of many confused by Essex's actions, especially given the strength of his forces. Pyne believed that Essex's departure had encouraged the rebels, hence their ambush during his resupply of Lysfinny. Pyne wrote Essex before the latter left for England, asking him to return. He assessed and summed up the Irish situation much as Ralegh would have—providing both the big picture and the important details, ranging from the prospects of Irish in the north joining forces with those in the south to the use of riverboats to transport supplies and the employment of Irish soldiers to man forts and conduct offensive operations. Pyne told Essex that all these things and more could be effected if he would just appear in person. Repeatedly, Pyne noted that the Irish needed to hear terms from Essex because no one else had his stature. Then Essex should issue a general pardon for the rebels and institute "a change of the Provincial Council or Magistrates." New men were needed, ones who could forget the wrongs of the past and begin a new era of peace.[10]

Sir Thomas Norris, president of Munster, was injured in a skirmish in late May and died in late August, a month before Essex returned to England. Ralegh's close friend and cousin Sir George Carew received appointment as president of Munster. The situation in the province appeared so dire to the English that Carew and his council reported to the Privy Council that none of the Irish leaders in Munster who alleged friendship with the English, including Patrick Condon, could be trusted, with the exception of Lord Barry, "the most of them having either their brothers, or next kinsmen in actual rebellion."[11] This assessment likely was accurate because Irish or Anglo-Irish had to maintain their ties with a wide swath of kinsmen and allies. Allegiance to the queen had to be balanced with allegiance to one's kin. The queen could not be counted on to guarantee justice.

Condon, for instance, had three Letters of Restoration ignored by the government in Ireland.[12] The inability of the English government to control its administration in Ireland, and by extension settle land disputes between Undertakers and those Anglo-Irish or Irish who owned the land rightfully under the English system, fanned hostilities. With the queen's sovereignty on shaky ground, Essex's desertion of his post—his inability to bring order to Ireland—negatively reflected on the queen. Essex's failure to understand the Irish situation and to act appropriately made things worse for all. Some historians believe that Essex was a friend to the Irish in the way he brought about an (alleged) ceasefire and refused to prosecute the war. As Elizabeth saw it, it was a surrender.

When Essex refused to take his forces north, the Irish in the north won two battles against English forces. In the south, Condon, the White Knight, and others were not necessarily discontented with English rule—they wanted justice and order. Once things did settle down, Condon, the White Knight, and other Anglo-Irish and Irish leaders in Munster returned to the English fold. Essex's actions in Ireland were not meant to uplift the dispossessed but resulted from his confusion over what could be done and how to do it. He lacked able advisors and was afraid to face Irish military power in the north. Though he retained his bravado, his confidence had been battered by his previous lack of military success and the berating of the queen. He hated taking orders from Elizabeth.

One of Elizabeth's especial grievances against Essex: she had warned him to confer knighthood only on men who had proved themselves in battle. From Cádiz to the Azores to Ireland, Essex indiscriminately created about half of the knights in England. One report to the English government from Ireland stated that Essex "never drew sword but to make knights."[13] He did so to create a power base from which to challenge the queen, Cecil, and Ralegh. Ralegh, it seems, took pleasure in reporting to the queen Essex's mass knighting in Ireland. But the deepest source of her anger was Essex abandoning Ireland against her express orders. He wasted England's foremost army on a senseless campaign that accomplished nothing—he had barely used it—and then had the gall to knight hundreds and claim victory! She would have to raise another army for Ireland, while dealing with Essex upon his return.

After only six months in Ireland, Essex reached England at the end of September 1599. He was charged not to leave his home and was almost immediately brought before the Privy Council and grilled for five hours. For abandoning Ireland and concluding a treaty with O'Neill, he was returned to house confinement. Over six months later, Essex was formally tried before a special commission, found guilty, deprived of his public positions, and returned to home confinement once again. He was permitted freedom by the end of summer, but the queen took away his monopoly on sweet wines, his major source of income. Essex and his followers blamed Cecil and Ralegh for his misfortune, though it was his own pride and failures that led to his fall from grace. Elizabeth had given him several chances to redeem himself, but his lack of humility before the Crown did him in.

Ralegh's star remained in ascension. He was "on call" as needed at court and by the queen. Ralegh and Cecil appear to have grown closer, which seemingly boded well for both of them. Cecil's son accompanied Ralegh to his Sherborne estate for vacation, and when the queen sent Cecil, to Cecil's dismay, on a diplomatic mission to France, Ralegh feted him with an elaborate going-away banquet and traveled with him to Dover to see him off. Cecil also lent Bridewell Palace to Ralegh, and the two frequently exchanged gifts. Ralegh also undertook a wide range of business for the queen, from being sent to the Netherlands on a mission to entertaining visiting ambassadors. Once he was assigned the task of giving the ambassador for the Archduke of Austria a personal tour of Westminster Abbey, "to see the tombs and singularities of that place." For several years, he pursued the post of Vice Chamberlain, which gave its bearer control of the court's accounts, but the queen eventually granted the post to another and instead rewarded Ralegh with the governorship of the Isle of Jersey in August 1600. Ralegh apparently received a hefty annual income as governor because part of his appointment included the stipulation that he pay another man who had vied for the position the yearly sum of £300. Ralegh's signal accomplishment as governor was rebuilding the island's fortifications.

Another marker of Ralegh's status with the queen occurred one night at dinner. Ralegh's good friend Lord Cobham, whose father had been the queen's chamberlain, the most important office in the queen's household, had the task of cutting the queen's meat. The queen would not eat meat cut by anyone: the person had to be high status and utterly trustworthy—monarchs worried about poisoning. Cobham wrenched his foot so badly that he could not make it to court, and Lady Kildare panicked that the meat would spoil. Fortunately for Lady Kildare, she was delighted to learn that Ralegh had just arrived at court because Ralegh performed well the "Carving of the Queens Meate."[14]

With Essex's fall from grace, his supporters suffered because he could no longer provide them with patronage. This left many discontented newly made knights in England. The distraught Essex fortified his estate, gathered his followers, and marched into London to force an audience with the queen. Declared a traitor (at Cecil's order), Essex retreated and was surrounded at his estate and forced to surrender. Ten days later he was tried for treason. A week after that he was beheaded at the Tower of London—the last person to be beheaded at the Tower. Allegedly, Essex did not bravely face his execution, nor did the axman perform well because it took three blows to completely sever the head. Rumors had it that Ralegh calmly smoked his pipe while watching the proceedings from a window, but he later denied that he gloated over Essex's death. Many of Essex's followers believed Ralegh responsible for the fall of Essex and held an abiding hatred for him. The rivalry was at an end, and yet it followed Ralegh into the next regime.

Soon after the execution, the Spanish again sought to undermine English power in Ireland. The new King of Spain, Philip III, sent six thousand men to County Cork with a great store of munitions for the rebels. Weather dispersed the fleet, but more than half landed at Kinsale, about forty miles southwest of Youghal; others landed at Baltimore, further southwest. In October 1601, Lord Mountjoy, who took control of English forces in Ireland, sieged the Spanish at Kinsale. Some Irish came from the north to support the Spanish, but the large army of Irish that the Spanish hoped for never arrived. The English navy hemmed in the Spanish, and by Christmas the Spanish and Irish troops took the fight to the English land forces. The Irish infantry proved no match for the English cavalry and were forced to flee. The Spanish, seeing their position as hopeless, surrendered. They were permitted to return to Spain with the other Spanish holed up along the coast. This was Spain's last significant attempt to help the Irish against England. Mountjoy's subsequent success in the north led to the surrender of the rebels shortly after Elizabeth's death in 1603. Many of the Irish leaders fled to Spain in the "Flight of the Earls," and the English initiated the Ulster Plantation's large-scale migration of English and Scottish Lowland Protestants to northern Ireland.

In Munster province, George Carew restored English authority. Carew and Pyne worked together to smooth ties with Irish and Anglo-Irish. Cecil and, to a lesser extent, Carew somewhat resented Pyne as an upstart, but both did what they could to help Pyne because he continued to be such a success on Ralegh's seignories. Even the queen sang Pyne's praises, rewarded him with more troops for stationing on Ralegh's seignories, and provided him funds for fortifications. The Irish and Anglo-Irish also praised Pyne. The Sugán Earl, after his capture by the White Knight, explained to Carew the "dislike of the Munster men against the English government." He cited differences in religion, the composition rent paid to support the garrisons, the "Undertakers en-croaching upon gentlemen's lands, the fears of English juries," which on scarce evidence condemned "Irishmen's lives," and the "general fear" that arose from the execution of leading men. But Henry Pyne he respected. Pyne met him after Essex's departure to convince him to lay down his arms, "so her Majesty would confirm unto him his earldom and lands." He claimed "he loved Henry Pyne exceeding well . . . and gave commandment to all his men not to harm him." At a second con-ference, Pyne again bade him to give up his arms and that he would return to him his corn, then stored at Mogeely.[15] If all English were like Pyne, and the Crown protected the Irish from injustice, then, the earl implied, the story of English colonialism would be very different.

Pyne remained in the good graces of many Irish and Anglo-Irish, but not with Sir Walter Ralegh. Ralegh and his partners Robert Bathurst and Veronio Martens and Pyne jointly owned Mogeely, including the castle, lands, tenements, and woods and a few adjoining parcels, and retained their "lawful interest for many years to come." Pyne, they al-leged, contrary to the covenants of their partnership had "raised great sums of money of the said works and lands" (the latter might refer to subleasing) "and gotten into his hands other sums" belonging to the partners amounting to £4,000 or more. The aggrieved partners insisted that Mogeely Castle was owned by all of them, but Pyne "doth con-vert the benefit of all the said works and lands to his own particular use." Pyne refused to provide accounts or to compensate Ralegh "for his woods felled and consumed." Dodge's estate, which Martens repre-sented, was in debt for bonds he had invested in the partnership, while "Martens is (by this occasion) brought to such distress as he is in some sort restrained of his liberty."[16]

The Privy Council ordered Carew to stop Pyne from shipping staves and to send him to England to settle the matter. Pyne did not reply to the charges until September 1601, probably because of the expected invasion of Ireland by Spain, which occurred that month. In a letter to Cecil, Pyne denied the charges against him, claiming Martens was the culprit who had "much wronged" Ralegh. Pyne had gone twice to England for long periods to "finish accounts," "which were delayed by the default in Martin and others in not rendering accounts." Pyne had requested the Lord President of Munster give warrants to two "agents and chief tenants" of Ralegh, "to examine the country and see if I offended" by cutting trees in his woods. Pyne said that the woods he used were his and that Ralegh "was in my debt for woods felled to the use of the company." Moreover, according to long-ago accounts made by Martens, Ralegh owed the company more than £1,000. On his last trip to England, Pyne reminded Ralegh of his debt and claimed he refused to pay because, Ralegh told Pyne, "he entered into a partnership to be a gainer and no loser." Pyne closed his defense by offering not to bother Cecil further in these "frivolous matters" while he had the Spanish to contend with. "These are times," he added, "for honest men," and he promised in a few days "to bring over an authentic testimonial of my well-doing."[17]

There is no record of how Pyne and his partners settled their financial differences. Ralegh was short of money, seemingly disinterested in Ireland, and adding responsibilities in England with his appointment as Governor of Jersey. He decided to sell his holdings in Ireland and be done with it. The sale of his Irish estates for relatively little—£1,500— shows how alienated from Munster and how needful of money he had become. Robert Cecil helped arrange the sale to Richard Boyle, an English bureaucrat in Ireland. Boyle made a fantastic financial success of the purchase. He followed Ralegh's lead and developed the iron and fishing industries, and pushed his weight around to control adjacent lands and build commercial networks, ultimately turning his attention to urban development. Boyle made great use of Ralegh's ties to the local Irish and Anglo-Irish, and even employed Henry Pyne, with whom he, too, fell into dispute. He ultimately bought out the claims of Pyne and other Ralegh colonists. Boyle became the richest man in Ireland by expanding Ralegh's projects.[18] He eventually received elevation to the peerage as the 1st Earl of Cork.

One might think that free of Ireland Raleigh would appear more often in the documentary record in England in 1602, but, in fact, that is the year for which there are the fewest traces of Ralegh since the late 1570s. It appears Ralegh focused his attention on developing his Sherborne estate, overseeing Jersey and the stannaries, and wrapping up the sale of his Irish lands—there was a lot of paperwork involved— with less interest in the affairs of state in London. That absence from

London hurt Ralegh. He played no role in the behind-the-scenes maneuvering taking place with James VI of Scotland to assume the English throne upon Elizabeth's death. This left Ralegh without ties to the next monarch.

Elizabeth refused to select or confirm a successor, though it was fairly clear that it would be her cousin James. There was understandable worry in England because, with no direct heir, civil war could occur with competing claimants to the throne. Elizabeth became listless in the new year and expectations grew that she would not be long for the world. She died March 24, 1603, at sixty-nine years of age.

—

ELIZABETH HAD REIGNED forty-four years. Ralegh marched in the funeral procession at the head of the queen's Guard. In May, the new king, crowned James I of England, chose a new Captain of the Guard, "whereunto in verie humble manner [Ralegh] did submit himself."[19] Ralegh also expected to lose his main source of income, the monopoly licensing the sale of wine. James made it clear he had no need for Ralegh's services. He eyed Ralegh suspiciously. When the two finally had opportunity to talk, Ralegh spoke of the desirability of pushing aggressively against Spain; Ralegh seems not to have realized that James was intent on ending the long Anglo-Spanish War.[20]

James's dislike of Ralegh might have stemmed from the fall of Essex, whose supporters whispered in the new king's ear that Ralegh was behind his fall. But it also likely resulted from Ralegh's reputation for unorthodox theology and thinking. Certainly, Ralegh represented Elizabethan England, and James expected everyone to move on from the past and respect him as the monarch. Instinctually, these two could not see eye-to-eye. They were temperamentally and intellectually polar opposites. Ralegh perceived the unseen universe as full of wonder, whereas James perceived it as full of danger and the place where the devil lurked. Ralegh was a pragmatic intellectual; James earned fame as "the wisest fool in Christendom."[21] Ralegh explored new worlds, while James was a pedant. Ralegh famously was associated with tobacco, which he delighted in smoking, while James wrote a treatise against the "stinking weed." Ralegh possessed a masculine and commanding presence, while James was viewed as dour and his masculinity was questioned. Historians have long suspected that Robert Cecil lay behind Ralegh's exclusion from the king's favor. Cecil had played a key role in smoothing the transition from Elizabeth to James. He likely recognized the king's hostility to Ralegh, though James and Ralegh had not met before James's arrival in England. Ralegh's personality, his larger-than-life persona, and his Hermeticism and lack of orthodoxy all combined to make him the perfect candidate for sacrifice on the funeral pyre of Elizabethan England.

In June 1603, word arose of a treasonous plot to kidnap James and force him to allow religious tolerance in the kingdom. The accused were both Catholics and Puritans, though the conspiracy is usually associated with Catholics because of the involvement of secular priests. Two Jesuit priests exposed the plot to the English government. The conspiracy itself lacked detail, and perhaps any real plan beyond talk. One of the conspirators was Sir George Brooke, younger brother of Ralegh's good friend Henry Brooke, Lord Cobham. His conspiracy is often called the Bye Plot because it was seen at the time as an offshoot of a greater conspiracy, the Main Plot, whose only association was that the Brookes were brothers and that the killing of James would lead to religious tolerance for Catholics. The Main Plot allegedly was a scheme hatched by Cobham and Ralegh to replace James on the throne with Lady Arbella Stuart.

The Main Plot encompassed Cobham meeting in England the ambassador of the Archduke of Austria, who would give him 600,000 crowns to fund the treason. Cobham would then visit Spain to procure Philip III's assistance, and he would convince Lady Arbella, a claimant to the throne, to write letters promising toleration of Catholics. She also would agree to a marriage arranged by Austria, Spain, and the Duke of Savoy. Cobham would carry the 600,000 crowns to Jersey to Ralegh, who would distribute much of the money to the discontented and keep 8,000 crowns for himself. It was a far-fetched plot, but it gave Ralegh's enemies a way to show their diligence in guarding the king against threats to his throne.

The trial took place November 7, 1603, in Winchester—the plague had struck London, which had forced a change in venue. A variety of justices sat as a commission over the proceedings and were joined by several important personages, including Robert Cecil, recently raised to the peerage by His Majesty. A king's sergeant, analogous to an attorney general, represented the king's interests, but most of the case was prosecuted by Sir Edward Coke, England's attorney general, who was actively supported by the Lord Chief Justice of England, Sir John Popham. Many years later, Coke's *Institute of the Lawes of England* and his *Law Reports* became foundational for the study and practice of English law. Coke also enjoyed a long career as chief justice, first of Common Pleas, and then of the King's Bench, and he also served as Speaker of the House of Commons. Popham, too, held office as Speaker of the House and attorney general. The trial pitted the leading jurists of England against Ralegh, who was denied the right to legal counsel. Many attended the trial, and some paid handsomely to do so.

Today the trial is still studied in law schools as an example of a treason case conducted entirely on hearsay evidence. Numerous transcripts of the proceedings survive in handwritten and published form. The prosecution portrayed Ralegh as the instigator of the Main Plot, who cunningly enlisted Cobham to do all the work. No other Englishman was connected to the conspiracy, presumably because it was snuffed out at such an early stage. The plotters' intent, according to the melodramatic rendering by the king's sergeant at law, was to kill King James and his "cubs." Ralegh pleaded not guilty.[22]

Coke held the lead role through most of the first half of the trial, beginning with a long-winded history of treason, of which he would prove Ralegh "the notoriest Traitor that ever came to the bar." The folly of asserting this as the worst example of treason in history is that if there was a plot, according to the government's own case, it never reached beyond discussion with the ambassador, whereas treasons existed that resulted in the murder of monarchs and the overthrow of governments.

Ralegh not only was denied legal counsel but also was prohibited from examining the only witness of his treason, Cobham. The witness never appeared in court. Ralegh protested that both the law and the Bible supported his right to cross-examine his accuser. The prosecution's response, supported by some of the justices, was that the accuser did not need to be brought to court in a treason trial. The justices argued that the charge of treason allowed them to disregard normal legal procedures and the rights of the accused. Ralegh repeatedly offered that if they brought Cobham to court and he asserted before everyone that Ralegh was a party to treason, then Ralegh would accept the charges against him and they would be done. Feeling harassed by Ralegh's repetition of this proposal, Lord Chief Justice Popham finally stated that he could not let Cobham appear because "then a number of Treasons should flourish." But there was no one else associated with the plot and no tentacles to spread. Popham feared that if Cobham testified in court, he might withdraw the accusation.

Ralegh also demanded the release of his friend Lawrence Kemys, who was held in prison for eighteen weeks for interrogation with nothing obtained from him. Ralegh complained that Kemys had been threatened with the "rack"—the infamous torture device. The Earl of Suffolk, one of the commissioners, stated that the king had pronounced that no torture should be used on Kemys. Ralegh asked why, then, was "the Keeper of the Rack sent for, and he threatened with it?" One of the other commissioners of the trial happened to be the Keeper of the Rack. Sir William Waad defended himself: "We told him he deserved the Rack, but did not threaten him with it," which indeed amounted to a threat.

Ralegh's main defense was that he could not be convicted of treason without two witnesses, citing the rule of law and biblical precedent. He asked again and again to be shown any evidence—a single shred—that proved his treason. Coke and Popham replied that Ralegh was so cunning that he purposefully did not tell anyone besides Cobham of the treason, so, if caught, there would not exist two witnesses. In court, "Cunning," "wit," and "Machiavellian" were repeatedly used to describe Ralegh's defense. Ralegh's use of words to defeat the arguments of the two foremost jurists in England frustrated them into an anger that scandalized observers. Ralegh ran rings around their arguments with simple replies that everyone could understand. Tiring of Coke's reference to Ralegh's "cunning," the defendant cogently observed of the prosecution, "Every thing that doth make for me is cunning, and every thing that maketh against me is probable."

Toward the end of the trial, Sargent Philips repeated the charges against Ralegh, and then Coke repeated the same hearsay evidence, adding in name-calling and personal attacks, including describing Ralegh as a "Spider of Hell." The defendant countered, "False repetition and mistakings must not mar my cause," and the "circumstance" the attorney described was not evidence. Even the court recorder made special note in the transcripts that Coke repeated his (empty) arguments. Cecil interrupted Coke's harangue, telling him to let Ralegh speak. The transcription reads:

> *Note*, Here Mr. Attorney sat down in a chase, and would speak no more, until the commissioners urged and intreated him. After much ado, he went out, and made a long repetition of all the Evidence, for the direction of the Jury; and at the repeating of some things sir Walter Raleigh interrupted him, and said he did him wrong.

> *Att*. Thou art the most vile and excorable Traitor that ever lived.

Raleigh. You speak indiscreetly, barbarously and uncivilly.

Att. I want words sufficient to express thy viperous Treasons.

Raleigh. I think you want words indeed for you have spoken one thing half a dozen times.

Att. Thou art an odious fellow, thy name is hateful to all the realm of England for thy pride.

Coke then produced a letter from Cobham stating that Ralegh agreed to accept a £1,500 per year pension from the Spanish to promote peace between England and Spain. Ralegh denied the charge, and Coke called him a "damnable atheist." Ralegh produced his own letter from Cobham saying, "I know no Treason by you." This created "much ado" in the court. The attorney retorted this was but a product of Ralegh's cunning, though he could not deny the letter was from Cobham. It did not matter: the jury departed and returned in fifteen minutes with a verdict of guilty.[23]

Many years later, a descendant of Sir Dudley Carleton produced a letter written soon after the trial by his ancestor to John Chamberlain. Carleton was with King James when he received news of the verdict. Carleton discussed the two men who delivered the news. The first "affirmed" Ralegh's performance at the trial, "that never any man spoke so well in times past, nor would do in the world to come"; the other, a Scot, said when he first saw Ralegh at the trial he "was so led with the common hatred" that he "would have gone a hundred miles to have seen him hanged." After Ralegh spoke, he would "have gone a thousand to have saved his life . . . never was man so hated, and so popular, in so short a time."[24]

Before passing judgment, Popham spoke at length of Ralegh's character. He lamented that he "thought it impossible that one of so great parts should have fallen so grievously." Ralegh could have served his king. In reference to Ralegh as an upstart, Popham lectured, "It is best for man not to seek to climb too high, lest he fall: nor yet to creep too low, lest he be trodden on." Popham claimed not to know why Ralegh had become so "discontented" as to commit treason. He had an income of £3,000 per year, and even if he "had been down, you know fortune's wheel, when it is turned about, riseth again." Ralegh was known as a "wise man" and had "shewed wit enough this day." The king had only deprived him of being Captain of the Guard. If the king took away his income from the wine license monopoly, it would have been for the public good. Popham thought Ralegh guilty of two vices: "an eager ambition" and "corrupt covetousness." The eager ambition Popham described as Ralegh's impatience to achieve the "grace and favour" under James that he enjoyed under Elizabeth. The covetousness was his willingness to become a spy in the pay of Spain. Ralegh had not, in fact, become a spy for Spain, though he might have considered it. Five or six of the august commissioners at his trial, including Cecil, were, or soon would be, accepting secret pensions from foreign governments—an ordinary feature of European diplomacy.

Popham repeated the hearsay: "You have been taxed by the world, with the Defence of the most heathenish and blasphemous Opinions," which he would not repeat so as not to offend Christian ears. He lectured Ralegh to not "let any devil persuade you to think there is no eternity in Heaven." Popham recalled how when Essex was to be executed, "he confessed his offences and obtained mercy of the Lord; for I am verily persuaded in my heart, he died a worthy servant of God. Your conceit of not confessing any thing, is very inhuman and wicked."

Popham passed judgment that Ralegh should be executed by hanging after being drawn through the streets but "cut down before death" so his body could be "opened, your heart and bowels plucked out, and your privy members cut off, and thrown into the fire before your eyes." This would be followed by beheading, and then the quartering of his body to be "disposed at the king's pleasure."[25]

Cobham was scheduled to die with the conspirators from the Bye Plot. Brought forward for execution, Cobham claimed that all that happened resulted from Lady Arbella seeking "his friendship," and his brother seeking hers. He painted the whole affair as a flirtation that swirled out of control, and the intrigue, he intimated, merely a game played in his mind. Then he blamed Ralegh, though it is unclear why if he had just invented the whole thing. According to Carleton, Cobham bravely faced death, "craved pardon," and received it. His brother was not so fortunate. When the executioner held up George's severed head and cried "God save the King," no one but the sheriff seconded the cry. This would have been unnerving for King James—the public seemed against him. Had he miscalculated?[26]

When the bishop of Winchester met with Ralegh, he refused to confess to the treason. The bishop found Ralegh "well settled, and resolved to die a Christian and a good Protestant." He "would yield to no part of Cobham's accusation," only that Cobham had "once mentioned, but never proceeded on" the Spanish pension.[27] On the day of execution, Ralegh was not called forth. It is possible that James determined there was no guilt, but, more likely, he did not want to make a martyr of Ralegh.

Ralegh and Cobham were both confined to the Tower of London. It would be a long imprisonment. But Ralegh was not confined to his room. Daily he would walk on the Tower walls and wave to the crowds, which grew to such numbers as to have Ralegh barred from making this public spectacle. Overnight, he had become a popular figure in England, and when the people grew discontented with their king and the new era of Stuart rule, and when they fondly looked back to Elizabeth and the dashing figures who had challenged Spain, they celebrated the king's prisoner Ralegh as the last of her generation, who carried the spirit of Elizabeth.

CHAPTER 29

The Great Cordial

By 1605, Ralegh had built a laboratory in the Tower of London. The Keeper of the Rack, Sir William Waad (also known as Wade), the Lieutenant of the Tower (and its highest-ranking official), rued that Ralegh had turned a "hen house" in the garden into a "still-house." Waad complained to Robert Cecil that this was "the only garden the lieutenant hath."

Waad and Ralegh held each other in mutual contempt, a personality clash magnified by the circumstances of their relationship. Though Ralegh was not tortured, Waad had been one of the investigators of the Main and Bye Plots, and thus played a role in Ralegh's incarceration. Now he was Ralegh's jailer. Ralegh's insults irked him. Shortly after Waad's appointment to oversee the prison, Ralegh "used some speech of his dislike of me." Ralegh apologized. But Waad could do nothing about Ralegh's privileges.

Several on the list of people allowed to visit him, including his servants and his wife and son, could stay the night. The extent of a prisoner's visiting privileges related to their class and other markers of status. An earl was allowed more servants than a baron. Ralegh was not allowed as many visitors as an earl because he was only a knight, but his status as Elizabeth's favorite carried into the Tower and was improved by additional circumstances of reputation and patronage. Waad learned that a garden door at the Tower had to be left open for Ralegh to access his laboratory, "where he doth spend his time all the day in distillations."[1] The lab consisted of a "furnace, with still [an apparatus heated to distill liquids and gases], retort [a container that is heated], and receiver [a tank or reservoir for holding liquids or gases]." Ralegh's connections at court ensured that his laboratory work proceeded unimpeded.

Ralegh's new patroness, whose influence at court carried into the Tower of London, was none other than Anne of Denmark, Queen of England. Anne had suffered from a disease that her physicians believed incurable; Ralegh stepped in and provided the cure. The queen sang Ralegh's praises at court, and he earned fame in England and other parts of Europe.

There were limitations on Queen Anne's power. She tenaciously fought with King James to bring their son Henry to England, whereas James insisted the prince remain in Scotland. Eventually, she prevailed. Behind the scenes, she lobbied for Ralegh's release from prison, at one point convincing Cecil and others to re-interview Cobham about his testimony against Ralegh. The story might be apocryphal. Published in 1651, but written earlier, the author asserted that Cobham claimed that his confession had not implicated Ralegh, but Waad afterward had added words to the signed confession insinuating Ralegh's guilt. (Recall how at his trial Ralegh was not permitted to examine Cobham.) The august committee that interrogated Cobham at Anne's request then kept secret what they had learned about the forged portions of Cobham's confession.[2] It is possible that the story is substantively true because Ralegh was restrained for a few days in the Tower when he refused to cease declaiming that Cobham had recanted his accusation.

As difficult as imprisonment was for Ralegh, this period of his life was characterized by incredible productivity—even triumph. He wrote a variety of tracts, authored a widely celebrated book, and became the most famous producer of medicines in England. All this activity influenced the development of pharmacology and modern chemistry, while epitomizing Hermetic thought on how America and empire fit into human history. From prison, Ralegh became one of the most important intellectuals of the English Renaissance.

—

WE KNOW LITTLE of Ralegh's early career in medicine but enough to trace the foundation for his practice. As early as 1592, over twenty years before supplying remedies for Anne, he had sent to the Countess of Shrewsbury two medicines of pearl and coral, staple ingredients in the alchemist's dispensary.[3] (Coral today has been praised for its potential to be one of "the medicine cabinets of the twenty-first century.")[4] Almost a decade earlier, before Ralegh sent the first expedition to Roanoke, John Hester dedicated his medical treatise *114 Experiments and Cures* to Ralegh.[5] Though a dedication does not prove that Ralegh was creating medicines at the time of publication, it does imply his interest. Hester claimed his book to be a translation of Paracelsus (1493/94–1541), the famed Swiss Hermeticist and physician who became highly influential for his use of mineral chemicals in medicine. His work led him to become the founder of the study of toxicology, for it assessed the degrees to which minerals could be poisonous or beneficial depending on their dosage. Paracelsus's teachings challenged medical orthodoxy on a number of fronts, but what likely made his work so attractive to Ralegh and other like-minded practitioners in the coming centuries was his natural philosophy: his emphasis on the harmony of man with nature, which included the healing power of crystals and other minerals and the experiential nature of scientific inquiry.

As noted earlier, Ralegh's brothers, Humphrey and Adrian Gilbert, were deeply interested in alchemy, and Adrian, in particular, was renowned for his work in the laboratory. Numerous records exist of Ralegh buying and selling ingredients for his medicines, including with his fellow Hermeticist and alchemist Henry Percy, 9th Earl of Northumberland, who spent years in the Tower of London conducting laboratory work at the same time Ralegh did. They carried over from freedom to imprisonment the study of chemicals and their friendship.

The medicines Ralegh produced were called cordials. *Cordial*, according to the *Oxford English Dictionary*, meant "of or belonging to the heart" and evolved to refer to a restorative beverage. Ralegh experimented with and produced many cordials. Numerous English archives, large and small, contain Ralegh's "recipes," the word for the list of ingredients in a medicine. The production of cordials brought Ralegh fame in his lifetime, but the recipes perpetuated his fame for centuries. Homeopathic remedies that included Ralegh's cordials were celebrated and used in the United States into the early twentieth century.

John Morgan Richard's 1888 overview of English medicine in Britain pronounced "that no medicine became so famous as Ralegh's 'Great Cordial.'"[6] This cordial was "everywhere regarded as the panacea for all diseases, and a large number of well-authenticated cures were really effected by its use."[7] The Great Cordial's association with royalty fueled its fame. Both Queen Anne and her son, Prince Henry, famously used the Great Cordial produced by Ralegh's own hands.

Almost a century later, England's Dutch monarch, William III, took the cordial as he neared death in 1702, and its usage was reported in the newspapers and elsewhere. Adding to the cordial's credibility was the publication of Nicaise Le Fèvre's *A Discourse upon Sr Walter Rawleigh's Great Cordial* (1664).

Le Fèvre was Royal Professor of Chemistry and Apothecary and conducted his experiments on the Great Cordial in the royal laboratory at the order of King Charles II. He possessed multiple copies of Ralegh's recipe, each with a slight variation, and noted in his text when subsequent generations made additions or changes. He analyzed not only the ingredients but also how Ralegh designed the processes to construct the cordial's many constituent parts, and then the blending of all together. It would be difficult to find a book so fawning in its praise of the genius of the inventor and his invention. A chemist, Hermeticist, and a follower of Paracelsus, Le Fèvre gushed that Ralegh was "the most worthily famous amongst the Moderns, by gathering together that which Nature furnishes" to produce the best of all cordials. It required of its inventor "so much Art and so much Experience" and "doth immortalize him," who attained "the sublime Knowledge . . . in this Incomparable Remedy."[8] Ralegh skillfully chose ingredients "above all those" who previously made cordials. But what he did with the ingredients shows "how much Art helps Nature."

Le Fèvre divided the three types of ingredients, as Paracelsus did, into animal, vegetable, and mineral. Only ambergris Le Fèvre could not place into one of the three categories because this material greatly changed under varying conditions, but there was no doubt to Ralegh or to Le Fèvre of its importance as one of the Great Cordial's "principal ingredients." Ambergris strengthened both "the Heart and the Brains" and could "recall, reestablish and augment the vital and animal spirits." Another ingredient notable for its inclusion was pearl, known to "rejoyce the Spirits, augment courage; resist Poisons, the Plague, and the corruptions of the Humors." Pearls must have been expensive, like ambergris, and so, too, was gold in its "purest" form. All these ingredients required transformation through chemical processes that took great skill, experience, and time.

Le Fèvre's analysis of Ralegh's processes took months. The processes Ralegh used were complicated, as indicated by a discussion of transforming gold. Gold had to be dissolved into a brown powder without a corrosive, a transformation initiated "by a simple digestion"— "simple" refers to a vegetative substance—and then lightly boiled "in a glass body in sand" with no "grain undissolved." The resin, called "Cro-cus of Gold," was divided and one part was precipitated with wine; the substance turned green and the gold moved "it self to the bottom of the vessel, into a brown Pouder." The powder was then improved by "several reiterated lotions" till it lost all flavor. Then it was placed for three days "in tartarized Spirit of Wine," in a gentle heat of Mary's bath—a dou-ble boiler—and then "must be kept during three days in Rose & Cin-namon-water," before it is filtered and dried. The liquid that remains is evaporated, the salts dried, further processed, and added to other spir-its, heated, dissolved, poured over new spirits in Mary's bath . . . creat-ing the "vitriolic Salt of the Gold." Those who use this "rare Remedy, have always seen and taken notice of its most surprising effects." Some-times it induces stools, sometimes vomiting, and sometimes neither, "but powerfully provokes Urines and Sweats; and most commonly no sensible operation at all." Its virtue lay in "augmenting the strength of the sick." All of this effort to prepare the gold represented but one of many processes that Le Fèvre described as Ralegh's method for produc-ing the Great Cordial. In documenting the care and forethought Ralegh applied to get things just right, Le Fèvre emphasized the contrast with those who used expensive ingredients just to make their cordials more expensive, but without the proper processing.

Le Fèvre's conclusions were glowing. He asserted that the Great Cordial "is absolutely necessary to the Maritime and Northerly Na-tions, and especially to the inhabitants of Islands" like the British Isles. The winds that strike the northern islands "agitate the Air in so many different manners" that it interferes with the "Heat of the Sun," hinders the "production of Vegetables," adversely affects animals and humans, and prevents the production of wine and "the ripening of Fruits." This cold, moist air promotes numerous ailments and diseases. "To combat all these evils . . . to preserve the Health of those that en-joy it, and to correct and re-establish the Health of those which do but linger and languish . . . the Great Cordial is wholly necessary." He recommended it for a huge array of diseases, from plague to consump-tion, and chronic ailments both pulmonary and digestive. The Great Cordial would ease childbirth, dissipate sleep disorders, combat poi-sons, heal epilepsy, end melancholy, fight venereal disease, and so on. As Le Fèvre and others described it, the Great Cordial was a panacea for all ailments and diseases. Ralegh had created a "remedy" to "all the defects." It is "powerful enough to seek out the Evil to the very centre of the Bloud and Spirits in which life doth reside."

So favorable was Le Fèvre's account that it sparked discussion of the government distributing Ralegh's Great Cordial the next time plague struck London. There is no record of government distribution—it would have been a huge and expensive undertaking. Just two years after Le Fèvre's publication, in 1666, a great outbreak of plague did strike London and people who could afford the Great Cordial reported that they did not succumb to the disease.[9] Because that was the last great outbreak of plague in England, no further experiments occurred to test the efficacy of the Great Cordial on that particular disease.

The curative power of the Great Cordial, real or not, was the product of its inventor's diligence, creative energies, and practical skills assessing and manipulating physical substances. The process involved the attempt to bridge the seen and the unseen. The "seen" was the Great Cordial and all that went into it. The seen also comprised some of the physical manifestations of illness. Ralegh believed that humans could know aspects of the unseen, in this case, the illnesses that debilitated, that arose (usually) from sources unknown and unseen. He and other Hermeticists imagined in the human body an *Archeus*, a portion of the spiritual world that lies closest to the material world, as a bridge or portal between the two. Disease or poison—the "Evil"—attacked life at the Archeus. If disease or poison prevailed, the material—the body—ceased to function and the soul moved through the Archeus, which had protected human life, into the spiritual realm.

The Renaissance scientist experimented, deduced, measured, and assessed the physical world in numbers of ways, then had faith and hope that the seen (the medicine) worked on the unseen (the internal body) to eliminate the poisons that threatened life. Contrary to many later generations that saw the spiritual and the material as separate, Ralegh, Le Fèvre, and others lived in a world where not only were the two connected, but portals existed, like the Archeus, marking the transition between life and death, but with the purpose of maintaining the living. Thus, one imbibed Ralegh's Great Cordial, which was envisioned as flowing to the Archeus to fight the disease or poison that entered the body. But it also could be prophylactic, taken to encourage the Archeus to protect the body from disease or debilitation from age.

Many hoped that human life could be extended to hundreds of years, as exemplified in the Old Testament. The long lives of the Old Testament patriarchs were not considered miracles, like the resurrection of Christ. Instead, the long lives seemed ubiquitous, obtainable, if people could find ways to fight disease and aging.[10] Ralegh's obsessive discussion of the ages of Old Testament patriarchs in his *History of the World* is testimony to his and others' belief that people could again enjoy extended lifetimes. Though Ralegh emphasized other factors to extend life, such as moderation in diet, there is no doubt that he, like many other seventeenth-century Europeans, thought that through careful analysis of physical substances, a cordial could be created to prevent people from being unnecessarily hurried through the Archeus to the spiritual realm. Eventually, there would be many more people like the Countess of Desmond, whose story Ralegh popularized in his *History of the World*, to illustrate that living to 140 years of age was more than possible—it had been accomplished in his lifetime.

Ralegh did not live to age 140, but his invention of the Great Cordial brought him centuries of fame after his death. His legacy in medicine and science can be seen in more subtle and, perhaps, more lasting ways when we examine the connection between him and Robert Boyle, for Ralegh's pursuit of medicine and science, and their relation to American colonialism, was passed on to Boyle. Ralegh and Boyle believed to an almost identical degree in the importance of the unseen universe, a worldview held by many Renaissance scientists, along with the belief that employing a scientific methodology to uncover the nature of the material universe would bring men closer to God. Both Ralegh and Boyle also believed that America held a special place in God's Creation.

Robert Boyle is known today for his work on gases, which resulted in the development of Boyle's law. He also earned renown for his writings on chemistry and natural philosophy, his inventions, his analysis of metals and crystals, and, particularly, his development of systematic methods to conduct chemical experiments, which has earned him consideration by many as the "father of modern chemistry." He was born in 1627 at Lismore Castle—Ralegh's castle—in Munster province, on estates Robert's father Richard had purchased from Ralegh in 1602. Robert Boyle never met Ralegh because he was born almost a decade after Ralegh's death, but Ralegh had significant impact on his life. As an alchemist, he helped overturn the same law that Humphrey Gilbert tried to sidestep in the establishment of the academy—the law against multiplication, the alchemical transformation of base metals into gold and silver. As a devout Christian, Boyle wrote numerous religious tracts. As a natural philosopher, he remained firm in his belief that the study of nature would reveal God's truths. He avidly contributed to missionary societies, financed the publication of a Bible in the Irish language, and tried to prove that the resurrection of the body was physically possible.

It is easy to see connections between Boyle and Ralegh—their lives at Lismore, their connection to Richard Boyle, their devotion to the laboratory and study of the nature of material things, their subscription to a worldview in which the discovery of nature's laws would bring one closer to God. The ties between them were not just parallels, or coincidences, they involved more palpable linkages. They shared an interest in America and in crystals, and in a specific American crystal, which Ralegh almost certainly obtained during his sojourn in Guiana in 1595.

Boyle described his connection to Ralegh in his extended essay "Some Considerations Touching the Usefulness of Experimental Natural Philosophy."[11] In the essay, Boyle explored "the virtues of American drugs," but his most effusive expressions he reserved for American minerals used for curing, and, in particular, "the admirable properties, not only in diseases, but even in wounds, of a certain mineral" that he had carefully examined but still could not readily identify as to "what species of stones" it belonged. This stone, which he first encountered as a child, "you cannot but have heard mentioned with wonder, under the name of Sir *Walter Raleigh's* stone, which my father . . . enjoyed, and did strange things with for many years."[12] In his will, Richard bequeathed the stone, "(as the highest legacy he could leave him), to his dearest friend, the most learned and famous, Bishop Ussher, Primate of Ireland." Richard Boyle, at the time of his death was the Earl of Cork and the richest man in Ireland. He died in 1643 when Robert was sixteen years old, and indeed he left this most precious of "jewels" to the bishop, though his will made no mention of its special character. The terms of Richard's will provided that the bishop could wear it during his lifetime, and then it would return to Boyle's heir. Robert Boyle never described what it looked like. He referred to it as if everyone would know the fame of Sir Walter Raleigh's stone. No matter how valuable the jewel because of its size and beauty, its greatest value, according to Robert Boyle, lay in its remarkable medicinal qualities.

Boyle specifically noted that the bishop would "wear" the stone, which meant it offered protection to whoever wore it. Its "admirable properties" extended to curing diseases, healing wounds, and providing antidotes to poisons. Boyle explained that special crystals like Ralegh's stone were placed in liquids to create curative beverages. Ralegh's stone, then, was a panacea, a wonder drug. That Boyle could not identify what kind of stone it was adds to the mystery because Boyle was one of the world's foremost scientific experts on stones, crystals, and jewels. Despite Boyle's ignorance of what it was and how it worked, its curative properties could not be overlooked. How the stone healed was the unseen. As Boyle aged, he increasingly devoted himself to spiritual matters, to the unseen, but he never lost his interest in the laboratory, issues of health, and the Archeus: the bridge between the physical and spiritual worlds. Boyle did not possess the Ralegh stone; after Bishop Ussher died it may have gone to one of Robert's five older brothers.

Robert Boyle turned his attention to Ralegh's Great Cordial. He recounted the example of a man kicked by a horse who subsequently suffered gangrene and whose condition grew "so desperate" that the physician and surgeon gave up on him for lost. The fellow looked elsewhere for help. "A large dose of Sir Walter Ralegh's cordial" saved the man's life by ridding him of his fever and delusion and restored "the limb . . . to its former soundness."[13] Boyle obtained the cordial recipe from Ralegh's son. Even if people did not know how it worked, experience, he asserted, showed that it did. The scientist must trust results even when he could not uncover the process. Boyle recounted another case where "skillful physicians" gave up on a patient, a renowned knight of almost seventy years of age, "long conflicted with a tedious ague, and fever." When given Ralegh's Great Cordial, "he neither was sensible . . . nor had known what he did, or what was done to him."[14] The knight enjoyed "a perfect recovery." John Aubrey, an English natural philosopher and writer, in referring to Ralegh's Great Cordial, recorded that "Mr. Robert Boyle haz the recipe, and makes it and does great cures by it."[15]

To Robert Boyle, Ralegh represented the Renaissance intellectual who pursued science through the laboratory, devoted himself to healing, and respected and attempted to reveal the unseen forces at work in the universe—the natural philosopher. Over a half century after Ralegh's death, Boyle, too, shared Ralegh's understanding that America existed, in part, to provide things the Old World needed to improve life, and that it possessed answers that the Old World needed to know about the unseen world. Boyle liked to make lists, and on one he included "two discoveries, trivial enough," that had altered the world. One was "the inclination of the needle, touched by the loadstone, to point toward the pole"—the invention of the compass. Without this, "those vast regions of *America*, and all the treasures of gold, silver, and precious stones, and much more precious simples"—medicinal plants—"they send us, would have probably continued undetected." Boyle did not devalue the precious metals and jewels and gemstones from America, but he knew that the medicinal plants were "much more precious." The second discovery, "but a casual discovery," was "the supposed antipathy between salt-petre, and brimstone." This led "to the invention of gunpowder, [which] hath quite altered the condition of martial affairs over the world by sea and land." Both inventions were of stupendous consequences, but, like Ralegh, Boyle turned to "Theological inquiries" and "natural philosophy" for answers to his speculations about the relative importance of empire. Which was more important, the compass or gunpowder? Boyle averred that physiology—by which he meant the physical and spiritual condition of the individual—exceeded all. Gunpowder had made possible "those great transactions, which make such a noise in the world, and establish monarchies or ruin empires, [but] reach not so many persons with their influence, as do the theories of physiology."[16]

Even if all of Boyle's and Ralegh's overlapping interests were purely coincidental, which they were not, their similar approaches to science, health, spirituality, and the physical realm and their mutual interest in natural philosophy and the seen and unseen worlds show that England had not changed so drastically from the Age of Elizabeth (1558–1603) to the Restoration (1660–1688). Boyle's and Ralegh's understandings of the universe were alike because they started from the same precepts and sensibilities and expected to end up in the same place: possessing a greater understanding of God's Creation.[17] One hundred years later, in the midst of the Enlightenment, Bacon, Ralegh, Boyle, and Shakespeare would not have recognized that "brave new world, That has such people in't!" For the intellectuals of Tudor and Stuart England, the wonders of discovering the unseen had been exchanged for an Enlightenment quest to *control* the physical world. The Swedish botanist Carl Linnaeus fed an extraordinary hunger to sort and to classify, whereby men might assert their mastery over living things. Intellectuals and many of the common folk, too, moved away from the unseen, eschewing faith in the unknown and the unknowable, which was blamed for causing the English Civil War, witchcraft hunts, and resistance to the notion that the Age of Miracles had ended with the last page of the Bible. Religion, for many, became a remnant of the past, a moral system to be maintained to keep the common people in line. The Enlightenment set aside imagination as quaint and fanciful.[18]

The Hermeticism and alchemy of Ralegh, Bruno, Boyle, Newton, and others have been explained as the hobbies or delusions of these men of science who had yet to become entirely modern. Their non-rational interests could not possibly have influenced their scientific work. Shakespeare's Hermeticism, too, was regularly dismissed, and still is dismissed, though it pervades his plays and poetry. There was no room in the rationalism of the Enlightenment for an unseen world. The physical and reason dominated the thought processes of intellectuals. And well they might. The phenomenal growth in the international trade in African slaves and the vast imperial wars fought on multiple continents and the crescendo of challenges to social hierarchies—all led to the belittlement of the unseen as a poor place to begin to imagine how to fix a world in desperate need of fixing. The concept of utopia survived as the idea of an orderly society without poverty, but instead of Spenser's medieval-style villages, where neighbors kept an eye on one another, new generations sought to remake not individual communities but society entirely.

CHAPTER 30

Prince Henry

S ometime around 1607–1608, it is believed that Queen Anne brought Prince Henry to the Tower to meet Ralegh. Though we do not know how many times they may have met, what we do know for certain is that Henry and Ralegh had contact with one another while Ralegh was imprisoned. Born in 1594, the eldest son and heir of King James, Prince Henry appears to have been quite taken with Ralegh as a great adventurer and warrior. In 1607, the thirteen-year old Henry invested in the colonization of Virginia with nephews of Ralegh and maintained active interest in America. Ralegh penned papers for the prince on statecraft, diplomacy, royal marriages, shipbuilding, and the navy. Some of these were published or circulated at court. In essence, Ralegh provided Henry lessons on kingship, both theoretical and practical.

Henry developed a huge entourage and was extremely popular in England. Athletic, handsome, bright, and charismatic, he had broad and entwined interests that led him to appreciate art, architecture, science, the military, and other areas of human expression, application, and inquiry, showing him to be a child of the Renaissance. Many envisioned him as a future monarch who would lead England to greatness. He looked upon his father's policies with suspicion at times. "No one but my father," Henry said of Ralegh's imprisonment, "would keep such a bird in a cage." When Ralegh wrote against a proposed marriage between Henry and the Duke of Savoy's daughter, Prince Henry rejected the marriage and then requested advice from Ralegh on whom he should marry.[1] Even from the Tower, Ralegh could influence public policy.

By 1612, the eighteen-year-old Prince Henry had convinced his father to free Ralegh from prison.[2] Two years earlier, Henry had convinced James to purchase Ralegh's former estate, Sherborne, from the
king's favorite, Robert Carr, for £20,000. The estate was to be given to
Henry, who would present it to Ralegh at his release from prison at
Christmas. At this time, Ralegh was finishing his massive *History of the
World* as a present to Henry. Ralegh's rise in the prince's and the king's
good graces is evident from the book's listing in the Stationers Register in 1611—it had been approved for printing. As historian Nicholas
Popper has noted, Ralegh's *History of the World* and his essays about
politics were designed in part to convince James of Ralegh's usefulness
as an advisor.[3] The wheel of fortune carried Ralegh not just into the
prince's affections and to the precipice of freedom but also, perhaps,
to a place in the king's administration. Yet soon, all this good fortune
was threatened.

In early October 1612, Henry fell ill with a fever—today it would be
diagnosed as typhoid fever, but at the time no one knew what ailed the
prince.[4] By late October, the illness had grown worse. Prince Henry
received the typical medical treatments practiced on the elite, which
emphasized ingestion of cordials and bloodletting. The latter was used
to balance the body's "humours" and had been practiced in Europe for
thousands of years. As with other treatments he received, the cures
tended to the dramatic, in part because of the seriousness of the illness
but also owing to the use of so many healers, each of whom had their
own special treatments to recommend. The array of physicians, surgeons, and apothecaries probably all agreed on the bloodletting, which
yielded a significant amount of blood. A detailed account of Henry's
illness and treatment reports seven to eight ounces drawn at a time,
though not more than once in a day, with the blood described as gold
colored, "thinner, corrupt, and putrid."[5] Henry's room was filled with
the emotion of healers, family, and well-wishers (and the curious) from
court, as the pendulum swung from deepest sorrow that his condition
was incurable to signs that the prince had turned a corner and was improving. When Henry fell into delirium, "hopes now began to vanish."

Panic led the healers to try ever more cures to accompany the
bleeding, including an array of cordials and "giving unto him a blister,
which brought away aboundance of corrupt and putrid matter." When
Henry experienced extreme pain in his head, they cut off his hair and
used cupping glasses to apply a mixture made of dead pigeons to "draw

away the humor of that suspicious Blood from the head." Through it all, the prince "endured with wonderfull and admirable patience." The disease's assault on his body took on greater force, striking his tongue, mouth, and throat, which gave the prince an intense thirst. On the eleventh day of his sickness, the physicians, surgeons, and apothecaries announced there was no hope for recovery: "the Chrisis was to be soon before a final dissolution." Parts of a dead rooster were applied "to the soles of his feet, but in vaine; the Cordials also were redoubled in number and quantities, but without any profit." The king came to see Henry, but his caretakers urged him not to look upon his son in this condition. James left, but not before ordering that those who came to see Henry only "out of Love" be turned away; only those necessary to attend his health were to be allowed with him. They also moved the prince to a "larger and greater chamber."

On the twelfth day of his sickness, the king was informed "there now remained noe hope or means of his Highnesse Recovery but with desperate and dangerous Attempt." The king's "cheife phisition," Dr. Théodore de Mayerne, was given leave to do as he may "without Advice of the others." Mayerne, worried that he could do nothing to help, became paralyzed to offer any treatment. He feared "to doe any thing of himselfe without advice of the rest," for if he failed, it would be said "that hee had killed the King's eldest sonne." The king, too, wiped his hands clean of his son's impending death. He "removed to theobolds (a house of his Majestie 12 miles from London) thence to expect the doleful event."[6]

Four doctors returned to bleed the patient: "they sayd the opening of a veyne was in their judgment the only meane left." Others came along and prescribed doubling or tripling the cordials and blistering his head. The archbishop of Canterbury arrived to prepare the prince for death, to discuss sin and whether the prince was ready to meet God. They had "this conference with a great deal more." On the fifth of November—the anniversary of the Gunpowder Plot of 1605, when English Catholic conspirators attempted to blow up the House of Lords and kill the king—the call went out to all the "Churches to pray for his Highnesse." In great pain, the prince called out for his friend David, who came but could not learn what the prince wanted to say to him. Two more physicians arrived and proposed bleeding and "did at last agree upon Diascordium," an opiate, "as the only meanes under God now remayning," and they also gave him "cooler Cordialls . . . in the presence of many honorable Gentlemen, about Ten o clock at night." None of this alleviated the prince's condition.

That evening the prince tried to speak to the surgeon at his bedside, but because "of the ratling of his throate that hee could not be understood," which filled the prince with anger so that he never spoke to anyone else "unless he were urged." (Rumor posited that at some point the prince said he was unhappy to die because he worried about Ralegh not being freed by his father.) About three o'clock in the morning, the prince suffered convulsions, his "spirite subdued," and two or three times they thought he had died. People wept, shouted, and cried, but they could not restore him. Rumor of his death spread through countryside and city—but he had not died. He lay in extreme pain. "All the world in this despaire were readie to bring" every cordial, diaphoretic (to induce sweat), and "Quintessentiall Spiritts" to be "given unto him," one of which succeeded in "forcing a small sweate; which (too late), was the first hee had during all his sicknesse."

For days, the queen had urged the physicians to obtain a cordial from Ralegh. When no hope was left, they deliberated and asked the "Lords of the Counsell there present" for advice on whether to use "the Cordiall sent by Sir Walter Ralegh." The lords debated: How could they turn to the king's prisoner to heal the king's son, notwithstanding the queen's use of the man's medicines. "As the last desperate remedie," the council allowed the cordial prepared by Ralegh, "after it had been tasted and proved" not to be poison, to be "given unto" the prince. John Chamberlain recorded Ralegh saying that they should have contacted him sooner, that it likely was too late.[7] The cordial induced "a gentle sweat" and allowed the prince to "Rest for a little while, But no remidie, Death would needs be conquered." Chamberlain noted it restored to the prince "some shew of sense and opening of his eyes," and some said he spoke, "but all faded again presently." His "sight and sense failing," these were "infallible signs of Death" nearing.

The archbishop called on Henry:

To prepare him to meet the Lord Jesus, with many other most excellent divine Exhortations: Thereafter calling more loude than ever thrice together in his Eare, Sir heare you mee, hear you mee, heare you mee, he sayd: If you heare me, in certaine signe of you

faith, and signe of the blessed Resurrections, give it for our comfort
a signe by lifting up both . . . hands together.

Henry complied, but the archbishop asked Henry for "another
signe by stirring his Eyes," which he did, while the others, receding
in the room, allowed Henry and the archbishop to continue praying.
Prayers extended from three that morning until the prince died at eight
o'clock on the evening of Friday, November 6, 1612. An autopsy was
performed, perhaps to prove he had not been poisoned, and a detailed
report was written.

The prince's death was unfortunate for all; he was mourned
throughout the land. His body was placed in state for an entire month.
James did not like funerals, so he refused to attend. The nation lost
its hope for a dashing, learned, and politique king, and instead would
receive his younger brother Charles, who would lose his head to the
executioner's ax in the English Civil War.

The most immediate loser, besides the prince and his mother, who
grieved deeply, was Ralegh. In less than two months he would have
been freed, his Sherborne estate restored, and the long nightmare of
imprisonment left behind. With Henry's death, James lost interest in
freeing Ralegh. He conveyed the Sherborne estate back to Carr for
£25,000. Some have thought James's refusal to release Ralegh owed
to Ralegh's failure to heal Henry, but no one blamed Ralegh because
he had not been called until it was too late. More likely, James was in-
different to Ralegh's fate and perhaps concerned that even in prison
Ralegh was highly influential on public opinion, given the many tracts
Ralegh wrote that made the rounds at court. James tried to halt publication of Ralegh's History of the World, but over the technicality that it
included a picture of Ralegh, who was civilly dead; James probably did
not yet know how very critical the book was of kings. He did not warrant that any king should be criticized—to criticize one was to criticize
all. James, indeed, loudly articulated the divine right of kings. Ralegh's
thoughts that James would come to his senses and release him to be
his advisor were chimerical.

With Henry's death, Ralegh returned to finishing his History of the
World. He already had made his mark as a courtier, colonizer, soldier,
sailor, and statesman. His cordials and scientific experiments won
him respect and a lasting legacy. But his History of the World brought
him into households throughout the kingdom. It had a remarkable

publishing history. In the seventeenth century, it went through at least fourteen editions and additional abridgements and remained popular in the eighteenth century, with numerous additional editions. The book brought together all of Ralegh's interests and experience and presented to readers the pervasive influence of colonialism on his thinking about the meaning of history.

CHAPTER 31

History of the World

The *History of the World* was published in 1614, when Sir Walter Ralegh was King James's prisoner. Written, he states, for Prince Henry, the work totals more than fourteen hundred pages and nearly one million words. Through the centuries, questions have arisen about how much of the book Ralegh wrote. Hariot likely assisted Ralegh with mathematical calculations because Ralegh was concerned with being precise in reporting distances, dates, and ages. Ralegh states that he had help with translations from Hebrew, but the voice, focus, and concerns throughout the book are all Ralegh. *History* reflects Ralegh's interests in politics, statecraft, geopolitics, lifestyle, and morality. The cynicism of his poem "The Lie" is evident throughout—the book provides a sustained condemnation of the abuse of power. *History* is also permeated by Ralegh's Hermeticism. He frequently cites Hermes as a source, and the book itself could be more aptly titled "A Hermeticist's History of the World." Its genius is in its presentation of Hermetic ideas and sensibilities in an easy-to-comprehend fashion. The entirety flows from Ralegh's interest in the relationship between the seen and unseen universes, with the natural philosopher's view of God, man, and nature. No random collection of facts, the book offers a focused conceptualization of world history that begins with Creation and ends before the story of Jesus, the first volume in what Ralegh suggested would be a two- or three-volume work "if the first receive grace and good acceptance."[1]

WE KNOW MUCH about Ralegh's sources—not only does he frequently cite his sources in the text, but also we know the contents of his library in the Tower of London—a collection of more than five hundred volumes. Historian Nicholas Popper has drawn on this library to show precisely where Ralegh obtained his material for constructing his history.[2] His constant citation of sources reassures his readers, and he often provides quotations in the original Latin and other languages, and then gives translations. Ralegh was self-conscious about how to educate and appeal to his audience, and thus purposeful in telling stories. He frequently referred to examples from contemporary society or his own life to illustrate historical points. This insertion of himself and the events he witnessed, or events and anecdotes drawn from his lifetime or within the early modern era, enlivens and contextualizes the text.

Personal experience shaped Ralegh's history in many ways. His knowledge of monarchy influenced his assessment of rulers (and their advisors), reflecting his experience at the English court and his interactions with government officials and foreign diplomats. Ralegh's military experience on land and sea, his political and military strategizing, his sensitivity to the relationship between military and domestic affairs, and his writing of pamphlets and state papers all illustrate how he could write an epic history that is so thoughtful in its critique of statecraft: for decades he contemplated rulers and the vast entwined issues they faced. The methods he employed in the laboratory carried over into his writing of history. Ralegh expertly harnessed his sources, weighed the evidence, and adroitly constructed his arguments.

At the root of Ralegh's book is God and man's relationship to history. God lives, so does history, and so does man. Referring to Creation in the preface, Ralegh explains "we plainly behold living now (as if we had lived then)." Humans inhabit the totality of history; "we live in the very time when" the world "was created." History "hath made us acquainted with our own dead Auncestors; and out of the depth and darknesse of the earth, delivered us their memory and fame. In a word, we may gather out of History a policy no lesse wise than eternall." God's existence is dynamic, as is man's, so Ralegh defines God's power by examining predestination, prescience, and God's judgments. In Ralegh's worldview, God is all-knowing, but humans bear responsibility for their actions. Ralegh shared this view of history with the Puritans—it is one reason his work remained so popular through the seventeenth century.

Because Ralegh's focus is ancient history, there is little discussion of Christianity and much reference to the Old Testament. King James was taken aback by how little Ralegh discussed Christ or used the traditional Christian references in the ancient world to point the way to Christ's arrival. Even more noteworthy is Ralegh's treatment of those with no knowledge of the Bible and who lived before Christ. Ralegh argues that God exists in people's consciousness: they lived with God even without knowledge of Judaism or Christianity. Many great thinkers of the ancient world, he argues, had no exposure to the Judeo-Christian religious traditions yet agreed there exists but one God. For Ralegh, this not only proved God's existence but also the eminent spirituality of those who had never been exposed to the Bible.

Ralegh never denigrates Christianity—he was a pious Christian—but he expresses that professed Christians are often poor Christians. Since non-Christians could grasp monotheism and no one—Christian or non-Christian—could ever know the unknowable, Ralegh promotes religious tolerance: while a human inhabits the "body," the heavens remain unsearchable; men cannot absolutely know God's will. Ralegh lamented "the perpetuall warre, massacres, and murders, for religion among Christians." In one of his many memorable quotes, he condemns religious bigotry: "We are all (in effect) become Comedians in religion." Christians cannot be trusted when they assert the certainty of their knowledge of God. In contrast, he praises those who without the Bible sought to become closer to the divine by understanding God's Creation—a Hermetic view of piety. Ralegh even excuses the heathen's worship of idols, for when Moses condemned images, the idols of men, he was referring to images of the living God; the idols of the long dead were inconsequential.

Ralegh's tolerance was reinforced by his concept of diversity. God is one. Nothing else can be singular. Everything that is not God is unique in and of itself. Of those now dust, and those still living, each has a unique face, "a divers picture of minde," a unique form and singular way of thinking. Nothing has so much triumphed in nature as "dissimilitude"—everything differs from everything else. "From whence it commeth that there is found so great diversity of opinions; so strong a contrariety of inclinations." Ralegh states that his own modus operandi has been tolerance. He claims that except in "defence of her excellent person, I never persecuted any man." Here he was not referring to any particular belief but a general view that no one should repress another, and that he only did so in the course of duty to the queen. "It is the power of Nature by diversity of meanes, or out of diversity of matter, to produce divers things." Without this diversity all would be the same— all that is not heaven would be earth . . . nature would be as much a "cause" as God—but, it is not so. Only God is unchanging.

The heavens cannot be known by mortal man, but humans can come closer to the divine by looking for it in material things. Ralegh mocks riches but celebrates the search for divinity in herbs, stones, and minerals. The quest to locate the secrets God cast into these useful things is pursued by a magus, "one altogether conversant in things divine." Against those who fear or condemn the search for the divine in material objects, Ralegh asserts, "the arte of Magicke is the arte of worshipping God." The magus has nothing to do with evil. Ralegh is careful to praise King James, who had written a book titled *Daemonology*, a study of black magic, reflecting James's obsession with the evil in the world, as opposed to Ralegh, whose cynicism about human behavior was tempered by his emphasis on the human ability, if not duty, to reach toward the divine. Ralegh claims to follow James in condemning "the Magick which His Majestie condemneth . . . that kinde whereof the Divelll is a partie." This "Unlawful magic" involved necromancy and the conjuring of devils. Despite his presumed support of James's fears, Ralegh claims that the alleged black magic was mere trickery. Ralegh defines witchcraft, which James especially condemned, and for which he had put so many alleged witches to death in Scotland, as the charming of beasts and birds and the drawing of serpents out of their dens—but Ralegh believed that people were fooled into thinking the witch controlled the animal. As for conjuring, he asserts that none had ever raised the dead.

In contrast, Ralegh has nothing but praise for the magi— magicians—and asserts there is no relation between their art and conjuring or witchcraft. The magus is not "familiar with evill." A magus "is one altogether conversant in things divine," his work "is in service of God." (Perhaps it was no coincidence that the King James Bible, published only a few years before Ralegh's *History*, translated the "magi" who visited Jesus after his birth as "wise men," to dissociate them from magic.) Ralegh praises magi as natural philosophers and cites Daniel in the Old Testament as confirming there are four kinds of wise men, of which the magi are one. The second sort are astrologers, who read the stars to show the natural tendencies that face each individual. The third are wise but do evil—witches or sorcerers. The fourth, translators, can do evil, too, and often are called Chaldeans, the fortune-tellers who rely on a sixth sense, but they also can contemplate the motions of the heavens. Ralegh's personal interest was the "Philosophie of nature," but he also respected astrology and the work of the Chaldeans. In both cases, Ralegh applauds the ancient practitioners: "the ancient Magicke is not to be condemned."

Ralegh claims to exalt the Chaldeans because Abraham was in their lands when he learned of God, and from them he learned other things, like astrology. When we think of astrology, we think of fate, but Ralegh understood fate and astrology through his understanding of God's powers to know all that is to come. He divides these into predestination, providence, and prescience. Prescience is the ability to foresee what will happen. Providence combines foresight with care for what will come in "respect to all creatures." Predestination, for which Ralegh relies on "Divines" for his interpretation, concerns "onely of man" and whether they will enjoy salvation; then he provides multiple opinions of "Divines" on the subject. How did astrology relate to God's power? The "Starres have great influence: and that their operations may be prevented or furthered." Just as the seasons may be followed to predict hot and cold, so, too, do the stars serve as "instruments" of great use. Since

> we cannot denie, but that God hath given vertues to Springs and Fountaines, to cold earth, to plants and stones, Mineralls, and to the excrementall parts of the basest living creatures, why should we robbe the beautifull Starres of their working powers.

Astrology, in Ralegh's mind, is an extension of God's power. Every star, Ralegh reveals, God has given a "peculiar virtue," just "as every herbe, plant, fruit, and flower . . . [is] for the use of man and beast, to feed them and cure them." The stars should not be read as "causes"— they do not bind people—but "as open Bookes." Humans can come to know their influences, but they will never understand them in their entirety. The stars are a part of God's universe that are both seen and unseen. We see them from afar, and special people learn how to read them, but we can never know them completely. When Man knows better the things of this earth, the "vertues of herbs and plants," for instance, then Man can better understand "heavenly things."

This leads Ralegh back to the question of fate. Ralegh agrees "with the Heathen" that God cannot be bound to his creatures, and man cannot be bound to the stars, for then humans would not bear responsibility for their actions. The stars influence individuals' sensibilities, appetites, moods, and passions, but "it is absurd to think" that the stars or the sun has "any power over the minds of men" or that men have power over celestial "bodies." Stars incline people certain ways at birth, but "Nature and Art . . . weaken their operation."

Ralegh's views of fate, destiny, astrology, magic, and other aspects of the unseen in his natural philosophy reflect belief in an all-powerful God who has endowed every bit of the natural world with forethought. Humans have taken advantage of this bounty but can do even more through study. To study nature is to draw closer to God because understanding Creation is to appreciate God's work and glory. Ralegh quotes the Roman poet Virgil, who expressed "God's spirit in all things . . . most excellently":

> *The heavens, the earth, and all the liquid main,*
> *The Moon's bright globe, and stars Titanian,*
> *A spirit within maintains: and their whole mass,*
> *A mind, which through each part infus'd doth pass.*
> *Fashions, and works and wholly doth transpierce*
> *All this great body of the universe.*

The unseen that can never be known by a mortal is God. But God's work can be identified within Creation, by the physical world God created. The human side of history is a story of folly, of humans' inability to transcend their folly, incompetency, and meanness. With his focus on rulers, Ralegh spends much of his book in criticism of monarchs. King James found the book "too saucy in the censuring of Princes." After a brief whirlwind tour of kings in his preface, Ralegh provides a litany of the moral shortcomings of kings:

> Oh by what plots, by what forswearings, betrayings, poysonings, and under what reasons of State, and politique subtlety, have these forenamed Kings, both strangers [foreigners], and of our owne Nation, pulled the vengeance of GOD upon themselves, upon theirs, and upon their prudent minsters!

Reformation of the world, as God would want humans to live, begins at the top of the hierarchy, with its rulers. "It is true, there was never any Common weale or Kingdom in the world, wherein no man had cause to lament. Kings live in the world, and not above it." The vanity of rulers blinds them to the needs of their kingdom. Even Elizabeth's vanity was noted, though the criticism subtle: she destroyed paintings of her "by unskillful and common Painters," but Ralegh implies that she spent too much effort destroying likenesses of herself that she did not find agreeable. Vanity not only blinds but enrages monarchs, whose self-love takes precedence over the needs of state. "Princes doe rather pardon ill deeds, than villainous words." In providing examples, Ralegh again calls on his experience and knowledge of Elizabeth and her punishment of Sir John Perot, not for his "counterfeit letter of the Romish Priest" but for "the contemptuous words" he "used against" Elizabeth. Ralegh did not highlight Elizabeth's faults; he barely refers to her in *The History*. But these contemporary examples were used to show that monarchs remained as riddled with faults currently as in the ancient past.

Ralegh's biting sarcasm in his *History* reflects the style of his poem "The Lie," especially when he references modern ages. In discussing the shortcomings of kings, he picks out Elizabeth's father, Henry VIII, as especially worthy of condemnation: "if all the pictures and patternes of a mercilesse Prince were lost in the World, they might all againe be painted to the life story of this King." Ralegh identifies a substantial list of abuses Henry committed against both men and women who were wrongly executed, including his wives, whom "he cutoff, & cast off, as his fancy & affection changed." Ralegh rues "the sorrowes" Henry inflicted upon the "Fatherlesse and Widowes at home" and the "vaine enterprises" he undertook abroad. These produced "causeless and cruel wars," especially against his nephew, King James V of Scotland, who did not deserve Henry's cruelty. By critiquing the ignoble past, Ralegh hoped that his revelations of the lives of kings and others who immorally and needlessly did not fill their charge from God would teach posterity, the children, that Christian "workes"—behavior—are necessary for indicating whether they are truly Christian or not. It would help if humans stopped lying, purposely perpetuating falsehoods. Children are not the problem in this regard, Ralegh notes, perhaps atypically, even as many people moralized that lying was inherent to the character of children. Ralegh notes instead that "every child could have told how much falsehood had been mingled with the truth." He regrets that in his own time,

There is indeed a certeine Doctrine of Policie (as Policie is now a-daies defined by falsehood and knaverie) that devised rumours and lies, if they serve the turne, but for a day or two, are greatly availeable. It is true that common people are sometimes mockt by them, as Souldiers are by false alarums in the Warres; but in all that I have observed, I have found the successe as ridiculous as the invention. . . . all men in general condemn the Venters of such trumperie, and for them feare upon necessarie occasions to entertain the truth it selfe.

Ralegh admits that his book might have been more exciting if he had chosen to write about the present. "I might have been more pleasing to the Reader," Ralegh explains, "if I had written the Story of mine owne times." After all, he knew so much firsthand, as he had "been permitted to draw water as neare the Well-head as another." But he had no need to write a modern history to "flatter" the world. Life is too short, he claims, at least for him, to waste his time when there was a more important story to tell. He preferred to write of the "eldest times," which still allowed him to "point at the present and taxe the vices of those that are yet living." If he offends people, so be it. He hardly needed to remind readers of his condition: his imprisonment provided him "eleven yeares leasure" to research and write.

The history he wished to document, that he felt compelled to tell, was ancient history, which provided the foundation for the world in which they lived: this was a history of plantation. God created the universe, then he created a "plantation of the world." Humanity inhabited different places, beginning with Adam, who "was first planted by God in one certaine place." But of greater importance than documenting Eden and Paradise, to which Ralegh devotes much discussion, is his extended analysis of what occurred after the flood—the plantation of the world by the descendants of Noah. As literary scholar Anna Beer touches on in a footnote to her study of the readers of Ralegh in the seventeenth century, Ralegh's analysis of the flood was unusual in not discussing it as "a complete analogue of the Fall" of man. Instead, as Ralegh says, it was a story to "truly teach the world's plantation, and the beginning of nations."[3]

This was the true foundation of history for Ralegh. He devotes about fifty thousand words to discussion of God's first plantation of the world after the flood. He follows that intermittently through the book with "teaching the worlds new plantation," including the Egyptian plantation, the plantation of Israel (and the ten lost tribes), and numerous other plantations that ended with "displantation" or replantation elsewhere. An exceptional historian, Ralegh recognized the importance of building a proper foundation for his book, which, after all, was *The History of the World*—so beginning with Creation was essential, but, so, too, the importance of specifying the who, what, and where that existed at the dawn of human history after the flood: Who were the world's peoples and where did they live?

God provided the what in that the planting of the world's people after the flood was his design: "the worlds plantation could not be effected without orders and conduction." That was why plantation proceeded relatively quickly. Italy, France, and Spain, for instance, according to Ralegh, all were planted within 140 years of the flood. Those whom God first sent out were not "discoverers," as in Ralegh's own time, nor were they "adventurers," because each received a designated place. Ralegh's concept of plantation and colonization surely was shaped by his own time, but he did not draw the conclusion that the modern movement and settlement of people was God-directed. That occurred only with the initial ancient plantations, which held no superiority over later plantations and colonies. By *plantation*, Ralegh meant people settling land where no one held sovereignty (as in the first plantations after Noah) or where one already held sovereignty but had not settled people. Hence, the English establishment of the Munster Plantation under Elizabeth or the Virginia Plantation and the Plymouth Plantation under James occurred on lands the monarch of England claimed sovereignty over. (Ralegh's Roanoke colony gave James sovereignty over all the lands that extended northward to Canada.) *Colony*, however, referred to people moving to the lands of other peoples. By the mid-seventeenth century, English no longer distinguished *plantation* from *colony*, and the latter became the preferred term for wherever English settled outside of England with government approval.

When God established plantations, all received bountiful land. Over time they also received knowledge from God on how to use their lands. This knowledge passed through generations, but what about knowledge of God and the world before the flood? Ralegh provides a Hermeticist's answer: Moses received this information from the Holy Ghost, but also, perhaps, Ralegh mused, through the Kabbalah, sacred mystical texts that Noah might have preserved.

The plantation of the world—that is, the world's history—was full of moral lessons for Ralegh's own time. Ralegh claims "that in all ancient storie[s]," the reader "finds one and the same beginning of Nations, after the flood; that the first planters of all parts of the World were said to be mighty, and Giant-like men," including in America, as Amerigo Vespucci reported on his second voyage. These giants lived simple lives eating "acorns and roots," living in humble cottages, wearing animal skins, wielding primitive weapons, and traveling in simple vessels on the water. Societies evolved by moving from oars to sails, learning the arts and husbandry, and establishing laws and government policies as God instructed them. This simplistic life was replaced by "greater Giants, for vice and injustice." Ralegh, as in his poem "The Lie," condemns what man has become—preoccupied by wealth. Cottages were replaced by palaces, and "men are rather knowne by their houses, than their houses by them." Humans had "fallen" from two dishes to two hundred, and drinking water was replaced by "wine and drunkennesse." Ralegh was not Spartan, but promoted moderation, particularly in eating. His years of imprisonment, it can be assumed, likely contributed to his bitterness toward excessive consumption. He had been confined to the Tower for over ten years before finishing his history. His castigation of the behavior of humans, especially kings, concerned both their mean-spiritedness and their abuse of the gifts God granted them. He did not, however, wallow in bitterness, and the moderation he preaches reflected his own moderation as a writer; he retained his focus and mindfulness.

The plantation of the world after the flood was so central to his book that Ralegh included maps to show who "planted" and where their "plantations" were located. (Ralegh's notebook in the British Library contains not only notes for his *History of the World* but also drafts of maps.) Not everyone remained at their original plantation. Subsequent history encompassed the movement of peoples, sometimes to start new plantations, but also colonies, or to build empires. Some colonies of the ancient world were shown on his maps, and he devotes much discussion to the formation of the first empire (Nimrod's) and what happened to that empire and others. Not all empires were established by force, such as that built peaceably by Belus—so empires, too, like colonies, were not inherently good or bad. Why did people not stay where they originally planted? The basic answer Ralegh provides: population growth forced people to plant new lands or to colonize or conquer. England, he rues, was no longer like the ancient lands, the "fruitfullest Vallies," but had become "barren and cold ground . . . where the dead and destroying winter depresseth all vegetative and growing Nature."

Migration, plantation, and colonization were natural processes of history. Ralegh held a nuanced view that there existed an array of contingencies for colonization. Sometimes peoples moved to barely inhabited lands, sometimes they mixed with the people already planted, other times they practiced removal or conquest. Colonization took on a qualitative factor when peoples were adversely affected. When he can, Ralegh describes what happened to those whose lands were colonized. The Assyrians, for instance, "transplanted" the colonized elsewhere. Sometimes Ralegh describes removal as "displanting." Sometimes the colonizers themselves were being punished by having to colonize. For instance, in Ralegh's recounting of the war between Greece and Troy, the Gods were upset with the victorious Greeks for having destroyed temples and thus forced them to become colonizers instead of allowing them to return home—the theme of Homer's great epic, *The Odyssey*. Perhaps Ralegh thought of English being driven overseas by their barren land as a form of punishment.

What mattered was not whether one was colonizer or colonized, but the character of the people. Ralegh cites the example of Alexander the Great dispersing his soldiers to plant colonies as a method "to bridle the barbarous nations." The men so disliked the unpleasant places and the "rude people, among whom they lived" that they departed for new lands. The fact of colonization was neither just nor unjust but was it conducted for everyone's benefit. The aforementioned situation could have been reversed—"barbarous nations" could attempt to colonize the lands of more socially advanced peoples. There is no sense in Ralegh's *History* that the colonizer was inherently superior to the colonized. Ralegh's limited discussion of manuring shows that he did not buy in to the views of so many other English that their knowledge of this "improvement" gave the English the right to take Native peoples' land. In a few of his examples, people who received land to plant or colonize would "manure," but he never uses manuring as an indicator that those who did not manure should lose their land to those who did. Ralegh's celebration of the simple life—pastoralism—ensured that he did not rate more "advanced" civilizations as superior to less developed ones. A people possess no right to colonize because of their cultural superiority or military strength.

Ralegh's lack of ethnocentrism did not make him egalitarian. He sometimes refers to the "vulgar" and "rude" people from whom special knowledge must be kept, presumably because their immorality and ignorance could lead them to abuse or misuse what they do not understand—like the Kabbalah—for evil or at least profane purposes. He shared this view with other Hermeticists, who feared the multitude obtaining, or at least misunderstanding, the divine knowledge available in natural philosophy texts; the ignorance and prejudice of the multitude had led to the destruction of Dr. John Dee's library at the hands of a mob. Thus, some sacred "knowledge" had to be "written in ciphers." But again, Ralegh's lack of ethnocentrism is remarkable. His condemnations of immoral behavior generally refer to the elite, not to non-Europeans, for instance. Not even the Spanish were considered inherently evil, and he praises the achievements of their empire. Ralegh almost invariably was interested in individual character; his history was not intended as one written by the victors to justify their conquests.

—

THE IRONY THAT RALEGH WROTE a history of the world from prison should not be passed over without comment. His mind took him to Paradise, Persia, Troy, America, and dozens of other places to answer some of the deepest questions about God, Creation, and humanity. He relived his own journeys and imagined those of others. We cannot imagine the intellectual and emotional investment, the sadness and joy, melancholy and elation, that he must have felt uncovering and explaining the glories and mysteries of the universe, as well as the abject misery and limitations of humanity.

But he had before him another great adventure in the physical world outside the confines of the Tower of London. Once again, he had the opportunity to become the new Columbus. If he failed, there would be no second chance.

CHAPTER 32

"He called to the Headman to shew him the Ax"

R alegh had several ways to earn release from the Tower. He could earn favor with those whom he healed with cordials and hope they would lobby for his release. He had come close to freedom and restoration of some of his estate through Prince Henry's intervention. After her son's death, Queen Anne continued to lobby for Ralegh, but this was not the only path out of the Tower.

He could also make himself indispensable to the king. James knew Ralegh was no ordinary man, that he possessed great political experience advising Elizabeth, had led men in battle, and had served as a governor and regional administrator. At one point, dismayed with his advisors, James proclaimed Ralegh was the only true knight in his kingdom. Later, although for political purposes, James had his ambassador inform the Spanish that Ralegh "upon all occasions, [was] as useful a Man, as served any Prince in Christendom."[1] James was not inalterably opposed to Ralegh, but Ralegh's influence made him a danger to the regime. A freed Ralegh could form an opposition to James's policies. The king had no one to rely on for counterarguments against Ralegh's perspicacity and wit. A freed Ralegh might use his popularity and pen to embarrass the king's advisors.

Fortunately for Ralegh, James had a weakness to exploit. The king had profligately lavished gifts on his favorites, and now he needed money. Over several years, Ralegh put forth proposals to make the king rich. Ralegh knew where untapped mines of gold in Guiana awaited. All he needed were ships, men, weaponry, food, and mining tools. Ralegh submitted proposals to Cecil (c. 1607), Thomas Hamilton (1610), and the Privy Council (1611). Ralegh was willing, at least in the last proposal, to have Kemys lead the expedition in his place; if Kemys brought home over a half ton of gold, then the king must release him.

One aspect of Ralegh's first proposals that worked against him was the propinquity of the mines to the Spanish in Guiana. The Spanish would not be pleased with English encroachment in South America, and any approach to the mines would risk combat. By 1615, Ralegh had remade the proposal to Secretary of State Ralph Winwood. Winwood shared Ralegh's anti-Spanish sensibilities, and they conveniently excised the Spanish presence in the area of the mines: there would be no Spanish to offend. Ralegh would lead the expedition, personally guaranteeing there would be no aggressive hostilities toward the Spanish. If Ralegh succeeded, the king could straighten out his finances and might very well become the richest man in Christendom.

The king assented. Having spent about a fifth of his life in the Tower of London, Ralegh again had opportunity to scale the heights of fame and fortune. All he needed to do was go to Guiana and find *El Madre del oro*, the great gold mines he had stood upon over twenty years before, but had not the tools, men, and time to exploit. It all seemed so easy.

—

To PREPARE THE EXPEDITION, on March 19, 1615/16, Ralegh was allowed to leave the Tower of London with an escort. He did not have to return. In the coming year, he raised about £30,000 for the building and leasing of ships and for food and supplies. He recruited sailors and gentlemen adventurers. He wined and dined his way through London and at the end of January was officially released as a prisoner of the Tower.[2] That summer he received official commission to lead an expedition to Guiana. Three earls gave bonds that Ralegh would return to England. The king granted Ralegh full power of life and death over the men. He was restricted from sailing to any lands under the sovereignty of a Christian prince.

There existed no agreement between England and Spain on where Spanish sovereignty began and ended in America, but the English certainly accepted that anywhere the Spanish settled belonged to them—until the English took it.[3] As was so often the case in colonial enterprises, the entire expedition was based on fictions. Nowhere was it stated in Ralegh's commission that he was going to a gold mine or that he would set up a colony. The king gave Ralegh permission to go to South American lands "possessed and inhabited by heathen and savage people, to the end to discover and find out some commodities and merchandises in those countries" of which the inhabitants "make little or no use" and that would be of use in "our kingdoms and dominions." By this trade, the Christian faith would be propagated "amongst those savage and idolatrous people." James made it sound like a trading venture, and no military purpose was stated. But one thousand men did not sign up for a voyage to South America to exchange goods. Those who invested and went as adventurers sought a percentage of the gold and any other wealth they might accrue. No one would be surprised if Ralegh went pirating along the way.

The minor problem remained that the public would need to support this expedition led by a man convicted of treason. James reassured everyone that by "our special grace, certain knowledge, and mere motion"—the same mystical terms Elizabeth employed in her colonial patent to Ralegh—the king and his "heirs and successors" granted to "Sir W. Ralegh full power and authority and free license and liberty . . . to take and lead . . . this intended voyage" to America. Ralegh and his people could carry whatever they needed to trade, or any other items, including what was necessary "for use and defence of him and his company." They could bring back to James's kingdoms anything they chose, and no one would molest their ownership of the said goods, as long as the king, his heirs, and his successors received one-fifth of all gold, silver, pearl, and precious stones, besides any customs duties. As with Elizabeth, James stated that Parliament could never make any law or take any other action that interfered with Ralegh's enterprise. Ralegh would be "sole governor and commander" over all who traveled with him, with full power to punish and pardon, including in capital cases. Those in charge of ports in the south of England were forewarned not to interfere with Ralegh and his people on their leaving or entering England.[4]

The Spanish ambassador was fully aware of English intentions and tried to convince James to stop Ralegh. James used the threat of Ralegh's expedition for negotiations with Spain on a range of diplomatic matters.[5] But James would not stop Ralegh from going. Too many had invested and the nation was excited by the prospect of recapturing past glories. James barred Ralegh from attacking Spanish settlements and informed the Spanish that Ralegh would go to the Orinoco to dig gold at a place not under their control.[6]

But the situation, indeed, had changed from when Ralegh journeyed to Guiana more than twenty years earlier: the Spanish had moved the town of San Thomé to the south bank of the Orinoco, directly in the way of Ralegh reaching the mines. James knew of the settlement from the frequent Spanish protests against Ralegh's expedition. If Ralegh reached the mines and procured their wealth, James would ignore Spanish claims to the area; if Ralegh failed, James could disavow him. As historian Samuel Rawson Gardiner observes, "For James there was to be everything to gain. For Ralegh there was everything to lose."[7] James was willing to challenge Spain in the New World—he had authorized the colonization of Virginia—and historian V. T. Harlow has made a convincing case that Ralegh and the king conferred together to enlist French aid in Guiana.[8] Ralegh made no secret to the government about San Thomé being a well-established settlement that was in the way of the English reaching the mine. In Ralegh's own time, some made the case that Ralegh never intended to go to Guiana, that all along he intended to attack the treasure fleet out of Mexico, but Ralegh did sail for Guiana and the English did seek out the mines—any jaunt against the treasure fleet would have occurred only if they failed at Guiana.

Six weeks before sailing, Ralegh issued *Orders to Be Observed by the Commanders of the Fleet*. "Divine service" was to be read twice daily, or once if the weather did not allow a second. The men should be admonished for blasphemy and Ralegh personally informed if a man refused to refrain. There can be no doubt Ralegh understood that force of arms would be necessary to secure Guiana: he ordered that all sailors should be trained to be soldiers on land in case they were needed. He warned the men against pirating the ships of any nation in amity with King James, barred card games and dice for purposes of gambling, and restricted smoking to certain areas. For the men's protection, he urged them not to eat any fruit they did not see birds or beasts eat, nor to swim in rivers where Indians did not swim, "because most of the rivers are full of alligators." Just as on the first expedition to Guiana, he barred abuse of the Native peoples. Any person who "shall force any woman, be she Christian or heathen," would suffer pain of death. He also warned the men to take nothing from "any Indian by force," explaining that all the English would then suffer at the Indians' hands: the Indians "must" be used "with all courtesy."[9]

A fleet of seven ships and about five hundred men sailed from Plymouth on June 19, 1617. The voyage was difficult from the very beginning. On departure, the wind blew them back to Plymouth. They set out again with the rest of the fleet, which doubled in size both the number of men and ships. The weather forced them into Falmouth, where Ralegh deposited some of the men he considered troublesome. Returning to sea, most of the fleet was blown into Ireland to Kinsale and Cork. The weather remained so bad that they stayed seven weeks. There, probably for the first time, Ralegh met Richard Boyle, who had purchased his Irish lands. Boyle later claimed to have given Ralegh 1,000 marks (about £675), and Ralegh declared that the leases Henry Pyne claimed to hold from Ralegh were forgeries. Both had their revenge on Pyne. Boyle found him a thorn in his side as he claimed complete control over the industries at Mogeely. The leases, indeed, might have been forgeries by John Meere, who had worked for Ralegh at Sherborne, where he perpetrated a string of forgeries. But allegedly, years later, Ralegh said that the leases to Pyne were not forgeries. Also, according to Boyle years later, Ralegh, who had his son Walter, known as Wat, with him on the expedition, said to Wat, "You see how nobly my Lord Boyle hath entertained and supplied me and my friends." After I am gone, "never question the Lord Boyle for any thing that I have sold him, for I do lay my curse upon my wife and children if they ever question any of the purchases his lordship had made to me."[10] This prescience on Ralegh's part—that the sale of Ralegh's lands to Boyle would be questioned by Ralegh's family after his death—is too good to be true. Not until Ralegh's wife, Elizabeth, and son, Carew, spent years suing Boyle for more compensation from the sale did Boyle claim that conversation took place. Ironically, John Meere was the one who spearheaded the dispute for Lady Ralegh against Boyle.

Boyle and Ralegh spent much time together while Ralegh waited out the weather. Boyle, Lords Roche and Barry, and others feted Ralegh and took him hunting. Boyle gave Ralegh a tour around Youghal to see all the work he had done on the town. They became partners in a copper mine.[11] Boyle also claimed to have given Ralegh oxen, beer, wine, and other foods.[12] We can presume that it was at this time that Ralegh gave Boyle the precious "Sir Walter Ralegh's stone" that he famously used in healing, likely as compensation for all that Boyle gave Ralegh.

When the winds finally changed, the fleet departed Ireland, August 19, 1617. By mid-September, they neared the Canaries, and an epidemic struck Ralegh's ship, *The Destiny*. Ralegh fell sick and could not eat solid food for almost a month.[13] Ten of the ships, including *The Destiny*, finally reached the Cayenne River, south of the Orinoco in modern-day Guiana, on November 14. The trip had taken more than three times as long as normal. Ralegh sent a skiff to look for local Native Leonard Regapo, who had been with Ralegh for three or four years in London. Ralegh also referred in his journal to a "Cassique" in the area who "was also my sarvant and had lived with mee in the tower 2 yeers." (*Servant* merely meant dependent. Ralegh, for instance, referred to all his men, including his soldiers, as servants.) Ralegh knew this Cassique by the name of Harry, "who had about forgotten his Inglish" and came "and brought mee great store of very good Casavi bread, with which I fed all my company some 7 or 8 dayes." Harry also "brought great plenty of roasted mullets," plantains, pistachios, and various fruits.[14]

Ralegh learned that the Spanish were waiting for the English at the Orinoco—after all, James had told them precisely where Ralegh was going. Ralegh had been expressly forbidden from assaulting the Spanish, but there was no way to get to the mines without passing their town. Ralegh preferred the Spanish to attack him, for then his response would be defensive. Nevertheless, in early December the English decided to attack at the town of San Thomé. Ralegh was still too ill to leave the ship, and those whom he ordinarily would rely on to lead the military had died of disease or remained ill. He had to trust his land forces to his nephew George Ralegh, who lacked experience. Kemys, being no military leader, was charged with locating the mine. Ralegh remained behind to command the fleet in case the Spanish entered the mouth of the Orinoco. Ralegh's son Wat, around twenty-four years of age, received command of one of the companies. Wat was something of a hothead and relished the chance to prove himself in battle—to gain the glory his father had attained. While Ralegh was in prison, Wat had taken his European tour with the famed writer Ben Jonson, who had his hands full with the rambunctious lad. After returning to England, Wat got into a dispute with a young man of one of England's leading families and challenged him to a duel in the Low Countries. Only Wat showed up. The government in London sent orders to English soldiers stationed there to seize and return the young man to England. Guiana gave Wat a chance to prove his mettle.

Five ships carried four hundred men up the Orinoco. Two of the vessels ran aground but eventually rejoined the others. Against the heavy current it took three weeks to reach San Thomé. The English marched into an ambush and Wat, who allegedly charged ahead, was killed. Even so, realizing that the English far outnumbered them, the Spanish abandoned the town.

But Kemys could not locate the mine. He had not been there for two decades. Frustrated, he went in search of a mine that the Spanish allegedly worked but fell into an ambush that frightened him so much that he ordered a retreat to San Thomé. Realizing he could not locate the mines Ralegh had found on his first trip, when they met Topiawari, the English retreated to their ships at the mouth of the Orinoco. The sailors and solders, as can be imagined, were irate that they had spent a nine-month journey from England to Guiana with nothing to show for their efforts. Some of the local Indians offered to take the English to other mines, but most everyone had had enough, and they worried about more Spanish forces supposedly on their way. When Kemys reported in person to Ralegh, his friend and commander berated him. "I told him," Ralegh later wrote, "that he had undone me by his obstinacy." Kemys returned to his ship's cabin and shot himself. When that did not end his life, he thrust a knife into his own heart.[15]

Ralegh considered leading an expedition to find the mine. The discovery of gold ingots at San Thomé convinced him that the mine must be nearby. He needed gold to prove to King James that the expedition had not been a lark, and that they should return the following year with forces large enough to permanently secure "the Countrie for his Majestie to whom it belongeth."[16] Yet the men had no intention of staying, and Ralegh could not force them.

They sailed out into the Caribbean to the Leeward Islands. Two ships abandoned Ralegh to go pirating, and Ralegh sent another home filled with "idle rascals." He considered going to Newfoundland for food and to freshen the ships, or to France, from which Ralegh might have held a commission. He feared returning to England empty-handed and thought about trying Guiana once again. He sailed toward Newfoundland but learned his flotilla intended to ransack the fishermen; some committed acts of piracy. Without landing, he set his own ship on a course for England. His men mutinied. They reached agreement to sail for Ireland with a promise from Ralegh that the men would not have to go to England until he had received a pardon for them. They landed at Kinsale, where most of the crew deserted; with the remainder he sailed to Plymouth and arrived in June. The entire expedition had taken one year.[17]

If Ralegh had returned with a large quantity of gold, James would have forgiven most anything. Failing that, Ralegh was eminently disposable. Once James made up his mind about Ralegh's fate, he warned his councilors that anyone who spoke in Ralegh's favor would be considered a traitor.[18] Under pressure from Spain, James issued a declaration denouncing the attack on San Thomé. Orders were issued for Ralegh's arrest. Ralegh wrote the king in defense of his actions, but James was intent on having Ralegh's head.

Sir Lewis Stuckley was sent on June 12 to arrest Ralegh, though there was no rush to bring him to London because the king and his advisors needed time to figure out how to proceed. Stuckley kept Ralegh under his eyes in the South West until he was ordered a month later to escort him to London. On the trip east, Ralegh considered fleeing to France. His return to England guaranteed that his friends would receive the return of their bonds, and the odds were high that he would be punished for attacking the Spanish without bringing home a substantial amount of gold. Ralegh stalled by feigning illness, and even convinced some physicians that he had leprosy by painting red spots on himself and substituting a black substance for his urine. He used the respite to write an *Apologie* in defense of his actions in Guiana—that the town of San Thomé had been moved, which was true, so they did not expect to come upon it; the Spanish had attacked the English, so they were merely protecting themselves; Guiana belonged to James, so Ralegh's men were defending the king's sovereign land. Once he finished writing, Ralegh recovered remarkably fast and the party continued on their way. Ralegh held on to the idea of escape to France and might even have paid bribes to that end. But he did not flee until he saw the Tower of London. Absconding in a small boat, Ralegh seems to have had some semblance of a plan to escape, but it had not been his primary choice—otherwise he would have fled earlier. By the inventory of items he carried with him to the Tower, we can assume that Ralegh expected incarceration and not flight. Seeing the Tower—remembering his long history there—likely broke his resolve. He was quickly captured.

The question remained for the king: What to do with the prisoner? Ralegh expected a trial to answer charges of having attacked the Spanish in a time of peace, but the king had no intent to let Ralegh run legal rings around his men now.

Ralegh remained under conviction for treason. He interpreted the king's assignment of him to lead an authorized expedition in the king's name as releasing him from his sentence—a pardon—for James had granted him power over the life and death of his subjects, and the king could not grant these powers to someone civilly dead. But the king's attorneys ignored Ralegh's argument. The king had made no explicit pardon. England's attorney general at Ralegh's treason trial, Sir Edward Coke, now one of the king's councilors, along with Sir Francis Bacon, wrote a paper laying out the king's legal position that Ralegh could not be tried for a new crime since he remained convicted of high treason: the civilly dead cannot commit crimes, though apparently they can perform the king's business. They recommended two possible courses. One, execute Ralegh under the old charge of treason and "publish a narrative in print of his late crimes and offenses."[19] Although the king was not "bound to give an account" for his actions, it would be politic, especially because fifteen years had elapsed since Ralegh's conviction. The second course, which they recommended, was to call a Council of State to charge Ralegh "with his acts of hostility, depredations, [and] abuse," including his attempt to escape, "and other misdemeanors." Ralegh could give a statement in response, and the council would then give advice to the king on whether Ralegh should be executed under his original conviction. James rejected bringing Ralegh before a public council, "because it would make him too popular, as was found by experiment at the arraignment at Winchester, where by his wit he turned the hatred of men into Compassion of him." James opted for "a middle course," in which Ralegh would be privately examined and "confronted" by witnesses "who were with him" on the expedition to Guiana.[20]

Keeping the proceedings against Ralegh behind closed doors made his case popular with the people. Many English were inclined to favor the hero who once again had taken on the Spanish, even if he had not returned with gold. We know little of the proceedings beyond that the council investigated Ralegh's "Faults committed" before, during, and after "his voyage." Some notes taken by Sir Julius Caesar have survived that record "Sir Walter's Answer" to the charges. These included Ralegh claiming that on his deathbed, Justice Gawdy said to a Dr. Turner at Ralegh's treason trial "that the justice of England was never so depraved and injured as in the Condemnation of Sir Walter Ralegh."[21] Ralegh also answered those who claimed he never intended to mine for gold by asserting that he had spent £2,000 for tools and "refiners"—why else would he have spent so much? He confessed that he did suggest capturing the treasure fleet from Mexico, but only "if the mine failed."[22] Ralegh denied other unspecified charges but "confesseth to have endeavoured to escape" when Stuckley brought him to the Tower. This he thought totally excusable based on biblical precedents. He also vehemently denied ever having made any "ill speeches about the King," which he insisted until his death.

Having gathered information about the expedition from Ralegh and witnesses, on October 28, 1618, the "judges of the King's Bench" had Ralegh brought before them to ask him if he could provide any reason why he should not be executed under the former sentence for treason. He failed to provide sufficient reason.[23] The Lord Chief Justice, Sir Henry Montague, pronounced that the king's commission to lead an expedition to Guiana did not absolve Ralegh of his earlier treason. Montague used the occasion to praise Ralegh's religiosity: "Your Faith hath heretofore been questioned, but I am resolved you are a good Christian, for your book which is an admirable work, doth testify as much." Ralegh begged the judges for one favor, that "I may be heard at the day of my death." This was granted. He also learned that he would be beheaded—not the more painful sentence from his treason trial of hanging until almost dead before being drawn and quartered.

Brought to Westminster for execution the next day, on the way to the scaffold Ralegh gave away his money to those who thronged around him. Taking notice of an elderly bald man who "pressed very forward," Ralegh asked what he wanted of him. The man said, "Nothing but to see him, and to pray God to have mercy upon his soul." Ralegh thanked him. "I have no better thing to return thee for thy good will; but take this night-cap . . . for thou hast more need of it now than I."[24]

Accepting the imminence of death, Ralegh retained his composure. Because he was being executed under the long-ago charge of treason, to the onlookers, and to much of England, the scene had a feeling of unfairness. He played his role for all it was worth. After studying many of the documents surrounding Ralegh's death, James Spedding has observed, "No tragic scene in real life was ever so finely acted." Sir Edward Harwood, who did not witness the execution but who wrote of the public impression the next day, wrote to Dudley Carleton that Ralegh died "with so much assurance, so Christianly and so like truth, as all his beholders were possessed he died innocent, not only of the treason, but of late new practices, and of ill speeches of his Majesty, and of [un]justly injuring the King of Spain."[25] John Pym and other future members of Parliament who played leading roles in the beheading of James's son Charles allegedly first awoke to Stuart tyranny and injustice at the execution of Ralegh.

At the scaffold, Ralegh gave his final performance. He rewarded his listeners with a scaffold speech that lasted about three-quarters of an hour. He entered the scene smiling and called friends closer so he would not have to shout. Several lords came near and shook his hand. Ralegh gave, according to one account, "a most grave, Christian, and elegant discourse," to clear himself of the charge of atheism.[26] After thanking God "that he hath sent me to Die in the sight of so Honourable an Assembly, and not in Darkness" in the Tower of London, where he had long suffered, he wished to clear his name on "two main Points of Suspicion, that his Majesty hath conceived against me." One was the belief that Ralegh "had some Plot with France," since he was going to flee there. There was no plot, he claimed, and he was not lying, for "to call god to Witness to a falsehood at the time of Death . . . there is no hope for such an one." Ralegh swore, "I never had any Commission from the King of France" or any "French Agent." Secondly, "his Majesty hath been Informed" that he spoke "Dishonourably and Disloyally of him." (This fear recalls Ralegh noting in his *History of the World* that monarchs cared more for what was said about them than any treason an individual might perform.) Ralegh denied the charge. He admitted to attempting to escape and to feigning sickness, "but I hope it was no sin."

Ralegh forgave those who had wronged him. He had "received the Sacrament this Morning," and now "I do forgive all the World." Although he forgave Stuckley by name, he maintained that Stuckley lied about the events surrounding his bringing Ralegh from Devonshire to London, particularly about the French plot that did not exist. Ralegh also explained the events surrounding the mutineers in Ireland, and the ridiculousness being spread that he had undertaken the expedition not to mine gold in Guiana but for other reasons. He discountenanced slanders made against him about the Guiana voyage and told his audience how he had kept his word to Lord Arundel by returning to England. Then he turned to the death of the Earl of Essex and swore that he did not smoke tobacco when the earl was executed: "I protest I shed Tears at his Death, though I was one of the contrary Faction." Ralegh claimed that at the execution he was so distant that he could barely see Essex, but he wished he had been closer, "for I heard he had a desire to see me and be Reconciled to me." Ralegh protested "that I lamented his Death . . . for it was the worse for me as it proved, for after he was gone I was little beloved."

Ralegh closed his speech, "I intreat you all to join with me in Prayer," for I have offended God with my "Vanity, and have lived a sinful Life, in all sinful Callings, having been a Souldier, a Captain, a Sea-Captain, and a Courtier, which are all places of Wickedness and Vice." After stating his hope to make "Peace with God," everyone but Ralegh was ordered off the scaffold, and Ralegh thanked them for their company.

Taking off his gown and doublet, "he called to the Headmen to shew him the Ax." The executioner refused. Ralegh scolded, "I pray thee let me see it, Dost thou think I am afraid of it!" Ralegh held it in his hands and "felt along upon the Edge of it, and smiling, spoke to the Sheriff, saying, *This is a sharp Medicine, but it is a Physitian for all Diseases.*" He then walked "to and fro upon the Scaffold, on every side he prayed the Company to pray to God to assist him and strengthen him." Asked which way he would lay "his Head on the Block," he replied, "*so the Heart be right, it is no matter which way the Head lieth.*" He forgave the executioner and gave him a sign to perform his office. "At two blows he lost both Head and Life, his Body never shrinking nor moving."[27]

—

THE PHYSICAL UNIVERSE has a way of leaving one breathless.

Given the above account of his last few years, one could easily see Ralegh's life coming to an end after a period spent consumed with the material aspects of existence. Gaining release from prison occupied his mind; he formed and led a massive expedition to South America to obtain gold; he returned to England a failure and lost his head.

But recall where we began, with the "Inventory" taken of the possessions on Ralegh's person during his third imprisonment in the Tower of London. Ralegh bore items indicative of his life, representations of the self who applied meaning to his universe. His pockets were filled with ores to test. He possessed ingredients, including the prized ambergris, for the cordials he made to treat illness. He brought his trusty "spleen stone" for his spleen or liver ailments. He drew from his pocket a "Guiana idol of gold," a symbol of his access to Native peoples in the remote Orinoco delta, that perhaps also bore spiritual meaning for Ralegh.

Symbols and fetishes are powerful statements of who we are and what we hope for. Most people display representations that others share, albeit with individualized alterations: one person wears a silver cross, another a gold, and a third chooses a Celtic. Ralegh was brash in representing himself and in emphasizing the uniqueness of each individual, as he profoundly related in his *History of the World*: each of us, each thing, was unique. Ralegh celebrated his own uniqueness by fearlessly wearing lace collars, jewels on his shoes, and an array of exotic gems and crystals that were as unique as he. He was unafraid of individuality and difference, the most substantive reason he had no interest in changing America's Native peoples, whom he appreciated like no one else in England. He found comfort in their keeping him company during his years of imprisonment in the Tower of London. Indeed, as he had hoped all along, he likely learned from them. Perhaps, too, he felt comfortable with America's Native peoples because they shared the view that physical things had unseen qualities, meaning, and power.

The "crimson ston set in gold," listed in the inventory, Ralegh likely wore into prison as Richard Boyle wore the stone Ralegh gave him, believing it possessed protective properties. Ralegh and others went far and wide to locate these precious objects. They believed crystals and stones could facilitate good health, and in alchemy could affect the transformation of one substance into another, or could connect the physical and spiritual worlds. These objects literally pointed the way to America and other distant lands. The most potent physical manifestation of European overseas expansion in Tudor and Stuart England was the ship, and, as Robert Boyle noted, the Europeans needed the compass to point the way. Ralegh carried with him into prison a lodestone—the grayish, seemingly unremarkable stone that possessed magical properties to manipulate particular objects with its unseen magnetic power. Properly placed, it identified the direction of the magnetic North Pole so that navigators could find their bearings. Ralegh and his peers did not need to know how the compass worked to use it; we cannot imagine how many times sailors and other travelers thanked their lucky stars—or God—for this gift.

The jacinth seal Ralegh carried into prison—likely a blue sapphire—"with a Neptune cut" into it, symbolized the importance of the sea in Ralegh's life. He could have chosen other features for his seal, but Neptune, the Roman god of the seas, was the most potent representation of the sea's power and mortals' need for supernatural assistance to survive the vagaries of the sailor's world.

Many items in Ralegh's possession reaffirm his preoccupation with Guiana. He bore maps of the land and waterways, a description of the Orinoco, a map of nearby Panama, five assays of a silver mine in Guiana, and, of course, the ores he brought back that required testing. All of this material bears witness to Ralegh's continued pragmatic interest in precious metals. His life was at stake and he needed proof that the mines of gold or silver existed. But it was illusory. Ralegh's faith and assertions did not make the mines real. There was gold and silver, but not in the vast amount that he sought. *Discovery of the Empire of Guiana*, he thought, was his ticket back to relevance with Queen Elizabeth; twenty years later, the promise of gold mines in Guiana opened the Tower's door to Ralegh's freedom. Monarchs were even more preoccupied with accumulating vast amounts of wealth than everyone else because they needed so much more. They had large courts to support and nations to defend. Ralegh had used his ships' capture of the *Madre de Dios* to earn his way out of the Tower of London during his incarceration for marrying the queen's lady-in-waiting without permission. With James, he had tried many ways, including winning the support of Queen Anne and Prince Henry. Once Henry died, there was nothing left but to convince James of the existence of Guiana's great mines.

Ralegh understood as few people did the centrality of wealth to political power because he had to maintain his own network of followers. Despite his many talents, once he lost the queen's affection, he needed new sources of income to buttress his network at court. Even though he had not lost the grants she gave him, he was on the outside looking in for access to patronage; he needed followers at court to constantly remind the queen of his value. His exploits in Guiana, he hoped, would increase his estate, and thus his network and power exponentially, but also the power of England against Spain.

America was the linchpin in Ralegh's career and in Tudor colonization. Ireland was of more immediate consequence than America, but the English grasp for empire extended beyond the British Isles, across the seas. England needed American sources of wealth to counter Spain's advantages in possessing an American empire. That empire had funded Spain's threatened domination over Western Europe. Ralegh and others, such as Gilbert, Grenville, and Drake, worked to reduce Spanish overseas power, siphon off its wealth, and insert England as the dominant power in America. By the mid-1590s, Spanish power had declined at sea, a result of the quagmire of the Dutch War and overextension of resources in multiple other ways. English and Dutch naval power were on a trajectory of ascension. Ralegh, who organized pirating expeditions, colonization in North America, South America, and Ireland, and who had led the way to victory at Cádiz, showed the English what they could accomplish. England's future depended on their mastery at sea and Ralegh both articulated this strategy and demonstrated, along with many others, how to succeed.

Ralegh's legacy as a colonizer, founder, architect, and exemplar of empire building has largely been misconstrued. Some applaud his celebrity as the first to plant English in America. Then they reference his failed colonial enterprises and note that the proper beginning of the English Empire was at Jamestown. This view skews and casts into shadows the centrality to later developments not only of Roanoke but also of Ireland, and the long history of England in the Emerald Isle. For four hundred years, the English gained experience as colonizers in Ireland and learned the difficulties of overseas planting. Beginning the story with Jamestown overlooks a basic factor in the Tudor mind-set: that the foundational story of England in the Age of Elizabeth lay in the Norman Conquest of 1066—England itself was a colonized nation where the colonizers had subjected the colonized. Some Elizabethans viewed this new stage of colonization in positive terms, as Spenser did, because it had brought civilization, modernization, order, and prosperity to the colonized in England.

Ralegh did not seek to use colonization as a makeover for Native peoples. His vision, planning, and thinking about colonialism ran much deeper and was more appreciative of Native cultures than the views of virtually any of his contemporaries. Like other Hermeticists, including Spenser, Ralegh did not portray the colonizing culture as inherently superior to that of the colonized. Despite their interest in discovery and the new, Hermeticists celebrated pastoralism and revered the ancient world. Ralegh and other Hermeticists appreciated Native peoples as they appreciated pre-Christian peoples' piety and were unconcerned with the speed with which Native peoples became Christian. Ralegh even denied that the English were the chosen people of God and, like other Hermeticists, believed that God had blessed non-Christian peoples. There was in Ralegh's *History of the World*, as in his life, an unusual breadth of openness and respect for non-Christians. Pious himself, he understood piety not in terms of Christianity but in terms of individuals seeking to understand the unseen universe through study of the infusion of the divine in the physical realm.

Ralegh sought answers in the natural world and in history. His legacy in the laboratory as a healer and chemist, as an author of a remarkable history that illustrated the importance of the unseen universe to the search for knowledge, for his ethnography of Guiana, for his promotion of art and literature about the Roanoke-area Indians—all these are the manifestations of the examined life that hoped to improve the physical circumstances of his country and humanity, while striving to grow closer to the divine.

Ralegh was not unusual in his holistic view of history and science. He typified the Renaissance intellectual in his broad-ranging interests and his quest to make connections among diverse areas of inquiry and represented the Renaissance scientist as a natural philosopher who relied on the experiential method to understand nature and the physical world. Nor was he unique in attempting to bridge the seen and unseen universes—the driving force among the leading Renaissance scientists who had rejected the view that all that mattered in science and mathematics had been discovered by the ancients. When Hariot viewed the moon through the telescope, what had previously been part of the unseen universe became part of the seen—the surface of the moon—and it gave him new appreciation of the wonders of the universe. These discoveries spurred the Renaissance scientists and filled them with confidence that other discoveries could be made. Hariot could not see the atom, but he imagined it. Ralegh imagined a world in which Native peoples would be treated as allies and English need not try to change them, a world where the future of both would improve through co-creation, where English women would be sent to intermarry with Native men to forge closer bonds.

Ralegh, Hariot, and others imagined an America that not only answered Europe's needs for precious metals but also offered lands for teeming populations to settle, plants for providing new cures for the sick, and answers to the mysteries of the universe. The fact that America possessed so many wonderful things proved God had blessed the land. Many Europeans believed that God intended that land for them and that the Native people were mere caretakers until the Europeans arrived to make better use of it. But Ralegh and others thought America's peoples should not be removed, enslaved, or killed, and that all could live in friendship amid a mutual sharing of knowledge and bounty.

Ralegh's openness to Native cultures was remarkable. He articulated to others, such as the queen, what should be the character of colonization and the importance of positive encounters with Native peoples. Ralegh had no need to present to the queen his radical views on not sending missionaries to Guiana, on Natives' justification in killing missionaries, and on having patience to wait until Natives requested missionaries unless he actually believed these ideas, which would not have been popular at court, were moral, correct, and mutually beneficial. Ralegh was a pragmatist and an idealist. He possessed a strong moral compass. He could not help but criticize the immoral behavior of bad kings in his *History of the World*, for fundamentally he was sure that all humans were subject to God and must answer for their behavior.

Ralegh was a man of faith. His descendants in science can be found among the many physicists who subscribe to string theory or the big bang theory on the origins of the universe. Both theories reflect Ralegh's excitement in connecting the unseen with the physical universe. Although neither of those theories requires the existence of God, modern physicists generally understand that they likely will never be able to prove them. These physicists possess faith in studying the unprovable because they perceive the process of study is key to unraveling the mysteries of the universe. Ralegh would have appreciated their confidence.

We could end the story here with a poem Ralegh wrote shortly before his death that closes with "And from which earth and grave and dust, the Lord shall raise me up I trust." But another poem he wrote at about the same time seems more to capture Ralegh's view of life as he faced death:

> *What is life? a play of passion.*
> *Our mirth? the Musick of division,*[28]
> *Our mothers wombs the tiring houses*[29] *be,*
> *Where we are drest for times short Tragedie.*
> *The earthe the stage; heaven the Spectator is*
> *Who still doth note who ere doth act amisse.*
> *Our graves, that hide us from the parching Sun,*
> *And but drawne curtaines when the play is done.*

ACKNOWLEDGMENTS

W hen I was in graduate school, I considered writing a book on Walter Ralegh and the initial stages of English colonization in America, but I realized that I was not up to this immense task. This book is the culmination of fifteen years of research. What began as an interest in Ralegh and English colonization grew into a project that spanned the Atlantic and the English Renaissance. I became immersed in Renaissance music, art, and theater; I discovered the importance of natural philosophy, Hermeticism, and alchemy. (My appreciation of the musicians who keep alive Elizabethan music— deepened.) In my exploration—voyages, if you will—I gained greater appreciation for Gershom Scholem's pioneering study of Jewish mysticism, *Kabbalah*; Francis Yates and her work on the Renaissance occult; and an interdisciplinary course I took at the University of Florida, taught by Taylor Scott, "Music, Eroticism, and Madness."

I am grateful to several archives and libraries whose collections provided much of the source base for this book, especially the British Library, the United Kingdom's National Archives, the National Library of Ireland, the National Archives of Ireland, the Library of Trinity College Dublin, the Bodleian Library of Oxford University, and the Folger Shakespeare Library in Washington, DC. Additionally, I found the material culture of the National Museum of Ireland, both at Kildare Street and Collins Barracks, useful for the study of sixteenth-century Ireland. Four trips to the town and environs of Youghal, to Ralegh's seignories, exploring the landscape, buildings, and waterways, were of importance for reconstructing the contours of colonialism on the local level. I also am grateful to the National Endowment for the Humanities for their generous support of this project, and to Texas Christian

University and The Ohio State University, which also generously supported this endeavor.

I thank my wonderful colleagues at Texas Christian University, an amiable collection of first-rate scholars who have attracted to the university an excellent cohort of graduate students. Two of my graduate students, Kallie Kosc and Brady Winslow, competently checked many of the quotations and footnotes in this book. Jennifer McCutchen, Jessica Webb, and Jeremy Albers provided additional research assistance.

At The Ohio State University, my esteemed colleagues John Brooke, Kenneth Andrien, David Cressy, and Matt Goldish allowed me to bend their ears on various questions related to Ralegh. John, who has written about Hermeticism, identified the Hermetic nature of smoke in the de Bry engravings, and Matt introduced me to other Hermetic engravings. David not only recommended bibliography but also facilitated the Early Modern Seminar discussing a play I wrote about Ralegh—I staged many of the main characters in Ralegh's life speaking their actual words as a way of trying to understand them and their relationships to one another. Ken, my friend and fellow explorer of Atlantic history, gave me the opportunity to develop and direct OSU's Center for Historical Research, where I enlarged my skills and vision of Atlantic studies.

Two former colleagues from Western Washington University—both dear friends—Leonard Helfgott and Nancy van Deusen, critiqued a number of chapters and spent many hours discussing the manuscript with me. My friend and former graduate student at Ohio State, now teaching at Western, Hunter Price, also read bits and pieces and discussed the work on numerous occasions.

Carolina Coleman always provided encouragement, frequently lent an ear to hear me work through intellectual problems, and provided a critical pen when I had a difficult piece that required assessment.

Don Critchlow of Arizona State University provided his friendship, support, and willingness to discuss this work—and the opportunity to share my thoughts with his students on several occasions. Isa Helfgott kindly invited me to the University of Wyoming to give a public lecture on Ralegh and to meet with several classes of students, from which I much benefited. Teresa Watkins introduced me to the ruins of several sites on Ralegh's lands in and about Youghal, and most every alleyway in her wonderful town.

Doug Egerton and Leigh Fought hosted me in Dublin during my first research trip to the Irish archives. Over the years, the three of us have had several occasions to read each other's work and discuss history and write at the same table—wonderful days spent together. Doug and Leigh even talked up my manuscript to Basic Books, which led to my publishing with them. I have known Doug since graduate school, so it is especially sweet to publish with the same press and editor, and to have our books appear in print the very same month.

Speaking of editors, I thank Dan Gerstle and Brandon Proia for their wise recommendations and suggestions. Carol Zuber-Mallison took my sketchy map of Ralegh's estates in Ireland and created a coherent and useful map.

I am grateful also—truth be told—to the baristas at my local Starbucks. Kaitlyn, Mary, Jeannet, Crystal, Annika, Ashley, Jay, Matt, Jordan, Erin, and the regional supervisor, Rose, have helped make the coffee shop my home away from home—much of this book was written there. Cheers, too, to my friends and fellow coffee shop devotees who are alternately kind enough not to interrupt my feeble train of thought and knowing enough about when to distract me from writing and editing: Jon van Winkle, Phil Poole (who, along with Mary Nell Poole, also waters my plants while I'm off doing research), Jeff Lerner, David Mercurio, Gary Glick, and David Ahearn. I've spent countless hours discussing Ralegh, writing, and the nature of the universe with Ahearn, who hasn't a clue what's going on, but then none of us do.

Need I say none of these people are responsible in any way for mistakes of fact or wrong-headed interpretations.

My daughter, Cyrana, also explored with me Youghal and its environs and contributed her formidable editing skills to several chapters. She allowed me to bend her ear on much of this book and did not complain—as far as I know. Her discussions of neuroscience influenced my conceptualization of historical process. Science and the humanities are much closer to each other in method than their practitioners usually recognize.

I dedicate this book to my sister Sandy, who has always been a rock in my life.

NOTES

The Inventory

1. For a copy of the inventory, see Edward Everett, *The Life of Sir Walter Ralegh . . . Together with His Letters*, vol. 2 (London: Macmillan and Company, 1868), 496–497; and Sir W. Ralegh, *The Discovery of the Large, Rich, and Beautiful Empire of Guiana*, ed. Robert H. Schomburgk (London: Hakluyt Society, 1848), 228. The inventory was included in a letter from Thomas Naunton, Secretary of State, to Thomas Wilson.

2. Stephen Greenblatt, *Sir Walter Ralegh: The Renaissance Man and His Roles* (New Haven, CT: Yale University Press, 1973) and *Renaissance Self-Fashioning: From More to Shakespeare* (Chicago: University of Chicago Press, 1980).

3. "The 21th and Last Booke of the Ocean to Scinthia," in Michael Rudick, ed., *The Poems of Sir Walter Ralegh: A Historical Edition* (Tempe: Arizona Center for Medieval and Renaissance Studies, 1999), poem 26.

4. *The Works of Edward Gibbon*, vol. 13, *Autobiographies* (New York: Fred de Fau & Company, 1907), 167–168.

Chapter 1: Toward an Empire

1. Cited in Anne McLaren, "Political Ideas: Two Concepts of the State," in *The Elizabethan World*, ed. Susan Doran and Norman Jones (New York: Routledge, 2010), 101–102.

2. The Normans were referenced several times in his book.

3. Much of the above discussion is drawn from John Patrick Montaño, *The Roots of English Colonialism in Ireland* (Cambridge: Cambridge University Press, 2011), 64–67, quotation from 66. For an overview of the first two centuries of English rule in Ireland after conquest, see Robin Frame, *Colonial Ireland, 1169–1369*, 2nd ed. (Dublin: Four Courts Press, 2012).

4. For instance, see The Composition Book of the province of Connaught and Thomond, where Irish in two counties surrendered their Irish names (CSP Ireland 2:582–583, October 3, 1585, item 2). The names of all were provided. This was part of the process called Surrender and Regrant.

5. Anthony M. McCormack, *The Earldom of Desmond, 1463–1583* (Dublin: Four Courts Press, 2005); Nicholas P. Canny, *The Elizabethan Conquest of Ireland: A Pattern Established, 1565–1576* (Hassocks, England: Harvester Press, 1976).

6. For discussion of coign and livery, see Ciaran Brady, *The Chief Governors: The Rise and Fall of Reform Government in Tudor Ireland, 1536–1588* (Cambridge: Cambridge University Press, 1994), 174–175. Brady notes that coign and livery were in decline in Ireland, but Desmond and Ormond had to maintain their armies out of "mutual distrust." For hostility toward Tudor centralization and taxation in Ireland, also see Brady, *Chief Governors*, 132–135. For English appointees' relationships with the Geraldines and Butlers, see Brady, *Chief Governors*, chapter 5, "Reform Government and the Feudal Magnates," especially 195–203, 207–208.

7. Colm Lennon, *Sixteenth Century Ireland: The Incomplete Conquest*, rev. ed. (Dublin: Gill & Macmillan, 2005), 213–217ff. On the history of coign and livery, see McCormack, *Earldom of Desmond*, 56–57, 129–132.

8. CSP Ireland 1:357; Lennon, *Sixteenth Century Ireland*, 215.

9. Thomas Churchyard, *A General Rehearsall of Warres, Called Churchyardes Choise* (1579). For analysis of the violence, see Rory Rapple, "Chapter 6: The Limits of Rhetoric: The Captains and Violence in Elizabethan Ireland to 1588," in *Martial Power and Elizabethan Political Culture* (Cambridge: Cambridge University Press, 2009), 200–249.

10. An excellent overview of the process of searching for new ways to Asia to obtain commodities is J. H. Parry, *The Age of Reconnaissance: Discovery, Exploration, and Settlement, 1450–1650* (London: Weidenfeld and Nicholson, 1963).

11. The best summary of initial English activities in the North Atlantic is Kenneth R. Andrews, *Trade, Plunder and Settlement: Maritime Enterprise and the Genesis of the British Empire, 1480–1630* (Cambridge: Cambridge University Press, 1984), chapter 1, "Early Ventures, 1480–1550": 41–63.

12. Andrews, *Trade, Plunder and Settlement*, 68.

13. The original definition of *adventurer* dates to the fifteenth century. The word referred to those who invested in an enterprise, and it came particularly to refer to investment of a speculative nature in overseas trade and settlements. The adventurer sometimes accompanied the expedition abroad to protect his investment and seek other opportunities as they became available.

14. For English encounters with the Inuit, see James McDermott, *Martin Frobisher: Elizabethan Privateer* (New Haven, CT: Yale University Press, 2001), 141–146. For more on the search for the Northwest Passage, see Peter C. Mancall, *Hakluyt's Promise: An Elizabethan's Obsession for an English America* (New Haven, CT: Yale University Press, 2007); Roger M. McCoy, *On the Edge: Mapping North America's Coasts* (New York: Oxford University Press, 2012); Robert McGhee, *Arctic Voyages of Martin Frobisher: An Elizabethan Adventure* (Québec: Canadian Museum of Civilization, 2001).

15. McDermott, *Martin Frobisher*, 151–152.

16. McDermott, *Martin Frobisher*, 176.

17. Harry Kelsey, *Francis Drake: The Queen's Pirate* (New Haven, CT: Yale University Press, 2000), 163.

18. Andrews, *Trade, Plunder and Settlement*, 142.

19. Kelsey, *Francis Drake*, 93–204.

Chapter 2:
Annoying the King of Spain:
Blueprints, Legalities, and Baby Steps

1. See Part Three for discussion of Ashley's relationship with Elizabeth.

2. Quoted in David Beers Quinn, *The Voyages and Colonising Enterprises of Sir Humphrey Gilbert*, 2 vols. (London: Hakluyt Society, 1940), 4.

3. See "Visions," British Library, Additional MS 36674 [59–62].

4. The treatise was published ten years later by George Gascoigne. Hakluyt reprinted it in *The Principal Navigations, Voiages, Traffiques and Discoueries of the English Nation* (1589 and 1600).

5. Lennon, *Sixteenth Century Ireland*, 215, 278. Gilbert had joined forces with Richard Grenville, who had purchased land along the coast, and together they planned to colonize in the vicinity of Baltimore below Cork. "Requests of Sir Warham St. Leger, Edward Saintloo, Richard Grenville, Thomas Leton, Humphrey Gilbert, Jacques Wingfield and Gilbert Talbot for Corporate Privileges in Munster," [1568–1569], in Quinn, *Voyages and Colonising*, 122–124; and for the fishing, and Gilbert's complaints about the Spanish and Basques, see Humphrey Gilbert, "The Discourse of Ireland," 1572, in Quinn, *Voyages and Colonising*, 124–128.

6. Eric H. Ash, *Power, Knowledge, and Expertise in Elizabethan England* (Baltimore: Johns Hopkins University Press, 2004), 93–94.

7. All quotations from Gilbert's paper on the academy are from a reprint found in Henry Ellis, *Archaeologia, or Miscellaneous Tracts Relating to Antiquity* (London: Society of Antiquaries, 1827), 506–520.

8. Christopher Hill, *Intellectual Origins of the English Revolution* (Oxford: Clarendon Press, 1980). Hill shows that mathematicians and artisans filled in the gap in education in London by offering a huge array of classes that promoted a wide range of needed expertise, from shipbuilding to road and house construction.

9. Humphrey Gilbert, "A discourse how hir Majestie may annoy the king of Spayne," November 16, 1577, in Quinn, *Voyages and Colonising*, 170–175. Gilbert reasoned that the wealthy in those countries would not invest in more ships, especially because they lacked seasoned timber.

10. Though I am unaware of how much fish Spain consumed from the cod fisheries in the late sixteenth century, about 150 years later the Spanish received enough cod from the fishery to supply about half of the nation's protein needs—in other words, fish were extremely important to the Western European diet. See John Robert McNeill, *Atlantic Empires of France and Spain: Louisbourg and Havana, 1700–1763* (Chapel Hill: University of North Carolina Press, 1985), 111.

11. Gilbert, "A discourse how hir Majestie may annoy the king of Spayne," 173.

12. Gilbert, "A discourse how hir Majestie may meete with & annoy the king of Spain," in Quinn, *Voyages and Colonising*, 176–180.

13. Gilbert, "A discourse how hir Majestie may meete with & annoy the king of Spain," 176–180.

14. Gilbert said the cost would be £20,000, which was better than spending £100,000 elsewhere. The actual foray, when led by Drake, cost £40,000. See discussion of Drake's foray in Part Four.

15. This idea is at least more than twenty-four hundred years old because it appeared in Kautilya's *The Arthashastra*.

16. See Ken Macmillan, *Sovereignty and Possession in the English New World: The Legal Foundations of Empire, 1576–1640* (Cambridge: Cambridge University Press, 2009), chapter 2, "Defining the Elizabethan Empire in America"; and Ken Macmillan, ed., with Jennifer Abeles, *John Dee: The Limits of the British Empire* (Westport, CT: Praeger, 2004).

17. Ralegh's elder brother Adrian Gilbert later partnered with Dee on New World exploration, and Dee consulted his crystals as to when Gilbert should sail.

18. Dee's activities with Humphrey Gilbert can be followed in the documentary collection published by Quinn, *Voyages and Colonising*, which includes Dee's map of the far north in America. Biographies of Dee include Deborah Harkness, *John Dee's Conversations with Angels: Cabala, Alchemy, and the End of Nature* (Cambridge: Cambridge University Press, 1999) and Glyn Parry, *Arch-Conjuror of England: John Dee* (New Haven, CT: Yale University Press, 2011).

19. Macmillan, *Sovereignty and Possession*, 56.

20. I base this assessment on Dee's detailed discussion of monarchical sovereignty in Europe, which revolved around how he perceived King Arthur treated lesser kings as vassals.

21. See Macmillan, *John Dee*.

22. Burghley was dismissive of Dee's claims over Spain's if they were to be based on the queen's descent from Arthur. See Glyn Parry, "John Dee and the Elizabethan British Empire in Its European Context," *Historical Journal* 49, no. 3 (2006): 643–675.

23. Quotation from *Holinshed's Chronicles* (1587, rev. ed.) *An Reg* 23 (1580).

Chapter 3: Ralegh and the Second Desmond War

1. Editors of the Privy Council Papers state that this might have been Warfleet Bay near Dartmouth. See May 28, 1579, APC 11:142–143.

2. Privy Council to Sheriff, etc., of Devonshire, in Quinn, *Voyages and Colonising*, May 28, 1579, 220–221.

3. Privy Council to Earl of Bedford, etc., July 13, 1579, in Quinn, *Voyages and Colonising*, 224–225.

4. Lennon, *Sixteenth Century Ireland*, 223.

5. Some of the Vatican documents are available on microfilm at the National Library of Ireland, Dublin. See Miscellaneous Documents Relating to English and Irish Affairs, 1578–1584, particularly Papers Relating to [Sebastian] B. di Giuseppi, commander of the garrison of Dunan Oir (Smerwick) 1579, vols. 2–3, 1965.

6. The most thorough exploration of the captains in Ireland is Rory Rapple, *Martial Power and Elizabethan Political Culture* (Cambridge: Cambridge University Press, 2009). See especially chapter 4, but the captains are discussed throughout this fine work. On the roles of captains in the Nine Years' War, see John McGurk, *The Elizabethan Conquest of Ireland: The Burdens of the 1590s Crisis* (Manchester: Manchester University Press, 1998), 197–199.

7. Agnes Latham and Joyce Youings, eds., *Letters of Sir Walter Ralegh* (Exeter: University of Exeter Press, 1999), 22 February 1580/81, 1–2. This would have been his return from London after traveling with Bingham for the latter to deliver his report on Smerwick to the Privy Council.

8. Rapple, *Martial Power*, 150–151.

9. All quotations above from Lord Grey to Queen Elizabeth, November 12, 1580, National Archives of the United Kingdom, calendared in CSP 2:267. "Diabolical fede" translates from the Latin as "diabolical faith."

10. Edmund Spenser, *A View of the Present State of Ireland* (written 1596, published 1633).

11. Grey to Queen Elizabeth, November 12, 1580.

12. Grey to Queen Elizabeth, November 12, 1580.

13. Unknown to Francis Walsingham, November 11, 1580, CSP 2:267.

14. There are many accessible copies of the original letter on the internet in various Google Book and ebook collections of Queen Elizabeth's correspondence. See Queen Elizabeth to Lord Gray, Lord Deputy of Ireland, December 12, 1580. The excusal of Elizabeth's role in perpetrating and increasing levels of violence in Ireland is ahistorical. Referring to the violence in Elizabethan Ireland, historian Rory Rapple observed of English operations in the north in the 1570s that one source of English brutality was the "decisive and unrelenting pressure towards severity [that] came from the monarch herself." Elizabeth berated one northern commander for not being severe enough, particularly in not executing enough of the "meaner sort" of rebels. Rapple provides numerous examples of Elizabeth urging her people to use untoward force in Ireland. Even in England she urged excessively violent measures against her people, not understanding that martial law could not be employed in England against those entitled to judicial process. Rapple, *Martial Power*, 205–206.

15. J. Stirling Coyne and N. P. Willis, "Dingle Bay," in *The Scenery Antiquities of Ireland*, vol. 1 (London: George Virtue, 1841 [but possibly 1842]). The Irish-born Coyne was a popular playwright of farces in England. Willis was a writer, editor, and publisher in the United States.

16. CSP Ireland 2:249, September 8, 1580, Dublin. I have quoted from the reproduction of the letter in Charles Paston Crane, *Kerry* (London: Methuen & Co., 1907), 170.

17. Cotton MSS, Titus A, xii, 313, British Museum. There's a complete copy in *The Complete Works in Verse and Prose of Edmund Spenser* by A. B. Grosart. The letter is undated and addressed "To the right worshipful, and my very good friend, Mr. Ralph Lane, at the Court, give this." Bingham also wrote Walsingham, "From Smerwicke roade, the 11 November 1580," providing the same information as in the Lane letter. It can be accessed through Google Books from *Queen Elizabeth and Her Times: A Series of Original Letters, Selected from . . .* by Adament Media. It is also in a free ebook, *Queen Elizabeth and Her Times* by William Cecil Wright (1838). This letter, actually dated November 12, is from Capt. R. Bingham to Walsingham, 120–122, in CSP Ireland 2:1574–1585, 267. The original is in vol. LXXVIII. #32. There are more documents listed in CSP 2:267.

18. The map is unlabeled No. 31 in the Dartmouth Collection, at the National Maritime Museum, Greenwich. I consulted the beautiful large reproduction at the National Library of Ireland, Dublin, titled "A Plan of the Battle of Smerwick," 16L 33(19).

19. Coyne and Willis, "Dingle Bay."

20. There are several manuscripts of the trial proceedings in the British Library. For published versions, see *Cobbett's Complete Collection of State Trials*, vol. II (London: T. C. Hansard, 1809), trial 74.

21. CSP Ireland 2:431, February 1582–1583, 84. Captain W. Rawley's first and second reckonings beginning July 13, 1580, and ending February 20, 1582/83.

22. For Hooker, see *Holinshed's Chronicles* (1587, rev. ed.) *An Reg 23* (1580). William Camden began writing *Annales* (1615) in 1607. The entry on Ralegh is for the year 1580.

23. The Spanish ambassador referred to the troops as "Romans" and iterates that they apparently were sent by the pope. Bernadino de Mendoza to the King, December 11, 1580, CSP, Spain, vol. 3, 1580–1586, 69.

24. Brady, *Chief Governors*, 210–211.

25. Lennon, *Sixteenth Century Ireland*, 228–230. Ralegh criticized Ormond to Lord Grey for not pursuing the rebels in Munster. See his letter to Grey of May 11, 1581, in Latham and Youings, *Letters of Sir Walter Ralegh*, 8–10.

26. Latham and Youings, *Letters of Sir Walter Ralegh*, Ralegh to Leicester, August 26, 1581, 11. Ralegh likely exaggerated that Fitzedmund of Cloyne was the only local elite who remained "true" in both rebellions.

27. Ralegh to Sir Francis Walsingham, February 23, 1580/81, in Edward Edwards, *Life of Sir Walter Ralegh*, 2 vols. (London: Macmillan, 1868), 2:10.

28. Ralegh to Walsingham, February 25, 1580/81, in Edwards, *Life of Sir Walter Ralegh* 2:11–13. Rapple notes that the English captains "generally received leases of the manors attached to the castles or forts they occupied and often received monastic lands adjacent to the fortifications. . . . They also, naturally, attempted to amass a portfolio of lands within these areas and further afield" (*Martial Power*, 145).

29. Ralegh to Walsingham, February 25, 1580/81.

Chapter 4:
"a man noted of not good happ by sea":
Humphrey Gilbert Prepares to Colonize America

1. For the planning of the Munster Plantation, see Part Six; Nicholas Canny, *Making Ireland British, 1580–1650* (Oxford: Oxford University Press, 2003); Michael MacCarthy-Morrogh, *The Munster Plantation: English Migration to Southern Ireland, 1583–1641* (Oxford: Oxford University Press, 1986).

2. Sir Thomas Smith to Lord Burghley, February 8, 1571/72, State Papers, National Archives of the United Kingdom, 70/146 f. 45.

3. The implication was that the English did not have to regard Native owners of the land, whereas Christian ownership would be respected.

4. For the terms of the settlement, see Quinn, *Voyages and Colonising*, 59–60.

5. Richard Hakluyt, *Divers voyages touching the discouerie of America and the Ilands adiacent . . .* (London: Thomas Woodcoke, 1582).

6. Carol Z. Wiener, "The Beleaguered Isle: A Study of Elizabethan and Early Jacobean Anti-Catholicism," *Past and Present*, no. 51 (May 1971), 27–28; William Haller, *Foxe's 'Book of Martyrs' and the Elect Nation* (London: Jonathan Cape, 1963).

7. John A. Wagner and Susan Walters Schmid, eds., *Encyclopedia of Tudor England*, 3 vols. (Santa Barbara, CA: ABC-CLIO, 2011), 1:927.

8. Quoted by Quinn, *Voyages and Colonising*, 72–73. Interestingly, the Catholic organizers of the colony also agreed to take to America one impoverished Catholic for every ten who migrated.

9. Quinn, *Voyages and Colonising*, 75.

10. See discussion below by Edward Hayes.

11. Humphrey Gilbert to Francis Walsingham, February 7, 1583, in Quinn, *Voyages and Colonising*, 339–341.

12. Ralegh to Humphrey Gilbert, March 16, 1583, in Quinn, *Voyages and Colonising*, 348.

13. Mendoza to Philip II, March 17, 1583, in Quinn, *Voyages and Colonising*, 349; and Mendoza to Philip II, July 11, 1582, April 26, 1582, and May 6, 1583, 278–279, 244, 364–365.

14. Quinn, *Voyages and Colonising*, 40.

15. Mendoza to Philip II, July 11, 1582, in Quinn, *Voyages and Colonising*, 278–279.

16. See "Additional Articles of Agreement Between Sir Humphrey Gilbert and the Adventurers, with His Instructions for the Voyage," in Quinn, *Voyages and Colonising*, 326–335.

17. Nicholas Faunt to Anthony Bacon, May 6, 1583, in Quinn, *Voyages and Colonising*, 365.

18. CSP Ireland 4:1588–1592, 170–171.

19. "Examinations of John Carter and Lancelot Clayton," August 6, 1583, in Quinn, *Voyages and Colonising*, 378–379.

20. Gilbert to Peckham, August, 2, 1583, in Quinn, *Voyages and Colonising*, 383.

21. The plots were granted in fee farm, which gave permanent ownership to the grantee, but they had to pay an annual rent (farm) to the grantor. The rent was high but fixed. The grantee would not owe to the grantor any of the feudal services normally associated with land ownership.

22. See Philip Edwards, "Edward Hayes Explains Away Humphrey Gilbert," *Renaissance Studies* 6, nos. 3–4 (1992): 273.

23. Edward Hayes, *Narrative of Sir Humphrey Gilbert's Last Expedition* (1583), in Quinn, *Voyages and Colonising*, 409.

24. See "Richard Clarke's Account of the Casting Away of the *Delight*," in Quinn, *Voyages and Colonising*, 423–426. It is possible that Gilbert was right and the two men blamed Gilbert after he was dead.

25. All quotations from Hayes's account are taken from Edward Hayes, *Narrative of Sir Humphrey*, 385–423.

26. For an interesting and thoughtful essay on Hayes's argument that it was God's will that Gilbert should die to leave for others the colonization of North America, see Edwards, "Edward Hayes Explains."

27. I used this calculator: http://www.moonsigncalendar.net/moonphase.asp. I doubt whether there was an earthquake that night because it would have affected the *Golden Hinde* as well.

28. For the popularization of Gilbert's penchant for terror, recorded by Thomas Churchyard, see his account published in *A general rehearsall of warres, called Churchyardes choise* (1579).

29. Sir Thomas Smith to Lord Burghley, January 9, 1572, State Papers, 70/146, and William Medlie to Lord Burghley, April 19, 1572, and May 19, 1572, State Papers, 12/86, 14 and 144, National Archives of the United Kingdom. David B. Quinn never considered that Gilbert was murdered by his men—and certainly not for raping his cabin boy. Quinn had a bit of trouble coming to terms with the evidence of Gilbert's predilections, but he was too good of a scholar not to note them in his work. In his two-volume *Voyages and Colonising* (1940), an extension of his dissertation, he mentions in a footnote "a possible leaning in Gilbert towards homosexuality." In Quinn's assessment of Sir Thomas Smith's and William Medley's comments on Gilbert's sexuality, the former, according to Quinn, was made "possibly in jest," while the latter was written "at a time when he had fallen out with Gilbert." See vol. 1:102n2. By the publication of Quinn's essay on Gilbert for the *Dictionary of Canadian Biography* (1966), he described him as "intermittently homosexual. (Sir Thomas Smith said that the only way to soothe his temper was to send a boy to him)." In 2003, Quinn again addressed Gilbert's predilection for boys as "an addiction to currently fashionable pederasty." See Quinn, *Explorers and Colonies: America, 1500–1625* (London: Bloomsbury Academic, 2003), 214. The gossiping of Smith and Medlie arose from their partnership with

Gilbert to produce copper from iron, earth, water, and fire. In France, as Elizabeth's ambassador, Smith urged Burghley to send his partner Gilbert to check up on Medlie, advising that Gilbert should take with him a "handsome man," otherwise he becomes "assotted [besotted] upon Mr. Medeley." February 8, 1571/72, Smith to Burghley, State Papers, 70/146f. 45. See also Mary Dewar, *Sir Thomas Smith: A Tudor Intellectual in Office* (London: Athlone Press, 1964), 151. Of course, homosexuality was not really the issue—Smith and Medlie both knew they could discuss Gilbert's proclivities with Lord Burghley—it is their discussion of Gilbert's need for boys to soothe his raging soul that reveals their separately offered assessments on how to handle Gilbert when he was in need of comfort.

30. Humphrey Gilbert's patent expired on June 11, 1584. Ralegh received his patent on December 12, 1584.

Chapter 5:
The Case for Genocide:
George Peckham Visualizes Colonization

1. George Peckham, *A True Reporte, Of the late discoveries, and possession, taken in the right of the Crowne of Englande, of the Newfound Landes: By that valiaunt and worthye Gentleman, Sir Humfrey Gilbert Knight* (London: John Hinde, 1583). The book was reprinted in Richard Hakluyt, *Principal Navigations*, vol. III (1589). For a modern reprint, see Quinn, *Voyages and Colonising*, 435–482.

2. *Dictionary of National Biography* entry for George Peckham by James McDermott.

3. John Rastell did promote colonization in his much earlier play, *A Merry Interlude of the IIII Elements* (1520). For discussion of the play, see Lydia Towns, "The Opening of the Atlantic World: England's Transatlantic Interests during the Reign of Henry VIII" (unpublished PhD diss., University of Texas at Arlington, 2019).

4. Modern Americans assume that United States sovereignty was obtained over Native peoples through conquest, though treaties were made with these sovereign peoples.

5. Robert A. Williams Jr. noted that Peckham's tract was the first in English to justify appropriation of American Indians' land. See *The American Indian in Western Legal Thought: The Discoveries of Conquest* (New York: Oxford University Press, 1990).

6. For a survey of how early English writers perceived Indians, see H. C. Porter, *The Inconstant Savage: England and the North American Indian, 1500–1600* (London: Gerald Duckworth & Co., 1979).

7. Ralegh's efforts recruiting men for the army are recorded in the CSP, Domestic Series. In 1597, it did take him longer than expected to recruit sailors for an expedition to the Azores.

Chapter 6: The Courtier

1. David Beers Quinn, ed., *The Roanoke Voyages 1584–1590. Documents to Illustrate the English Voyages to North America Under the Patent Granted to Walter Raleigh in 1584*, 2 vols. (London: For the Hakluyt Society, 1955), 1:82–89. I used this copy of the patent reproduced in *Roanoke Voyages*. Quinn made this copy from *Patent Roll*, 26 Eliz, pt. 1, National Archives of the United Kingdom C66/1237, and collated it with the copy reproduced in Richard Hakluyt, The *Principall Navigations* (1589). Hakluyt's version came from the "original patent (not extant) or a copy of it." See Quinn, *Roanoke Voyages*, 89n1.

2. Patricia Seed discussed the significance of this phrase in her important essay, "Taking Possession and Reading Texts: Establishing the Authority of Overseas Empires," *William and Mary Quarterly* 49, no. 2 (April 1992): 183–209.

3. Patricia Seed recognized that in the English patents, God is the author of the queen's rights. I generally follow her line of thought in "Taking Possession" on the phrasing, though I think that the "science" refers to knowledge instilled by God, and that "motion" also originated from God. Ken Macmillan noted the repetition of the phrases in colonial charters and that the Stuarts replaced "science" with "knowledge." Both Seed and Macmillan also acknowledge that no one could colonize who was not already an "imperial" prince. Ken Macmillan, *Sovereignty and Possession in the English New World: The Legal Foundations of Empire, 1576–1640* (Cambridge: Cambridge University Press, 2009), 106–107.

4. Seed, "Taking Possession," 187.

5. The key works on Elizabethan perceptions of sovereignty, especially in regard to overseas possessions, are Ken Macmillan, *Sovereignty and Possession*; Patricia Seed, *Ceremonies of Possession in Europe's Conquest of the New World, 1492–1640* (Cambridge: Cambridge University Press, 1995); and Laura Benton, *A Search for Sovereignty: Law and Geography in European Empires, 1400–1900* (New York: Cambridge University Press, 2009).

6. See Macmillan, *Sovereignty and Possession*, 40–41.

7. The poem is "Now we have present made." For the full poem, see poem 23 in Michael Rudick, ed., *The Poems of Sir Walter Ralegh: A Historical Edition* (Tempe: Arizona Center for Medieval and Renaissance Studies, 1999). For its use as a song, see Katherine Butler, *Music in Elizabethan Court Politics* (Woodbridge, England: Boydell Press, 2015), 213.

8. Paul E. J. Hammer, *Elizabeth's Wars: War, Government and Society in Tudor England, 1544–1604* (Houndmills, England: Palgrave Macmillan, 2003), 103.

9. Elizabeth A. Brown, "'Companion Me with My Mistress': Cleopatra, Elizabeth I, and Their Waiting Women," in *Maids and Mistresses, Cousins and Queens: Women's Alliances in Early Modern England*, ed. Susan Frye and Karen Robertson (New York: Oxford University Press, 1998), 132.

10. For Elizabeth's relation to Ashley and other women, see Susan Doran, *Elizabeth I and Her Circle* (New York: Oxford University Press, 2015), 193–215.

11. Doran, *Elizabeth I*, quotation from 213.

12. Thomas Morgan to the Queen of Scots, April 19, 1585, in *Calendar of the Cecil Papers in Hatfield House: vol. 3, 1583–1589* (London, 1889), Part III: 97.

13. D. C. Peck, "Raleigh, Sidney, Oxford, and the Catholics, 1579," *Notes and Queries*, new series 23, nos. 5–6 (October 1978): 427–431.

14. Ralegh's relations with Catholics in Ireland are elaborated below in Parts Six through Eight.

15. Steven W. May, *The Elizabethan Courtier Poets: The Poems and Their Contexts* (Columbia: University of Missouri Press, 1991), 13–15, based on David Starkey, "Introduction: Court History in Perspective," in *The English Court from the Wars of the Roses to the Civil War*, ed. David Starkey (London: Longman, 1987), 9.

16. The numbers I have provided come from John Guy, "Introduction," in John Guy, *The Reign of Elizabeth I: Court and Culture in the Last Decade* (Cambridge: Cambridge University Press, 1995), 1–2.

17. Quoted in James M. Boyden, *The Courtier and the King: Ruy Gómez, Philip II, and the Court of Spain* (Berkeley: University of California Press, 1995), 41.

18. On the importance of merchants to the extension of English interests overseas, see Alison Games, *The Web of Empire: English Cosmopolitans in an Age of Expansion, 1560–1660* (Oxford: Oxford University Press, 2008).

19. For a recent discussion of Devon and Cornwall as a breeding ground for Elizabethan pirates, see Mark G. Hanna, *Pirate Nests and the Rise of the British Empire, 1570–1740* (Chapel Hill: University of North Carolina Press, 2015), chapter 1, "The Elizabethan West Country: Nursery for English Seamen . . . and Pirates, 1570–1603."

20. These tilts were theatrical but important nonetheless—and rated. See Roy Strong, *The Cult of Elizabeth: Elizabethan Portraiture and Pageantry* (London: Pimlico, 1999), 133. Original work published 1977.

21. Roy Strong's tilt list for the Accession Day celebrations from 1581–1602 includes none of the Devonshire men noted above. See Strong, *Cult of Elizabeth*, 206–211.

22. Joan Thirsk, *Economic Policy and Projects: The Development of a Consumer Society in Early Modern England* (Oxford: Clarendon Press, 1978), 57–60. Frobisher was something of an exception, but his right came through association with influential London merchants, and the purpose was to open a trade route, not to colonize.

23. It is usually assumed that Ralegh was appointed to the position in 1587, but Hakluyt's dedication of one of his volumes to Ralegh implies his appointment in 1586, and others, too, note that he held the office in the summer of 1586.

24. Butler, *Music in Elizabethan Court Politics*; Susan Watkins, *Public and Private Worlds of Elizabeth I* (London: Thames & Hudson, 1998); Jane Elizabeth Archer, Elizabeth Goldring, and Sarah Knight, eds., *The Progresses, Pageants, and Entertainments of Queen Elizabeth I* (Oxford: Oxford University Press, 2007).

25. Jennifer Richards, *Rhetoric and Courtliness in Early Modern Literature* (Cambridge: Cambridge University Press, 2003), 33.

26. Frank Whigham, *Ambition and Privilege: The Social Tropes of Elizabethan Courtesy Theory* (Berkeley: University of California Press, 1984), 30.

27. Richards, *Rhetoric and Courtliness*, 44–46.

28. Joan Sion, *Education and Society in Tudor England* (Cambridge: Cambridge University Press, 1979), 167, 340. But also see Whigham, *Ambition and Privilege*, chapter 1. For other courtesy texts, see Whigham, *Ambition and Privilege*, 28.

29. Quote from Richards, *Rhetoric and Courtliness*, 61.

30. Catherine Bates, *The Rhetoric of Courtship in Elizabethan Language and Literature* (Cambridge: Cambridge University Press, 2006).

31. I am grateful to Reverend Dr. Taylor Scott for his undergraduate course at the University of Florida, "Music, Eroticism, and Madness," which first exposed me to the Arthurian literature and its sexual dynamics. Dr. Scott also introduced me to interdisciplinary study, which has greatly influenced this book. For a theoretical study of the relationship/conflict between marriage and love, which sees the Arthurian literature as central in shaping modern conceptualizations in Western Europe, see Denis De Rougemont, *L'Amour et l'Occident* (1939), often translated as *Love in the Western World*.

32. For studies of clothing of the period, see Ann Rosalind Jones and Peter Stallybrass, *Renaissance Clothing and the Materials of Memory* (Cambridge: Cambridge University Press, 2000). Chapter 1, "The Currency of Clothing," discusses the market and circulation of clothing, even at the court level. See also Susan Vincent, *Dressing the Elite: Clothing in Early Modern England* (New York: Berg, 2003).

33. May, *Elizabethan Courtier Poets*, 53.

34. On the use of ruffs, see Vincent, *Dressing the Elite*, 19–20, 32–33, 170–71.

Chapter 7: The Cult of Elizabeth

1. May, *Elizabethan Courtier Poets*, 132–133; on Elizabeth's flute playing, see Butler, *Music in Elizabethan Court Politics*.

2. May, *Elizabethan Courtier Poets*, 53.

3. May, *Elizabethan Courtier Poets*, 31–57, quotations from 53, 55.

4. May, *Elizabethan Courtier Poets*, 69.

5. May, *Elizabethan Courtier Poets*, 77.

6. Katherine Duncan-Jones, *Philip Sidney, Courtier Poet* (New Haven, CT: Yale University Press, 1991).

7. May, *Elizabethan Courtier Poets*, 101.

8. May, *Elizabethan Courtier Poets*, 103–112.

9. May, *Elizabethan Courtier Poets*, 117.

10. Early in his career, Ralegh's melodramatic poetry questioned the steadfastness of Elizabeth's love—the great composer William Byrd turned one of these poems into a song by 1588, "Farewell, False Love." Part Eight examines an example of Ralegh's and Elizabeth's use of poetry as political statements about their relationship.

11. The poem appeared as a commendatory poem for George Gascoigne, *The Steele Glas* (1576).

12. The best edition of Ralegh's poems is Rudick, *Poems of Sir Walter Ralegh*.

13. The tract was titled *The Cabinet-council containing the chief arts of empire and mysteries of state*. Martin Dzelzainis described Milton's presentation of Ralegh as reverent. See "Milton and the Protestants in 1658," in *Milton and Republicanism*, ed. David Armitage, Armand Himy, and Quentin Skinner (Cambridge: Cambridge University Press, 1995), 206. See also Angelica Duran, "Walter Raleigh through John Milton, according to William Carlos Williams," *William Carlos Williams Review* 31, no. 1 (Spring 2014): 15–31.

14. For a study that explores Machiavelli's influence on Ralegh, see Ioannis D. Evrigenis, "Sir Walter Raleigh's Machiavelli," in *Machiavellian Encounters in Tudor and Stuart England: Literary and Political Influences from the Reformation to Restoration*, ed. Alessandro Arienzo and Alessandra Petrina (New York: Routledge, 2016), 59–74.

15. Greenblatt dismisses Ralegh's authorships of the poem as beneath Ralegh's abilities, but perhaps his dismissal comes from his refusal to see the depths with which Ralegh distrusted the court and societal institutions that he simultaneously exploited and buttressed for his own ends. Stephen J. Greenblatt, *Sir Walter Raleigh: The Renaissance Man and His Roles* (New Haven, CT: Yale University Press, 1973), 171–176. For discussion of Ralegh's authorship of "The Lie," and of poems written in response, see Rudick, *Poems of Sir Walter Ralegh*, xlii–xlvii; see xliii for discussion of the venom against Raleigh—quite enlightening. Lefranc also questioned Ralegh's authorship of "The Lie," but Rudick questions his assessment (Rudick, *Poems of Sir Walter Ralegh*, xliii–xliv). Pierre Lefranc, *Sir Walter Raleigh écrivain: l'œuvre et les idées* (Paris: Librarie Armand Colin, 1968), 86–94.

16. A. L. Rowse, *The Elizabethan Renaissance: The Cultural Achievement* (New York: Charles Scribner's Sons, 1972).

17. See Anthony Rooley, "New Light on John Dowland's Songs of Darkness," *Early Music* 11, no. 1, Tenth Anniversary Issue (January 1983): 6–21. Also see discussion of Dowland's melancholy and Hermeticism in Robin Headlam Wells, *Elizabethan Mythologies: Studies in Poetry, Drama and Music* (Cambridge: Cambridge University Press, 1994), 195.

18. For Elizabeth's healing through touch, see Anna Whitelock, *The Queen's Bed: An Intimate History of Elizabeth's Court* (New York: Farrar, Strauss and Giroux, 2013), 159–160. The Gheeraerts portrait is in the National Portrait Gallery, London.

19. Elizabeth was the sun and the moon—in many depictions the moon is more associated with Elizabeth because the sun also represented the pope, and the moon allegedly possessed ethereal qualities, like Elizabeth did.

20. Doran, *Elizabeth I*, 195. Anna Whitelock, *Queen's Bed*, notes that there is no way to definitively know whether Elizabeth died a virgin, but she makes a good case that everyone would have known if she romped promiscuously, as had been portrayed by her enemies.

21. Carole Levin, *The Heart and Stomach of a King: Elizabeth I and the Politics of Sex and Power* (Philadelphia: University of Pennsylvania Press, 1994), 27.

22. For Elizabeth's self-promotion as the Virgin Queen, see chapter 2, "Elizabeth as Sacred Monarch," in Levin, *Heart and Stomach of a King*, quotations from 27, 30. On the evolution of the cult of the Virgin, see Helen Hackett, *Virgin Mother, Maiden Queen: Elizabeth I and the Cult of the Virgin Mary* (New York: St. Martin's Press, 1995).

23. Quoted in Strong, *Cult of Elizabeth*, 15, from John Nichols, *The Progresses of Queen Elizabeth* (London, 1823).

24. Much has been written on the relationship between Hermeticism and science. Francis Yates is generally considered to be the first to make a strong connection between the two. See her books, *Giordano Bruno and the Hermetic Tradition* (Chicago: University of Chicago Press, 1964); *Astraea: The Imperial Theme in the Sixteenth Century* (London: Routledge and Kegan Paul, 1975); *The Occult Philosophy in the Elizabethan Age* (London: Routledge and Kegan Paul, 1979); and her essay, "The Hermetic Tradition in Renaissance Science," in *Art, Science, and History in the Renaissance*, ed. C. S. Singleton (Baltimore: Johns Hopkins University Press, 1967), 255–274. For a challenge to Yates, see Robert S. Westman and J. E. Mcguire, *Hermeticism and the Scientific Revolution* (Los Angeles: William Andrew Clark Memorial Library, 1977). An excellent balanced assessment with very useful footnotes is Brian P. Copenhaver, "Natural Magic, Hermetism, and Occultism in Early Modern Science," in *Reappraisals of the Scientific Revolution*, ed. Robert S. Westman and David C. Lindberg (Cambridge: Cambridge University Press, 1990), 261–302. The famed physician, botanist, and toxicologist of the early sixteenth century, Paracelsus, followed hermetic teachings on illness and health in formulating his approach to the treatment of the body. See Allen G. Debus, *The Chemical Philosophy: Paracelsian Science and Medicine in the Sixteenth and Seventeenth Centuries* (New York: Science History Publications, 1977).

25. Yates, *Astraea*, 121.

26. Glyn Parry, "John Dee and the Elizabethan British Empire in Its European Context," *Historical Journal* 49, no. 3 (2006): 652, 665–666, 669. I am grateful to David Cressy for recommending this essay to me. Ralegh provided patronage to Dee at various times. See Glyn Parry, *The Arch-Conjuror of England John Dee* (New Haven, CT: Yale University Press, 2011).

27. Yates, *Astraea*, 75.

28. Yates, *Giordano Bruno*, 289.

29. Yates, *Giordano Bruno*, 289.

30. Yates, *Giordano Bruno*, 169–189. Parry discusses Dee's eschatology as nonsectarian in "John Dee," 643–675, but see especially 648–649, 658–659, and 671.

31. Yates, *Occult Philosophy*, 99–101, and *Astraea*, 38. Burghley found dubious Dee's claims about Elizabeth's rights in America and Europe based, as they were, on her descent from Arthur. Parry, "John Dee," 669.

32. Yates, *Astraea*, 118–119.

33. Yates, *Astraea*, 119.

34. Yates, *Astraea*, 49–50, and *Occult Philosophy*, 99–100; Peter J. French, *John Dee: The World of the Elizabethan Magus* (London: Routledge, 1972), 56.

35. Yates, *Astraea*, 66–68.

36. Although the first three books of the *Faerie Queene* were not published until 1590, Spenser began the work in 1580. See Yates, *Occult Philosophy*, 112. Yates believed that Spenser's exposure to Hermeticism and the Arthurian imagery associated with Elizabeth came from his close association with the circle of intellectuals around Dee. Yates, *Occult Philosophy*, 122. See also Yates, *Astraea*, 69–70.

37. Quotations taken from Yates, *Astraea*, 70–71.

38. Yates, *Astraea*, 114–115.

39. *De modo Evangelli Jesu Christ publicandi, propgandandi, stabilendi inter Infideles Atlanticos*. See Harkness, *John Dee's Conversations with Angels*, 150.

Chapter 8: Planting a New World Colony

1. Two insightful books about the two Richard Hakluyts engaged in English overseas expansion are Peter Mancall, *Hakluyt's Promise: An Elizabethan's Obsession for an English America* (New Haven, CT: Yale University Press, 2007), and George Bruner Parks, *Richard Hakluyt and the English Voyages* (New York: American Geographical Society, 1928).

2. The discourse is reprinted in E. G. R. Taylor, *The Original Writings and Correspondence of the Two Richard Hakluyts*, 2 vols. (London: Hakluyt Society, 1935), 2:211–326.

3. Hariot might also have earned a master's degree at Oxford.

4. Jon V. Pepper, "Harriot's Calculation of the Meridional Parts as Logarithmic Tangents," *Archive for History of Exact Sciences* 4, no. 5 (1968): 359–413; "Some Clarifications of Harriot's Solution of Mercator's Problem," *History of Science*, no. xiv (1976): 235–244; and "Harriot's Earlier Work on Mathematical Navigation: Theory and Practice," in *Thomas Harriot: Renaissance Scientist*, ed. John W. Shirley (Oxford: Clarendon Press, 1974), 54–90. See also John W. Shirley, *Thomas Harriot: A Biography* (Oxford: Clarendon Press, 1983), 87.

5. Eric V. Ash, *Power, Knowledge, and Expertise in Elizabethan England* (Baltimore: Johns Hopkins University Press, 204), 172–173.

6. Ash, *Power, Knowledge, and Expertise*, 174–175.

7. Pepper, "Harriot's Earlier Work," 54–55.

8. Shirley, *Thomas Harriot*, 95.

9. The French also erected a pillar in claiming Florida. Quotations from Richard Hakluyt, *Principal Navigations*, vol. III (1600), cited in Patricia Seed, *Ceremonies of Possession in Europe's Conquest of the New World, 1492–1640* (Cambridge: Cambridge University Press, 1995), 1. Seed's book is seminal on European ceremonies to claim the lands of the New World. For the original account of Gilbert's performance of ceremonies in Newfoundland, see Edward Hayes, *Narrative of Sir Humphrey Gilbert's Last Expedition (1583)*, in David Beers Quinn, *The Voyages and Colonising Enterprises of Sir Humphrey Gilbert*, 2 vols. (London: Hakluyt Society, 1940), 2:402–403.

10. Barlowe's account was made available to members of the court and other prospective investors in manuscript form before publication by Richard Hakluyt in *Principal Navigations* (1589), 728–732. It is titled "The Firft Voyage Made to the Coaftes of America."

11. Seed, *Ceremonies of Possession.* Seed notes that the Roanoke expedition of 1585 was unusual in negotiating "consent" for settlement. Only Maryland, among English colonies, did likewise before 1640. I assume that English consultation with Indians for land on Roanoke Island was directed by Ralegh.

12. Alan Gallay, *The Indian Slave Trade: The Rise of the English Empire in the American South, 1670–1717* (New Haven: Yale University Press, 2002), 106–121.

13. For the Jesuit mission, see Clifford M. Lewis and Albert J. Loomie, *The Spanish Jesuit Mission in Virginia, 1570–1572* (Chapel Hill: University of North Carolina Press, 1953).

14. Barlowe almost certainly presented in person additional information to Ralegh, perhaps sharing doubts and warnings about the Roanoke, which he would not have put in the written report because it would have frightened potential investors. Michael G. Moran, *Inventing Virginia: Sir Walter Raleigh and the Rhetoric of Colonization, 1584–1590* (New York: Peter Lang, 2006), 34.

15. Barlowe must have sent barks along the coast because he noted there was over two hundred miles of islands extending to Chesapeake Bay. He could not vouch for the mainland, which he assumed was as fertile and full of wildlife as the islands, evincing that he had not sent parties overland.

16. The English make no mention of it, but a Spanish observer reported that the English left two of their men in exchange for Manteo and Wanchese. See the report of the testimony of an English prisoner in Jamaica recorded in Licentiate Francisco Marqués de Villalobos to the Crown, Jamaica, Document 39, in Irene A. Wright, ed., *Further English Voyages to Spanish America, 1583–1594. Documents from the Archives of the Indies at Seville Illustrating English Voyages to the Caribbean, the Spanish Main, Florida, and Virginia* (London: For the Hakluyt Society, 1951), 175.

17. On Native Americans in England, see Alden T. Vaughan, *Transatlantic Encounters: American Indians in Britain, 1500–1776* (Cambridge: Cambridge University Press, 2006). See also A. L. Rowse, *Sir Richard Grenville of the "Revenge": An Elizabethan Hero* (Boston: Houghton Mifflin, 1937), 212.

18. Vaughan, *Transatlantic Encounters,* 21–23.

19. David Beers Quinn, *Set Fair for Roanoke: Voyages and Colonies, 1586–1606* (Chapel Hill: University of North Carolina Press, 1985), 167.

20. David Beers Quinn, ed., *The Roanoke Voyages 1584–1590. Documents to Illustrate the English Voyages to North America Under the Patent Granted to Walter Raleigh in 1584,* 2 vols. (London: For the Hakluyt Society, 1955), 1:126. (Hereafter referred to as *Roanoke Voyages.*)

21. *Roanoke Voyages,* 1:127–128.

22. Quoted in Quinn, *Set Fair,* 43.

23. *Roanoke Voyages,* 1:123.

24. "Parliamentary Proceedings on the Bill to Confirm Ralegh's Patent," from Thomas Cromwell's diary, in *Roanoke Voyages,* 1:123–125. Quinn believes the Commons' provisos to Ralegh's bill were "unwelcome" to him. But if this were so, Ralegh would have withdrawn the bill from Commons. Quinn also posits that the bill was "wholly unacceptable to the Queen," because it interfered with her powers in issuing letters patent.

25. Parliamentary historian John Neale asserts that the queen was behind the rejection of the bill by the lords, but again, though this is possible, it is not necessarily probable. See *Roanoke Voyages,* 1:126n1.

26. This was Ralegh's first Parliament and he represented Devon, as he would again in 1586. He also represented Mitchell in 1593, Dorset in 1597, and Cornwall

in 1601. According to the website History of Parliament online, Ralegh was unique in representing three different counties. In his career, Ralegh placed friends in pocket borough parliamentary seats, though there is no way to know for sure just how many.

27. For Parliament during the reign of Elizabeth, see J. E. Neale, *Elizabeth I and Her Parliaments*, 2 vols. (London: Jonathan Cape, 1952, 1957); G. R. Elton, *The Parliament of England, 1559–1581* (Cambridge: Cambridge University Press, 1986); Jennifer Loach, *Parliament Under the Tudors* (Oxford: Clarendon Press, 1991).

28. *Roanoke Voyages*, 1:125–126; for Journal of the House of Lords, see *Roanoke Voyages*, 2:74.

29. He was knighted January 6, 1584/85.

Chapter 9: Summer of Discontent

1. Rowse, *Sir Richard Grenville of the "Revenge,"* 10.

2. The makeup of the colonists is drawn from Quinn, *Set Fair*, 87–90.

3. Anonymous, *The Voyage Made by Sir Richard Greenuille, for Sir Walter Ralegh, to Virginia, in the yeere 1585*, in Hakluyt, *Principal Navigations* (1589), 786.

4. *Roanoke Voyages*, 192n2.

5. Michael Leroy Oberg, *The Head in Edward Nugent's Hand: Roanoke's Forgotten Indians* (Philadelphia: University of Pennsylvania Press, 2008), 67.

6. Grenville's widowed mother married Thomas Arundel, and John Arundel was born thereafter. Little is known of this John Arundel—there were many in Cornwall by that name—but he became a ward of his much older half brother Richard in 1580. Rowse, *Sir Richard Grenville*, 169.

7. *Roanoke Voyages*, 169–171, including footnotes.

8. Drake was cousin to Richard Grenville and claimed to be a cousin to Francis Drake, though if true, he likely was a distant cousin. He was knighted for his expedition to Newfoundland but died the following year. For biographical information, see Julian Stafford Corbett, *Papers Relating to the Navy During the Spanish War, 1585–1587* (London: Printed for the Navy Records Society, 1898), 297.

9. *Roanoke Voyages*, 171–173, for the activities of Drake and George Raymond, commander of the *Lion*.

10. Grenville to Walsingham, October 29, 1585, in *Roanoke Voyages*, 218–221.

11. Henry Talbot to the Earl of Shrewsbury, October 6, 1585, in David Beers Quinn, *New American World: A Documentary History of North America to 1612*, 5 vols. (New York: Arno Press, 1979), 3:294.

12. *Roanoke Voyages*, 244.

13. *Roanoke Voyages*, 245. A copy of the map is inserted between pages 460 and 461, in *Roanoke Voyages*.

14. Quinn, *Set Fair*, 104. Hariot noted that many of the men never left the island—see discussion in Part Five.

15. Barlowe reported in his account of hearing of this great chief, but the first expedition did not meet him.

16. "Ralph Lane's Discourse on the First Colony," in *Roanoke Voyages*, 279–280.

17. For starvation at Jamestown, see Edmund S. Morgan, *American Slavery, American Freedom: The Ordeal of Colonial Virginia* (New York: W. W. Norton, 1975), and "The Labor Problem at Jamestown, 1607–1618," *American Historical Review*, June 1971, 595–611.

18. "Ralph Lane's Discourse," in *Roanoke Voyages*, 276.

19. "Ralph Lane's Discourse," in *Roanoke Voyages*, 280.

20. "Ralph Lane's Discourse," in *Roanoke Voyages*, 282–283.

21. "Ralph Lane's Discourse," in *Roanoke Voyages*, 281–282.

22. Quinn believes that the casada was actually cassava, a root. *Roanoke Voyages*, 283, 349n4.

23. "Ralph Lane's Discourse," 277.

24. The best discussion of Lane's attack on the Roanoke is in Oberg, *Head in Edward Nugent's Hand*, chapter 4.

Chapter 10: Singeing the Spaniard's Beard

1. McDermott, *Martin Frobisher*, 297–298, from Corbett, *Papers Relating to the Navy During the Spanish War 1585–1587*.

2. John Maynard Keynes, "Economic Possibilities for Our Grandchildren (1930)," in *Essays in Persuasion* (New York: W. W. Norton, 1963), 362.

3. All quotations from the plan for the campaign come from "A discourse of Sir Francis Drake's voyage, which by God's grace he shall well perform," in Corbett, *Papers Relating to the Navy During the Spanish War 1585–1587*, 69–74.

4. During his 1579 assault on Spanish settlements in the New World, Drake frequently feted the captains he held for ransom. The best biography of Drake is Harry Kelsey, *Sir Francis Drake: The Queen's Pirate* (New Haven, CT: Yale University Press, 1998).

5. Wright, *Further English Voyages*, xxviii and Document 13, "Licentiates Fernández de Mercado and Baltazar de Villafañe to the Crown, La Española, Jan. 14, 1586," 19–22.

6. Wright, *Further English Voyages*, xxv.

7. See McDermott, *Martin Frobisher*, 310.

8. The ransoms were not included in the official tally of the booty of the expedition, because those were considered the personal property of the captor.

9. Kelsey, *Sir Francis Drake*, 273–274.

10. Walter Biggs, *A Summarie and True Discourse of Sir Frauncis Drake's West Indian Voyage*, in Mary Frear Keeler, *Sir Francis Drake's West Indian Voyage, 1585–86* (London: Hakluyt Society, 1975), 270. Although Biggs is noted as the author of this journal, he died during the expedition and the journal was completed by Lieutenant Crofts.

11. McDermott, *Martin Frobisher*, 315.

12. See also Biggs, *Summarie and True Discourse*, 209.

13. Quotation from Wright, *Further English Voyages*, Document 51, "Alonso Sancho Saez and Miguel de Valdés, depositions made at San Agustin," 200. For the English attack on St. Augustine, see the documents collected in Keeler, *Sir Francis Drake's West Indian Voyage*.

14. Source on cannon shot Wright, *Further English Voyages*, Document 54, 205.

15. Wright, *Further English Voyages*, Document 51, "Alonso Sancho Saez and Miguel de Valdés, depositions made at San Agustin, Aug. 12, 1586," 200.

16. Wright, *Further English Voyages*, Document 54, "Posada to Crown from San Agustin, Aug. 12, 1586," 206.

17. Wright, *Further English Voyages*, Document 51, "Deposition of Saez and Valdés," 200.

18. Wright, *Further English Voyages*, Document 54, "Juan de Posada to the Crown, San Agustin, Sept. 12, 1586," 205.

19. Alonso Suarez de Toledo to the Crown, Havana, July 3, 1586, Document 45, in Wright, *Further English Voyages*, 187.

20. Paul E. Hoffman, *The Spanish Crown and the Defense of the Caribbean, 1535–1585: Precedent, Patrimonialism, and Royal Parsimony* (Baton Rouge: Louisiana State University Press, 1980), chapter 4: "1564–1577. A System Takes Shape."

21. Wright, *Further English Voyages*, Document 45, "Alonso Suarez de Toledo to the Crown, Havana, July 3, 1586," 187; also in *Roanoke Voyages*, 722.

22. "Ralph Lane's Discourse," in *Roanoke Voyages*, 289.

23. The only mention of Towaye is in Hakluyt's *Principal Navigations* (1589), 587, where he is listed with Manteo among those who "safely arrived in Virginia, 1587," with the others who joined John White on the famous Lost Colony expedition. Manteo and Towaye were described as "Savages. That were in Englande and returned home into Virginia with them." See "The names of all the men, women and children, which safely arrived in Virginia, and remained to inhabite there."

24. Discussed in Quinn, *Set Fair*, 141.

25. APC, May 8, 1587, 15:76.

26. For the assets of the voyage, see Corbett, *Papers Relating to the Navy During the Spanish War*, 85–96.

27. Biggs, *Summarie and True Discourse*, 44; "Drake's Account to the Queen for her Share," in Keeler, *Sir Francis Drake's West Indian Voyage*, 57.

28. Wright, *Further English Voyages*, Document 49, "Don Pedro de Lodeña to the Crown, Cartagena, July 30, 1586," 192. Lodeña was governor and claimed that the English "did the city more than 400,000 ducats of damage," including 107,000 ducats they paid in cash, 86 artillery, 250 burned houses, damage to the cathedral, booty, and loss of galleys.

29. Wright, *Further English Voyages*, lxvi. For Spain's reaction to Drake (and English assistance to the Dutch), particularly in Philip's European strategies, see Geoffrey Parker, *The Army of Flanders and the Spanish Road: 1567–1659: The Logistics of Spanish Victory and Defeat in the Low Countries' Wars* (Cambridge: Cambridge University Press, 1972), 206ff.

30. *Roanoke Voyages*, 312–313.

31. *Roanoke Voyages*, 312–313.

32. Corbett, *Papers Relating to the Navy During the Spanish War*, 85–96; Keeler, *Sir Francis Drake's West Indian Voyage*, 50–62.

33. CSP Foreign, 1581–1586, 711.

34. *Roanoke Voyages*, 254–255, and Keeler, *Sir Francis Drake's West Indian Voyage*, 32n1.

35. Wright, *Further English Voyages*, Document 22, "The sack of the city of Cartagena, done by Francis Drake Englishman," [unknown author, place, and date. Author might be Sargento Mayor Bartólome Lopez], 51.

36. Wright, *Further English Voyages*, Document 38, "Alonso Suarez de Toledo to Crown, Havana, June 27, 1586," 173. Pedro Sanchez, a seaman who was captured and then escaped, reported that Drake at Cartagena and Santo Domingo "carried off" 200 "Moors from the galleys . . . whom he promised to send to their own country, for they would pass through the Strait of Gibraltar." Also, "150 negroes and negresses from Santo Domingo and Cape Verde—more from Santo Domingo." Wright, *Further English Voyages*, Enclosure no. 2, 212.

37. *Roanoke Voyages*, 254–255.

38. Wright, *Further English Voyages*, Document 53, "Diego Fernández de Quiñones to the Crown, Havana, September 1586," 204.

39. Wright, *Further English Voyages*, Document 46, "Pedro de Arana to the House of Trade, Havana, July 4, 1586," 189.

40. Wright, *Further English Voyages*, Document 44, "Gabriel de Luxan and Diego Fernández de Quiñones to the Crown, Havana, July 1, 1586," 185.

41. *Roanoke Voyages*, 255.

42. Joyce Lorimer, ed., *Sir Walter Ralegh's Discoverie of Guiana* (London: Hakluyt Society, 2006), xxiii.

43. "Introduction," in Clements R. Markham, ed. and trans., *Narratives of the voyages of Pedro Sarmiento de Gambóa to the Straits of Magellan*, vol. XCI (London: Hakluyt Society, 1895). For the magic rings and ink, see Owen Davies, *Grimoires: A History of Magic Books* (Oxford: Oxford University Press, 2009), 85–86, and the biographical introduction included with Sarmiento's *The History of the Incas*, trans. Brian S. Bauer and Vania Smith, introduction by Bauer and Jean-Jacques Decoster (Austin: University of Texas Press, 2007), 6.

44. An *escudo* was the standard gold coin in sixteenth-century Spain. A university professor made about 100 escudos per year—so this equaled ten years' salary. See Frances Luttikhuizen, *Underground Protestantism in Sixteenth Century Spain: A Much Ignored Side of Spanish History* (Göttingen, Germany: Vandenhoeck & Ruprecht, 2017), 202n38.

45. Markham, *Narratives*, 342–343.

46. Lorimer, *Sir Walter Ralegh's Discoverie*, xli.

47. Deposition of Jean Retud in Lorimer, *Sir Walter Ralegh's Discoverie*, 248.

48. Deposition of Jean Retud in Lorimer, *Sir Walter Ralegh's Discoverie*, 248–250.

Chapter 11: *A Briefe and True Report*

1. Kim Sloan makes a good case that White likely was not "base-born" and was indeed a gentleman, but I believe that he likely did not appear a gentleman to others, hence the need to bolster his authority with a coat of arms. Sloan, ed., *A New World: England's First View of America* (Chapel Hill: University of North Carolina Press, 2007), 25–26. The seal is now in the collections of the Folger Library, Washington, DC.

2. White's journal of the voyage expresses dismay at Fernandes's choices and the ignoring of White's opinions.

3. Quinn, *Set Fair*, 270.

4. Quinn, *Set Fair*, 269.

5. E. G. R. Taylor, *The Original Writings and Correspondence of the Two Richard Hakluyts*, 2 vols. (London: Hakluyt Society, 1935), 2:377.

6. The number of non-Iberian ships pirated is unknown. Kenneth R. Andrews, *Elizabethan Privateering: English Privateering during the Spanish War, 1585–1603* (Cambridge: Cambridge University Press, 1964), 224.

7. Frankfurt, where the book was published, "was the center of the international book trade via its annual fair." Peter Stallybrass, "*Admiral narration*: A European Best Seller," in Thomas Hariot, *A briefe and true Report of the new found land of Virginia: The 1590 Theodor de Bry Latin Edition* (Charlottesville: University of Virginia Press for the Library at the Mariners' Museum), 11.

8. Only seven copies of the original exist. A private edition without identification of the printer or publisher, the folio went unrecorded at Stationer's Hall. For information on the first edition, see the introduction to the facsimile edition by Luther S. Livingston (New York: Dodd, Mead, & Company, 1903).

9. The original quarto also noted at the end of the text February 1588, which almost assuredly meant 1589. Henry Stevens in 1885 noted the book's actual publication was 1589. My guess is that Hariot composed a draft in 1588, hence his noting in the beginning of the text that Ralegh had replanted a colony the previous year. The text likely went through several drafts, and not until Ralegh and Hariot were in Ireland did they have the time to confer closely and brainstorm precisely what they wanted the text to convey.

10. Deborah E. Harkness discusses European interest in the New World in *The Jewel House: Elizabethan London and the Scientific Revolution* (New Haven, CT: Yale University Press, 2007). See also Vanita Seth, *Europe's Indians: Producing Racial Difference, 1500–1900* (Durham, NC: Duke University Press, 2010).

11. Amir Alexander, *Geometrical Landscapes: The Voyages of Discovery and Transformation of Mathematical Practice* (Palo Alto, CA: Stanford University Press, 2002), overemphasizes Hariot's reference to silver.

12. Hariot apparently was unimpressed with Lane's belief in pearls northwest of Roanoke Island.

13. The medicinal qualities of tobacco had been noted for centuries until the discovery in the twentieth century of its cancer-producing qualities, which steered physicians and researchers away from studying whatever benefits it may possess. Tobacco was used in the treatment of dozens of conditions and illnesses either through its smoke or in pill form. Indeed, it may possess curative properties when used in limited amounts for short periods.

14. On Ralegh and tobacco in England, see Raleigh Trevelyan, *Sir Walter Raleigh* (New York: Henry Holt, 2002), 143–144.

15. See discussion in Alan Gallay, *The Indian Slave Trade: The Rise of the English Empire in the American South, 1670–1717* (New Haven, CT: Yale University Press, 2002), 23–24.

16. Edmund S. Morgan, *American Slavery, American Freedom: The Ordeal of Colonial Virginia* (New York: W. W. Norton, 1975).

17. Much of the English public, particularly outside London, remained skeptical of the existence of the New World and American Indians. Alden Vaughan, *Transatlantic Encounters: American Indians in Britain, 1500–1776* (Cambridge: Cambridge University Press, 2006), 1–10. For Native Americans in London, see Coll Thrush, *Indigenous London: Native Travelers at the Heart of Empire* (New Haven, CT: Yale University Press, 2016).

18. "Fear" refers to the Indians behaving properly toward the English. See further discussion below.

19. Two eighteenth-century examples of promotional tracts downplaying the danger of Native people in North Carolina to prospective settlers are John Lawson, *A New Voyage to Carolina* (London, 1709) and *An Impartial Hand, Information Concerning the Province of North Carolina* (Glasgow, 1773).

20. See, for instance, Bartolomé de las Casas, *Apologetic and Summary History Treating the Qualities . . . (1559)* (New York: Columbia University Press, 1946).

21. Anthony Pagden, *The Fall of Natural Man: The American Indians and the Origins of Comparative Ethnology* (Cambridge: Cambridge University Press, 1982); Nancy E. van Deusen, *Global Indios: The Indigenous Struggle for Justice in Sixteenth-Century Spain* (Durham, NC: Duke University Press, 2015); Neil L. Whitehead, *Lords of the Tiger Spirit: A History of the Caribs in Colonial Venezuela and Guyana, 1498–1820* (Dordrecht, the Netherlands: Royal Institute of Linguistics and Anthropology, 1988).

22. Hariot was not alone in his thinking. Publishing nearly simultaneously, the Jesuit missionary José de Acosta made similar propositions. Acosta spent seventeen years in Peru and Mexico. In 1590, he published his *Historia natural y moral* in Seville. Acosta's work is much more detailed than Hariot's in analyzing many of the same themes, and additional ones as well. Like Hariot, Acosta discusses Native ceremonies and rituals, as well as spiritual beliefs and religion. He praises Native intellect and spiritual capabilities. Acosta sought to understand the Natives and their culture on their own terms and possessed a keen scientific interest in the Americas. For Hariot and Acosta, the European possession of the Bible did not bespeak superiority—it was but one truth that the Indians had yet to receive. Acosta published in Seville two main books. *De Natura Novi Orbis* (1588) [*On the Nature of the New World*]. For a modern translation of his renowned *Historia natural y moral* (1590), see *Natural and Moral History of the Indies*, ed. Jane E. Mangan, trans. Frances López-Morillas (Durham, NC: Duke University Press, 2002).

23. Anthony Pagden analyzes sixteenth-century European understanding of Indian mythology in *Fall of Natural Man*.

24. Ironically, Europeans believed that technological superiority proved the legitimacy and superiority of their religion.

25. See Part Eight for further discussion of Protestants retaining belief in the spiritual power of objects.

26. Keith Thomas, *Religion and the Decline of Magic: Studies in Popular Beliefs in Sixteenth and Seventeenth Century England* (London: Weidenfeld & Nicolson, 1971).

27. For a fascinating study of Euro-Americans calling on African religious beliefs and practices for health benefits, see James H. Sweet, *Domingo Álvares, African Healing, and the Intellectual History of the Atlantic World* (Chapel Hill: University of North Carolina Press, 2011). Also see Erik R. Seeman, *The Huron-Wendat Feast of the Dead: European Encounters in Early North America* (Baltimore: Johns Hopkins University Press, 2011).

28. On African understanding of the sources of misfortune, see John K. Thornton, *Africa and Africans in the Making of the Atlantic World, 1400–1800*, rev. ed. (Cambridge: Cambridge University Press, 1998); Mechal Sobel, *The World They Made Together: Black and White Values in Eighteenth-Century Virginia* (Princeton, NJ: Princeton University Press, 1987).

29. It is typical in the historiography of the Americas for historians to claim that Native peoples blamed the Europeans for their sickness and to attribute Native conversion to Christianity as a hope to procure a cure. For Indians blaming animals for their sickness, see Calvin Martin, *Keepers of the Game: Indian–Animal Relationships and the Fur Trade* (Berkeley: University of California Press, 1978).

30. Myra Jehlen recognized that Hakluyt was referring to the marriage vow and that "fear" implied proper behavior on the part of the Indians. Thomas Scanlan, on the other hand, avers that Hariot was describing the relationship between a parent and child, and that the child should honor, obey, fear, and love the parent. Jehlen, "The Natural Inhabitants," in *The Cambridge History of American Literature, Vol. 1: 1590–1820*, ed. Sacvan Bercovitch and Cyrus R. K. Patell (Cambridge: Cambridge University Press, 1994), 38. Scanlan, *Colonial Writings and the New World, 1583–1671: Allegories of Desire* (Cambridge: Cambridge University Press, 1999), 55.

31. For the mutual idea of incorporation of the other at Roanoke and Jamestown, see Karen Ordahl Kupperman, *Indians and English: Facing Off in Early America* (Ithaca, NY: Cornell University Press, 2000), especially chapter 6.

32. Hariot did not mention those (allegedly) starving on the way to Virginia, who were abandoned at Jamaica, but he was referring only to the health of his men in Virginia, not during the voyage over.

33. "The adventure of his person" meant he paid his own way to Virginia. This reference to grants of land likely referred to the colonists on the third expedition.

34. Hariot, who rarely published anything, likely because he feared the political consequences, appears to have taken pride in the fact that his work published by de Bry appeared in four languages. David B. Quinn, "Thomas Harriot and the New World," in *Thomas Harriot: Renaissance Scientist*, ed. John W. Shirley (Oxford: Clarendon Press, 1974), 47.

35. See Sandra Young, "Narrating Colonial Violence and Representing New-World Difference: The Possibilities of Form in Thomas Harriot's *A Briefe and True Report*," *Safundi: The Journal of South African and American Studies* (2010), 4:343–360, on the altered context of Hariot's *Briefe*.

36. I should elaborate on a few points made murky by scholars assessing the cultural production generated by Hariot, White, and de Bry. Scholars have long heaped praise on Hariot's *Briefe* as the first book about Virginia, for its account of the Native peoples, and for its influence on later accounts. But not all scholars have celebrated Hariot's *Briefe*. The most notable critic is literary scholar Stephen Greenblatt, a "new historicist" who blasts all writings of colonizers as irredeemable propaganda. The new historicists claim that nothing can be learned about Native peoples from the colonizers, whose self-serving writing only leaves clues about themselves. In contrast, B. J. Sobel argues that despite the propaganda elements, Hariot transcended colonialism as a scientific observer doing his honest best to objectively report on Indians. Sobel overemphasizes Hariot's objectivity, whereas Greenblatt's dismissiveness of the colonizer's ability to report facts of Native life is utter nonsense. Even as colonizers failed to understand Native life, they could still report objectively on material conditions and folkways. A house can be identified as a house, a dance as a dance, and a ritual as a ritual. More troublesome, however, is Greenblatt's, Sobel's, and other scholars' failure to distinguish Hariot's *Briefe* from the captions he provided for White's paintings. Most scholars ignore Hariot's captions. In Greenblatt's defense, if I pointed out to him that the *Briefe* and the captions were two separate constructions, produced to different ends, he would dismiss this as irrelevant because both were the work of the colonizer. On the other hand, Sobel would have made a better case for the significance and accuracy of many of Hariot's observations by accepting some of Hariot's limitations and by analyzing Hariot's elaborations of White's pictures. The Greenblatt essay on Hariot was originally published in the journal *Glyph* in 1981. There are several revised versions, including in *Shakespearean Negotiations: The Circulation of Social Energy in Renaissance England* (Berkeley: University of California Press, 1988), chapter 2, "Invisible Bullets," 21–65. For B. J. Sokol's criticism, see "The Problem of Assessing Thomas Harriot's *A briefe and true report* of His Discoveries in North America," in *Annals of Science* 1 (1994):1–16.

37. For the impact of the Dutch Revolt on the Black Legend, see Benjamin Schmidt, *Innocence Abroad: The Dutch Imagination and the New World, 1570–1670* (Cambridge: Cambridge University Press, 2001). The impact of the massacre of French Protestants in Florida on Western European Protestants is a major theme of Jonathan Hart, *Representing the New World: The English and French Uses of the Example of Spain* (New York: Palgrave Macmillan, 2001).

38. Acosta's near simultaneously published *Historia natural y moral* showed readers a sympathetic and insightful Spanish account of Native peoples. But the de Bry

engravings, the large format of the volume, and the multiple languages of initial publication would have spread the English accounts faster and more broadly in Europe. Publication in Frankfurt and display at the book fairs led to great dissemination.

Chapter 12: Publicizing Ralegh's Virginia

1. See *"Admiranda narratio:* A European Best Seller,"* in the facsimile of *A briefe and true report*, 9.

2. See *John Nichols's The Progresses and Public Processions of Queen Elizabeth I: A New Edition of the Early Modern Sources*, ed. Elizabeth Goldring, Faith Eales, Elizabeth Clarke and Jayne Elisabeth Archer (Oxford: Oxford University Press, 2014), and Elizabeth Goldring, "The Funeral of Sir Philip Sidney and the Politics of Elizabethan Festival," in *Court Festivals of the European Renaissance: Art, Politics and Performance* (Aldershot, England: Ashgate Press, 2002), 199–224.

3. Stallybrass points out that the English market was rather limited. The French market might have been unstable because of the Wars of Religion. Latin publication of de Bry's work would have satisfied the needs of the intelligentsia in England and France.

4. Michiel van Groesen, *The Representations of the Overseas World in the De Bry Collection of Voyages, 1590–1634* (Leiden, Netherlands: Brill Academic Publishers, 2008), 116.

5. The most commonly copied engravings were from the Virginia volume, though other volumes also had their engravings copied, particularly in the eighteenth century. On the influence of the engravings, see van Groesen, *Representations*, 373–376; Stallybrass, *"Admiranda narratio,"* 9–30; Michael Gaudio, *Engraving the Savage: The New World and Techniques of Civilization* (Minneapolis: University of Minnesota Press, 2008), xiii, 108–109; Surekha Davies, *Renaissance Ethnography and the Invention of the Human: New Worlds, Maps and Monsters* (Cambridge: Cambridge University Press, 2016), 268–274.

6. On Jefferson, see van Groesen, *Representations*, 1–2.

7. The Calvinist Jean de Léry had offered a sympathetic, sober, and intimate portrayal of the Tupi of Brazil in *Historie d'un voyage facit en la terre du Brésil* (1578). The book was republished in 1580 and 1585, with four more editions in the coming decades. A modern English translation of the original publication is *History of a Voyage to the Land of Brazil, Otherwise Called America*, trans. and introduction by Janet Whatley (Berkeley: University of California Press, 1990).

8. The publication of André Thevet in the 1550s probably provided for de Bry the precedence of multivolume travel accounts. Thevet published a volume on Asia and another on Brazil based on his own travels, and both included illustrations. For Thevet's influence on Hakluyt, see Peter C. Mancall, *Hakluyt's Promise: An Elizabethan's Obsession for an English America* (New Haven, CT: Yale University Press, 2007), 115–121. For a brief history of the publication of collections of overseas travel narratives before de Bry, see van Groesen, *Representations*, 23–41. I suspect the success of Hans Staden's account of his captivity in Brazil (1557) also influenced de Bry, who published his own version of Staden in 1593. Other texts that likely influenced de Bry include Benzoni's text, which is marred by his inveterate disgust for the Spanish. On the other hand, he covers an array of Indian activities, including dancing and fishing, and in this way reflects interests held by Hariot and White. See also Pedro de Cieza de Léon, who published the first part of his chronicle of Peru in 1553; the other parts

were not published until long after his death. For a modern translation, see *The Discovery and Conquest of Peru*, ed. and trans. Alexandra Parma Cook and Noble David Cook (Durham, NC: Duke University Press, 1999).

9. The Protestant Le Moyne had moved to London around 1580, where he met White and shared his paintings with him. Le Moyne was a talented artist. For Le Moyne's skills as an artist, see Paul Hulton, *America 1585: The Complete Drawings of John White* (Chapel Hill: University of North Carolina Press, 1985), 36–37. See also the collection of Le Moyne drawings and engravings of his work in Paul Hulton, ed., *The Work of Jacques Le Moyne de Morgues: A Huguenot Artist in France, Florida, and England*, 2 vols. (London: British Museum Publications, 1977). For questioning of the engravings' accuracy, see Jerald Milanich, "The Devil in the Details," *Archaeology*, May/June 2005, 26–31. Also consult Christian F. Feest, "Jacques Le Moyne Minus Four," *European Review of Native American Studies* 2, no. 1 (1988): 33–38.

10. For background on the published collections of voyages, see van Groesen, *Representations*, 23–49.

11. The engravings in many volumes were tinted before their sale (often through the use of stencils), animating Virginia by adding color to flesh, clothing, and fauna.

12. Ralegh gets two mentions—as part of the title of the book and again where John White is introduced as the person who "Diligentlye Collected and Draowne" the illustrations, who "was sent thiter speciallye and for the same purpose by the said Sir Walter Ralegh the year abovesaid 1585."

13. Shannon Miller, *Invested with Meaning: The Raleigh Circle in the New World* (Philadelphia: University of Pennsylvania Press, 1998), 120–126. Not to be left out of the credits, de Bry notes that White's work is "now cut in copper and first published by Theodore de Bry att his wone [own] chardges."

14. Miller, *Invested with Meaning*, 120.

15. The originals of White's paintings are at the British Museum. The best reproductions of White's paintings can be found in Hulton, *America 1585*, and Sloan, *New World*. Both volumes provide commentary on the paintings and engravings. Sloan also provides reproductions of the copies made of White's paintings in the seventeenth century when the original by White is no longer extant. Hulton includes black-and-white reproductions of these. Both volumes also include de Bry's engravings of White's paintings, along with White's captions.

16. Joyce Chaplin addresses European conceptualization of the differences between American Indian and European bodies. She argues that when the English were at Roanoke, they admired Native physicality and technology. As the colonial mind frame altered in the seventeenth century, so, too, did views of Indian bodies and skills. As Indian bodies declined, because of disease, for instance, the Europeans took this as a mark of inferiority; simultaneously, they held less esteem for Native technology and skills. Chaplin, *Subject Matter: Technology, the Body, and Science on the Anglo-American Frontier, 1500–1676* (Cambridge, MA: Harvard University Press, 2001). For additional analysis of how English "read" Indian bodies in this time period, see Kupperman, *Indians and English*, 41–76.

17. Miller, *Invested with Meaning*, 144.

18. See particularly Louis Montrose, "The Work of Gender in the Discourse of Discovery," *Representations*, no. 33, Special Issue: The New World (Winter 1991): 1–41; Margarita Zamora, *Reading Columbus* (Berkeley: University of California Press, 1993), 152–179.

19. Miller, *Invested with Meaning*, 86–113, especially 108–112.

20. Miller, *Invested with Meaning*, quotations from 115–116.

21. From Hakluyt's dedication to *De Orbo novo Petri Martyris . . . [Peter Martyr's Decades]* (1587), translated in Taylor, *Original Writings*, 2:367–368. Also quoted in Miller, *Invested with Meaning*, 134.

22. The classic study is Henry Nash Smith, *Virgin Land: The American West as Symbol and Myth* (Cambridge, MA: Harvard University Press, 1950).

23. See Hulton, *America 1585*, 8, for White as a member of the Frobisher expedition.

24. For definitions of counterfeiting in sixteenth-century England, see the *Oxford English Dictionary*.

25. German artist Christoph Weiditz created a wonderful compendium of scenes of everyday life around the world in 1529, which included depictions of Native Americans. His *Das Trachenbuch des Christoph Weiditz von seinen Reisen nach Spanten* has been reproduced as *Authentic Everyday Dress of the Renaissance: All 154 Plates from the "Trachenbuch"* (New York: Dover Publications, 1994), plates xi–xxiv. I thank Nancy E. van Deusen for bringing this work to my attention.

26. Christian F. Feest, "John White's New World," in Sloan, *New World*, 70.

27. Hariot's and White's details about the care for the dead (see discussion below) at Secota, and Hariot's assertion in his *Briefe* of conferring with priests and others about religion and cosmology, show that Hariot must have returned to these towns in the course of his year in Virginia.

28. Hariot calls the tattoos "pounce," which refers to the contemporary sixteenth-century technique of hole-poking to make a template for producing multiple copies of a picture. Hans Holbein, for instance, used this method for repetitious use of the face of Sir Thomas More. On the use of pouncing, see Susan Foister, "The Production and Reproduction of Holbein's Portraits," in Karen Hearn, ed., *Dynasties: Painting in Tudor and Jacobean England, 1530–1630* (London: Tate Publishing, 1995), 21–26.

29. Interestingly, many of the websites that reproduce the paintings and engravings fail to include Hariot's accompanying text. Virtual Jamestown is perhaps the best website for exploring the changes made by de Bry's engravings, offering textual discussion of de Bry's alterations. Inexplicably, the site excludes Hariot's text that accompanied the engravings. www.virtualjamestown.org/images/white_debry_html/jamestown.html.

30. One important exception, believed by scholars to be the work of de Bry and not Hariot, occurs when the captions occasionally editorialize that Europeans would do well to copy the Indians' self-control and moderation, especially in eschewing gluttony.

31. For the tolerance of Hermeticism in the sixteenth century, see Florian Ebeling, *The Secret History of Hermes Trismegistus: Hermeticism from Ancient to Modern Times*, trans. David Lortai (Ithaca, NY: Cornell University Press, 2007), 84–89; and Frances A. Yates, *Giordano Bruno and the Hermetic Tradition* (Chicago: University of Chicago Press, 1964), 186–187.

32. Hart, *Representing the New World*.

33. Benjamin Schmidt, *Innocence Abroad: The Dutch Imagination and the New World, 1570–1670* (Cambridge: Cambridge University Press, 2001).

34. André Thévet published a remarkable portrait of a Florida Indian, Satouriona, in 1584, in *Vrais portraits et vies des hommes illustres* (8 vols.). The engraving likely was based on a painting by Jacques Le Moyne, because he was the French painter in Florida at the time. The portrait is notable for the clothing as much as for the individual, as it displays the subject clothed in animal pelts. The eight volumes are devoted to no-

table people around the world. For a modern reproduction of the engraving, see *André Thevet's North America: A Sixteenth-Century View*, trans. and ed. Roger Schlesinger and Arthur P. Stabler (Montreal: McGill-Queen's University Press, 1986), 128.

Chapter 13: Fire and Smoke: The Hermeticists' Indians

1. Verse from Taylor, *Original Writings*, 2:349.

2. Taylor, *Original Writings*, 2:365–366.

3. Taylor, *Original Writings*, 2:366–367.

4. Hariot's text accompanying the engraving, *Town of Secota*.

5. For a general discussion of Hariot's appreciation of Indian ingenuity, see Karen Ordahl Kupperman, *Roanoke: The Abandoned Colony*, 2nd ed. (Lanham, MD: Rowman & Littlefield, 2007), 56–57.

6. Text from *The Manner of Makinge Their Boates*.

7. See Hariot's caption for engraving 18 in de Bry's *A briefe*.

8. The exception is the painting and engraving of Indian fishing, in which the depiction of fire and smoke is roughly equivalent—and relatively subdued.

9. Art historian Michael Gaudio devoted an entire chapter of his book *Engraving the Savage: The New World and Techniques of Civilization* to the smoke produced by the fires in de Bry's engravings, noting the differences from White's originals. Gaudio argues that White's intent was to show the "fact" of fire. He asserts that in the engravings, smoke represents less the product of fire than the "visible traces of the engraver's hand."

10. The de Brys moved their publishing operation to Oppenheim, a city that attracted Hermeticists, where they published several hermetic tracts, particularly those of Englishman Robert Fludd, who had the same hermetic mentor at Oxford as Thomas Hariot, Thomas Allen. (See van Groesen, *Representations*, 88, 93, on the move to Oppenheim from Frankfurt.) Interestingly, they handsomely paid Fludd for a book, which thrilled and surprised him, because English printers wanted *him* to pay the printing costs. On the importance of the de Bry firm for printing alchemical texts in the seventeenth century, see Stanislaw Klossowski de Rola, *The Golden Game: Alchemical Engravings of the Seventeenth Century* (New York: George Braziller, 1988), 14–15. By coincidence, when de Bry first displayed the Virginia volume at the Frankfurt Book Fair in September 1590, Giordano Bruno, Europe's most famous Hermeticist, was in attendance. See Dorothea Waley Singer, *Giordano Bruno: His Life and Thought* (New York: Henry Schuman, 1950), chapter 7.

11. For instance, he altered the title of White's painting of the "flyer" to the "Conjuror"—the latter term applied by Hermeticists to Moses and others who possessed the power to tap into God's universe through magic.

12. Van Groesen believes that de Bry's son Johan actually produced the engraving, for which his father took credit, because the son added his signature to the engraving for a subsequent edition published after his father died. Nonetheless, the father would have chosen or approved of opening the volume with the Adam and Eve picture. Van Groesen, *Representations*, 71, 413.

13. Theodore de Bry, *INDORVM Floridam provinciam inhabitantium eicones . . .* (1591).

14. The engraving, for instance, was excluded from the English translation of *Narrative of Le Moyne, An Artist who accompanied the French Expedition to Florida*

under Laudonnière, 1564 (Boston: James R. Osgood and Co., 1875) and from Stefan Lorant, *The New World: The First Pictures of America* (New York: Duell, Sloan & Pearce, 1946). The most surprising exclusion is in the British Museum's publication of the Hulton collection, *Work of Jacques Le Moyne*. This grand two-volume work of Le Moyne's paintings and the engravings of his work by de Bry leaves out the Noah engraving, arguably because Le Moyne did not provide the model for it, but other engravings are included that are not by Le Moyne. More to the point, eliminating the Noah engraving ahistorically alters the Florida volume by leaving out the engraving that makes a statement about the significance of the subject matter that readers will want to know: that America's Natives are part of the family of man and have been blessed by God. Websites devoted to the Le Moyne de Bry volume, produced by the National Humanities Center (http://nationalhumanitiescenter.org/pds/amerbegin /exploration/text4/text4read.htm), the University of Florida (http://ufdc.ufl.edu/UF0 0067341/00001), and the University of South Florida (https://fcit.usf.edu/florida/photos /native/lemoyne/lemoyne0/lemoy0.htm), also exclude the Noah engraving. The University of Miami Special Collections used to place many images from an original copy of the book online—it excluded the image as well. The "Florida Memory" site of the State Library and Archives of Florida (https://www.floridamemory.com/collections /debry/) also reprints the engravings without Noah. In contrast, booksellers and book catalogs of auction houses tend to include the Noah engraving in their descriptions when they have a copy of the volume for sale.

15. My thanks to Matt Goldish for confirming the typicality of this depiction of Noah to Renaissance Hermeticism and showing me additional copies.

16. *The Jewish Alchemists: A History and Source Book* (Princeton, NJ: Princeton University Press, 1994), 22.

17. Van Groesen, *Representations*, 381, states that the de Brys did not attribute "prelapsarian notions" to the Indians despite the Adam and Eve engraving, but he bases this assessment on the overall depiction of Indians in the entire series of volumes on the Americas, whereas I argue that de Bry's Hermetic association of Indians with the divine is apparent only in the first two volumes.

18. William Bourne in 1578 addressed the issue of Indian origins by dismissing two theories that provided "offense before God," that there were two Adams or that some people not of Noah's family survived the flood. Bourne posited that there were descendants of Noah who inhabited a "great Ilande called Atlantida," whose kings were the sons of Neptune, a trading people. When the island sunk, the survivors boarded ships and moved to America. See chapter 10 of the fifth book of *A booke called the Treasure for traveilers . . .* (London, 1578).

19. For an overview of sixteenth-century European concern with Indian origins, see Olive Patricia Dickason, *The Myth of the Savage and the Beginnings of French Colonialism in the Americas* (Edmonton: University of Alberta Press, 1984), 32–34.

20. Gaudio, *Engraving the Savage*, 18.

21. For the Curse of Ham, see Winthrop D. Jordan, *White over Black: American Attitudes Toward the Negro, 1550–1812* (Chapel Hill: University of North Carolina Press, 1968); David M. Goldenberg, *The Curse of Ham: Race and Slavery in Early Judaism, Christianity, and Islam* (Princeton, NJ: Princeton University Press, 2003); Rebecca Anne Goetz, *The Baptism of Early Virginia: How Christianity Created Race* (Baltimore: Johns Hopkins University Press, 2012).

22. Quotations translated from the Latin text in de Bry, *INDORVM Floridam*, 121.

23. This engraving, along with a few others, was produced for de Bry by Gysbert van Veen.

24. One can easily argue that Europeans came to see scalping as the single most important difference between themselves and American Indians, certainly by the late seventeenth century, but the sixteenth-century volumes on America's Native peoples emphasized all sorts of body mutilation without singling out scalping. Native nudity also constituted a perceived difference. Christianity was the third great difference. Over time, however, even when Indians converted to Christianity, dressed in European clothing, and ceased scalping, racist Euro-Americans still asserted that differentiation was too strong to include them in their society.

25. From the caption of engraving XXI.

26. For the use of comparative ethnology to understand sixteenth-century Americans, see Pagden, *Fall of Natural Man*.

27. White was inspired by Le Moyne, on whose work he based one of the females covered in tattoos. For the Le Moyne painting, see Hulton, *Work of Jacques Le Moyne*, 2: plate 7.

28. Display of genitalia was common in the early engravings of Native peoples. See, for example, the works by Jean de Léry and André Thévet.

29. De Bry substituted a Pict daughter for one of the Pict men, perhaps to show the savagery passing on to the next generation, because there was little difference in the pictures.

30. The painter appears to have used the exact same models for two of the Pict paintings.

31. *The Tempest*, Act 5, Scene 1.

32. *The Tempest*, Act 2, Scene 2.

33. Taylor, *Original Writings*, 2:368.

34. Richard Hakluyt to Sir Walter Ralegh, 1586, in Taylor, *Original Writings*, 2:353–356.

Chapter 14: Planning the Munster Plantation

1. The best study of English colonial policies in Ireland from the reign of Elizabeth through the English Civil War is Nicholas Canny, *Making Ireland British, 1580–1650* (Oxford: Oxford University Press, 2001).

2. Sir Francis Walsingham to Sir H. Wallop, [January] 1585/86, CSP Ireland 2:550, item 53.

3. The Privy Council, December 1585, CSP Ireland 2:589, item 54.

4. See Michael MacCarthy-Morrogh, *Munster Plantation*, 117–118, including footnotes.

5. June 21, 1586, CSP Ireland 3:84–85.

6. St. Michael marked the beginning and end of the husbandman's year on September 29.

7. June 21, 1586, CSP Ireland 3:86.

8. May 14, 1587, APC 15:76.

9. This is taken from *Carew Manuscript 625*, para. 369, in the Carew Collection of Lambeth Palace Library, London, England. The text has been placed online as "The Desmond Survey," by University College Cork at http://www.ucc.ie/celt/published/E580000-001/. Hereafter referred to as "Desmond Survey."

10. "Desmond Survey," para. 370.

11. [December 1585], CSP Ireland 2:589, item 54. For another example of the attempted exclusion of Irish, see August 23, 1585, CSP Ireland 2:576–577, which repeats a note of December 1583.

12. For "Carew's estimate," which he composed in December 1585, see *Calendar of the Carew Manuscripts preserved in the Archiepiscopal Library at Lambeth, 1575–1588*, 6 vols. (London: Longmans, 1868), 2:413, item 591.

13. See *Acta Cancellariae, or Selections from the Records of the Court of Chancery . . . Part First*, ed. Cecil Monro (London: William Benning, 1847), 178–179. Adrian sued Ralegh in 1613 for repayment of thousands of pounds of debt while Ralegh was in prison. The court apparently dismissed the case.

14. "Desmond Survey," para. 374.

15. For copies of the surveys, see "Desmond Survey." See also "Survey of Attainted Lands," in National Library of Ireland, Dublin, Public Record Office, series 63, October 5, 1586, No. 52; "Abuse of the Surveyors and Undertakers Against the Queen," December 19, 1587, CSP Ireland 3:450–451, item 40; APC, 14: February 7, 1585/86, 15; March 20, 1585/86, 39; July 17, 1586, 187; July 24, 1586, 193. Robyns began surveying October 8, 1585. Also see APC, 16: June 19, 1588, 119–120.

16. For other sources, see Robert Dunlop, "Sixteenth Century Maps of Ireland," *English Historical Review* 20 (1905): 309–337; and Dunlop, "The Plantation of Munster, 1584–89," *English Historical Review* 3 (1888): 250–269. The surveyors faced little opposition from the Irish, in part owing to the size of the party but also because of the devastation of the war and famine.

17. For example, Mogeely by the Bride River is now Lower Mogeely and Upper Mogeely (with the name *Mogeely* currently designating a separate place several miles to the south).

18. For other problems with the surveying of the tracts and the Undertakers' hiding some of the lands they claimed, see Anthony J. Sheehan, "Official Reaction to Native Land Claims in the Plantation of Munster," *Irish Historical Studies* 23, no. 92 (November 1983): 297–318.

19. The tracts often were labeled as waste, not because they were infertile but because they required much clearing and labor to become arable.

20. Hariot used the phonetic alphabet he had invented for recording Algonkian in Virginia to say on the map, "Copid UWT [out] of Descripshen of Arti Robins by Tomas Haryots of Yohal, 1589 August 28th." For Hariot's adaptation of the Robyns map, see W. A. Wallace, "John White, Thomas Harriot and Walter Ralegh in Ireland," The Durham Thomas Harriot Seminar, *Occasional Paper No. 2*, 1985. (A Thomas Hariot seminar also meets at Birbeck College, University of London.) Wallace mistakenly places White's parcel of Ballynoe only a few miles from Molana Abbey, turning White into a neighbor of Hariot. Ballynoe is over ten miles away by how the crow flies.

21. Some of these maps include Francis Jobson, *The Province of Mounster* (1592) NLI, MS 16.B. 13, and another copy at the National Maritime Museum, Greenwich, England, Dartmouth Collection of maps and charts, P/49 (20); unknown artist, *The Province of Movnster* (circa 1595), National Maritime Museum, Dartmouth Collection, p/49 (27). There also are many copies of John Speed, *The Province of Mounster* (1611). See also the unpublished [Ireland south of Limerick] (1590), National Maritime Museum, Dartmouth Collection, p/49 (22).

22. See, for example, the claims examined by the Privy Council on January 2, 1587–1588, in APC 15:316–321.

23. September 10, 1593, referring to events of January 8, 1582–1583, CSP Ireland 5:145.

24. MacCarthy-Morrogh, *Munster Plantation*, 106.

25. See discussion of John Fitzedmund Fitzgerald, the Seneschal of Imokilly, in chapter 17.

26. July 8, 1587, APC, 15:158.

27. See C. Monro, ed., *Acta Cancellariae* (London: Benning, 1847), 176–177; Fleet prison, February 7, 1579–80, APC 11:384. They gave sureties not to fight and were released February 13, 1579/80, APC 11:388–389.

28. John Perrot to Francis Walsingham, March [15] 1588, on mf in NLI, March 18, 1588, CSP Ireland 3:498; Burghley to Perrot, October 12, 1587, cited in MacCarthy-Morrogh, *Munster Plantation*, 52.

29. Nicholas Canny, *The Upstart Earl: A Study of the Social and Mental Worlds of Richard Boyle, First Earl of Cork, 1566–1643* (Cambridge: Cambridge University Press, 1982).

Chapter 15: Bloodlines:
Captain Ralegh and the Desmonds

1. *The first and second volumes of Chronicles comprising 1 The description and historie of England, 2 The description and historie of Ireland, 3 The description and historie of Scotland: first collected and published by Raphaell Holinshed, William Harrison, and others . . .* ([London]: [Henry Denham], Finished in Januarie 1587), 3:174.

2. For Ralegh's views of treating with the Irish rebels during the Second Desmond War, particularly by bolstering the elite below the Desmonds, see Burghley's notes on Ralegh's recommendations, October 25, 1582, National Archives of the United Kingdom, vol. 96, no. 30 and 31 [CSP Ireland 2: 406]; Ralegh to Walsingham, February 23, 1580/81 in Latham and Youings, *Letters of Sir Walter Ralegh*, 3–5; Ralegh to Walsingham, February 25, 1580/81, in Latham and Youings, *Letters of Sir Walter Ralegh*, 5–7. Grey's hardline policy was opposed by the queen, and by 1582 he spoke against Ralegh's recommendations. See Lord Grey to Burghley, January 12, 1581/82, CSP Ireland 2:340. Grey's resentment of Ralegh became personal. See Grey to Walsingham, May 7, 1582, National Archives of the United Kingdom, Series 63, vol. 92, no. 10.

3. *First and second volumes of Chronicles*, 3:173.

4. *First and second volumes of Chronicles*, 3:174.

5. This is from the papers of the Villiers-Stuart Family, NLI, A 17 11–10.

6. *First and second volumes of Chronicles*, 3:61. The *Oxford English Dictionary* (*OED*) defines *breakdanse* as "disturbing, turbulent." Incidentally, the *OED* uses this quote by Hooker to illustrate the word's usage.

7. *First and second volumes of Chronicles*, 3:61.

8. *First and second volumes of Chronicles*, 3:62.

9. *First and second volumes of Chronicles*, 3:62.

10. *First and second volumes of Chronicles*, 3:63.

Chapter 16: Ralegh in Youghal

1. Eric Klingelhofer, *Castles and Colonists: An Archaeology of Elizabethan Ireland* (Manchester, England: Manchester University Press, 2011), 88, 106n7.

2. Niave Gallagher, "The Irish Franciscan Province: From Foundation to the Aftermath of the Bruce Invasion," in *Franciscan Organization in the Mendicant Context*, ed. Michael Robson and Jens Röhrkasten (Berlin: LIT Verlag, 2010), 19–42.

3. The carving is now the centerpiece of an altar in Saint Mary's Church attached to the Franciscan Friary of Cork City.

4. The Irish history section of Turtlebunbury.com has much information on these religious institutions, but the speculation about all these things being connected is my own.

5. MacCarthy-Morrogh, *Munster Plantation*, 226.

6. The Irish also exported much leather to England, whereas New England exported cattle to the West Indies.

7. Ralegh economically connected the Canaries to his seignories and England through the wine trade—see Part Eight. From the trade through the Canaries he learned about El Dorado, though the key information about the city he obtained from Sarmiento—see Chapter 10.

8. Among those referring to Spenser as a Radical Protestant are Thomas Herron, "Reforming the Fox: Spenser's 'Mother Hubberds Tale,' the Beast Fables of Barnabe Riche, and Adam Loftus, Archbishop of Dublin," *Studies in Philology* 105, no. 3 (Summer 2008): 336–387; Philippa Berry, *Of Chastity and Power: Elizabethan Literature and the Unmarried Queen* (London: Routledge, 1994); David Mickics questions the radical Protestantism of Spenser in *The Limits of Moralizing: Pathos and Subjectivity in Spenser and Milton* (Lewisburg, PA: Bucknell University Press, 1994).

9. The first law of this sort was passed in 1536. See Eamon Duffy, *The Voices of Morebath: Reformation and Rebellion in an English Village* (New Haven, CT: Yale University Press, 2001), 91, who throughout his excellent book on Morebath discusses the application of Tudor laws to force English towns to display the Bible and to use the Book of Common Prayer.

10. See Part Ten.

11. One recent student of Hermeticism and art has shown how closely Spenser's use of Hermetic symbolism parallels that of John Dee, particularly the latter's *Monas Hieroglyphica*. Jill Delsigne, as did Francis Yates before her, argues that a Catholic understanding of holiness and devotion permeates *The Faerie Queene*. Delsigne, "Reading Catholic Art in Edmund Spenser's Temple of Isis," *Studies in Philology* 109, no. 3 (Spring 2012): 199–224.

12. Delsigne, "Reading Catholic Art," 201, 208.

13. See Part Nine.

14. Little is known of Ralegh's activities during the arrival of the Armada, except that he was by the queen's side. No heroic activities have been documented. For a brief discussion of Ralegh and the armada, see Agnes Latham and Joyce Youings, eds., *The Letters of Sir Walter Ralegh* (Exeter, England: University of Exeter Press, 1999), 45n3.

Chapter 17:
Preparing the Plantation: Establishing Authority

1. For the Peyton and Desmond Surveys, see *Carew Manuscript 625* in the Carew Collection of Lambeth Palace Library, London, England. The text has been placed online as "The Peyton and Desmond Surveys" at http://www.ucc.ie/celt/published/E580000-001/. Peyton's Survey, in "The Peyton and Desmond Surveys," para. 34.

2. T. C. Croker quoted in *The Parliamentary Gazetteer of Ireland* . . . (Dublin: A. Fullarton, 1846), 13.

3. See *Oxford English Dictionary*.

4. The archbishop, Miler Magrath, was one of the most colorful figures in colonial Irish history. A member of the Franciscan order who rose to become a bishop, Magrath

switched to the Protestant Irish Church and ever after has been viewed unfavorably by Catholics as a turncoat and by Protestants as financially corrupt.

5. Meyler [Magrath], Archbishop of Cashel, to Sir Robert Cecil, May 15, 1601, CSP Ireland 10:339–343. For more on Nuse as Ralegh's man, see CSP Ireland 11:90.

6. Capt. George Thornton to Sir Robert Cecil, October 5, 1595, CSP Ireland 5:413. "Russel's Journal," October 1597, *Calendar of the Carew Manuscripts, Preserved in the Archiepiscopal Library at Lambeth, 1589–1600,* ed. J. S. Brewer and William Bullen (London, 1869), 237.

7. For Moyle as Carew's cousin, see Lord Deputy (Fitz-William) to Sir George Carew, October 24, 1588, in *Calendar of the Carew Manuscripts . . . 1601–1603,* 494. References to Moyle's captaincy in Ireland are scattered throughout the *Carew Manuscripts.* Fitz-William was also cousin to Carew.

8. CSP Ireland 3:341, 404, 470.

9. CSP 3:94. This is noted in a letter from James Myagh to Burghley of July 6, 1586.

10. Myagh to Burghley, July 6, 1586, in CSP Ireland 3:94–95.

11. For examples of the Irish lord deputy and council repeatedly disregarding the English Privy Council in this period, see Anthony J. Sheehan, "Official Reaction to Native Land Claims in the Plantation of Munster," *Irish Historical Studies* 23, no. 92 (November 1983): 297–318.

12. John Meade to Sir F. Walsyngham, January 31, 1587/88, CSP Ireland 3:470.

13. Lord Deputy Fitzwilliam to the Privy Council, [November 2] 1588, CSP Ireland 4:71; Mr. Chief Justice Anderson and Mr. Attorney General to the Privy Council, [November 2] 1588, CSP Ireland 4:71.

14. John Miaghe, [1588], item 25, CSP Ireland 4:18.

15. James Myaghe to Burghley, December 8, 1592, CSP Ireland 5:30–31.

16. See also Ralegh to Walsingham, February 23, 1580/81, in Edward Edwards, *The Life of Sir Walter Ralegh: Based on Contemporary Documents,* 2 vols. (London: Macmillan, 1868), 2:9–10.

17. Privy Council to the Lord Deputy, September 12, 1588, CSP Ireland 4:34.

18. For Fitzgerald's imprisonment in Dublin Castle, see CSP Ireland 4:12, August 18, 1588.

19. "Memorial," January [21], 1588–89, CSP Ireland 4:110; Pa. Foxe to Walsyngham, February 26, 1588–89, CSP Ireland 4:126. Patrick Foxe, a frequent correspondent of Walsingham, described Fitzgerald as a great man.

20. Lord Deputy Fitzwylliam to Walsyngham, January 6, 1588–89, CSP Ireland 4:106.

21. "Memorial of things resolved on, touching the Province of Munster by the Privy Council to be put in execution by the Lord Deputy of Ireland," January [21] 1588/89, no. 33, CSP Ireland 4:110ff.

22. Michael MacCarthy-Morrogh, *Munster Plantation,* 42.

23. For wardships, see Daphne Pearson, *Edward De Vere (1550–1604): The Crisis and Consequences of Wardship* (Aldershot, England: Ashgate, 2005).

24. See June 7, 1597, *Calendar of the Patent and Close Rolls of Chancery in Ireland from the 18th to the 45th of Queen Elizabeth,* ed. James Morrin (London: Longman, 1862), 2:497.

Chapter 18: Resistance to Plantation

1. Captain Rawley to Lord Deputy Grey, May 1, 1581, enclosed with Lord Deputy Grey to Walsyngham, May 14, 1581, in CSP Ireland 2:304.

2. See Mary Hickson, "Lord Grey of Wilton at Smerwick in 1580," in *The Antiquary: A Magazine Devoted to the Study of the Past*, no. 31, New Series (July 1892): 20.

3. In particular, I refer to her two-volume work, *Ireland in the Seventeenth Century or The Irish Massacres of 1641–42* (London: Longmans, 1884), which includes a hefty introduction by Hickson that runs to well over 150 pages. The renowned Anglo-Catholic historian James Anthony Froude, according to historian Ciaran Brady, "persuaded his friend Lord Carnavan to fund" Hickson's collection and transcription of depositions of the massacres of 1641. R. Dunlop's review of the work in the *English Historical Review* suggested that perhaps the documents should not have been published because the facts they contained were questionable. Dunlop, *English Historical Review*, October 1886, 740–744. Subsequent issues of the *EHR* include Hickson's cogent defense of her work.

4. "Answer of Sir Walter Rawley to certain articles to be answered unto by the Undertakers for the peopling of Munster," item 27, May 12, 1589, CSP Ireland, 4:170.

5. Walter Ralegh, *The History of the World* (London, 1614), book 1, chapter 5.

6. Leicester recorded the story in his Commonplace book while residing in France as an English ambassador. The story was later retold by Sir William Temple around 1688, attributing the story to Leicester, "who was a person of great learning and observation, as well as truth." *The Works of Sir William Temple, Bar*, 2 vols. (London: A Churchill et al., 1720), 1:276.

7. Hariot had been long gone from Ireland when Eleanor went to court.

8. Miss Joan Hickson, "The Old Countess of Desmond: A New Solution of an Old Puzzle," *The Reliquary and Illustrated Archaeologist* 22, no. 1 (1881): 33–39; no. 2 (1881): 69–75; no. 3 (1881): 169–176; no. 4 (1881): 233–277.

9. Hickson, "Old Countess," no. 2, 70ff.

10. Hickson seems to greatly overestimate the value of the land and was unaware that so many of his tenants had died in the war.

11. See *Annals of the Kingdom of Ireland, by the Four Masters, from the Earliest Period to 1616*, vol. 5, ed. John O'Donovan (Dublin: Hodges, Smith, and Co.,1856), 1840–1841; *Carew Manuscripts*, Acts of Parliament, Lambeth Palace Library, London, MS 632:88.

12. Hickson, "Old Countess," no. 3, 169.

13. Hickson, "Old Countess," no. 3, 161–170.

14. "Book of the Proceedings in Munster," September 3, 1588, CSP Ireland 4:16.

15. Hickson, "Old Countess," no. 3, 172.

16. "Book of the Proceedings in Munster," 16. If the husband committed treason but the wife brought the land to the marriage, then the land was protected in her lifetime.

17. *A Repertory of the Inrolments on the Patents of Chancery in Ireland*, vol. 1, ed. John Caillard Erck (Dublin: James McGlashen, 1846), 1:92–96, 98–99. This printing does not include the entirety of either the inquisition or the inspection. Thus, I used the originals and later copies that can be found in the Lismore Papers at the National Library of Ireland, MS 43, 584/2.

18. Paul McCotter, "The Carews of Cork," part 2, *Journal of the Cork Historical and Archeological Society* 99 (1994): 71–72. These Carews appear to be unrelated to Sir George Carew and the Ralegh family, according to McCotter.

Chapter 19: Ralegh's Colonists

1. "A note or abstract of the names of all such freeholders, fee farmers, lessees for years, copyholders, and cottagers, as are inhabiting upon the lands and possessions of Sir Walter Ralegh, knight . . . ," item 28, [May 12, 1589], CSP Ireland 4:170.

2. It appears that most of the colonists brought their wives and families. It is difficult to tell exactly how many families because the census does not always indicate which men brought a wife and family. My guess is that somewhere between half and two-thirds of the men brought family members.

3. "A note or abstract."

4. Peter Elmer, *The Miraculous Conformist: Valentine Greatrakes, the Body Politic, and the Politics of Healing in Restoration Britain* (Oxford: Oxford University Press, 2013), 20 nn24–25.

5. It is possible that Greatrakes, like his neighbor Robert Boyle, was influenced indirectly by Ralegh to become a healer. See discussion of Ralegh's influence on Boyle in Chapter 29, with discussion of Greatrakes's and Boyle's connection in note 12 in Chapter 29.

6. Latham and Youings, *Letters of Sir Walter Ralegh*, appendix 1, for the letter from Ralegh to [James Gold or Goold] that notes the accusation by Jewell.

7. The will was discovered in 1971 and is printed in Latham and Youings, *Letters of Sir Walter Ralegh*, appendix 2.

8. Latham and Youings, *Letters of Sir Walter Ralegh*, July 27, 1603, 247–251, discusses his "poore daughter" in a letter to Ralegh's wife.

9. Bernard Burke, *Romantic Records of Distinguished Families . . .* , 2nd ed., 2 vols. (London: E. Charton, 1851), 1:212. The author reported that the deed signed by Ralegh was still intact. See also the leases in Lismore Papers, NLI, MS 43, 142/2.

10. For more on the Crokers in Ireland, see the detailed research of Nick Reddan, "The Irish Crokers," unpublished manuscript. http://members.iinet.net.au/~nickred/croker_research/The_Irish_CROKER.pdf.

11. *The Itinerary of Fynes Moryson*, 4 vols. (Glasgow: University of Glasgow Press, 1907), 2:172. Original work published 1617.

12. J. K. Floyer, "Two Devonshire Papists in the Time of Queen Elizabeth," *Devon County Association Transactions* 50 (1918): 611–620.

13. Ralegh to Cecil, April 21, 1600, in Latham and Youings, *Letters of Sir Walter Ralegh*, 190–191.

14. *Bibliotheca Manuscripta Landsdowniana* (London, 1807), 280. The report was made July 29, 1592. Another Carew colonist related to Ralegh, Robert, to be discussed below, stayed permanently in Ireland, but I cannot determine whether he was Catholic or Protestant. An additional Catholic colonist was Henry Darrell, who probably did not stay more than two or three years, because his recusancy was later reported to Lord Burghley and I assume this took place in England.

15. Quinn, *Voyages and Colonising*, 41–47.

16. The NLI has a microfilm copy (n.4763) of the records from the John Rylands Library in Manchester, England. It includes the receipt from Anne Thickpenny to Stanley for the rent. The original receipts are for a yearly rent paid for the castle, May 16, 1584, then half a year's rent paid four more times, the last on May 13, 1586. The library has other Stanley papers, including Stanley's assignment of Lismore to John Egerton (his in-law) and two others on December 1, 1585. There's another letter from Anne Thickpenny to Lady Stanley, February 24, 1587/88, as well as Egerton's two petitions to the Privy Council (n.d.) and Ralegh's answer by Andrew Colthurst (n.d.) and

Egerton's reply (n.d.) and a "Note recording goods left with Mr Whyeth in Waterford" (n.d.).

17. For Elizabeth's consideration of sending Stanley to Ireland, see APC, April 10, 1586, 14:62.

18. See *Cardinal Allen's Defense of Sir William Stanley's Surrender of Deventer, January 29, 1586–87* (1851), xli.

19. The archbishop of Cashell in 1592 was still trying to collect rent money owed by Stanley—20 marks sterling per year plus interest—and had "destrained" his goods until payment was made. APC, July 18, 1592, 23:34–36. APC, July 28, 1587, 15:171–172.

20. Quoted in David Beers Quinn, *Ralegh and the British Empire* (London: Hodder & Stoughton, 1947), 148.

Chapter 20: The Plantation Economy

1. Lismore Castle, Papers, NLI, MS 22,068.

2. W. A. Wallace, "John White, Thomas Harriot and Walter Raleigh in Ireland," *Thomas Harriot Seminar Paper* (London: Historical Association, 1985), 10.

3. Eric Klingelhofer, *Castles and Colonists: An Archaeology of Elizabethan Ireland* (Manchester, England: Manchester University Press, 2010), 73–77. Quotation from Joe Nunan, "New English Settlement on the Bride River," *Blackwater Archaeology*, chapter 4.2: http://www.jpnunan.com/sitebuildercontent/sitebuilderfiles/joenunaneast indiacompany4.pdf.

4. September 1599, CSP Ireland, 8:164.

5. Colin Breen, *An Archaeology of Southwest Ireland, 1570–1670* (Dublin: Four Courts Press, 2007), 105, from August 1, 1586, CSP Ireland 3:126. This directive could not have applied to the other Mogeely in County Cork because it had yet to take that name, which came centuries later.

6. See Part Ten.

7. Ralegh reminded Burghley in 1593 that the queen had granted the Undertakers this right. See *Historical Manuscript Commission, Calendar of the Manuscripts of the most Honourable Marquis of Salisbury*, Part IV (London, 1892), 464.

8. Breen, *An Archaeology*, 89–90. For analysis of the Irish trade with Bristol, see Susan Flavin, "The Development of Anglo-Irish Trade in the Sixteenth Century" (master's thesis, University of Bristol, 2004), and "Consumption and Material Culture in Sixteenth-Century Ireland" (PhD thesis, University of Bristol, 2011). Sources for the trade between Bristol and Ireland in the sixteenth century are available in Susan Flavin and Evan T. Jones, eds., *Bristol's Trade with Ireland and the Continent, 1503–1601: The Evidence of the Exchequer Customs Accounts* (Dublin: Four Courts Press, 2009).

9. Arthur E. J. Went, "Fisheries of the Munster Blackwater," *Journal of the Royal Society of Antiquaries of Ireland* 90, no. 2 (1960): 97–131.

10. On the use of light, see Arthur E. J. Went, "The Pursuit of Salmon in Ireland," *Proceedings of the Royal Irish Academy: Archaeology, Culture, History, Literature* 63 (1962–1964): 193–195.

11. Went, "Fisheries of the Munster Blackwater," 117–118. On salmon in Europe, see Fynes Morison, *An Itinerary Written by Fynes Morison, the Itinerary of Fynes Moryson*, 4 vols. (Glasgow: University of Glasgow Press, 1907), 159 (original work published 1617), cited in Keith Pluymers, "Taming the Wilderness in Sixteenth- and Seventeenth-Century Ireland and Virginia," *Environmental History* 16 (October 2011): 622.

12. Parliament treated the subject on several occasions but especially in the 1860s and 1870s. For the continued dispute over ownership of the river, see "Youghal Council Dukes It Out," *Irish Echo*, January 13–19, 1999. In this particular episode, the estate of the Duke of Devonshire was blocking development of Youghal harbor on the basis of his owning the riverbed as originally obtained by Ralegh through permanent lease.

13. Went, "Fisheries of the Munster Blackwater," 100–101.

14. Went, "Fisheries of the Munster Blackwater," 128.

15. Ralegh's father sued Roger Slade, to whom he leased fishing rights, for not paying the tithe on fish. See Court of Chancery Papers, Series II, 1558–1579, National Archives of the United Kingdom, C 3/152/3.

16. Roger also later leased the weir at Lysfinny on the Bride River from Richard Boyle. Alexander B. Grosart, ed., *The Lismore Papers*, First Series, 10 vols. (London: Chiswick Papers, 1886–1889), 2:255–256. The agreement provided that Roger would pay £5 sterling per year, but Boyle could cancel the contract if it interfered with his nearby ironworks.

17. The Desmond and Peyton Surveys mention yearly rents of £13 on the Dell River, £2 on the Phele River, 10 s. on the Deyle River, and another of £1 on the Phele River. For the Peyton and Desmond Surveys, see *Carew Manuscript 625* in the Carew Collection of Lambeth Palace Library, London, England, and online as "The Peyton and Desmond Surveys" at https://celt.ucc.ie/published/E580000-001/index.html. For the grant to Carew, see NLI, 43,153/1 Salmon Fishery.

18. The largest salmon today are chinook, which can reach about 125 pounds, though 30 pounds is more common. Scattered references refer to Atlantic and Irish salmon in the early modern period as being well over 100 pounds.

19. Went, "Fisheries of the Munster Blackwater," 117–118, quoting R. H. Ryland, *Topography and Antiquities of the County and City of Waterford* (London, 1824), 351.

20. An interesting aside: Arthur Conan Doyle's maternal great-grandfather, Thomas Foley, acquired the salmon rights for an eleven-mile stretch of the Blackwater at Lismore in the mid-eighteenth century. Andrew Lycett, *The Man Who Created Sherlock Holmes: The Life and Times of Sir Arthur Conan Doyle* (London: Weidenfeld and Nicolson, 2007), 10–11.

21. For Ralegh's Lismore lease, and grants from Elizabeth, as well as sale and leasing of land, see Lismore Castle Papers, MS 43, 142/1, MS 43, 087/5, and MS 43,087/6; "An Inquisition taken at Tallagh . . . ," in John Caillard Reck, ed., *A Repertory of the Inrolments on the Patent Rolls of Chancery in Ireland* (Dublin: James McGlashan, 1846), vol. 1, part 1, no. 43, 169–170; "Grant from the King to Sir Richard Boyle, Kn^t," in *Calendar of the Patent Rolls of the Chancery of Ireland* (Dublin: 1800), xxi, no. 27, 41–43, and "Inquisition held at Tallagh," xliii, no. 11 in *Calendar of the Patent Rolls of the Chancery of Ireland*, 66.

22. Lismore Papers, MS 41, 985/3. The weirs were reported ruined in the lease of Molana to John Thickpenny in 1577. See Fiant 3161 in *The Thirteenth Report of the Deputy Keeper of the Public Records in Ireland* (Dublin: Alex. Thom, 1881), 57–58.

23. The tract is reproduced in Raymond Gillespie, "Plantation and Profit: Richard Spert's Tract on Ireland, 1608," *Irish Economic and Social History* 20 (1993): 71.

24. Jean Farrelly, "From Sand and Ash: Glassmaking in Early Seventeenth-Century Ireland," in John M. Hearne, ed., *Glassmaking in Ireland: From the Medieval to the Contemporary* (Dublin: Irish Academic Press, 2010), 36. See also Nessa Roche, "Seventeenth-Century Irish Flat Glass: Its Makers and Their Markets," in *Glassmaking in Ireland*, 55–82.

25. Nunan, "New English Settlement," 17.

26. Nunan, "New English Settlement," 18.

27. Nunan, "New English Settlement," 19.

28. Nunan, "New English Settlement," 18.

29. The tin workers' rights were confirmed and reconfirmed under many monarchs, beginning with a charter granted by King John I. They possessed an unusual array of rights that extended from exemptions to taxation to the jurisdiction of their own courts with fellow tin miners comprising half their juries.

30. Colin Rynne, *Industrial Ireland, 1750–1930: An Archaeology* (Cork: Collins Press, 2006), 111. See also Rynne, "The Social Archaeology of Plantation-Period Ironworks in Ireland: Immigrant Industrial Communities and Technology Transfer, c. 1560–1640," in *Plantation Ireland: Settlement and Material Culture, c. 1550–c.1700*, ed. James Lyttleton and Colin Rynne (Dublin: Four Courts Press, 2009), 248–264. Rynne notes that Norreys's workers "may well have dwelt in the small Elizabethan village created near Mogeely Castle, on the estate of Sir Walter Raleigh" (253).

31. Later, one Englishman reported that Ralegh and his partners in the lumber industry barred the overseer of lumber production, Henry Pyne (who was also a partner), from selling lumber in Ireland—Ralegh focused instead on shipping staves and planks abroad. "Examination of Geffrey Galway of Kinsale," April 28, 1593, item 39 iii, CSP Ireland 5:151.

32. For cask and pipe stave production, see Sarah Fawsitt, "Casks & 16th Century Trade in Northern Europe: A Study of the Cargo from the Drogheda Boat" (master's thesis, University of Southern Denmark, 2010); S. M. Lough, "Trade and Industry in Ireland in the Sixteenth Century," *Journal of Political Economy* 24, no. 7 (1916): 713–730; K. Kilby, *The Cooper and His Trade* (London: John Baker, 1971); M. Manders, "Wood, Casks, and Baltic Trade: Analytical Prospects of a Sixteenth-Century Shipwreck," *Avista Forum Journal* 12, no. 2 (2001): 25–29.

33. See volume 2 in Andre Simon's three-volume work from the early twentieth century, *History of the Wine Trade in England* (London: Wyman & Sons, 1906, 1907, 1909).

34. Edward Williams, *Virginia, more especially the south part there of . . .* (London, 1650).

35. Ralegh to Sir George Carew, December 28, 1589, Latham and Youings, *Letters of Sir Walter Ralegh*, 50–51.

36. Sir George Carew to Lord Deputy [Fitzwilliam], July 18, 1591, *Calendar of the Carew Manuscripts Preserved in the Archiepiscopal Library at Lambeth,1589–1600*, ed. J. S. Brewer and William Bullen (London, 1869), 58.

Chapter 21: Of Friendship, Marriage, and Goddesses

1. "Fortune hathe taken away my love," in Michael Rudick, ed., *The Poems of Sir Walter Ralegh: A Historical Edition* (Tempe: Arizona Center for Medieval and Renaissance Studies, 1999), poem 15.

2. A copy of the poem with notations can be found in May, *Elizabethan Courtier Poets*, 319–321.

3. A. L. Rowse, *Ralegh and the Throckmortons* (London: Macmillan & Co., 1962), 125–128.

4. Ralegh to Sir Robert Cecil, March 10 [1592], Latham and Youings, *Letters of Sir Walter Ralegh*, 62–63.

5. Raleigh Trevelyan, *Sir Walter Raleigh* (New York: Henry Holt, 2002), 171.

6. Trevelyan, *Sir Walter Raleigh*, 165–187, provides a fairly full account of the events leading up to Ralegh's marriage, some of it drawn from A. L. Rowse's *Ralegh and the Throckmortons*, 150–164, but both miss the significance of Essex standing as godfather, and the very real possibility that Elizabeth did not know of the marriage when placing them under house arrest.

7. "My boddy in the walls captived," in Rudick, *Poems of Sir Walter Ralegh*, poem 25.

8. Scholars long have thought that the first twenty books of the poem were missing since the poem begins with the twenty-first, but it seems clear that Ralegh meant by starting at Book 21 that his earlier poetry to the queen, his life worshipping the goddess, comprised the first twenty books, and he was writing a conclusion to all that came before. For discussion of the controversy over the number of books in the poem, see Stacy M. Clanton, "The 'Number' of Sir Walter Ralegh's *Booke of the Ocean to Scinthia*," *Studies in Philology* 82, no. 2 (Spring 1985): 200–211; Steven W. May, *Sir Walter Ralegh* (Boston: Twayne Publishers, 1989), 45–46.

9. "The 21th and last booke of the Ocean to Scinthia," Rudick, *Poems of Sir Walter Ralegh*, poem 26.

10. "The end of the boockes, of the Oceans love to Scinthia, and the beginninge of the 22 boock, entreatinge of Sorrow," Rudick, *Poems of Sir Walter Ralegh*, poem 27.

11. For Ralegh as a poet, see May, *Sir Walter Ralegh*. For the context of Ralegh's poetry with other poets and court life, see May, *Elizabethan Court Poets*.

Chapter 22:
A Courtier's Disgrace and the Shipping of Staves

1. Ralegh to Sir Robert Cecil, [Late July?] 1592, Latham and Youings, *Letters of Sir Walter Ralegh*, 68–69.

2. "Order by the Lord Deputy, Fytzwylliam, and Council to the local authorities . . . ," June 4, 1590, CSP Ireland 4:350.

3. He was a juror on Ralegh's attainder in Ireland 1603. *Calendar of the Patent Rolls* xliii, no. 11 (1603): 66.

4. See Ralegh to Sir Robert Cecil, Latham and Youings, *Letters of Sir Walter Ralegh*, [Late July?] 1592, 68—69, and notes 6 and 12. The dispute over Ardmore appears to have been ultimately settled in March 1637/38. See Grosart, *Lismore Papers*, 5:41.

5. Sir John Dowdall to Lord Burghley, March 9, 1595/96, CSP Ireland 5:484–485.

6. Ralegh to Sir Robert Cecil, [Late July] 1592, Latham and Youings, *Letters of Sir Walter Ralegh*, 68–69.

7. Ralegh received the lease to Ardmore in January 1591/92 and was ejected two years later, likely by some ad hoc court that the lord deputy put together.

8. Dowdall is referred to in the inquisitions taken at Tallagh, in County Waterford, on April 2, 1604, after Ralegh's attainder of November 17, 1603, as "late of Piltowne," since he might have moved by then to another locale, as he seems to have not died until 1606. *Calendar of the Patent Rolls* xliii, no. 11 (1603): 66.

9. A summary of the events surrounding the *Madre de Deos* can be found in Trevelyan, *Sir Walter Ralegh*, 184–187.

10. APC January 7, 1592/93, 24:6–7.

11. Sir Henry Wallop to Sir Robert Cecil, July 24, 1596, CSP Ireland 6:46.

12. Lord Deputy to Burghley, March 18, 1592/93, CSP Ireland 5:82.

13. Sir Henry Wallop to Sir Robert Cecil, July 24, 1596, CSP Ireland 6:46–47.

14. Lords of the Council to Lord Burghley, January 6, 1592/93, *Calendar of the Manuscripts of the . . . Marquis of Salisbury*, Part IV (1892), 278.

15. For Condon's leases of land to Pyne October 10, 1592, see Lismore Papers, MS 43, 156/1. These included Ballynecomas, Killioran [Kilcoran] and Ballneglass [Curraglass?]. For the examinations against Pyne, see Lord Deputy to Burghley, September 22, 1593, with six enclosures from March to July 1593, CSP Ireland 5:150–151. Condon's enemies were the Roches, and his main ally was the White Knight, Edmund FitzGibbon. His principal castle was Cloghleigh, near the village of Kilworth, just above Fermoy and about 10 miles overland from Mogeely.

16. See Christopher Maginn, *William Cecil, Ireland, and the Tudor State* (Oxford: Oxford University Press, 2012), 59n18.

17. September 21, 1593, CSP 5:150.

18. See Part Six.

19. See Part Nine for more attacks on Pyne.

20. All this is from Ralegh to Sir Robert Cecil, May 10, 1593, Latham and Youings, *Letters of Sir Walter Ralegh*, 93–95.

21. Ralegh to Lord Burghley, June 15, 1593, Latham and Youings, *Letters of Sir Walter Ralegh*, 96–97.

22. Ralegh to Sir Robert Cecil, August 27, 1593, Latham and Youings, *Letters of Sir Walter Ralegh*, 99–100.

23. All the above from APC 24:335–340.

24. November 27, 1593, APC 25:514, appendix.

25. Lord Deputy to Sir Robert Cecil, January 30, 1593/94, CSP Ireland 5:201–202.

26. The new lord deputy was William Russell, 1st Baron of Thornhaugh.

27. See, for example, letters numbered 68, 73, 76, 83, 94 in Latham and Youings, *Letters of Sir Walter Ralegh*.

Chapter 23: The Search for El Dorado

1. For the history of the search for El Dorado, see John Hemming, *The Search for El Dorado* (New York: E. P. Dutton, 1978), 97–100, quotation from 99.

2. *The Travels of Pedro de Cieza de León, A.D. 1532–50, contained in the First Part of his Chronicle of Peru*, trans. and ed., with notes and an introduction, Clements R. Markham (London: Hakluyt Society, 1864); *Civil Wars of Peru, by Pedro de Cieza de Léon: The War of Chupas*, ed. and trans. Clements R. Markham (London: Hakluyt Society, 1917), 55.

3. Markham, *Civil Wars of Peru*, 55–56.

4. Hemming, *Search for El Dorado*, 100.

5. Hemming, *Search for El Dorado*, 107.

6. Hemming, *Search for El Dorado*, 111.

7. V. T. Harlow, ed., *The Discoverie of Guiana by Sir Walter Ralegh* (London: Argonaut, 1928), lxxxvii.

8. Lorimer, *Sir Walter Ralegh's Discoverie*, 29.

9. Sir Walter Ralegh, *The Discoverie of the Large, Rich, and Bewtiful Empyre of Guiana*, transcribed, annotated, and introduced by Neil L. Whitehead (Norman: University of Oklahoma Press, 1997), 72ff.

10. Ralegh, *Discoverie*, 75–80.

Chapter 24: The Discovery of Guiana

1. Sir W. Ralegh, Knight, Captaine of her Maiefties Guard, Lo. Warden of the Stanneries, and her Highneffe Lieutenant generall of the Countie of Cornewall, *THE DISCOVERIE OF THE LARGE, RICH, AND BEWTIFVL EMPYRE* . . . (London: Robert Robinson, 1596). In the dedication of the book, Ralegh notes one reason for writing was that people said he had not gone to sea and had "hidden in Cornewall, or else where."

2. Joyce Lorimer, ed., *Sir Walter Ralegh's Discoverie of Guiana* (London: Hakluyt Society, 2006), xl. The Hakluyt Society has published the drafted text side by side with the published text in a wonderful edition edited by Joyce Lorimer.

3. Lorimer, *Sir Walter Ralegh's Discoverie*, 155, 157.

4. Lorimer, *Sir Walter Ralegh's Discoverie*, 63.

5. Lorimer, *Sir Walter Ralegh's Discoverie*, 63.

6. Lorimer, *Sir Walter Ralegh's Discoverie*, 65.

7. Lorimer, *Sir Walter Ralegh's Discoverie*, 221.

8. Rowland Whyte to Sir Robert Sydney, October 15, 1595, in *Historical Manuscripts Commissions, Report on the Manuscripts of Lord De L'Isle and Dudley*, 2 vols. (London, 1934), 173.

9. Lorimer, *Sir Walter Ralegh's Discoverie*, 79, 81, 83.

10. Lorimer, *Sir Walter Ralegh's Discoverie*, 131.

11. Lorimer, *Sir Walter Ralegh's Discoverie*, 147.

12. By *breed*, Ralegh is referring to Topiawari not possessing royal or noble blood. Lorimer, *Sir Walter Ralegh's Discoverie*, 139, 141, 143, 145.

13. Lorimer, *Sir Walter Ralegh's Discoverie*, 151, 153, 155.

14. Lorimer, *Sir Walter Ralegh's Discoverie*, 165, 167.

15. Ralegh was so impressed with the military strategy of burning grasses to subdue an enemy that he repeated the story almost twenty years later in his *History of the World*.

16. Lorimer, *Sir Walter Ralegh's Discoverie*, 171, 173, 175, 177.

17. Of the four boys sent in 1586, who arrived in 1587, we have record, perhaps, of only one of them, and he eventually returned to Europe. Eighteen years after being left at Trinidad, this nameless Englishman talked some merchants visiting Trinidad into carrying him to England in 1605. When asked what country he belonged to "he pretended himselfe to be a Dane and sometimes a portingall & sometymes a Dutche." The English captain who carried him, Joice Waus, called him a stranger, meaning foreigner, but he apparently was hiding his identity for reasons unknown. He did mention that he had been there for seventeen years—close to the precise time that the four boys had been left there. Waus gathered that he lived on the mainland in or on the Orinoco River. (The Italian had dropped him on an island in the river.) And Waus noted that the young man could speak Danish, Flemish, Spanish, "and some englishe."

The young man's reticence likely arose from his suspicion of all Europeans, as Trinidad remained in dispute for some years among Spanish, Portuguese, and English. It is possible that when he approached Waus, he knew that England and Spain had just made peace in August 1604. Had this been his first chance to return home? His refusal to reveal his name and nationality might simply have been a matter of survival, because he would have hidden his true identity for many years so that the Spanish, who predominated in the area, did not imprison or kill him. But he also might have feared for his life at English hands for reasons unknown. The whole experience might have traumatized him, but he had the wits of survival, as evidenced by his accumulation of tobacco for trade, his foreign language skills, and his ability to keep mum about his true identity. On return to England, Waus's ship docked at Devon, and the unnamed young man stored the tobacco he had brought to pay his expenses in England, and "was Ridinge to Exceter from Topsham and by the way was death strooke & dyed at Exceter but never spake." A young man in his twenties could die of stroke, but the timing is odd, to say the least. He had not been robbed for riches and killed because he had warehoused the tobacco. Perhaps he was poisoned—thus the appearance of a stroke—but why he had an enemy after all these years is unknown. Certainly, he might have been identified by one of the sailors in Devon because he likely was from Devon—as we have seen, Ralegh usually recruited from South West England, because that was his home. Ralegh, himself, was in prison at the time of the young man's return, so he could not have ordered his murder so soon after the young man came ashore. Perhaps someone thought the newly returned man knew some secret about El Dorado and saw fit to silence him. We most likely will never know. But we do know that no one onboard the merchant ship claimed to have known the identity of the man and no blood relative stepped forth to claim the tobacco. "Instruccions for the Tobacco at Apsham," in Lorimer, *Sir Walter Ralegh's Discoverie*, 250–251.

Chapter 25: The Benevolent Empire

1. For an excellent discussion of the meaning of gold in the search for El Dorado, which includes Native conceptualizations, see Sir Walter Ralegh, *The Discoverie of the Large, Rich, and Bewtiful Empyre of Guiana*, transcribed, annotated, and introduced by Neil L. Whitehead (Norman: University of Oklahoma Press, 1997), 70–91. Though Whitehead does not discuss Hermeticism, he notes the importance of alchemy and mysticism to Ralegh and sees that as contributing to his interest in gold. See also Mary C. Fuller, "Ralegh's Fugitive Gold: Reference and Deferral in *The Discoverie of Guiana*," *Representations*, no. 33, Special Issue: The New World (Winter 1991): 42–64.

2. See V. T. Harlow, Robert H. Schomburgk, and Joyce Lorimer, all of whom reproduced "Of the Voyage for Guiana" and refrained from commenting on Ralegh's direction that the English Empire in Guiana should be a benevolent one. Benjamin Schmidt's recent edition of the *Discoverie* includes excerpts of the documents, as he excerpted other documents, and excises much of the discussion of cooperation to be fostered between English and Natives. Neil Whitehead's edition of *Discoverie* does not include the document—though his analysis of the published *Discoverie* is excellent.

3. "Of the Voyage for Guiana," in Lorimer, *Sir Walter Ralegh's Discoverie*, 253.

4. "Of the Voyage for Guiana," in Lorimer, *Sir Walter Ralegh's Discoverie*, 254.

5. "Of the Voyage for Guiana," in Lorimer, *Sir Walter Ralegh's Discoverie*, 254–255.

6. It is possible that Ralegh believed the prophecy that an Inga would return and conquer Peru and that this was why the English should not conquer Guiana—because it would forestall the prophecy—but Ralegh did not offer this reasoning.

7. In the margins of the text, Ralegh placed numerous biblical citations to his sources.

8. "Of the Voyage for Guiana," in Lorimer, *Sir Walter Ralegh's Discoverie*, 256–257.

9. "Of the Voyage for Guiana," in Lorimer, *Sir Walter Ralegh's Discoverie*, 258.

10. "Of the Voyage for Guiana," in Lorimer, *Sir Walter Ralegh's Discoverie*, 258–259.

11. "Of the Voyage for Guiana," in Lorimer, *Sir Walter Ralegh's Discoverie*, 259–261.

12. "Of the Voyage for Guiana," in Lorimer, *Sir Walter Ralegh's Discoverie*, 261.

13. David Northrup, *Africa's Discovery of Europe, 1450–1850* (New York: Oxford University Press, 2002).

14. None of the editors of the *Discoverie* cited above comment on the significance of Ralegh's offer of English women to Native men.

15. "Of the Voyage for Guiana," in Lorimer, *Sir Walter Ralegh's Discoverie*, 261–263.

16. "Of the Voyage for Guiana," in Lorimer, *Sir Walter Ralegh's Discoverie*, 263.

Chapter 26: Wheel of Fortune

1. See the third edition of Ralegh's *History of the World* (1621), published for Walter Burre.

2. John Gilbert to Ralegh, January 17/27, 1595/96, in Lorimer, *Sir Walter Ralegh's Discoverie*, 266.

3. "The examinacion of Thomas Saunders," February 19/March 1, 1596, in Lorimer, *Sir Walter Ralegh's Discoverie*, 266. Gilbert also confirmed Spanish interest. Sir John Gilbert to Ralegh, March 16/26, 1596, in Lorimer, *Sir Walter Ralegh's Discoverie*, 267.

4. Ralegh to Robert Cecil, November 10, 1595, in Latham and Youings, *Letters of Sir Walter Ralegh* (Exeter: University of Exeter Press, 1999), 125.

5. Ralegh to Robert Cecil, November [12], 1595, in Latham and Youings, *Letters of Sir Walter Ralegh*, 126–127.

6. Ralegh to Robert Cecil, November [12], 1595, in Latham and Youings, *Letters of Sir Walter Ralegh*, 126–128.

7. Ralegh to Robert Cecil, November [26], 1595, in Latham and Youings, *Letters of Sir Walter Ralegh*, 133.

8. Ralegh to Charles Lord Howard, November 30, 1595, in Latham and Youings, *Letters of Sir Walter Ralegh*, 134–135.

9. Lady Ralegh to Robert Cecil, July 1596, in Lorimer, *Sir Walter Ralegh's Discoverie*, 287; Ralegh to Robert Cecil, November [12], 1595, in Latham and Youings, *Letters of Sir Walter Ralegh*, 127.

10. She would have learned this from Kemys on his return to England. Lady Ralegh to Robert Cecil, July 1596, in Lorimer, *Sir Walter Ralegh's Discoverie*, 287.

11. The documents on Francis Sparrow are reproduced in Lorimer, *Sir Walter Ralegh's Discoverie*, 267–278.

12. Lawrence Kemys, *A Relation of the Second Voyage to Guiana. Perfourmed and written in the yeare 1596* (London, 1596).

13. Thomas Hariot to Robert Cecil, July 11/21, 1596, in Lorimer, *Sir Walter Ralegh's Discoverie*, 285–286; George Trenchard and Ralph Horsey to Robert Cecil, July 31/August 10, 1596, and August 10/20, 1596, in Lorimer, *Sir Walter Ralegh's Discoverie*, 287–288.

14. The background and course of the expedition can be found in R. B. Wernham, *The Return of the Armadas: The Last Years of the Elizabethan War Against Spain, 1595–1603* (Oxford: Clarendon Press, 1994); M. Oppenheim, ed., *The Naval Tracts of Sir William Monson in Six Books*, 2 vols. (London: Printed for the Navy Records Society, 1902); Walter Ralegh, "A Relation of Cadiz Action, in the year 1596, transcribed from a manuscript in the hands of his grandchild, Mr. Ralegh," in *The Works of Sir Walter Ralegh, Kt.*, 8 vols. (Oxford: Oxford University Press, 1829), 8:667–674.

15. *A Declaration of the causes mouing the Queenes Maiestie of England, to prepare and send a Nauy to the Seas, for the defence of her Realmes against the King of Spaines Forces . . .* (London: By the deputies of Christopher Barker, 1596).

16. CSP Domestic, 1595–7, April 24, 1596, nos. 41 to 44, 207–208.

17. Wernham, *Return of the Armadas*, 104, cites the Spanish who commented with surprise how the women were not mistreated by the English. Gonçalo Vaz Coutinho, governor of São Miguel Island in the Azores, observed, "It may well be that if we invaded England we might not show the same restraint." Quoted by the editor (Oppenheim) of Monson's account of Cadiz, in *Naval Tracts of Sir William Monson*, 2:72.

18. Although not on that expedition, Ralegh gained some notoriety in England by writing an account of his cousin Grenville's death, *A Report of the Trvth of the fight aboue the Iles of Açores, this last sommer. Betwixt the Reuenge, one of her Maiesties shippes, And an Armada of the King of Spaine* (London: Printed for William Ponsonbie, 1591).

19. Wernham, *Return of the Armadas*, 85.

20. Quoted in Wernham, *Return of the Armadas*, 87.

21. Wernham, *Return of the Armadas*, 89.

22. Quotations from Ralegh, "Relation of Cadiz Action," 8:670.

23. Ralegh, "Relation of Cadiz Action," 8:673–674.

24. Ralegh, "Relation of Cadiz Action," 8:674.

25. Documents translated in Nabil Matar, *Europe through Arab Eyes, 1578–1727* (New York: Columbia University Press, 2009), 159–162.

26. Wernham, *Return of the Armadas*, 108–109.

27. John Donne, who later gained fame as one of the great English poets of the seventeenth century, and who was a member of the Cadiz expedition, wrote short poems in real time about the events at Cadiz and penned one in support of the earl's desire to pursue the treasure fleet. He wrote another for Ralegh. *The Variorum Edition of the Poetry of John Donne*, Vol. 8, *The Epigrams, Epithalamions, Epitaphs, Inscriptions, and Miscellaneous Poems*, ed. Gary A. Stringer (Bloomington: Indiana University Press, 1995).

28. Oppenheim, *Naval Tracts of Sir William Monson*, 1:355.

29. Wernham, *Return of the Armadas*, 111.

30. Oppenheim, *Naval Tracts of Sir William Monson*, 2:56.

31. Cited in Oppenheim, *Naval Tracts of Sir William Monson*, 2:15.

32. Adrienne Laskier Martín, *Cervantes and the Burlesque Sonnet* (Berkeley: University of California Press, 1991), 102.

33. Howard Mancing, *The Cervantes Encyclopedia*, 2 vols. (Westport, CT: Greenwood Press, 2004), 2:576. The poem at Philip's tomb is titled, "Al túmulo del rey que se hizo en Sevilla."

Chapter 27:
Reincarnation: Ireland and the Course of Colonialism

1. See M. Oppenheim, ed., *The Naval Tracts of Sir William Monson in Six Books*, 2 vols. (London: Printed for the Navy Records Society, 1902), 2:67–68n81; Sir Walter Rawleigh, "A Discourse of the Invention of Ships, Anchors, Compasse, &c.," in *Judicious and Select Essayes and Observations, by that Renowned and Learned Knight, Sir Walter Raleigh* (London: Printed by T. W. for Humphrey Moseley, 1650), 1–42; Sir Walter Rawleigh, *Excellent Observations and Notes, Concerning the Royall Navy and Sea-Service . . . Dedicated to the Most Noble and Illustrious Prince Henry Prince of Wales* (London: Printed by T. W. for Humphrey Moseley, 1650).

2. Rowland Whyte to Sir Robert Sydney, September 22, 1596, in *Historical Manuscript Commission, Report on the Manuscripts of Lord De L'Isle & Dudley*, vol. 2 (London: His Majesty's Stationary Office, 1934), 218.

3. "A larger Relation of the said Hard Voyage, written by Sir Arthur Gorges Knight . . . ," in Samuel Purchas, *Hakluytus Posthumus or Purchas His Pilgrimes . . .* , 20 vols. (Glasgow: James MacLehose and Sons, 1907), 20:69–70.

4. APC 25:453–454, June 13, 1596. Goring was a member of Parliament in 1593 and 1601 from Lewes and died in 1602. How he managed to extend his debts and keep his land is unknown.

5. CSP Ireland, 1598, 7:429.

6. The land itself was owned by Fitzgerald and leased by Pyne for the trees. Pyne later sued Fitzgerald to harvest the wood. R. J. Hunter, "The Disruption of a Munster Plantation Enterprise, 1598," *Journal of the Cork Historical and Archaeological Society* 75 (1970): 158–160.

7. Wallop had enjoyed the same rights as Pyne when they first shipped staves abroad—before Pyne and others were barred from doing so. When Pyne had his rights restored, he seems to have been the only one. Wallop continued to produce boards and other lumber. The Nine Years' War also created a severe shortage of barrels in England, which Wallop tried to fill. CSP Ireland 6:260, April 6, 1597; APC 28:141, November 23, 1597.

8. APC 25:445.

9. See "What the rebels of Munster have done to get Moghelly Castle, since the beginning of their rebellion," in CSP Ireland, September 1599, 8:161–165, quotation from 162.

10. Edmund Spenser, *A View of the State of Ireland*, ed. Andrew Hadfield and Willy Maley (Malden, MA: Blackwell Publishers 1997), 47, 70.

11. Spenser, *View*, 84–85.

12. Spenser, *View*, 153.

13. Spenser, *View*, 20.

14. Spenser, *View*, 42–55.

15. In medieval England, counties and shires were divided into hundreds, each possessing a court.

16. Spenser, *View*, 145–146.

17. Spenser, *View*, 144–145.

18. Spenser, *View*, 148.

19. Spenser, *View*, 144–145.

20. Spenser, *View*, 145.

21. Spenser, *View*, 84, 151.

22. Spenser, *View*, 149–150.

23. Spenser, *View*, 70–71.

24. Spenser, *View*, 92–93.

25. Spenser, *View*, 100–101.

26. Spenser, *View*, 101–102.

27. Spenser, *View*, 102–104.

28. Spenser, *View*, 152.

29. Spenser, *View*, 107.

30. There are multiple versions of the poem readily available. A few of the versions can be compared in *The Poems of Sir Walter Ralegh: A Historical Edition*, ed. Michael Rudick (Tempe: Arizona Center for Medieval and Renaissance Studies, 1999), 42–44.

Chapter 28: Treasons

1. Rowland Whyte to Sir Robert Sydney, April 18–19, 1597, in *Letters and Memorials . . .* 2 vols. (London, 1746), 2:42.

2. Oppenheim, *Naval Tracts of Sir William Monson*, 2:24.

3. Discussion of the Azores based on Oppenheim, *Naval Tracts of Sir William Monson*, 2:17–82, including the editor's additional information and assessment.

4. October 1598, CSP Ireland 7:326 and October 21, 1598, 292.

5. November 17, 1598, CSP Ireland 7:350.

6. Queen to Sir Thomas Norreys, December 3, 1598, CSP Ireland 7:390–391; Robert Cecil to Thomas Norreys, December 3, 1598, 391–392.

7. John McGurk, *The Elizabethan Conquest of Ireland: The 1590s Crisis* (Manchester, England: Manchester University Press, 2009), 201.

8. This information is from "A Journal of the Occurrences of the Camp from the 21st of May until the last of the same month, and thence continued till the 22nd of June 1599," *Carew Manuscripts*, Lambeth Palace Library, MS 621.

9. The ambush is also mentioned in a letter from Henry Pyne to the Earl of Essex, October, 27, 1599, in CSP Ireland 8:201–203.

10. Pyne to Essex, October 27, 1599, CSP, Ireland 8:201–203, October 27, 1599.

11. George Carew to the Privy Council, April 30, 1600, CSP Ireland 9:128.

12. See Patrick Condon to Robert Cecil, 1594, *Calendar of the Manuscripts of the . . . Marquis of Salisbury*, Part V (1894), 68.

13. Robert Napper to Robert Cecil, November 18, 1599, CSP Ireland 8:260.

14. Rowland Whyte to Sir Robert Sydney, February 25, 1599/00, in *Letters and Memorials . . .* , 2 vols. (London, 1746), 2:172.

15. James Thomas Fitzgerald, Confession, June 3, 1601, *Calendar of the Carew Manuscripts: 1601–1603*, ed. John Sherren Brewer (London: Longmans, 1870), 79.

16. Martens might have been barred from leaving his community because of debt. Privy Council to Sir George Carew, July 18, 1601, in *Calendar of the Carew Manuscripts: 1601–1603*, 109. The Privy Council also wrote directly to Pyne to register his partners' complaint—their letter was pretty much identical to the one written to Carew but included a warning of Pyne's need to come to England: "Hereof fail you not." July 12, 1601, APC 32:57–59.

17. September 26, 1601, CSP Ireland 11:90.

18. Boyle's biographer Nicholas Canny assessed the transition: "All of the achievements of Richard Boyle are as much a tribute to the initial efforts of Ralegh as they are to the energy and astuteness of Richard Boyle." See "Ralegh's Ireland," in *Ralegh and Quinn: The Explorer and His Boswell*, ed. H. G. Jones (Chapel Hill: North Caroliniana Society, 1987), 98.

19. May 18, 1603, APC 32:498.

20. Mark Nicholls and Penry Williams, *Sir Walter Raleigh: In Life and Legend* (London: Continuum International Publishing Group, 2011), 190–194.

21. Many have been associated with having first defined James in this way—which shows how widespread was the belief.

22. There are numerous handwritten copies of the trials in archival collections. All quotations are taken from a published version, *Cobbett's Collection of State Trials*, 33 vols. (London, 1809–1826), 2:2–31.

23. For discussion of a document, which one historian believes implies Ralegh's legal guilt of treason, see Mark Nicholls, "Sir Walter Ralegh's Treason: A Prosecution

Document," *English Historical Review* CX, no. 438 (September 1995): 902–924. The document is included at the end of Nicholls's essay.

24. Dudley Carleton to John Chamberlain, November 27, 1603, in *Cobbett's Collection of State Trials*, 46–47.

25. Popham quoted in *Cobbett's Collection of State Trials*, 30.

26. Dudley Carleton to John Chamberlain, December 11, 1603, *Cobbett's Collection of State Trials*, 51–54.

27. Dudley Carleton to John Chamberlain, December 11, 1603, *Cobbett's Collection of State Trials*.

Chapter 29: The Great Cordial

1. Sir William Waad to Earl of Salisbury, August 17, 1605, and August 19, 1605, in Cecil Papers, vol. 17.

2. Sir Anthony Weldon, *The Court and Character of King James I* (London, 1651), 12–13. There is some question whether Weldon actually wrote the book or someone else did under his name. Weldon had been part of James's court. He died in 1648.

3. Edmund Lodge, *Illustrations of British History . . .* , 2nd ed. (London, 1838), 2:442–43.

4. National Ocean Service, https://oceanservice.noaa.gov/facts/coral_medicine.html.

5. Charles Nicholl, *The Creature in the Map: A Journey to El Dorado* (London: Jonathan Cape, 1996), 279.

6. John Morgan Richards, ed., *A Chronology of Medicine* (London: Balliere et al., 1880), 103–104.

7. Richards, *A Chronology*, 99.

8. N. Le Fèbvre, *A Discourse upon Sr Walter Rawleigh's Great Cordial*, trans. Peter Belon (London, 1664). The original French version was not published until 1665.

9. David Boyd Haycock, "'A Thing Ridiculous'? Chemical Medicines and the Prolongation of Human Life in Seventeenth-Century England" (Working Papers on the Nature of Evidence, Department of Economic History, London School of Economics, No. 10/106, July 2006); Stephen Porter, *The Great Plague* (Chalford, England: Amberley, 2009), 39.

10. For the sixteenth-century belief that life could be greatly extended, see Haycock, "'A Thing Ridiculous'?"

11. The essay was originally published in 1663, and again with additions in 1671. It is reprinted in the new edition of *The Works of the Honorable Robert Boyle*, 6 vols. (London: W. Johnston et al., 1772), 2:23.

12. Another connection at Lismore worthy of exploration is between Robert Boyle and Valentine Greatrakes, the great healer of Restoration England. Greatrakes's family worked for Boyle's family for many years. Robert Boyle and Valentine Greatrakes were born a year apart in the same neighborhood and would have known each other as children. Boyle later became a great supporter of Greatrakes in England. One can easily imagine that Greatrakes, like Robert Boyle, was exposed to the stone that Ralegh gave Richard Boyle. The best biography of Greatrakes is Peter Elmer, *The Miraculous Conformist: Valentine Greatrakes, the Body Politic, and the Politics of Healing in Restoration Britain* (Oxford: Oxford University Press, 2013).

13. *Works of the Honorable Robert Boyle*, 2:116.

14. *Works of the Honorable Robert Boyle*, 2:206.

15. John Aubrey, *"Brief Lives," Chiefly of Contemporaries, Set Down by John Aubrey, Between the Years 1669 and 1696*, 2 vols., ed. Andrew Clark (Oxford: Clarendon Press, 1898), 2:182.

16. *Works of the Honorable Robert Boyle*, 2:65.

17. A bridge between the two, whom Ralegh knew personally, was Francis Bacon, often called the founder of empiricism, the modern scientific method. Bacon looked to Ralegh, Thomas Hariot, and the Earl of Northumberland—the Wizard Earl—as three models as scientists, "themselves being already inclined to experiments," but also because of their understanding that scientific inquiry led to better understanding of the purpose of the divine. See his essay "The Great Instauration" (1620) and *The Works of Francis Bacon . . .* , 15 vols., ed. James Spedding (London: Longman, 1857–1874), 13:343n1.

18. Linnaeus, himself, possessed a wonderful imagination and succeeded in so many different endeavors, from medicine to poetry to zoology.

Chapter 30: Prince Henry

1. See Joyce Lorimer, ed., *Sir Walter Ralegh's Discoverie of Guiana* (London: Hakluyt Society, 2006), 296–297n4.

2. See "Paper from our Ambassador in London . . . " in Lorimer, *Sir Walter Ralegh's Discoverie*, 297; John Chamberlain to Dudley Carleton, November 12, 1613, CSP Domestic, *James, 1611–1618*, 155.

3. Nicholas Popper, *Walter Ralegh's "History of the World" and the Historical Culture of the Late Renaissance* (Chicago: University of Chicago Press, 2012).17. Even after Henry died, Ralegh still held out hope that James would make him an advisor, particularly after the death of Henry Howard and the king's obvious need for a wise political strategist.

4. For the early stages of Henry's illness, see Roy Strong, *Henry Prince of Wales and England's Lost Renaissance* (London: Pimlico, 2000), 166–167.

5. The eyewitness account of the illness can be found as "The manner of the Sicknesse and Death of Henry Prince of Wales, sonne to King James, Anno 1612," IETCD, MS 732, Manuscripts & Archives Research Library, Trinity College, Dublin, Ireland. There is another copy at Cambridge University.

6. This was also confirmed in Sir Thomas Lake to Dudley Carleton, November 10, 1612, CSP Domestic, *James I, 1611–1618*, 155.

7. John Chamberlain's letter quoted in *The Gentleman's Magazine, and Historical Chronicle* 96, part 2:615.

Chapter 31: History of the World

1. All quotations from Ralegh in this chapter are taken from his *History of the World* (London: Walter Burre, 1614).

2. Nicholas Popper, *Walter Ralegh's History of the World and the Historical Culture of the Late Renaissance* (Chicago: University of Chicago Press, 2012).

3. Anna R. Beer, *Sir Walter Ralegh and His Readers in the Seventeenth Century: Speaking to the People* (London: Macmillan, 1997), 58n31.

Chapter 32:
"He called to the Headman to shew him the Ax"

1. *Historical Collections of Private Passages of State*, Vol. 1, *1618–29* (London: D. Browne, 1721), 1–10.

2. For copies of the royal warrant permitting Ralegh to travel outside the Tower with a "Keeper," and his subsequent official release from the Tower "notwithstanding any attainder or judgment given against him," see Alfred John Kempe, ed., *The Loseley Manuscripts and other Rare Documents . . .* (London, 1836), 378–379. For many years it has been asserted that Pocahontas visited Ralegh in the Tower of London during her visit to England in 1616–1617. But Ralegh no longer resided in the Tower after his March release. Most likely, she visited the Wizard Earl. She knew the earl's brother in Virginia, and the earl's family hosted Pocahontas in England.

3. This remained the English view of Spanish possessions in the New World—to take from the Spanish lands they desired, disregarding Spanish claims to sovereignty. The United States inherited this disposition, purchasing the Louisiana Territory from France when it belonged to Spain, and sending troops into Florida in disregard of Spanish sovereignty. This was followed by seizure of the Philippines and Puerto Rico at the end of the nineteenth century.

4. The document was signed July 28 and sealed and delivered August 26, 1616. A full copy exists in James Spedding, ed., *The Works of Francis Bacon . . .*, 15 vols. (London: Longman, 1857–1874), 13:387–390.

5. V. T. Harlow, *Ralegh's Last Voyage* (London: Argonaut Press, 1932), 24–29.

6. Harlow, *Ralegh's Last Voyage*, 35.

7. *History of England from the accession of James I . . .*, 10 vols. (London: Longman, 1883–1884), 3:43.

8. Harlow, *Ralegh's Last Voyage*, 38–44.

9. Reprinted in *The Works of Sir Walter Ralegh, Kt.*, 8 vols. (Oxford: Oxford University Press, 1829), 8:682–688.

10. Quoted in Nicholas Canny, *The Upstart Earl: A Study of the Social and Mental World of Richard Boyle, First Earl of Cork, 1566–1643* (Cambridge: Cambridge University Press, 1982), 20–21.

11. Entries August 1617, *The Lismore Papers (First Series) . . . of Sir Richard Boyle . . .*, 5 vols., ed. Alexander B. Grosart (Privately Printed, 1886), 1:162–163.

12. Dorothea Townshend, *The Life and Letters of the Great Earl of Cork* (London: Duckworth, 1904), 122–124.

13. Harlow, *Ralegh's Last Voyage*, 55.

14. For a printed version of Ralegh's journal of the voyage, see the Schomburgk edition of Ralegh's *The Discovery of the Large, Rich, and Beautiful Empire of Guiana* (London: Hakluyt Society, 1848), 177–208, with discussion of Leonard and the Cassique on 197–200.

15. "Sir Walter Rawleigh his apologie for his voyage to Guiana," reprinted as *Apology*, in *Works of Sir Walter Ralegh, Kt.*, 8:494–495.

16. "Sir Walter Rawleigh his apologie," 494.

17. Harlow nicely summarizes the return from Guiana to England in *Ralegh's Last Voyage*, 82–86.

18. Raleigh Trevelyan, *Sir Walter Raleigh: Being a True and Vivid Account of the Life and Times of the Explorer . . .* (New York: Henry Holt, 2002), 516.

19. Spedding, *Works of Francis Bacon*, 13:361–62.

20. The king's letter is reprinted in Spedding, *Works of Francis Bacon*, 13:363. It likely was written with the assistance of the Duke of Buckingham.

21. Spedding, *Works of Francis Bacon*, 13:366.

22. Spedding, *Works of Francis Bacon*, 13:366–367.

23. Ralegh's reply can be found in Harlow, *Ralegh's Last Voyage*, 302–304.

24. Letter from Thomas Lorkin to Thomas Puckering, in Harlow, *Ralegh's Last Voyage*, 312–313.

25. Quoted in Spedding, *Works of Francis Bacon*, 370.

26. Lorkin to Puckering, in Harlow, *Ralegh's Last Voyage*, 312.

27. The scaffold speech has been reprinted many times. For the quotations, I used the version in Harlow, *Ralegh's Last Voyage*, 306–311.

28. Here *division* might refer to its connotation in the sixteenth and seventeenth centuries of transforming one long note into a rapid succession of shorter notes—that life begins slowly, then moves rapidly.

29. A *tiring house* is the dressing room for a play.

INDEX

Alan Gallay is the Lyndon B. Johnson chair of United States history at Texas Christian University and the author of several books, including *The Indian Slave Trade*, which won the Bancroft Prize. Gallay lives in Fort Worth, Texas.